A House of Prayer for All Peoples

Congregations Building Multiracial Comunity

SHERYL A. KUJAWA-HOLBROOK

The Alban Institute

Copyright © 2002 by the Alban Institute. All rights reserved. This material may not be photocopied or reproduced in any way without written permission. Contact: Permissions, The Alban Institute, 7315 Wisconsin Ave., Suite 1250W, Bethesda, MD 20814-3211.

Library of Congress Catalog Number 2003105600
ISBN 1-56699-282-6

07   06   05   04   03   VG   1   2   3   4   5   6   7   8   9   10

Contents

God Beyond Borders

God beyond borders
we bless you for strange places
and different dreams

for the demands and diversity
of a wider world

for the distance
that lets us look back and re-evaluate

for new ground
where the broken stems can take root,
grow and blossom.

We bless you
for the friendship of strangers
the richness of other cultures
and the painful gift of freedom

Blessed are you,
God beyond borders.

But if we have overlooked
the exiles in our midst
heightened their exclusion
by our indifference
given our permission
for a climate of fear
and tolerated a culture of violence

Have mercy on us,
God who takes side with justice,
confront our prejudice
stretch our narrowness
sift out our laws and our lives
with the penetrating insight
of your spirit
until generosity is our only measure.
Amen

—Kathy Galloway, *Maker's Blessing*
(Glasgow: Wild Goose Publications, 2000)

Foreword

SOMETIMES I CAN BECOME TOO PESSIMISTIC ABOUT OUR
progress on issues of race and racism in the life of the church and more
broadly in our society. With regard to these issues it seems that American culture, at least in the United States, thrives on a steady diet of
hypocrisy. In several of the larger Protestant denominations especially,
there are too many pronouncements about valuing racial inclusiveness
that are not backed up by a commitment to realizing that vision within
the local churches. Of course this pattern in the church reflects a more
general trend.

In general, our leaders have become increasingly skillful at generating propaganda, with proclamations about moral values that we must
continue to cherish, such as building a nonracist, multiracial society.
But it seems as if these proclamations about moral values, cleverly
worded by speechwriters and public relations specialists, are created
to distract the public from noticing the vast majority of policies that
subvert those values. This is a common political strategy by high-level
government officials and media commentators. It provides us with
daily lessons on how to feel good about proclaiming community-
affirming values for public life while being committed to actions that
do the opposite.

Churches mimic this pattern by using theological language about
the loving, just relationships that God desires for all human beings in
our interactions with one another, while perpetuating racially and
socioeconomically segregated congregations as well as discriminatory
practices related to sex/gender access to ordination and pastoral leadership. For the church, this way of operating is not just a problem of
hypocritical organizational practices. It represents a spiritual crisis, a
loss of genuine connection with Christ's call to discipleship.

It is fortunate that resources such as this one by Sheryl Kujawa-
Holbrook save me from descending into complete pessimism and

despair about the possibility of improving public moral life within our churches and society. This book offers specific details about how local churches maintain commitments to including a racially diverse body of members as well as to building racial justice among the membership of their churches and within their local communities. The churches described here develop creative theological, programmatic, and organizational responses to the unique cultural dynamics that arise within each setting. While confronting some of the most challenging aspects of building racial justice, they also address related problems of heterosexism and socioeconomic inequalities in their communities.

The challenge that this work represents must not be minimized. It means resisting the strong pull of major cultural influences such as the denial of racism. The desire to deny the existence of racism in oneself and in one's everyday relationships is an extremely stubborn trait to remove.

For instance, to break through denial in an attempt to build racial justice requires churches to challenge multiculturalism as their main goal. This means interrupting the "good feeling" that abounds after successfully forming a group that includes persons with multiple racial identities. This "good feeling" is interrupted by insisting on the further task of creating antiracist ways of relating to one another. Especially among whites there is sometimes a tendency toward self-congratulation when they make the choice to gather together with persons of color in informal settings such as faith communities. It is true, of course, that in our current racist culture, when whites choose to be associated with people of color, informally "hanging out" with them, certain possibilities for social status are reduced for them. Similarly, congregations that are made up predominantly of people of color may have a tendency to boast when they have "some white folks" attending and joining their churches. However, even to glimpse racial justice within such congregational relationships, one must acknowledge the racist realities that order our social environment and attempt to redirect these realities. Racist realities are ugly and painful; acknowledgment of them almost always brings tension and conflict.

It is not just the opportunity to "feel good" that may be cut short if denial is overcome. Racial justice threatens most of our existing arrangements of power, privilege, and status. It challenges biased values of the broader society such as white domination, which is evident in many ways, for instance, in the exclusive racial/ethnic composition of many churches, racial paternalism in church mission projects, or stained glass windows in the sanctuary depicting Jesus and all other biblical characters as white. Shifting from domination by one social group to shared power and privilege among multiple cultural groups is hard. It involves a loss of power and privilege, which are not easily given up by those who are accustomed to being able to dominate boards of trustees, to having their cultural traditions dictate the music for worship, or to seeing their own racial group reflected in the faces of the pastor and his/her family.

For whites, this shift often means that the social rewards are diminished. White privilege, the most common manifestation of racist rewards in our society means that, for instance, whites are always seen as "the normal ones," or assumptions about what is considered "classical" studies in academia or "classical" music in the arts is always European-centered. In making a shift toward racial justice, rewards of racism that white/European Americans receive would have to be diminished in favor of a more just distribution of cultural worth and status that includes Latinos/Hispanics, African Americans, Asian Americans, and Native Americans and their rich cultural heritages.

For people of color, this shift can mean that lessons often learned at great personal cost about the need to earn and maintain the approval of whites have to be unlearned. Shifting away from denial about how racism—a belief in white superiority—has been internalized creates a significant challenge for persons of color. Yet racism and the other forms of oppression with which it is interlocked cannot be dismantled without searching out the entrapping ways that all community members uphold it. Destructive competitive patterns between racial/ethnic groups of color will have to be acknowledged and confronted. In addition, mixed cultural identities that defy the boundaries of recognized racial/ethnic group categories will need to be honored instead of resisted.

As the stories of faith communities that are presented in this book demonstrate, church acceptance of these challenges requires a definite process. Theological, biblical, and spiritual approaches are needed that specifically respond to these complicated dynamics. To create change, every detail of the structuring of church boards and committees, as well as the designation of leaders, will need scrutiny. Particular attention to the management of, and decision-making power over, the use of money and other resources has to be included. The relationship between the values held by the church and those of the broader society will have to be closely monitored as the church embraces the vital the task of helping to build shared communal values in their communities and across global boundaries.

Brave Christians have already accepted this challenge. Sheryl Kujawa-Holbrook's study has gathered a myriad of concrete examples of how they have done it. This volume offers a bold witness to the ability of faith communities to enter this struggle of building racial justice.

TRACI C. WEST
Associate Professor of Ethics and
African American Studies
Drew University Theological School

Acknowledgments

THE EXTENSIVE TRAVEL REQUIRED FOR THIS BOOK WOULD NOT have been possible were it not for the gracious hospitality provided at each location. Special thanks in this regard is extended to Joyce Clark, Joe Ellwanger, Gwen Gutierrez, Larry Hamil, Charlene Higbe, Ann Hinz, Marv Hinz, Elaine Kujawa, Richard K. Miller, Jim Robinson, Chip Stokes, Susan Stokes, Fredrica Harris Thompsett, and Phillip Wilson.

Interviews with clergy, staff, and members of each congregation and its wider community featured here contributed greatly to the stories collected in this book. Many interviewees drove long distances or came after long days at work in order to share their insights, candor, and humor. The interviewing process was deeply engaging for me, and I hope the same for the marvelous people I met during the process:

St. Matthew's and St. Paul's, Delray Beach, Florida
Janet Aguhob, Mike Brennan, Bob Chapin, Bonnie Davis, Janet Davis, Sherry Fleming, Chris Herin, Bill Hurd, Connie Impert, Keith Johnson, Tim Kilpatrick, Jacqueline J. Lewis, Jeff Perlman, Mary McCarty, Rosalind Murray, Edie Quinn, Chip Stokes, Mary Beth Wells, Edward W. White, Douglas Williams.

Quincy First Presyterian Church, Quincy, Washington
Candy Bennett-Houston, Mike Blakely, Judy Bryant, Joyce Cook, Sally Curran, Jackie Flinn, Ann Hinz, Marv Hinz, Mark Koenig, Roxa Kreimeyer, Kari McFarland, Ellen Mead, Lea Patterson, Pat Patterson, Lynn Rowse, Isabel Saldana, Diana Santiago, Mary Schramm, Lynn Snyder, Teri Wilson, Bill Wurl, Sylvia Wurl, Mary Ybarra-Vega.

Cross Lutheran Church, Milwaukee, Wisconsin
Jessie Andrews, Paulette Barr, Kaylynn Blackwell, Bounheua Bouakongxaya, Khamphanh Bouakongxaya, Frances Bryant, Rick Cesar, Denise Davis, Guy Davis, Jr., Rick Deines, Joseph W. Ellwanger, Horatio Glover, Lois Glover, Bradley Hauser, Ann Hogan, Reynolds Honold, Johnson Hunter, Judi Hunter, Carolyn Jackson, Tom Jackson, Lisa B. Jacobsen, Marguerite Kelley, Betty Marx, Jovanna Miller, Lillian Miller, Sammie Miller, Fred Moss, Ever Lee Porter, Wayne Porter, Lisa Quam, Lillie Robinson, Marty Schneider, Mary Steppe, Katherine Wilcher, Lula Williams, Teri Woodley, Gloria Wright.

Delhaven Christian Church, LaPuente, California
Pete Aranda, Shirley Aranda, Patsy Barrios, Roy Bullock, Jody Bullock, Bob Cantrell, Christine Cantu, Kathy Cantu, Renee Cantu, Richard Cantu, Britany Carlock, Deirdre Carlock, Mark Carlock, Matthew Carlock, Mavis Davenport, Art DeBry, Dora DeBry, Bert DeYoung, Mildred DeYoung, Betty Franklin, Dave Genung, Gwen Gutierrez, Mittie Hanson, Kelly Harrison, Lonnie Harrison, Roberta Harrison, Glenn Johnson, Frances Landers, Otis Landers, Kimberlie Manager, Gabrielle McClure, Richard K. Miller, Marie Morgan, Kate Moyer, Tom Nevarez, Alice Peace, Fannie Powell, Maurice Powell, Gayle Schoepf, Doug Smith, Hank Smith, Janice Vance, Dorothy Wells, Willie Wells.

Church of the Redeemer, Morristown, New Jersey
Charles W. Dickerson, Larry Hamil, Carol King, Marcia Liotard, Janice Paran, Phillip Wilson; Bert Jones (Diocese of Newark), Richard Horsley, Kathy Seabrook (St. Peter's, Morristown), Traci C. West.

First Parish, Brewster, Massachusetts
Carlos Barbosa, David Billings, Joseph Daluz, Jeanne Denike, Bill Gardiner, Elizabeth Goodrich, Mykel Johnson, Carie Killam, John Mother Bear Myers, Frances Perkins, Pancheta Peterson, Jim Robinson, Marilyn Watson, Michele Wolfson, Tom Wolfson.

Besides those who contributed to this project through site visits, numerous other individuals and congregations responded to questionnaires, telephone queries, and e-mail requests and interviews,

ACKNOWLEDGMENTS   xiii

including the following: Brian Grieves, Martha E. Hedberg, Phyllis
Joan Leopold, Joan Martin, Fred Williams, George Yancey, Eric H. F.
Law, Patricia Dorsey, Kenyetta Aduma, Rosemarie Davidson-
Gotobed, Denise Scott, Fletcher L. Tink, Bob Forsberg, Jessica Sippel,
Caroline Kelly, Greg Van Dunk, Jerry Stromberg, Brenda Zook
Friesen, Chuck Ruehle, Sue Ruehle, Steven Charleston, Alcena Boozer,
Terrance Kelshaw, Davette Turk, Edward Lee, Julia Sibley Juras, G. J.
Weltsek, Jr., Jeannette Brown, Peggy Ornell, Ginny Wagener, Hugo L.
Piña-Lopez, Mary Sauerheber, Mimi Dortch, Kevin Tripp, Tom Sulli-
van, Tom O'Brien, Susan Simons, George Read, Elizabeth Keaton,
Mark Beckwith, Sandy Hampton, Beth Turner, Bob Carter, Kristi
Philip, Bert Jones, Jerry Folk, Barbara Dua, David Lamarre-Vincent,
Ron L. Keller, Kahu Tom Van Culin, Louie Crew, John Kater,
Geoffrey Little, Claire Cohen, Connie S. Spitack, Betty Sue Sherrod,
Dan Polish, Mark Koenig, Nozomi Ikuta, Alan Dennis, David G.
Smith, Richard M. Turk, Louis Schoen, Betsey Haren, Dru Green-
wood, H. Gerald Knoche, Don Stahlhut, Jess Delegencia, Tim Tseng,
Keith A. Russell, Joel Soffin, Fred Wedemeyer, D. Motto, Jeff Green-
way, Dori Englehardt, Wyvetta Bullock, Darline Balm-Demmel,
Cheryl Edwards, Marian Ronan, Wait Perry, Jody LeFort, LeeAnn
Parry, Dan Krutz, Barrie M. Tritie, Ken Hoke, Vicki Wallace, Laura J.
Collins, Hector Cortez, Grace Basham, Paul Leichty, Roz Hall, Dan
Di Domizio, Scott Fisher, Dennis Sparks, David Kolberg, Mike
Mather, Tony Pappas, Gary Fancett, Dori Engelhardt, Amy Philbrick,
Katie Day, William Barnwell, Gary Reierson, Ben Richmond,
Makanah E. Morriss, Kenneth L. Couchman, John Harvey, Curtiss
Paul DeYoung, Gibson Stroupe, Kathy Ketcham, Rock Dillaman,
Brian K. Bauknight, Tammerie Spires, Andrea Baker, Hope Eakins,
Connie Casebolt, Burton Garlinda, Tony L. Colson, Lyle E. McKee,
J. L.Wolf, Terry Van Hook, C. Albert Wagaman, Michael L. Pfleger,
Andrew Ekblad, Kenneth L. Carder, Jessicah Krey, Kurt Crays, Britt
Marshall, Richard Taylor, Mary Lyman Jackson, Kenneth J. Brucks,
Mark Milligan, Eva Brooks, Don E. Peavy, Sr., Tony Campolo, Lee
Van Ham, Carla Schultz, Lawrence E. Johnson, Jerrett L. Hansen,
Janet Storts, Currie Burns, K. Gordon White, Marcel Welty, Robert
Edgard, Tina Whaley, Caese Levo, Richard K. Taylor, Laura J. Collins,
Jack Eastwood, Beth Turner, Judith Conley, Carlos Zervignon, Jim
Dougans, Nibs Stroupe, Jan Swanson, Nancy Lee Atkins.

Research for this project was generously assisted through grants from the Conant Sabbatical Grant Fund, the Episcopal Church Center; the Theological Writing Fund, Episcopal Divinity School; and the Alban Institute. Jennifer Morazes assisted with site research at the early stages of the project. Jayne J. Oasin, Social Justice Ministries Officer at the Episcopal Church Center, gave generously of her time and talents throughout the development of this book, as did my colleagues on the Anti-Racism Committee of the Executive Council of the Episcopal Church: Hilario Albert, Don Betts, Carol J. Gallagher, Anita George, John Kitagawa, Harriet Kollin, Ed Leidel, John L. Rabb, Al Rodriguez, Chip Stokes, and Tina Lynch. David Lott of the Alban Institute blessed this project with his keen editorial insights and skills. Janet Landis Barrett and the Denver Anti-Racism and Reconciliation Team dedicated a meeting to the project: Sandy Vizina, Hamilton Jenkins, Sherry Flynn, Fannie Harris Fiddmont, Elva Bankhead, Jean Nelson, and Charles Jenkins. Jacqueline J. Lewis and colleagues of the Cultural Boundaries Conversations Group of the Alban Institute provided inspiration and vision: Andreia Foster, Jeffrey Haggray, Karen Hernandez-Granzen, Joseph W. Daniels, Jr., Gil Rendle, John Janka, Chris Hobgood, Ian Evison, Suzanne Stier, and David Lott. Angela Bauer of the Episcopal Divinity School provided invaluable assistance with scripture passages.

Mentor and colleague Edward W. Rodman not only agreed to read the manuscript, but also provided his suggestions and challenges throughout the project. Without Ed's support of this project, my own eyes would have only seen part of the story. Lastly, I want to thank my dear husband, Paul Holbrook, for his enduring support and patience during the long hours of travel and writing that it took to complete this project.

Introduction

A House of Prayer for All Peoples

*And as for the foreigners who join themselves to the Holy One, to min-
ister to God and to love the name of the Holy One, and to be God's ser-
vants, all who keep the sabbath, and do not profane it, and hold fast to
my covenant—these I will bring to my holy mountain, and let them
rejoice in my house of prayer; their burnt offering and sacrifices will be
accepted on my altar; for my house shall be called a house of prayer for
all peoples.*

*Thus says the Holy One God, who gathers the outcasts of Israel, I
will gather others/still more to those already gathered.*

Isaiah 56:6-8[1]

D R. MARTIN LUTHER KING JR. CALLED ELEVEN O'CLOCK ON
Sunday mornings the most segregated hour in America. Dr. King
believed that churches should play a fundamental role in shaping the
morality and changing the prejudices of the nation. Our churches have
long been divided by confessional differences, but some of the deepest
and most painful separations in American congregations have resulted
from the experience of racism. In general, American congregations
have historically mirrored rather than transformed the racism of our
society. For the most part, the experience of genuine multiracial community within congregations is illusive. Racism has prevailed as an
organizing principle of religious life throughout our congregations.
Racism is not confined to a fringe group of religious life, persons who
subscribe to a faith based on hate and who have not grasped the core
of Scripture. Such people and groups are flagrant in their racism and
bigotry and are therefore fairly easy to disavow. Rather, the racism

1

that is the subject of this book is at the very core of our faith communities. At a time when racism and race relations are a major national concern, how can congregations—some of the most segregated institutions in North America, but perhaps the only institutions with clear moral authority—be catalysts for religious and social change? How can congregations actively build multiracial community? How can we incarnate the vision of the prophet Isaiah of a "house of prayer for all peoples"?

Not surprisingly, recent studies have suggested that although mainline churches argue the importance of inclusiveness, there are comparatively very few integrated congregations—only 2 to 3 percent on average—and that racially mixed congregations account for only 8 percent of total American congregations.[2] These studies suggest that multiracial communities are not organic; that is, without intervention we instinctively build our congregations according to assumptions of racism and racial division rather than on a vision of justice and reconciliation. Though it can be argued that there are many individuals within congregations who seek racial justice through their personal vocations, and while individuals can and do make a difference, their impact is short-lived and temporary if not supported by a committed faith community of believers empowered by God's healing presence. More than secular political movements, economic theory, or social analysis (although all three are essential), congregations can be sources of both change and authentic racial reconciliation on the personal, interpersonal, institutional, and cultural levels of human society.

The development of a church tradition beyond racism depends on a multiple-strategy approach to change in congregations. The challenge is to promote personal and structural change at the level of individual believers, congregations, judicatories, and daily expressions of congregational life. In order to accomplish these changes, the spirit of multiracial community needs to embrace the whole of congregational life—worship, hospitality, evangelism, formation for all ages, pastoral care, and community witness. We need to push beyond seeing racial justice as a "program" to seeing it as integral to the vocation and mission of the congregation. This vision of congregational life must encompass moral practice as well as public policy making through which the congregation relates to other religious traditions and to the broader community. Finally, congregations must develop a theological perspective based on multiracial community that offers people a sign of hope in an enduring culture of oppression. As the population of the United States grows increasingly diverse, the need for a greater awareness of cultural and racial differences is a challenge facing all people of faith who will live, work, and pray in this changing context. For European Americans this challenge includes understanding the power dynamics inherent in "whiteness" and how the resultant social power affects persons of other races and cultures. For people of color, this will include understanding how internalized oppression impacts individuals and communities within a church and society where the dominant culture remains white. In order to build multiracial communities, both white people and people of color must grow more culturally competent and aware of how the history of racism in the United States has impacted our faith communities.

This is a book based in hope. As imperfect as our congregations may be, I am confident we can bring about the changes necessary to make the vision of the prophet Isaiah a reality. To be sure, raising issues of race in many congregations can be risky, but the question is whether or not we believe that our faith communities are resilient enough to confront the evils of our era. I believe that congregations are in fact one of the few places in our society where people of very diverse backgrounds can work together constructively for the good of humankind. This conviction comes from seeing congregations that have confronted the racism in their midst, have struggled with it, and have moved closer to the reality of multiracial community. In facing racism, these congregations have faced death. That confrontation itself is hope embodied. William Stringfellow wrote that "hope is known only in the midst of coping with death. Any so-called hope is delusory and false without or apart from the confrontation with the power of death. . . . Resistance to death *is* the only way to live humanly in the midst of the Fall."[3]

This book is aimed at clergy, congregational leaders, seminarians, and concerned religious folk. Its primary goal is to encourage congregations to participate actively in the building of multiracial community, and to provide a context and resources for local churches to pursue this work on a long-term basis. The congregations featured here are not perfect; rather, they have found that there is much to learn and to *unlearn* when it comes to racism. Yet they have all experienced a glimpse, a foretaste, of what building multiracial community means for them. Represented here are the stories of a variety of congregations: large, small, affluent, poor, of different denominations and different geographical contexts. They each have faced pain and loss as they have struggled with what it means to confront racism, yet they have chosen to live in hope. In reading this book, you will, I hope, see something of yourself and your congregation in their stories and will be challenged to live more fully as a multiracial congregation in your own context.

Suggestions for Talking about Race and Racism in Congregations

- Begin with yourself.
- Reflect and discern your call to multiracial community from a faith perspective.
- Honor your own experience and the experience of others.
- Be honest about your feelings.
- Look for understanding on several levels: emotional, intellectual, and spiritual.
- Develop intercultural communication skills.
- Learn about other cultures.
- Identify resources and networks in the community.
- Face conflicts and the people who disagree with you openly.
- Prepare yourself for the mistakes you will make and learn from them.
- Seek support and assistance from within and outside the congregation.
- Pray and celebrate!

WHY FOCUS ON "RACE" AND "RACISM"?

This book focuses on building *multiracial* community; it examines the impact of racism on communities of faith and looks at what some congregations are doing to address it. This is not in any way to minimize other forms of oppression. Certainly, sexism, classism, homophobia, ageism, ableism, and other "isms" also impact congregational life. Indeed, because of the interlocking nature of oppressions, it is not possible fully to address one form of oppression and not another. None of us is free until all God's people are free. In other words, in order to examine our racism fully, we must also examine sexism, classism, and so on. The congregations featured here have focused on racism *and* have also sought to address other forms of oppression. It is crucial, however, for communities of faith to recognize the persistence of racism in predominantly white religious institutions. Many predominantly white congregations would describe themselves as "progressive" and might see themselves as "justice-centered," but they have often done little or nothing to address their own racism, particularly on a structural level. In fact, in many cases such congregations would deem to minister in particular with one or several groups of marginalized persons. This book in no way wants to discount these efforts. Yet racism is embedded in the history of the United States from the colonial era, and the structures that maintain it remain in place. Though the demographic reality of the United States has changed, the historical legacy of racism remains.[4]

An important goal of this book, then, is to examine how congregations deal with the impact of racism on their lives, how this learning leads to greater cultural appreciation of all groups, and how racism harms us all. This book is also predicated on the belief that racism is a profoundly *spiritual* concern and central to the proclamation of the gospel. Racism robs us of our wholeness as the body of Christ. Though churches often refer to the need for racial reconciliation today, authentic multiracial community can only be built on a foundation that recognizes the impact of centuries of racism and discrimination on people of color, and the relative and unequal impact of this legacy on white people. Further, part of the task before us, as people of faith, is to learn to look at the reality of racism and other forms of oppression with "gospel eyes."[5] The gospel of Jesus Christ is the story of the liberation of all people. Inherent in this view is the assertion that the church is intended to be a vehicle for human freedom, rather than an instrument of oppression. One of the most frequently heard forms of resistance to building multiracial community are comments that reduce antiracism training and racial justice efforts to "social issues" or exercises in "political correctness." Turning to our communities with "gospel eyes," however, demands nothing less than re-envisioning our common life through the eyes of Jesus Christ. Some of the questions that need to be asked in this regard, include: What is the connection between my attitudes and behaviors that perpetuate racism? Who are members of this congregation and who are not? What are we prepared to give up to make multiracial community a reality? What are the obstacles to our vision of multiracial community? How are the ways we hold on to a racist vision of our congregation sinful? Though often resisted as a "negative" term, "antiracism," when looked at from the perspective of "gospel eyes" is indeed a positive term. In this context, "antiracism" becomes an intentional turning away from a racist vision of community to a vision of multiracial community where one group is not dominant over another.

LEARNING AND UNLEARNING HISTORY

Integral to building multiracial community is both the learning and the *unlearning* of how our histories are a source of freedom as well as oppression to ourselves and others. The truth sets us free. One of the roots of prophetic action is history. Knowing and coming to terms with our own history and the history of our congregations and denominations are vital for those who purport to lead the church into the future. "History has its flexible side," says African American author Toni Morrison. "And each time we critique and examine it, we can deliver other information and insight that in fact changes what we already know about it." Morrison further asserts: "My point is that you are not bound by the future, and, more important, you are not bound by the past. The past can be more liberating than the future if you are willing to identify its evasions, its distortions, its lies, and unleash its secrets and truths."[6]

In his "Letter from Birmingham City Jail," Dr. Martin Luther King Jr. refers back to the earliest Christians as a source for prophetic action:

> There was a time when the church was very powerful. It was during that period when the early Christians rejoiced when they were deemed worthy to suffer for what they believed. In those days the church was not merely a thermometer that recorded the ideas and principles of popular opinion; it was a thermostat that recorded the mores of society. . . . Things are different now. The contemporary church is often a weak, ineffectual voice with an uncertain sound. It is so often the archsupporter of the status quo. Far from being disturbed by the presence

of the church, the power structure of the average community is often consoled by the church's silent and often vocal sanction of things as they are. But the judgment of God is upon the church as never before. If the church of today does not recapture the sacrificial spirit of the early church, it will lose its authentic ring, forfeit the loyalty of millions, and be dismissed as an irrelevant social club with no meaning for the twentieth century. . . .[7]

It has been forty years since these words of Dr. King, yet his challenge to the twenty-first-century church is unmistakable and his vision remains unlived. How can we as faithful people free the church, in a sense, from a history of racism and complicity to capture more fully the values of the earliest Christians? How do the identities, beliefs, ideas, and actions of persons living in the past support or resist a vision of multiracial community? How has God spoken to us, as a faith community, and how has God formed us, challenged us, nurtured us, and allowed us to change over time?

One of the first steps of building multiracial community is the telling of stories, which not only unmasks the various levels of history within a congregation but shows how the experience of an institution differs when it is told from varying perspectives. Further, our personal experience is at the root of how we experience difference, as well as how we experience God. "Telling my story is not itself theology but a basis for theology," writes Jung Young Lee. "Indeed the primary context for doing my theology. This is why one cannot do theology for another. If theology is contextual, it must certainly be at root autobiographical."[8]

My family of origin, as Polish Americans, has a distinct racial, ethnic, cultural, and class heritage. I was born and raised in a large Midwestern city, and attended primary and secondary schools there during the 1960s and 1970s. My grandparents and parents both worked in a variety of agricultural and then factory and service occupations. The reality of ethnic discrimination against Polish people—even when we comprised a large portion of the white population—combined with discrimination based on economic class, served to reinforce among the Polish Americans in my community a fierce determination to survive and to keep the culture alive. My grandparents spoke little English and were still studying for United States' citizenship at the time of their deaths. Throughout their lives, they held on to the hope that their grandchildren—because it did not happen for their children—would have access to higher education, professional advancement, and leisure pursuits. Another by-product of the discrimination my family and neighbors experienced was the growth of our own prejudices against other European-American ethnic groups, as well as a deeply ingrained racism against people of color.

It was not until I attended graduate school at an elite, predominantly white eastern college, without another Polish American in sight, that I began to notice that many of my white peers had little sense of distinctive ethnicity or culture. Conversations about ethnicity or class would evoke such responses as, "Oh, we're American," or, "I guess my great-great-great grandparents came from England." Mostly, the young adults I met just looked at me strangely for even asking the question. It had never occurred to me that it was possible for a person of European descent to be raised in the United States with little or no ethnic or cultural identification.

Though my academic success is partially due to my abilities, I am also aware that it has everything to do with my whiteness. My ability to "pass" as someone from middle-class, white "American" culture assured my acceptance in classrooms defined by the dominant culture, while my Polish American, working-class inner voice always felt like a fraud. Although I felt isolation because of my economic marginalization, I know I had personal support and access to resources that were not shared by the small number of students of color in the program. The experience taught me a lesson about the privilege of whiteness and at the same time gave me a "window" into what it might be like for those who experience racial oppression. Though I have experienced oppression and marginalization, as a white person I will never experience racism first-hand. My whiteness means that I do not have to face the unremitting racial oppression that people of color face all the time.

As an ordained minister and faculty member at a denominational seminary, I continue to ask myself how racial privilege impacts my ministry and how I can better use my institutional power to enhance the lives of all peoples. In particular, as a European American professor, I see it as part of my particular responsibility to challenge white students in a way that assists them to identify their unearned racial privilege and that offers examples of how they can use that privilege within the context of ministry. After more than twenty years of anti-racism training among many predominantly white church groups, I have seen the fear, the anxiety, and the hostility expressed when the need to address our racism is raised. European Americans raised with little cultural education or vocabulary may feel inadequate to discuss their own racial and cultural heritage or that of other persons. Discussions of racism often evoke feelings of shame and guilt in white people. Still others fear differences in intercultural communication and feel as if they "are walking on egg shells," when as European Americans they attempt intercultural dialogue. Yet the fact remains that neither white people nor people of color are *personally* responsible for racism. Racism is an oppressive system that predates our personal histories. We *are* responsible, however, for perpetuating racism and internalized oppression through our complicity and our failure to take action against them. Those of us who are European American must take responsibility for our racist attitudes and behaviors. We must develop the skills necessary for interracial dialogue. If we do not, we are guilty of neglecting our part in leading our congregations toward multiracial community.

Twenty-first-century society is global and highly mobile. Until fairly recently most American historical writing either minimized or denied racial differences. The theory of the "melting pot" envisioned that racial, ethnic, class, regional, and other cultural differences could be subsumed under the inclusive identity "American." Although the theory has proved untenable, its assumptions continue to influence the way racial differences are approached. Many European Americans are raised to believe in the well-intentioned but misinformed "melting-pot" vision of American society. They believe that racial differences are negative and that the ideal American society would not consist of discrete racial groups. All such groups would somehow become melded into one coherent whole. Recent work in multicultural studies has pointed to the limitations of this perspective, including its racist bias. As Edward W. Rodman notes:

> All this adds up to a situation in which the so-called majority in this country is really to be understood as a coalition of European ethnic groups who have dropped their ethnic identity, and have chosen to become that homogenized "American" that we call white. This in turn is then portrayed as the norm for the society, and is identified as the

melting pot. The only problem is that those who are not European cannot melt, and that the numerically average person in the world is an eighteen-year-old Asian woman.[9]

The effect of this racist perspective on whites is illustrated also by Mary Elizabeth Hobgood:

> The race system is a complex web of social institutions that devastates people of color economically, politically, and culturally. The race system, which gives whites dominance over other racialized groups, also restricts whites emotionally and damages us morally. White dominance, or white supremacy, harms people socially constructed as white in ways most whites neither see nor understand. That said, the truth is that whites gain at the expense of communities of color, which is the primary reason for the construction of whiteness and the racial system.[10]

The automatic privileges received by European Americans within United States' culture were the topic of an influential study by Peggy McIntosh entitled, "White Privilege: Unpacking the Invisible Knapsack." McIntosh argues that she was taught about racism as a phenomenon that puts others at a disadvantage, but not taught how it gave her, as a white person, personal and societal advantages. These advantages are what McIntosh calls "white privilege." McIntosh uses the metaphor of white privilege as an invisible, weightless knapsack of special provisions, maps, code books, visas, tools, and blank checks. White privilege is given to us because we are born white; we do not choose it. Similarly, white privilege is experienced as oppressive to people of color, whether we beneficiaries choose to be oppressive or not. White people are socialized, according to McIntosh, "to think of themselves as mentally neutral, normative, and average, and also ideal, so that when we work to benefit others, this is seen as work that will allow "them" to be more like "us."[11]

Most of the privileges McIntosh lists in her article are things that a European American living in the United States can and does take for granted. For instance, we can, if we wish, arrange to be in the company of our own race for most of the time. We are educated knowing that the accomplishments of our own race will be included. We can go to any shopping mall and find the music we listen to, the food we eat, and someone who can style our hair. We can extrapolate the privileges received by individual white people and extend them to congregational life. For instance, those of us who are white can enter our congregation and expect to hear the hymns that we like to sing, eat the food we like to eat, and listen to sermons relevant to the way we operate in the world. It is possible for white seminarians to have role models of their racial background outside their immediate family. Seminary classes and libraries hold up many aspects of white culture, whereas it is not yet a given that a person of color will learn anything about their own culture within a formal educational setting. The impact of white privilege on people of color is so pervasive that it is experienced even in contexts where no white people are present. As bell hooks illustrates:

> Nowadays, it has become fashionable for white and black folks alike to act like they do not have the slightest clue as to why black folks might like to separate, to be together in some corner, or neighborhood, or even at some dining table in a world where we are surrounded by whiteness. It is not a mystery. Those of us who remember living in the midst of racial apartheid know that the separate spaces, the times apart from whiteness, were for sanctuary, for re-imagining and re-membering ourselves. In the past separate space meant down time, time for recovery and renewal.

Letting go of white privilege in congregations means acknowledging that our churches are not as welcoming as we would like to believe, and perhaps too that our ministries need to be examined and reshaped if authentic multiracial community is to be a reality. Since the liberalization of immigration legislation in 1965, even relatively remote communities have increasingly diverse populations. Increasing mobility and access through international travel and electronic communication have opened the way to increased cultural diversity throughout the United States. Although there are individuals and groups within European American culture who have undeniably suffered from negative prejudice and discrimination, whiteness carries with it unearned entitlements that make the domination of institutions like the church possible. Rather than holding onto the vision of a melting pot, we are called to a new vision of a "mosaic," or "salad bowl," or "symphony." In these visions difference is considered valuable and enriching for communities. Although we, as European Americans, are born into racial privilege without a choice, what we decide to do with these advantages *is* a matter of choice.

CULTURAL COMPETENCE

European American religious leaders and congregations will be better prepared for ministry in multiracial contexts if they are challenged to become "culturally competent." The ability to recognize and respond to varying aspects of cultural difference, and to remain thus engaged for the long term, is an important prerequisite for the eradication of white racism. On the other hand, religious leaders who are people of color are also challenged to become more culturally competent as the demographic diversity of the population increases. Further, cultural competence is an integral skill for communities of color in responding to the effects of racism on their communities. Cultural competence is a *learned skill*, not an automatic part of theological education. Though it is not often incorporated into practice, research has shown that sound mental health is correlated to strong ethnic identification, and by extrapolation the same holds true for congregations.[13] One of the most rewarding aspects of community can be to learn about other racial and cultural groups. Such work provides opportunities for lasting relationships between individuals of diverse racial and ethnic backgrounds and confronts the isolation of those outside the dominant culture. Marginalized groups have a history of courage in the midst of racism that can strengthen communities of faith when recognized. Further, an inadequate understanding of how race and ethnicity work in a religious context hampers multiracial coalition building in the larger community. African Americans, Asian Americans, Hispanic Americans, American Indians, and European Americans bring distinctive cultures and contributions to the larger community.

For the purposes of establishing some common terminology throughout this book, the following definitions are operative.[14] Congregational leaders should keep in mind when sharing definitions that not all persons in any given congregation are necessarily from the United States in terms of national origin. While racial and ethnic oppression exists worldwide, how it impacts persons living in a specific context varies. For instance, racism as it is experienced in the United States is a result of a particular set of historical circumstances that may be similar, but not identical, to the oppression experienced elsewhere. Moreover, people of color who come to the United States from other countries will face racism in this context even if they are members of "the majority" in their home counties. Diversity in national origin can greatly enrich congregational discussions on race, ethnicity, and culture, but only if there is an openness to information and critique from those born in a country other than the United States.

African American or black (not of Hispanic origin)—Persons who are of African descent or who have African ancestry. Though the terms are used interchangeably, some prefer reference to geographic origins rather than skin color.

American Indian/Alaskan native—Persons who have descended from or who have ancestral connections to any of the original (indigenous) peoples of North America. In some contexts, the term *Native American* is preferred.

Anglo or Anglo-American—Pertains to English-rooted culture in the United States; refers to a language group, not an ethnic identification. Because of the fundamental nature of the English language in American culture, this term is often used to signify the mainstream or dominant culture.

Asian American/Pacific Islanders—Persons who have origins in the people of the Far East, southern Asia, or the Pacific Islands.

bigotry—An intensive and negative form of prejudice usually marked by fear, intolerance, hatred, or suspicion.

cross-cultural—The interaction, communication, or connection between people from two or more different cultures.

cultural identity—The part of each of us that relates to the cultural groups to which we belong, also referred to as social location. Individual persons, in fact, encompass multiples identities in that they relate to a variety of cultural groups, including race, ethnicity, gender, nationality, sexual identity, and so on.

culture—The body of learned beliefs, traditions, behavior patterns, communication styles, concepts, values, institutions, and standards that are commonly shared among members of a particular group. These elements are socially transmitted to individuals, and individuals are expected to conform to them.

Persons belong to a variety of cultural groups simultaneously, for example, racial cultures, ethnic cultures, religious cultures, regional cultures, and so on.

diversity—Differences among people or peoples reflected in a variety of cultural forms, included but not limited to race, ethnicity, gender, age, religion, class, and so on. Technically, to state that a group or a congregation is "diverse" does not assume that there are relationships between people across differences.

dominant culture—That which is considered mainstream American culture; used synonymously with white culture; the historic and institutionally recognized set of cultural patterns.

ethnic or ethnicity—Refers to a people who share a group identity because of common racial, national, tribal, religious, linguistic, or cultural characteristics.

European American—Persons who are of European descent or have their origins in the peoples of Europe.

genocide—The destruction of or conspiracy to destroy a group because of its cultural, racial, ethnic, national or religious identity.

Hispanic American or Latino/Latina—Persons of Spanish-speaking cultures of origin such as Mexican, Puerto Rican, Dominican, Central or South American. Latino/Latinas, or Hispanic Americans, are from a variety of racial groups. The terms *Hispanic* or *Latino* are sometimes used interchangeably; often particular locations or ethnic groups favor one of the terms.

internalized oppression—The response of a marginalized individual or group that reinforces the oppressor's view of that individual or group. Because of the systemic nature of racism and the fact that racism is primarily about social power, people of color are continually challenged by internalized racism. Similarly, women struggle with internalized sexism, or a patriarchal view of their identity.

multicultural—The coexistence of a variety of distinct cultures within a given context. Technically, the term *multiculturalism* alone does not assume that a group or a congregation is antiracist, or has worked to correct the power imbalance between whites and people of color in a given context.

oppression—The use of power by one group against another.

people of color—A collective term that includes African Americans, Asian Americans, American Indians, and Hispanic Americans. Though commonly used, the term *minorities* is a misnomer; persons within these groups are the numerical majority in the world and in parts of the United States. Though this term continues to be a source of debate, it is preferable to *non-white*, which only describes what other racial groups are *not*.

pluralism—A state where members of diverse groups maintain autonomous participation in both a common society and separate cultural groups.

power—The capacity to have control, authority, or influence over others. In the context of cultural competence and white racism awareness, social power refers to the capacity of the dominant (white) culture to have control, authority, and influence over people of color. Social power plus prejudice equals oppression.

prejudice—A pre-judgment that is directed against others before one has all the facts. Prejudice can be positive or negative.

race—A social (rather than biological) construction based on differences in skin color and facial features imposed by Europeans in North America in order to justify colonization.

racism—The systematic oppression of one race by another. In the United States, racism operates on the personal, interpersonal, institutional, and cultural levels and, as a system, differentiates between whites and people of color. Because the social systems and institutions within the United States are controlled by white people, they have the social power to make and enforce decisions and have greater access to resources. Racist attitudes and behaviors can be intentional or unintentional. A shorthand definition for racism is prejudice + social power.

stereotype—An oversimplified and usually inaccurate belief about a group that is projected onto all members of that group.

white—A political (rather than cultural) construct used to describe the racial identity of European Americans. It was first used in seventeenth-century Virginia by upper-class persons (the numerical minority) in an effort to have lower-class "whites" identify with their group rather than with blacks or indigenous persons. Previously, legal documents referred to "ethnic" identities such as English, German, Dutch, African, and so on.

Promoting multiracial community in congregations requires a commitment on all levels of institutional life. While workshops on "diversity" may assist congregations in gaining a greater knowledge of other cultures, as well as of their own, cultural competence suggests a long-term educational process as well as a systemic intervention into the life of the community. Before such work can even begin, congregational leaders themselves must be prepared to make a long-term commitment to become culturally competent. Though the support of colleagues of color is crucial in this process, the eradication of white racism is not their responsibility. White congregations and religious institutions have relied too long on people of color to take the lead concerning racism. Institutional change will occur only when whites take responsibility to end the mono-cultural bias that underlies the racism within our congregations and denominations.

Cultural competence is the outcome of engaging in a multilevel process of change in multicultural and antiracism awareness, which enables individuals and congregations to do the following:[15]

1. *Know the difference between race, ethnicity, and culture; that culture is more than race and ethnicity, and be able to apply this knowledge within theological contexts.* While the focus of this book is on racism and building multiracial community, which to a large degree remains the most divisive issue in United States society, other dimensions of culture include ethnicity, gender, geography, age, ability, social class, sexual identity, religion, and so on. We need to acknowledge that cultural differences are real. On a personal level, this means that European Americans must understand how culture shapes white identity, how whiteness dominates our culture and the

church, and how the reshaping of our identities is a life-long process. We also need to recognize the multitude of cultural differences among people of color. Here members of congregations may be assisted through exercises designed to help them get in touch with their individual cultural backgrounds, with the goal of building a multiracial experience through a process of shared pride in commonness and differences. Person-to-person sharing of stories in congregations, as well as exercises designed to elicit experiences of "belonging" and "otherness," are also helpful.

2. *Get in touch with issues of prejudice and stereotypes.* Cultural competence requires each person and each congregation to examine their own traits and to develop an understanding about how these characteristics impact relationships with persons of different cultures. When dealing with issues of race and culture, feelings of anxiety, awkwardness, fear, and discomfort are natural. Often one has a sense that discussing differences is wholly negative, or that if one lacks a multicultural vocabulary it can cause uncomfortable feelings in discussions of raising cultural differences. Biases about different racial and cultural groups are often apparent at the level of feeling rather than on a cognitive level. At this stage it is important for congregations to provide people with an opportunity to discuss the effects of racism and prejudice in their own lives. Here members of congregations may benefit from a discussion about their families of origin and what their own background has taught them about racial and cultural differences.

3. *Challenge the myth of color blindness, and be aware of the reality of color consciousness as it pertains to race and theological institutions.* People of color have suffered many injustices at the hands of white people and continue to do so within institutions. These factors of oppression are present whether the church chooses to recognize them or not. Thus, individuals and congregations concerned with gaining cultural competence need to be aware of how our racial identity informs the power relationships within our congregations. Further, it is important for European Americans to learn how to communicate accurate information on behalf of communities of color, as well as when and how it is appropriate to advocate in behalf of persons from different racial groups. Here individuals may benefit from inventories designed to evaluate their cultural skills.[16]

4. *Understand that race, ethnicity, gender, economic class, sexual identity, age, ability, religion, and so on are organizing principles for good or ill in everything they do.* It is important for those working for systemic change within churches to have a grasp of the interlocking nature of oppressions. That is, oppression, the use of power by one group against another, is expressed in many different contexts. Racism, sexism, classism, homophobia, ableism, and ageism are terms used to describe various types of oppression. All too frequently persons concerned with social inequities focus on only one or two of these "isms," often at the price of disregarding the others. *Everyone* has experienced some form of oppression, and all forms of oppression damage not only those in marginalized groups (people of color, women, disabled people, and others) but also those in the dominant culture as well. Cultural competence suggests a knowledge of the complex nature of interlocking oppressions, rather than focusing on all forms of oppression through the lens of a single issue. Here the members of congregations would benefit from case studies that examine multiple forms of oppression and that ask them to make their own decisions and name their own biases.

5. *Recognize that there are multiple centers of truth, whose legitimacy is often determined by the amount of power any given perspective may have in a particular context.* The human tendency to universalize our own experience notwithstanding, it is important to understand that what we value as the "objective" truth may not be perceived the same way by persons of different racial groups who have their own experiences of truth. For those of us who are European Americans, this means that we can never *really* know what it means to be anyone other than a white person, and that some of the skills needed are those that help us identify how to be an effective ally to people of color, given our own experiences, attributes, and limitations. Although people of color generally know more about white culture than whites know about theirs—because it is critical to their survival—they too need to develop strategies to recognize and cultivate helpful allies. Here it is important for individuals and congregations to consider questions such as: What experiences have you had in changing your perception of a person from another racial group? How did this happen? How did your relationship change with people from other racial groups? Out of this discussion where are you most challenged?

My experience of teaching and training antiracism in religious contexts has suggested to me that individuals and congregations who are introduced to the concepts of cultural competence and make a commitment to work toward multiracial community, undergo a long-term process of change. To be sure, raising the issue of racism in a congregation elicits emotional responses that range from guilt and shame to anger and despair. Yet, when faithful people are given the opportunity to examine issues related to race in an environment where both their emotional and intellectual responses are acknowledged, the possibilities for interracial understanding and change expand.[17]

If we examine the *actual* level of diversity that exists in the United States today, the critical nature of building understanding between racial groups becomes obvious, and increased cultural competence becomes an essential ingredient to our survival and participation in our own communities and the world:

- By the end of the twentieth century, five billion of the earth's six billion people are people of color.

- There are over five thousand living languages in the world; there are more bilingual than monolingual people, and more people speak English as a second language than as a first language.

- In the United States, according to FBI statistics, 40 percent of bias crimes are against blacks and 13 percent are antiwhite crimes. The highest growth in hate crimes in recent years is against Asians and homosexuals. Every hour someone commits a hate crime; every day eight blacks, three whites, three gays, three Jews, and one Latino become hate crime victims; every week a cross is burned.

- Thirty percent of African Americans and Hispanics live in poverty, compared to 12 percent of European Americans. For African Americans, unemployment is twice as high, and their paychecks are half as much as those of their white counterparts. Infant mortality in African American babies is more than double that of European Americans.

- Presently, there are over a million students in the New York City school system representing the following groups: 38 percent black, 35 percent Hispanic, 19 percent white, and 7.9 percent Asian. In some California school systems, twenty languages are represented. In the rural community of Hall County, Nebraska, with a population under 50,000 people, thirty different languages are spoken in homes.

- If recent trends continue, whites will no longer be the voting majority in several states between 2025 and 2050. By 2050, Asians, Hispanics, non-Hispanic blacks and American Indians together will account for almost half the total population of the United States.[18]

BUILDING MULTIRACIAL COMMUNITY

Building multiracial community is much more than a congregational "program." What ultimately distinguishes authentic multiracial community from congregational life rooted in diversity or multiculturalism is power analysis. Power, both personal and corporate, is necessary for persons to feel truly human. Power is integral for shaping self-identity and healthy self-esteem. "Powerlessness breeds a sense of anomie which is a major source of psychological distress among those who lack power."[19] Though organizational theories differ slightly, most suggest a five- or six-stage process of change leading to a fully inclusive multicultural organization, with full participation and shared power at the final stage. Application of several schema suggests the following stages of change leading to multiracial community:[20]

The *exclusive congregation* perpetuates the domination of one racial group over another. Such congregations intentionally exclude or segregate racial groups on all institutional levels, including decision making, policies, religious teaching, and so on. Leaders of such congregations maintain that either one race is inferior to the other or that to challenge the racism of the church would be to hinder the life of the congregation or jeopardize their own position in it.

The *passive congregation* maintains the privilege of those who have traditionally held power in the church, with the exception of a very limited number of people of color who have the right credentials and do not threaten the established order. The organizational model of this congregation resembles that of a private club. The fear in this congregation is that it will have to change to accommodate persons of other races and cultures if they join. In other words, the majority culture's history, worship, language, and other cultural forms will be lost if those outside "the club" are allowed in.

The *compliant congregation* values multiculturalism on a symbolic level, yet essentially reflects an assimilation model. That is, the congregation may welcome persons from various racial backgrounds, and it may even hire a staff member in order to identify with an incoming racial group. However, most other aspects of the church's ministry remain the same, and there is often an unconscious assumption that the incoming group should make the effort to "fit in." This model is essentially conflict avoidant and, though often nominally antiracist, has put the burden for change on the marginalized group. One fairly common manifestation of this model is to invite "ethnic" congregations to share a church facility or occasionally to participate in joint worship services. Though the invitation is usually expressed to demonstrate a desire for more cross-cultural relationships, it does not necessarily also include an invitation to share in the power and ownership of the church. Another group in this category is congregations that claim to be multicultural but will address race only from the perspective of "racial unity" in the belief that to do otherwise is contentious and divisive. The limitation of this approach is that the racism and prejudice of the members are not addressed but are suppressed for the sake of an artificial "unity" that only exists when the congregation is gathered.

An *antiracist congregation* is one that has grown in its understanding of white privilege and of racism as a barrier to multiracial community. Such churches benefit from specific antiracism training on all levels of the congregation and have developed an increasing commitment to eliminate racism in the congregation. At the same time such congregations begin to develop relationships with communities of color, as well as increasing sensitivity to the effects of other forms of oppression. An antiracist congregation can envision an alternative multiracial community, but its institutional structures continue to maintain white privilege and white culture.

A *redefining congregation* makes intentional choices to rebuild its congregational life according to antiracist analysis and identity. By this stage congregations are prepared to recognize and acknowledge: (1) that racism is inherent in all institutions; (2) that racism is instrumental in both past and current institutional contexts; (3) the need for a commitment to change; (4) the need to put mechanisms in place to facilitate change; and (5) that action is a necessary step in the process of change. Congregations engaged at this stage of the change process understand that the purpose of antiracism education and training is not only to enhance individual awareness but also to enable multiracial community. In these congregations, members acquire the pastoral support and challenge they need, while at the same time keeping the focus appropriately on sustainable community action. This type of congregation seeks to address issues and differences so that they can be processed in a healthy manner. Congregations at this stage of development undertake regular "audits" of all aspects of institutional life in order to ensure full participation of people of color. Here the congregation has transformed their means of organizing structures, policies, and practices in order to distribute power among all of the diverse groups in the congregation. Further, through their commitment to antiracist action, such congregations are intentionally accountable to communities of color and work to dismantle racism in their wider community.

A *transformed congregation* upholds a *future* vision of a new reality where racial oppression no longer sets limits on human growth or potential. A transformed congregation is a fully multicultural organization that has overcome systemic racism and all other forms of oppression. A congregation within this context would reflect the contributions and interests of diverse racial and cultural groups in its mission, ministries, and institutional structures. Here people of color are full participants in the congregation. Moreover, the boundary between the wider community and the congregation is porous; the congregation works to form alliances and networks in support of efforts to eliminate social oppression and to educate others to do the same.

RESISTANCE TO CHANGE

Often the most difficult step for individuals and congregations to take is to move beyond viewing racism solely from the perspective of personal and interpersonal attitudes and behaviors and to examine the structural (institutional and cultural) aspects of racism through power analysis. In fact, most religious institutions stop or drastically curtail antiracism efforts that move beyond personal and interpersonal awareness of racism. Comparatively few congregations have ventured into the "antiracist church" stage of the change process described here. This is partially why there are relatively few congregations engaged in building multiracial communities. Racism is ultimately only a social construction, and while personal and interpersonal change is positive for individuals, without structural change racism will be perpetuated in congregations and religious institutions, as it is in society as a whole. In other words, racism is bigger than any one of us alone. The institutionalization of racism occurs at a *structural* level when the beliefs and behaviors of the dominant culture are reinforced through social power. Social power is that which allows members of one group to maintain a system of disadvantages against another. However, the Spirit of hope suggests that if racism is a social construction, it can be *deconstructed*. Here skills in social analysis can equip congregations to see the connections between the sources of power that have historically maintained the status quo in terms of access to basic human needs and rights and the sources of power that continue to do so. Ultimately congregations seeking to build multiracial community must confront the challenge of envisioning a new way of being: a congregation where social power is shared and where one racial group does not dominate another.

One of the reasons this stage of the process of change is difficult for individuals and congregations committed to social change is that it is here personal experience meets historical context. It becomes obvious that we need to go beyond appreciation of others' music and food— as rich positive as these experiences are—and look at the way we do business. Who does a congregation serve? What values, beliefs, and cultural norms govern community life? How are the assets expended and who makes those decisions? Who is in the leadership structure of the congregation and who is not? Racism exists in contexts that are, technically, diverse and multicultural. It is quite common for congregations to include persons of different races in a congregation and not to address who has the power to dominate and who does not. What is learned as history is not in fact objective truth, but is shaped by the dominant culture. What are respected religious beliefs and traditions for some are the source of degradation and oppression for others in the same congregation.

There are clearly many implications for European American congregational leaders involved in the change process. As members of the dominant culture, we are often reluctant and ill-equipped to give up power, and our forays into "sharing" power often remain within our own context, where we comfortably control the outcome. After all, white privilege often remains invisible to those who benefit from it. If European Americans control the agenda in congregations, what impact does this have on people of color? Or on the white members of the congregation? How do white clergy, trained in predominantly white theological institutions, become equipped to minister in multiracial congregations? How do white ministers educated within the limitations of white experience respond to the changing communities they will encounter in their professions? How does the way we have historically defined our congregations oppress those who are of different races and cultures? And lastly, how can we use our social power for good within congregations, as well as within denominations and other communities of faith? The reality of internalized oppression is also integral to the change process and is often ignored in discussions on racism, just as interracial discussions of racism are often avoided. However, without an analysis of the learned behaviors of people of color that also perpetuate oppression, these behaviors can continually be used by predominantly white congregations as a justification for racism.

WHERE DO WE BEGIN?

In his book *The Color of Faith: Building Community in Multiracial Society,* Fumitaka Matsuoka offers advice to people of faith compelled to build multiracial communities: "The starting point is not to find ways of uniting people divided by fear and violence, but to recognize, celebrate, and learn from God's gift of one creation embodied in varied cultures, languages, religions and races. It is to restore moral integrity in the midst of the culture of decay by restoring freedom and dignity to the captives we held."[21]

The congregations featured in this book continue to work toward their own transformation as multiracial communities. No two congregations have shared the same history or the same struggles. The congregations selected for this book were chosen not because they have all the answers, but because they have consciously chosen to engage in the long-term process of building multiracial community.

They all are engaged in the call to a life of rich diversity, yet they continue to question, to struggle, to evaluate this vision.

Though each congregation here exists in its own context and has a different approach to building multiracial community, their stories suggest several common elements that are supportive for those interested in introducing cultural competence and antiracism in communities of faith:

- Build on an analysis of power and privilege.

- Continually tie together action and reflection.

- Create a "democratic" place for the healthy expression of feelings.

- Reserve time for cultural sharing and discovery.

- Discourage discussion that suggests polarities, for example, "good people and bad people."

- Encourage the study of history.

- Show how oppression harms everyone.

- Resist attempts to define one objective reality.

- Be gentle but firm in the face of resistance.

- Make connections between a vision of multiracial community, congregational life, and the practice of faith.

Finally, all the congregations featured here uphold and celebrate the joys and the struggles of their journey toward multiracial community through their corporate worship. Choosing to stand against racism requires a great deal of spiritual stamina. An enriching spiritual life is perhaps the greatest support for the challenges faced by those who choose to open up their lives in this way. A great variety of people can become a community if they heed the Spirit, which constantly calls for us to expand our boundaries. The story of Pentecost suggests that in our various cultural identities and through our linguistic differences we can understand each other. It is ultimately our resistance to the Spirit that divides us as peoples—not race, or ethnicity, or religion, or nationality. May we all continue in the hope that the church will call us into multiracial community so that we may become "a house of prayer for all peoples."

1

The God of Difference

St. Matthew's and St. Paul's
Delray Beach, Florida

Our humanity is caught up in that of all others. We are human because
we belong. We are made for community, for togetherness, for family, to
exist in a delicate network of interdependence. Truly, "it is not good for
man to be alone [Genesis 2:18]," for no one can be human alone. We
are sisters and brothers of one another whether we like it or not and
each one of us is a precious individual. It does not depend on things
such as ethnicity, gender, political, social, economic or educational sta-
tus—which are all extrinsic. Each person is not just to be respected but
to be revered as one created in God's image.

—Desmond Mpilo Tutu[1]

"THE EVIL OF RACISM IS AN EVIL THAT WE MUST ROOT OUT OF
this church and out of this community." Calls to repentance and self-
examination are common expressions in Lenten sermons, but it is
doubtful that many people at St. Paul's Church in Delray Beach,
Florida, expected to hear their rector, William "Chip" Stokes, focus
these calls so directly and forcefully on the issue of racism on the First
Sunday of Lent in March 2001. However, when opposition arose to
calling an African American seminarian, Keith Johnson, as the congregation's curate, Stokes found that the racism he heard within that
opposition left him with little choice but to speak these words.

Articulating the matter as a "battle of good and evil" within the
hearts, minds, and souls of the people of St. Paul's, Stokes believed
that the spiritual health of the community was at stake. His sermon

27

addressed what he saw as the spiritual challenges of white racism and the need for a call to justice within the congregation.[2]

> I did not set out to find a black candidate. . . . This candidate was placed before us to consider. . . . I believe God was at work in this . . . that God wanted to place this particular candidate in front of us at this particular time in our church's life.
>
> Racism is evil. . . . It is a great sin and scar on the soul of America and the soul of our church. . . . I understand that many of you are from a generation that was raised with these notions of the inferiority of the races and the need to keep them separate. But I have to tell you, these notions are wrong, morally wrong, spiritually wrong. . . . They are an offense against God and his church. . . . They have no place in our souls. . . . They have no place in our church.
>
> The search committee is doing its work. It is considering this candidate and it is considering other candidates, but I want to be clear. . . . I will not allow questions of this candidate's race or his interracial marriage to be considered as negative factors in this consideration by the search committee or by the vestry. To allow this to occur would be to succumb to Satan, the adversary. . . . It would be to succumb to evil . . . and the evil of racism is an evil that we must root out of this church and out of this community. . . . It is a part of our baptismal commitment. . . . It is a part of our Christian calling.

Despite receiving a standing ovation from the congregation for preaching this sermon, Chip Stokes admits that personally and spiritually the experiences in St. Paul's concerning racism have brought him the "most painful Lent and the most powerful Easter" he has ever known. "I just prayed, 'Where's the power? How do I reach it?'" he says.[3] Though some members of St. Paul's feel that Chip Stokes has gone overboard in keeping the issue of racism before the congregation, they also report that most in the congregation are positive about the results. St. Paul's is a congregation that has confronted its own racism and has been profoundly changed. St. Paul's and its partner congregation, St. Matthew's, have forged a joyful and challenging partnership with a commitment to building a multiracial community.

A TOWN OF "TWO CITIES"

In struggling through a difficult history of racism marked by the failure to open their hearts to one another, the parishioners of St.

Matthew's and St. Paul's, two historic Episcopal churches located four blocks apart in the small resort town of Delray Beach, Florida, have begun the reconciling work described by Archbishop Desmond Tutu. The emergent partnership of these two parishes and their leadership in racial dialogues in the community represent one way in which congregations can begin to see the image of God in each other and become catalysts for racial justice.

Located fifty miles north of Miami, Delray Beach is a town of "two cities"; its residents live in neighborhoods divided by both race and class. The African American and Haitian residents live on the west side of town, and the European American residents live on the east side. St. Matthew's has historically been an African Caribbean congregation, while St. Paul's has served primarily white Episcopalians. Although the ministries of the two congregations are intertwined, they differ significantly in terms of membership and resources.

Two Episcopal Congregations in Delray Beach, Florida (2002)		
	St. Matthew's	St. Paul's
Membership	115	1,100
Average Sunday worship attendance	78	345
Sunday worship services	1 service (10:00 A.M.)	3 services (7:45, 9:00, and 11:15 A.M.)
Racial/ethnic makeup of congregations	African American Caribbean American Bahamian	Predominantly white
Total budget	$118,400	$1,091,570

St. Matthew's Episcopal Church

A family-size congregation, St. Matthew's takes pride in its catholic liturgy and lovingly maintained small church building and parish hall.

St. Matthew's choir and stunning soloists sing a diverse selection of music from the Episcopal hymnals and from the African American tradition. Music is central to the spirit of celebration in St. Matthew's liturgy, which also features incense, processions, and special blessings for birthdays and anniversaries. The family feeling of the congregation is further enhanced as members share information on events such as graduations and hospitalizations during the announcements. St. Matthew's shares in a rotating Tuesday-morning Bible study with St. Paul's and sponsors service and devotional groups for men and women. Integral to St. Matthew's vision statement is "love and compassion for all of God's children, cultural richness and flavor, music and song, spirit and faith. . . ."

The pride that the members of St. Matthew's feel about their church is palpable on a Sunday morning. Yet, as is the case with many small and struggling congregations, money is tight and the leaders are tired. The ancestral ties within this congregation are strong, yet there remains a continuing concern about the need for new members, better stewardship, and more leaders. Some current leaders have numerous responsibilities and in the past have had to do hours of work at the church during the week with little pastoral care or spiritual sustenance for themselves. The leaders of St. Matthew's are firmly committed to the distinct identity and mission of the congregation, but the church benefits from outside resources offered in a spirit of partnership.

St. Paul's Episcopal Church

Less than a quarter mile away is St. Paul's, which was founded in 1898 when Sunday school classes for the Episcopal Church were begun in a local schoolhouse. Though the church is located on what has been described as the "racial fault line" of the town, the congregation made the decision to remain at its present location when other Delray Beach congregations were moving to the suburbs. As a thriving corporate parish, St. Paul's sponsors a wide range of programs for its members and for the greater community. The mission of St. Paul's "is to be a steadfast source of God's love, faith, grace, joy and inspiration through worship, fellowship, education, and compassion for others." By the year 2006 the parish aims to be a "spiritual community leader providing for personal faith development with doors open to all, a champion of justice and diversity, and a loving teacher of God's Word in the Anglican tradition based on the Baptismal Covenant and Christ's Summary of the Law. . . ."

In addition to a thrift shop, St. Paul's operates a day school for pre-school children regardless of religious affiliation and has recently renovated space for its youth and children's programs. Education for all ages is an important part of the life of St. Paul's, as are prayer and service groups for women. Besides the weekly Bible study with St. Matthew's, there are classes for newcomers, confirmands, special Advent and Lenten programs, Parent Effectiveness Training, walking the labyrinth, icon painting, and poetry. The programs for children and youth formation offer a variety of opportunities for nursery-age children through high school, including a pilgrimage to Canterbury Cathedral. Laypersons are active in many aspects of the liturgical life of the congregation, and there is an extensive music program with a monthly concert series. The laity at St. Paul's are also integral to pastoral care through Stephen Ministry, lay eucharistic ministry, and the transportation committee. The mission and outreach committee coordinates the parish's participation in a soup kitchen on a regular basis, as well as various walks and outreach projects.

Another dimension of St. Paul's work in the Delray Beach community is an burgeoning after-school program for twenty Haitian American children and adolescents. The streets immediately surrounding St. Paul's house a significant population of Haitian Americans. Given the history of conflicts between Bahamians—the predominant ethnic group at St. Matthew's—and Haitians, the Haitian Americans did not gravitate to St. Matthew's even though it is a black congregation. St. Paul's, on the other hand, has continued to provide support for the Haitian community, and gradually the young people have become members of the congregation. Though initially some members of St. Paul's experienced difficulty with inviting children and youth to worship services without their parents in attendance, the congregation has worked to overcome the differences in child-rearing styles between the generations and the cultures. Since many of the children have working parents, the parish provides a real service to Haitian families. Janet Aguhob, St. Paul's parish administrative assistant, explains, "They felt safe and comfortable here." Aguhob, a Filipino American, feels that she is in a unique position to see several sides of racial issues within the congregation. "Maybe that's why God put me here," she says.[4]

Ministry with the Haitian Community

In 1998, Evans Delva, a Haitian American youth who was then thirteen years old, crossed the street from his home and attended worship at St. Paul's. In the weeks that followed, Evans's sister and her friends also began to attend the church to pray and to learn how to read the Bible. "I liked coming to church," said Delva. "The people were nice to me." Soon Chip Stokes realized that the congregation could be more helpful to the children of the Haitian community surrounding St. Paul's through an organized effort, and he instituted a formal after-school program. The vestry granted $25,000 for the project, and St. Paul's sought additional funding through grants. Two part-time teachers were hired for daily shifts from 2:30 to 7:00 P.M. shifts. Daily sessions for the twenty young people ages 2 through 16 include tutoring and an afternoon meal. "God put this child in front of us," said Chip Stokes in reference to that first visit of Evans Delva. Now many of the children from the after-school program continue to attend St. Paul's on Sunday and are often part of the visitors from the parish to worship services at St. Matthew's.

Source: Linda Reeves, "Act of Faith: A Delray Teen's Interest in the Church Sparks a Growing After School Program," *Sun-Sentinel Community News*, Delray Beach Section (March 16, 2001), 6.

Though St. Matthew's and St. Paul's worked together occasionally on educational programs, they largely performed separate ministries from their inception. A few members of each congregation met each other through participation in a community choir, Cursillo, and an adult education program of the Episcopal Church called Education For Mission (EFM). Tim Kilpatrick, junior warden at St. Paul's, who had met parishioners from St. Matthew's through Cursillo and EFM, noted that earlier there had been some interest among the laity of both congregations in sharing resources and sponsoring joint activities but believes that the enthusiasm was not shared by some leaders who wished to maintain their individual ministries and congregations.

The community of Delray Beach, Florida, in which both congregations are located, is at the southern end of Palm Beach County, directly on the Atlantic Ocean. Voted an All-America City by the National Civic League in 1993 and again in 2001, Delray Beach was first settled as an agricultural community in 1895. More than 90 percent of the 15.37 square miles of land that comprises Delray Beach has been developed. Retail trade and service industries are the largest employers, comprising over 67 percent of the employment base. Property values have skyrocketed since 1994, yet over 32 percent of the households in Delray Beach have an income under $25,000.[5] The city operates under a commission-manager form of government, and has nineteen active advisory boards and committees. Delray Beach has over ninety congregations of different denominations. Within the Episcopal Church, St. Matthew's and St. Paul's are part of the Episcopal Diocese of Southeast Florida, which encompasses seven counties in the southeastern portion of the state and includes over eighty-five congregations.

Delray Beach, Florida	
Settled	1895
Incorporated	1911
Population (1920)	1,015
Population (2000)	60,645
Population makeup (2002)	
White	66.5%
Black/African American	26.6%
Asian	1.1%
American Indian	0.2%
Native Hawaiian	0.1%
Two or more races	4.0%
Median age	46.2 years
Fastest growing population	0-14 years
Area (square miles)	15.37

Source: Planning & Zoning Department of the City of Delray Beach, Florida, and the U.S. Census Bureau (2000).

In a number of ways, Delray Beach is a town of contrasts. If one were to walk or drive primarily through the downtown area or neighborhoods with newer housing, the town would appear to be prosperous and bustling. Boutiques, restaurants, and banks line much of the

well-manicured commercial district. Yet, in some of the neighborhoods near St. Matthew's and St. Paul's, the grinding poverty of many
of the people of color in the community is evident, and it is obvious
that these residents do not share in the resources of other areas of the
city. St. Paul's is located on South Swinton Avenue, which lies south of
Atlantic Avenue, an area of significant redevelopment. Additional
redevelopment that is planned for areas surrounding both St. Paul's
and St. Matthew's has raised concerns about the effects of gentrifica-
tion on the people of the neighborhood, most of whom have limited
financial resources and who are people of color.

COMMUNITY DIALOGUE ON RACISM, JUSTICE, AND RECONCILIATION

The partnership between St. Matthew's and St. Paul's grew slowly
around social and educational activities and without immediate plans
for a formal team ministry. William "Chip" Stokes, the primary
visionary of the team ministry between the two congregations arrived
as rector of St. Paul's in January 1999, at a time when the congregation was aging and accumulating a growing deficit—the annual budget of $546,000 included a deficit of $56,000. Chip Stokes describes
St. Paul's at the time of his arrival as a "white, privileged, aging church
in a black community." Aware of the potential for partnership
between St. Paul's and St. Matthew's soon after his arrival in Delray
Beach, Stokes nonetheless saw the importance of providing for the
pastoral needs of the members of St. Paul's before instituting change.
"I felt called to the context," he says, "and I felt that it was important
to make clear to the people here that I was going to be with them. It
is important to be clear about who you are."

   In the fall of 1999, Chip Stokes and Thomas Shepherd, the rector
of St. Matthew's Church initiated a "St.Matthew's–St.Paul's Community Dialogue on Racism, Justice and Reconciliation" to address the
issues of racism in Delray Beach.[6] (The Episcopal Diocese of Southeast
Florida had sponsored a similar dialogue for congregations the previous year.) The dialogue's mission was to examine and to respond to
the call of both St. Paul's and St. Matthew's to bring racial reconciliation to their community.

The elected officials and business and community leaders who met once a month for the community dialogue sponsored by St. Matthew's and St. Paul's spent a great deal of time during early sessions telling their personal stories, which opened doors to deeper dialogue.[7] Eventually the group addressed particular issues of concern within the community; some brought news articles to the sessions for distribution and conversation. In June 2000 the city dialogue sponsored a retreat that hosted parishioners from both congregations, community leaders, and representatives from local and county government, to engage in discussions on racial reconciliation in their community.

The ten participants in the community dialogue, some of whom lived in white neighborhoods, heard about incidents in Delray Beach where black residents experienced racism. Black residents had long expressed their frustrations that city managers seldom provided their neighborhoods with the same benefits as the mostly white downtown and beachfront areas. The Haitian community, estimated at approximately one-quarter of the Delray Beach population, lacked representation in the city government. Though few denied that racism existed in Delray Beach, the subject had not been discussed openly with a representative group of participants. Further, the church-based dialogues opened communication between white officials and people of color and began to forge relationships to seek the common good. Among other benefits, the group worked together to obtain a grant to sponsor workshops on improving race relations.[8]

Chip Stokes hopes to continue hosting groups for the community dialogue. Mary McCarty, who is the chair of the Republican Party for Palm Beach County, saw in the community dialogue an opportunity to "refrain from the too obvious point of view, and listen to a variety of opinions." Through the process of dialogue, Commissioner Jeff Perlman saw "people pushing to make the right decisions." Rosalind Murray, an African American woman who is on the staff of the Delray Beach Community Redevelopment Agency (CRA), says that she was surprised about the spiritual depth of the group, and that factor helped her to become less skeptical of white politicians. "I saw and heard these people talk about their pain and rejection and their struggles to balance the public self and what's in their heart, " she says. "If you can change this place," says Murray, "then there is hope for other people. I did see people changed; I did see people transformed."[9]

A Model for Dialogue

The model for the St. Matthew's–St. Paul's community dialogue was drawn from *The National Dialogues on Anti-Racism* developed through the Episcopal Church. First published in 1996, and revised in 1999 and 2003, the dialogue process was developed to respond to concerns about racial justice in local contexts and has been adapted both within and beyond the Episcopal Church by congregations, regional church governing bodies, and community groups. The dialogue is intended to lead groups through a five-level change process that begins with diversity awareness and concludes with examining institutional racism. Generally, the five levels of the change process correlate to the following frameworks:[10]

1. Appreciating Diversity—Deconstruction. This first level of the process explores the history and contributions of different races and cultures. The goal is to appreciate and value racial and cultural differences. At this level of the process in the Delray Beach dialogue, the participants from the different congregations, community organizations, and government were given ample opportunity not only to share their own stories and encounters with difference but also to hear the stories of other participants. At this level of the process participants learn to recognize difference as valid and move to trust and value difference as a positive dimension of human society. "People are equal but not the same." Here participants also come to identify the various cultural groups in which they participate and how diversity impacts their lives. The key to this level in the change process is deconstruction. That is, participants must first unlearn the misinformation they have absorbed that reinforces bias and prejudice. In order for deconstruction to occur, false assumptions need to be exposed as do the realities of oppression that people of color have endured. Genuine appreciation of diversity can be accomplished only in relationship with people from other racial, ethnic, and/or cultural groups. The purpose of this level of the process is to provide an opportunity for people to begin to form relationships across the human boundaries that have keep them apart. Here there may be resistance and conflict on the part of participants of the dominant culture—in racial and ethnic terms, white culture—to the influence of other cultures.

2. Prejudice Reduction—Behavior Analysis. This level of the process examines the nature and consequences of prejudice and stereotyping. The goal is for individuals to move toward reducing their prejudicial attitudes and behaviors. Participants enter this level of the change process with some cultural sensitivity and appreciation of diversity, as well as with some awareness of the nature of prejudice. It is at this level that participants are first able to distinguish between "appreciating diversity" and "racial justice," because it is the behaviors that justify prejudice and reinforce white privilege that support the perpetuation of racism. Here in the midst of a supportive environment participants are asked to examine their prejudices in an effort to change oppressive attitudes and behaviors. At this stage for Delray Beach, as well as other communities, participants encounter, many for the first time, the differences in perception across racial boundaries. They also often struggle with the reality that while one does not *intend* to be racist, the *impact* of an action, attitude, or behavior is experienced as racist. The last step—one of the most difficult in the change process—challenges participants to go beyond identifying the negative and construct a reality where European Americans are no longer a racially privileged group. It is at this level where many educational efforts directed toward racial justice stop and never enter into the realm of power analysis.

3. Power Analysis—Social Constructivism. This level examines how people are socialized into racism and calls for visioning antiracist structures. The goal is for participants to recognize the power shifts necessary for an antiracist reality to exist. Here it is particularly important to ensure, as did the organizers of the community dialogue in Delray Beach, that the people within a community who actually have the power and resources to effect change are participants in the process. This third step in the change process moves participants beyond the realm of interpersonal behaviors and beliefs and introduces them to power analysis. Given that racism is a social construct, it is imperative for participants to realize that while interpersonal change is positive, without structural change racism will continue to be perpetuated within our (religious) institutions and in society as a whole. Here it is emphasized that institutional racism occurs on the structural level, where the beliefs and behaviors of the dominant culture are reinforced through social power. Ultimately, participants need to identify those social structures within their own context that need to be challenged in order to impact racism.

The third level of the change process is often the most difficult for individuals and groups committed to social change; participants are challenged with the reality that what they learned as objective history is in fact racist and has been shaped by the dominant culture. What are considered respected beliefs and traditions for some are the sources of degradation and oppression for others in the same context. How does the way white denominations historically define our congregations oppress those of different races and cultures? How do white clergy and laity in changing contexts respond to the community? And lastly, how can we use our social power for good within the church and the community? One indication that a group has integrated the work of the first three levels of the change process is their ability to envision an alternative to the status quo: What would our congregation or community look like without racism? Or in the case of the community dialogue discussed here, what would Delray Beach without racism look like?

4. Visioning—Anti-Oppression. This fourth level in the change process examines the interrelationships between various forms of oppression and challenges participants to change oppressive systems. While envisioning a reality without racism in church or community can give participants the opportunity to utilize skills in power analysis, the experience often brings with it a degree of fear. It can be much more difficult to envision a positive experience without racism than to imagine a situation where existing social roles are simply reversed. Bigotry and racism are fueled by the fear of those in the dominant culture that as white people become a statistical minority they may lose social power and invite the kind of oppression that has been perpetrated on people of color for centuries. The heart of the question really is: What would racial justice look like, and how might we overcome our history of violence and oppression? In the case of a community such as Delray Beach, this stage of the process is an opportunity for those who are leaders in the town and in congregations to sit down together and look at how they, at times inadvertently, perpetuate oppression.

The goal of level 4 is to look at the interrelationship of the numerous forms of oppression. Level 4 of the change process instructs members of the dominant culture on how they perpetuate racism and people of color on how they are complicit with racism in the form of internalized oppression. The reality of internalized racism among people of color is often ignored in discussions of racism, just as interracial discussion on racism is often avoided. Yet without an analysis of learned behaviors that perpetuate racism, these behaviors can continually be used by the dominant culture as a justification for racism. Participants who have reached this level of understanding are equipped to envision a new reality where racism no longer sets limit on human potential.

5. Reconstruction—Institutional Racism. This final level of the change process calls for people to ask questions of their institutions and to change racist structures. Who is included or excluded? Who holds power and who does not? This stage is focused on the implementation of a new vision in concrete terms. Participants realize that racism is inherent in our institutions and that to facilitate change action is necessary. Focusing on sustainable action, participants at this level of the change process acquire the personal support they need to work toward a true multiracial community.[11] For the Delray Beach community dialogue, this stage entailed the construction of a plan of action.

A SHARED MINISTRY

A pivotal opportunity for the partnership of the two congregations occurred in the fall of 1999 after Thomas Shepherd, the rector of St. Matthew's, resigned to take a position in Kansas City. At this time the Episcopal Diocese of Southeast Florida requested that a shared ministry committee comprised of members from both St. Matthew's and St. Paul's be formed. The work of the shared ministry committee was to look for ways to build bridges between the two congregations and to explore ways in which they could combine resources and work together in the community.

The shared ministry committee met for more than a year and developed a number of ways in which members of both congregations could begin to come together to get to know each other better. In addition to a calendar of regular exchange Sundays, the committee proposed additional ways that the European American and African American Episcopalians could join together and represent their community as members of the same denomination. Members from both congregations walked together in the Delray Beach holiday parade under the banner "St. Matthew's and St. Paul's—The Episcopal Churches of Delray Beach." In February 2001 the shared ministry committee hosted a Mardi Gras picnic attended by approximately seventy-five people from both congregations. Member of both parishes marched for the second time in the Martin Luther King Jr. Day Walk in Delray Beach in January 2002. At the Martin Luther King Jr. Community Church Service sponsored by Christ Missionary Baptist Church that same afternoon, St. Paul's clergy and laity were the only white participants from the community.

Though the shared ministry committee had some noteworthy successes, the level of participation from both congregations in the activities was not great, and there was some concern about how the two congregations might share in ministries on a deeper level. A turning point in the development of the relationship between St. Matthew's and St. Paul's came in October 2000 when a team of consultants from the Alban Institute was retained by the Episcopal Diocese of Southeast Florida and the two congregations to determine the future of the shared ministry project. The Alban Institute team included Jacqueline J. Lewis, an African American woman, and Edward W. White, a European American man, as consultants to the project. After meeting extensively with representatives of both parishes during site visits, and after examining data concerning their hopes, fears, and expectations of the partnership, the team advised that the first level of work involved strengthening the congregation of St. Matthew's and assisting them in identifying with more clarity their hopes for the future of their congregation.

The consultants returned to Delray Beach to work with the vestry of St. Matthew's over a weekend in December 2000 to determine some of the issues and concerns of the congregation and the implications for the future of a shared ministry with St. Paul's. The congregation's leaders were concerned about the impact of the congregation's size on their finances, and in particular, on their ability to finance a full-time rector's salary. There had also been some informal discussions between leaders at both congregations about the possibility of St. Paul's assisting St. Matthew's with funding for a full-time rector, perhaps as a grant, with decreasing payments over a period of years until St. Matthew's would eventually absorb the whole cost of the salary.

Though they were interested in shared ministry with St. Paul's, leaders at St. Matthew's wanted to maintain the autonomy of their congregation. "I felt this was a chance; we can't let this chance [for funding a full-time rector] go by us," says Douglas Williams, a member of St. Matthew's for over thirty years. Edie Quinn, then treasurer at Matthew's, believed the partnership was a positive idea because, "both sides didn't want to leave their nest." Mike Brennan, a chemist originally from the Bahamas on St. Matthew's vestry, believes that the essence of the partnership lies in relationships and change: "It is easier to set up a program," he says. "But to get to the core of what we are supposed to be about—response to the gospel—that is change and change is hard. Quantum physics and spiritual growth are very similar."

Ed White says that throughout the consultation with the shared ministry committee, St. Matthew's leaders were clear that they did not want a merger of the two congregations on any level. They were both actively concerned about stewardship and ambivalent about potential growth. St. Matthew's was particularly weak in terms of organizational structures: "If they want to grow they will have to face it," he says. Consultant Jacqui Lewis concurs with these observations on St. Matthew's and adds several questions of her own relating to race and class. "How can they expand their identity to include others in the diaspora?" "How are they addressing the race and class differences between themselves and the people at St. Paul's?" Throughout the consultation, Lewis was impressed with the energy and the gifts brought forward by both congregations, and urged them "to look at ways to use their gifts to create a new, shared culture."

Both consultants agreed that important developmental areas for St. Matthew's include enhancement of ministries with children and youth, growth to include two Sunday services (and thus need for a full-time clergy person), and with St. Paul's a joint partnership in community housing and economic development. Moreover, both consultants stressed the need for St. Matthew's leaders to "speak the truth in love," rather than to value harmony at all costs, in an effort to gain genuine community among themselves and with leaders at St. Paul's.

While the shared ministry committee examined the partnership between the two congregations, St. Paul's had begun its own ambitious strategic planning process. The goal was to include every area of St. Paul's common life in a process of collaborative thinking and decision making concerned with how the congregation could increase its service, stature, and financial health in the coming five-year period. The areas explored were expansive, including organizational, physical plant, faith issues, and communications. Internally, St. Paul's exhibited the attitudes and behavior of a pastoral-sized church when they were actually a corporate or resource-sized church. The effectiveness of committee leadership and structures needed to be enhanced, and internal and external communications needed to be reconfigured. Physically, the congregation sought major physical improvements in order to expand ministries with children and youth and in the community. Overall, leaders at St. Paul's were concerned that the congregation needed to move from a vision of the church as "an institution" to a vision of the congregation as the church in the world, from maintenance to mission, and from membership to discipleship.[12]

As the expanding ministries of St. Paul's suggested the need for additional clergy staff, the congregation at the same time began a search for a curate and also a strategic planning process. As a way to honor and recognize the work of their shared ministry committee, they included a member from St. Matthew's on the search committee from the beginning of the process. After over a year without a satisfactory ordained candidate, the search was suspended in the spring of 2000 and the funding was used to create two new positions at St. Paul's to respond to the congregation's need for staff in two key areas—a full-time lay pastoral assistant and a full-time director of children and youth ministries.

Despite the addition of two professional lay staff, the vestry of St. Paul's continued to feel strongly that their rector needed clergy assistance, and the search committee was reactivated for that purpose in December 2000. Douglas Williams from St. Matthew's was again on this search committee; the members from St. Paul's represented a range of age groups and a variety of interests. One person that came to their attention was Keith Johnson, a candidate for ordination in the Diocese of Southeast Florida in his last year of seminary. Johnson was invited to visit St. Paul's for a series of interviews with the search committee, staff, and vestry in January 2001.

Though Keith Johnson was considered by many in the parish to be an excellent candidate for the position, a vocal minority of parishioners, some in vestry leadership positions, opposed his election. Some long-standing members of St. Paul's believed that calling Johnson would divide the parish; others felt that his presence on the staff would be a financial drain on the congregation. As often happens in predominantly white congregations who take a stand for racial justice, several people, some of whom were significant financial contributors, left the congregation. Chip Stokes was personally attacked and was told by one member of the congregation that he should be ashamed of himself for considering Johnson a candidate for the position. Still others believed that all Stokes's recent "good work" would be undone. Though many on the search committee and vestry believed that Johnson should be called as the curate, others believed that the church should interview at least one other candidate. At least four other candidates were considered. Perhaps the most vehement personal attacks were directed at Keith Johnson's interracial marriage: his wife, Virginia Johnson is white. Still others at St. Paul's had difficulty accepting the Johnson's disabled child. One lay eucharistic minister at St. Paul's remembers seeing some members of the congregation cringe after receiving the chalice following a black person.

Connie Impert, an eighty-six-year-old white woman who had never seen a black person until she was a teenager in Evanston, Illinois, was a member of St. Paul's vestry and the search committee that called Keith Johnson, She sees the events at the parish as a "catalyst" and believes that the partnership between the two parishes "does a lot for everybody, even though a few people will never give up what they believe." Sherry Fleming, a white member of St. Paul's strategic planning committee, whose grandmother started one of the first black kindergartens in the country, believes that overall "people were ready for the changes." Bonnie Davis, a member of St. Paul's vestry and the search committee that called Keith Johnson, is a Sunday school teacher who has experienced some conflicts in the parish concerning the shared ministry with St. Matthew's, as well as over the Haitian American children who attend services. Yet she remains optimistic: "If you give people a safe place to work it out—an opportunity to grow— then it will happen."

Though aware of the opposition of some of the people at St. Paul's, Keith Johnson continued to feel called to ministry there. The potential for innovative and creative work in the community and in the congregation appealed to him more than other options." I liked the idea of working in a living laboratory," he says. "I am not just interested in changing laws, but changing hearts and minds." Though a few people walked out of his sermon at St. Paul's during the interviewing process, Johnson maintains that most of the congregation were welcoming. "I can't help you with your perceptions, but I'm not going to hate you for them," Johnson told the congregation. "I am just going to show you the person I am. God loves us all regardless."[13]

THE CLERGY TEAM MINISTRY

In June 2001, Keith Johnson was ordained a transitional deacon at his home parish in Key West and the following week moved to Delray Beach. Convinced that "God may be calling St. Matthew's and St. Paul's to explore a whole new life and ministry together," Chip Stokes discerned that confluence of various factors—the shared ministry relationship between St. Matthew's and St. Paul's already in process, the absence of a rector at St. Matthew's, and the protracted search for a curate at St. Paul's, as well as Keith Johnson's obvious ministerial gifts—presented an immense opportunity for both congregations, "a kairos moment." He was encouraged by Edie Quinn, a lifelong member of St. Matthew's, who had read Johnson's resume and told Chip Stokes that if St. Paul's didn't want him, St. Matthew's did. "His resume didn't say if he were black or white," says Quinn, "but I knew he belonged here."[14]

Chip Stokes subsequently drafted a proposal to create a clergy team ministry for St. Matthew's and St. Paul's. The proposal was for the clergy staff only and did not affect the autonomy, independence, or canonical status of either congregation. Besides Stokes and Johnson, original members of the clergy team included another assistant at St.

Paul's and Mary Beth Wells, a psychotherapist who served as St. Paul's lay pastoral minister until her ordination as a deacon in May 2002. Wells saw the depth of the spiritual issues facing St. Paul's at the time: "I felt we needed to give it a try and give it time. It would be sinful not to do this—not to go forward in this day and age."

As senior rector in the clergy team, Chip Stokes is the designated team leader and is largely responsible for mentoring the clergy team. All members of the clergy team share responsibility for the administrative and pastoral oversight of the churches and rotate worship and preaching responsibilities in both congregations for weekday and Sunday services. The clergy team ministry of St. Matthew's and St. Paul's is not technically a yoked congregation; rather, each retains its historical identity and legal status, while each benefits from the other's distinct gifts, traditions, and resources. The parish calendar on St. Paul's Web site now includes the services and events of both congregations. Chris Herin, a member of St. Paul's vestry and the search committee, says that while there is still some concern when members of St. Matthew's need to leave St. Paul's for their own Sunday worship service, overall "we have creative leaders who can develop the relationship further." As Chip Stokes wrote announcing the formation of the new ministry:

> The formation of the clergy team ministry affords the people of both St. Matthew's and St. Paul's the opportunity to discover that they are the mother and father, sisters and brothers of one another in Christ. Formation of the clergy team will not solve the problems of race that affect our nation, our community, our communion or even our two churches. It does, however, present an opportunity for the people of both parishes to work seriously at reconciliation in their corporate life as the Church and as members of the community of Delray Beach.[15]

The Rt. Rev. Leo Frade, bishop of the Episcopal Diocese of Southeast Florida, is also supportive of the arrangement and encourages creative ideas that address the issues facing congregations: "One of the most [racially] discriminating places left in this country is our churches," says Bishop Frade. "Our schools, our city halls, our businesses are integrated because the government tells us we must, but nobody tells the churches anything. So you go to church and you see everybody of one kind." Frade believes that broader acceptance of multiracial community will come as more people of color move into leadership positions. Some congregations "are willing for them [people of color] to show up in the pews but not share the power," says Frade. "Let's start making room for our new people to have access to decision making. The only solution is to put our pride aside and work together. We must be willing to wash the feet of anybody in the love of Christ."[16]

Once the proposal for the clergy team ministry was accepted by both congregations in July 2001, it was decided that Keith Johnson would be interviewed by the vestry of St. Matthew's and, if approved, would be called as rector after his ordination to the priesthood in December 2001. (He served as deacon-in-charge until that time.) Simultaneously, Johnson was accepted by consent of St. Paul's vestry and called as associate rector. Stokes and the other clergy staff at St. Paul's were also voted by the vestry of St. Matthew's as associate clergy of that congregation. In the future, upon the vacancy of either rector's position, the rector with the most years of service at either St. Matthew's or St. Paul's will become the senior clergyperson of the team. The agreement also stipulates that Keith Johnson, as the rector of St. Matthew's, will have office space and office hours in both churches, and that each church will cover one-half of his salary package. The clergy team ministry is to be evaluated annually for effectiveness by both congregations, and after three years, in July 2004, the overall agreement will be reevaluated.[17]

GOD'S RECONCILING WORK THROUGH MULTIRACIAL COMMUNITY

Although a practical arrangement in terms of the deployment of ordained clergy between one prosperous congregation and one with fewer financial resources, the clergy team ministry also presents a model for a ministry of racial justice within a community context. Though the model respects the cultural heritage and autonomy of both congregations, it also raises the issues of racial justice in the community and has broken through barriers between people. Such a model also attempts to support the smaller, poorer, congregation without "swallowing it up." Initially, some vestry members of St. Matthew's were justifiably concerned that to enter into such an arrangement would mean the end of their distinctness and autonomy. The life experience of the African American and Caribbean American people of St. Matthew's did not offer many examples of partnerships with European Americans where power and resources were actually shared equitably. Yet the clergy team ministry provides members of both congregations with the opportunity to work and worship regularly with persons of different racial and ethnic heritage, as well as with persons from different economic backgrounds and nationality.

The focus of the clergy team ministry of St. Matthew's and St. Paul's is on God's reconciling work; the different worship styles, the different music, the different worship spaces of the two congregations are held up as opportunities for celebration. At St. Matthew's and St. Paul's the underlying message is that differences are good; in these congregations "the God of difference" is not to be feared but is to be celebrated in the church and in the wider community. The clergy team ministry of St. Matthew's and St. Paul's seeks to address significant theological and well as social challenges within the life of congregations concerned with racial justice:

> How can two churches less than half a mile apart, historically divided by race, preserving two distinct heritages, live the mandates of the Gospel and live into the primary mission of the Church "to restore all people to unity with God and with each other in Christ?" How can they do this while trying to live into our Lord's hope and prayer for his followers "that they all may be one, as we are one" (John 17:11)? How can two churches live into those mandates of the Baptismal Covenant that call upon each Christian to "seek and serve Christ in all persons loving your neighbor as yourself" and to "strive for justice and peace among all people and respect the dignity of every human being" (*The Book of Common Prayer*, 293-294) while they continue to worship in two separate buildings and operate as two distinct and separate entities?[18]

Soon after Keith Johnson's arrival at St. Matthew's, the struggling congregation was reenergized. Sunday attendance grew to close to ninety persons, and the sanctuary itself benefited from new paint, tile, carpet, and pews. The congregation also obtained a new computer and has plans for a Web site. "I basically want St. Matthew's to not think of itself as a second-class church, because it isn't," says Johnson. "It never was. And now they're starting to realize their place. There's a lot of more energy here." Janet Davis, senior warden at St. Matthew's and a member of the Delray Community Choir, values the opportunity she has gained from the partnership to learn about people from other cultures. "It is an opportunity to share your culture and to appreciate other cultures," she says. Davis also believes that some of the resistance to change she previously experienced at St. Matthew's has been broken and that the stability brought by the clergy ministry team has given the congregation the needed stability to "thrive, survive, pass it down, and pass it on," she says. Bob Chapin, the senior warden of St. Paul's says the partnership is a "step forward that has eliminated the separateness," but that there is still not complete integration. For instance, there is still only limited visiting between members of the two congregations in each other's homes. Chip Stokes believes that the partnership allows for a healthy cultural exchange. "We cannot just become one homogeneous blob. That's not what pluralism is about. Pluralism is about honoring the distinct identity and celebrating the differences of culture and people," he says.[19]

During this past year the partnership between St. Matthew's and St. Paul's has deepened and matured. Moreover, the partnership has given St. Matthew's an opportunity to continue work on unresolved issues that if ignored will hinder the congregation's growth in the future. Keith Johnson reports that while one family continues to walk out of the service when he is at St. Paul's, the rest of the congregation is not only welcoming but wishes he could be there more often. During Holy Week, St. Matthew's hosted Tenebrae for both congregations. Also during Holy Week the two congregations coordinated the Stations of the Cross. Almost one hundred people from both churches walked the stations along the four blocks that separate the congregations. St. Matthew's has also starting a weekly youth group. Plans are in the works for the congregations to sponsor another round of community dialogues in the future and to ask Alban Institute consultants to return to assist in the clergy team evaluation process.

SUMMARY

The clergy team ministry and the "St. Matthew's–St. Paul's Community Dialogue on Racism, Justice and Reconciliation" are examples of congregational racial justice ministries based within both the church and the large community. The clergy team ministry offers a means by which both congregations can receive the benefits of a culturally diverse, highly skilled ordained staff while at the same time maintaining their individual autonomy and historical distinctness. The effectiveness of this model in terms of efforts to achieve racial justice is heavily dependent on strong ordained leaders who will continue to keep the issue alive within the congregations. Though white clergy need to be constantly aware of how they use their racial privilege within a congregation, a benefit is that the burden of naming racism in the context of St. Matthew's and St. Paul's is not solely the responsibility of people of color.

One challenge at St. Matthew's and St. Paul's will emerge if and when the senior member of the clergy team is a person of color. Does the depth of the congregations' commitment to racial justice make allowances for a senior clergyperson who is African American? Would an African American senior rector be fully supported by St. Paul's, or is there a tacit belief that clergy of color will always be in the junior position? How do clergy transitions impact the clergy team ministry? Is some sort of antiracism training or experience with communities of color a requirement for membership?

Beyond the clergy team ministry, the needs of laity in both congregations need to be continually reassessed. While in the case of both St. Matthew's and St. Paul's the lay leadership is mostly supportive of the partnership, what about other laity in the congregations? Both congregations benefit from the activities of a shared ministry committee, such as social and educational events and participation in worship at the partner congregations. These types of activities allow for members of both congregations to meet informally and build relationships, and they require little additional planning. However, laity in both congregations expressed the need for more participation in shared activities. Here, as is the case in all strategies involving racial justice in congregations, continuing education and reeducation for the entire parish, including children and youth, is an important component of the change process.

Finally, the "St. Matthew's–St. Paul's Community Dialogue on Racism, Justice and Reconciliation" is an important model of how congregations can organize to have an impact on an entire community. Certainly this type of model is built on the host congregations' ability to bring to the table community leaders with a high degree of influence and social power. Here patience and persistence are the rule. For community dialogue to be beneficial on this level—or within congregations for that matter—members of the group have to commit to a level of participation and frequency of meeting that will allow them to become more open with each other on a deeper level. As Archbishop Desmond Tutu suggests, for those who endure the struggle, much becomes available to us when we greet each other as created in God's image.

2

Capirotoda—Hearing Each Other's Stories

Quincy First Presbyterian Church
Quincy, Washington

While religion is promoting "inculturation," none of the religious groups I know are dealing with the issues on the growing intercultural reality that is rapidly emerging through the process of mestizaje. *This could be the greatest contribution and challenge of the churches as they baptize the new mestizo children into the family of their churches. Does the church really want them and value them as they are—as the carriers of the various races and ethnicities of their parents and grandparents? . . . In the very blending of the differences into a new whole, everyone can be enriched, can become more human, and I dare to say, can become more divine.*

—Virgilio Elizondo[1]

AFTER MORE THAN TWO YEARS OF PARTNERSHIP WITH QUINCY First Presbyterian Church in Quincy, Washington, Centro Christiano Fuente de Vida Nueva (Fountain of New Life Christian Church) dedicated their new church building in July 2002. Fifteen members of Quincy First Presbyterian attended the three-and-one-half-hour service with fellowship time afterward—and some stayed for the entire event. "We had talked the previous Sunday about it being okay for them to come and go as they needed to. It's pretty difficult for Anglos to sit through a three-and-one-half-hour service," says the Rev. Dr. Ann Hinz, pastor of Quincy First Presbyterian Church since 1999. Hinz was invited to sit up front during the dedication with six Latino pastors from the community. The Hispanic congregation honored members of Quincy First Presbyterian during the celebration with special certificates. One member of Quincy First Presbyterian, Norman White, was especially honored for his assistance in helping the Hispanic congregation with the necessary building permits. "I was a bit overwhelmed, but felt honored and delighted," says Hinz. "As I sat up there in this new church building reflecting on a partnership that began over two years ago, I was humbled and very grateful to God."[2]

THE CREATIVE PROCESS OF *MESTIZAJE*

Statistics suggest that if it is not already the case, at least within the next decade Hispanics will be the largest "minority" group in the United States, which is already the fifth largest Spanish-speaking nation in the world. In his book *The Future Is Mestizo: Life Where Cultures Meet,* Virgilio Elizondo responds to the question, "Is the frontier between the United States and Mexico the border between two nationalities or is it the frontier zone of a new human race?" When Elizondo uses the phrase "the future is mestizo," he is referring to the creative process of *mestizaje,* whereby peoples become not only genetically mixed but culturally and religiously transformed. Studies on the "browning" of America have predicted that within two decades Latinos will be the largest group of people of color in the United States. Still, Elizondo argues, the "white–black" paradigm continues to dominate the racial and cultural discourse in the United States, further rendering those who live outside that paradigm invisible. He enlarges the discussion with a vision of many-hued American people who enrich and challenge current notions of democracy. As a priest-theologian-activist of Mexican ancestry from San Antonio, Texas, Elizondo raises integral questions for Christians attempting to life their faith within the context of a multicultural society: "How can I best live out the gospel in the midst of these particular circumstances? Can the gospel show me a way to help build a world in which 'all may be one'? Does the gospel have something to say to the pressing questions of today's shrinking planet?"[3]

Quincy First Presbyterian Church, a small congregation founded in the rural community of Quincy, Washington, in 1905, is a place where the joys and struggles of living out the gospel in the midst of the creative process of *mestizaje* is palpable. The town of Quincy is located in a desert region of Grant County, in the center of Washington State. Like many rural communities across the country, Grant County and Quincy itself experienced rapid growth in the 1990s. In 1998 there were an estimated 6,889 people in the area. The projected population for the area in 2003 is 7,975, with a growth rate exceeding that of the rest of the country. Though the area was once settled by German American farmers, the demographics of Quincy and Grant County are quickly changing to reflect a rapidly growing Hispanic population.[4]

Before 1950 the area around Quincy was primarily desert with less than eight inches of rain annually. But in 1950 "the water came" with the Columbia Federal Reclamation Project, turning desert land into excellent soil. European and European American farmers moved in and built the community. By the 1960s Hispanic families began to move to Quincy to assist in harvesting produce; as the farms grew, so did the numbers of Hispanic workers. Though confronted with racism and bigotry—some Quincy residents would not rent to them or employ them—some Hispanic families began to remain throughout the year. Food processing plants were soon established in Quincy, and many of the Hispanics who formerly worked in the fields filled the demand for workers. Though white residents are the plant mangers, 85 percent of the workers in the processing plants today are Hispanic.

Though Grant County, Washington, was at one time a predominantly white region, the population is "browning," and the Anglo population is in decline. Estimates vary, but the current Hispanic population of Quincy, Washington, is between 50 and 65 percent of the overall population and is growing. Nevertheless, positions of power in the community are still held overwhelmingly by whites. Most of the Hispanic population of Quincy is of Mexican American ancestry, and many are themselves migrant workers from Mexico, Texas, or California or are the descendents of such workers. There are also a few Hispanic families from El Salvador. Ann Hinz, pastor of the Quincy First Presbyterian Church, notes that Hispanics in Quincy break down into three groups: persons whose families have lived in Quincy since the 1960s, many of whom were born in the area and who now form a middle-class Hispanic population; persons who have lived in Quincy for fifteen to twenty years and who own local shops and businesses; and those who are seasonal workers.

Population of Grant County and Quincy, Washington

Grant County
  Population
    1990   54,168
    1999   68,438

  Growth rates in Grant County
    People of color, 1990–1999
      Hispanics   90%
      American Indians   14%
      Asians   35%
      African American/black   50%
      White   0%

Quincy
  1990
    Population   7,422
    Hispanic population   1,888

  1999
    Population   9,133
    Hispanic population   3,562

  Growth rate in Quincy, 1990–1999   89%

  Overall Hispanic population
    in state of Washington in 1999   16%

Source: Presbyterian Church Locator, Neighborhood Democratic Report, Quincy First Presbyterian Church.

Today, 85 percent of public elementary school students in Quincy are Hispanic, though it has been only six years since students were allowed to speak Spanish in school. The school district still struggles to meet the needs of the children of the community. There is only one Hispanic teacher and one Hispanic school counselor in the school district; both women, whom we will introduce below, are members of the first Mexican family to move into the town. Bilingual aides assist children in their transition from Spanish to English. Most of the Hispanics with teaching degrees in the Quincy school system are employed as aides or janitors. White families have largely fled the public school system, particularly on the elementary level, opting instead to home-school or to send their children to a 95-percent white Christian school twenty miles away. "My board sees things through the eyes of white farmers," says Lynn Rowse, Quincy school superintendent. As a participant in antiracism trainings hosted at Quincy First Presbyterian Church, Rowse continues to encourage attendance at the training sessions by teachers and school administrators. Though Rowse sees some improvements, she also recognizes the failures of the school system to address the needs of the Hispanic population. Among her critical concerns are improving the participation of Hispanic parents in the school system and finding a way to reach children lost in the school system. "How do we help the whole family?" asks Rowse. "If we're not, then we are sending them [the children] to the fields," she says.

Mary Ybarra-Vega, a member of the first Mexican family to purchase a home in Quincy, works as a school counselor in the district. Remembering the racism she faced as a young person in the community, Ybarra-Vega now works to link the Hispanic community with public services. "There are some good people here," she says of the school district, "but there are others who are resistant, who make no effort to learn Spanish, or the cultural pieces." Her sister, Isabel Saldana, a transitional bilingual/migrant teacher who is currently involved in a dispute with the school district, is keenly aware of how the system perpetuates racism. Housed in a portable classroom outside the school building, Saldana is concerned that the facility will further inculcate feelings of inferiority in the children. "We try to make it like a home for them, we do the best we can," she says. "But we should be able to have them inside, for these reasons. What is going on here?" Lynn Snyder, another teacher in the Quincy school system, sees the need "to find a better way to talk about the needs" of the majority of the children within the school system."

Sally Curran, who has worked in cooperation with Quincy churches through Language Partners, and with the Quincy Diversity Council, sees the importance of building multiracial community in the town through a variety of means, including Spanish- and English-language groups, believes that there is motivation in the community to build bridges between cultures. "There are motivated people out there, and we take advantage of people like that," she says.

The Community of Quincy, Washington

Within a three-mile radius of Quincy First Presbyterian Church:

- 19.4% live on farms; 79.2% in rural nonfarm areas; 1.4% "urban," or with at least 2,500 people in the surrounding area.
- 39% of the residents of Quincy are unchurched.
- 31% are employed in farming, forestry, or fishing—well above the 2.5% national average in these fields.
- The average commute to work is less than ten minutes.
- 33.3% are in the community's largest income group, earning between $15,000 and $29,999 per year; the next largest income group (27.1%) earn between $30,000 and $49,000 per year.
- 74.3% of Quincy adults age 25 years or older have a high school diploma or some college; 11.9% of this same age group did not complete high school, below the national average of 14%.
- Most Quincy residents live in houses built between 1950 and 1979 or in mobile homes.
- Over 77% are married couples with (38.14%) or without (39%) children.

BUILDING RELATIONSHIPS ACROSS CULTURES

As an Anglo pastor, Ann Hinz knows that the language and cultural issues between European American and Hispanic residents of Quincy are deeply ingrained, as is the systemic racism. "About 75 percent of what we do is working on relationships," she says. Quincy First Presbyterian Church is a warm and welcoming family-size church of about nineth-eight people discerning how to live the gospel in their community. Presently, it is a predominantly Anglo congregation "working on our own issues," according to Hinz. She sees the congregation's response to the language and cultural issues in their community as "organic" and rooted in creative partnerships with churches, schools, agencies, and organizations. Before to her move to Quincy, Ann Hinz ministered in Gold Beach, Curry County, in southern Oregon, an area with very few people of color. Though called to Quincy with the intention of building bridges with the Hispanic community, Hinz recognized the fear among the white members of the congregation and community, as well as the denial about the actual numbers of Hispanics.

(Some white residents of the community believe that the community is still "changing" or that the population is about one-third Hispanic. The latest U.S. Census estimates that the population is at least 65 percent Hispanic. Quincy *has* changed!) "My growing edge is realizing that my work for now is with white folks—to have compassion for them and to keep the conversation going," says Hinz. "I know that God is working with my sisters and brothers, but God's call is not always simple, and hardly ever easy. As a pastor, I am called to be both a prophetic voice and to gently care for the people of the congregation; It's not always an easy task," she says. Hinz also believes that she herself as well as members of the congregation need to enter into relationships with Hispanic people in the community, as one step toward "naming the oppression of white racism that has caused so much pain and fear." This view is shared by many members of the congregation: "Ann has helped our church so much in realizing our potential—helping us to 'see more clearly—face to face' in ways that we can further our relationships with our Hispanic neighbors. . . . This is to understand and appreciate another's culture, to value people as individuals and collectively," says Roxa Kreimeyer.

Quincy First Presbyterian Church is located on one of the main streets in town. Like many rural communities, Quincy has its share of churches, and Quincy First Presbyterian is situated between a Roman Catholic congregation and the Church of the Nazarene. As happens in many congregations that attempt to build multiracial community, a few members left the congregation after Hinz's proactive leadership on issues of racial justice became apparent—"because we don't want Mexicans in our church"—yet the congregation has also experienced some minor growth. "It was hard for some people in the congregation to hear about racism," says Roxa Kreimeyer. "They didn't like being preached to," she says. "But if we are going to be more inclusive in the community, we are going to have to open our hearts to each other," she added. Candy Houston, who works with young people at Quincy First Presbyterian Church, says she learned through her participation in workshops held at the church "that there was a lot more racism going on than I knew about." Mike Blakely, a vocational educator, says that there are some "older" members of Quincy First Presbyterian church who do not understand the dynamics within the community, or why the church should be involved in projects that bring in

new members. "But at least the church is working hard to do something," he says.

Though Ann Hinz was called to the congregation specifically to
build bridges with the Hispanic community, few in the small, aging
congregation understood the type of changes this work would bring.
"People have said to me that I am the kind of pastor that they prayed
for, but now they are scared," says Hinz. "The majority of the Anglos
in Quincy, who have done very little traveling outside of the United
States, have little understanding of the difficulties Latinos face in coming to this country, particularly those Latinos who come as political
refugees," says Hinz.

Still, members of Quincy First Presbyterian Church are active in a
variety of social justice ministries in the community and give very generously of their time and resources for a small church. These ministries
include the Language Partners program, Habitat for Humanity, a
thrift shop, and a community food bank. Conscious of the need to
nurture and support members of congregations in time of change, the
parish newsletter is replete with affirmations for birthdays, anniversaries, and graduations. "This congregation is rooted and grounded in
prayer," says Ann Hinz. The principal service is held on Sundays at
10:30 in the morning; most members greet each other by name for the
small, informal gathering. The congregation regularly sponsors a
choir, a men's early morning worship group, a children and youth program, and an adult Bible study program. Similarly, the prayers and
worship life of the congregation reflect its variety of personal, interpersonal, and global concerns. The congregation prays for individuals
and families, for the congregation's vision, for a Hispanic youth minister, for local communities of color, and for national leaders. Quincy
First Presbyterian Church also sponsors a missionary in Guatemala.

Notably, as an outgrowth of its growing relationship with the Hispanic community, Quincy First Presbyterian Church also hosts a regular Tuesday evening study group entitled "Dismantling Racism."
(Similar groups have also begun in the nearby towns of Wenatchee
and Leavenworth.) The simple format of the group meetings includes
a book study and discussion on how to apply what has been learned.
The group that meets at Quincy First Presbyterian Church includes
several teachers from the Quincy school district and the community
college in Moses Lake, a woman who works for Habitat for Human-

ity, and Ann Hinz. The group is convened by one of the Quincy teachers and has read and discussed books such as *A Promise and A Way of Life: White Racism Activism*, by Becky Thompson, and *Crossing Over: A Mexican Family on the Migrant Trail*, by Ruben Martinez.[5]

Though the growth and excitement among many of members of Quincy First Presbyterian Church as a result of their deepening commitment to form meaningful relationships with their Hispanic neighbors are almost palpable, this stage was reached only after many painful and soul-searching conversations, recounts Ann Hinz:

> Painful racist comments have bubbled to the surface, pouring out of the mouths of congregational members. I have wondered if I will be able to remain in this congregation after some of the stories and some of the comments I have shared about racism in conversations and sermons. I have refused to walk this journey alone, consistently asking the question of the board members, "I will lead you, but I won't walk this journey alone; are we in this together or not?" Over and over again, the board members have said they are in this process for the long haul. They remind each other and me that in the pastor search process, they were looking for a pastor who could lead them in building bridges with their Hispanic neighbors. At this point, they usually laugh and say, "but we didn't know it was going to be this much work!"[6]

Ann Hinz believes that it is the essential health of the congregation that allows the members of Quincy First Presbyterian Church to take risks, even when the result is painful. "This is not a crash and burn place," she says. "Yet that doesn't mean that it isn't sometimes painful to listen with love to what is going on." For Hinz, emotional and spiritual struggle are part of efforts to build multiracial community—"like the Israelites in the desert." "We may never have a significant Hispanic membership," she says, "but we can build relationships with white folks and Latinos who want to be part of this kind of work. We are not looking for Latinos to become white." Jackie Flinn, an elder of the congregation, concurs. "I wonder if it is realistic for Hispanic people to come here," she says. "I don't think we are peppy enough," says high school teacher Judy Bryant, also a supporter of the congregation's efforts to build relationships with the Hispanic community. Teri Wilson, a member of Quincy First Presbyterian Church since childhood, questions what she perceives as the congregation's switch from building bridges with the Hispanic community as one of the ministries of the congregation's to "the main focus. I wonder if we are taking enough time to watch out for our own," she says.

CAPIROTADO: FORGING A PARTNERSHIP

A focal point of the deepening awareness of racial justice within Quincy First Presbyterian Church is its emergent partnership with Centro Christiano Fuente de Vida Nueva (Fountain of New Life Christian Church), a Spanish Assembly of God congregation. The partnership between the two congregations began in January 2000 and is slowly developing as one example of how a predominantly white congregation can form a relationship with a Hispanic congregation that can effect a transformation for both churches.

Pastor Felix Pacheco of Centro Christiano Fuente de Vida Nueva in Quincy describes the relationship between his congregation and Quincy First Presbyterian as *capirotada* or coming together as different peoples yet united in Christ. *Capirotada* is a Mexican dish made from the blending of many kinds of foods—bread, bananas, olives, hot peppers, cheese, milk—served during Holy Week. Though the mixture is blended together, Pacheco emphasizes that the importance in the symbolism is the reality that each ingredient retains its individual flavor and contributes to the beauty of the whole. In this way, both congregations have shared in a variety of ministries yet retained their own culture and distinctiveness. Ann Hinz and Felix Pacheco now serve as president and vice-president, respectively, of a revived Quincy ministerial association, thus modeling a multicultural leadership beyond their individual congregations.

As the recent recipient of a doctor of ministry degree from San Francisco Theological Seminary with a concentration in preaching, Ann Hinz sees the relationships between Hispanic and European Americans as deeply rooted in the call to hear each other's stories: "We are called to listen to the stories of our Hispanic sisters and brothers who are neighbors," says Hinz. "It sounds so simple, but listening is difficult, because we have to lay aside our own agendas and endeavor to identify deeply with people who are different from us. We have to honor these differences rather than rush to unify and reconcile. We have to move from an ideology of the 'melting pot' in which the goal is to blend everyone together, to an ideology of *mestizaje* in which differences are honored and celebrated."[7]

The opportunity for a relationship between Quincy First Presbyterian Church and Centro Christiano Fuente de Vida Neuva came when a friend of Ann Hinz from Bethany Presbyterian Church in Grants Pass, Oregon, contacted her to suggest the possibility of a youth and adult mission project between their two congregations with a local Hispanic congregation. The Spanish Assembly of God congregation had just purchased land in Quincy for the construction of a new church. Pastor Felix Pacheco agreed to meet with representatives of the two Anglo congregations to discuss the possibility of a construction project and a Vacation Bible School. After this initial meeting, representatives of all three congregations agreed to begin exploring the possibility of the three congregations working together. For Quincy First Presbyterian this meant first meeting with the congregation's Mission/Outreach Committee and then having that group make a recommendation to the board (or session). Though the congregation had never entered into this kind of partnership before, they agreed to move forward and to work toward a construction project and a Vacation Bible School.

The first meeting for representatives from all three congregations took place in April 2000 in a Mexican-owned restaurant in Quincy. Three men and Pastor Ann Hinz from Quincy First Presbyterian Church, two men from Bethany Presbyterian in Grants Pass, and Pastor Felix from Centro Christiano Fuente de Vida Nueva. The Anglo participants thought that this would be a relatively short meeting, yet it lasted for three hours. The Anglos learned that it was important for the group to take time to build a relationship before doing work together. In addition, the meeting gave Felix Pacheco an opportunity to voice his concerns about getting the needed building permits from the city for the construction project. Two of the men from Quincy heard his concerns and agreed to help the Hispanic congregation acquire the necessary permits. Finally, the representatives of the three congregations agreed to a sidewalk construction project and a Vacation Bible School in July 2000. As part of the joint project, two services of "unity" were planned on two different Sundays, one at Quincy First Presbyterian and one at Centro Christiano Fuente de Vida Nueva, as well as a joint "fiesta" at the site of the future Hispanic church on the last day of the Vacation Bible School.

Quincy First Presbyterian Church and Centro Christiano Fuente de Vida Nueva continued to meet regularly during the months between their gathering and the July start date for the projects. Among whites, time is sometimes viewed as one of the most precious commodities— if not most precious commodity—but other cultures hold different views of time and work. In some cultures, the quality of the time spent together is as important as, if not more important than, the number of tasks accomplished. For them, "the journey is the destination." For members of Quincy First Presbyterian Church and Centro Christiano Fuente de Vida Nueva, time together in advance of the project was a crucial element to its overall success. How else would trust begin to develop between such culturally divergent congregations? For example, both congregations had the opportunity to experience their neighbor at worship: Quincy First Presbyterian has a large modern facility complete with an underutilized Sunday-school wing, while the Spanish Assembly of God congregation worshiped in an overcrowded space without classrooms for the sixty to seventy children in regular attendance.

Common prayer and worship between the two congregations, in Spanish and in English, was also an integral component of their growing relationship. And as the fellowship deepened, members of Quincy First Presbyterian Church began to understand aspects of the experience of Hispanics in their community that previously had been invisible to members of white culture. As the white members of Quincy First Presbyterian saw how Pastor Felix and his congregation faced innumerable obstacles with architects, builders, and city officials— many of which would not have been encountered by a white congregation seeking to build a church in the community—they entered into a compassionate solidarity with Hispanic people. The encounter gave members of the white congregation a glimpse of the oppression experienced on a daily basis by Hispanic people in Quincy, and how white people participate and are complicit in this racism.[8]

In a similar way, the two congregations integrated relationship building, prayer, and celebration into the creative partnership that birthed the Vacation Bible School program. Hosted at the Quincy First Presbyterian Church for four days from 4:00 to 6:00 P.M. for children from preschool through sixth grade, the program attracted eighty participants in the first year and 120 in the second year. Both congregations took ownership of the program and worked hard to promote it. Though the Spanish Assembly of God congregation and the wider

Hispanic community of Quincy had many more children in the program, the congregation of Quincy First Presbyterian Church provided volunteer teachers, kitchen helpers, snack organizers, and publicity workers.

In July 2002 another collaborative Vacation Bible School program was held in Quincy, this time coordinated by Diana Santiago through the efforts of four congregations: Quincy First Presbyterian, Redmond Presbyterian Church in Seattle, Centro Christiano Fuente de Vida Nueva, and the Foursquare Hispanic Church in Quincy. There were 120 children in the program, 90 percent of whom were Hispanic. Diana Santiago herself had faced the racism of the Quincy community as a child when she first enrolled in the all-English school system. "At first they would say, 'why don't you go back to where you come from?' But gradually we got more accepted," she says. Of more than fifty youth and adult leaders for the program, approximately half were Hispanic and half were Anglo. Carefully designed on a shared-leadership model, the program was conducted in Spanish and in English, including Bible stories, worship, music, games, and arts and crafts. Though published curricula for authentically bilingual Vacation Bible School programs are fairly scarce, the leadership in Quincy made creative use of available materials. For example, for two days the Bible story was told in Spanish and translated into English; and for the other two days the story was told in English and translated into Spanish.

Through the experience of the Vacation Bible School and the construction project, members of Quincy First Presbyterian Church have had the opportunity to form relationships with members of the Hispanic community and engage in vital ministry opportunities. Diana Santiago sees her work as coordinator of the Vacation Bible School as a mission, and herself as a missionary in the broader community. "We [Hispanic people] need to get involved, to do things for God," she says. "I think that God has a plan for everybody." Bill and Sylvia Wurl, both longtime members of Quincy First Presbyterian Church were active in both the construction project and the Vacation Bible School with the Spanish Assembly of God congregation. Though originally hesitant about working with Hispanic people, Bill Wurl was urged by Ann Hinz to get involved with the project. "Sometimes we have to do things out of our comfort zone," he says. "The kids got so much out of the Vacation Bible School," says Sylvia Wurl. "We can

work well together; and the Hispanic people went out of their way,"
she says. Both believe that some members of the congregation are still
adapting to the partnership, but "many people are willing to help;
they begin with curiosity and then a relationship develops," says
Sylvia.

NEW MINISTRY OPPORTUNITIES

Energy from their first projects with the Hispanic Community has
branched out into other possibilities for building multiracial community at Quincy First Presbyterian Church. Though it remains an Eng-
lish-speaking congregation, music in both Spanish and English is
included in Sunday services. To help the congregation assess possibilities for future ministry, a Hispanic person was hired part-time during
the summer of 2001. The next summer, a ninety-two-year-old member
of the congregation pledged $1,000 to support hiring a Hispanic staff
person at Quincy First Presbyterian. The Sunday after the dedication
of the new Spanish Assembly of God church in September 2002, the
Christian Education Committee at Quincy First Presbyterian made a
motion at the board meeting to hire a Hispanic person to work part-
time with an emerging junior high youth group. The congregation has
also applied to the synod for $5,000 to fund this position. Parish sec-
retary Ellen Mead sees great potential for the congregation if a bilingual Hispanic minister were hired. "It would be a real draw in the
community," she says, "and would open the doors to more people."

Other new ministry initiatives include a language program began
by intern Kari McFarland from Columbia Seminary in Atlanta.
McFarland started a basic English and Spanish group for the community; the group was attended by several Hispanic and Anglo women.
Another woman in the community is applying for grant money to
institute an ESL (English as a Second Language) class at Quincy First
Presbyterian Church. Besides language instruction, members of the
congregation have begun to build bridges through music. A community
mariachi band has formed and sometimes meets at Quincy First
Presbyterian Church. Pat and Lee Patterson, both educators who have
attended antiracism workshops in the community, see the mariachi
band as an opportunity to do something for the youth of the region

that instills self-esteem. In addition, a member of the congregation has given $1,000 toward the formation of an ecumenical interracial youth choir. As a congregation with limited financial resources and many members on fixed incomes —the congregation's budget for 2002 was $98,768—the members of Quincy First Presbyterian Church are generous and creative about seeking funds for their expanding ministries. Money is sought from local sources as well as from their presbytery, synod, other Presbyterian congregations, and ecumenical organizations to finance various partnerships.

MODELING AUTHENTIC PARTNERSHIPS

The partnership between Centro Christiano Fuente de Vida Nueva and Quincy First Presbyterian Church, along with occasional participation from other congregations, avoids many of the traps of the model of partnerships known as "theological tourism"—that is, experiences designed wholly by members of the dominant culture *for* the marginalized, which serve only to reinforce the status quo rather than offer an opportunity for transformation. Rather than patronize the oppressed, these partnerships give members of the dominant culture opportunities to recognize how God is already at work among those encountered.

How then can congregations model authentic partnerships with others from different cultures to form multiracial communities? From the perspective of racial justice, how can predominantly white congregations better participate in antiracist partnerships with other congregations? Though neither Centro Christiano Fuente de Vida Nueva nor Quincy First Presbyterian Church began their partnership with a formal set of criteria, some useful guidelines for similar ventures in other communities can be extrapolated from their experiences:[9]

First, the partnership between Centro Christiano Fuente de Vida Nueva and Quincy First Presbyterian Church is built on the premise of forming a long-term *relationship* between people. Though many congregations engage in one-time work projects, such isolated experiences tend to favor task over relationship and are not nearly as likely to produce lasting change as are ongoing partnerships where relationships are formed over time.

Another important aspect of the partnership between these two congregations is that the projects undertaken by the churches have a direct relationship to the needs of the home community. Further, the relational process entered into by the two congregations gives Centro Christiano Fuente de Vida Nueva the opportunity to define their own needs. Rather than having the predominantly white congregations decide what they would like to do *for* the Hispanic congregation, the representatives of the two congregations enter into a mutual education process that allows both groups to define what they want from the partnership. The emphasis is on listening, identifying, and sharing. Thus members of both congregations are empowered; neither is left feeling dis-empowered or dependent. The importance of a shared discernment process contributes to the overall success of the partnership for both congregations, says Marv Hinz of Quincy First Presbyterian Church. "No one church had to carry the project, and no one had to give up their culture to be accepted," he says.

Through an ongoing relationship members of both Quincy congregations learned what kind of assistance was actually needed and what kind of projects they could do together. The emphasis throughout the construction project and the Vacation Bible School was on the mutual relationship between people within a community, not simply on one congregation doing work *for* another. Further, the partnership between these two congregations in Quincy demonstrates a "systems approach" to issues in the community, which focuses on issues of mutual empowerment, the development of networks, and community organizations, rather than simply giving time or money for immediate satisfaction. For instance, members of Quincy First Presbyterian Church have invested more than time and money in the construction project and the children's program. They have participated in a *process* whereby they have glimpsed of the kind of oppression their Hispanic neighbors experience daily. What is it like for a Hispanic person in Quincy to try to get a building permit? What kind of barriers are experienced by persons whose first language is not English, even though Spanish-speaking persons are the numerical majority in the community? These and similar questions are key insights for predominantly white groups engaged in partnerships with communities of color.

One common mistake made by predominantly white congregations is to "consume" the other congregation, often unintentionally and in the name of good will. Generally speaking, models of white groups undertaking projects *for* people of color should be avoided. Rather, both Quincy First Presbyterian Church and Centro Christiano Fuente de Vida Nueva made every effort to share in the work that needed to be done. For instance, approximately equal numbers of Anglo and Hispanic people worked together on the construction project, as well as in leadership for the Vacation Bible School. Visiting youth groups applying to work with the partnership in Quincy are asked about the ethnic and racial diversity of their group, as well as their level of Spanish language ability.

Finally, integral to the vitality of the partnership between Quincy First Presbyterian Church and Centro Christiano Fuente de Vida Nueva is the intentional community building and spiritual formation that is incorporated into their common life. How is God present in the experience? What are the possibilities and plans for future action? The prayers in Spanish and English, as well as the numerous celebrations/fiestas, are crucial to building community within the partnership and are opportunities for members of the congregations to experience the interconnectedness of humanity. Moreover, praying and celebrating together sets the stage for a mutual understanding that allows different communities to work together for change. Certainly, the cultural differences are there, as are denominational differences. The congregation of Quincy First Presbyterian Church clearly was not used to services that were almost three hours in length or to singing in Spanish, nor were members of Centro Christiano Fuente de Vida Nueva used to a woman pastor or to praying in English. Yet through the power of the Spirit working in community, both congregations have grown to see the power of God working within each group. And that is what the spirit of true partnership is about!

It is significant that Quincy First Presbyterian Church has received denominational support for their racial justice work. The Presbyterian Church (U.S.A.) has made a commitment to become a more ethnically and racially diverse church. Ann Hinz first participated in an antiracism workshop at a "Peacemaking" conference in 1997 sponsored by the Presbyterian Church (U.S.A.), and she participated in a denominational antiracism trainers conference in spring 2002 and continues to draw on those resources for her local racial justice work. W. Mark Koenig, formerly with the Antiracism Program of the Presbyterian Church (U.S.A.), says that the work of Quincy First Presbyterian Church is an example of work that "is ahead of the denominational curve (thus challenging our vision and drawing us into something new) and of benefiting from denominational support." Ann Hinz also arranged to do an introductory training event for Central Washington Presbytery and to meet with Presbytery leaders. Conversely, Koenig and other Presbytery leaders were able to teach and preach at Quincy Presbyterian Church. "Thus [Ann Hinz's] denominational connections became a source of support and further learning for the people in Quincy and her work in Quincy brought the challenge of working on antiracism to the entire presbytery . . . a very nice circle," says Koenig.[10]

THE IMPACT IN THE REGION: NORTH CENTRAL WASHINGTON COALITION TO DISMANTLE RACISM

Efforts at building multiracial community and for racial justice that began at Quincy First Presbyterian Church have also impacted the wider region. Ann Hinz, as pastor of Quincy First Presbyterian, is also an active board member the North Central Washington Coalition to Dismantle Racism, a grass-roots organization composed of representatives from four area counties committed to working together for racial justice. Active coalition members include clergy and laity from Presbyterian, Methodist, Lutheran, Roman Catholic, Unitarian, and United Church of Christ congregations; teachers, counselors, parents, and administrators from the school districts of Quincy, Cascade, Wenatchee, Chelan, and Seattle, Washington; as well as representatives from the United States Forest Service, Americorps, the Girl Scouts, Habitat for Humanity, Washington State University, Big Bend Community College, the regional library, and others. Members of the North Central Washington Coalition to Dismantle Racism are committed to "inform and strengthen our respective institution's efforts to dismantle racism; report to the group our struggles and successes in the process and thus maintain accountability to one another; network and serve as resources to one another based on our relationships and common experiences; and, organize within our institutions to dismantle systemic racism."

The coalition began two and one-half years ago with some funding from Faith Lutheran Church in Leavenworth, Washington, and it has been working with Crossroads Ministry, an interfaith and community-based antiracism training organization that was established in 1986 and has offices in Chicago, Milwaukee, and Racine, Wisconsin. Crossroads trains teams within institutions to help them "analyze racism and to develop and implement strategies to dismantle racism within their structures." These teams develop skills in analysis of systemic racism, research and evaluation, teaching and racism, and organizing for change. The Crossroads Ministry model of education and training to dismantle racism follows seven key organizing principles:

1. The task is organizing for systemic change.
2. The organizing task is to develop an antiracist institutional identity.
3. The organizing task is an "inside" job.
4. The specific model for change is needed for each specific situation.
5. Trained, equipped leadership teams are needed.
6. Antiracism transformation is long range, even generational.
7. Institutional change is a component of community change.

Since its inception, the North Central Washington Coalition to Dismantle Racism has held a variety of antiracism workshops, including a half-day workshop for seventy-five people, and three two-and-one-half-day workshops in different communities, including one at Quincy First Presbyterian Church in March 2001. The workshop in Quincy was filled to capacity—forty-five persons, of whom at least half were required to be people of color. Further grant money has been made available to the North Central Washington Coalition to Dismantle Racism through the Presbyterian and Lutheran churches to order to make additional workshops possible. Two one-day workshops were scheduled for November 2002: one day for school administrators, teachers, and staff, and one for participants from churches, social service organizations, and counseling agencies; another two-and-one-half-day workshop was sponsored in March 2003.

Crossroads Ministry has sent a diverse team of women and men to assist members of the coalition in their efforts. Crossroads Ministry cofounder Joseph Barndt, the author of *Dismantling Racism*, has worked with many groups across the country, with a particular emphasis on "equipping Christians to dismantle racism in church and society." "The primary thesis about racism," he writes, "is that we are all—people of color and white people alike—indoctrinated and socialized in such a way as to be made into 'prisoners of racism.' Every leader in the struggle against racism, from Frederick Douglass to Dr.

Martin Luther King Jr. [has] emphasized that racism is as debilitating to white people as it is to people of color, and that the goal is freedom for all people."[12]

The Crossroads Ministry antiracism model is built around a long-term organizing process made up of programs, workshops, curricula, consultations, and training for different constituencies. The process is developmental and organized into sets, so that the organization can move forward, over time, toward a long-term commitment and plan of action to dismantle racism. Predicated on long-term developmental goals for overall institutional transformation, the Crossroads Ministry model sets out twenty-year plans, with five-year goals, and two-year objectives. Crossroads Ministry trainers recognize that while many congregations are racially and culturally homogeneous, they too can become transformed through building an antiracist identity and that such an identity is not dependent on people of color within a congregation. Rather, congregational transformation and greater diversity are the outcome of a congregation's antiracist identity and action in a community.[13]

For white congregations such as Quincy First Presbyterian Church, Joseph Barndt and Charles Ruehle recommend five practices necessary for European Americans in order to begin the transformation to a racially just society: First, they suggest that European Americans must strive to understand white racism and make a commitment to dismantle it. This includes working with other white people to combat racism, as well working with people of color to focus on specific acts of resistance. The second practice suggested by Barndt and Ruehle is for European Americans to link their identities as people of faith with the challenge of racism in our society. Far too often our churches support the racist assumptions and beliefs of our culture. Here Barndt and Ruehle link faith and action as integral to the third practice, that is, to build relationships based on God's vision of justice. The people of God in white congregations are challenged both to build trusting relationships within the congregation and to continue to challenge each other.[14] As Ann Hinz wrote in reflection on her role at Quincy First Presbyterian Church:

> As I begin as a pastor in a new congregation, I am very aware that I have to first of all build trust with the people God has called me to serve, which means visiting and getting to know them. I need to hear their stories, their joys and challenges. I also need to share about myself, so they

can begin to know me as more than just "Pastor Ann." It is the on-going balance of being pastor/prophet! I have to intentionally work on building relationships, while at the same time, keeping the "edge" of challenging myself and the people God has called me to serve with the gospel message! We have to walk together in this process.[15]

The fourth practice for European Americans interested in antiracist transformation according to Barndt and Ruehle is to discover those in the present and the past who have worked to dismantle racism. Who are other white people who have fought for justice? How can we uncover the history of those in the past who have fought for justice? How can we become united with those in the present and gain support in the journey? Finally, European Americans need to make a commitment to a multicultural identity and to building a multicultural society. Though white people are traditionally accustomed to setting the agenda and then "inviting" others to participate, in a church and society without racism all would participate equally. According to Barndt in *Dismantling Racism*, building multiracial, multicultural institutions is as important as eradicating racism. How can a congregation more accurately reflect a pluralistic society? As Barndt reflects, "Is there not within each of us a deep longing for the community that was lost or never realized? This longing becomes even more intense as we begin to remove the barriers that have prevented such a sense of community from being fulfilled."[16]

In general, according to Barndt, a multiracial, multicultural organization (such as a congregation):

- reflects the contributions and interests of diverse cultural and social groups in its mission, operations, and product or service
- acts on a commitment to eradicate social oppression in all forms within the organization
- includes the members of diverse cultural and social groups as full participants, especially in decisions that shape the organization
- follows through on broader external social responsibilities, including support of efforts to eliminate all forms of social oppression and to educate others in multicultural perspectives[17]

Similarly, the members of Quincy First Presbyterian Church are on a journey toward building multiracial community by reflecting on their own culture and the contributions of the Hispanic community; by acting against racism in Quincy and beyond; by working to include members of the Hispanic community as full participants in decisions that shape their common life; and by following through on efforts to eliminate social oppression in the community and to educate others in multicultural perspectives. Though some members of Quincy First Presbyterian Church date their involvement with the Hispanic community from the beginning of Ann Hinz's ministry there, she is quick to point out that the first stages of the work began to take shape in the congregation twenty years ago under a succession of other pastors. "Many of you have personal relationships with Hispanic folks," said Hinz in September 2002, "but God has placed the burden specifically on you as a church community to be a model for other churches in the community about what it means to model Christian love with neighbors who are very different from you. Most people run from doing this kind of work, and I know that some of you want to run away from it. In fact, I think a few people have run away."[18]

Ann Hinz's direct, gentle, and confrontative pastoral leadership style has served to move the congregation to a deeper relationship with their Hispanic neighbors than they thought possible. Though most members of the congregation are devoted to Ann Hinz, some signs of resistance, such as a fear that "things are moving too fast," emerge from time to time. Recently such fears were voiced after it appeared that the congregation's goal of hiring a part-time Hispanic staff person might indeed be achieved. Hinz's response in the congregation's newsletter was anchored in prayer, pastoral in tone, yet unequivocal in its challenge to the congregation to move forward in its commitment to building a multiracial community: "We have groups for singles, couples, and children. This is all part of the vision to have Hispanics and people of other races worshipping with us. We have to be intentional about this if it is going to happen. We have been taking many gentle steps in this process. Part of this process is to have a Hispanic person on staff who is bilingual and can more easily relate to some of the Hispanic people in the community. . . . Let us rejoice in the work God is calling us to do!"[19]

SUMMARY

The story of Quincy First Presbyterian Church is one that bespeaks the commitment of white people to work against white racism. It is also the story of an authentic multicultural, multiracial partnership between two congregations working to make a difference in a small, rural community. The congregation struggles to find ways to maintain traditions that nurture its current members *and* move them into the future. Though individual members of the congregation continue to struggle with the realities of change, overall the members of the congregation have moved forward toward building an antiracist identity in the spirit of prayer, study, and action in the community. The movement of Quincy First Presbyterian Church toward multiracial community is deeply grounded in the spiritual life of the congregation, as evidenced in their depth of prayer and the presence of Spanish-language elements during worship. Indeed, the entire spiritual formation of the largely adult congregation is strongly intertwined with their journey toward multiracial community. Although a small and aging congregation might face issues of multiculturalism and white racism more easily as issues of survival, in this case the more obvious struggle is around vocation and calling. What is God calling us to do? What is the ministry of Quincy First Presbyterian Church in this community? This faith-based identity is one of the strengths in the process of Quincy First Presbyterian Church as it moves toward making multiracial community a reality.

The leadership of Ann Hinz has been critical to the ability of Quincy First Presbyterian Church both to discern its vocation in the midst of its own unique context and to keep the issues of multiracial community in the forefront of the congregation even in the midst of conflict. No "lone ranger," Hinz has been clear with the congregation and its leaders that she was called to Quincy to do this work, and that her role is to lead them, but not to do the ministry alone. Hinz's ability to assume and balance the roles of pastor and prophet and her gifts as an imaginative networker have enhanced the ministerial scope of the congregation beyond their size and resources. She also continues to struggle with the question of how to minister to those in the congregation who feel "left out" or who are resistant to the path Quincy First Presbyterian Church has taken toward antiracist, multicultural community. Moreover, the creative partnerships that the congregation has forged within Quincy and beyond have provided their pastor with a rich network of support that both enhances her effectiveness and provides her with helpful allies in the struggle.

Partnerships beyond the congregation, such as that with the North Central Washington Coalition to Dismantle Racism, have provided resources to Quincy First Presbyterian Church and have equipped the congregation for leadership in the broader church and throughout the region. Membership in the coalition has also provided Quincy First Presbyterian church with connections to people and institutions beyond the congregation. The creative partnership undertaken by Quincy First Presbyterian Church with Centro Christiana Fuente de Vida Nueva, the Spanish Assembly of God congregation in Quincy, has provided individual members and both congregations an opportunity to engage in deep and lasting relationships with their neighbors across the boundaries of difference. The commitment to equal partnership between the two congregations builds trust and serves as a model to the broader community. Further, the projects undertaken serve the people of Quincy and open the door to further opportunities for ministry. Hispanic leadership in the Vacation Bible School program has also given Quincy First Presbyterian Church the opportunity to experience firsthand the advantages of having bicultural and bilingual workers in order better to serve the needs of the community.

The next steps for Quincy First Presbyterian Church include the need for bilingual Hispanic staff persons to bring about a deeper impact on the community and perhaps a greater diversity within the congregation itself. Though Quincy First Presbyterian Church may remain predominantly white, what it means to have a multiracial identity *within* the congregation, as well as through external partnerships, needs to be explored more fully. Though the immediate environment supports a number of all-Hispanic congregations, some Hispanic persons may want the option of worshiping in a diverse and/or smaller congregation that welcomes them. Certainly, the congregation does attract white people who are looking for a supportive faith community and who are also interested in building multiracial community in the region. In this way, Quincy First Presbyterian may have an opportunity to continue to form partnerships and share leadership with Hispanic people within and beyond the congregation itself. Even if the numbers of people of color in the congregation never grow substantially, Quincy First Presbyterian Church can be transformed through redefining all its relationships from the perspective of building multiracial community.

3

This Far by Faith

Cross Lutheran Church
Milwaukee, Wisconsin

Empowered by the Holy Spirit not to lay their religion down, African American Christians by the grace of God have overcome. They have overcome cultural marginality by finding family in the church. They have overcome dehumanization and oppression by knowing themselves to be God's children. They have overcome trials and tribulations, storms and tempests, to find joy and peace in believing. Hear them as they worship and sing the triumph of trust in God, having come **This Far by Faith.**
—"Worship and Culture: An African American Lutheran Perspective"[1]

DESPITE THE MILWAUKEE FIRE DEPARTMENT'S BEST EFFORTS TO save it, Cross Lutheran Church's building was nearly destroyed in February 1995 when a devastating five-alarm electrical fire spread through the church and devoured all but one of the original walls. Considered "a rock of support" and "a sign of hope" for the North Side community, the congregation secured a temporary location within a week and held Sunday services at the usual time. "The reason for making the decision quickly was so that people would know that immediately this Sunday we'd continue our ministry," says Joseph W. Ellwanger, now pastor emeritus of the congregation. In the aftermath of the fire, with the help of hundreds of congregations and friends, the people of Cross Lutheran Church gained a renewed strength and built a new building that was dedicated in June 1996. The theme of the dedication service was "Rising from the Ashes—Strengthened by the Refiners Fire." A new organ was designed and built in 1997. "People

here really hold together," says Marguerite Kelly, a neighborhood resident for thirty-six years. "The church isn't the building—it's the people." Though the new building looks similar to the old one from the
outside, the inside not only features more efficient usage of space, but
is more reflective of the African American cultural background of
many of the present congregation.[2]

Though originally situated in a stone church reminiscent of gothic
architecture and the German American roots of the congregation, the
members of Cross Lutheran Church now worship in a light and airy
space, with plenty of modern stained glass windows representing the
predominantly African American congregation and neighborhood. In
addition, the modern design of the new church building provides the
congregation with movable educational space within and around the
sanctuary itself. The open and simple design and appointments of the
new Cross Lutheran Church building allow for the fluid and highly
participatory liturgical style of the congregation. Key to Cross Lutheran
Church's efforts to build multiracial community is the spirit of hospitality across cultures that pervades the congregation. Cross Lutheran
Church encapsulates the dialogue between culture and the Christian
faith expressed in worship and shaped by the African Americans,
European Americans, Asian Americans, and Hispanic Americans who
consider the congregation their spiritual home. A recent Lutheran
study presents four categories for understanding this dialogue:

> The reality that Christian worship is always celebrated in a given local
> cultural setting draws our attention to the dynamics between worship
> and the world's many local culture. Christian worship relates dramati-
> cally to culture in four ways. First, it is *transcultural,* the same sub-
> stance for everyone, everywhere, beyond culture. Second, it is
> *contextual,* varying according to the local situation (both nature and
> culture). Third, it is *counter-cultural,* challenging what is counter to the
> gospel in a given culture. Fourth, it is *cross-cultural,* making possible
> sharing between different local cultures.[3]

INTERGENERATIONAL CELEBRATION AND EDUCATION

The liturgical life of Cross Lutheran Church is an intergenerational
celebration; the gifts of people of all ages from preschool children to
elders are visible and utilized in the congregation. Worship at Cross

Lutheran Church is led by different choirs every Sunday. The congregation sponsors three choirs, including the Cross Praise Choir for adults, a twenty-five-voice Youth Choir, and the Angel Choir for children. Though the overall format of the liturgy is from the *Lutheran Book of Worship*, the order of worship has been adapted to offer hospitality across races, ethnicities, and cultures and to support the members of the congregation who came to Cross Lutheran Church from other denominations. Indeed, non-Lutherans are attracted to Cross Lutheran Church not so much because of its denominational affiliation as because the congregation is a multiracial community committed to a multiplicity of social justice ministries within its neighborhood, the city, and the wider world. "We can take someone from any religion and make them Lutheran," says Lois Glover, a member of the congregation since 1967.[4]

Of the 875 baptized (572 confirmed) members of Cross Lutheran Church, the weekly worship attendance is approximately 205 people. Over the last two years the congregation has celebrated over seventy baptisms of children and adults.[5] A transportation committee is in place to offer rides for services and church events to those who need them. "I drive someone from here somewhere almost everyday," says Ever Porter, who came to Cross Lutheran Church from a Methodist congregation twenty-five years ago and is now one of the drivers. "I trust Cross," he says. "They helped me a lot and they don't keep you here all day on Sunday." "If I don't come here, I feel like I miss something," says Lula Williams, an elder who came to Cross Lutheran Church from the Sanctified Church over thirty years ago. A self-proclaimed "doer not a talker," Williams says she appreciates the way the congregation has assisted her in raising her grandchildren. "There is always someone there when you need it," she says. Jovanna Miller, a student who received a scholarship from the congregation for college appreciates the congregation from the perspective of a young adult who was raised there. "I am very conscious of the 'Cross legacy,'" she says. "I know that it is my role to take that legacy with me wherever I go." Lisa Jacobsen, a young adult member of the congregation who also works with youth as a social worker, says that "the investment in youth is central here."

On a typical Sunday, members and visitors alike are welcomed to a liturgy that features music from a variety of hymnals, including

African American Lutheran and Roman Catholic. In 1980 Cross Lutheran Church and four nearby Lutheran congregations published an *Urban Hymnal Supplement,* incorporating four community liturgies and 115 hymns from various traditions. In 1988 an additional supplement was published in cooperation with the Milwaukee Area Lutheran Coalition.

Worship at Cross Lutheran Church is structured according to the ancient pattern of scripture lessons, sermon, offering, and communion. Besides a sermon by the pastor, Sunday worship includes a "contemporary witness," typically by a member of the congregation, as well as a children's sermon, also contributed by members. There is a high priority at Cross Lutheran Church for laypersons of all ages to have the opportunity to share with the entire congregation how their personal faith intersects with their work in the world. For example, at the confirmation service in May 2002, the sermon consisted of "witness talks" from the twelve young people who were confirmed, as well as one from the pastor who helped prepare them.

The spirit of the worship at Cross Lutheran Church is fluid and moving. Participation of as many people as possible is valued over precision. "We believe the Bible is the living, transforming message of the loving God," claims a brochure for Cross Lutheran Church. Typically, a "call to discipleship" is offered before the sermon hymn to give people an opportunity to confess their faith, or to find spiritual direction, or to ask for prayer. Elders and caregivers are available to pray and talk with those who ask for support.

Just as Cross Lutheran Church's worship and music reflect the generational, racial, ethnic, and cultural diversity of the congregation, so does the community's education program. For adults there is a Sunday morning Bible class, as well as a rigorous fifteen-week pastor's class for adults considering joining the church or for those who want an opportunity to study the Christian faith in depth. The congregation supports a variety of programs for children and youth of all ages and with differing needs.

The congregation's Sunday school currently serves approximately 142 children with the assistance of twenty-one leaders and teachers. Outreach and service are integral to the education of children and youth of all ages at Cross Lutheran Church. Last year the theme of "caring" was developed through participation in the Heifer Project.

Emily Ballew, a member of Cross Lutheran Church and a finalist in a poetry contest sponsored by Strive Media Institute and Gumbo Magazine, wrote the following poem inspired by the worship and music at the congregation.

Church Sunday

Loud powerful music
Jingle jangle of the tambourine
Rattle and thump of the drum
Clang clang of the piano
Clap clapping of the hands
The voices of the people

African spirituals, passed down from generation to generation,
Sung by everyone.
From the respected elders
Down to the young children.
The music fills everyone's soul and explodes upwards
And outwards into the sweet air.
Young and old,
Male or female,
Black or white,
No matter, just let the music come into your body.

Music is a hypnotizing force that moves you in indescribable ways.
Songs contain so much history
History of who we are,
Where we came from,
How we got here,
And how we're gonna get back home.

Time changes a lot of things,
But not the effect music can have on you.

Music is a very powerful force of nature

Especially on Church Sunday.

"Poetry Corner," Cross Lutheran Church. Used by permission.

Kindergarten through fifth-grade students have also focused their energy and creativity on the congregation's shut-ins. Each month the children learned about a person who was not able to attend services, and they created a care package for that person. "We work hard to care for the children who come here," says Kaylynn Blackwell, one of the directors of the Angel Choir, "and to help the kids learn to care for each other."

The twenty-five-voice Cross Youth Choir has performed across the country in over a dozen summer tours, including a nine-day tour in 1998 with stops in Indianapolis, Birmingham, Pensacola, Orlando, Atlanta, Lincolnton (NC), Columbia, Chicago, and at the congregation's "sister" church in Naples, Florida. Choir director Marilyn Miller does the work as a labor of love and to help build the self-esteem of the young people. Choir practice is held every Saturday, and the choir has sung every month since its inception in 1969. Miller, who has been a member of Cross Lutheran Church since she was ten years old, is now the director of the Lutheran Human Relations Association and vice-president of the Greater Milwaukee Synod of the Evangelical Lutheran Church in America (ELCA). "The choir ministry's goals are helping youth feel comfortable with the gospel, expanding awareness of the world and to help them become more disciplined," she says.[6]

Cross Lutheran Church's commitment to young people in the congregation and throughout the community is demonstrated in programs that go beyond Sunday mornings. In addition to the Cross Youth Choir, there is a variety of other educational programs designed to empower the mostly African American young people of the congregation and the neighborhood. For instance, Cross Lutheran Church sponsors weekly meetings of PEPCI (Persons Expressing Problems Challenging Ideas), a support group for middle and high school youths who have family members who are addicted. Project RETURN (Returning Ex-offenders To Urban Realities and Neighborhoods), a program for ex-offenders initiated by and based at Cross Lutheran Church for twenty years, offers a six-week summer enrichment program for children ages 6 through 12. "Come Together With Project RETURN" provides the children with six weeks of recreation and classes in basic learning skills and social skills for $25. In addition, free tutoring in all subjects is offered every Saturday at Cross Lutheran Church for students in grades 4 and above, and the congregation supports post–high school scholarship funds through the "Martin Luther King All-a-thon" held in May each year.

Cross Lutheran Church also sponsors a summer program for children entering Kindergarten through sixth grade. The 2002 program,

Shalom High School, an alternative school, now occupies the building that formerly housed the school of Cross Lutheran Church. The congregation continues to maintain a relationship with many of the young people in the school, and graduation ceremonies are held at Cross Lutheran Church. Simmie Booker, a young man who graduated from Shalom High School in 2002, wrote the following poem and recited it at graduation.

If I Can Do It, So Can You

The restraints of my environment holding me down,
Evil that was present pulling me down.
Label another fool like homie the clown.
Anytime I'm recognized, it's only with doubt.

And when the odds has stacked against me,
While my back was against the wall.
I cracked against the pavement,
And my ego started to fall.

I walked a different path,
I felt a need for change.
I finally did the math
My soul called my name.

It spoke of my foul living,
And my misguided ways,
He said I should be now giving,
Cause I gook so much away.

Now I walk the narrow road,
I'm one of the chosen few.
And if I can do it,
So can you.

"Poetry Corner," Cross Lutheran Church. Used by permission.

entitled "What a Beautiful World This Would Be," was an academic program that explored the word's diversity through social studies, geography, reading, and artistic expression. For six weeks the children studied the array of people and cultures in the world; the kindergarten studied Japan, Mexico, and Africa; the first and second grade studied South America; and the third and fourth grade focused on Africa. The program, which cost $25 for the entire period, stressed the need to respect differences.

Girls from throughout the neighborhood participate in the CHOICES program, which is devoted to celebrating the joys and struggles of being created female. Eight years ago, Venice R. Williams, director of youth ministry at Cross Lutheran Church from 1989 to 1997, Gloria Wright, a member of the congregation for forty years, and Lynn Erickson, campus pastor at Marquette University, had a heart-to-heart talk about what it was like to grow up female. "We asked ourselves how life might have been different if we'd had a safe place as girls, where we could talk about the changes we were going through and all the questions we had about life. So we decided to create that space for other girls," says Venice Williams.[7]

Cross Lutheran Church was the site for the first CHOICES group, and Ericka Copeland, now one of the adult women facilitators, was enrolled in that first group of girls as a participant. What began as a week-long camp for girls is now a multi-site mentoring program for girls of all ages and racial and ethnic backgrounds throughout Milwaukee. The groups are facilitated by congregational volunteers and Marquette University students. Some sites have separate groups for elementary students and for junior high and high school students. The goal remains to help girls sort through the complex and conflicting messages sent by society and to offer a nurturing environment in which to make life decisions. Venice Williams is now the director of the program run by the Greater Milwaukee Area Synod's Seedfolk Youth Ministry, along with sponsoring congregations and healthcare organizations. "This kind of nurturing doesn't happen enough," says Williams. "But that's the beauty of this. Unlike other ministries where you have to get people involved, CHOICES draws women to fill their own voids—voids of intergenerational female nurturing." Gloria Wright also believes in the importance of the girls seeing women in leadership: "I only hope and pray that they see the good they can do," she says.[8]

"These young women come for the fulfillment they get here," says Ericka Copeland. "The girls support each other and help each other make good choices. When they talk, they know they're not the only one going through situations with peer pressure, drugs, sex, and parental relationships." Williams has designed a curriculum that builds self-esteem in girls, equips them with decision-making skills, and includes cultural and recreational opportunities. "It's what many of them don't get otherwise," says Williams. "We also talk about nutrition, self-care, and sexuality—there's nothing we won't talk about. And what we talk about stays here. That's part of safety." She adds, "Part of what we do is unlearn the negative, and create positive images of being women. God said we were good, not just that man was good."[9]

Venice Williams and Seedfolk Youth Ministry has developed a program similar to CHOICES for boys called the Simba Circle. The weekly gatherings for Milwaukee-area African American males ages 8 to 18 create a place for boys, young men, and adult mentors to explore daily challenges, growing up male in the city, the challenges of being a black man, and teaches a variety of life skills. A similar weekly group for boys, CHALLENGES, has been formed at Cross Lutheran Church. "We think it is important for us to have something for young men here," says Wayne Porter, who is a parole officer and assists with the confirmation class. "I think it is important that they have an opportunity to give back, and do something for someone else," he says.[10]

In an effort to strengthen all the youth programs at Cross Lutheran Church, the youth education committee instituted a new program focus in 2002 called "Working Together in Peace." To start the program the congregation held four training sessions and recruited a team of leaders with complementary skills. The first session was led by Gloria Wright on the themes of limit setting and active listening. Wright described active listening as essential to limit setting and composed of the following elements: Concentrate, Acknowledge, Respond, and Empathize. In the second session, Kristen Geenen-Powers emphasized ways to prevent behavioral crises. The last two sessions were on behavioral levels and corresponding staff responses, and nonverbal and paraverbal communication. Throughout its programs for children and youth, Cross Lutheran Church seeks to build multiracial community across generations, throughout the neighborhood, and in the greater Milwaukee area.

FIFTY YEARS OF CONTINUOUS CHANGE

The last fifty years in the history of Cross Lutheran Church have been marked by continuous change within the congregation and the neighborhood. To respond to those changes in the spirit of the gospel, the congregation has launched many creative ministries that uphold a vision of multiracial community within wider Milwaukee. The demographic history of Cross Lutheran Church marks its movement from an all-white, predominantly German American congregation with 2,500 baptized members in 1955, to a predominantly African American (80 percent) congregation with 875 members in 2001. The congregation was founded in 1870, when thirteen men gathered to form "Cross Evangelical Lutheran Congregation, Unaltered Augsburg Confession." The congregation arrived at its current site—the third location in its history—in 1931. Cross Lutheran Church supported a Christian day school from its inception until it was forced to close in 1965 because of financial pressures. Cross Lutheran Church was a Lutheran Church–Missouri Synod Congregation (LCMS) from its inception in 1870 until 1976, when it joined the Association of Evangelical Lutheran Churches (AELC). In 1988, Cross Lutheran Church joined in the founding of the Evangelical Lutheran Church in America (ELCA). Since its founding, Cross Lutheran Church has been served by six senior pastors—the seventh having arrived in September 2002— and numerous assistant, part-time, and volunteer pastors. The congregation has helped train parish interns since 1969, and since 1988 the congregation has been part of the Horizon Intern program of the ELCA which trains pastors for urban and rural ministry. The first African American members of the congregation joined after 1958, at the invitation of members of the congregation who visited throughout the neighborhood and opened the parish school to children in the neighborhood. The Midtown area of Milwaukee, where Cross Lutheran Church is located, is now 95 percent African American; 70 percent of the people in the area live below the poverty level; and all of the children in the neighborhood public school qualify for free or reduced-price lunch.

Gloria Wright became one of the first African American members of the congregation after she was invited to church by a German

Milwaukee, Wisconsin

Total population	508,824

Metro population makeup

European American	74.0%
African American or black	15.5%
American Indian	0.5%
Asian	2.0%
Other	0.1%
Racially mixed	1.2%
Hispanic	6.3%

The majority of the Hispanic population
self-describe as Mexican or Mexican American.

Families below poverty level	17.0%

Of these families, 57% have children under 18
years of age, and 35% are families where the
householder is female.

Grandparents raising grandchiildren	7,000
Households where first language is other than English	15.0%
Unemployment rate	6.0%

Sources: U.S. Census Bureau, 2000; CensusScope for Milwaukee, Wisconsin; Lewis Mumford Center.

American neighbor. Though her first experience of Sunday worship at Cross Lutheran Church was listening to the service in German while seated in the last pew, Wright felt that it was "a welcoming church." Wright's children also attended the parish school. "It was obvious that part of the church wanted us here," she said. "The church recognized that this community would become all-black," says Wright. "They realized that their future was here. Many left, others stayed." A descendent of the German American founders of the congregation, Betty Marx was baptized in the congregation seventy-six years ago and has remained with the congregation through many of its transitions. "As black families moved in and the others moved out, distance became an excuse to leave," says Marx who commutes a long distance

Cross Lutheran Church, 2001

Current membership   875

Congregation makeup (self-described)
    African American   758
    Asian/Pacific Islander   11
    Hispanic   4
    European American   102

Peak membership year: 1953, with 2,638 members
Lowest membership year: 1971, with 266 members
    (The congregation lost an average of 100 persons per
    year from 1953 to 1971.)

Average growth rate, 1994–2001   26.8%
Percent attending worship   23.4%
Confirmed membership   28.8%
Size of Sunday school   142 pupils and 21 leaders

Total income $263,363
Total disbursements $264,216

Source: Evangelical Lutheran Church in America Trend Report, Department
for Research and Evaluation

to the church. "I taught Sunday school for thirty-nine years," she says, "and I got to know people through their children. There are wonderful, dedicated people here. I don't always agree with everything, but this is my home, I am not leaving now." As treasurer for over twenty years, Marx maintains that some of the greatest struggles of the congregation have been financial. Though the congregation always pulled out of times of financial hardship, Marx recalls one time when she initiated an "adopt a bill" program. That is, she laid all the congregation's bills out on a table after the service in the hope that members of the congregation would select one to pay!

Over the years from 1994 to 2001, Cross Lutheran Church experienced a fairly steady 26.6 percent rate of growth. The mission of the congregation is summed up in the following statement from the brochure for Cross Lutheran Church: "We believe that part of following Christ means standing in solidarity with those who often find themselves on the 'outside" because of race, gender, age, sexual orientation, disabilities, economic status or addictions." Though Cross Lutheran Church is a predominantly black congregation numerically, almost all the members describe the congregation as "racially integrated." Belief in the need to dismantle racism and to live in a congregational model that reflects racial, ethnic, and class diversity and that strives for justice, including faith-based community organizing, are deeply held values among those who find Cross Lutheran Church to be their spiritual home. Many of those who have joined Cross Lutheran Church during the last thirty-four years—including the 20 percent who are of European American, Asian American, or Hispanic heritage—have joined the congregation because of their desire to be part of a multiracial community.

Joe Ellwanger arrived in Milwaukee in 1967 after serving congregations in Missouri and Alabama and remained at Cross Lutheran Church until his retirement in 2001. Throughout much of his thirty-four-year pastorate, "Pastor Joe"—as he is called by many in the congregation—was a chief architect and visionary for Cross Lutheran Church's development as a multiracial and justice-oriented community. "It's got to be from the heart and it's got to be real," he says. "Then people come back." Joe Ellwanger's leadership style—both deeply pastoral and deeply prophetic—has nurtured and challenged Cross Lutheran Church to be able to take on controversy and to remain a spiritual community. "Any congregation not walking with people on the edges will miss some of the gospel. The church has to be involved in the transformation of the society." His ability to negotiate the balance between the more traditional aspects of pastoral care and social action are key to the ability of this congregation to parlay change into transformation. "As opportunities beckon we live out the call of the Spirit," he says. We value spiritual growth first, and numerical growth comes after that." Ellwanger considers his long pastorate "not a burden, but a great blessing." Both Joe and Joyce Ellwanger believed it was crucial to their ministry at Cross Lutheran Church to live in the community and to send their children to the local schools. "I can't serve this community if I can't live here," says Joe.

Several African American families were drawn to Cross Lutheran Church in 1969 with the formation of the Youth Choir by Gloria Wright, which added to the diversity of Sunday worship. Two years later, the congregation had begun to develop the "community liturgies" that are still a feature of its worship today. Before the publication of the ELCA's African American hymnal *This Far By Faith*, members of Cross Lutheran developed the congregation's own *Urban Hymnal Supplement,* drawn from African American, folk, as well as traditional Lutheran sources, in an attempt to make worship more relevant and accessible to the people of the neighborhood and beyond. Also in 1969 the congregation hosted the People's Committee for Model Cities. The mass meetings that ensued not only helped set the course for the current strong focus on social justice that is part of Cross Lutheran Church today; it also pushed the congregation to live with controversy, to work with the poor, to network with community groups, and to negotiate power structures, and to live with the pluses and minuses of media attention.

Throughout the early 1970s, Cross Lutheran Church lived under the threat of expulsion from the Lutheran Church–Missouri Synod district president, because of the congregation's ecumenical relationships and its commitment to the leadership of women. In 1972 the congregation chose to continue its practice of women elders, including high school youth, rather than uphold the LCMS's male-only tradition. The year 1973 brought another threat of expulsion, this time because of Cross Lutheran Church's decision that it would better serve the neighborhood if it strengthened its relationship with Christ Presbyterian Church. By 1976 the congregation chose to join the Association of Evangelical Lutheran Churches, an ELCA ancestor body, as a sign of solidarity with others who believe in women's leadership in the church and in the spirit of ecumenism.

FAITH-BASED INITIATIVES

Besides negotiating its denominational identity in the 1970s, Cross Lutheran Church was beginning to build on its history of racial and cultural diversity and neighborhood action in a more concerted, focused way. Moreover, the congregation began to join and launch a variety of faith-based initiatives that would serve to move the congregation into deeper relationship with a variety of local and international justice concerns.

In an effort to reach out to persons from other cultures who do not speak English as well as recent immigrants, Cross Lutheran Church decided in 1979 to sponsor two Laotian refugee families. The relationship that was formed with these families—who later chose to join the congregation—opened the door later for further outreach within an apartment complex three blocks from the church that has a large Laotian and Hmong population. Khamphanh Bouakongxaya, the daughter of one of the Laotian families sponsored by Cross Lutheran Church and a graduate of Carthage College in Kenosha, Wisconsin, is now a neighborhood public school teacher and a member of the congregation's board of elders. Bouakongxaya said she first experienced American racism when she was seven years old. Yet participation in the congregation taught her "to be open-minded, and that diversity can take place." Her parents Bounheua and Thongba moved into the parsonage with their four small children in 1961. "These people were good people to our family," says Bounheua. "They became like brothers and sisters." The positive experiences and the challenges of sponsoring refugees encouraged Cross Lutheran Church later to sponsor one Guatemalan refugee as part of the sanctuary movement as well as two Haitian refugees and three Sudanese families.

In 1981 a growing concern within Cross Lutheran Church for those incarcerated in four minimum-security prisons within a mile and a half of the church led the congregation after almost a year of study to start Project RETURN. Under the leadership of Mary Steppe, the ecumenical, church-based program, currently serves the minimum-security prisons located near the church, as well as several state prisons. Though in some ways the ex-offenders are on the margins of the congregation, two to four prisoners participate in Sunday worship at Cross Lutheran Church. The offices for Project RETURN were located in the parish house until space limitations forced the staff to move several blocks from the church. Several ex-offenders have joined the congregation through their relationship with the project.

Besides providing support group services for ex-offenders, Project RETURN offers job placement and housing assistance. A Certified Alcohol and Drug Counselor (CADC III) is available through Project RETURN to provide confidential assessments and to assist clients if services are needed. "We work on all levels together for healing," says Mary Steppe. Perhaps most importantly, Project RETURN seeks "to walk with each individual. We attempt to give every client the confidence it takes to be a healthy member of society, to be the best one can be. We act as the support many of our clients have never had." A Jobs Task Force at Cross Lutheran Church also provides job placement services to anyone in the community on a twice-weekly basis.

Lois Glover, a member of Cross Lutheran Church, was vice-president of MICAH (Milwaukee Inner-city Congregations Allied for Hope), an ecumenical and interfaith community-based organization made up of forty-eight congregations from fifteen denominations concerned with local justice issues. Cross Lutheran Church joined MICAH in 1989 and joined with 48 congregations from 15 denominations concerned with local justice issues, such as the closing of a drug-related tavern. "MICAH is about people working together," says Glover, "denominations are not as important." Members of Cross Lutheran Church are key leaders in MICAH as the organization continues to address problems related to public education, affordable housing, drug treatment availability, fair labor practices, and immigration issues.

In May 2002 MICAH sponsored a summit on immigration issues for faith communities. Concerned that current immigration laws separate families and treat working people unfairly, the summit was organized to enable people to lobby their legislators for action. MICAH is affiliated with an umbrella organization called WISDOM, of which Lois Glover is currently president, which connects faith-based groups throughout southern Wisconsin. Together MICAH and WISDOM are working to reduce the negative impact of the continuing cutbacks in public education, which might not be necessary if tax loopholes were closed. For instance, legal services, along with other businesses are not taxed. The Cross MICAH Core Team worked to organize members of the congregation to participate in a demonstration at a major Milwaukee law firm to focus on a tax loophole, and to make it known that if the firm had paid taxes there would have been an additional $30 million in state revenue in 2001. Other objectives of MICAH members have been the removal of red-lining in the central city, securing funding for drug treatment for uninsured persons, providing affordable housing, and increasing the number of accessible, family-supporting jobs.

In the early 1990s, when the congregation became aware that ten blocks from the church was another underserved community,

Plymouth Manor Nursing Home, members of Cross Lutheran Church developed a strategy to provide pastoral services and to build relationships there on an intergenerational basis. The installation of an elevator and wheelchair-accessible bathrooms in the church facility in 1994 allowed for participation of persons from the nursing home in the worship and programs of the congregation. As part of Cross Lutheran Church's rebuilding effort after the fire, the bathroom on the sanctuary level was also made wheelchair accessible. These modifications in the congregation's physical plant paved the way for the opening of an Adult Center in 1994 at Cross Lutheran Church. The purpose of the center, which has grown every year since its inception, is to provide positive growth experiences for older adults and younger adults in need of enrichment opportunities, as well as leadership opportunities for adults in the congregation. Gloria Wright was the founding director, assisted by Dolores Riley as nutrition coordinator, Betty Marx as treasurer, and a twelve-member planning council. The current director is Joyce Briley. The Adult Center also provides a forum for intergenerational dialogue between older adults and youth at Shalom High School, an alternative high school that occupies the building adjacent to Cross Lutheran Church. Open every Tuesday morning, the Adult Center offers people—many of whom are senior citizens who attend the program whenever possible—meals, fellowship, and opportunities for recreation such as Bible study, discussion groups, and arts and crafts. "We never try to let new people feel left out," says Sammie Miller, an active participant in the Adult Center program. Cross Lutheran Church's Caregivers work constantly to reach out to persons with disabilities within the congregation, at Plymouth Manor Nursing Home in Jackson Center, and in neighborhood group homes.

Cross Lutheran Church provides additional services to the community through the Bread of Healing/Empowerment Program, a community-based hunger-prevention program that offers emergency food and also seeks to get at the root causes of poverty. Also housed in parish facilities, the program was founded in 1992, offers holistic healthcare and assists the congregation in forming relationships with the hundreds of individuals and families who come to the church for emergency food. The parish food ministry was coordinated by Annie Porter and Johnnie Mae Phillips from 1980 through 1999. When Bread of Healing was founded in 1992, the food was purchased, cooked, and served by Nellie Davis. In 1999, Teri Woodley became the coordinator of the weekly program, which now provides many services and spiritual guidance. Woodley sees the eradication of oppression as a "spiritual problem." "It is time to stop discriminating, living in the past, and better to try to make the world a better place," she says.

The Bread of Healing/Empowerment Program takes place every Wednesday at noon and offers clients a meal, Bible study, substance abuse counseling, a clothing and food bank, men's and women's support groups, and a medical clinic staffed by a physician from Sinai Samaritan Medical Center in Milwaukee. Thanks to a collaboration with the medical center through Aurora Healthcare, Cross Lutheran Church added a parish nurse, Rick Cesar, to the staff in 1993. Cesar serves Cross Lutheran Church for twenty hours per week coordinating the holistic healthcare program on Wednesday and working with people in physical and spiritual need. Cesar sees the purpose of his ministry as a public health nurse "to live the word and love of Jesus." "The work involves me with justice issues in the community—with people who live on the fringes and who are denied access, and who are suffering from injustice," he says. Cesar also became a member of Cross Lutheran Church, and two of his four foster sons were baptized there. "Cross could be held up as a very human church," says Cesar. "It struggles as a community just as an individual would. But to see the gospel living is its own evangelism." As well as providing AIDS/HIV testing and information, the Bread of Healing Empowerment program at Cross Lutheran Church is the only church program in Milwaukee to provide free needle exchange through the AIDS Resource Center of Wisconsin. "Our hope is to empower those who come to live into their potential for the sake of themselves, their family and their community," says Joe Ellwanger.

A "RECONCILED-IN-CHRIST" COMMUNITY

Some of the most difficult issues for some members of Cross Lutheran Church to negotiate have been in relationship to the congregation's decision in 1989 to become a "Reconciled-in-Christ" congregation after months of Bible study, dialogue, and prayer. "Reconciled-in-

Christ" congregations seek to be "welcoming communities for gay and lesbian people through the ministry of Word and Sacrament, sharing God's truth and love with all people."[11] The educational process that preceded this decision was rooted in the study of Scripture and challenged the congregation to struggle with issues of sexual identity in a positive way. A LGBT (Lesbian, Gay, Bisexual, Transgendered) committee was formed at Cross Lutheran Church in 2000. Several gay and lesbian people, including couples, chose to become members of the congregation because of this stand, and out of a desire to belong to a multiracial community. Additional members of the gay and lesbian community were attracted to Cross Lutheran Church after 1993, when the congregation agreed to the celebration of same-sex commitment ceremonies.

The story of the struggles of Cross Lutheran Church in its effort to become a "Reconciled-in-Christ" congregation is significant also because it is an example of the broad range of attitudes and beliefs within multiracial communities. Too often efforts to build community within diverse contexts assume (without analysis) a broad "fellowship of the oppressed," without taking into account the multiplicity of opinions, beliefs, and attitudes held by individuals within a given community. For instance, within the congregation of Cross Lutheran Church neither all the African Americans nor all the white members were prepared to accept gay and lesbian people into the congregation. In both racial groups some members still do not agree with the congregation's decision to become a "Reconciled-in-Christ" congregation. Conversely, there are also African Americans and European Americans in the congregation who are supportive of the decision and who do perceive the systemic connections between all marginalized persons. Rather than polarize the issue across racial lines—a possibility, given that most of the lesbian and gay members of the congregation are white and most of the rest of the membership is black—the answer to try to avoid this polarization was to set up opportunities for structured education and dialogue that allowed for the diversity of perspectives to be heard. The pastor and other key leaders of the congregation were unequivocal in their support of lesbian and gay people, and they continued to hold up the biblical principle that it is the gospel of Christ that is at the heart of the Christian faith. They encouraged all who would commit to continuing dialogue and education to remain together for the sake of the gospel and the mission of the church.

Though Cross Lutheran Church lost six to eight members after the vote to become a "Reconciled-in-Christ" congregation, and about the same number after it began to celebrate same-sex commitment ceremonies, Joe Ellwanger maintains that the overall gain for the congregation was worth the struggle. "Our homophobia is more culture driven than scripture driven," he says. "The gospel mandate is to reach out to all people and particularly those at the edges. In our society gays and lesbians often are at the edges, especially if they come out." "'Coming out' services have become annual events at Cross, so "gays and lesbians do not have to hide themselves and wonder every Sunday whether somebody's going to find out and condemn and attack them," says Joe Ellwanger. Cross Lutheran Church member Bradley Hausler, a lifelong Lutheran, believes that his sexual identity is "just one of God's diversities." He chooses to belong to a multiracial congregation because he sees the membership as a "huge blessing." The challenge of participating in the congregation has moved him to realize his "own issues with racism." Lisa Quam and Ann Hogan were drawn to Cross Lutheran Church as a congregation where they could attend together and would be treated as a couple. Welcomed by the congregation, they each are involved with different activities and have felt the need on occasion to stretch some member's perception of gender roles. Similarly, Fred Moss and Marty Schneider stayed at Cross Lutheran Church after a Christmas visit. Heavily involved in the life of the congregation, the couple were drawn to the Cross community because issues such as racism, classism, and homophobia were raised from the pulpit.

PARTNERSHIPS BEYOND THE LOCAL COMMUNITY

The many partnerships of Cross Lutheran Church are more than part of the congregation's history; they are integral to the ongoing life of the congregation and its commitment to multiracial community. Though served for over thirty years by a white pastor, the congregation's overall leadership reflects the diversity of its membership, as does the leadership of its programs. Moreover, the congregation's commitment to racial justice has led the community to a network of relationships that transcend many boundaries beyond race, including social class, national origin, gender, generation, and sexual identity. Not all members of the congregation agree universally on all justice issues, but the underlying sense of care and concern within the membership knits the community together across differences. One of the reasons that Cross Lutheran Church is able to remain active in such a variety of justice-oriented ministries lies in its creative receptivity to forming partnerships—in the neighborhood, ecumenically, throughout the denomination, and even globally. This ability to form alliances with other congregations and faith-based organizations has increased the witness of Cross Lutheran Church and multiplied its opportunities for ministry. Further, the story of Cross Lutheran Church also illustrates how the nature of "interlocking oppressions" is lived out in a congregation committed to multiracial community. In other words, congregations truly committed to an antiracist vision of justice will eventually encounter the oppression experienced by other groups and will again have to discern their relationship as a community with these people. Ultimately, justice cannot be partitioned.

Cross Lutheran Church has relationships with partner Lutheran congregations in the Wisconsin communities of Sheboygan (First United), Neenah (St. Mark's), Watertown (Immanuel), Bowler (Church of the Wilderness), and Waukesha (Ascension). Proximity allows the members of Cross Lutheran Church and these predominantly white congregations to get beyond stereotypes and tackle issues of racism, classism, and heterosexism. All the partner congregations have visited one another and have shared educational experiences through adult forums and Bible study. These exchanges have helped the other congregations see that the members of Cross Lutheran Church "are not poor stepdaughters and sons," says Joe Ellwanger. "We have our financial difficulties, sure, but in many ways we are *so rich* and we have much to share with the larger church."

Always seeking ways to network with other Lutheran congregations, Cross Lutheran Church has also formed some partnerships with a "sister" congregation in another part of the United States. Emmanuel Lutheran Church in Naples, Florida, originally "adopted" Cross Lutheran Church to lend their financial support to the congregation, but it soon became clear that the partnership offered opportunities for relationship and learning that benefited both congregations. Though originally not looking for a cultural exchange, members of Emmanuel Lutheran Church declared after a Sunday worship visit that the Cross Lutheran Church congregation was the "huggingest" they had ever experienced. The Sunday schools of both congregations have instituted a pen-pal program, and the Cross Youth Choir has appeared at Emmanuel Lutheran Church in Naples.[12]

In 1983 Cross Lutheran Church further extended the boundaries of its ministries by developing partnerships within Central America. After over six months of prayer and Bible study the congregation voted to become a sanctuary site for Central American refugees. Not only did the community declare itself a sanctuary congregation. It formed a relationship with a partner congregation, Resurrection Church, in San Salvador, and provided support for a missionary. A "sister synod" relationship was formed also between the Greater Milwaukee Synod and the Lutheran Church in El Salvador, as a result of the recommendation of Cross Lutheran Church in 1989. Carolyn Jackson, a member of Cross Lutheran Church since 1972 along with her husband, Tom, served on the ecumenical Milwaukee Sanctuary Committee from 1982 to 1990. Carolyn Jackson remembers that the "contemporary witness" talks during worship were especially effective in challenging the congregation to take on the sanctuary movement. Jackson was instrumental in inspiring six congregations in metropolitan Milwaukee, including Cross Lutheran Church, to become sanctuary congregations.

Cross Lutheran Church is a member of the Milwaukee Area Lutheran Coalition of the Greater Milwaukee Synod, ELCA, which seeks to eradicate racism within the larger church and the community. The Coalition has worked with the Crossroads Ministry and the Lutheran Human Relations Association in the area of antiracism training and strategies.[13] In May 1988, the Milwaukee Area Lutheran Coalition founded the Milwaukee Outreach Training Network (MOTN) to train leaders for the mission of the church in the city and to establish new local ministries. Some of ministries connected with MOTN, and through this organization to Cross Lutheran Church, include Abundant Life Ministry, which offers life skill training, vocation and career counseling, and job placement services; and Serenity Inns, a new treatment ministry that will provide a twenty-eight-day inpatient recovery program and housing for men and women in recovery, and Kujichagulia youth center, with programs for youth, women, and men, with a special relevance for African Americans living in the urban context.[14]

Cross Lutheran Church's commitment to racial justice and cultural diversity anticipated a larger movement within the Evangelical Lutheran Church in America (ELCA). In 1987 the denomination adopted the following goal: "It shall be a goal of this church that within 10 years of its establishment the membership shall include at least 10 percent people of color and/or whose primary language other than English."[15] The ten-year period has passed and the overall percentage of membership of people of color and/or whose primary language is other than English has reached 2.13 percent, which falls short of the stated goal. But the numbers of people in these groups increased by 23.7 percent between 1987 and 1994.

Today the ELCA has 2.3 percent people of color and is trying to overcome its "hyper-segregation." In 1998 only 564 of its 6,673 congregations had 10 percent or more people of color.[16] "God calls us to a better life and a radically new way of being human. We can't continue with business as usual," says Pastor Joseph A. Donnella II, of Gettysburg College in Pennsylvania. "Lutherans can't afford to continue using their central theological confession that they are justified by God's grace through faith as an excuse for doing nothing, idly waiting for God to repair the world's disorder."[17]

Cross Lutheran Church provides leadership for denominational racial justice efforts. "Sometimes when things happen to me, I don't know if it's because of my race or because I'm a woman," says Marilyn Miller of Cross Lutheran Church. "You know in your heart that racism is not from all white people, but you're in an environment where white people make decisions that make you so angry, decisions that are keeping institutionalized racism in place." Miller serves as the director of the Cross Youth Choir and also as executive director of the Lutheran Human Relations Association in Milwaukee. For over ten years, Miller and a white colleague, Joyce Caldwell, have offered workshops to help congregations confront prejudices and work to eradicate the racism in society's institutions. As a white ally, Caldwell sees her role as "carrying Marilyn's story and the stories of so many other people in my heart. My role is to be aware when, in an all-white group, people feel safe saying stuff that is awful. As an ally, I can't get away with not interrupting them." "Many people are comfortable with saying nothing," says Miller. "But that is not what the Lord call us to do. You can't just say, 'I'm a Christian and I love all people.' Your actions have to go with that."[18]

Over the last decade, the ELCA has renewed its affirmation of the commitment to 10 percent growth and the Multicultural Mission Strategy adopted at the Churchwide Assembly in 1991. The Multicultural Mission Strategy Action Plan calls for:

- All baptized members of the Evangelical Lutheran Church in America to reflect, confess, and act on our personal commitment for ministries with African American, Black, American Indian and Alaskan Native, Arab and Middle Eastern, Asian, and Hispanic people;

- All members of the Evangelical Church in America to support and encourage the ministry of congregations with predominantly African American, Black, American Indian and Alaska native, Arab and Middle Eastern, Asian, and Hispanic members;

- All congregations to learn about their communities, develop, and implement plans for outreach in their neighborhoods with African American, Black, American Indian and Alaska Native, Arab and Middle Eastern, Asian and Hispanic people;

- All ELCA congregations to become partners in this effort;

- All synods in cooperation with churchwide units to identify congregations in racially changing communities and assist them to develop strategies for outreach;

- All synods to provide leadership to congregations that are engaged in or exploring ministry with African American, Black, American Indian and Alaska Native, Arab and Middle Eastern, Asian, and Hispanic communities;

- All ELCA pastors, rostered lay ministers, and persons in leadership positions to accelerate efforts to develop and support leaders to serve in multicultural ministries;

- All schools, colleges, universities, seminaries, and affiliated organizations to accelerate efforts to recruit, develop and support leaders to serve in multicultural ministries;

- All synodical bishops, pastors, rostered lay ministers, pers(leadership positions, and congregation members to receive ing sessions in order to combat racism and classism;

- All synodical bishops, pastors, rostered lay ministers in leauer-ship positions to work with pastors and African American, Black, American Indian and Alaska Native, Arab and Middle Eastern, Asian, and Hispanic people to address the issues of jus-tice and advocacy on behalf of people living in poverty, in prison, and discriminated against due to race, ethnicity or gender.[19]

As in efforts throughout the ELCA, the members of Cross Lutheran Church are concerned with systemic questions that address institu-tionalized racism, such as, Who in our community has access to ser-vices, opportunities, and education? Who doesn't? Also, who are the leaders and decision makers? Are the voices of the community, includ-ing the poor, represented in decision making? Lastly, are the policies of the institutions within the community written and interpreted so that they promote equality, accessibility, and social justice to people of color and those whose primary language is other than English? Joe Ellwanger says that one of the reasons those at Cross Lutheran belong to organizations such as MICAH and have formed other partnerships is "that there are major changes in the urban scene that we could never bring about by ourselves, or by simply being the sign of hope and transformation that our very existence signals." The experiences of Cross Lutheran Church as a multiracial community have, over the years, opened the congregation to relations and ministries that have brought change where structures and patterns don't change easily. As Joe Ellwanger says:

> One learning is that the majority of European Americans, including Christians, are racist and classist in terms of where they live and with whom they associate. When African Americans moved into the Cross neighborhood, whites moved out. Some of this movement was due to sheer racism and classism. Some of it was due to fear of the higher crime rate in pockets of poverty. Some of it was due to the cultural mood of the times to move to better housing, nicer neighborhoods, more spa-cious yards, that is very much the thought pattern of whites and blacks, as they secure jobs that permit them to purchase or rent such housing.

It is all of the above that accounts for the fact that only one "old guard" member remains at Cross. However, it is to be noted that 20 percent of the membership at Cross is European America. These are the people who have come to Cross after the "old guard" members left—most of them living outside the immediate area, but some living within ten minutes of Cross. They have joined Cross for any number of reasons, including: Desire to be part of a racially and income diverse congregation, for the sake of the gospel; appreciation of a musically diverse liturgy; commitment to social justice; commitment to inclusion of gays and lesbians; commitment to being part of the solution to urban problems instead of the cause; readiness to be part of a "can-do" missional congregation that is ready to take risks because of what it means to live the gospel in these times.

SUMMARY

Though Cross Lutheran Church has been through a great deal of change over its history, it now stands poised for more change as it moves from a long-term pastorate to the leadership of a new pastor. In June 2002 the congregation voted to call the Rev. Robert W. Crabb, who began his ministry in Milwaukee in September of the same year. Previously the pastor of St. Stephen's Lutheran Church in Brooklyn, New York, and founder of New Hope Lutheran Church in the Bronx where he served as managing director for Lutheran Family Community Services, Pastor Crabb's work in diverse communities has provided him with a wealth of ministry experience for pastoring Cross Lutheran Church. Lay leaders who have worked hard to support the congregation's ministries during the interim period are looking forward to having a pastor. As is the case with most long pastorates, most of the current congregation has significant experience with only one pastor. Though there is hope and excitement about a new pastor, there is also some anxiety about changes he may bring to the congregation.

Almost universally noted among those interviewed for this study among the membership of Cross Lutheran Church are the warmth and caring of the congregation. As a multiracial community, Cross Lutheran Church has continued to reinvent itself and knit together a diverse group of people. The diversity of the worship and the visibility of young people, as well as the witness of the congregation in the neighborhood and in social justice ministries, are also consistently recounted as the congregation's strengths. Patsy Coleman, 2002 president of the congregation, notes: "We have very committed people who do an enormous amount of work for the church. It is now time for us to take charge during this transition." "Some people were devastated when Joe [Ellwanger] retired," says Lisa Jacobsen. "We are working hard to overcome that." "This community expects a lot out of a pastor," says Katherine Wilcher, who has been a member of the congregation for four years, "but we will also need to support our new pastor a lot."

Still, Cross Lutheran Church faces challenges as they seek to build a multiracial community. Funding for the congregation and its many efforts, though always a concern throughout its history, is a source of anxiety now that donations are down. This is not uncommon during an interim period, but the decrease in funding has put further stress on lay leaders. "We need more people," says Guy Davis, who with his wife, Denise, have been part of Cross Lutheran Church for thirty-three years. "We have recruited people from other communities. But we may also have to be honest about what we can and cannot do." The Davises, as well as others who have been leaders in the congregation for a long time, also emphasize the need for new leadership and a more steady Sunday congregation, particularly adults in their twenties and thirties, who now form only a small part of the congregation. Johnson and Judy Hunter, who have held numerous leadership roles since 1976, are concerned about the aging pool of current leaders as well as about the issues involved in the maintaining an urban and highly-used building. "Joe had a lot of energy to do things," says Johnson Hunter, "but now we have to fill in those gaps, like managing to keep the building locked after hours." "We have ongoing struggles with maintaining the physical plant," echos Paulette Barr. Reynolds K. Honold, former president of the congregation and chair of the calling committee for the new pastor agrees. "There has been a real willingness of the laity to take charge and reduce our dependence on Joe," he says, "but we also need to look at recruiting new leaders and dealing with our recurring maintenance issues." Frances Bryant, a member of the congregation for twenty-five years, suggests that she is very involved in the congregation because when "I come here on empty, I go home full." Yet Bryant and other lay leaders suggest that the congregation needs to continue to build trust and to communicate honestly with each other, especially in the face of conflict. "Sometimes it is more loving to confront each other," says Bryant. "We are loving but sometimes we need to understand that it is important to speak the truth in love."

Among the next steps for Cross Lutheran Church will be to deepen the bonds of love already strong within the multiracial congregation and to strengthen them for the future.

4

Mulligan Stew

Delhaven Christian Church
La Puente, California

Clearly, God is more comfortable with diversity than we are. After all, She made it! We, on the other hand, tend to fear our differences more than celebrate them. In fact, diversity may be the hardest thing for a society to live with and perhaps the most dangerous thing for a society to be without. . . . The challenge, then, is to recognize that the world is about two things: differentiation and communion. The challenge is to seek a unity that celebrates diversity, to unite the particular with the universal, to recognize the needs for roots while insisting that the point of roots is to put forth branches.
—William Sloane Coffin, "Civility, Democracy and Multiculturalism"[1]

THE POTLUCK LUNCHEONS AT DELHAVEN CHRISTIAN CHURCH in La Puente, California, are legendary. One such fabulous affair occurred on a Sunday in April 2002, when after a worship service featuring hymns in English and Spanish and a liturgical dance by Erica Villapondo of Chapman University, the "Delhaven family" and guests feasted on a remarkable spread of foods representing African American, Latino, Asian, and European American favorites. The feast was reminiscent of William Sloane Coffin's suggestion that the world is about both "differentiation" and "communion." Here in this small Disciples of Christ congregation, the sumptuous and multicultural potluck luncheons are but one symbol of both the differentiation and the communion of the multiracial community that is Delhaven Christian Church. "We taste all nationalities here," says congregation member Marie Morgan.[2]

With the pride of knowing that the family feast will be a spectacular banquet, members of Delhaven Christian Church make sure to invite family and friends from far and near to worship and dine with them on potluck Sundays. Charlotte D. Harris, an ordained African American Disciples minister and member of All Peoples Christian Church and Christian Center in Los Angeles, says "black folks are historically good at hospitality. At church they got strokes because they did not get them from the world outside."[3] At Delhaven Christian Church African American members, as well as European American, Hispanic, and Asian members, know that their gift of hospitality will provide guests with an experience of communion across the boundaries of difference, yet support each one for who they are as individuals, and for the races and cultures they represent.

Throughout Scripture there are many incidents of people of faith gathering together to share a meal. The vision of God's banquet in Isaiah 25:6-8 suggests a vision of "a feast of rich food" and a vision where all people of the earth who will respond are invited as guests and are delivered from death. Throughout the Gospels, Jesus feeds his followers on several occasions, with no barriers to participation. Indeed, many of the stories about Jesus' public ministry include a vision of open and inclusive table fellowship where all are welcomed as they are, including some of the most marginalized within his society. Marcus Borg wrote in *Meeting Jesus Again for the First Time*, "One of his [Jesus'] most characteristic activities was an open and inclusive table. . . . The inclusive vision incarnated in Jesus' table fellowship is reflected in the shape of the Jesus movement itself. . . . It included women, untouchables, the poor, the maimed, and the marginalized, as well as some people of stature who found this vision attractive."[4]

On this mountain the Lord of hosts will make for all peoples a feast of rich food, a feast of well-aged wines, of rich food filled with marrow, of well-aged wines stained and clear. And the Holy One will destroy on this mountain the shroud that is cast over all peoples, the sheet that is spread over all the nations; God will swallow up death forever. Then the Lord God will wipe away the tears from all faces, and the disgrace of God's people will be taken away from all the earth, for the Lord has spoken.

Isaiah 25:6–8

In many ways the small congregation of Delhaven Christian Church reflects a multiracial banquet. The table fellowship began soon after the congregation was founded almost fifty years ago. As the community turned from rural to suburban to urban, the congregation discovered the rich heritage of food traditions in their midst. Many of the congregation's members had moved to California from the South and from the Midwest bringing delicious fried chicken, casserole, sweet potato pie, and other recipes with them. Through the years the foods have changed with the racial and ethnic diversity of the congregation, yet the feasts remain unplanned potlucks with many individuals bringing their special dishes. When there are special guests, the meat dish will be prepared by one or more of the best cooks of the congregation.

The congregation at Delhaven Christian Church enjoys inviting guests and sharing other people's food and recipes, but the potlucks are not just about food, as important as food is to us. The potlucks are about sharing a valuable part of community identity. The festive meals develop intimacy, strengthen relationships, reach out into the neighborhood, and celebrate the joy of being in a place that strives to make a difference in the community and in the world. "I love the food," says Roberta Harrison, who lives in a convalescent hospital but maintains frequent contact with Delhaven Christian Church. "Religion should be fun and not about pious people sitting around telling other people how good they are." As a white woman with five Mexican American grandchildren, Harrison finds the congregation of Delhaven Christian Church to be "a welcoming family in good times and bad."

Sometimes Delhaven Christian Church plans outdoor barbeques to share with the neighborhood. On these occasions two of the congregation's members, Maurice Powell and Hank Smith, prepare the meat just as they have for the last fifteen years using their own original recipe. "We moved here from Maryland in the 1960s," says Maurice Powell, an African American member of the congregation, "and we always have felt comfortable here. The Lord has been good to me and has seen us through lots of troubles. We believe in giving back and the people here do things everywhere and are not afraid to go out into the community." Hank Smith, also African American and a retired military officer, has held many leadership roles in the congregation over twenty-three years, including deacon, treasurer, and elder. Smith also cleans the church on the weekends. Throughout his career on active duty Hank Smith was moved by the poverty and oppression faced by the poor in all parts of the world. "God led me to Delhaven," he says. "We are *inclusive*, not just *integrated*—we struggle together wherever we go."

The sentiments of Maurice Powell and Hank Smith about the strength of Delhaven Christian Church as a multiracial community are echoed through the congregation's membership. Kimberlie Manager commutes almost an hour to the congregation. As a young African American woman, Manager feels that Delhaven Christian Church "is a living example of what Christ really wanted. The people who stay in this congregation learn what it means to love people who are different from them, Delhaven draws it out." Kathy Cantu and her daughters, Christine and Renee, share a vision of Delhaven Christian Church as a place where they can truly be both "recognized and belong." "When I went to other churches I left feeling just as empty as when I started," says Patsy, a new deacon in the congregation. "Here they accepted me and drew off my strength." Pete and Shirley Aranda, an interracial couple, both came to Delhaven Christian Church looking for a place to belong. "As lay people get involved here their strengths come out," says Pete Aranda, who is of American Indian descent. "This was a welcoming congregation for interracial couples, and the demographics exceeded what I was looking for." "This is a neighborhood church and we want all people—all ages—to feel that there is something here for them," says Alice Peace who is of African American and American Indian ancestry and who joined the church after she was widowed in 1996.

Delhaven Christian Church describes itself as a multiracial "family" where open hospitality and "love not rules" reign. Gathered here are the representatives of several generations of members from different races and cultures, as well as newer members attracted to the multiracial ethos of the congregation and its conscious effort to become "one family." "This church changes the color line" says Bert DeYoung, a white member of the congregation. Richard (Dick) Miller, pastor of the Disciples of Christ congregation since 1999, describes the community as "Mulligan Stew." As he says, "a stew of any ingredients that are available." The multiracial pastoral-size congregation continues to struggle with the challenge of how to continue to respond to the diversity of their context. "Our concern for social justice can't be watered down by multiculturalism," says Dick Miller. "It has to be intensified by it."[5]

Delhaven Christian Church (Disciples of Christ), 2002

Total Membership	76
Participating Membership	71
Average Sunday Attendance	55
Baptisms	3
Transfers	4
Average Church School Attendance	25
Racial/Ethnic Makeup of Congregation	
African American	29
Asian and Pacific Islanders	2
Hispanic	9
American Indian	1
White/Caucasian	30
Other	0
Membership by Age	
Birth to 5 years	4
6–11	20
12–14	6
15–18	9
19–25	4
26–50	20
51–64	20
65+	29

Communities Served
La Puente, West Covina, Hacienda Heights of greater Los Angeles, California.

Source: Statistical report 2002 for Delhaven Christian Church, filed by Gayle Schoepf, for the denominational yearbook.

Demographics by Census, 2000

La Puente, California
Hispanic	83.1%
Black or African American	2.0%
American Indian and Alaska Native	1.3%
Asian	7.2%
Native Hawaiian	0.2%
Multiracial	5.2%
White	39.1%
Other	45.0%

West Covina, California
Hispanic	45.7%
Black or African American	6.4%
American Indian and Alaska Native	0.8%
Asian	22.3%
Native Hawaiian	0.2%
Multiracial	4.9%
White	49.9%
Other	21.2%

Hacienda Heights, California
Hispanic	38.3%
Black or African American	1.6%
American Indian and Alaska Native	0.7%
Asian	36.1%
Native Hawaiian	0.1%
Multiracial	3.9%
White	41.0%
Other	16.6%

Sources: *Los Angeles County Almanac,* Los Angeles Newspaper Group, 2002; also, Gregory Rodriguez, "Don't Mistake the Parts for the White in L.A.," *Los Angeles Times,* July 6, 2001, B5; Robin Fields and Ray Herndon, "Segregation of a New Sort Takes Shape," *Los Angeles Times,* July 6, 2001, A1, A17.

FORMATION AND CHANGE

Delhaven Christian Church was founded in September 1956 and met in a small house until the first building, later known as Charles Hall, was completed in 1957. Though the founding congregation included two interracial couples, the balance of the group was classified as "Anglo" in their Southern California context. The most influential charter members of the congregation were committed members of the Christian Church (Disciples of Christ), who attended the denomination's regional church camp and young adult fellowship and became friends with people of color from All Peoples Christian Church in Los Angeles. All Peoples Christian Church and Christian Center was founded in 1942 as a multiracial community in the inner city at a time of deep division between people of different races and cultures. As Dan B. Genung, founding pastor of All Peoples recalls:

> We must remember what U.S. Society was like in the '40s and '50s. The Civil Rights movement did not exist; Martin Luther King was a schoolboy. Churches were segregated. Restrictive covenants denied housing to nonwhites. Restaurants, skating rings, swimming pools as far north as Detroit, Chicago, and Columbus either barred or embarrassed minority persons. Washington, the nation's capital, had separate taxis for whites and blacks. . . . In addition to these societal conditions, the West Coast was also affected by the evacuation of a segment of its population. Following Pearl Harbor in December 1951 all persons of Japanese ancestry, including American-born citizens, were forced to leave their homes and belongings to live in internment camps for three years.[6]

Gwen Barrow Gutierrez, a former administrator at All Peoples Christian Church and now one of the leaders of the congregation at Delhaven Christian Church, remembers that one of the strengths of her former congregation was "accepting people as they are, with no push to conform. Gwen writes of the founder, Dan Genung, "you started with love and concern for the neighborhood people; therefore, you began with their 'felt' needs; you determined those needs by calling on every home and talking with the families; you talked with the young people on the playground, ones who were surprised to find someone who listened."[7]

Still, though the founding families of Delhaven Christian Church were receptive to people of other races and nationalities, there was no intentional strategy to build a multiracial community between the years 1957 and 1959. The site for the church was chosen at a time when the strawberry and cabbage fields in the La Puente area were being sold to make room for inexpensive housing developments. At that time there were very few homes in the area immediately south and

west of the church. The name "Delhaven" came from the large housing development northeast of the church. When the church was
formed, the properties to the south of the church were still in five- and
ten-acre parcels. When these were divided into parcels for single-fam-
ily dwellings, the population of the area soon exploded and new
homes were quite affordable. Subdivisions began developing in the
areas south and west of the church, and people of color started moving
into the houses. Housing discrimination, or "redlining," determined
that a specific area was set aside for housing African Americans. This
area was directly across the street from Delhaven Christian Church.
Before the building of the sanctuary had even begun, the congregation
was faced with the decision either to stay in the neighborhood and
include African American members or to relocate.

Delhaven's first full-time minister, Bill Tolliver, with his wife,
Mildred, initiated the congregation's first contact with people of color
in the community in 1958 and thereafter aggressively welcomed
African American families into the congregation. Bill Tolliver was the
type of minister who insisted on cutting his own lawn around his
home on the corner of the church property. As the story goes, while
Bill Tolliver was mowing the lawn one day an African American man
by the name of Sam Steverson was returning home from the market.
Bill stopped mowing and engaged Sam in a conversation, asked him
about his family and invited him to church. At the same time, Sam's
son, Sammy, told his father that he was tired of spending all Sunday
driving into Los Angeles to go to church and asked why they could not
go to church in La Puente. Sam directed his son to find a neighborhood church that the family could attend, and he would consider
changing his membership. Sammy visited several churches but did not
feel welcome at any of them until he attended Delhaven Christian
Church. Sam and Eunice Steverson and their two children were soon
taking part in the various activities at Delhaven Christian Church,
including the choir, and they brought their neighbors into the church
as well. In October 1965 Sam Steverson was the soloist at the service
of dedication for the new sanctuary. After several months, another
African-American family, Emmett and Wilda Terrell and their two
children, started attending Delhaven and became members, as did
other families.[8]

Though there was conversation before 1964 among some white
members of Delhaven Christian Church about the "changing nature

of the congregation" after the arrival of African American families, the leadership of Bill and Mildred Tolliver and several charter members convinced the congregation to stay in the neighborhood and to form a multiracial congregation. When asked by a member of the congregation what he would do if one of "them" walked down the aisle to join the church, Bill Tolliver replied unequivocally that he "would welcome him and encourage him to become active." Though several families did leave Delhaven Christian Church when the first African American family joined, the congregation as a whole was happy to have the community involved and assisted the Tollivers in calling on families in the neighborhood. "Some in that first generation were for integrating the church," says Roy Bullock, pastor of the congregation from 1963 to 1970, "but they were not integrated in their hearts and minds. It took time living together to accomplish relationships and a sense of community."

The first African American members to join Delhaven Christian Church walked into a white congregation of about two hundred members. Many of these African American families had just moved from all-black communities in Los Angeles where they had attended black congregations. They were adjusting to living in a new community, and many commuted to black congregations before joining Delhaven Christian Church. "I think it is significant that in those early days the first African Americans to join Delhaven Christian Church felt confident enough to take leadership roles immediately—sing in the choir, teach Sunday school—later of course, become elders. I sometimes wonder if the outcome would have differed had they been welcomed but not affirmed," says Gwen Gutierrez. She also recalls that on the night when the Rev. Dr. Martin Luther King Jr. was murdered, Sam and Eunice Steverson invited members of the Delhaven congregation for a night of prayer and reflection. Similar community gatherings occurred when President John F. Kennedy and Senator Robert Kennedy were killed.

Delhaven Christian Church's commitment to multiracial community extends to other forms of diversity as well. In August 2000, a year after calling its first openly gay pastor, the congregation officially became "An Open and Affirming Congregation." Though initially Delhaven Christian Church members assumed that the words "Disciples of Christ" on their sign meant to everyone who read it that *all* were welcome, the congregation recognized their complacency and realized that sexual identity was an issue that needed to be confronted. In voting to become officially "An Open and Affirming Congregation," affiliated with the GLAD (Gay, Lesbian and Affirming Disciples) Alliance of the Disciples of Christ, members of Delhaven Christian Church officially proclaimed what they had quietly been practicing. "As the mother of a gay son I know how important it is to show support," says Betty Franklin. "Here I can pray for him, love him, whatever."[9]

Dedication to welcome *and* affirm all people has been the cornerstone of Delhaven Christian Church since its earliest days, and that same spirit continues through to the present day. The excitement in the church on Sunday mornings in this small congregation is palpable, and the greeters have the uncanny ability to remember names of even intermittent visitors. Delhaven Christian Church has been able to avoid one of the main obstacles churches face in attempting to become multiracial communities by not only welcoming persons of all racial and ethnic groups, but welcoming their *cultures* as well. Thus, during a "typical" Sunday service at Delhaven Christian Church "Amens" can be heard throughout the service. Clapping often follows the choir anthem. There is a variety of music, and sometimes voices can be heard singing the hymns in Spanish as others sing in English. Leaders of worship are drawn from a diversity not only of racial and ethnic backgrounds, but of ages as well. "I personally cannot clap after the anthem because I have not been able to let go of my past training that put so much emphasis on everything contributing to the flow of the worship service," says Gwen Gutierrez. "But I have learned to rejoice when I hear others clap because I know they have learned to worship with their bodies as well as their minds and spirits. It seems to me that too often our churches say that all are welcome when what they really mean is that all are welcome who are willing to become like us," she says. "Don't expect to interrupt the service with 'Amens' or change the music we sing or serve mochi or pan dulce during refreshment time. These churches may even say that gays are welcome, meaning all sinners are welcome, but don't ask them to 'affirm' those whose sexual orientation is not heterosexual. If I sound disappointed in much of what goes on in the name of Christianity, I am."

The multiracial and multilingual worship at Delhaven Christian Church is supported by Gayle Schoepf, an ordained Disciples of Christ

pastor who serves the congregation as organist and minister of education and youth. Schoepf commutes thirty miles from her home in Long
Beach, California, because she is excited by the opportunity to serve
such a diverse congregation. "This is a real hands-on kind of place,"
says Schoepf, and we have to find a way to use all the gifts we've got.
The congregation's youth program is open to participation from any
young person in the community, and is based on a model of educational experiences, sharing, and fellowship. The youth group also
holds regular projects to serve the community, and regularly takes
charge of the worship service including the sermon and communion.
Young people are incorporated not only into the service, but are
"expected to participate and enjoy it," says Glenn Johnson, a member
of the congregation. "We try to involve whole familes," says Shirley
Aranda. Kimberlie Manager feels that the youth group is the biggest
asset of the congregation. "It makes life a little easier," she says.
Because of her commitment to building multiracial community, Janice
Vance left an affluent white congregation to direct the preschool at
Delhaven Christian Church, which serves families in the community
surrounding the church. Aware that prejudice develops in children at
an early age, Vance designs the program to "help the children to learn
to live multiculturally." This commitment is demonstrated in a variety
of ways in the preschool program, including such things as snacks,
holidays, and prayers.

In an effort to maintain the multiracial character of the congregation, leaders of Delhaven Christian Church have decided not to organize a parallel congregation with a Spanish-language service. "We
would like to extend into the neighborhood and worship together,"
says Art DeBry of the congregation. "We offer who we are and not a
comfort zone." Though the congregation provides worship space for
a group of Filipino Seventh-Day Adventists, Delhaven Christian
Church members have decided to continue to support their vision of
multiracial community through worship and community life that
upholds a variety of languages and cultures within the same congregation. "It is still difficult for us to have the involvement we would like
because we are not representative of the community," says Mark Carlock, choir director and chair of the board for seven years. "We are
comfortable as a small congregation, but we need to get our voice a
bit louder," he says. Carlock, who grew up in All People's Christian

Church in Los Angeles, is committed to the vision of multiracial community at Delhaven Christian Church "because we have a commitment here to challenge people to be even greater than they think is possible." He agrees with the decision to continue as a multiracial community rather than begin a parallel Latino congregation. "I believe we can be a real community center," says Carlock. "The saddest thing in the world is an empty church building. We can use the building as a way to invest in the future." "As a multiracial community we are stronger than racism," says Deirdre Carlock, also a leader of the congregation. "For me this has been a place to deal with people on a human level and to heal from Rodney King and the O.J. Simpson trial. We seek to understand each other here. I would really miss out without the richness of people from other cultures." The Carlock's two children, Matthew, a college student, and Britany, a high school student, also articulate what they have learned at Delhaven Christian Church. "We don't turn people away with hidden messages," says Britany Carlock. "God is large and we need to not box God in," says Matthew. "We need to think about what Jesus really did and do that in the community," he says.

RESPONSE TO THE COMMUNITY

The first step taken by members of Delhaven Christian Church to respond to the needs of the community was calling on homes. Instead of holding complicated mission strategy sessions or long outreach committee meetings, the members of Delhaven Christian Church have remained flexible and built their response to the community on specific needs as they discerned them over time. Thus, the focus of social justice activities has changed over the years. "We are a poor church that does a lot," says Gabrielle McClure, a member of the congregation. "We are 'just folks,' not glitzy, but we give to families and to the community and this makes us bigger and broader than what we are." Throughout the history of the congregation, the members of Delhaven Christian Church have focused on the Disciples' mission "to serve" through multiracial community action and the pursuit of justice. Their ability to integrate the prophetic vision of multiracial community with spirituality and pastoral care has not only continued to keep justice as a focal point of community life, but has sustained the congregation during periods of transition and change. "Here people have a face and issues are enfleshed; they are not an abstraction" says Dave Genung, an educator and a board member of the Eastmont Community Center, an organization that serves a primarily low-income Latino community. Genung hopes that Delhaven Christian Church continues to work "to exceed our comfort level."

Throughout the 1960s and 1970s, Delhaven Christian Church was very active in the San Gabriel Valley chapter of the National Association for the Advancement of Colored People (NAACP). Soon after the church was founded, members of the congregation noted that "redlining" was still in effect and that overt racism was prevalent throughout the community. The NAACP chapter president and several members of the executive board were members of Delhaven Christian Church. The group, which continues to meet and hold activities in the fellowship hall for several years, worked for the end of housing discrimination in the community adjacent to the church. As houses were built and young families moved into the community, the high school youth of Delhaven Christian Church saw a need and began to develop a tutoring program for children in the neighborhood. By the early 1970s, this response to children and their families became the Delhaven Community Center, housed in church facilities. Staff as well as volunteers were members of the congregation and supported this rapidly growing program. Still known as Delhaven Community Center, the award-winning program rapidly outgrew church facilities and became a separate entity. The organization continues to serve children and families in the east San Gabriel Valley. In a similar manner, as it became apparent that the community surrounding the church needed quality daycare, Delhaven Christian Church opened a preschool. At the present time, the board of the preschool is made up of members of the congregation who continue to work to provide care and education for the young children in the community. The congregation hosts the preschool graduation to honor the children and to give the congregation an opportunity to meet their families.[10]

In addition to these major projects, Delhaven Christian Church has responded to the community in a myriad of small ways. Members of Delhaven Christian Church wrestle with the meaning of the gospel in their time and place through Bible study and prayer. In a prominent place in the fellowship hall stands an "Awareness Table" stocked with pamphlets, brochures, articles, buttons, and other goods designed to keep the congregation aware of local and global needs and how they can work to bring racial and social justice to their community and the larger world. Further, the congregation's willingness to try something new has given them the flexibility to respond to the community, to change, and to experiment. For many years the congregation has maintained a food pantry and an emergency fund for anyone who telephones or stops by the church for assistance, and cooperates with other congregations in the area to provide food for the homeless. The congregation also distributes food at Thanksgiving through the public school system. Members of Delhaven Christian Church are concerned neighbors and thus host a variety of food-related events—the congregation's specialty—including Thanksgiving baskets, an ourdoor barbecue, and a chili meal on the Fourth of July. These activities help to build community inside and outside the congregation, as well as to raise funds for additional community projects. Through its annual "Alternative Christmas" emphasis, the congregation contributes to such organizations as Church World Service, Habitat for Humanity, Heifer Project, Third World Handarts, and Homie Accents, which is a job- and skills-training program for gang-involved young people. At Christmas 2002, the congregation spent more than $3,000 on alternative gifts for families and friends to the organizations listed above. Throughout the history of Delhaven Christian Church the congregation has sought ways to relate to local and global needs and to change oppressive systems. Presently, the congregation is focusing on how to better serve the growing Latino population of their neighborhood. Overall, Delhaven Christian Church is a multiracial community where people's needs are met. Spiritual hunger is fed through study and worship. Physical needs such as food and clothing as well as educational needs are also met. Members of the congregation feel wanted and needed and loved.

For the members of Delhaven Christian Church building multiracial community takes the form of countless small gestures and events conducted by its members to witness to the possibilities inherent in such a congregation. For Bob Cantrell, who joined Delhaven Christian Church from another congregation, one of the most powerful symbols of the multiracial community is the moment at the end of the service when the entire congregation encircles the church and holds hands for prayer. "At that moment you can visualize how we connect with everyone here," he says. The closing circle, the equivalent of "passing the peace" in other congregations, though it follows communion rather than precedes it, is a time at Delhaven Christian Church for meeting and greeting visitors, for anyone in the circle to share what is important to them in their life at that moment, and a time for thanksgivings. "As we touch one another by holding hands and are able to see each other's face, it becomes a safe and inclusive way of receiving love and acceptance before we go forth to give," says Gwen Gutierrez. For Dick Miller, the closing circle reminds him of the poem "Outwitted" by Edward Markham, a late-nineteenth- and early-twentieth-century poet who once belonged to the First Christian Church (Disciples of Christ) in San Jose, California:[11]

> He drew a circle that shut me out –
> Heretic, rebel, a thing to flout.
> But love and I had the wit to win
> And we drew a circle that took him in.

In all aspects of community life, people of color and European Americans work side by side at Delhaven Christian Church, and witness to the community together. Though the congregation's leaders are familiar with market charts and surveys, their strategy of evangelization is more focused on upholding a presence in the diverse community surrounding the congregation. For instance, when the congregation hosts the graduation ceremony of its preschool, all parents, extended family, and friends of the graduates are greeted. The congregation sponsors a chili booth in a West Covina Park on the Fourth of July in order to greet the people who wander through the park. This emphasis on building multiracial community through witness and social action in the local community characterizes the approach of Delhaven Christian Church to working atainst racism.

Significantly, the multiracial congregation at Delhaven Christian Church is one of the attractions that the church holds for those who consciously choose to become members. As the most multiracial Disciples of Christ congregation in southern Califorinia, Delhaven Christian Church has attracted several pastors to its membership. Doug Smith, a pastor who works for Church World Service, claims that

Delhaven Christian Church will always be "an edge place," part of a "theology of the remnant" in exile. "Dick Miller has laid a good foundation for a healthier, larger church," says Smith. "We have a new image of ourselves and we are no longer in crisis mode. But I don't see Delhaven ever very much bigger given our ethos or setting." Gayle Schoepf, affirms this perspective. "Here the differences between people are constantly in your face," she says. Kate Moyer, a nursing home chaplain, notes that besides racial and cultural diversity, there is also a wide range of theological perspectives in the congregation. "I choose to live in a more diverse community," says Moyer. "Real life—that is my choice."

"PROGRESSIVE" CHRISTIANITY AND MULTIRACIAL COMMUNITY

As a way of reflecting on its life as a multiracial community, Delhaven Christian Church voted to affiliate with the Center for Progressive Christianity, an ecumenical organization pledged "to offer the message of Christianity to those for whom organized religion has proved ineffectual, irrelevant, or repressive; to uphold evangelism as an agent of justice and peace; to give a strong voice in the churches and the public arena to the advocates of progressive Christianity; and, to support congregations embracing search, not certainty." The organization defines "Progressive Christianity" as an orientation toward the faith which affirms the variety and depth of human experience, the promotion of serious conversation, learning and teaching, and a commitment to work to ease the suffering of society. Further, the organization stresses the need to support congregations, like Delhaven Christian Church, who embrace search, not certainty, and those who may have faced rejection by the church, or have not had a meaningful connection between the church and their daily lives.[12]

A key aspect of the Center for Progressive Christianity's approach to issues of multiracial community and change is its critique of congregations who claim to welcome all people but in reality expect their new members eventually to look like themselves. "They assume that doubters and skeptics will become believers, that gays and lesbians will become straight or at least celibate, that everyone will appear to be cheerful, and that people in the church will adopt the same manners and develop similar tastes."[13] However, Progressive Christians, including the congregation at Delhaven Christian Church, interpret the gospel to mean that the followers of Jesus are called to "welcome all people without imposing on them the necessity of changing their attitudes, their culture, their understanding of the faith, or their sexual orientation."[14] Further, the community at Delhaven Christian Church believes that it is the *established* members of the church who are called to do the changing. At Delhaven Christian Church there is an openness and an awareness that a congregation must be ready to adapt to the people they hope to welcome. These values are articulated in the vision statement of Delhaven Christian Church, where the congregation states its commitment to "follow the teaching and example of Jesus by:

- Deepening our connection with God.

- Recognizing and valuing individual spiritual paths.

- Staying open to new insights.

- Discovering ways to express love, compassion, peace, and justice at home and throughout the world.

- Welcoming and affirming all people who would share this vision with us regardless of age, sexual orientation, race, ethnicity, or talents."

DISCIPLE OF THE YEAR AWARD, 2001

Part of the appeal of Delhaven Christian Church as a multiracial community is the congregation's ability to make it a spiritual home, as well as a place where people are challenged to connect their faith with their daily lives. The congregation's ability to proclaim consistently the vision of multiracial community rooted in the gospel was recognized by the Pacific Southwest Region of the Christian Church (Disciples of Christ) when Delhaven Christian Church was granted the Disciple of the Year Award in 2001. It was only the second time in the award's twenty-seven-year history that a group and not an individual was granted the honor for "living the essence of the Rev. Dr. Martin Luther King Jr.'s vision." "Perhaps the strongest argument [against racism] is a good example," said Mark Carlock at the time of the award. "When a multiracial and multi-ethnic congregation can not only peacefully co-exist but thrive and grow, we are only talking about the economics of scale when we envision the same for the community, the country, the world."[15]

All are welcomed to become full partners in the life of Delhaven Christian Church without an imposing sense that they need to meet some unspoken standard. Newcomers are tended and promised that they will not be embarrassed by anything that will happen. The feelings of warmth and the testimonies to the sense of community are genuine, as is the sense that building multiracial community takes more than discussing racism and other forms of oppression from a solely intellectual perspective. "This was taught to me personally by a black friend almost fifty years ago," says Gwen Gutierrez. "From a loving place within me and from a desire to promote racial integration and justice in our Disciples [of Christ] churches, I expressed opinions regarding what we could do. I had no clue as to what was important in his life at that time. Actually, as difficult as it is for me to acknowledge, I was being racist."

The importance of building relationships across differences is a strong emphasis throughout the "typical" Sunday service at Delhaven Christian Church, where "welcome," "belonging," and "participation" are common themes. Here a relaxed and nonhierarchical style of community and leadership seems to be the norm. As the minister of the congregation, Dick Miller is known for his ability as a preacher and a teacher to bring the gospel into modern-day terms and make it relevant to the lives of Christians. "The pastor relates to all members of the congregation," says Otis Landers, an African American a member of the congregation. "If you want to go to a pastor that knows what he is talking about, in everyday life, I recommend that you go to him." Dick Miller does not dominate the congregation, although he provides strong direction. The sins of racism and classism, the oppression of gay and lesbian people, and international concerns are regularly the focus of sermons. Because of its small size, the congregation devotes limited attention to program activities—although there are ample opportunities in this area. Social events celebrating the multiracial character of the congregation are an important aspect of community. The overall message conveyed by Delhaven Christian Church is deeply incarnational; that is, each person is fashioned in the image and likeness of God and is intended to share in God's mission in the world. As Deirdre Carlock, said in a sermon in March 2002:

> Here is where I learned the strength of God's power. Here is where I learned forgiveness and what it really means to forgive. Here is where I learned to let go. Here is where I learned to step out on faith. Here is where I learned that my family was bigger than just my husband, kids, parents and siblings. Here is where I feel cared for and loved. Here is where I feel good. I get that feeling . . . but here I learned the name of that feeling. THIS IS IT! We have the Spirit of the Lord here at Delhaven. It's in each and every one of us. . . .[16]

EVOLVING LEADERSHIP

As pastor of Delhaven Christian Church, Dick Miller draws on his prior history in the Student Christian Movement and the civil rights movement in order to assist the congregation in finding its renewed purpose. Miller sees his role at Delhaven Christian Church as a "transitional" ministry, with the goal of leaving the congregation less clergy-dependent and more invigorated when he retires in January 2003, than when he arrived. Though the congregation has historically been adaptive to the needs of those who entered its doors, Miller's concern has been to keep the small congregation out of "survival mode" and looking toward future possibilities. "This is a deep community; they really are more exciting than they realize," he says.

As in many pastoral-size congregations, the core leadership group of Delhaven Christian Church is loyal and tenacious, concerned with growth yet equally concerned about the impact of that growth on the intimacy of the community. One goal held almost universally, however, is the desire on behalf of the congregation's leaders to groom new leadership to see Delhaven Christian Church into the future. "People here are hard-working, but we do not want to have elders elected for life," says Dick Miller. He also is concerned with the lack of diversity among the congregation's ordained leadership. "All the pastors and clergy who have served here are white," says Miller. "Not only does that have implications for the pastoral care of the African American members, as well as other people of color, but I am wondering if we have not reached the point where we need the skills of someone who can really reach out into the Latino community." Miller hopes that the congregation will remain multiracial and multicultural yet continue to strengthen its ties with the neighborhood and become "more Latinized" in areas such as worship and outreach.

Dick Miller's pastoral leadership is deeply rooted in social justice, and he addresses the ministries of preaching, teaching, and pastoral care from this perspective. "Our Rev. speaks to all sorts of issues—he really *goes there*," says Mittie Hanson, who came to Delhaven Christian Church from the African American Methodist tradition. Miller also envisions the multiracial community at Delhaven Christian Church as part of the larger diversity of the Disciples of Christ and the denomination's multicultural mission strategy. Miller refers to the summary of the gospel that has been adopted by the Disciples of Christ nationally—"The Good News is that God's unconditional love has been offered to each and to all"—as a way to examine issues of oppression. One of the challenges he faces in a multiracial community like Delhaven Christian Church is how to preach and teach on forms of oppression that have not been as directly addressed within the congregation as have racism and homophobia. For instance, how can a community such as Delhaven Christian Church address divisions based on social class, income levels, education, and cultural interests? "One of the most perplexing issues for me in viewing the aspirations and values of this church," says Dick Miller, "is that it is hard for me to caution people who are just coming into the middle class about the dangers of consumerism and the seductive temptations which come from aspiring for a better standard of living for themselves and for their families."

Dick Miller's response to addressing classism, as told in a sermon preached a week after the congregation launched into a capital fund campaign, is to challenge people to live the gospel "in our relationships with each other regardless of social status or social class so we can never be accused of showing more regard for the rich than for the poor." "I would also confess that since ideas about what is good taste and bad taste also get associated with class distinctions—and I see this especially as it applies to the kind of music various people like—we will try not to impose the taste of any one class of people on the rest," he says. "And in this area especially as it applies to worship, we have more that needs to be done in order to incorporate in practice the full diversity of cultures and tastes that are present in our congregation in this very time."[17]

Gwen Gutierrez, who was awarded the Disciple of the Year Award with her late husband, Rudy, in 1978, has been active in numerous social justice ministries since she arrived at All Peoples Christian Church and Christian Center in 1948. Her husband was an educator and school principal who, despite fierce opposition, developed inter-cultural programs that were eventually accepted throughout the school district. Gwen Gutierrez believes that it is important for faithful people not to limit their efforts against racism to legal justice, but rather to also embrace the need to change attitudes and behaviors. "Justice, as we usually use the word, does not necessarily affirm, value, respect, and view as equal. Actions are extremely important, but it seems to me that attitudes, especially attitudes that create actions, need to be the underlying basis of racial and social justice." As a white person, Gwen Gutierrez believes that some of the ways she can change attitudes and support actions against racism, include:

- I must be aware of and admit to myself that I benefit from racial injustice.

- I must acknowledge that I have never nor do I now walk in the moccasins of a person who is not white; therefore, I may not have the answers that are needed in a particular situation.

- If I am willing to acknowledge my lack of personal experience [of racial injustice], then I can become willing to listen and to learn.

- On the other hand, using sensitivity does not mean that as a white person I do not take a stand.

- My role is to take a stand in all personal situations including racial jokes, unequal treatment, etc.

- My role is to take advantage of every opportunity to educate myself, my contacts, and my church by attending seminars or by inviting seminars to come to my church.

- My role is to keep aware of appropriate legislation, write letters, make telephone calls, and to bring it to the attention of my contacts and my church.

- My role is to keep aware of local opportunities and to act appropriately.

- My role is to help myself and others understand the importance of attitude [in resisting racism].

In a similar way, other members of Delhaven Christian Church recount how the congregation lives its vision of multiracial community. Tom Nevarez, a fairly new member of the congregation who is still learning about the denomination, attends Delhaven Christian Church because it is "where I can be who I am. "I can't imagine not being here," says Kathy Cantu. "I can't imagine living another way." Though Christine Cantu and Renee Cantu would like to see more people in their twenties through forties in the congregation, they feel close to many members of the congregation. Mavis Davenport, who recently came to Delhaven Christian Church from a conflicted congregation, appreciates the healing she has found as well as the "caring from all directions."

REGIONAL ANTIRACISM EFFORTS

Though the Christian Church (Disciples of Christ) has decried the sin of racism for years, the denomination renewed and expanded its commitment to the eradication of racism in 2000 when the General Board called for the church to engage in "ministries of reconciliation, compassion, unity and justice" and to "be an antiracist/pro-reconciliation church." The Pacific Southwest Region of the Christian Church (Disciples of Christ), of which Delhaven Christian Church is a part, has made an ongoing commitment to become "a transforming antiracist, inter-generational institution where brothers and sisters of all races, cultures and languages share fully in the leadership of the region." Further, the region has committed to the eradication of racism within all communities and partnerships. Driven by the biblical and spiritual mandates of inclusiveness, the region has envisioned a church "where all have a place at the table and none shall be turned away."[18] The Regional Anti-Racism Committee has contracted with Crossroads Ministries to assist in providing training for local teams and in developing and evaluating the strategic plan. One of the initial steps of the strategic plan is a series of ninety-minute presentations throughout the region. One such session was presented at Delhaven Christian Church by Don Shelton, regional minister-president of the Pacific Southwest Region of the Disciples of Christ, and Charlotte D. Harris. "If racism is true then Pentecost is a lie," says Charlotte D. Harris. "Racism distorts the image of God. We need to put feet to our dreams and move institutions," she says.[19]

The antiracism session at Delhaven Christian Church centered on the sin of racism as well as the biblical mandates against it. The Crossroads Ministry model stresses the importance of using the common definition of "race prejudice + the misuse of power by systems and institutions = racism." The model emphasizes organizing for systemic change, developing antiracist, multicultural identity, organizing from *within* institutions, equipping leadership teams, developing long-term plans (twenty to thirty years), and participating in social change.[20] Members of Delhaven Christian Church have joined with their regional team and will continue to participate in antiracism training across the church. The work on this level has just begun and it remains to be seen what larger contributions—beyond Delhaven Christian Church—its members can make to denominational antiracism efforts.

SUMMARY

Delhaven Christian Church is a banquet that envisions a life in multiracial community with vitality and purpose. The rich feasts that are shared by the members of this congregation, and which they share with others, do much to build and maintain bonds between people of diverse backgrounds. As a small church, the congregation recognizes the importance of fellowship and spiritual nurture, yet does not divorce these from the rest of life. Examples of faithful ministry abound in this congregation; leadership is shared and all people regardless of racial or ethnic background, from children through elders, are encouraged to share their gifts with the greater community. Overall, the congregation works to interpret its context and to respond to the challenges of its urban environment. In so doing, they continue to face the challenge of adapting their worship to meet the needs of the local community and to respond to the needs of local people. Delhaven Christian Church has historically stood for justice, and it continues to wrap this history within the metaphor of a family that both nurtures and challenges its members to fully live out their vocations within the church and the world. As Anthony Pappas notes:

> Small churches that care have a future. The personal nature of the small church is its divine gift to humanity. In the small church each person is important, each person can make a difference to someone else, each person can experience unconditional love, each person is called to live up to his or her potential, each person is of infinite worth. The people-centered quality of small-church life makes it necessary in each generation.[21]

To be sure, Delhaven Christian Church faces the many challenges that occur in small churches. Money is often in short supply, and the congregation's dedicated core leadership is stretched. As in many small churches, it is a challenge to fund a full-time minister, yet it is difficult to "grow" a congregation without one. Though every person interviewed for this book stressed the need to expand as a congregation, they almost all were concerned that numerical growth would change the degree of intimacy members currently experience. There may also be a temptation, at times, for such a historically committed congregation to rest on its having "done enough" active witness in previous years. This tendency would be particularly serious if Delhaven Christian Church were to stop looking seriously at how it might extend membership to the surrounding Latino community just as it visited and welcomed African Americans over forty years ago. In terms of addressing racism specifically, there is the temptation in congregations such as Delhaven Christian Church where everyone sees each other as "family," to deny the political significance of race and the impact of racism in the church and in the community.

The strength of Delhaven Christian Church is the sense of hope and joy embodied in the congregation, even in uncertain times. It is hoped that a recently initiated capital fund drive will raise enough money to complete long-needed repairs to the buildings and the parking lot. As Dick Miller retires in January 2003, he leaves a stronger congregation than when he arrived and with an increasing level of shared leadership. A youth group that is a source of pride for the whole congregation is a sign that the legacy of Delhaven Christian Church will be known to future generations. Presently, the congregation is continuing to undertake life-changing ministries and to prepare for a new pastor, Maria Tafoya, who will begin her relationship with Delhaven Christian Church on Pentecost Sunday in June 2003. The faithful remnant of Delhaven Christian Church, with little sense of their own uniqueness, continues to be praised for their openness and blended multiracial community. "It's very exciting because it shows that the whole church is interested in peace and justice and the value of all people," says Gwen Gutierrez. "[As our pastor said], we want our church to be a headlight and not a taillight, to lead the way."[22]

5

A Liberation Community

Church of the Redeemer
Morristown, New Jersey

Only through an inner spiritual transformation do we gain the strength
to fight vigorously the evils of the world in a humble and loving spirit.
The transformed nonconformist, moreover, never yields to the passive
sort of patience which is an excuse to do nothing. And this very trans-
formation saves him from speaking irresponsible words which estrange
without reconciling and from making hasty judgments which are blind
to the necessity of social progress. He recognizes that social change will
not come overnight, yet he works as though it is an imminent possi-
bility.

—Martin Luther King Jr.[1]

T HE SIGN IN FRONT OF THE CHURCH OF THE REDEEMER IN MORRIS-
town, New Jersey, reads: "We Are One Family," and lists the groups
that make up this diverse congregation—"male, female, children,
seniors, gays, straight, infants, liberals, dreamers, white, black, Christian, non-Christian, questioner, partnered, single, conservatives, in
recovery, searching, youth." The congregation refers to itself as a family united by questions and dreams "rather than our answers." Visual
representations of the parish's commitments include a banner that
reads, "It is a Come as You are Party," a rainbow flag, the Black Liberation flag, and a portrait of Dr. Martin Luther King Jr. "We're *not*
the only parish that shares and promotes these values," says Phillip
Dana Wilson, rector of the congregation since 1987. "I know many
other communities who endorse them. As for Redeemer we are clear

about our vision, and we act on it in our own way." At Redeemer, "liberation" is experienced on several levels:

- Personal: reclaiming our identities as daughter/son of God;

- within church community creating a safe place to be who we are;

- within immediate community dealing with social and economic liberation;

- within larger liberation movements: African American, women's, gay and lesbian, economic, etc.

The Church of the Redeemer in Morristown, New Jersey, is a congregation committed to the work of building multiracial community that bespeaks the Rev. Dr. Martin Luther King Jr.'s vision of the "transformed nonconformist," in its spiritual vigor and belief in the imminent possibility of social change. Church of the Redeemer calls itself "a Christian Liberation Community in the Episcopal tradition." One of the primary vehicles for Church of the Redeemer's witness for racial justice is its innovative and transformative liturgical life. Through the efforts of a team of creative and gifted liturgists, musicians, and artists that comprise the congregation's worship committee, the liturgical year of the congregation both proclaims and interprets racial justice as a mandate of the gospel. While Church of the Redeemer offers a "traditional" worship service early Sunday morning according to the rites in *The Book of Common Prayer*, a later inclusive-language Eucharist is the principal Sunday worship service. Throughout the liturgy, male and female images of God exist side by side by design.

RECONCILIATION SEASON

Members of the Church of the Redeemer Racial Dialogue Group, along with congregation's worship committee, collaborate on a series of Sunday worship services known as the "Reconciliation Season." The season begins with the Rev. Dr. Martin Luther King Jr. Day in mid-January and ends with the feast of Absalom Jones, the first African American priest ordained in the Episcopal Church, in mid-February. The series of worship services is designed to focus on the

evils of racism as the starting place for looking at all issues of liberation, and the responsibility of the people of God to work for its eradication. Though the focus of the liturgies is specifically on the theme
of racial reconciliation, the worship notes for the season state: "we
know that all areas of oppression support each other and work
together to keep people separated and afraid of each other. Were we
to name only one oppression and to ignore all others, we would miss
this point. This liturgy seeks to address the need for reconcilition in
a broad range of life experience."[3]

Each Sunday of Reconciliation Season in 2001 focused on the life
and work of a person who answered God's call to "Let my people go."
In 2001 the Sunday themes focused on Martin Luther King Jr., Harriet
Tubman, Ida B. Wells, Absalom Jones, Jonathan Daniels, an Episcopal seminarian and civil rights activist killed protecting a child from a
bullet, and the Rev. Pauli Murray, the first African American woman
ordained in the Episcopal Church. Colors for the vestments during the
season include all colors of the rainbow and all human skin tones.
Similarly, the color of the worship books reflect the skin tones of people of color.

Quilts displayed in the interior of the church during Reconciliation
Season were made by Colleen Hintz of the Church of the Redeemer
from fabrics from all over the world. Using the book *Hidden in Plain
View: A Secret Story of Quilts and the Underground Railroad* by
Jacqueline Tobin, Raymond Dobard, and others, Hintz stitched
together patterns based on the traditional codes that were used as
secret signals on the Underground Railroad. During the nineteenth
century, quilting was allowed on plantations; however, slaveholders
were unaware that the quilts were used as mnemonic devices to assist
slaves in fleeing their captors. For instance, the symbol of a bear's paw
communicated the importance of using bear tracks in order to confuse
dogs following a scent. Similarly, wagon wheels symbolized the
advantage of not following a straight route, but rather a zig-zag trail
to elude trackers. Flying geese suggested the best times to leave for the
north, normally in the spring or summer months. While most log
cabin quilts of the era had red centers, those on the Underground Railroad had yellow or black centers to alert slaves that the particular
house was a safe haven. At Church of the Redeemer during Reconciliation Season, the log cabin quilt rests on the altar, symbolizing that
"this is a safe house."[4]

Each liturgy of Reconciliation Season begins with a choral introit, "Tear down the walls that divide us," from the "Liberation Mass," composed in 1994 by Robert Demmert, a former organist of the congregation, or with the lament "Steal Away to Jesus," another "code" song, written at a time when preaching by black ministers was illegal on plantations, and thus secret worship meetings were held by enslaved people in the deep woods at night. The song was a coded message that such a gathering would be held that evening. As the worship notes for Reconciliation Season at Redeemer in 2001 suggest: "As the choir sings the refrain, we reflect on our unity with all humankind, for in all ages and all places humans have heard in thunder the Divine Voice. Once again, though, there is a double meaning. For slaves who did not intend to stay long on the plantation, the instruction to make an escape during a storm offered a good strategy for eluding bloodhounds."[5]

Like all the worship services at Church of the Redeemer, liturgies for Reconciliation Season are painstakingly researched in terms of content and historical accuracy. All aspects of worship—prayers, music, readings, vestments, banners, quilts, and other visuals around the church, as well as the leaflets themselves—are created by the worship committee to coordinate with the central themes of the season. After the choral introit during Reconciliation Season, the congregation bursts into song in celebration of the freedom to gather for public worship. Music for the season is not only Eurocentric, but also reflects the African American and Hispanic heritages. The metaphors of "Exodus," the "Underground Railroad," and "following the North Star" are prevalent throughout the worship services. Responses to the readings, one of which is a lesson from a contemporary source such as Dr. Martin Luther King Jr., include the refrains "Let my people go," "Here I Am, Lord," and "No turning back." At the center of the liturgy during Reconciliation Season at Church of the Redeemer is the "Litany of Reconciliation and Confession," focused on the themes of inequality of power and the abuse of power, often unknowingly.

During Reconciliation Season in 2001, on the Sunday that focused on Harriet Tubman, the service featured a twenty-minute performance by Gloria Lowery Tyrrell. As she played freedom fighter Harriet Tubman, Tyrrell walked from the back of the church to the front, rhythmically tapping her walking stick as the spiritual, "Go Down

Litany of Reconciliation and Confession

Leader: In a world where prejudice and power have joined hands to elevate one people at the expense of another,

People: We pray for reconciliation.

Leader: In a world where the heritage of slavery is still active in people's lives,

People: We pray for reconciliation.

Leader: In a world where the evils of racism infect public discourse and private thought,

People: We pray for reconciliation.

Leader: In a world where women live overt and subtle violence at the hands of men,

People: We pray for reconciliation.

Leader: In a world where gays and lesbians are denied the freedom to love, to live and to create a family,

People: We pray for reconciliation.

Leader: In a world where we see only the disability and the person remains invisible,

People: We pray for reconciliation.

Leader: In a world where people, just because they are different, evoke fear and contempt,

People: We pray for reconciliation.

Leader: Like those who traveled the Underground Railroad we too are on a journey to freedom and wholeness. It is a journey that beings within as we name and confess that which separates us from ourselves and each other.

Let us pray:

O God, Giver of Life
Bearer of Pain
Maker of Love,
You are able to accept in us that which we cannot acknowledge;
You are able to name in us that which we cannot speak;
You are able to hold in your memory that which we try to forget.

People: Forgive us when out of fear we heart each other and ourselves.
Forgive us our silence when we could have spoken out.
Forgive us the abuse of our power and privilege.
Forgive us the prejudice and bigotry that live within our hearts
Reconcile us to all that we have rejected in ourselves.
Reconcile us to the others we have ignored, rejected or abused.
Let us find no part of your creation to be alien or strange to us,
That we ourselves will be made whole.

Minister/Leader: God forgives us and offers us wholeness and reconciliation, continually calling us into new relationships.

Source: Church of the Redeemer, "Reconciliation Season," 2001. Closing
collect adapted from Janet Morley.

Moses" was played. Dressed in authentic Civil War costume, Tyrrell presented the story of Tubman's life from her birth as a slave to her role in the establishment of the Underground Railroad as a network of activists pledged to help African Americans escape slavery. Tyrrell is director of the Sickle Cell Anemia Fund and executive director of Dramatic Interpretations, a New York-based theater company founded in 1982. The actor has brought over seventeen African American characters to the stage and is the only woman approved by the King family to play Dr. Martin Luther King Jr.[6] In the same year, Church of the Redeemer also hosted Fred Morsell as abolitionist Frederick Douglass in "Why I Became A Woman's Rights Man."

In 2002 Reconciliation Season at the Church of the Redeemer was expanded to include, in addition to racial reconciliation, sexism, elitism, and oppression against undocumented people. Working with an immigrant advocacy group in Morristown, Winds of the Spirit, the liturgy explored the human cost for those leaving native lands and what it means to live as an undocumented person in the United States. Phillip Wilson says that while the congregation on the whole is supportive of the racial justice emphasis in worship during the Reconciliation Season, it remains the one season of the liturgical year at Church of the Redeemer that continues to cause anxiety and anger. "Racism is still alive," he says. "It is one season where some people are happy when it is over. Which is all the more reason why we have to keep doing it." Phillip Wilson's experience with the reactions at the Church of the Redeemer against confronting racism within the context of worship, is echoed in other predominantly white "Progressive" congregations.

"Sometimes I think that we want to say we 'have done' racism and want to move on far too quickly," says Phillip Wilson. "The challenge in a congregation like this is not in raising justice issues, but in finding ways to help people go deeper. I have to always remind myself that as a white person I am never forced to face racism every day, which is why I have to be intentional about challenging myself to stay focused," he says.[7]

Although it is an Episcopal congregation of the Diocese of Newark, the Church of the Redeemer has rejected traditional forms of Christian formation and church membership, choosing instead to widen its embrace and actively evangelize those underserved by institutional religion. "We live in tension with belief, book, structure," says Phillip Wilson. "The experience of God as liberation is the primary experience by which we make decisions and order our life." As Wilson notes, "It's not written in stone. We're not after some absolute standard for Christianity. . . . We're living in a world with no absolutes. The church gives principles, *not* absolutes."[8]

Carol King, a leader in the congregation, says that the coordination of Church of the Redeemer's worship life is "very time consuming and very life giving." Though some members of the congregation have struggled with the liturgical innovations at Church of the Redeemer, "sometimes the pace is too slow for me," says King. The worship committee "grows" each service and season individually and has instituted a series of "liberation holy days" alongside traditional Christian holy days, to underscore God's work of reconciliation and liberation in the present day. Among other holy days, the congregation celebrates Dr. Martin Luther King Jr. Sunday, Recovery Sunday, Women's Journeys Celebration (in place of Mother's Day), Holocaust Sunday, and Gay and Lesbian Pride Sunday every year. The liturgical year at Church of the Redeemer concludes with an eight-week "Creation Season" celebrating the presence of God in all creation.

All are welcome to receive the Eucharist at Church of the Redeemer regardless of age, instruction, or tradition. Unlike most Episcopal congregations, grape juice and wine are consecrated in an attempt to fully include both children and people in recovery; the celebrant receives the Eucharist last as a symbol of servant leadership and to discount images of hierarchy. In addition, in lieu of reciting the Nicene Creed, the congregation has adopted "the first Christian creed"—"Jesus is Lord"—as a way of expressing their relationship to Christ. The acclamation "Jesus is Lord and we are the Body of Christ" has been put to music and is sung three times during the service as the congregation's affirmation of faith. Believing that "ordination comes in all shapes and sizes," the worship committee at the Church of the Redeemer has rewritten the Eucharistic Prayer so that all present say the words of Jesus over the bread and wine, rather than reserving those words for the presider.

Church of the Redeemer, Morristown, New Jersey	
Founded	1852
Total Membership	
1987	40
2002	400
Average Sunday Attendance	180–400
Composition of Congregation	
Adults	80%
Children and Youth	20%
Heterosexual	57%
Gay/Lesbian	43%
Living in committed relationships	50%
Single	50%
Children living with opposite-sex parents	61%
Children living with same-sex parents	39%
European/American/White	92.3%
African American/Black	5%
Hispanic	2.7%
Total Budget (2003)	$370,000

Sources: Church of the Redeemer, and the Rev. Phillip Dana Wilson

The social justice themes that deeply pervade the worship of Church of the Redeemer also communicate the agenda of the congregation. "We look around to see who is still marginalized," says

Marcia Liotard, a leader in the congregation. "Who is there and who is not?" The former rectory adjacent to the church on a main commercial street in Morristown, houses a program for homeless persons with HIV/AIDS; an AIDS chapel and AIDS quilt reside in the church. The parish house is occupied by a community soup kitchen and hosts the homeless for a month each year as part of the local hospitality network. The Racial Dialogue Group meets monthly. Church of the Redeemer proactively extends hospitality to the gay and lesbian community; the parish has blessed same-sex unions since 1991.

CROSSROADS BETWEEN LIFE AND DEATH

According to Phillip Wilson, "the Holy Spirit found Redeemer" through the life and death of Eric Johnson. Johnson, the son of life-long church members, contracted AIDS and died of the disease in 1990. Through their relationship with Eric and his family during his illness, members of the Church of the Redeemer gained a renewed sense of compassion for the oppressed and passion for action. The congregation was spiritually transformed. The congregation had dwindled to about forty members by 1987 when Wilson arrived. Yet, "AIDS gave new life to these bones," says Wilson. "The community found a reason to live: to welcome and to serve Eric and others living with AIDS." By 1999, church membership was about 150-200; by 2002, membership was nearly 400, with 180-200 present for Sunday worship. "*Really* being Christian attracted people," says Wilson, "and they responded to that integrity." Now leaders at the Church of the Redeemer are concerned with how to accommodate all the growth of the congregation. Presently, a broad cross-section of church leaders collaborate on a wide range of ministries within and outside the parish, and the buildings are used by a variety of social-justice–oriented local groups and as performing arts space. Today the Eric Johnson House assists persons with HIV or AIDS with employment assistance, substance-abuse treatment, mental-health counseling, transportation, daily-living skills training, and access to medical care, among other services.

Today members of the Church of the Redeemer make their stewardship commitments in the form of a financial pledge and a ministry pledge. Larry Hamil, lay pastoral assistant, says that Church of the Redeemer is a congregation that "values liberation and really tries to become a family." The role of the rector, he adds, "is to be the vision, the leadership, to hold us together." Like other parishioners, Hamil, who studied theology at Drew University in preparation for the Methodist ministry before beginning a thirty-year career as an educator, says that he probably would not be in the church at all without the Church of the Redeemer: "Even here the church is not God—but we do have a ministry of reconciliation, says Hamil. "I know what resurrection is in my personal life and I know there is a force beyond me that is there and a source of new life." Hamil observes that when members of Church of the Redeemer refer to themselves as a "family," they mean "the conscious show of solidarity" evident within the congregation. "We see God wherever we see people," says Hamil. "Liberation is from whatever is holding them down, and the community facilitates, supports, and provides a window where that can happen."

Presently, the Church of the Redeemer enjoys the support of its judicatory leaders, though the congregation's identity is focused beyond its denomination in a conscious effort to welcome and attract those outside the boundaries of organized religion. Church of the Redeemer was named Church of the Year in 1996 by the Episcopal Diocese of Newark, as "an ecclesiastical haven for those who have felt themselves to be outside the scope of traditional religious care. . . . If you are the victim of prejudice, whether that prejudice is based on race, gender, or sexual orientation, you are welcomed here, and this congregation will walk beside you to help achieve the glorious liberty of the Children of God, promised to all God's people."[9]

Significantly, Church of the Redeemer is located in Morristown, New Jersey, which is both a commercial and a residential area in close proximity to New York City, with its major Fortune 500 companies. Morristown is located in Morris County, where African American residents have a higher per capita average income than anywhere else in the United States. Church of the Redeemer was founded in 1852 by a group who decided to leave St. Peter's Church, another Episcopal church just two blocks away in Morristown. The first wooden church was built a year later, and the congregation moved to its present location in 1885. The first "golden years" of Redeemer's history were during 1919–1952. During this period the parish built its

current stone church with a seating capacity for 400. One of the
largest congregations in the Episcopal Diocese of Newark at this time,
Redeemer also built the parish house with a full gym and became a
community center in Morristown. Always concerned with the community and social issues, the parish hosted the first Alcoholics Anonymous meeting to be held in a church hall in New Jersey in 1940.
During the 1960s and 1970s Redeemer hosted civil rights groups and
Anti-Vietnam War groups. The first woman to celebrate the Holy
Eucharist at Church of the Redeemer was the Reverend Nancy Wittig,
one of the first women ordained to the priesthood in the Episcopal
Church, ordained in 1974.[10]

Population of Morristown, New Jersey, 2000	
Total Population	18,544
European American/White	12,452
African American/Black	3,144
Asian	700
American Indian/Alaska Native	41
Native Hawaiian/Pacific Islander	12
Hispanic/Other	1,572
Two or more racial groups	623
Average Household	2.43
Average Family Size	3.19
Age Range for the Highest Number of Residents	25–54
Percentage over 18 Years of Age	75.5%

Sources: Morris County, New Jersey; Census 2000

By 1985 Church of the Redeemer was at a "crossroads between life
and death." Wilson arrived in 1987 as the congregation's fifteenth rector and had a terrible first year before the events surrounding Eric
Johnson and his struggle with AIDS led to the spiritual transformation
of the small congregation. "People who live in a dysfunctional community are people who *like* it," says Wilson in reference to his first
year at the congregation. "People said they wanted a leader—they
wanted a target!" Yet only a year afterwards the congregation held

their first annual Dr. Martin Luther King Jr. Sunday as a major parish liberation celebration. By 1990 the congregation's emphasis on liberation liturgies became a focus through the initiation of "Creation Season" in October and November, and with the commitment to use inclusive language at all its principal Sunday services. By 1998 the congregation had its first budget surplus without going into the endowment for operational expenses.

Today Church of the Redeemer is a "magnet congregation" that draws its membership from a thirty-mile radius. In 2001 the Church of the Redeemer in Morristown was named one of three hundred "Excellent Protestant Congregations" as a result of a two-year study funded by the Lilly Endowment. Though racial-justice ministry in particular or social justice in general were not specific criteria of this study, Redeemer was selected for a standard of excellence that included a joyful spirit, awareness of diversity, being welcoming and accessible, true spirituality and a deep relationship with God, innovativeness, thoughtful worship, and collaborative leadership.[11] In response to this honor, Wilson explained part of Redeemer's spiritual appeal. "I think people are spiritually hungry," says Wilson. "They hunger for values. The church is the perfect place to embrace people from different backgrounds."[12]

The major criterion that governs the congregation of the Church of the Redeemer is its vision of life from the perspective of human liberation as a reality, as if God's reign were enacted here on earth. The congregation considers itself a work in progress: "if we think we are finished, we start to die. [We] must constantly rename God in our midst," says Phillip Wilson. Theologically, Redeemer is not interested in creating a new liberal orthodoxy; rather, they choose to embody a model that values "both/and" thinking over "either/or" thinking. "[We believe] that which connects us is stronger than that which divides us," says Phillip Wilson.

As a congregation, the Church of the Redeemer strives to rejoice in difference and to embody values that hold that one does not have to understand what another thinks or does to value that person. The imagery of "fall and redemption" is largely absent from the liturgy. Formal divisions between clergy and laity are discouraged, and all members are challenged to see their vocation in the world as ministry. At Church of the Redeemer pastoral care is considered as much the work of the people as it is of the priest, and it is enacted within the context of the congregation and the wider community. Laity of diverse backgrounds tell their stories as sermons and homilies is common in the congregation. While many of the members of Church of the Redeemer do not have a strong affiliation with the Episcopal Church, the congregation continues to honor and support (15% of its budget) its diocese, whether they are in total agreement with its positions or not. At Church of the Redeemer, the diocesan bishop is viewed as a "symbol of inclusivity" connecting the congregation with other Episcopal congregations, some of whom are vastly different both theologically and culturally.[13]

RACIAL JUSTICE INITIATIVES

Church of the Redeemer's commitment to multiracial community is lived out in a variety of ways that intersect with different groups and ministries in the congregation, the wider church, and the community. Parish leaders see their approach as complementary, rather than competitive; part of the goal is to utilize the best of the antiracism and racial-justice resources available through the local diocese, the national Episcopal Church, the local seminary (Drew University School of Theology), other local educational institutions, and the community. Overall, Church of the Redeemer remains a predominantly white congregation; about 5 percent of the congregation are of black or African American descent; 2.7 percent are Hispanic. Aware of the growing Hispanic population throughout Morris County, Church of the Redeemer has recently begun to include more Spanish-language elements in the principal Sunday worship service. Otto Maduro, professor of World Christianity at Drew University, preached at the parish and has attended Church of the Redeemer on a regular basis. Maduro also serves as co-director of the Hispanic doctorate of ministry at Drew University. His sermon at Church of the Redeemer in February 2002 challenged the congregation on a global level to consider the implication of the United States lifestyle on the people in other parts of the world who manufacture our products and services. Maduro thus raised the important connection between personal liberation and the need not to forget the oppression that continues throughout the world.

One of Church of the Redeemer's wardens, Lyle Timpson, commented on the continuing struggle within a "Liberation Community" "for the liberated to become liberator" in the congregation's newsletter, *Crossroads:*

> But while we rejoice in our own personal liberation, many still languish under the yoke of oppression, many continually suffer the humiliation of inequality and our world struggle to endure the burden of human excess. Redeemer is a magnet that draws many of us great distances each week because we're unable to find parishes closer to home that embody Redeemer's vision. Perhaps our beloved congregants' relocation would not have been so traumatic—for them and us—if the reality we relish every Sunday were more than a vague possibility in the larger world. Inherent in Redeemer's vision is the call to extend the message of justice and liberation outside these walls; to foster its development and apply its wisdom in the larger world. While much work is already done in our local community, larger social and environmental issues require our attention.[14]

Church of the Redeemer's response as a congregation to the issue of racism is in part due to a 1993 initiative of the Episcopal Diocese of Newark Anti-Racism Committee report that challenged every congregation in the diocese to establish a racial dialogue group with the assistance of a diocesan consultant. The congregation implemented the challenge, and several years later participated in a diocesan training program using the *National Dialogues on Anti-Racism,* developed through the national Episcopal Church. At the present time, the Episcopal Diocese of Newark continues to use the *National Dialogues on Anti-Racism* model throughout the diocese and has one of the most active antiracism committees of the Episcopal Church as part of its "Mission to Dismantle Racism." Bert Jones, the coordinator of the diocesan antiracism efforts, has appreciated working with leadership from Church of the Redeemer over the years. "Redeemer-Morristown has done some good work,' says Bert Jones. "Phillip Wilson has really tried to put his church on the map by pushing the issue of racism. They started a few years ago, and still continue to do the work. Just last year, they had a joint [antiracism training] session with St. Peter's-Morristown. . . . Phillip [Wilson] has tried to cut deep into the issue of power."[15] This session that Jones refers to had about forty participants from the two congregations combined. Richard Horsley, a member of St. Peter's, is a member of the diocesan antiracism facilitators team. As an African American, Horsley sees the value of both local and judicatory antiracism efforts. "I think that we have an excellent opportunity to learn from each other in a deep way," he says. "The parish and the diocesan programs support each other."

THE RACIAL DIALOGUE GROUP AND THE ERACISM GROUP

Central to Church of the Redeemer's efforts to build multiracial community is the congregation's Racial Dialogue Group (RDG). As of September 2002, the group has been meeting for five years once a month on Saturday mornings. A considerable time commitment, the sessions run for approximately three hours each. A year ago the Racial Dialogue Group joined with a similar group at St. Peter's Episcopal Church in Morristown, a few blocks down the street from Church of the Redeemer. (The parish buildings are within sight of each other.) Each group uses a slightly different name within its own congregation: Racial Dialogue Group, or RDG, at the Church of the Redeemer, while St. Peter's group calls itself the Eracism Group. The names are used interchangeably, and the group alternates the location of monthly meetings between the two congregations. Approximately eighteen to twenty-five people attend the group regularly. Phillip Wilson notes that the shared group model has proved helpful to Redeemer's racial-justice efforts for several reasons. First, St. Peter's has more people of color in its membership and thus is more able to provide the leadership of people of color for the combined group. As in so many predominantly white congregations, people of color in leadership at Church of the Redeemer have suffered from burnout as a result of the isolation and racism that are inevitable in white institutions. In addition, a continuing group devoted to the eradication of racism was a concrete project that the two congregations could undertake together and thus was a way to boost their collegiality and profile in the community.

Charles "Chuck" Dickerson, one of the co-chairs of the Racial Dialogue Group at Church of the Redeemer and an African American, agrees that the partnership with the neighboring congregation is a fruitful one. Chuck Dickerson teaches African American history at the

County College of Morris and estimates that there are about fifteen to twenty African American members of the congregation at Redeemer, and twenty-five to thirty at St. Peter's. He estimates that about five people of color regularly participate in the Racial Dialogue Group, and that they are of African American ancestry. Though some Hispanic people have attended in the past, the group has had difficulty in retaining their participation. About 50 percent of group members are Episcopalian; as is the case with all groups that Church of the Redeemer sponsors, persons from all religious backgrounds are welcome. Chuck Dickerson deeply appreciates the shared partnership he has with the co-facilitators of the group: Janice Paran, a white woman from Redeemer; Gregory Cobbs, an African American man from St. Peter's; and Kathy Seabrook, a white woman from St. Peter's.

Janice Paran, a co-facilitator from Church of the Redeemer, has been a member of the congregation since 1980 and a member of the Racial Dialogue Group since its second year of operation. Besides an interest in the subject matter since her childhood in Detroit in the 1960s, Janice Paran, who is white, says she "liked the idea of a place where people could tell the truth to each other about race." The word "dialogue" found in the group's name also appealed to her, and "regardless of what was going on in the room I knew I had to be there," she says. She found group exercises based on Wellesley professor Peggy McIntosh's work on "white privilege" both transformative for herself, and a source of deep resistance for other white people.

The automatic privileges received by European Americans within the United States is the focus of Peggy McIntosh's work. In an important article, "White Privilege: Unpacking the Invisible Knapsack," McIntosh argues that as a white person she was taught about racism as a phenomenon that puts others at a disadvantage, but not taught to see how it gave her, as a white person, personal and societal advantages. These advantages are what McIntosh calls "white privilege," or "an invisible package of unearned assets," that white persons "can count on cashing in each day," but about which we are oblivious. McIntosh uses the metaphor of white privilege as an invisible, weightless knapsack of special provisions, maps, codebooks, visas, tools, and blank checks. White privilege is given to us because we are born white; we do not choose it. Similarly, white privilege is experienced as oppressive to people of color, whether we beneficiaries choose to be oppressors or not. Many of the privileges McIntosh lists in her articles are those things that a European American living in the United States can and does take for granted. For instance, we can, if we wish, arrange to be in the company of our own race most of the time. We can go shopping most of the time without being harassed. We are educated knowing that the accomplishments of our race will be included. For European Americans, letting go of white privilege means both to confront the reality of our privilege and to let go of assumptions we once considered time-honored truths. While as European Americans we are born into racial privilege, what we do with these advantages is a matter of choice.[16]

Though Janice Paran admits some frustration with the small number of people of color who attend the shared racial dialogue group—feeling that the depth of learning is greater in a more multiracial group—she also acknowledges the increased personal cost for people of color who are placed in the position of having to retell repeatedly the stories of the impact of racism on their lives, and thereby having perpetually to educate white people. "What happens to the quality of the conversation when it is an increasingly white conversation?" she asks. "There is no end to the richness and the stimulation of hearing a different experience of the same issue." In this regard, Janice Paran found hearing people of color discuss their experiences of internalized racism extraordinarily powerful, and feels she would have missed these insights completely in an all-white group.

This sense of the extraordinary depth of sharing within the shared racial dialogue group is echoed by Kathy Seabrook, a co-chair of the Eracism Group at St. Peter's, who is also white. Like the leadership at Church of the Redeemer, she also frequently encounters resistance to the group from other white parishioners. "Resistance is so high," says Kathy Seabrook. "[White] people would say that they just feel like they are beaten over the head." For this reason, she sees the need to find ways to introduce white people to discussions about race and racism that open up rather than close down the conversation. "This is hard and heart-wrenching work," says Kathy Seabrook. "It's not like being on the altar guild. It's not about other people—it's about me—how I face my own 'isms.'"

A continuing issue within the shared racial dialogue group between the two congregations regards the degree to which it is proactive or not. Is the group a place for people to do their own internal work on racism and then move from there into the community, or are members of the group responsible for taking a public stand against racism in the community? Presently, members of the existing group have varying opinions on these questions. The overall aim of the shared racial dialogue group is not so much to provide resources relating to racial justice to both congregations—though they do so on occasion—but to provide members with an in-depth and consistent multiracial community in which to explore and discuss the personal implications of racism and internalized racism in their daily lives. The long duration and consistency of the group, as well as the quality of the relationships formed, have allowed members to discuss with candor and intensity both the effects of white power and privilege and the effects of internalized rage and oppression in their lives and on their spirits. Though participants discuss racism from the perspective of their own life experiences, the focus of the shared racial dialogue group is not behavioral as much as it is structural. The intimacy and trust that have been built in the group over time have supported both the quality of the confrontation and degree of risk that members are willing to commit, as well as the level of transformation potentially achieved. To strike a balance between personal antiracism work and collective action, many of the topics that the shared racial dialogue group has planned for 2003 are more connected to the larger community than ever before.

The organization of the shared dialogue group between the Church of the Redeemer and St. Peter's depends on the subject for discussion, which is chosen by the co-chairs, and leadership is rotated according to the topic selected. A wide variety of media are selected for the group to experience together: books, film, theater, speakers, and the like. Phillip Wilson at one time assisted in developing the topics, but the program is now developed by the co-chairs of the group. Past films shared by the group, include *The Problem of Color in the African American Community*, *Psychological Residuals of Slavery*, *The Color of Fear*, and *Race in America*. Topics proposed for 2002–2003 include the film *Nothing But a Man*; a trip to see *Crowns*, a musical at the McCarter Theatre in Princeton adapted from the best-selling book which celebrates black women and their church hats; a lecture at County College by Professor Peggy McIntosh on "white privilege";

the Morristown Martin Luther King Jr. celebration; a panel of church and community leaders for black history month; a round-table forum on the question, "How is race lived in our community?"; and a meeting on issues of privilege and power facilitated by Dr. Traci C. West, associate professor of ethics and African American studies at Drew University School of Theology.[17]

Traci West has also served as a consultant to the shared racial dialogue group. She notes that, although the two congregations work together on racial justice issues, they are really very different as congregations, and this factor is part of their joint process. On the whole, St. Peter's is the more traditional congregation of the two, and more people of color attend St. Peter's. While the Church of the Redeemer would consider itself more progressive theologically, it remains a predominantly white congregation. As a congregation, Church of the Redeemer is more consistent about confronting homophobia, for which they are criticized in the larger community, yet Traci West observes that the congregation of St. Peter's seems generally more open to examining classism. She believes that the shared dialogue between members of the two congregations is a good example of "how complicated it is to raise the issues of interlocking oppression within churches." As a facilitator, I have been clear that the racism piece matters to me," Traci West says. "But I have been equally very clear about the homophobia piece, and that you have to talk about it when issues about oppression are raised." She also sees the advantage of a shared leadership model. Isolation is a common factor among leaders in antiracism work within congregations, and sometimes the people who are willing to serve in the role do not have the stamina, owing to other personal factors, to serve in a consistent and long-term capacity. "The shared leadership here," says Traci West, "has allowed people to share their strengths and not carry the whole group all the time."

Overall, the shared racial dialogue group of Church of the Redeemer and St. Peter's uses designated facilitators only on some occasions. Individual Saturday reflection sessions by the group are conducted without an assigned facilitator—the group self-facilitates. Still, they find it important to bring in "outside" consultants on occasion for presentations and as process consultants. Occasionally, members of the group have homework to do such as viewing a film or some advance reading. The session always begins with some food and a check-in, or "how are we doing" time with the members, and ends with a time spent on "walking the talk," or "how can we better live or change lives with what we have learned today."

Chuck Dickerson says that he has seen people with "a total lack of understanding [about racism] come to a different place," through participation in the shared racial dialogue group. A longtime member of the Church of the Redeemer, Chuck Dickerson stays in the congregation because of its commitment to diversity and the practical obstacle of a long drive to more diverse or predominantly black Episcopal congregations in other communities. He admits that he and his wife "have walked away [from Church of the Redeemer] twice. We had had it." Why as an African American would he return to a predominantly white parish and openly discuss the experience of racism, the pain of which he experiences everyday? "Some of us had to be there," he says, referring to the need to have both people of color and white people in a group for effective interracial dialogue. "I felt the deep pulls of obligation and I came back."

Chuck Dickerson feels that much of what is discussed by white participants of the shared racial dialogue group focuses on the reality of white privilege, the pain around letting it go, and the need to learn to share power with people of color. He feels that many of the reflections of the people of color in the group, like his own reflections, focus on the lack of progress [for racial justice], the rage and anger they are feeling, and the "lack of understanding about why there is no understanding [about racism]" among so many white people. Though sometimes, Chuck Dickerson admits, he comes to the shared racial dialogue group with "doubts that it will make a difference" and with little belief in the potential for change, he sees his role and participation as a person of color in the group as crucial in order to go about "chipping away at the mountain."

The shared racial dialogue group receives approximately $1,500 from each congregation annually as a budget, as well as occasional grants and income from a bequest from a former member. Though a great deal of personal time and resources are donated by the co-chairs and other members of the group, the budget funds are used to cover program costs and to pay for occasional outside facilitators and consultants for the group.

A recurring challenge for the shared racial dialogue group of the Church of the Redeemer and St. Peter's is the incorporation of new group members. Rather than advertising themselves as a strictly open or closed group, the leadership attempts to design the schedule with multiple entry points. While new members are integral to the group's longevity and survival, they have had difficulty determining what the incorporation process for newcomers should be. Longtime members of the shared racial dialogue group miss the intensity of the experience when they have to "slow down" for newcomers and sometimes feel impatient "with having to wait until people catch up." Conversely, it is difficult for newcomers to participate fully when they have not had similar group experience, significant antiracism training, or the same depth of relationship as longtime group members.

In past years, the shared racial dialogue group has provided a type of "orientation" for newcomers by offering two sessions on the history and background of the group, with limited success. This year, the co-chairs of the shared racial dialogue group have committed to offering the *National Dialogues on Anti-Racism* training on one night per week for people who might be interested in joining the racial dialogue group in the future. It is hoped that such training will serve as a helpful initial experience for those interested in exploring racism further, as well as provide some basic definitions and structure. Though this is an additional time commitment for the co-chairs, it is hoped that these extra sessions will help both broaden the membership of the existing racial dialogue group and provide an additional educational opportunity for racial justice within the congregations and the wider community.

WHAT DOES A WHITE PERSON HAVE TO SAY ABOUT RACISM?

Phillip Wilson sees it as integral to his role as rector of the Church of the Redeemer to keep the issue of racism in front of the congregation. "The absolute cancer in American society is racism. If the Christian church can do anything, it needs to name the sins of the past, hold out the hope for healing and break down the barriers that exist today," he says. Phillip Wilson keeps the issue in front of the congregation through supporting the Reconciliation Season in the congregation's worship life, the work of the racial dialogue group, as well as by using other entry points to reach members of the congregation and community. Phillip Wilson summed up his views on racial justice in a sermon in January 2002 on the day of the Dr. Martin Luther King Jr. Breakfast. Entitled "What Does a White Person Have to Say about Racism?" the sermon traces the development of Phillip Wilson's own racial consciousness from the 1960s to the present. "As a white person," says Wilson, "I believe I must learn to live with the fact that racism lives within me and that the best I can be is a recovering racist. And, if you know anything about recovery programs, you know that recovery is a lifelong process. . . . And, like the alcoholic, if I do not work on this problem, it will kill me." Though concerned with the personal and interpersonal dimensions of racism, Wilson makes clear that racism will not be eradicated without changing the balance of power between white people and people of color. He suggests that there are five things (at least) that a white person can say about racism:

1. For me to join the fight against racism, I must first get in touch with what it feels like to be white. I must name and own my own white privilege.

2. Racism is a mixture of prejudice and fear joined with power. The imbalance of power within our society is what keeps the racism firmly in place.

3. For my commitment to be more than theoretical and for me to be a real ally, I must first revisit experiences in my life when I was abused by the combination of power and prejudice.

4. The fight against racism is going to be a difficult struggle because power concedes nothing without demand. It never has and it never will.

5. Finally, racism is as much my problem and that of every white person as it is that of my black sisters and brothers.

When the Church of the Redeemer in Morristown, New Jersey, was recognized by the Rt. Rev. John Shelby Spong of the Episcopal Diocese of Newark in January 1996 with the Bishop's Banner for Congregational Excellence, he praised the integrated approach toward justice issues that has characterized the congregation's approach to racism as well as to other forms of oppression. "Issues of human justice have defined the liturgy that is used, revised the hymns that are sung and determined the witness that the congregation makes."[18] This intensely focused and integrated approach to antiracist inclusivity in the liturgy and in congregational life and action characterizes the Church of the Redeemer today. As the closing prayer from a Reconciliation Season liturgy states:

> We leave hearing the call to act with justice, love tenderly, to serve one another and to walk humbly with God. We hear the call to reconciliation and are strengthened in our resolve to be its agents. Like the slaves on the Underground Railroad we are on a journey to freedom and wholeness.

SUMMARY

Though the Church of the Redeemer in Morristown, New Jersey, is not the only congregation to move beyond the concept of "outreach" toward the vision of a liberation community where racial justice is threaded through several dimensions of its corporate life, its story suggests several factors that support this transformation. Through its worship life, Redeemer continually calls the congregation to reevaluate and reinvent their symbolic life and systems of metaphors. Such worship is indigenous and emerges from the concerns of the community. This congregation sees language itself as a justice issue, and it is sensitive to the need for inclusive images and metaphors from a racial, ethnic, and cultural perspective, as well as from a gender-inclusive perspective. The vibrant worship of Redeemer is both a powerful witness and a model of formation. Further, the congregation's expansive worship committee is integral to the congregation's life; they do a great deal of intentional planning to prepare extensive service booklets, create works of art, and write hymns and prayers. The spirituality of the Church of the Redeemer is connected to its Christian and denominational heritage, yet they continue to reinterpret this heritage within their emergent social context.

As a liberation community, Redeemer welcomes all persons, especially those who otherwise feel excluded from organized religion. This congregation evaluates their openness as a community by *who is not included*, by who is not present in their midst, and their response to the spiritual hunger of the marginalized. Though Redeemer continues to struggle as a white congregation with issues of white power and privilege, the congregation's multiple approaches allow them to experience the call to multiracial community in a variety of contexts, including worship, education, and ministry in the greater community. Moreover, the congregation is challenged by the small number of people of color in its membership, but the remaining diversity of the congregation provides an opportunity to examine racial justice from the perspective of multiple and interlocking oppressions. The congregation continues to struggle to build a perspective beyond viewing racism as a "black and white" problem and needs to continue to strive to include additional voices, such as Hispanic and Asian representation. Helpfully, the shared racial dialogue group of Redeemer is rooted in a systemic approach to oppression and to social change.

The leaders of Church of the Redeemer, lay and ordained, are conversant about the dynamics of power and teach it as part of religious formation. Moreover, members of the Church of the Redeemer are urged first to recognize the racism in their midst, rather than among persons who live elsewhere. Leadership in this liberation community requires vision as well as the capacity to cope creatively with conflict, ambiguity, and risk. Skill in collaboration, the ability to hold multiple perspectives on truth, and the capacity for discernment are important charisms. Leaders in this congregation are media savvy and effectively communicate the mission of the congregation as part of their overall strategy of evangelism.

Finally, within the vision of the Church of the Redeemer as a "liberation community," ministry and stewardship are inextricably linked. All members are challenged to root their lives in worship and social justice as spiritual disciplines. Redeemer strives to use all wealth for the transformation of church and society. The varied ministries of the Church of the Redeemer as a liberation community are an important models for the transformation of today's congregations in the midst of diversity and great human need. This congregation strives to deepen the personal and corporate dimensions of faith through working for justice for all.

6

The Sea Captains and Slavery

First Parish Brewster
Brewster, Massachusetts

> *You, the Turk, the Arab, the Swede,*
> *The German, the Eskimo, the Scot,*
> *The Italian, the Hungarian, the Pole,*
> *You the Ashanti, the Yoruba, the Kru, bought,*
> *Sold, stolen, arriving on a nightmare,*
> *Praying for a dream.*
>
> *Here, root yourselves beside me.*
> *I am that Tree planted by the River,*
> *Which will not be moved.*
> *I, the Rock, I, the River, I, the Tree.*
> *I am yours—your passages have been paid.*
> *Lift your faces, you have a piercing need*
> *For this bright morning dawning for you.*
> *History, despite its wrenching pain,*
> *Cannot be unlived, but if faced*
> *With courage, need not be lived again.*
> > —Maya Angelou,
> > "On the Pulse of the Morning"[1]

A CONGREGATION THAT HAS FACED WITH COURAGE ITS PAST IN order to address a history of racism is First Parish Brewster in Massachusetts. Known as "The Church of the Sea Captains," the Unitarian-Universalist congregation of over 700 members is one of the oldest churches in North America. Founded in 1700 as a Pilgrim Church, it became identified with sea captains in the nineteenth century because of the many clipper-ship captains and their families that worshiped there. The current meetinghouse was built in 1834 and looks like a traditional New England church with white clapboard siding, a tall steeple, and wooden box pews. (The congregation became Unitarian-Universalist in 1961 when the two denominations merged.). A sign that the congregation was proud of this heritage was seen in the prints of clipper ships on the walls of the meetinghouse. The local historical society and several historians in Brewster assured the senior minister, James "Jim" Robinson, that the particular sea captains and ships affiliated with First Parish were not involved with slavery.

Jeanne Denike, a former social worker and activist and a member of First Parish Brewster, became concerned about the possible connection between the sea captains and the slave trade after an incident in the congregation's cemetery in 1998. The old cemetery immediately adjoining First Parish is the final resting place of many of Brewster's first residents, including the sea captains. On Halloween, Jeanne Denike was asked to lead a worship service or ritual experience before the weekly staff meeting. Given the time of year, she decided it would be good for the group to go into the cemetery and honor the ancestors of the congregation. Equipped with a history of the cemetery, and some stones, shells, and pine cones to place near the graves, Jeanne Denike led the group into the southwest corner of the cemetery. As the staff would gather around a particular grave, Denike would read excerpts about the sea captains and their families. For instance: "Godfrey Lincoln, son of Silvanus Lincoln, and Rhode Snow Lincoln, died at St.. Thomas, Africa, march 1819, Age 11 [sic]. He accompanied Gen. Elijah Cobb and Capt'n Issac Clark on a trading expedition to the west coast of Africa. Capt'n Clark, Capt'n Nickerson, and Capt'n Joseph Mayo also lost their lives from African fever on this disastrous voyage."[2]

One member of the staff who remained close to the group but who did not place offerings next to the gravestones was the Rev. Pancheta Peterson, a Jamaican who serves as community minister at First Parish Brewster. After the service, Jeanne Denike says she "had one of those heart-in-the-throat feelings as I understood that I had just invited Pancheta and the staff to honor the memory of sea captains whose business in Africa was quite unknown to us. What exactly were they doing there? Who was benefiting and who was suffering from their presence in Africa? Had they been involved in the slave trade? Later that day I telephoned Pancheta to acknowledge that without her silent reminder I might have continued on with my unexamined admiration of our sea captains."[3]

Before this incident, First Parish Brewster was extensively involved in the Unitarian-Universalist antiracism programs. Afterwards, the history committee of First Parish—with Jim Robinson's urging—began to research more thoroughly the history of the sea captains and the vessels prominently displayed in their meetinghouse. Although comparatively few sources relate directly to Brewster's participation in slavery, a visit to the Heritage Library on Hilton Head, South Carolina, revealed to Jeanne Denike some strong connections. In W. E. B. Dubois's book *Suppression of the Slave Trade*, Jeanne Denike was able to identify three ships engaged in the slave trade between 1841 and 1864 that were commanded by members of First Parish Brewster, the *Charlotte,* the *Sophia,* and the *Senator.* House Executive Document #61 stated that the *Senator* was once owned by the a man who lived just a few houses away from First Parish. In January 1847 the *Senator* sailed from Brazil to four ports on the west coast of Africa, where the ship was sold and 914 slaves were put on board. By the time the ship cast anchor again in Brazil twenty-three days later under the command of a Portuguese captain, 246 black Africans were dead, mostly due to the lack of water. Though it is not clear if the *Senator* was sold before it became a slave ship, and while the information on the *Charlotte* and the *Sophia* was limited, the members of First Parish Brewster chose to face up to the implications of their history, rather than to deny the significance of the information they uncovered. "While the specifics of direct participation by Brewster sea captains in the slave trade still require more research into hard-to-find documents, the indirect involvement and economic benefit are painfully clear," says Jeanne Denike. "I realized that I have preferred to think of slavery as a mostly southern institution, and as somewhat periphral to the development of this country, rather than as a central to our economic success. Now I recognize that the much revered stately sea captain's homes and even this beautiful sanctuary were built at least in part from the profits of a trade which supported slavery."[4]

The Atlantic slave trade was one of the most successful commercial ventures in history. By the second half of the eighteenth century, the colonies included several commercially successful seaports, among the largest of which were Boston, New York, and Philadelphia. The mercantile activities of the northeastern seaports brought a degree of prosperity hitherto unknown. The United States, as well as other colonial nations, built unprecedented economic prosperity on the enslavement of black Africans. Though the imported merchandise varied, merchants rarely specialized. The "triangular trade" of molasses, rum, and slaves was inextricably linked to the shipping industry. At least eleven million black Africans were brought from their homelands to a port in the Americas between the years 1492 and 1870. Although participation in the slave trade was made illegal by action of the United States Congress in 1808, the laws were seldom enforced. The illegal slave trade was extensive, particularly during the period from 1850 to 1860. Many of the clipper ships that brought slaves across the Atlantic were built in New England and fitted with second decks in order to disguise their cargo should the ship fail to evade naval patrols. The people transported across the Atlantic to be sold as slaves endured horrible conditions, and many died in transit.[5]

What is to be gained by researching the painful aspects of a congregation's history? How do we benefit in the present from the study of the moral complexities of our forebears? How does exposing the racism of the past support individuals and congregations striving for multiracial community?

For congregations interested in building multiracial community, one of the most important areas of exploration is history. Multiracial community does not happen without intentional leadership and this requires that we explore not only our personal and interpersonal racial history but also our corporate histories, including the histories of our congregations. Certainly each community of faith has at the very least an unspoken sense of its own history. Congregations interested in becoming multiracial communities are further challenged to examine their history on a deeper level from the perspective of the history of racial oppression in the United States. A major challenge to forming multiracial communities is that many white Americans do not consider that the history of racism and discrimination in this country and in the church is relevant to congregational life and change. In many predominantly white congregations, the racism of ancestors in the faith either goes unexamined or is considered part of a past that should be forgotten. Conversely, history is very relevant to people of color, who still know and feel the pain that the past brings to bear on their lives. Generally, people of color know more about white America than white people know about communities of color. Further, as white people continue to benefit from a history of unearned privileges, so do people of color continue to struggle because of a history of racial oppression. Building a multiracial community, then, requires sensitivity to the history of a congregation, as well as resolve to challenge the dominant narrative in an effort to uncover and reinterpret the past from the perspective of different races and cultures.

"I believe we limit ourselves as a welcoming church unless we acknowledge all the contributors to our history," says Jeanne Denike.

> If we don't talk about the African trade as part of our past, we may deny a whole people the sense of belonging to our history and therefore to our present. Understanding how the sea captains were men of their times, intent on making a living and wittingly or unwittingly supporting what would have been against their religious principles, may help us see more clearly our relationship to the disturbing questions of our times. In our quest for truth where are there other walls with openings to discover?

Jeanne Denike also realizes that the encounter in the cemetery was with herself: "I had not wanted to expose any part of my own racism, ignorance, denial, or insensitivity," she says. "Yet there it was, and it prodded me into a year-long process of searching. That has opened me to a deeper appreciation of the richness of our history and a stronger conviction that bringing out what has been hidden also reveals new strengths. I hope that I can grow in compassion in other places where I have been quick to gloss over reality or to make judgments."[6]

In an effort to share what was learned from this investigation of the history of "The Church of the Sea Captains," First Parish Brewster drafted a statement that discusses the significance of their history. This statement, "The Sea Captains and Slavery," was approved by the First Parish Board of Trustees in November 2000 and is now displayed in the meetinghouse:

> In the course of researching our history for our Tricententennial, questions were raised about the trading activities of the First Parish sea captains. Although specific evidence is lacking, it can be reasonably assumed that some of our captains and crews were involved, at least

indirectly, with the slave trade. First Parish deeply regrets this involvement. It is also clear that some of our sea captains were vocal abolitionists. The American economy, North and South, were dependent on the system of slavery to a degree that has never been widely acknowledged. We believe that an awareness of our past is an integral part of our on going commitment to racial justice in the present and in the future.[7]

Besides an awareness of how the economic benefits of slavery were related to the congregation's history, First Parish Brewster continues both to take pride in its heritage and to confront those aspects of it which have been racist and have enforced white supremacy. First Parish also sees as necessary integrating the genocide of Native Americans on the Lower Cape into the congregation's history. Further, members recognize that historically, Unitarian-Universalism within the United States and Canada has largely been white, middle-class, highly educated, and professional in membership. The Anti-Racism Task Force of First Parish Brewster continues to urge and support church leaders to create opportunities for members of the congregation "to both celebrate their history and to be honest about it."[8]

RACIAL JUSTICE AND SPIRITUAL VALUES

First Parish Brewster is a vibrant and predominantly European American congregation in an affluent community on Cape Cod, Massachusetts. *The Cape Cod Times* calls the area one of the five most expensive places to live in the United States. An estimated 3 percent of the congregation's membership is of color, comparable to 2 to 3 percent on Lower Cape Cod as a region. First Parish's membership is economically diverse in part because of the unusual economy on Cape Cod. A third of members and friends of the congregation are retired, and another third are employed in tourist-dependent small businesses or service jobs. Jim Robinson, who has served the congregation for twenty years, estimates that roughly one-third of the congregation is especially challenged by the Cape's high cost of living. The congregation's motto of "Diversity with Unity" is lived out through the religious values of love, truth, service, compassion, peace, justice, and reverence for life. Christians, Jews, Buddhists, humanists, Hindus, and pagans worship together and participate in a wide range of programs for all ages. "Love is the doctrine of this church," says the Affirmation of First Parish Brewster. "The quest for truth is its sacrament and service is its prayer. To the end that all souls shall grow into harmony with the divine." The antiracism efforts of First Parish grow out of these values, and the congregation seeks intentionally to be a meeting place that affirms these values.[9]

Historically, First Parish Brewster has been a congregation with strong opinions about the way the marginalized should be treated. The congregation's social-justice work has included work with low-income families, the Unitarian-Universalist Service Committee, battered women, the homeless, Habitat for Humanity, environmental issues, and people with AIDS/HIV. First Parish is also a partner church to a Romanian congregation. In the 1980s First Parish became a sanctuary congregation for eighteen Salvadoran refugees, becoming one of the first congregations in the northeast United States to do so.

In 1990 First Parish Brewster was the first congregation to complete the UUA's "Welcoming Congregation" program, thereby officially welcoming gay, lesbian, and transgender people. In the present the members challenge themselves to let their actions speak their values. "We need truthfulness and a willingness to acknowledge the current as well as three-and-a-half centuries of wrongs committed against people of color, born out of ignorance, intolerance, and a sense of superiority, i.e., power, professed by the white society and taken for granted as the norm." Members see the importance of moving from "fixing" wrongs to working for systemic change. "For me this next step of understanding and confronting white privilege is the most difficult," says Jeanne Denike. "I see it now as deeply spiritual work. Although this level certainly involves individual self-examination, I believe that working together is essential, and that the full support of your church leadership is crucial."[10]

First Parish Brewster is part of the larger "Journey Toward Wholeness" movement within the Unitarian Universalist Association to eliminate racism. Dr. William Sinkford, the newly elected president of the UUA, stated, "The election of a black person to be head of this association has symbolic value, clearly, and it is part of the story we tell about who we are. But a more important element for me is that this is not only a symbol, but a sign that reconciliation is actually possible across the lines of race."[11] Though First Parish has succeeded in attracting some people of color to worship, the congregation's long-term goal toward building multiracial community is to become anti-racist in every aspect of organization and community. Some of the particular steps that First Parish has taken toward this goal, include the following:

- A two-year (1996–1998) evaluation of racism in worship services, religious education, and other events.

- Participation of two hundred members of First Parish Brewster in "Study Circles"—small group, highly participatory dialogues that focus on how people make a difference in their community—to examine racism and increase members' understanding of racism as individuals.

- Formation of ongoing alliances with people of color on Cape Cod. These include a fourteen-year relationship with the Cape Cod Chapter of the National Association for the Advancement of Colored People (NAACP); an ongoing alliance with the Wampanoag People; alliances with the Brazilian and Latino communities through the English as a Second Language (ESL) project; and an alliance with the Jamaican migrant community through the "Welcoming to Cape Cod Project."

- Hiring and ordaining Pancheta Peterson, a person of color, to serve as community minister at First Parish Brewster.

- Continuing to advocate for hiring more teachers of color in the Nauset School District, and participation in FREED (Fighting Racism and Educating for Ethnic Diversity), an organization that works for racial and ethnic diversity in public schools.

- Send representatives to meetings of Cape Codders Against Racism to report back to the social justice committee of the parish and to explore the possibilities of joint projects.

- Formation of an Anti-Racism Task Force, which meets regularly for mutual support and regularly audits the congregation's activities and programs.[12]

There are about sixteen members of the First Parish Anti-Racism Task Force, who meet regularly as a group to support each other as well as to monitor and audit the congregation's work in this area. The time commitment for members of the task force is considerable; the group met once weekly during its first year—remarkable in a resort community! All members of the task force have participated in training on several occasions. Though the membership of the task force has remained fairly stable, anyone who wants to attend the group's meetings is urged to come. "We try to find ways we can help each other *and* deliver this ministry," says Michele Wolfson, a member of the group. "Part of our strategy has been to pick achievable goals, and explore the spiritual dimensions of anti-racism," says Jim Robinson. "Yes, we approach it [racism] in bits," says Pancheta Peterson, First Parish's community minister. "We also have a number of leaders—no solos— and look at this work as a long-term commitment," she says. "We will be seated at this table for a long time."[13]

Pancheta Peterson has lived on Cape Cod since 1975. Her husband, Burnham Peterson, who is white, is involved in the tourist business, and the couple raised four children on the Cape. "I have found living here one of the loneliest lives God could deliver," she says. A racist incident against her daughter moved Pancheta Peterson to speak up, and since that time she has been involved as a community activist. Pancheta Peterson started the group FREED with other women and started training in the local public schools. "To hear people tell it there is no racism on Cape Cod. We started to educate the Cape one person at a time," says Peterson. She was also trained in the Study Circles method and adapted the model for wider use. Pancheta Peterson joined the staff at First Parish Brewster at the invitation of Jim Robinson in 1997 and has been ordained almost three years. Besides her work in the community, and with the Anti-Racism Task Force, Peterson is a regular presence in worship life of First Parish Brewster and conducts Bible studies. She cautions other white congregations who hire people of color to make sure that enough support is in place to make it work. "I have a mentor and an advocate in Jim [Robinson]," says Pancheta Peterson. "It is his commitment that has helped make this work. I am not left out to twist in the wind." Though she feels called to her ministry at First Parish Brewster, she also admits that it is hard work. "This is a call, yet I'm not sure that this is a real healthy way of living. I have to constantly educate."

Pancheta Peterson is frank about the loneliness she has experienced as a person of color living in a predominantly white community. "He has feared for my life sometimes," she says in reference to her husband, "but I have not been able to give it up." A couple of years ago, a student from Senegal who was living with the Petersons was held at gunpoint by the police after walking off a bike path. The incident once again raised the issue of racial profiling on Cape Cod. "It is institutional racism, a racism so deep that, for many people, it is unrecognizable," says Pancheta Peterson. "There were other people on the bike trail that day. Did the police stop them? Did the police go after them? No. They went after Mamadou, the only black man on the trail that day. In my heart I always felt my children were at risk of being accidently shot. That is every black mother's fear."

Pancheta Peterson is "relieved and pleasantly surprised that a church wants to do this [anti-racism] work." However, she is clear that it is not her role, as one of the few people of color in the congregation, to put the issue of racism before the congregation on her own. "I'm here because I am committed to change and to keep the relationship going," says Peterson. "But white people have to carry this, and that they keep coming to a group like this is rare." Frances Perkins, an African American member of the Anti-Racism Task Force, says: "This is the only group that gives me that sustained feeling of nurture. When I first came here it was the first time I was in a group of white people who acknowledged racism in their behavior. I felt I could so something for them, and I knew there would be enough for me."

The feeling that there is always more to do, or that they are not doing enough, frequently runs through the conversation of the First Parish Brewster Anti-Racism Task Force. "It's like waking up a sleeping elephant," says Jim Robinson in reference to the pervasiveness of white privilege. "Sometimes I feel that we're doing next to nothing." Mykel Johnson, assistant minister of First Parish Brewster, draws on skills gained through antiracism training when working with other marginalized groups. She asks: "How do we make links between all these different struggles?" David Billings, a member of the Anti-Racism Task Force and an early childhood educator, similarly "is interested in how people engage difference," and makes the connection between anti-bias education and his role on the First Parish Brewster children and youth ministries committee.

First Parish Brewster is known throughout the region as a congregation that challenges people and that is engaged in the community.

Members of the parish who are not official members of the Anti-Racism Task Force, also participate in antiracism trainings and events and are, on the whole, supportive of the group. "Jim [Robinson] challenges people to be honest and to look deeper," says membership volunteer coordinator Carie Killam. "Everybody has work to do. This is a place to be real about racism and to let the raw emotions hang out there. The community will hold you through it." Marilyn Watson, president of the board, believes that it is part of her role to keep the issue of racism out in the forefront of the congregation. "Once you draw back it becomes silent again," she says.

Members of First Parish insist that what this congregation on Cape Cod has done to build multiracial community and eliminate racism could be duplicated in other communities. The congregation has been a leader in forming small groups where members can make a connection with a more intimate circle of people and become more deeply involved in the congregation's life. The fact that the congregation was known for its social-justice activism is also helpful. "The community of Cape Cod looks to us for a conscientious response to issues," says First Parish Brewster board member Karen Estell. "If something happens that has ethical and moral dimensions, people on the Cape expect that we will take a stance." Karen Estell and others in the congregation are clear that leadership is key to the congregation's ability to impact the community. "The secret is a minister who is visible in the community and a congregation that takes a role in community issues." "First Parish is a known commodity in the region," adds board member John Myers. Says board vice-president Kevin Lowey: "What I've witnessed here could easily happen elsewhere. Three things are needed: intent, focus, and action. This is not a sit-back place." Still, one of the challenges of building multiracial community is the need for keeping people connected over the long haul. "We have looked at how we can proceed without paralyzing people," says Jeanne Denike, a member of the Anti-Racism Task Force. "In this work the journey is the destination. How do we keep the work fresh, rather than going on to the next hot topic? We have had to challenge ourselves to work in a holistic way; to be respectful and dialogical," says Jeanne Denike. "And we have to be careful not to assume what people think.[14]

First Parish Brewster was not always the bustling congregation that it is today. When Jim Robinson first arrived over twenty years ago, the congregation had a membership of 130. William Zelazny, district

---

First Parish, Brewster, Massachusetts

Current Size: 700+ members, 171 children and youth

Size Five Years Ago: 573 members, 200 chldren and youth

Sunday Service Attendance: 370 adults, children, and youth

Annual Budget: $450,000

———

Statistics from the Unitarian Universalist Association and *Interconnections* 5, no. 3 (summer 2002): 1–2.

---

executive for the UUA's Ballou Channing District, of which First Parish is a part, credits the congregation's growth to strong leadership that is committed to the church and the larger community. "Time and again, research has shown that people come to churches that are exciting and involved and the Brewster church is surely exciting and involved." "This truly is a remarkable congregation," says Mykel Johnson. "Jim [Robinson] has created a spirit of welcome for people that has changed lives. People talk about this church as something that has been life-transforming for them. Sometimes I think the sparks caught fire a while back, and then a momentum happened that carried itself forward. Once it was burning it spread and spread. . . . But the central core is what catches people."[15]

ALL CHURCH RACISM PROJECT

Though historically committed to serving the marginalized, First Parish Brewster's "All Church Racism Project" began in 1996. In that year the congregation unanimously voted to commit itself to assertively work to eradicate racism within their own church community and the larger human community. In a sermon entitled "Freedom," Jim Robinson, who is white, related his reaction to a workshop given in the congregation where members were asked to give ways in which white or black people have special privileges in our society. "The answers for white privilege were perceptive, and accurate," says Robinson. "We know what it is like to be white. The answers for black privilege were stereotypical. Here are some of the answers we gave for

black privilege: better teeth, fewer wrinkles, better singers and ath-
letes, more emotional, don't get sunburn, etc. We did not list privileges, we listed stereotypes. . . . It was the most painful moment I have
ever had in this sanctuary. I said to the person next to me: 'This is *so*
painful.' And the person said: Oh why?"[16]

In the same sermon, Jim Robinson confronted the racism experienced by people of color who live on Cape Cod. One such person,
William Brown, an African American Cape Codder, believes that
blacks there are the targets of stereotypical harassment. "Perhaps this
is because, for many whites, we are lacking in detail," says Brown.
"We are seen as a monolith, countless replicas. This singular vision of
us centers on color, which leads to a focus on exterior, resulting in us
being seen as little more than cardboard figures or conceptual sketches
on a movie director's storyboard."[17] Jim Robinson also shared a story
about his own racism toward Asian Americans:

> My brother married a Taiwanese Chinese woman. Everyone in the
> extended family went to the wedding. Everyone treated her with
> respect. Why was it then, after five years of marriage, that she began to
> confront the extended family about racism towards Chinese? It took me
> years to understand what she was telling me. I had unconscious pictures
> in my head, from childhood onward, about what Chinese people are
> like: quiet, inscrutable, well-behaved, good at math. First of all, she
> taught me that there are hundreds of ethnic Chinese cultures, each one
> different than the others, and none of them fit my stereotypes. Even
> more importantly, she showed me, that most white educated Americans
> have a subtle but definite superior attitude when relating to Asians.
> Well, I finally got it, and my sister-in-law felt heard and accepted. It was
> hard, humbling work for me. But I am very glad I did it. My friends,
> there are two things we white people need to do in this culture: *we need
> to listen to people of color, and we need to be more honest about our
> own racism.*[18]

At the congregation's annual meeting in June 1996, the members of
First Parish Brewster committed to some practical actions to explore
racism within the congregation and larger community. The congregation also agreed to the following:

- Every identifiable and ongoing group at First Parish (choir, hiking
  group, youth, men's group—all parish groups) was asked commit
  at least one of their meetings during the year to the subject of

racism and race relations. The groups could design their own program or ask for assistance from the Social Justice Committee.

- The congregation set a goal that at least one-quarter of its membership (180) would participate in the Circle Study Discussion Program on racism and race relations.

- The staff, officers of the church, board of trustees, and chairpersons of all committees were to attend a one-day workshop by the Social Justice Committee on the subject of racism and race relations.

- Worship leaders were asked to schedule at least six services on either the subject of race and race relations, or a celebration, in style and content, of an ethnic/cultural occasion that is not European American. (In the case of either option, guest artists, speakers, or resident ministers or speakers may participate.)

- Leaders of worship would make a further commitment to include readings, music, and other elements that are non–European American in origin throughout Sunday services during the year.

- The Religious Education Committee was asked to create programming for all levels on the subject of race and race relations to be used during church school, during family homily, or at special programs.

- First Parish youth groups (grades 7 and 8 and grades 9–12) were asked to explore the subjects of race and racism during at least three meetings during the year.

- The Social Justice Committee was asked to strengthen the alliances between First Parish Brewster and Cape Cod groups working in the area of race and race relations, by appointing members of the congregation to attend the groups' meetings, as well as to explore the possibility of joint projects. Specifically, these groups included the NAACP, FREED, and Cape Codders Against Racism.

- The Social Justice Committee was asked to initiate a new project in the area of race and race relations and to encourage First Parish members to participate.

- The ministers of First Parish were asked to meet with clergy from other Cape Cod churches that are not predominantly European American in membership to explore possible exchanges between the church communities.

- In regard to parish administration, the board of trustees was requested to study the organizational structure of the congregation to determine what forms of racism exist and to make suggestions for change.[19]

After affirming these guidelines for action, the congregation agreed to hold open hearings the next year to evaluate how fully First Parish Brewster met each specific action criteria and to make suggestions for further action. The Social Justice Committee was asked to report these results to the congregation's board of trustees, and the wider congregation through the newsletter. Further, the ministers were encouraged to frame a dialogue among church members on the congregation's progress during a Sunday service.

STRUCTURAL CHANGE—A TRANSFORMING INSTITUTION

In 1997 the UU General Assembly called for a commitment to develop an antiracist multicultural religious community on all levels of the UUA. (The United States Commission on Race rated the UUA program one of the top one hundred programs on racism in the country.) Members of First Parish Brewster participated in this assembly, which gave the congregation an opportunity to evaluate the first stage of their antiracism work and continue in the educational process toward change. Crossroads Ministry serves as the outside consultants with the UUA in its goal to develop an antiracist multicultural religious community; it bases its work on a "Continuum on Becoming an Anti-Racist Multicultural Institution." The continuum depicts the evolution from a monocultural, to a multicultural, to an antiracist, to an antiracist multicultural institution through a series of six levels: (1) exclusive, (2) passive, (3) symbolic change, (4) identity change, (5) structural change, and (6) fully inclusive.[20]

After reflection on their antiracism efforts for the years 1996–1998, members of First Parish determined that they had moved from level 3, symbolic change, or from a stage of intentional multiculturalism with little change in decision making, policies, or patterns of privilege, to level 4, identity change, or to an antiracist institution, with an increasing commitment to dismantle racism, yet with structures and culture that maintain white privilege. With this learning and a commitment to work toward level 5, twenty-five members of First Parish Brewster attended the UUA's Anti-Racism Jubilee II training in June 2001. Level 5 of the continuum focuses on structural change for "A Transforming Institution." Such an institution is built on shared power at all levels of the institution and redefines all relationships from the perspective of antiracist commitments. The training commitment at this level required that members of First Parish Brewster undertake an analysis of the congregation from the perspectives of individual, institutional, and cultural racism. Additionally, participants were asked to engage in a historical analysis of First Parish Brewster within the context of the history of racism within the United States.

Stage 5. Structural Change

A Transforming Institution:

- Commits to a process of institutional restructuring, based on antiracist analysis and identity;
- Audits and restructures all aspects of institutional life to ensure full participation of people of color, including their worldview, culture, and lifestyles;
- Implements structures, policies, and practices with inclusive decision making and other forms of power sharing on all levels of the institution's life and work;
- Commits to struggle to dismantle racism in the wider community, and builds clear lines of accountability to oppressed communities;
- Antiracist, multicultural diversity becomes an institutionalized asset;
- Redefines and rebuilds all relationships and activities in society, based on antiracist commitments.

Source: Excerpted from Continuum on *Becoming an Anti-Racist Church,* © Crossroads Ministry, adapted from original concept by Bailey Jackson and Rita Hardman, and further developed by Andrea Avazian and by Ronice Branding. Used with permission.

First Parish Brewster defines its commitment to building multiracial community as spiritual in context. After the UUA training, the Anti-Racism Committee and staff began to evaluate the work they felt that the congregation needed to do to move toward becoming an anti-racist, multicultural organization. Their report says:

> Racism destroys the body, mind and spirit. To shape an identity is a spiritual act. As a faith community with a clear commitment to love, truth, service and harmony we want to explore, in a deep and spiritu-ally supportive way, how racism is affecting our identities and our lives, as individuals and in community. As we approach this work together in a spiritual context, we will open to new understandings and our actions will be guided by compassion.

Some of the premises upon which First Parish built their continuing efforts to become an antiracist, multicultural community, as a result of the UUA training experience, include the following:

- The purpose of systemic racism is to keep control in the hands of the dominant white culture.

- White privilege is so all-pervasive that it seems "normal," and we have to educate ourselves to become aware of it.

- None of us has had choice or control over how we were taught to be racist.

- This kind of awareness and self and institutional awareness is a painful process, but necessary for growth.

- Racism involves three misuses: power over people of color; power to preserve and maintain control for white society; ulti-mate power to shape all our identities, and to control and destroy everyone.

- Antiracism is the deliberate and intentional act of examining and dismantling racism in all its forms.[21]

Beginning in June 2001, First Parish Brewster developed a timetable extending until 2003 to explore key areas of community life for ves-tiges of white privilege. During 2002, the overall goal of the First Parish Anti-Racism Task Force was to undertake this self-assessment, an "audit," of all aspects of the congregation's life in the following areas: *worship*, including language, sources, symbolism, format, music, readings, and themes; *governance*, including the composition, style of governance, committees, decision making, and planning processes; *programming*, including educational programs for all ages, fund-raising, small groups, and outreach; and *communication*, including the parish newsletter, Web site, bulletins, and overall networking. During this evaluation process, education was provided to all members of First Parish Brewster on two levels. Each committee of the church and all staff were offered a workshop explaining the goals of becoming an antiracist, multicultural church, and each committee was challenged to develop a plan for implementation in its own area of programming. Further educational opportunities were provided to all members of First Parish in the areas of understanding racism, reduction of personal prejudice, and the vision of a truly multicultural First Parish. Further, the committee pledged to continue to deepen the congregation's "ally work" with communities of color on Cape Cod, including the NAACP, the Wampanoag community, the Brazilian and Latino communities, and the Jamaican community.[22]

The UUA "Journey Toward Wholeness" program recommends that each congregation take a public vote to become "An Anti-Racist Congregation," in the hope that this will encourage the community, particularly its leaders and leading committees, to continue its work in this area. In June 2002 the following motion was passed by the congregation: "First Parish commits itself to being an antiracist, multicultural church community, and encourages all members and committees at First Parish to explore how they can implement that intent of this proposal."[23]

At the annual meeting of First Parish Brewster, the results of the 2002 antiracism audit were reported to the congregation, along with recommendations for further action from the Anti-Racism Task Force, including the following:

- The mission statement of First Parish Brewster does not make reference to the eradication of racism or other forms of oppression as integral to the purpose of First Parish. It was recommended that such a statement be added.

- The worship at First Parish draws mostly from the European American tradition. It was recommended that worship leaders develop more multicultural Sunday worship.

- Though First Parish has made significant progress in making language free of gender bias, and by providing an interpreter for the deaf, the congregation has not effectively included languages other than English. Worship leaders were urged to consider how other languages, especially Portuguese and Spanish, could be integrated into Sunday worship.

- Children and youth ministries at First Parish draw from a variety of spiritual traditions. It was recommended that programs for children and youth create more opportunities for young people to meet and dialogue with persons from different ethnic, racial, and religious backgrounds. Also, it was stressed that programs for young people should respectfully "share" other religious traditions, rather than "appropriating" other religious traditions.

- With the exception of cultural events such as concerts, most of the large number of adult education programs at First Parish are reflective of European American models. It was recommended that new educational opportunities be developed to bring into deeper contact with people, ideas, and cultures other than European American.

- The Anti-Racism Task Force recommended that First Parish Brewster encourage a policy of affirmative action in the recruiting and hiring of staff, and in the recruitment and placement of parish volunteers. The intent of these recommendations was to intentionally bring people from different ethnic and racial backgrounds into leadership positions at First Parish.

- "Does this institution exist to maintain white privilege and superiority, or does it exist to equally strengthen all ethnic and racial groups?" is the key question in terms of governance and accountability for antiracist institutions. Here the Anti-Racism Task Force recommended that the First Parish Board of Trustees, and other key committees experience ongoing anti-racism education, and make contact with people of color in the community for the purposes of evaluation and feedback.

- Given that understanding racism is a life-long process, it was further recommended by the Anti-Racism Committee that a variety of ongoing programs that address racism be offered to the members of First Parish.[24]

ALLY PROJECTS

Key efforts in building multiracial community at First Parish Brewster are the "ally projects" sponsored by the Social Justice Committee with other ethnic communities on Cape Cod, specifically the NAACP, the Wampanoag Tribe, the Brazilian community, and Jamaican migrant workers. Given that Lower Cape Cod is 97 percent European American, and that the UUA has historically been a white denomination in the United States and Canada, specific, long-term "ally projects" are an intentional way for a congregation such as First Parish to deepen its connections with people of color. First Parish Brewster has "a great history in doing social justice work in the community in general," says William Gardiner, director of the UUA Social Justice Empowerment Program. They have a "strong desire to be accountable to those leaders [in communities of color]," he says."

The long-standing relationship between First Parish Brewster and the Cape Cod chapter of the NAACP has provided a model of how such relationships between white congregations and communities of color can become mutually beneficial. First Parish Brewster has supported the NAACP through special events, an annual membership drive, and standing with the organization on human rights campaigns such as a recent petition to the town regarding the need to hire more people of color as teachers. "My wife and I feel like we are part of the family," says Joseph Daluz, former president of the Cape Cod chapter of the NAACP. "When those people commit to something, they don't shy back," he says. Another current project with the NAACP is to challenge a local radio station that has maligned the NAACP local leadership.

The ally projects of First Parish Brewster are not about membership recruitment—though the congregation is committed to welcoming people of color as members—as much as they are about building multiracial relationships and addressing racism throughout the community. "We are going to do this work whether or not another black person comes through these doors," says Pancheta Peterson. "Those who have decided to catch the vision here have decided to do the work because it is the right thing to do. Every time I see this sort of commitment it makes my heart sing." The furtherance of these ally projects is an important element in the congregation's overall antiracism strategy. "When I grew up in the 1950s it was a Jim Crow South with legal segregation, and polite segregation in the North and West," says Jim Robinson. "The tremendous advance is, blatant discrimination is unacceptable. The racism now is more personal and each of us will have to struggle with that inside ourselves to keep the movement going forward."[25]

Learning their history was again the first step toward First Parish Brewster's ally project with the Mashpee Wampanoag, one of the last remaining Native American tribes in Massachusetts. "I believe that what's happening to the Wampanoag community is still part of three hundred years of genocide and is still happening in a more quiet way," says Jim Robinson. Through the One Earth One People Project, First Parish Brewster reminds the congregation and the community of the true history of Cape Cod and whose land it was originally. Though the tribe survived European occupation, it owns less than one hundred acres of the Town of Mashpee's fifteen thousand acres. Increasing property values and taxes threaten even the small number of homes that belong to members of the tribe. The One Earth One People Project, headed by Tom and Michele Wolfson of First Parish Brewster, brings together people of the congregation who seek healing and reconciliation with the native people of Cape Cod. The group, which meets monthly, also raises funds for the Homes of Seven Generations program, designed to assure the minimum survival of the tribe on their own land. The overall goals of the Homes of Seven Generation program are to preserve and expand tribal ownership of land, to conserve open space, and to guarantee the capacity for traditional hunting, fishing, and farming. Last year the One Earth One People Project through First Parish Brewster sponsored a 3,200-mile cross-country bicycle adventure (from San Diego, California, to St. Augustine, Florida) to raise money for Homes for Seven Generations, and the project hopes to coordinate a similar event through the United Way on Cape Cod. An educational event open to the community and led by tribal educators is scheduled at First Parish Brewster in March 2003. "There is a certain kind of collective awareness and collective guilt shared by white Americans for our history of slavery and genocide," says Tom Wolfson. "To do something positive for them and for ourselves is important for everybody that wants to be a loving people."[26]

The One Earth One People Peace Prayer

We are One People on One Earth. All Life is sacred. The Earth is sacred. We cherish and protect our Mother Earth, Father Sky, and Sacred Waters. The generations of humankind from the Four Directions must live in harmony and balance with each other and all living things. We are all related. We respect and honor the sacredness of life and all creation so Seven Generations from each generation, unborn future generations, will live. Seven eagle feathers represent future generations and sacred ceremonies. They carry our prayer to Creator. We pray that Mother Earth and all of her children will live. It is one prayer: PEACE.

Source: Sonne and Elayna Revna, see www.fpbuu.org/biketrip/index.htm.

There is a deep spirituality at the core of the One Earth One People Project: "The spiritual center is the primary focus of the group," says Tom Wolfson. "We remember the sufferings of the native people, and we remember the earth, and we give thanks." The One Earth One People Project is named after "The One Earth One People Peace Prayer," an important spiritual focus for the group.

Like the One Earth One People Project, other First Parish Brewster ally projects are integrally linked to the changing economics of Cape Cod. With home prices rising drastically across the region, it is becoming increasingly difficult for middle- or lower-income people to live on Cape Cod. Yet the tourist industry brings a demand for workers. As the gap widens between what a worker can earn and housing costs, the result is a shortage of affordable housing and labor. This labor shortage is currently being met by Brazilians and Jamaicans, who are recent arrivals to Cape Cod. Some remain on the Cape all year, while some return home after the tourist season ends. Though some of these "new Cape Codders" bring their families with them, many have to leave their families behind. The ally project entitled Celebrating Cape Cod Diversity is designed to build relationships between members of First Parish Brewster and people of the Brazilian and Jamaican communities.

Community Minister Pancheta Peterson meets with and helps provide support for Jamaicans on the Lower Cape. This "ministry of welcome" eases the adjustments for Jamaican workers new to Cape Cod by providing information on healthcare resources and community services. At the same time, Jim Robinson has organized ESL (English as a Second Language) classes for the Brazilian community. Currently 140 people are taking ESL classes at three levels, taught in the evening by members of First Parish Brewster in space donated by the Cape Cod hospital. By January 2003 over 200 students will be expected in the expanding program, and day classes will be added to the schedule. Students pay for the book, but otherwise the classes are free. "Without Jim and the people from the church we couldn't do anything," says Carlos Barbosa, a businessman who helps identify students for the program. "This is the best thing for the Brazilian community here in a long time." Both projects are opportunities for members of First Parish Brewster to form relationships with persons of color. For members of First Parish Brewster the project is also a way to learn cross-cultural communication skills, and to extend themselves across the boundaries. "It is important for white people in cross-cultural situations not to get stuck in the shame and fear," says Pancheta Peterson. "Learning conversational skills can help prevent people from stepping into that place."[27]

Like many of the members of First Parish Brewster, white people committed to building multiracial community have an integral role as allies of people of color. In becoming white allies they commit themselves to take action on behalf of people of color, and at the same time make a commitment to come to terms with the history of racism. While individuals did not create the racial oppression of the past, white allies realize that white people have a responsibility to do something about racism in the present. White allies need always to remember that there is a difference between being an effective ally and presuming to know the reality of another's experience. People of color are the experts on their own experience, and white people can never fully know the impact of racism. Rather, the role of white allies is to learn to stand *with* communities of color, to listen to them and learn about their issues, and then to use white privilege to intervene with other white people whose attitudes and actions are racist. White people will often be heard on the subject of racism where a person of color in the same situation will be discounted. Further, the role of the white ally is a moral and spiritual choice. It requires a commitment to living in multiracial community and, on the part of white people, to expand intentionally the world beyond the cocoon of white privilege. For the past twenty years, First Parish Brewster has become a congregation of allies committed to authentic diversity and multiracial community. As Jim Robinson observes:

> This [authentic diversity] is why we have grown in membership. How-
> ever the work never ends, and there is much for us to do in all areas.
> This work is liberating for us as a community, and as individuals. Each
> time we open up our community to authentic diversity, we open up
> some constricted place inside our individual selves. This is the hard, yet
> joyful, work of liberating the spirit of love.[28]

SUMMARY

First Parish Brewster is a predominantly white congregation in a pre-dominantly white community and denomination, and yet the congregation has made a vision of multiracial community integral to its common life. In facing its own history, this congregation has uncovered its racism and complicity and thus has begun the process of *unlearning* racial oppression. Through the work of an active Anti-Racism Task Force and committed clergy leadership, the congregation continues to deconstruct *and* reenvision itself in the mold of an anti-racist, multicultural congregation. A detailed and monitored strategy that includes all levels and programs of the congregation, as well as the deliberate use of denominational resources has supported First Parish Brewster in the journey toward multiracial community. Further, the congregation has provided a broad assortment of resources for training, educational, organizing, and spiritual growth in an effort to meet the needs of all the members of the congregation as they deepen their commitment to live as a multicultural, antiracist congregation.

A noteworthy aspect of First Parish Brewster's growth as a mul-tiracial congregation is the intentional ally projects undertaken by members of the community. The care with which these ally relation-ships are formed and the focus on the needs of the marginalized com-munities are important examples of how white privilege can be exercised for the benefit of people of color. Further, the deep relationships forged through the First Parish Brewster ally projects are mutually transformative, changing individuals, the congregation, and the wider community. Such partnerships move the congregation beyond service to organize for action and social change. As First Parish Brewster continues its journey toward transformation, the spiritual core of its antiracism commitments will continue to sustain its members through future challenges and struggles.

Conclusion

Love and Power

Power without love is reckless and abusive, and love without power is sentimental and anemic. Power, at its best is love implementing the demands of justice, and justice at its best is power correcting everything that stands against love.

—Martin Luther King Jr[1]

ALL LOVE AND POWER ARE CENTRAL TO GOD; SO TOO THEY MUST be central to all who walk in God's way and strive for justice. When Dr. King spoke of love and power, he was talking about the "connective tissue" that holds all of Christian life together. As the stories of the congregations featured in this book suggest, to build multiracial community is also an exercise in love *and* power. To bring people together across racial differences not only requires sharing in God's great love; it also necessitates the power to accomplish human community, hopefully and intentionally, despite inner turmoil or outside conflict. Love on its own does not form healthy multiracial congregations. But love and power give congregations the ability to transform themselves and impact the larger community. One of the reasons why so many attempts at multiculturalism fail is that white culture often does not recognize or strive to correct the deep power imbalance that exists in many congregations. Multiracial communities emanate from the collective concern that we are all, despite the divisions we perpetuate, part of one human community; if life is improved for one person, all benefit. Justice does not admit of partitioning. In the Jewish tradition this practice is known as *tikkum olam*, or the healing and repair of the world. Christians are called to live in communion with each other, to be transformed for the sake of one another and the world.

Congregations are rooted in their local context, and thus it is not possible to suggest a "recipe" for building multiracial congregations. Multiracial community can be found in congregations of all sizes and all economic levels; what is critical is that the congregation sees multiracial community as integral to the work of the church and in its own self-interest. As the stories featured here suggest, each congregation has been transformed through the process of building multiracial community; yet each has had its own successes and failures along the way, and each has different challenges to face in the future. Though each congregation featured here has grown as a result of building multiracial community, each has also experienced the loss of members as a result of the changes and conflicts that ensued. But for each of these congregations "growth" means more than increased members. The congregations experienced profound spiritual growth, growth in community involvement, and growth in relationships between members.

Without minimizing the distinctiveness of each congregation, it is possible to point out some of the characteristics of healthy multiracial congregations that are applicable in a variety of contexts.

Assessment
Characteristics of Multiracial Community

Does your congregation respect the dignity of all human beings, treat all people with respect, and encourage relationships based on mutuality?

Has your congregation investigated its history from the perspective of people of various races and cultures? Who is reflected in the historical discourse and who is not? What has the congregation learned from its history, and how does this learning impact the future?

Does the worship of your congregation include a diversity of cultures in language, symbols, music, readings, and content? Is there an openness to work in languages other than English? Are officiants and worship planners respectful and inclusive of other cultures, and do they avoid appropriating others' traditions out of context? Is racism challenged through sermons and worship?

Do people from different racial, ethnic, and cultural groups share their stories during worship and programs in the congregation? Do the religious education programs for all ages—adults, youth, children—include material reflective of and relevant to people of various races and cultures? Does the pastoral care of the congregation blend both the pastoral and the prophetic?

Is your congregation genuinely grounded in the local community? Are projects planned with, rather than for, the local community? Are there opportunities for dialogue between members of the congregation and local community leaders? Does the congregation seek new members from the local community through outreach, including notices in targeted media? Does the congregation participate in community celebrations and events related to racial justice, for instance, Dr. Martin Luther King Jr. Day events, Cinco de Mayo celebrations, black history month programs, "alternative" Thanksgiving celebrations, or Chinese New Year?

Does the congregation provide structured opportunities for all members to explore racism? Are those in leadership required to participate in antiracism training? Does the congregation utilize denominational and community resources and networks in this area? Does the congregation have relationships with organizations for people of color for information, referrals, and support? Does the congregation advocate at the judicatory and denominational level for racial justice for all persons? Are the congregation's leaders in antiracism well chosen, and is there provision for their continuing training?

Is the congregation's commitment to multiracial community evident in all publications, including newsletters, Web sites, etc.? How is the "sacred space" of the congregation reflective of multiracial community?

Do the governance structures of the congregation include people of various races and cultures in leadership positions? Do the hiring practices and bylaws of the congregation explicitly state that no one should be denied access on the basis of race, ethnicity, or cultural background? Is the ordained leadership of the congregation diverse racially, ethnically, culturally? Is the congregation's committee membership reflective of all identity groups?

Does the congregation regularly monitor and evaluate its antiracism efforts? Are there clear indications of long-term commitment? Does the congregation utilize the media to make its commitment to multiracial community and racial justice known?

CHARACTERISTICS OF
HEALTHY MULTIRACIAL CONGREGATIONS

1. *Build on Health.* Congregations that build multiracial community are those that strive on all levels to affirm the dignity of every human person and to sustain relationships based in mutuality and respect. All congregations experience transitions, including all of the congregations detailed in this book, but those that seek to build multiracial community should do so from the perspective of congregational health. Though "health" is a relative term, a congregation that is riddled by unresolved conflicts, lacks coherent leadership, is plagued by mismanagement, fails to provide pastoral care to its members, or is avoidant of or hostile to the surrounding community will not be in a good position to build a strong community across racial differences. In congregations that are always in process, health denotes a community where people interact with each other in respectful and appropriate ways, where feelings and ideas are expressed directly and openly, where the gifts of all are welcomed and utilized appropriately, where clergy and laity use power justly and constructively for the common good and recognize the abuse of power, where there is an openness to ongoing education and issues in the community, and where the spiritual concerns and pastoral care of the members are addressed. In several of the congregations featured in this book, in situations where leaders of the congregation were without pastoral care for some time, clergy leaders opted to spend time assuring members of the congregation that their pastoral needs would be met before implementing major changes.

2. *Know Their History.* The study of history reveals both the heritage and traditions of a given congregation and leads to further discernment of a church's mission and ministry in the present. The members of the congregations studied here were conversant with their congregation's history and were willing to reinterpret that history not only from the perspective of the dominant culture but also from the perspective of communities of color. If a congregation is destined to be something more than a museum, the study of spiritual ancestors is a means to transforming the members' sense of where they have been

and where they wish to go in the future. Certainly, in terms of building multiracial community, the study of history is imperative in order to understand the dynamics of institutions and who is included or excluded in the present. Otherwise, the community is built on the premise, "We want to include more people who are just like us." Denial of the negative, and in this case, racist aspects of a congregation's history will not only prevent the formation of authentic community; it will serve to maintain social oppression. Just as it is crucial for individuals engaged in antiracism work to continue to delve into their own personal history for the sources of racist attitudes and beliefs, it is critical for congregations to undergo a similar process of investigation, interpretation, and ultimately, of renewal. Such a study of history unmasks the duality of the "American Dream" of freedom, justice, and liberty for all, which excludes those who are not in the dominant cultural group. If truth be told, all congregations, just as all human institutions, share a history of heroism and courage alongside a history of failure and fear. The words of author Toni Morrison bear repeating here:

> History has its flexible side. Of course it can be repeated disastrously, or it can be reformed in new guises, but it can also be critiqued. . . . My point is, you are not bound by the future, and, more important, you are not bound by the past. The past can be more liberating than the future if you are willing to identify its distortions, its lies, and unleash its secrets and truths.[2]

3. Seek Committed Leadership. Leadership is a key variable for congregations concerned with building multiracial community over the long haul. Clearly, clergy and laity who understand the dynamics of power and oppression and who are committed to change are integral. Such leaders tend to view building multiracial community more in terms of *process* than as *product* or *program*. Many of the clergy and laity interviewed for this book experienced a strong sense of vocation or "call" to antiracism, racial justice, or to multiracial community itself. At the most basic level, they experience building multiracial community as a call from God. They tend to share a sense of long-term and "sacrificial commitment." They strive to "walk the talk knowing the risks." Leaders in multiracial communities come from different backgrounds, yet many share common experience in that they express some "turning point" or "conversion" in their lives resulting from a direct and personal encounter across the boundaries of race, ethnicity, and culture. Grounded and nourished spiritually, these leaders have challenged their own racism and resistance to change and thus are better equipped to lead a congregation through a similar process. All of the leaders interviewed for this project envision leadership as a "partnership" rather than as a relationship of domination. Moreover, the ministry within the congregations featured here blends the pastoral with the prophetic; pastors in these contexts are acutely aware that pastoral care, in the prophetic sense, relates to individuals as well as whole communities Moreover, they understand the impact of racism and other forms of oppression on those within their communities from a pastoral perspective. On the skill level, such leaders are good listeners, knowledgeable about power dynamics, reflective preachers and teachers, effective process facilitators, experienced in community advocacy, skilled with the media, and able to communicate across cultural differences. They are willing to take risks, are open to the possibility of failure, and perhaps most importantly, are persistent. Because authentic multiracial community is difficult to achieve and sustain, it is crucial that leaders in these congregations are able to withstand criticism and periods of frustration and disillusionment. Most of the leaders interviewed for this book reported that they were criticized for "talking about racism too much," or that they were "going overboard" when it came to evaluating the congregation's antiracism efforts. A small minority in each congregation reported that while they chose to remain members, they felt that their minister's emphasis on multiracial community served to exclude other worthy concerns and meant that the church was not "taking care of its own." Obviously, change is personally painful to people in congregations, and any leader seeking multiracial community should be prepared for periods of resistance, conflict, doubt, and disillusionment. Yet those leaders who find joy in the challenge of working for change tend also to be the type of people who cultivate support systems for themselves, and who can accept care from individuals and from the community.

4. *Share a Rich Symbolic Life.* Though congregations have different "entry points," those committed to building multiracial community eventually experience change on all levels of the organization:

education, worship, governance, pastoral care, outreach, and so on. Part of the challenge of building multiracial community is adapting the symbolic life of the congregation in terms of worship, music, education, and even architecture to reflect various cultures. Do the worship and music of the congregation reflect racially and culturally diverse language and content? Is the multiracial character of the congregation upheld through religious education programs for all ages? Are people from different races and cultures welcomed to share in leadership? Does the congregation reserve time for cultural sharing and discovery? Does the community regularly celebrate holidays and heroes of the faith reflective of the racial diversity of the congregation? Does the "sacred space" of the congregation—architecture, seating, windows, art—reflect a multiracial, rather than a homogeneous reality? Many of the congregational leaders interviewed for this book adapted to the challenges of making the symbolic life of the church reflective of varying races and cultures. For some, it was the challenge of introducing Spanish-language hymns or prayers into worship. For others, it was the task of including symbols, texts, and rituals reflective of other races and cultures and at the same time avoiding the insensitive appropriation of others' traditions. All have had to reexamine their worship, music, education, and all other aspects of congregational life from the perspective of an antiracist, multicultural vision.

5. Develop Community and Denominational Relationships. Theologically, the congregations and leaders included in this book are from diverse backgrounds, yet they share a vibrant faith that is ecumenical and interfaith in nature. Though all have a denominational home, these congregations do not confine their mission within the context of one particular church, nor do they relate solely to other like congregations. Rather, the congregations featured here have sought to reinterpret their mission and ministry within the context of their local communities and with the aim of building multiracial community. These congregations have developed skills in community advocacy and have built alliances across churches and local agencies. Further, the congregations included here have benefited from denominational support and resources: all continue to participate on some level in denominational antiracism initiatives, and all have provided leadership beyond the local congregation. Not only are these congregations knowledgeable about their denomination's work in antiracism and racial justice, but each contributes leadership and seeks opportunities to collaborate with others on these issues within their own denomination and with allied organizations. The congregations featured in this book have utilized the training and resources from a variety of sources. Though there is no single way to structure experiences in antiracism, the effective programs mentioned here share several common elements:

- For Christian programs, biblical and theological doctrine that names racism as a sin

- A dual focus on teaching and experiential activities

- Clearly stated definitions of racism as prejudice plus power, bias, discrimination, and other forms of exclusion; and discussions of culture and ethnicity

- Activities that focus on institutional and systemic racism as well as individual racism

- Explicit connections between racism and other forms of exclusion and oppression

- Strategies and plans for a long-term implementation of a comprehensive antiracism program in organizations and communities of various sizes and complexities in a variety of contexts and settings and practical tools and resources for implementing this process

- After examining racism within the church, a focus that extends beyond the organizational church to civil society

- An approach that fosters ecumenical and interfaith connectedness[3]

6. *Implement an Action Plan; Monitor and Evaluate.* All the congregations in this study, regardless of size or resources, have implemented some formal action plan designed to build multiracial community, and they continue to monitor their progress and evaluate how they are doing. In any successful community-building effort, there should be a clarity of purpose and a clear plan of action. As you gauge your congregation's needs and capacities for multiracial com-

munity, and discover what has worked for others engaged in similar efforts, you will begin to develop the strategies and tactics best suited to your context. Without ongoing evaluation, discernment, reflection, adjustments, and modifications, any plan of action will soon lose its relevance, energy, or direction. As long as injustice remains, so does the need for goals and strategies, action and analysis. Clearly, the congregations featured here are aware that building multiracial community is a long-term commitment.

7. Cultivate Spiritual Stamina. God calls all humankind to a life of rich diversity. Our spirituality reflects the relationships we have with God, other people, and the world and is consistent with our racial, ethnic, and cultural heritages. Throughout the New Testament, Jesus is frequently found in relationship with and in communication with persons of cultures different from his own. The process of living out multiracial community impacts our hearts, our minds, and our lives and brings about new attitudes and behaviors about God, oneself, and our larger society. Choosing to live in multiracial community is countercultural, given the monocultural bias of American culture, and requires a great deal of spiritual stamina. A disciplined life of prayer and reflection rooted in a multiracial community of faith is perhaps the greatest source of support for the challenges faced by those who choose to open up their lives in this way.

We, as the people of God, are called to respond to a world that is groaning under the weight of injustice and broken relationships. Our differences and our interdependence are intended to be a source of strength and a gift from God. As people of faith, we know that the reign of God will not ultimately be built on separatism or political arguments, but on the transformation of hearts—*new* life, not just reordered life. As the people of God who believe in justice, forgiveness, and reconciliation, we can resist the temptation to stop at the political, social, or even emotional level of racial awareness. Rather, through building multiracial community, we can be about the healing and wholeness that the world craves.

Annotated Bibliography and Resource List

The resources listed below were consulted in preparation for this book and represent only a fraction of those available. The list here is not intended to be exhaustive, but rather highlights those resources that might prove useful to congregations interested in building multiracial community. The categories here are somewhat arbitrary in that many of the resources could be listed under several categories. Most of the resources listed here are available through on-line sources, major book- stores, denominational offices, or organizations. Although every effort has been made to ensure accuracy upon publication, bear in mind that addresses, phone numbers, and e-mail addresses grow obsolete quickly. Since the needs of particular contexts vary, in all instances resources should be read or previewed before recommended for use in a congre- gation.

I. BOOKS AND PUBLICATIONS

African Americans

Barnes, Annie S. *Say It Loud: Middle-Class Blacks Talk about Racism and What to Do about It.* Cleveland: Pilgrim Press, 2000. Based on the stories of 150 middle-class black college students, who discuss their frequent encounters with racism. Featuring many personal testimonies and stories, this book is an excellent resource for groups who wish to discuss the inter- section of race and social class.

Brandt, Eric, ed. *Dangerous Liaisons: Blacks, Gays, and the Struggle for Equality.* New York: The New Press, 1999. A collection of articles by high- profile writers on issues pertaining to the relationship between African Americans and homosexuals, which could profitably be read individually, or collectively as a whole. An excellent resource for groups who wish to explore the intersection between race and sexual identity.

Collins, Lynn Arentha. *Afro-Anglican Youth Facilitators Training: Preparing Future Leaders.* New York: Episcopal Church Center, 2001. Leadership development curriculum for youth of African descent. Designed particularly for Episcopal and/or Anglican contexts, this curriculum is a useful resource for groups interested in exploring racial identity formation and empowerment. The resource also includes useful group exercises and information on group process. The curriculum upholds the premise that youth development should be a primary concern for churches and communities. Available through the Episcopal Church Center (*see* Denominational Resources).

Dash, Michael I. N., et al. *Hidden Wholeness: An African American Spirituality for Individuals and Communities.* Cleveland: United Church Press, 2000. Individual and group activities designed for spiritual wholeness. Traces the spirituality of the African American community from slavery through the economic and social issues faced today. What is particularly helpful about this book is the manner in which it links spiritual wholeness and healthy community. The exercises are suitable for many spiritually based groups within congregations.

Douglas, Kelly Brown. *Sexuality and the Black Church: A Womanist Perspective.* Maryknoll, N.Y.: Orbis, 1999. Discusses the interplay between black sexuality and the black church within the context of white culture. Douglas's book not only explores the intersection of racial identity and sexual identity from the perspective of the black church, but frankly assesses the impact of white racism on the church and black community as a whole. An expansive and well-integrated study.

Gill, LaVerne McCain. *Daughters of Dignity: African Women in the Bible and the Virtues of Black Womanhood.* Cleveland: United Church Press, 2000. Discusses the ethnic roots and moral heritage of African American women, and discusses the religious leadership from the perspective of scripture. This book would be a helpful resource for any individual or group interested in examining the role of women in the African American community.

hooks, bell. *Killing Rage: Ending Racism.* New York: H. Holt, 1995. Twenty-three essays written from a black and feminist perspective on race and racism in the United States. bell hooks is a prolific writer and educator who skillfully addresses the intersection of racism and sexism, classism, and homophobia. The essays are fairly brief and would be suitable for discussion groups and as part of training sessions.

Martin, Joan M. *More than Chains and Toil: A Christian Work Ethic of Enslaved Women.* Louisville: Westminster John Knox, 2000. Shows how the Christian religion was used both to enslave and strengthen slave women. Martin is a social ethicist and skillfully uses a variety of narrative sources designed to "give voice" to enslaved women. This book shows both the liberating aspects of Christianity and the complicity of the church with racism.

Myers, William H. *God's Yes Was Louder Than My No: Rethinking the African-American Call to Ministry.* Lawrenceville, N.J.: Africa World Press, 1994. A study of call narratives of African American clergy, this book looks at the formation of spiritual leaders. The helpful stories and narratives from those included give insights into the nature of ministry and leadership within the African American community. This book would be helpful for those concerned with spiritual formation and ministry development, including judicatory leaders.

Myers, William R. *Black and White Styles of Youth Ministry: Two Congregations in America.* Cleveland: United Church Press, 1991. Weaves together theory and practice as it tells the story of youth ministry in a black congregation and in a white congregation. This book is helpful because of Myers's insightful perspectives on congregational life and because of his obvious respect for young people. This is a helpful source for congregations interested in "partnerships" with persons of congregations of other cultures.

Oglesby, E. Hammond. *O Lord, Move This Mountain: Racism and Christian Ethics.* St. Louis: Chalice Press, 1998. Argues for a notion of covenant-*harambee* that is at once faithful to African conceptuality and Christian theology. This visionary work points to a beyond-racism Christian ethic.

Smith, Archie, Jr. *Navigating the Deep River: Spirituality in African American Families.* Cleveland: United Church Press, 1997. Discusses pastoral care for African American families from the perspective of spiritual resources. Examines the African American family within the context of history, racism, democracy, and multiculturalism. The strength of this work lies in its straightforward approach and advice on care and support for African American families.

West, Traci C. *Wounds of the Spirit: Black Women, Violence, and Resistance Ethics.* New York: New York University Press, 1999. Discusses the causes and cost of sexual violence against black women, as well as the effect on the whole community. West also shows the sources of women's hope and resistance.

Wimberly, Edward P. *Relational Refugees: Alienation and Reincorporation in African American Churches and Communities.* Nashville: Abingdon Press, 2000. Contends that pastoral counselors need to address the historical and social contexts of clients. An important premise of this book is the author's belief of the importance of social location for the care of individuals and communities. He also raises issues of pastoral significance in African American communities, such as the importance of mentors.

American Indians/Native Americans

Anderson, Owanah. *400 Years: Anglican/Episcopal Mission among American Indians.* Cincinnati: Forward Movement, 1997. This evocative book presents the history of American Indians within the Episcopal Church. Throughout, Anderson presents the faith and struggles of American Indians from the colonial era to the present day. Importantly, this work corrects the historical record in that it claims the role of American Indians within North American Anglicanism. Contact: Forward Movement Publications, 412 Sycamore Street, Cincinnati, OH 45202-4195. Phone: 513/721-6659 or 800/543-1813. Web site: www.forwardmovement.org

Deloria, Vine Jr. *God Is Red: A Native View of Religion.* Golden, Colo.: Fulcrum Press, 1994. Describes the basic tenets that underlie Native American religion. Part of the value of this book is that it describes the diversity within Native American religion from the perspective of indigenous people themselves, rather than from the perspective of "appropriation."

First Peoples Theology Journal. Articles on theology and ministry written by indigenous people, mostly from a North American Anglican/Episcopal perspective. The short articles respond to a variety of topics and concerns. Contact: Indigenous Theological Training Institute, 1730 Clifton Place, Suite 202, Minneapolis, MN 55403.

Gossen, Gary H., ed. *South and Meso-American Native Spirituality: From the Cult of the Feathered Serpent to the Theology of Liberation.* World Spirituality, vol. 4. New York: Crossroad, 1993. Offers a historical and contemporary portrait of the diverse spiritual traditions in South and Central American and the Caribbean. This survey highlights the major themes and symbols contextually, and from a perspective of liberation theology.

Hampton, Carol. "A Heritage Denied: American Indians Struggle for Racial Justice," *Sojourners,* January 1991. This is a key article on the effects of racism from the perspective of American Indians within the United States. Hampton is an Episcopal priest and she writes with clarity and passion. This brief article is helpful for any group studying racism within the United States. Contact: *Sojourners,* 2401 15th Street NW, Washington, DC 20009. Phone: 202/328-8842. Web site: www.sojo.net

Hummelen, Remmelt, and Kathleen Hummelen. *Stories of Survival: Conversations with Native North Americans.* New York: Friendship Press, 1985. A collection of shared stories from Native peoples that is rich and evocative. The stories can be used individually with individuals and groups, or as a whole.

Lewis, Bonnie Sue. *Creating Christian Indians: Native Clergy in the Presbyterian Church.* Norman: University of Oklahoma Press, 2003. This book relates how the Nez Perce and the Dakota Indian became Presbyterian yet incorporated Native culture and tradition into their Christian identities. This book is helpful to groups interested in the relationship between religion and culture.

Negative Stereotyping of Native Americans Resource Packet. Cleveland: Justice and Witness Ministries, The United Church of Christ, n.d.. This resource packet relates directly to stereotyping, prejudice, and racism targeted by Native Americans. The packet includes helpful background information, articles, exercises, and so forth. Contact: Justice and Witness Ministries, The United Church of Christ (*see* Denominational Resources).

Noley, Homer. *First White Frost: Native Americans and United Methodism.* Nashville: Abingdon Press, 1991. A history of Native Americans in the denomination. This book provides a helpful survey and is written in an accessible style suitable for a variety of audiences.

Smith, Huston, et al., eds. *One Nation Under God: The Triumph of the Native American Church.* Santa Fe: Clear Light Publications, 1998. Discusses both the challenges faced by American Indian religion and spirituality within a white culture, as well as the conditions of its cultural survival. The book speaks to the importance of a variety of cultural expressions within the church.

Treat, James, ed. *Native and Christian: Indigenous Voices on Religious Identity in the United States and Canada.* New York: Routledge, 1996. An anthology on contemporary Native American spirituality, including articles on Native American churches, liturgy, culture, and community. This is a comprehensive and well-researched anthology of accessible articles on religious identity written from the perspective of indigenous people.

Asian Americans

Eng, Phoebe. *Warrior Lessons: An Asian American Woman's Journey into Power.* New York: Pocket Books, 1999. This book presents an Asian woman's experience and transformation. This would be a helpful book for anyone interested in the intersection between race, culture, and gender.

Kwok Pui-Lan. *Introducing Asian Feminist Theology.* Cleveland: Pilgrim Press, 1995. Feminist theology written from the perspective of an Asian theologian and biblical scholar, this evocative book is designed as a survey and is accessible for those without formal theological training. This book is also a helpful introduction for those who have little background in Asian studies.

Lee, Jung Young, ed. *Journeys at the Margin: Towards an Autobiographical Theology in American-Asian Perspective.* Collegeville, Minn.: Liturgical Press, 1999. This anthology of articles presents differing perspectives on Asian American theology. The premise of the collection is based on the importance of personal narrative and theology. The essays show the deep connection between spiritual identity and racial/cultural identity and would be helpful for individuals or groups interested in spiritual formation and spiritual development.

Lee, Stacey J. *Unraveling the "Model Minority" Stereotype: Listening to Asian American Youth.* New York: Teachers College Press, 1996. Relates the Asian American experience from the perspective of youth. This book poignantly relates the racism and other challenges faced by Asian Americans from the perspective of the "model minority" stereotype. Though written specifically from the context of young people, this work raises the negative impact of racism on all ages.

Matsuoka, Fumitaka. *Out of Silence: Emerging Themes in Asian American Churches.* Cleveland: Pilgrim Press, 1995. Discusses the growth of Asian American presence and participation in churches, and presents a description and an analysis of Asian American Christians of Chinese, Filipino, Japanese, and Korean ancestry. This book presents an important overview of Asian Christianity from the perspective of a variety of ethnic groups, as well as important insights on congregations. An important resource for those interested in the participation of Asian Christians within congregations.

Ng, David, ed. *People on the Way: Asian North Americans Discovering Christ, Culture, and Community.* Valley Forge, Penn.: Judson Press, 1996. Throughout this book the author discusses the growing numbers and impact of Asian people on North American churches. The book highlights the relationship between Asian culture and religious faith and how these relate to faith communities.

Ng, Donald, ed. *Asian Pacific American Youth Ministry: Planning Helps and Programs.* Valley Forge, Penn.: Judson Press, 1988. This resource is a practical manual for those interested in working with young people of Asian Pacific background within congregations. Ng's wealth of experience in youth ministries is evident in his insights into young people, as well as the specific needs and cultural context of Asian Pacific young people. The book discusses various ethnic communities within Asian culture, and gives some useful program ideas and planning sessions. The programmatic advice of this manual could be adapted for working with other age groups.

Sunoo, Brenda Paik, ed.. *Beyond the Crucible: Responses to Anti-Asian Hatred.* New York: Episcopal Church Center, 1994. A resource book of materials designed to educate individuals and congregations about the rising incidents of hate crimes against Asians that could be used in a variety of contexts. This resource contains background information on hate crimes, as well as materials designed to encourage community action. Though designed specifically in response to hate crimes perpetrated against Asians, the format could be adapted to raise issues of racial profiling and hate crimes against other groups. Available through the Episcopal Church Center (*see* Denominational Resources).

Wu, Frank H. *Yellow: Race in America Beyond Black and White.* New York: Basic Books, 2002. Examines racism from the perspective of Asian American experience. This evocative book challenges the "bipolar" perspective in the United States that frames racism as a predominately black–white issue. Wu's narrative powerfully shows how racism impacts the Asian community.

Yep, Jeanette, et al. *Following Jesus without Dishonoring Your Parents: Asian American Discipleship.* Downers Grove, Ill.: Intervarsity Press, 1998. This book examines many of the issues and conflicts Asian Americans face within churches, particularly those that do not come from Christian families. Yep's book illustrates key issues and concerns that relate directly to the discipleship of Asian American young people. This book is a useful resource for all those who are concerned with ministry with Asian American youth and young adults.

Bible and Bible Study

De La Torre, Miguel A. *Reading the Bible from the Margins.* Maryknoll, N.Y.: Orbis, 2002. An introduction to reading and understanding the Bible from the perspectives of race, class, and gender. De La Torre's concise and highly readable book argues for the impact of social location on how we read scripture. He shows how racism, classism, sexism, and homophobia have influenced the reading of texts, and also shows how the marginalized have used the Bible as a source of liberation. This is an excellent book for groups first exposed to reading the Bible from the perspectives of race, class, gender, and sexual identity.

DeYoung, Curtiss Paul. *Coming Together: The Bible's Message in an Age of Diversity.* Valley Forge, Penn.: Judson Press, 1995. Communicates what the Bible teaches about the oneness of humanity in light of the gospel. This book both raises the challenges of human diversity, such as racism, and compellingly makes the case for the key role of the Christian community in reconciliation. Written from a biblical perspective, the book is both realistic and hopeful.

———. *Reconciliation: Our Greatest Challenge—Our Only Hope.* Valley Forge, Penn.: Judson Press, 1997. This book seeks to clarify what biblical reconciliation is and what precipitates it within human community. One of the strengths of DeYoung's work is his ability to portray the challenges of the church's role as an agent of racial reconciliation from a biblical, theological, and practical perspective. Throughout, DeYoung is clear about the cost of change, and the difficult, painful, and ultimately liberating process called reconciliation. In an age where the need for racial reconciliation is widely spoken, this book is a source of practical advice and thoughtful challenge.

Felder, Cain Hope. *Race, Racism, and the Biblical Narratives.* Minneapolis: Fortress Press, 2002. Shows how the Bible has been used to trivialize African contributions and demean and enslave black people. Challenges scholars and church people alike to a more honest and informed engagement with the biblical text. This small book is a helpful resource for those interested in more challenging Bible study.

González, Justo L. *Santa Biblia: The Bible through Hispanic Eyes.* Nashville: Abingdon, 1996. Brings the Hispanic/Latino/a experience to bear on biblical interpretation, and gives the reader insights into reading the Bible through "Hispanic eyes." González's work is an excellent resource for those interested in relating to scripture from a Hispanic perspective.

Hines, Samuel George, and Curtiss Paul DeYoung. *Beyond Rhetoric: Reconciliation as a Way of Life.* Valley Forge, Penn.: Judson Press, 2000. This book presents reconciliation from the perspective of biblical theology and life in the world. The authors both draw on their extensive experience in ministry and urge individuals and the church to go beyond the rhetoric of inclusiveness to encompass reconciliation as portrayed by the gospel.

Kwok Pui-Lan. *Discovering the Bible in the Non-Biblical World.* Maryknoll, N.Y.: Orbis, 1999. A multidimensional reading of the Bible that draws on traditions outside of the West, as well as contemporary feminist and third world theologies, this book is an excellent resource for those interested in biblical interpretation from a multicultural perspective.

McKenzie, Steven L. *All God's Children: A Biblical Critique of Racism.* Louisville: Westminster John Knox, 1997. Throughout this book the author makes a compelling case for the biblical call for the eradication of racism. McKenzie supports his arguments with sound scholarship and a wide variety of texts. This is a great secondary source for those interested in the relationship between racism and the Bible.

Congregations

Angrosino, Michael V. *Talking about Cultural Diversity in Your Church: Gifts and Challenges.* Walnut Creek, Calif.: Altamira Press, 2001. A workbook on cultural diversity for a local congregation, this resource provides a wealth of material, including articles, exercises, and resource guides. For congregations who have never done work on multiculturalism, this is a very helpful text.

Barndt, Joseph. *Dismantling Racism: The Continuing Challenge to White America*. Minneapolis: Augsburg, 1991. This book is one of the key resources on the impact of racism in the United States and the challenges of dismantling racism. Widely used by antiracism trainers, this book provides a useful practical and theoretical background for those interested in looking at white racism. Barndt's book powerfully illustrates the impact of racism throughout our communities, including churches, and addresses the role of the white community in both perpetuating and eradicating it. This book is an important fundamental resource for antiracism work in churches and other communities.

Branding, Ronice E.. *Fulfilling the Dream: Confronting the Challenge of Racism*. St. Louis: Chalice Press, 1998. An in-depth analysis of contemporary racism for churches and people of faith. Branding points to the insidious nature of racism and the ways it has negatively affected all of humanity. The book includes a wealth of practical suggestions and appendices, including ways to make a difference in church leadership, worship, church communication, stewardship, Christian education, and community action.

Cenkner, William, ed. *The Multicultural Church: A New Landscape in U.S. Theologies*. Mahwah, N.J.: Paulist Press, 1995. A theology of multiculturalism in the local church, this book raises up a new vision of community life. The author draws from a variety of contexts to describe church communities where cultural differences are not only recognized, but celebrated.

Davies, Susan E., and Sister Paul Teresa Hennessee, S.A., eds. *Ending Racism in the Church*. Cleveland: United Church Press, 1998. Three case studies pertaining to churches and community agencies that strive to end racism, with articles on related themes, such as baptism, eucharist, and so forth. An appendix designed to assist local groups to work for racial justice in their communities is included. These short articles helpfully raise the issue of racism within a variety of contexts in a congregation, and offer practical assistance.

Day, Katie. *Difficult Conversations: Taking Risks, Acting with Integrity*. Bethesda, Md.: Alban Institute, 2001. This useful book provides leaders with a proven process for engaging congregations in transformational conversations on difficult topics. The book features captivating congregational stories and practical tools for institutional change.

DeYoung, Curtiss Paul, et al. *United by Faith: The Multiracial Congregation as an Answer to the Problem of Race*. New York: Oxford University Press, 2003. A multiracial team argues that multiracial Christian congregations offer a key to racial reconciliation in the United States. The result of a major research project, this book supports the role of churches in the eradication of racism and the building of a more just society.

Foster, Charles R. *Embracing Diversity: Leadership in Multicultural Congregations*. Bethesda, Md.: Alban Institute, 1997. Discusses the complex interpersonal dynamics and institutional realities of becoming a multicultural organization. Foster's ability to read congregations, along with his valuable insights into leadership and change, provide an excellent resource for those interested in developing skills for multicultural leadership.

———, and Theodore Brelsford. *We Are the Church Together: Cultural Diversity in Congregational Life*. Valley Forge, Penn.: Trinity Press International, 1996. Features several specific congregations and discusses how cultural diversity forms and renews communities of faith. Throughout this book the authors richly describe the life of culturally diverse congregations, and in so doing, show the challenges and rewards of their community life. This book is an excellent companion to the book listed above and this volume.

Hagen, June Steffensen, ed. *Rattling Those Dry Bones: Women Changing the Church*. San Diego: Luramedia, Inc., 1995. Twenty-two prominent women church leaders and theologians from diverse racial and ethnic backgrounds answer the question, "What holds you in the church?" Throughout this book the respondents are honest and provocative in their views on the pain, struggle, hope, and joy in church life. The experience of racism, as well as other forms of oppression, figures in these stories.

Harmer, Catherine M. *The Compassionate Community: Strategies That Work for the Third Millennium*. Maryknoll, N.Y.: Orbis Books, 1998. A call to compassion for churches and community organizations, this book offers a new vision of the human community. Harmer identifies several major issues, including poverty, violence, and homelessness; the root causes, including racism; and then offers strategies for action that involve the whole community. This book is an important text for congregations or groups that work with the marginalized.

Kujawa-Holbrook, Sheryl A. "Beyond Outreach: Worship, Justice, and Hospitality." *Congregations*, July/August 2002. This article focuses on how two different congregations embody and express their support for social justice through the ministries of worship and hospitality. In each congregation, the carefully designed worship life of the congregation is enmeshed in the ministries of social action: spiritual formation and social justice are interrelated. Contains some helpful characteristics of congregations that practice "radical hospitality." Available through the Alban Institute (www.alban.org).

Law, Eric H. F. *Inclusion: Making Room for Grace*. St. Louis: Chalice Press, 2000. Details a biblical and theological process for multicultural inclusion. Law draws on his extensive experience as a consultant for congregations involved in change processes, and has designed models that value cultural differences and strengthen communication skills. Throughout he argues against "inclusion" models based on assimilation, and promotes multicultural dialogue and community building.

———. *Sacred Acts, Holy Change: Faithful Diversity and Practical Transformation*. St. Louis: Chalice Press, 2002. Offers practical guidelines for the transformation of congregations attempting to become multiculturally inclusive, including a suggested change process. This book is also a deeply theological interpretation of change from the perspective of discernment, conversion, and grace. Throughout Law's carefully articulated process for "planned change," he stresses the need for group discernment and prayer. This is a very helpful book for congregations going through planning processes, and interested in faithful diversity and practical transformation.

———. *The Wolf Shall Dwell with the Lamb: A Spirituality for Leadership in a Multicultural Community*. St Louis: Chalice Press, 1993. A book on multicultural leadership for congregations, including specific sections on the Bible, liturgy, and the process of "mutual invitation." This is the first of Law's books and an important introduction to the tools and themes he develops in his later work. His process of "mutual invitation" is adaptable to a wide variety of congregational groups and situations where greater participation, especially among those historically silenced, is advocated.

Lo, Jim. *Intentional Diversity: Creating Cross-Cultural Relationships in Your Church*. Indianapolis: Wesleyan Publishing, 2002. This is a book of practical advice on bridging cultural differences in a local church. Topics include how to learn to appreciate, rather than fear, diversity in a congregation; the differences between tolerance and compromise; cross-cultural ministry opportunities; and how the church can become more cross-culturally sensitive.

Peart, Norman Anthony, and John Perkins. *Separate No More: Understanding and Developing Racial Reconciliation in Your Church*. Grand Rapids, Mich.: Baker Books, 2000. This book provides concrete models for racial reconciliation in congregations. Peart examines the historical problem of racism, the biblical mandate for reconciliation, as well as the possibilities for congregational change. Peart developed an important "reconciliation continuum" that explains the relationship between various models of racial reconciliation within congregations today, from segregation to "inHIMtegration," the model closest to the biblical ideal. The author interviewed pastors and used many sources for his analysis. This is a help-

ful book for those interested in various models of congregational development as it is related to racism reconciliation.

Stroupe, Nibs, et al. *While We Run This Race: Confronting the Power of Racism in a Southern Church.* Maryknoll, N.Y.: Orbis, 1995. The story of Oakhurst Presbyterian Church in Decatur, Georgia, this moving and inspiring book provides a glimpse of multiracial congregational life. The authors examine the congregation for both historical and historical perspectives.

Tate, Gloria J. "Journey toward a Multicultural Congregation." *Congregations,* July/August 1999. This is an excellent and brief article that raises key issues for congregations that desire to become more multicultural. Available through the Alban Institute (www.alban.org).

"Vision or Afterthought? Racial, Ethnic and Immigrant Evangelism and Church Growth." *Church & Society,* January/February 2002. This issue of a journal published by the Presbyterian Church (U.S.A.) discusses new church development from the perspective of several racial and ethnic groups, and raises important issues about church growth strategies. Contact: *Church & Society* Magazine, 100 Witherspoon St., Louisville, KY 40202-1396. Phone: 888/728-7228, ext. 5810. Web site: horeb.pcusa. org/churchsociety

Williams, Cecil. *No Hiding Place: Empowerment and Recovery for Our Troubled Communities.* New York: HarperCollins, 1992. Another important congregational history, this book is the story of the transformation of Glide Memorial Church, San Francisco, an intentionally multiracial and multicultural congregation. The book makes a strong case for the role of the church in the midst of racism and other forms of oppression.

Education, Training, and Leadership

Adams, Maurianne, et al. *Teaching for Diversity and Social Justice: A Sourcebook for Teachers and Trainers.* New York: Routledge, 1997. Addresses the need to facilitate communication and understanding between members of diverse and unequal social groups, and provides both learning theory and practical suggestions from a variety of perspectives. This resource would be most helpful to those leading training sessions of seminars on antiracism.

Advocates for Youth. *A Youth Leader's Guide to Building Cultural Competence.* Washington, D.C.: Advocates for Youth, 1994. A resource book for youth leaders on different forms of cultural diversity that is intended to provide them with background and resources related to young people. Available for download at www.advocatesforyouth.org

America's Original Sin: A Study Guide on White Racism. Washington, D.C.: Sojourners, 1992. A study guide for examining racism in groups, featuring background articles by renowned authors and reflection questions. Contact: *Sojourners,* 2401 15th Street NW, Washington, DC 20009. Phone: 202/328-8842. Web site: www.sojo.net

Batts, Valerie. *Modern Racism: New Melody for the Same Old Tunes.* Cambridge, Mass.: Episcopal Divinity School Occasional Papers, 1998. Offers a model for identifying and changing modern racism. Based on consultation and training offered by the VISIONS groups since 1984 (*see* Organizations). Available at www.episdivschool.edu

Beauboef-Lafontant, Tamara, and D. Smith Augustine, eds. *Facing Racism in Education.* 2nd ed. Cambridge, Mass.: Harvard Educational Review, 1996. Sixteen articles concerning the experience of racism in an educational context, and the practice of anti-racism. The authors and topics reflect a variety of racial backgrounds, and would be useful background for anti-racism trainers and congregational leaders.

Bell, Linda A., and David Blumenfeld, eds. *Overcoming Racism and Sexism.* Lanham, Md.: Rowman & Littlefield, 1995. An interdisciplinary collection of seventeen articles concerning the intersection of race, gender, racism, and sexism. These articles are brief enough to be used during antiracism training sessions, particularly with groups concerned with interlocking oppressions.

Building Bridges with Reliable Information: A Guide to Our Community's Races, Religions and Cultures. New York: National Conference for Community and Justice, 1997 (2nd edition). Published through the National Capital Area office of the NCCJ (*see* Organizations), this resource provides histories, beliefs, and self-descriptions of various ethnic groups. Very helpful for congregations and organizations interested in community action.

Center for Democratic Renewal. *When Hate Groups Come to Town: A Handbook of Effective Community Responses.* Atlanta: CDR, 2000. This helpful manual supports organizations in their fight against hate groups, and proposes action and response plans. Contact: Center for Democratic Renewal (*see* Organizations).

Colorlines. A multiracial magazine for communities of color, published quarterly by the Applied Research Center. For more information, write P.O. Box 3000, Denville, NJ 07834; or call GrassrootsFundraising.org at 1-888-458-8588. Web site: www.colorlines.com

Crossing the Racial Divide: America's Struggle for Justice and Reconciliation. Washington, D.C.: Sojourners, 1998, 2000. A four-session study guide on institutional racism from the perspective of the gospel. Each session features several articles by renowned authors with study and reflection questions. The articles are suitable for use in a variety of contexts, individually and as part of the curriculum. Contact: *Sojourners*, 2401 15th Street NW, Washington, DC 20009. Phone: 202/328-8842. Web site: www.sojo.net

Derman-Spark, Louise, and Carol Brunson Phillips. *Teaching/Learning Anti-Racism: A Developmental Approach*. New York: Teachers College Press, 1997. Manual of teaching methods and educational designs focused on antiracist identity, awareness, and behavior. This guide describes a process that leads students from proracist consciousness to active antiracism. Throughout, the book integrates methodology and course content with student writings and analyses of students' growth.

Freire, Paulo. *Pedagogy of the Oppressed*. New York: Continuum, 2000. Based in his work on adult literacy in Brazil, Freire discusses the type of education that liberates the oppressed. This book is not a practical manual; its strength is in talking about the process and value of transformational education.

Hogan-Garcia, Mikel. *The Four Skills of Cultural Diversity Competence: A Process for Understanding and Practice*. Pacific Grove, Calif.: Brooks/ Cole, 2003. This is a process-based manual for intercultural skill-building designed to increase awareness and understanding about mainstream United States culture, personal culture and core identity, theories of diversity, and culturally centered communication skills in interpersonal and group settings.

Jackson, Bailey, and Evangelina Holvino. "Developing Multicultural Organizations." Brattleboro, Vt.: Reprinted by the authors, 1994. This concise article outlines the stages of multicultural development in organizations, and is directly applicable to congregations and other religious organizations. Contact: bailey.jackson@educ.umass.edu

Kiselica, Mark S., ed. *Confronting Prejudice and Racism during Multicultural Training*. Alexandria, Va.: American Counseling Association, 1999. Fifteen scholars provide multiple perspectives on understanding and responding to resistance and the issues of racism, sexism, homophobia, ableism, and ageism as they emerge during multicultural training. The authors provide multiple perspectives on understanding and responding to resistance and offer effective recommendations for confronting prejudice in compassionate and nonagressive ways.

Kujawa, Sheryl A., et al. *Resource Book for Ministries with Youth and Young Adults in the Episcopal Church*. New York: Episcopal Church Center, 1995. Section IV of this resource contains eight articles relating to race, ethnicity, culture, and young people. The overall intent of the section is to provide background for those who work with youth on racial identity development and the effects of racism, as well as ways to address the topic of racism, with young people of color, as well as with European American young people. Available through the Episcopal Church Center (*see* Denominational Resources).

Kujawa-Holbrook, Sheryl A. "Beyond Diversity: Cultural Competence, White Racism Awareness, and European-American Theology Students." *Teaching Theology & Religion*, July 2002. Discusses the need for greater awareness of cultural and racial differences for those who work in church contexts, and raises specific ways to introduce the topic of racism, as well as antiracism training, into the seminary curriculum.

McCoy, Martha, et al. *Toward a More Perfect Union in an Age of Diversity: A Guide for Building Stronger Communities through Public Dialogue.* Brattleboro, Vt.: The Learning Center, 1997. A discussion guide to aid participants in community dialogue on issues such as racism and advance to collaborative action. This helpful work provides a basic framework for those who want to structure a dialogue in the community. Contact: The Learning Center at 289 Fox Farm Road, 05031. Phone: 802/254-1234, ext. 130.

Moving Toward Racial Healing: A Guidebook. Philadelphia: St. Vincent de Paul Church, 2002. Facilitator's manual for a small-group-based racial reconciliation process based at this congregation. The manual provides the outlines for eight sessions, as well as supplementary worship resources, community-building exercises, and articles. Contact: 109 East Price St., Philadelphia, PA 19144-2145. Phone: 215/438-2925.

National Immigration Forum. *Together in Our Differences: How Newcomers and Established Residents Are Rebuilding America's Communities.* Washington, D.C.: National Immigration Forum, 1993. This report documents community-based programs in the United States that bring together newcomers and established residents from different racial and ethnic groups to address common concerns. Available through The National Immigration Forum, 50 F Street NW, Suite #300, Washington DC 20001. Phone: 202/347-0040. Web site: www.immigrationforum.org

Poverty and Race. The newsletter of the Poverty and Race Research Action Council is a collection of articles and resource listings on race and racism geared toward nonprofit organizations. Contact PRRAC, 3000 Connecticut Avenue NW, Suite 200, Washington, DC 20008. Phone: 202/387-9887. Web site: www.prrac.org

The Race Relations Reporter. Monthly publication and database with news headlines addressing racism across the country. Contact: CH II Publishers, Inc., 200 West 57th Street, 15th floor, New York, NY 10019. Phone: 212/399-1084. E-mail: info@jbhe.com. Web site: www.jbhe.com/jbhe

Turning the Tide: Journal of Anti-Racist Action, Research, and Education. Quarterly journal published through People Against Racist Terror (PART). Contact: PART, P.O. Box 1055, Culver City, CA 90232. E-mail: part2001@usa.net. Web site: www.people.we@mediaone.net

West, Cornel. *Race Matters*. Boston: Beacon Press, 1993. This book addresses the crisis in black leadership today and is an important core text for those interested in race and racism in America. Arguing that racism breaks down the democratic order, West provides strategies for multiracial democracy.

General—Racism and Multiculturalism

Adams, Maurianne, et al., eds. *Readings for Diversity and Social Justice: An Anthology on Racism, Anti-Semitism, Sexism, Heterosexism, Ableism, and Classism*. New York: Routledge, 2000. The first anthology to cover the scope of social oppression from a social justice standpoint, these readings on a variety of subjects, including racism, are valuable resources for group discussions and training events.

Anderson, David, and Brent Zuercher. *Letters Across the Divide: Two Friends Explore Racism, Friendship, and Faith*. Grand Rapids, Mich.: Baker Books, 2001. A dialogue between two friends—one black and one white—on racism. The movement of the dialogue between the two friends opens up some major themes in interpersonal cross-cultural relationships, as well as institutional racism. The book is useful for individuals and groups exploring racism on a personal level.

Blackwell, Angela Glover, et al. *Searching for the Uncommon Common Ground: New Dimensions on Race in America*. New York: W. W. Norton, 2002. The authors address the real and material steps necessary for economic and social equality. The authors argue that today's racial divide cannot be healed through mere conversation and understanding; rather, practical issues must be addressed for material gains to be achieved.

Bowens-Wheatley, Marjorie, and Nancy Palmer Jones, eds. *Soul Work: Anti-Racist Theologies in Dialogue*. Boston: Skinner House Books, 2003. These nine articles written by a diverse compliment of authors are the result of a major consultation on antiracist theologies. The essays are powerful, insightful, and mark an important contribution to the field. These articles can be used in a variety of ways with faith-based antiracism training, and for discussion in their own right.

Bullard, Robert D., et al., eds. *Confronting Environmental Racism: Voices from the Grassroots*. Boston: South End Press, 1993. This collection of essays studies the impact of environmental racism in local contexts. Part of the power of this book lies in its powerful indictment of environmental racism and its effects. Recommended for those interested in exploring racism and other forms of oppression from the perspective of the environmental movement.

Ellis, Anne Leo, ed. *First, We Must Listen: Living in a Multicultural Society.* New York: Friendship Press, 1996. A collection of articles, speeches, and stories from a variety of racial and ethnic groups, assembled to provide material for dialogue and action in congregations. A leader's guide by Marilyn Winters is also available. This creative collection is a helpful resource for congregations engaged in multicultural exploration.

Ford, Clyde. *We Can All Get Along: 50 Steps You Can Take to Help End Racism.* New York: Dell Publishing, 1994. Practical projects for individuals and groups to help end racism in the world. This pragmatic book will appeal in particular to those who are seeking some specific actions that they or their congregation can do to dismantle racism.

Lee, Jung Young. *Marginality: The Key to Multicultural Theology.* Minneapolis: Fortress Press, 1995. Proposes a framework for doing contextual theology by redefining marginality itself as central to the theological enterprise. Lee helps the reader find the connections between their identity and their "voice." This book is helpful to those working on antiracism and multiculturalism in a theological framework.

Nash, Kimberleigh A., and Jorge Velazquez. *Cultural Competence: A Guide for Human Service Agencies.* Washington, D.C.: Child Welfare League of America, 1999. Guidelines for organizations on cultural competence. This manual is a helpful discernment tool for use with individuals or groups in discerning levels of multicultural awareness within organizations. While it is designed for human service agencies, the categories and commentary are readily adaptable to congregations and religious organizations. Available through the Child Welfare League of America, 50 F Street NW, 6th Floor, Washington, DC 20001-2085. Phone: 202/638-2952. Web site: www. cwla.org

"Race & Power." *The Nonprofit Quarterly,* Summer 2002. This issue of the magazine, published by Third Sector New England, features several articles on the impact of racism in nonprofit organizations. Though written for development professionals, the insights gained apply to many nonprofits. Contact: Third Sector New England, 8 Tremont St., Suite 700, Boston, MA 02108. Web site: www.nonprofitquarterly.org

Robins, Kikanza Nuri. "Cultural Proficiency: The Next Wave." Project Equality of Delaware Valley, April 2002. This article is an interesting overview of recent trends in cultural competency written by a diversity consultant. Available from knurirobins@earthlink.net

Rodman, Edward W. "9/11 and Race: One Christian Perspective." *All Things New: The Newsletter of the Episcopal City Mission,* Winter 2001–2002.

This article is a reflection on the changing context of antiracism training and racial justice after September 11. A brief piece that puts forth some helpful connections about why it is important to address racism in our congregations and in the community. Available through the Episcopal Diocese of Massachusetts, 138 Tremont St., Boston, MA 02111. Phone: 617-482-4826. Web site: www.diomass.org

Rowing Together. Episcopal Diocese of Southern Virginia. Resource Packet compiled by St. Cyprian's, Hampton, Va. and St. Martin's, Williamsburg, Va.. This packet of materials is a compilation from a variety of sources of some of the resources these two congregations have found helpful in their explorations of racism. The packet is also an example of a partnership model between two congregations. Contact: 600 Talbot Hall Road, Norfolk, VA 23505-4361. Phone: 757/423-8287 or 800/582-8292. Web site: www.southernvirginia.anglican.org

Thompson, Herbert, Jr. *Let My People Go: A Statement to Cincinnati and the World.* Cincinnati: Forward Movement Publications, 2001. This booklet is really an address on racism and the justice system by an African American Episcopal bishop. The author raises key issues of institutional racism and institutional violence. Contact: Forward Movement Publications, 412 Sycamore Street, Cincinnati, Ohio 45202-4195. Phone: 513/721-6659 or 800/543-1813. Web site: www.forwardmovement.org

Tutu, Desmond. "Why As Christians We Must Oppose Racism." *St. Mark's Review,* Winter 1995. This short article argues that racism is evil and that reconciliation is at the heart of the gospel message. Along with vivid examples from his own experience, Archbishop Tutu challenges all Christians to oppose racism. Contact: 15 Blackall St., Barton ACT, 2600 Australia. E-mail: scowdell@csu.edu.au

Washington, Raleigh, and Glen Kehrein. *Breaking Down Walls: A Model for Reconciliation in an Age of Racial Strife.* Chicago: Moody Press, 1993. This book outlines eight principles of racial reconciliation. The authors recount how God acted in their own lives and the lives of a struggling congregation to create a vital multiethnic community of faith.

The Witness. This magazine and Web site feature frequent articles about racism and other social justice concerns. The articles are brief, readable, and expertly written and thus useful to a wide audience. Contact: The Witness, P.O. Box 1170, Rockport, ME 04856. Web site: www.thewitness.org

Hispanics and Latinos/as

Deck, Allan Figueroa, et al., eds. *Perspectivas: Hispanic Ministry.* New York: Sheed and Ward, 1995. This book is on the topic of pastoral ministry from a Hispanic perspective. It is a particularly helpful for its insights into ministry with Hispanic persons.

Elizondo, Virgilio. *The Future Is Mestizo: Life Where Cultures Meet.* Revised edition. Boulder: University of Colorado Press, 2000. This book offers a distinctive Hispanic perspective on Jesus as a *mestizo*, and thus a bridge between persons of different cultures. Elizondo's work upholds the uniqueness of Hispanic culture, and at the same time shows the strength of cultures coming together in Christ.

González, Justo. *Mañana: Christian Theology from a Hispanic Perspective.* Nashville: Abingdon Press, 1990. A concise and introductory study of Latin American liberation theology, this book is an excellent introduction to the subject. González writes in a compelling style and draws the reader into Hispanic culture and theology.

Martinez, Elizabeth, ed. *500 Years of Chicano History: In Pictures.* Albuquerque: Southwest Organizing Project, 1991. This resource book on Chicano history is well written and engaging. Available through the Southwest Organizing Project (*see* Organizations).

Martinez, Ruben. *Crossing Over: A Mexican Family on the Migrant Trail.* New York: Picador, 2001. This book is focused on a migrant family and journeys with them from Mexico, to California, Wisconsin, Missouri, and Arkansas. Martinez richly and compassionately captures the lives—joys, struggles, faith—of the family and educates on migrant issues at the same time.

Ortiz, Manuel. *The Hispanic Challenge: Opportunities Confronting the Church.* Downers Grove, Ill.: Intervarsity Press, 1994. Explores the needs and concerns of Hispanics in the United States, describing models for effective ministry and leadership training. This challenging book is a helpful resource for congregations engaged in or interested in ministries with Hispanic people.

Recinos, Harold J. *Who Comes in the Name of the Lord? Jesus at the Margins.* Nashville: Abingdon Press, 1997. This is a theological work on Jesus written from a Hispanic perspective. Throughout the author proclaims the solidarity of Jesus with marginalized persons.

Rodriguez, Albert. "Proposed Implementation Plan for the Mexican American Evangelization Initiative." Austin Episcopal Convocation, July 2002. This article, written by an Episcopal priest, describes Mexican-American culture and details an evangelization plan. Contact the author at: alpadre@yahoo.com

Valentin, Benjamin. *Mapping Public Theology: Beyond Culture, Identity, and Difference.* Harrisburg, Penn.: Trinity Press International, 2002. Examines Hispanic/Latino/a theology from the perspective of social justice. Importantly, this work takes up the importance of theology within the public sector.

Vila, Pablo. *Crossing Borders, Reinforcing Borders: Social Categories, Metaphors, and Narrative Identities on the U.S.–Mexico Frontier.* Austin: University of Texas Press, 2000. Draws on over 200 group interviews with 900 persons to discuss how Mexican nationals, Mexican immigrants, Mexican Americans, African Americans, and Anglos describe their experience and perceive their differences from others.

Ybarra, Lea, et al., eds. *Americanos: Latino Life in the United States.* New York: Little, Brown, 1999. This publication and its accompanying Web site present some of the newest data and research on Latinos in the United States. Web site: www.americanosproject.com

Identity

Bivens, Donna K. "Internalized Racism: A Definition." *Women's Theological Center Quarterly Newsletter,* June 1995. This brief article is an insightful discussion of internalized oppression and its effects. It could be used as the starting point of a major group discussion on the topic. Contact: P.O. Box 1200, Boston, MA 02117-1200. Phone: 617/536-8782.

Lipsky, Suzanne. "Internalized Oppression." Paper presented at the National Association of Black and White Men Together, Washington D.C., April 25, 1994. This article is a transcript from a major address and outlines a definition and framework for analysis of internalized oppression. The strength of this articles lies in its discussion of the impact of internalized oppression. Contact: NABWMT, P.O. Box 81236, Pittsburgh, PA 15217-4236.

Pinderhughes, Elaine. *Understanding Race, Ethnicity, and Power: The Key to Efficacy in Clinical Practice.* New York: The Free Press, 1990. Written for clinicians from the perspective that an understanding of race, ethnicity, and culture are integral to human wholeness. Discusses how bias is learned, what causes discomfort, and how to address inequities in power. Helpful for all who are concerned with human identity and culture.

Sharma, Arvind, and Kathleen M. Dugan, eds. *A Dome of Many Colors: Studies in Religious Pluralism, Identity, and Unity.* Harrisburg, Penn.: Trinity Press International, 1999. A collection of essays that discusses the intersection of multiple identities and religious pluralism. What is helpful about this collection is its assertion of the positive aspects of difference.

Tatum, Beverly Daniel. *"Why Are All the Black Kids Sitting Together in the Cafeteria?" And Other Conversations about Race: A Psychologist Explains the Development of Racial Identity.* New York: Basic Books, 1997. Focuses on constructive racial identity development and facilitating communication across racial and ethnic lines. Goes beyond the black–white paradigm to discuss issues pertaining to Asians, Latinos,

American Indians, as well as biracial youth. Though the book certainly pertains to youth, it also is useful in understanding racial identity in persons of any age group.

Thompson, Becky, and Sangeeta Tyagi, eds. *Names We Call Home: Autobiography on Racial Identity.* New York: Routledge, 1966. Twenty-seven authors analyze how they define themselves, what they were taught about race as children, and how various social movements have shaped their activism. The strength of this book lies in the stories it tells about the identities of the authors, how they experience them, and what shaped them. This book is a wonderful conversational starter and is helpful as a way to assist others tell their own stories, and to learn from others with different life experiences.

Wright, Marguerite A. *I'm Chocolate, You're Vanilla: Raising Healthy Black and Biracial Children in a Race-Conscious World: A Guide for Parents and Teachers.* San Francisco: Jossey-Bass, 1998. Teaches those concerned about children how to reduce racism's impact on the development of black and biracial children. Though the focus of this book is on teachers, the book is important reading for pastors, and other who care for young people.

Legacies

Bell, Derrick. *Faces at the Bottom of the Well: The Permanence of Racism.* New York: Basic Books, 1992. This book speaks to the inevitability of racism in America and the author's response to that reality. Bell believes that racism is so ingrained in American life that no matter what blacks do they are doomed to fail unless the majority of whites begin to see themselves threatened by the status quo. The book is a good resource for groups who have been engaged in racial justice work for a time and would benefit from a deeper look at how racism permeates American society.

Cone, James H. *Martin & Malcolm & America: A Dream or a Nightmare.* Maryknoll, N.Y.: Orbis Books, 1991. Examines the relationship and the historical legacy of the two African American leaders. This book provides an important corrective to some of the informal assumptions about the two leaders and shows their impact to the present day.

Emerson, Michael O., and Christian Smith. *Divided by Faith: Evangelical Religion and the Problem of Race in America.* New York: Oxford University Press, 2000. Relates the history of racial division in American religion and how white evangelicals perpetuate the racism they publicly oppose. Part of the book's importance lies in its revelations about the relationship between religion and racism; that is, how religion has been used historically as both a source of oppression and a source of liberation.

Guinier, Lani, and Gerald Torres. *The Miner's Canary: Enlisting Race, Resisting Power, Transforming Democracy.* Cambridge, Mass.: Harvard University Press, 2002. Identifies racial literacy as a new way to think about social change in the United States. Calls us to rethink old lines of division, rethink outdated systems, and transform democracy. The authors envision people of all races struggling together as the grassroots level, to improve the lives of everyone who has been "raced" black, regardless of skin color.

Gottlieb, Roger S. *Joining Hands: Politics and Religion Together for Social Change.* Cambridge, Mass.: Westview Press, 2002. Gottlieb argues that religious belief and spiritual practice are integral to social change. He provides fresh interpretations of the civil rights struggle, feminism, the environmental movement, and fighting against breast cancer, to assist the reader in looking at the political role of religion and the spiritual component of politics.

Ivory, Luther D. *Toward a Theology of Radical Involvement: The Theological Legacy of Martin Luther King, Jr.* Nashville: Abingdon, 1997. Interprets the radical and prophetic legacy of Dr. King's message for our time. This book is an important resource for all who seek to interpret Dr. King's legacy.

Takaki, Ronald. *A Different Mirror: A History of Multicultural America.* Boston: Little, Brown, 1993. Comprehensive text on American history written from the perspective of different racial and ethnic groups. This book reveals the many peoples who compose our culture and provides an important corrective to more "traditional" histories of the United States.

Tutu, Desmond. *No Future Without Forgiveness.* New York: Random House, 1999. A bold spirituality that recognizes both the reality of oppression and the idealism of reconciliation. Throughout this work, Archbishop Tutu addresses what he has learned about forgiveness from the perspective of his own life and ministry in South Africa. The book dramatically speaks to the interrelationship between justice, forgiveness, and reconciliation.

Young, Josiah Ulysses III. *No Difference in the Fare: Dietrich Bonhoeffer and the Problem of Racism.* Grand Rapids, Mich.: Wm. B. Eerdmans, 1998. From an African American perspective, Young shows how Bonhoeffer's thought is inimical to racism and suggests ways to move society from divisive bigotry to inclusive community. This book is important in that it brings a new interpretation to Bonhoeffer's theology.

Young-Bruehl, Elisabeth. *The Anatomy of Prejudices.* Cambridge, Mass.: Harvard University Press, 1996. Surveys the development of "prejudices"—anti-Semitism, racism, sexism, and homophobia—since World War II, and discusses their differences and similarities. This book is not an easy read, yet is the most comprehensive of its kind. At its core, the book shows how prejudice is learned and the result of social conditioning.

Pastoral Care

Bell, Peter. *Chemical Dependency and the African American: Counseling and Prevention Strategies*. Center City, Minn.: Hazelden, 2002. Written by an expert on chemical dependency and African Americans, this book contains several helpful assessment tools on cultural diversity and racial identity. Though the book is focused on the treatment of chemical dependency, its resources on culture and identity have many uses outside of the topic area.

Chinula, Donald M. *Building King's Beloved Community: Foundations for Pastoral Care and Counseling with the Oppressed*. Cleveland: United Church Press, 1997. A scheme on the pastoral care of the oppressed based on the theology of Dr. Martin Luther King Jr. This book is important because it dramatically demonstrates the effects of power and powerlessness on oppressed persons. Important reading for anyone who ministers with the marginalized, this book shows the shortcomings of traditional models of pastoral care for the oppressed, and suggests ways of healing and transformation.

Culturally Competent Practice: A Series from Children's Voice Magazine. Washington, D.C.: Child Welfare League of America, 1995–1997. A pamphlet with articles discussing the care of Asian, African American, Latino, and American Indian families. This resource is focused on the care of families from a social-science perspective, yet provides important insights for anyone interested in multiculturalism. Contact: CWLA, 50 F St. NW, 6th Floor, Washington, DC 20001. Phone: 202/638-2952. Web site: www.cwla.org

Gleich, Patricia K. "Caring Outside the Comfort Zone." *Church & Society*, March/April 2002. A call to extend the care of the church beyond human boundaries. The author asserts that it is central to the work of the church to work with those traditionally outside institutional structures, and it is in doing that work that transformation occurs. Contact: *Church & Society* Magazine, 100 Witherspoon St., Louisville, KY 40202-1396. Phone: 888/728-7228, ext. 5810. Web site: horeb.pcusa.org/churchsociety

Poussaint, Alvin F., and Amy Alexander. *Lay My Burden Down: Unraveling Suicide and the Mental Health Crisis among Black Americans*. Boston: Beacon Press, 2000. Examines the increasing rates of suicide among young African Americans from the perspective of pervasive racism; defines suicide as direct intention and as the result of high-risk behaviors. This book is an important resource for any discussion of internalized racism and its affects on people of color.

Willie, Charles V., et al., eds. *Mental Health, Racism, and Sexism*. Pittsburgh: University of Pittsburgh Press, 1995. A collection of articles on diagnosis, treatment, training, and contemporary issues impacted by racial and gender oppression. Focused on the mental health system, this book provides important background on the factors that bear upon marginalized persons everywhere.

Wimberly, Edward P. *Relational Refugees: Alienation and Reincorporation in African American Churches and Communities.* Nashville: Abingdon, 2000. Wimberly identifies the alienation of individuals among the root causes of violence, domestic strife, racism, and addiction. He suggests that pastoral caregivers need to address the larger historical and social contexts of their clients, and challenges the church to provide relational environments to re-create strong families and communities.

Spirituality and Theology

Cone, James H. *Risks of Faith: The Emergence of a Black Theology of Liberation, 1968–1998.* Boston: Beacon Press, 1999. An anthology of Cone's essays, this work also shows the progression of his work over a thirty-year period.

Davis, Kortright. *Serving with Power: Reviving the Spirit of Christian Ministry.* Mahwah, N.J.: Paulist Press, 1999. Explores the power of God's Word and Spirit in an attempt to shape a new spirituality of ministry. Davis addresses what he sees as the need for a radical new spirituality to reshape and transform the lives of those called to minister in the world today.

Jarrett, Emmett, ed. *To Heal the Sin-Sick Soul: Toward a Spirituality of Anti-Racist Ministry.* Boston: Episcopal Urban Caucus, 1996; reprinted, 2003. Six essays on antiracist spirituality and ministry written from an Anglican perspective. These brief essays address in a compelling manner the connections between the spiritual life and the pursuit of racial justice. Contact: Episcopal Urban Caucus, P.O. Box 2247, New London, CT 06320-2247. Phone: 860/437-8890. Web site: www.episcopalurbancaucus.org

Kujawa, Sheryl A. "Love and Power: Spiritual Formation and Racial Justice." *Journeys,* Winter-Spring 2002. This article connects spiritual formation with the pursuit of racial justice, and attempts to respond to the question, What does antiracism have to do with spirituality? Contact: American Association of Pastoral Counselors, www.aapc.org

Leech, Kenneth. *The Eye of the Storm: Living Spiritually in the Real World.* San Francisco: HarperSanFrancisco, 1992. Contains essays on Christian spirituality related to liberation themes. Leech's approach to spirituality is rooted in gospel and in the local context.

———. *Through Our Long Exile: Contextual Theology and the Urban Experience.* London: Dartman, Longman and Todd, 2001. This book is written from a British perspective and engages the question, What kind of theology is relevant in a multicultural and multiracial community of communities?

Matsuoka, Fumitaka. *The Color of Faith: Building Community in a Multira-cial Society.* Cleveland: United Church Press, 1998. Provides a theological perspective on racial and ethnic plurality, and on the role Christian faith communities play in a multiracial society. Throughout the book the author asserts the importance of faith communities in transforming the racial oppression of society.

Poling, James Newton. *Deliver Us from Evil: Resisting Racial and Gender Oppression.* Minneapolis: Fortress Press, 1996. Defines evil as the abuse of bodies and spirit and relates these to the societal evils of racial and gen-der oppression. Poling constructs a Christology of resistance. Written as a formal theological work, the book provides helpful connections between theology and social justice.

Ruffing, Janet K., ed. *Mysticism and Social Transformation.* Syracuse: Syra-cuse University Press, 2001. A collection of essays that looks at how mys-tical empowerment can serve as a catalyst for acts of justice and long-term social change. Rather than viewing mysticism as a source of detachment from the world, the author focuses on the connections between spiritual and social empowerment.

Soelle, Dorothee. *The Silent Cry: Mysticism and Resistance.* Minneapolis: Fortress Press, 2001. Explores mysticism in major religious traditions and the connections between the passion for wisdom and social justice. Throughout the book, Soelle emphasizes the importance of spiritual growth, discernment, and the zeal for justice.

Whiteness

Feagin, Joe R., and Hernán Vera. *White Racism: The Basics.* Routledge: New York, 1995. Focuses on the dynamics of white-on-black racism in con-temporary society. The book focuses on racism from the perspective of lesser-known settings: at a small midwestern college, in the farmbelt, in family restaurants, and on the job.

Fine, Michelle, et al., eds. *Off White: Readings on Race, Power, and Society.* New York: Routledge, 1997. A collection of articles on whiteness. Both the differences and the similarities found in these diverse stories contribute to the authenticity of the collection.

Frankenberg, Ruth. *White Women, Race Matters: The Social Construction of Whiteness.* Minneapolis: University of Minnesota Press, 1993. Racism dis-cussed from the perspective of white women. This book is interesting in that it discusses white women as both the oppressed and the oppressors in the context of racism.

Hitchcock, Jeff. *Lifting the White Veil: An Exploration of White American Culture in a Multiracial Context.* Roselle, N.J.: Crandall, Dostie &

Douglass Books, 2002. Written in response to the question, What do white people want? The author's premise is based on the assertion that people are more likely to be motivated to create something positive—a multiracial world—and discusses the role white people might play in a multiracial society.

Hobgood, Mary Elizabeth. *Dismantling Privilege: An Ethics of Accountability.* Cleveland: The Pilgrim Press, 2000. Examines systemic, unearned race, class, and gender privilege from an ethical and spiritual perspective, and offers chapters on "dismantling whiteness" and the politics of solidarity.

Ignatiev, Noel. *How the Irish Became White.* New York: Routledge, 1996. Traces the history of how European immigrant ethnic groups assimilated into American culture and became "white." This book shows the development of race as a social construction historically. It is a good resource for predominately white groups to use as the focus of a discussion on the origins of "whiteness."

Jacobson, Matthew Frye. *Whiteness of a Different Color: European Immigrants and the Alchemy of Race.* Cambridge, Mass.: Harvard University Press, 1998. Traces the history of race formation among European immigrant groups in the United States. Though this book is academic in format, this is an invaluable resource for those interested in the historical construction of race in the United States.

Katz, Judith H. *White Awareness: Handbook for Anti-Racism Training.* Norman: University of Oklahoma Press, 1978. Antiracism training manual for working with white groups. This is an excellent handbook that provides a complete collection of training exercises.

Kivel, Paul. *Uprooting Racism: How White People Can Work for Racial Justice.* Philadelphia: New Society Publishers, 1996. Basic primer on racism written for white people, this book can be used with a variety of groups as an introductory text.

Leon-Hartshorn, Iris, et al. *Set Free: A Journey toward Solidarity against Racism.* Scottsdale, Penn.: Herald Press, 2001. A collaborative project dedicated to dismantling racism, written from the perspectives of an African American woman, a Mexican Amerindian woman, and a white male. This book discusses how white people can be effective allies with people of color. Written for faith communities, this book is an excellent resource for white congregations interested work in solidarity with communities of color.

McIntosh, Peggy. "White Privilege: Unpacking the Invisible Knapsack." *Independent School,* Winter 1990. This groundbreaking article explores the realities of white privilege, and is a must for any group interested in exploring white racism. In a clear and concise manner, McIntosh unlocks the unearned privileges of whiteness for the reader. Contact: National

Association of Independent Schools, 1620 L St. NW, Suite 1100, Washington, DC 20036-5695. Phone: 202/973-9700. Web site: www.nais.org

Rothenberg, Paula S., ed. *White Privilege: Essential Readings on the Other Side of Racism.* New York: Worth Publishers, 2002. A series of essays on whiteness, including perspectives from a diversity of groups. The book explores the themes of the power of invisibility, the power of the past, the power of privilege, and the power of resistance.

Shearer, Jody Miller. *Enter the River: Healing Steps from White Privilege toward Racial Reconciliation.* Scottdale, Penn.: Herald Press, 1994. Resources devoted to the problem of white privilege and white racism from a Christian perspective. Shearer writes from the perspective of his own experience, and clearly and poignantly addresses key issues in correlation to the relationship between racism and the churches.

Thandeka. *Learning to Be White: Money, Race, and God in America.* New York: Continuum, 1999. This book directly exposes the relationships between racism and classism, as well as the forms of resistance in relationship to the two. The book is important because it is one of the comparatively few books available that address classism.

Thompson, Becky. *A Promise and a Way of Life: White Antiracist Activism.* Minneapolis: University of Minnesota Press, 2001. The life histories of thirty-nine people who have placed antiracist activism at the center of their lives. This book shows some of the important patterns of development, and gives a glimpse into the journey of antiracist leadership.

White Racial Awareness Process. Inglewood, Calif.: Holy Faith Episcopal Church, n.d. A workbook for trainers working with groups of white people on racism, this resource provides training designs, exercises, and other materials. The resources can be used with church groups from most areas. Contact: Holy Faith Episcopal Church, 260 North Locust Street, Inglewood, CA 90301. Phone: 310/674-7700.

Worship and Preaching

Aghahowa, Brenda Eatman. *Praising in Black and White: Unity and Diversity in Christian Worship.* Cleveland: United Church Press, 1997. A comparison of European and African American worship styles, this work celebrates the strengths of both. This is an excellent resource for congregations engaged in discernment about their worship styles and who desire to become more multicultural.

Arias, Miguel, et al. *La Navidad Hispana: At Home and at Church.* Chicago: Liturgy Training Publications, 2000. Bilingual Spanish/English Advent and Christmas worship resource, this very practical booklet is easy to use in a variety of settings.

Bell, John L. *One Is the Body*. Glasgow, Scotland: Wild Goose Publications, 2002. Fifty songs used in public worship across Britain, whose focus is on themes related to diversity and pluralism.

Black, Kathy. *Culturally-Conscious Worship*. St. Louis: Chalice Press, 2000. Discusses how to plan more culturally sensitive worship, from a variety of perspectives. This is an excellent resource for congregations interested in evaluating their worship and looking at ways to make their worship more culturally sensitive and inclusive.

————. *Worship Across Cultures: A Handbook*. Nashville: Abingdon Press, 1998. A practical guide to worship in many cultural settings, including the major ethnic and cultural groups present in North American Protestantism. This is a practical handbook, and is filled with many creative concepts and approaches.

Blain, Susan, et al., eds. *Imaging the Word: An Arts and Lectionary Resource*. 3 vols. Cleveland: United Church Press, 1994–99. Culturally diverse art, stories, photography, music, drama, scripts, liturgies, and commentary based on the Revised Common Lectionary. This is an artistically diverse and appealing collection of materials that could enhance the worship and visual life of a congregation.

Boyd, Malcolm, and Chester Talton, eds. *Race and Prayer: Collected Voices, Many Dreams*. Harrisburg, Penn.: Morehouse Publishing, 2003. This resource is a collection of prayers written on themes related to race and racism, including pluralism, racial profiling, racial identity, seasons of the church year, and so forth. An excellent work that contains many prayers, litanies, and meditations which could be used on a variety of occasions.

Costen, Melva Wilson. *African American Christian Worship*. Nashville: Abingdon, 1993. Charts the history and development of African American worship, especially in regard to preaching, prayer, and music. This resource provides a historical and descriptive overview for the reader.

Galloway, Kathy, ed. *The Pattern of Our Days: Liturgies and Resources for Worship from the Iona Community*. Glasgow, Scotland: Wild Goose Publications, 1996. Contains a variety of readings, litanies, blessings, and prayers related to racism and justice. The style of the collection is highly participatory, responsive, and adaptable to various parts of a worship service.

González, Justo L. *¡Alabadle! Hispanic Christian Worship*. Abingdon: Nashville, 1996. Highlights the cultural, generational, and denominational elements that compose Hispanic worship. This work gives the reader a broad historical and descriptive overview.

Haskins, James, ed. *Keeping the Faith: African American Sermons of Liberation*. New York: Welcome Rain, 2002. An anthology of sermons and other texts by great African American preachers. This book also comes with a supplementary CD that gives a sense of the delivery of the sermon. The preachers represented are men and women, from the colonial era to the present.

The Iona Abbey Worship Book. Glasgow, Scotland: Wild Goose Publications, 2001. This adaptable book of services from the Iona Community has liturgies for morning, evening, and Sunday, all with a specific social justice emphasis. The additional prayers, litanies, and blessings can also be used to augment worship.

Lee, Jung Young. *Korean Preaching: An Interpretation.* Nashville: Abingdon, 1997. Preaching discussed from the perspective of reformulating Christian theology on the basis of marginality. Part of the importance of this work is Lee's perspective on the importance of "voice" within the context of preaching and marginalization. Though the focus is on Korean preaching, the lessons of this book are helpful in reference to other marginalized groups.

Lift Every Voice and Sing. New York: Church Publishing, 1993. Hymnal in the African American tradition published by the Episcopal Church. This resource provides a variety of hymns for the various seasons of the church year, and on a number of themes.

Nyberg, Anders. *Freedom Is Coming: Songs of Protest and Praise from South Africa: Songbook.* Glasgow, Scotland: Wild Goose Publications, 1990. Fifteen a capella songs from the South African church. These powerful songs can be adapted to a variety of settings and contexts.

Smith, Christine M., ed. *Preaching Justice: Ethic and Cultural Perspectives.* Cleveland: United Church Press, 1998. Brings together eight distinct ethnic/cultural voices to articulate the justice concerns of their own community toward "transformed preaching." This book is one of the most comprehensive in terms of its focus on preaching and social transformation.

This Far by Faith: An African American Resource for Worship. Minneapolis: Augsburg Fortress, 1999. Hymnal and worship resource published by the Evangelical Lutheran Church in America that contains a variety of hymns from various occasions and seasons. The front part of the book also contains a helpful essay on African American worship and music in the Christian tradition.

Tirabassi, Maren C., and Kathy Wonson Eddy. *Gifts of Many Cultures: Worship Resources for the Global Community.* Cleveland: United Church Press, 1995. A collection of worship resources from the global community. These resources are particularly useful for weddings, funerals, and other rites of passage. The resources are from the Christian tradition, as well as other religious traditions.

Tutu, Desmond. *The African Prayer Book*. New York: Doubleday, 1990. A collection of prayers, readings, and other spiritual resources from Africa that can be used for private prayer as well as in public worship.

II. VIDEOS

Beyond Hate. With Bill Moyers. Produced by International Cultural Programming Inc. and Public Affairs Television. 88 min. 1991. This film chronicles the impact of hate on its victims and those who are victimized by it. Features world figures, gang leaders, and young people. Available from Mystic Fire Direct. Phone: 212/941-0999.

Beyond the News: Racism. Produced and directed by Mennonite Board of Missions Media Ministries. 25 min. 1993. Looks at the effects of prejudice and racism on jobs, education, the judicial system and the church; includes study guide. Available from the Mennonite Central Committee (*see* Organizations).

Black Is . . . Black Ain't. Produced and directed by Marlon Riggs. 87 min. 1995. Discussion of the diversity of black identities by bell hooks, Cornel West, and others. Study guide included. Available from the Western States Center (*see* Organizations).

Chicano! History of the Mexican American Civil Rights Movement. Produced by NLCC Educational Media. 1996. Four videos on Chicano history and culture. Available from the National Latino Communications Center, P.O. Box 39A60, Los Angeles, CA 90039. Phone: 800/722-9982.

A Class Divided. Produced by Yale University Films. 60 min. 1985. From the PBS "Frontline" program, this film documents an exercise in discrimination based on eye color in an Iowa classroom. Discussion guide included. Available from the Mennonite Central Committee (*see* Organizations).

The Color of Fear. Produced and directed by Lee Mun Wah,. 90 min. 1994. This film is a dialogue among men of Asian, European, African, and Latino descent about race and racism. The film comes with a printed study guide. *Walking Each Other Home: The Color of Fear 2* is also available (see below). Available from Stir Fry Seminars and Consulting (*see* Organizations).

Conscience and the Constitution. Produced and directed by Frank Abe. 56 min. 2000. Film on the American internment camps for people of Japanese ancestry during World War II. Available from the Western States Center (*see* Organizations).

Different and the Same. Produced by Family Communications, Inc. 1993–94. 9 videos, 15 min. each. A series of videos designed to help first through third graders discuss and understand racism. A teachers guide and professional development video are also offered. Available from Great Plains National, Box 80669, Lincoln, NE 68501-0669. Phone: 800/228-4630. E-mail: gpn@unl.edu

Domino: Interracial People and the Search for Identity. Produced by the National Film Board of Canada. 45 min. 1994. Discusses race and racism from the perspective of interracial people. Available from Films for the Humanities, P.O. Box 2053, Princeton, NJ 08543.

Ending Racism: Working for a Racism-Free 21st Century. Produced by Crossroads Ministry. 35 min. 1996. An introduction to antiracism and the need to address the reality of racism in the 21st century. Available from Crossroads Ministry and the Mennonite Central Committee (*see* Organizations).

The Family of God: Helping Pre-Adolescents Respond to Racial Stereotypes. Produced by the Evangelical Lutheran Church in America. 1995. Video and five-session study guide geared for young people, ages 8–12. Available from Crossroads Ministry (*see* Organizations).

Facing Difference: Living Together on Campus. Produced by the Anti-Defamation League. 10 min. 1990. A video that addresses cultural understanding among students. Available from the Anti-Defamation League (*see* Organizations—World of Difference Institute).

Fires in the Mirror. Produced by Anna Deavere Smith. 82 min. 1993. A film of Smith's play on the riots between the Jewish and African American communities in Crown Heights, Brooklyn in 1991, features a collage of interviews with individuals who were connected with the events. Available from PBS Learning Media, 1320 Braddock Place, Alexandria, VA 22314-1698. Phone: 800/645-4727.

Forgotten Fires. Produced and directed by Michael Chandler. 57 min. 1997. Film on the black church burnings. Produced through the Independent Television Service and distributed through PBS. Web site: www.pbs.org

Free Indeed: Of White Privilege and How We Play the Game. Produced by the Mennonite Central Committee. 30 min. 1995. This video discusses white privilege and includes a study guide. Suitable for youth and well as adults. Available from the Mennonite Central Committee (*see* Organizations).

Jefferson's Blood. Produced by Thomas Lennon. 90 min. 2000. This film from the PBS "Frontline" series looks at the white and black descendents of Thomas Jefferson and their struggle with the question of their own racial identity. Available from PBS Video, P.O. Box 751089, Charlotte, NC 28275. Phone: 877/PBS-SHOP. Web site: www.shop.pbs.org. A PBS learning Web site based on the video is located at www.pbs.org/wgbh/pages/frontline/shows/jefferson

Lift Every Voice: The Bible in an Age of Diversity. Produced by Seraphim Communications. 2 tapes, 128 min. 1994. A five-part video Bible study with professors Cain Hope Felder and Tony Campolo. Designed to help people understand the dynamics of a diverse society from a biblical perspective. Includes discussion guide. Available from Seraphim Communications, 1568 Eustis Street, St. Paul, MN 55108. Phone: 651/645-9173 or 800/733-3413. Web site: www.seracomm.com

Long Night's Journey into Day: South Africa's Search for Truth and Reconciliation. Produced by Frances Reid and Deborah Hoffman. 94 min. 2000. A film that examines the short- and long-term impact of the Truth and Reconciliation Commission on the lives of victims and perpetrators of apartheid in South Africa. Also explores the meaning of healing, forgiveness, justice, and reconciliation. Available through Iris Films, 2600 10th Street, Berkeley, CA 94710. Phone: 510/845-5414. Web site: www. irisfilms.org

Making Peace: Facing Racism. Produced by Tom Weidlinger. 57 min. 1996. A session of a multiracial group in an Unlearning Racism workshop. The film illustrates the intensity and personal investment needed to face racism. Available from Films for the Humanities and Sciences, P.O. Box 2053, Princeton, NJ 08543-2053. Phone: 609/275-1400. Web site: www.films. com

Myth of Race. Produced by Damascus Road, a program of the Mennonite Central Committee. 19 min. 2002. This video traces the history of the social construct of race. Discussion guide included. Available through the Mennonite Central Committee (*see* Organizations).

Nobody's Born A Racist. Produced by Students Commission. 20 min. 1996. A Canadian film produced for youth by youth, this film features interviews and stories from young people on how racism has personally affected them. Includes study guide. Available through the Mennonite Central Committee (*see* Organizations).

Not in Our Town, I, II, III. Produced by California Working Group. 3 tapes, 30 min. each. 1995. The first video tells the story of how the residents of Billings, Montana, step up to hate violence in their community; the second two continue to tell the stories of other communities inspired by the Billings story to do the same. A viewing guide is included. Available through The Working Group, Not in Our Town videotapes, Box 10326, Oakland, CA 94610. Phone: 510/268-9675. Web site: www.notinourtown.org

People Like Us: Social Class in America. Produced and directed by Louis Alvarez and Andrew Kolker. 124 min. 2001. Through a variety of segments this video discusses the relationship between race and class in America. Available through CNAM Film Library, 22-D Hollywood Avenue, HoHoKus, NJ 07423. Phone: 800/343-5540.

A Place at the Table: Struggles for Equality in America. Produced by Teaching Tolerance. 40 min. 2000. Stories about racial identity told by young people. Available through Teaching Tolerance, a project of the Southern Poverty Law Center (*see* Organizations).

Racism Didn't End. . . . Produced by corVISION Media. 20 min. 1996. This documentary features eight American leaders of color and how racism impacts their lives. The video helps clarify the consequences of organizations doing business when institutional racism prevails. Available from Enterprise Media, 91 Harvey Street, Cambridge, MA 02104. Phone: 800/423-6021. Web site: www.enterprisemedia.com

Rights and Wrongs in America: Building Tolerance in America. Produced by Globalvision. 3 tapes, 78 min. 1995. A three-segment video production that investigates the roots of intolerance and the rise in hate crimes, racial violence, and attacks on civil rights in the United States today. Available from The Video Project, 5332 College Avenue, Oakland, CA 94618. Phone: 800/4-Planet. Web site: videoproject@igc.apc.org

The Shadow of Hate: A History of Intolerance in America. Produced by Teaching Tolerance. 40 min. 1995. This film documents the legacy of prejudice and intolerance in the United States. Available through Teaching Tolerance, a project of the Southern Poverty Law Center (*see* Organizations).

Stolen Ground. Produced and directed by Lee Mun Wah. 40 min. 1993. This documentary shows how racism has affected six Asian men and their healing responses. Available from Stir Fry Seminars and Consulting (*see* Organizations).

Troubling Behind. Produced and directed by Robbie Henson. 56 min. 1990. A film based in a Kentucky community featuring white residents and their explanation of why no black people live in the town. Addresses systemic racism and whites' denial. Order from California Newsreel, 149 Ninth Street, San Francisco, CA 94103. Phone: 415/621-6196.

Traces of the Trade. Produced and directed by Katrina Browne. Forthcoming, 2003. This documentary details the journey of an old New England family as they come to terms with the reality of their ancestors' participation in the Atlantic Slave Trade. The final film is in production but an insightful and useful short version is now available from KBrowne@ TracesoftheTrade.org

True Colors. Produced by ABC. 19 min. 1989. An episode from ABC's "Prime Time," hosted by Diane Sawyer, that follows two college men of different races in daily situations. Available through the Mennonite Central Committee (*see* Organizations).

Twilight: Los Angeles, 1992. Produced by Anna Deavere Smith. 90 min. 2001. A film adaptation of Smith's play that revisits the 1992 Los Angeles riots after the Rodney King trial. Events are seen through the perspective of various community members. Order through Hipster Entertainment, 18 Maplewood Avenue, Dobbs Ferry, NY 10522. Phone: 914/674-0842. E-mail: cfortis@twightlightlosangeles.com

Two Towns of Jasper. Produced and directed by Whitney Dow and Marco Williams. 87 min. 2002. A PBS film about the murder of a black man by three white men in Jasper, Texas. James Byrd, Jr. dragged to his death from the back of a truck. The film documents the aftermath of the murder by two different film crews, one black and one white. See the Web site: www.twotownsofjasper.com. Available from PBS Home Video. Web site: www.shop.pbs.org

Walking Each Other Home: The Color of Fear 2. Produced and directed by Lee Mun Wah. 55 min. 1998. This film is the sequel to *The Color of Fear* (see above). The film explores in greater depth the dialogue between eight men of different and ethnicities. Produced by Stir Fry Seminars and Consulting (*see* Organizations).

The Way Home. Produced and directed by Shakti Butler. 92 min. 1998. Stories of sixty-four women from eight different ethnic groups and cultural councils on the subject of racial oppression. Available through New Day Films, 22-D Hollywood Avenue, HoHoKus, New Jersey, 07423. Phone: 888/367-9154. Web site: www.newday.com

What Makes Me White? A film from Aimee Sands Productions about white racial identity. The final film is in development, but a shorter version is available from Aimee Sands Productions, 1 Paul Gore Terrace, Boston, MA 02130. Phone: 617/522-3294. E-mail: amsproductions@earthlink.net

White Shamans and Plastic Medicine Men. Produced by Native Voices Public Television. 26 min. 1995. This film is a critique of the appropriation of Native American culture and spirituality by white people who make a living from selling indigenous spiritual ritual and symbols. Available from Western States Center (*see* Organizations).

Work in Progress: The Web of Institutional Racism. Produced by Albuquerque Project Change. 60 min. 1996. A series of community leaders share their experience of institutional and individual racism. Available from Albuquerque Project Change, Box 25881, Albuquerque, NM 87125. Phone: 505/242-9536. Web site: www.projectchange.org

III. DENOMINATIONAL RESOURCES

The Anglican Church of Canada

Anglican Council of Indigenous Peoples (ACIP). This organization provides program and resources to indigenous persons and communities throughout the Anglican Communion. Web site: www.Anglican.ca/acip/

General contact information: 600 Jarvis Street, Toronto, Ontario, Canada M4Y 2J6. Phone: 416/924-9192. Web site: www.anglican.ca

Christian Church (Disciples of Christ)

Reconciliation Mission. Provides leadership for the Anti-Racism/Pro-Reconciliation Initiative of the Christian Church (Disciples of Christ). Provides some basic resources and training opportunities for the denomination. Web site: www.reconciliationmission.org

General contact information: 130 East Washington Street, Indianapolis, IN 46204-3645. Phone: 317/635-3100. Web site: www.disciples.org

Episcopal

House of Bishops Pastoral Letter on the Sin of Racism. March 1994. This document presents the social and pastoral teaching of the bishops of the Episcopal Church on racism, and presents the theological stance of the denomination on the subject. Available from the office of Social Justice Ministries. Web site: www.episcopalchurch.org/peace-justice/

Seeing the Face of God in Each Other: Anti-Racism and the Episcopal Church. This title includes a variety of resources for use with groups on the theme of antiracism. Included in the series is a comprehensive video on the theme of racism in the church, featuring a variety of persons discussing their experience of racism in the church. Also in the series is a video of case studies, a study guide for use with the videos, and a guide for holding an antiracism hearing/forum. Available from the office of Social Justice Ministries (see above).

Stop Hate: A Guide to Selected Anti-Hate Resources. This is a basic guide to anti-hate resources available from a variety of sources. Available through the office of Peace and Justice Ministries (see above).

The National Dialogues on Anti-Racism. New York: Episcopal Church Center, 1999. To be revised in 2003 under the title, *Seeing the Face of God in Each Other: A Manual for Anti-Racism Training and Action in the Episcopal Church.* This manual, designed for anti-racism trainers, presents a process based on five levels of awareness, as well as supplementary resources, handouts, and worship materials. Available from the office of Social Justice Ministries (see above).

General contact information: The Episcopal Church Center, 815 Second Avenue, New York, NY 10017. Phone: 212/716-6000 or 800/334-7626. Web site: www.episcopalchurch.org

Evangelical Lutheran Church in America (ELCA)

Even the Stones Will Cry Out For Justice. Chicago: Evangelical Lutheran Church in America, 1998. This resource is a bible study curriculum for adults on the themes of racism. The lesson plans are concise and adaptable to a variety of contexts and for denominations other than the ELCA. Available through the ELCA Distribution Service. Phone: 800/328-4648.

Freed in Christ: Race, Ethnicity and Culture: Social Teaching Statement Congregational Study Guide. Chicago: Evangelical Lutheran Church in America, 1993. This concise study guide is designed to assist church leaders to process the ELCA social teaching on racism within the context of congregations. Available through the ELCA Distribution Service (see above) or for download at the ELCA Division for Church in Society Web site at www.elca.org/dcs/diversit.html

Multicultural Mission Strategy: Congregational Study Guide. Chicago: Evangelical Lutheran Church in America, 1992. A pamphlet that details the biblical and theological foundations of a multicultural church, how to become a multicultural congregations, and, a process towards building a multicultural mission strategy. Available through the ELCA Distribution Service (see above) or may be read on the ELCA Commission for Multicultural Ministries Web site at www.elca.org/cmm/stragedy.html

General contact information: 8765 W. Higgins Rd., Chicago, IL 60631. Phone: 773/380-2700 or 800/638-3522. Web site: www.elca.org

Presbyterian Church (U.S.A.) (PCUSA)

Facing Racism: A Vision of the Beloved Community. This resource is the policy statement for the Presbyterian church. The theologically based statement presents a compelling case for the church's role in the eradication of racism, and is suitable in itself for use as a study document. Web site: horeb.pcusa.org/oga/racism/

Lee, Lonna Chang-Ren. *Facing Racism: In Search of the Beloved Community.* A Presbyterian Peacemaking Offering Packet and five-study session for youth, this resource provides detailed lesson plans and facilitator assistance. Web site: www.pcusa.org/marketplace

General contact information: 100 Witherspoon St., Louisville, KY 40202-1396. Phone: 800/872-3283. Web site: www.pcusa.org

Unitarian Universalist Association (UUA)

James, Jacqui, and Judith Frediani. *Weaving the Fabric of Diversity: An Anti-Bias Program for Adults.* Boston: Unitarian Universalist Association,

1996, this comprehensive curriculum offers complete lessons plans for adult learns on the subjects of ableism, racism, heterosexism, ageism, classism, and "becoming a more inclusive congregation." Handouts for each session, as well as process and worship notes are included. Web site: www.uua.org/bookstore

Journey Toward Wholeness Anti-Racism Program. This comprehensive anti-racism program provides a wealth of on-line and print resources, including study guides, training tools, evaluation instruments, articles, etc. Web site: www.uua.org/re/reach/justice/jtw.html

General contact information: 25 Beacon St., Boston, MA 02108. Phone: 617/742-2100. Web site: www.uua.org

United Church of Christ (UCC)

A New Church/A New World. A Racial Justice Resource of Justice and Witness Ministries, United Church of Christ. This basic denominational resource provides an overview on racism from the perspective of the faith community. Contact the Reverend Ben Guess; phone: 216/736-3704; e-mail: guessb@ucc.org

General contact information: 700 Prospect Ave., Cleveland, OH 44115. Phone: 216/736-2100. Web site: www.ucc.org

United Methodist Church (UMC)

Jenkins, Elaine. *Anti-Racism: Confronting the Sin.* An Anti-Racism Study/Action Guide from the General Commission on Religion and Race, General Board of Church and Society of The United Methodist Church. This basic resource provides an overview for congregational and community leaders on racism from the perspective of the faith community. The booklet provides questions for reflection as well as resource and video suggestions throughout. Two other related booklets in the series are *The Gift of Diversity,* by Eric Law and *Overcoming Racism's Economic Legacies,* by J. Philip Wogaman. Web site: www.gcrr.org/Resources

General contact information: Information Services UMC, P.O. Box 520, Nashville, TN 37702. Phone: 800/251-8140. Web site: www.umc.org

IV. WEB SITES AND RESOURCE GUIDES

AntiRacismNet. Provides assistance to antiracism organizations and contains information on antiracism from around the world. Maintained by Project Change (*see* Organizations). www.antiracismnet.org

Beyond Race and Class Bibliography. Edward W. Rodman, ed. Comprehensive annotated bibliography available through the Episcopal Divinity School, Cambridge, Mass. E-mail: erodman@episdivschool.edu

Beyond Racism: Embracing an Interdependent Future. A Web site of the Comparative Human Relations Initiative that offers information, research, resources, and links for people who want to learn how and why racism persists. www.beyondracism.org

Community Building Resource Exchange. A Web site managed by the Aspen Institute that provides links to a variety of organizations concerned with racism. www.Commbuild.org

Crosspoint Anti Racism/U.S.A. A Web resource with links to many organizations worldwide that focus on antiracism, antifascism, and human rights. www.magenta.nl/crosspoint/us.html

Denouncing Racism: A Resource Guide of Faith-Based Principles. New York: The National Conference for Community and Justice, n.d. This guide provides the text of the NCCJ's statement on racism, as well as texts and policy statements on racism from eight different faith groups, and a dozen Christian denominations. Available for download: www.nccj.org/faithbook.pdf

Dialogue to Action Initiative. A Web site that supports community dialogue and provides valuable lists of resources and training opportunities. www.thataway.org

Facing Racial and Cultural Conflict: Tools for Rebuilding Communities. A resource guide for resolving intergroup conflicts. Available through the National Civic League, PCPS Publications, 1319 F Street NW, Suite 204, Washington, DC 20004. Phone: 202/783-2961. E-mail: dcpcps@aol.com

Intergroup Relations in the United States—Programs and Organizations. New York: The National Conference for Community and Justice, n.d. An annotated directory of over 300 national and regional programs that focus on race and racism and related issues. Available through the National Conference for Community Justice. Web site: www.nccj.org

Justice and Peace Action Network. A grassroots advocacy network in the United Church of Christ that provides ideas related to advocacy and education for congregations, as well as legislative updates. www.ucc.org/justice/jpan.htm

Mennonite Central Committee. Offers a variety of videos and other resources on racism and multiculturalism to rent and purchase, many of which are faith-based and useful in a variety of contexts. 21 South 12th Street, Box 500, Akron, PA 17501-0500. Web site: www.mcc.org

Project Change. *Anti-Racism Resource Guide.* Oakland: Project Change, 2000. A comprehensive guide for antiracism resources. Available for download at www.projectchange.org/publications/guidetext.pdf

President's Initiative on Race. *Pathways to One America in the 21st Century: Promising Practices for Racial Reconciliation.* Washington, D.C.: Government Printing Office, January 1999. Government study on racial reconciliation.

RaceMatters.org. A Web site with a wealth of information on articles, resources, conferences, and other points of interest in regard to racism. www.racematters.org

Recovering Racists Network (RRN). Database of organizations that have antiracism, anti-hate, unity, nonviolence, or overcoming intolerance as the primary focus. Address: 670 W. Washington Ave., Kirkwood, MO 63122. Phone: 925/682-4959. Web site: www.rrnet.org

Schoene, L., and M. DuPraw. *Facing Racial and Cultural Conflict: Tools for Rebuilding Community.* Washington, D.C.: Program for Community Problem Solving, 1994. Resource guide for communities experiencing racial and cultural conflict.

Shapiro, Ilana. *Training for Racial Equity and Inclusion: A Guide to Selected Programs.* Washington, D.C.: The Aspen Institute, 2002. This recently published resource gives comprehensive information on ten different antiracism training programs, related organizations, as well guidelines for selecting an antiracism training program. The text identifies five "theories of practice": prejudice reduction, healing and reconciliation, antiracism, diversity/multiculturalism, and democracy building.

Signs of Hope—Promise of Change: In Celebration of the Inauguration, Churches Uniting in Christ, January 2002. Cincinnati: Forward Movement, 2002. Statements on racism from the various churches in Churches Uniting in Christ, as well as denominational resource lists.

Tolerance.org. A Web site of the Southern Poverty Law Center that provides resources for teachers, parents and young people interested in strategies to combat racism. www.tolerance.org

Viewing Race. A free resource guide comprised of information on seventy-four films that explore the topics of racism, diversity, and tolerance. From National Video Resources (NVR), 73 Spring Street, Suite 606, New York, NY 10012. Web site: www.nvr.org. The *Viewing Race* Web site contains articles and information on films about racism, as well as useful background information for those who may want to use these resources in training or programs. www.viewingrace.org

White Privilege.com. A Web site that features articles on how white privilege is connected to racism and prejudice, as well as additional notices and materials. www.Whiteprivilege.com

Williams, Loretta. *History of Racism and Resistance in the Americas: An Annotated Bibliography.* n.d. This hardcopy bibliography prepared for the

Consultation on Church Union (now Churches Uniting in Christ) highlights a variety of resources and media on racism and the history of race in America. Available from the Racial Justice Working Group, National Council of Churches, 475 Riverside Drive, Room 572, New York, NY 10115. Phone: 212/870-2298.

V. ORGANIZATIONS

Center for Democratic Renewal. Founded in 1979 as the National Anti-Klan Network, this multiracial organization advances the vision of a just society free of racism and bigotry. It helps communities eliminate groups, movements, and government practices that promote hatred and bigotry. P.O. Box 50469, Atlanta, GA 30302. Phone: 404/221-0025. Web site: www.thecdr.org

Center for the Study of White American Culture. This center supports cultural exploration and self-discovery among white Americans, and encourages dialogue among all racial and cultural groups. It provides publications, conferences, and library resources. 245 West 4th Avenue, Roselle, NJ 07203. Phone: 908/241-5439. Web site: www.euroamerican.org

Center for Third World Organizing. Provides training and resources for collective action in communities of color across the country by training organizers, sponsoring an activist apprenticeship program, establishing model multiracial community organizations, and building active organizations with activists of color. 1218 E 21St St., Oakland, CA 94606. Phone: 510/533-7583. Web site: www.ctwo.org

Challenging White Supremacy Institute. The Institute provides several workshops with the goal to create social change by building mass-based, multiracial grassroots movements led by radical activists of color. The workshops offered include: "Anti-Racism for Global Justice," "Becoming an Anti-Racist Activist," and "Becoming An Anti-Racist Organizer." 2440 16th Street, PMB #275, San Francisco, CA 94103. Phone: 415/647-0921. Web site: www.cwsworkshop.org

Changework. This organization is a group of trainers, organizers, and educators working to strengthen the organizational capacity of grassroots groups. 3948 South Third Street, Jacksonville Beach, FL 32250. Phone: 904/241-0488. Web site: www.changework.net

The Christian Council of Metropolitan Atlanta. This organization has worked to bring diverse communities of faith together since 1879. They provide training, a congregational exchange initiative, and provide links between diverse congregations and communities of faith. 465 Boulevard,

S.E., Suite 101, Atlanta, GA 30312. Phone: 404/622-2235. Web site: www.christiancouncil.org

Churches Uniting in Christ (CUIC). A relationship among nine denomina-tions that have pledged to live more closely in expressing their unity in Christ and in combating racism together. Provides publications, including, "Appeal to the Churches to Seek God's Beloved Community." 700 Prospect Avenue, Cleveland, OH 44115. Phone: 216/736-3294. Web site: www.eden.edu/cuic/cuic.htm

Congress of National Black Churches. An ecumenical coalition of eight his-torically black denominations. The organization provides services in theo-logical education and leadership development, community development, child and family development, and health and wholeness. 1225 I Street NW, Suite 750, Washington, DC 20005. Phone: 202/371-1091. Web site: www.cnbc.org

Community Change, Inc. An organization committed to serving as a center for action and collaboration among individuals and multiracial groups to achieve racial justice and equity. Provides an extensive resource library and events information. 14 Beacon Street, Room 605, Boston, MA 02108. Phone: 617/523-0555. Web site: www.communitychangeinc.org

The Community Renewal Society. Assists groups of clergy, seminarians, and other community workers with understanding issues relevant to urban life in order to strengthen ministry programs. 332 South Michigan Avenue, Suite 500, Chicago, IL 60604. Phone: 312/427-6130. Web site: www.crs-ucc.org

Crossroads Ministry. The mission of this organization is to dismantle sys-temic racism and build multicultural diversity within institutions and com-munities. This mission is accomplished primarily by training institutional transformation teams. 425 South Central Park Avenue, Chicago, IL 60624; also, 600 21st Street, Racine, WI 53403. Phone: 773/638-0166 (Chicago). Web site: www.crossroadsministry.org

Cultural Boundaries Conversation Group. An Alban Institute–sponsored group of pastors, seminary faculty, and others concerned with developing leaders who can effectively negotiate cultural boundaries. Specific pro-grams focused on leadership development in this area are in the planning stages. The Alban Institute, 7315 Wisconsin Avenue, Suite 1250 West, Bethesda, MD 20814-3211. Consultant contact: Jacqueline J. Lewis (e-mail: jlewis@alban.org). Web site: www.alban.org

Denver Area Anti-Racism and Reconciliation Team. A local team of antiracism advocates and facilitators committed to dismantling racism in the Denver area and beyond. Provides events, workshops, and other resources. Presbytery of Denver, 1710 South Grant Street, Denver, CO

80201. Phone: 303/777-2453. Contact: J5Barrett@aol.com. Web site: www.denpres.org

Damascus Road Anti-Racism Process. The Damascus Road training process is designed to equip participants with the theological, educational, and organizational antiracism skills they need to begin the process of transformation in their own institutions. Antiracism educating and organizing training, and introductory workshops provided. Mennonite Central Committee, 21 South 12th Street, P.O. Box 500 Akron, PA 17501. Phone: 717/859-1151. Web site: www.mcc.org

Dismantling Racism Institute. A key training program of this regional office of the National Conference for Community and Justice, the organization also provides an "Inclusive Community" workshop, and a specific dismantling racism institute for educators. National Conference for Community and Justice, 721 Olive Street, Suite 915, St. Louis, MO 63101. Phone: 314/241-5103. Web site: www.nccj.org

Episcopal Divinity School. An Episcopal seminary with students from a variety of denominational background, EDS provides educational opportunities for students and ministers in the vicinity on antiracism, including an annual class for academic credit. 99 Brattle Street, Cambridge, MA 02138. Phone: 617/868-3450. Web site: www.episdivschool.edu. Contact: Sheryl Kujawa-Holbrook, skujawa@episdivschool.edu; or Edward W. Rodman, erodman@episdivschool.edu

Facing History and Ourselves. A national education organization whose mission is to engage students of diverse backgrounds in an examination of race, prejudice, and anti-Semitism. Provides workshops and publications. 16 Hurd Road, Brookline, MA 02445. Phone: 617/232-0281. Web site: www.facinghistory.org

Fisk University Race Relations Institute. The Institute is committed to heighten the awareness among all people about the divisive and insidious nature of racism. Provides roundtable discussions, critical dialogues, and publications. 1000 17th Avenue, North, Nashville, TN 37208. Phone: 615/329-8578. Web site: www.fisk.edu

Fresh Ministries. Seeks to bring into relationship groups that have been typically separated by barriers of age, gender, economics and especially race. Offers a congregational exchange program, preaching ministry, study circles, and consult with pastors. 1131 North Laura Street, Jacksonville, FL 32206. Phone: 904/355-0000. Web site: www.freshministries.org

The Greenlining Institute. Empowers communities of color and other disadvantaged groups through multiethnic economic and leadership development, civil rights, and anti-redlining activities. Sponsors a multicultural leadership training program in low-income advocacy and community economic development. 785 Market Street, Suite 300, San Francisco, CA 94103. Phone: 415/284-7200. Web site: www.greenlining.org

Healing the Heart of Diversity. A professional leadership development program and change process that fosters a deeper understanding of diversity issues for professions. Offers retreats for professional leaders engaged in organizational, social, and cultural change. 712 Staunton Avenue, NW, Roanoke, VA 24016. Phone: 540/343-5192. Web site: www.healingtheheart.org

Highlander Research and Education Center. Works with grassroots leaders on variety of social concerns, including racial, gender, and sexual discrimination. Also provides programs for youth and children, and a grassroots think tank for progressive southerners. 1959 Highlander Highway, New Market, TN 37820. Phone: 423/933-3443. Web site: www.hrec.org

Hope in the Cities. Connects communities through honest conversations on race, reconciliation, and responsibility. Provides consultation services, publications, and videos. 1103 Sunset Avenue, Richmond, VA. Phone: 804/358-1764. Web site: www.hopeinthecities.org

The Institute for Global Leadership. Their Reconciliation Leadership Program provides consultation, training, and mentoring services to develop and support leaders who facilitate, mediate, and reconcile highly stressful situations. P.O. Box 20044, Worcester, MA 01609. Phone: 508/753-1004. Web site: www.global-leader.org

Interfaith Action for Racial Justice, Inc. A coalition of roughly 110 organizations in the Baltimore area based on the idea of racial reconciliation. Sponsors community dialogues and a youth initiative. 325 East 25th St. Baltimore, MD 21218-5303. Phone: 410/889-8333. Web site: www.iarj.org

Law, Eric H. F., Consulting. Dr. Law consults with The Kaleidoscope Project does workshops, training, and consulting for Episcopal, United Methodist, Roman Catholic, Lutheran, and Presbyterian churches. 35A Sandpiper, Palm Desert, CA 92260. Phone: 760/837-0468. E-mail: ehflaw@aol.com

Leadership Conference on Civil Rights. A progressive coalition of over 180 national organizations for equal opportunity and justice. Their Civilrights.org Web site posts numerous program opportunities and publications in addition to an action center, a research center, and a career center. 1629 K Street, NW, 10th Floor, Washington, DC 20006. Phone: 202/466-3311. Web site: www.civilrights.org

Leadership Development in Interethnic Relations Program. Equips people with the skills and background to address race relations in their own communities effectively. The program consists of three major elements: adult training, alumni activity, and youth training. 1145 Wilshire Blvd. 2nd level, Los Angeles, CA 90017. Phone: 213/977-7500.

The Lutheran Human Relations Association. Provides educational resources and events related to justice, peacemaking, racism, and multicultural issues. 5233 N. 51st Blvd., Milwaukee, WI 53218. Phone: 414/536-0585. Web site: www.lhra.org

Multicultural Center of NW Arkansas. Provides programs, services, and outreach within the community. 614 East Emma, 231 Box 22, Springdale, AR 72765; and PO Box 778, Rogers, AR 72765. Phone: 501/927-1111.

Multicultural Collaborative. Provides a variety of programs, trainings, a newsletter, and other publications. Founded after the 1992 civil unrest in Los Angeles, the organization promotes the elimination of intergroup strife, violence, and bias through collaborative action. 1010 S. Flower Street, #304, Los Angeles, CA 90015. Phone: 213/748-2105. E-mail: grancirco@aol.com

The National Immigration Forum (NIF). Founded to embrace and uphold America's tradition as a nation of immigrants. Provides a strategic communications training for refugee leaders and advocates. 200 I Street NE, Suite 220, Washington, DC 20002-4362. Phone: 203/544-0004. Web site: www.immigrationforum.org

National Coalition Building Institute. An international training organization that provides a variety of training conferences and seminars designed to teach the range of skills that are necessary for providing leadership to end discrimination, reduce intergroup conflict, and build multigroup coalitions. Included are a one-day prejudice reduction workshop, a five-day leadership training institute, and a three-day train-the-trainer seminar. 1835 K Street NW, Suite 715, Washington, DC 20006. Phone: 202/785-9400. Web site: www.ncbi.org

National Conference for Community and Justice (NCCJ). A human-relations organization dedicated to fighting bias, bigotry, and racism. NCCJ has many chapters and programs nationwide, as well as publications and other resources. 475 Park Avenue South, 19th Floor, New York, NY 10016. Phone: 212/545-1300. Web site: www.nccj.org

National Council of Churches Racial Justice Working Group. Supports fifty projects within denominations and in community-based organizations in areas such as racist violence, prison industrial complex, police brutality, self-determination, antiracism education and training, and resource coordination and development. 475 Riverside Drive, Suite 880, New York, NY 10115. Phone: 212/870-2298. Web site: www.ncccusa.org

National Council of LaRaza. Organized to reduce poverty and discrimination, and improve life opportunities for Hispanic people. Provides capacity-building experience, applied research, media activities, and international projects. 1111 19th St. NW, Suite 1000, Washington, DC 20036. Phone: 202/785-1670. Web site: www.nclr.org

National Multicultural Institute. With a focus on "leading with diversity," this organization provides training and consulting, conferences, executive coaching, assessment, publications, and special projects. 3000 Connecticut Ave. NW, Suite 438, Washington, DC 20008-2556. Phone: 202/483-0700. Web site: www.nmci.org

The National Network of Anti-Racism Community Organizing Institutes. A collaboration of four regional social justice groups to address institutional racism and intercultural tensions in the United States. Provides information and resources, including "A Community Builders Tool Kit," that can be downloaded for use. The tool kit includes fifteen tools for creating healthy, productive, interracial/multicultural communities. Institute for Democratic Renewal, McManus 225, 170 East 10th St., Claremont Graduate University, Claremont, CA 91711. Phone: 909/607-9220. Contact: John Maguire; e-mail: john.Maguire@cgu.edu. Also, Project Change, 678 13th Street, Oakland, CA 94612. Phone: 510/663-0148. E-mail: sstrong@projectchange.org

The People's Institute for Survival and Beyond. A cooperative training institute that provides not only community organizing skills, but analysis, principles, and values that make these skills useful. The flagship program is the "Un-doing Racism Workshop." In addition, the Institute offers a variety of services and trainings to diverse communities. 7166 Crowder Blvd., New Orleans, LA 70127. Phone: 504/944-2354. Web site: www.thepeoplesinstitute.org

Poverty and Race Research Action Council. Links social science research to advocacy work to address the intersection of race and poverty. Provides newsletters and publications. 3000 Connecticut Avenue NW, Suite 200, Washington, DC 20008. Phone: 202/387-9887. Web site: www.prrac.org

The Prejudice Institute. A resource for activists, lawyers, and social scientists, the Institute is devoted to research and education on all dimensions of prejudice, discrimination, and ethnoviolence. Provides fact sheets on the Web site, a newsletter, publications, speakers, and internships. Center for Applied Study of Ethnoviolence, 2743 Maryland Avenue, Baltimore, MD 21218. Phone: 410/366-9654. Web site: www.prejudiceinstitute.org

Project Change. Works to strengthen the antiracism infrastructure and networks through technical assistance training, networking, publications, and online resources. Sites in Albuquerque, El Paso, Knoxville, and Valdosta, Georgia. P.O. Box 29919, San Francisco, CA 94129. Phone: 415/561-4880. E-mail: antiracism@projectchange.org. Web site: www.projectchange.org

Reconciliation Studies. Bethel College and Seminary is developing an academic minor in reconciliation studies. Bethel College & Seminary, 3900

Bethel Drive, St. Paul, MN 55112-6999. Phone: 651/638-6400. Web site: www.bethel.edu

Seeking Educational Equity & Diversity [S.E.E.D.]. An inclusive curriculum project that offers seminars and issue papers. Wellesley College Center for Research on Women, Wellesley, MA 02481. Phone: 973/763-6378. Web site: www.wcwonline.org/seed

Social Justice Ministries Office, Anti-Racism Training, Episcopal Church Center. A denominational office that provides a broad network of antiracism trainers, sponsors training conferences (as well as train-the-trainers events), publishes resources, and produces video resources. 815 Second Avenue, New York, NY 10017. Phone: 800/334-7626. Contact: Jayne J. Oasin; e-mail: joasin@episcopalchurch.org. Web site: www.episcopalchurch.org/peace-justice/antiracism.asp

Southern Poverty Law Center. An organization that combats hate, intolerance, and discrimination through education and litigation. Sponsors a number of print and video resources on racial justice for use with children, youth, and adults through the "Teaching Tolerance" project as well as online resources through their Web site, www.Tolerance.org. 400 Washington Avenue, Montgomery, AL 36104. Phone: 344/956-8200. Web site: www.splcenter.org

Southwest Organizing Project. A statewide multiracial, multi-issue, community-based organization that provides organizing training and promotes the exchange of ideas. 211 10th Street SW, Albuquerque, NM 87102. Phone: 505/247-8832. Web site: www.swop.net

Stir Fry Seminars & Consulting. An organization of multicultural trainers and facilitators available to work with corporations, agencies, educational institutions, and other organizations. The organization offers a range of antiracism and multicultural workshops and training events, and also produces superb video resources. 3345 Grand Avenue, Suite 3, Oakland, CA 94610. Phone: 510/419-3930. Web site: www.stirfryseminars.com

Study Circles Research Center. An organization dedicated to finding ways for all kinds of people to engage in dialogue and problem solving on critical issues. Sponsors community dialogues, youth dialogues, school dialogues, etc. The Studies Circles method and publications are also used in congregations. Of particular importance is the five-session study guide, "Facing the Challenges of Race and Race Relations." P.O. Box 203, Pomfret, CT 06258. Phone: 860/928-2626. Web site: www.studycircles.org

Tools for Diversity, Technical Assistance for Community Services. Dedicated to providing affordable trainings that address timely issues for nonprofit leaders; also included are workshops, on-site technology trainings, and customized training. 1903 SE Ankeny, Portland, OR 97214. Phone: 503/239-4001. Web site: www.tacs.org

Tools for Tolerance for Professionals/Simon Wiesenthal Center. Through interactive workshops, exhibits, and videos, participants in the day-long workshops explore the issues of prejudice, diversity, tolerance, and cooperation. The New York Tolerance Center is scheduled to open in May 2003. 9760 West Pico Blvd., Los Angeles, CA 90035. Phone: 310/772-7611. Web site: www.wiesenthal.com

VISIONS, Inc.—Vigorous Interventions Into Ongoing Natural Settings. An organization committed to the belief that a multicultural environment can be created by understanding and eliminating racism, sexism, ageism, classism, heterosexism, anti-Semitism, adultism, ableism, violence, and other forms of oppression. Offers a four-day "Changing Racism" workshop, consultative services, and customized services. 17 Spring Valley, Arlington, MA 02476. Phone: 781/642-2291. Web site: www.VISIONS-inc.com

Western States Center. The organization sponsors the RACE (Research and Action for Change and Equity) program that developed a "Dismantling Racism" project, which offers workshops and resources geared to individuals and organizations. In addition to training, the project offers assistance through caucus development, organizational assessment, and strategic planning. P.O. Box 40305, Portland, OR 97240. Phone: 503/228-8866. Web site: www.westernstatescenter.org

White People Working On Racism. Training for Change, an organization that is committed to justice, peace, and environmental harmony sponsors this multiracial improvisational theatre troupe, "Whites Confronting Racism" workshops (beginning, intermediate, and advanced), and training for social-action trainers. Training for Change, 1501 Cherry Street, Philadelphia, PA 19102. Phone: 215/241-7035. Web site: www.TrainingForChange.org

Woodrick Institute for the Study of Racism and Diversity. This Institute at Aquinas College, an undergraduate institution, provides a two-day institute for "Healing Racism," allies luncheons, and an "Addressing Race in the Workplace" workshop for any interested participant. Aquinas College, 1607 Robinson Road SE, Grand Rapids, MI 49506. Phone: 616/457-8281, ext. 4424. Web site: www.woodrickinstitute.org

World Of Difference Institute. This Institute, sponsored by the Anti-Defamation League, is designed for groups of people who share a community and desire to explore diversity, improve intergroup relations, recognize bias, and dismantle racism, anti-Semitism, and all forms of prejudice and bigotry. Anti-Defamation League, 823 United National Plaza, New York, NY 10017. Phone: 212/885-7700. Web site: www.adl.org

Notes

INTRODUCTION

1. Translation by Dr. Angela Bauer of the Episcopal Divinity School.

2. For a synopsis of recent studies, see John Dart, "Hues in the Pews: Racially Mixed Churches an Illusive Goal," *Christian Century,* February 28, 2001, 6–8.

3. William Stringfellow, *An Ethic for Christians and Other Aliens in a Strange Land* (Waco, Tex.: Word Books, 1973), 138.

4. "Race as a Target Variable," VISIONS, inc., Arlington, Massachusetts, n.d.

5. The term "gospel eyes" was, to my knowledge, first used by the Rt. Rev. Mark L. MacDonald, bishop of the Episcopal diocese of Alaska.

6. Toni Morrison, Commencement Address, Duke University, Durham, North Carolina, 1992.

7. Martin Luther King Jr., "Letter from Birmingham City Jail" (1963), in *My Soul Looks Back, 'Less I Forget: A Collection of Quotations by People of Color,* ed. Dorothy Wimbush Riley (New York: HarperCollins, 1991), 213.

8. Jung Young Lee, *Marginality: The Key to Multicultural Theology* (Minneapolis: Fortress Press, 1995), 7.

9. Quoted in Sheryl A. Kujawa, *Resource Book for Ministries with Youth and Young Adults in the Episcopal Church* (New York: Episcopal Church Center, 1995), 155.

10. Mary Elizabeth Hobgood, *Dismantling Privilege: An Ethics of Accountability* (Cleveland: Pilgrim Press, 2000), 36.

11. Peggy McIntosh, "White Privilege: Unpacking the Invisible Knapsack," *Independent School* (Winter 1990): 31–36.

12. bell hooks, *Killing Rage: Ending Racism* (New York: Henry Holt, 1995), 5–6.

13. For example, see Elaine Pinderhughes, *Understanding Race, Ethnicity and Power: The Key to Efficacy in Clinical Practice* (New York: Free Press, 1990).

14. These definitions have been developed from a variety of sources and over years of experience in teaching and training in antiracism; see *The National Dialogues on Anti-Racism: Expanded Version* (New York: Episcopal Church Center, 1999), 17–20; see also Valerie Batts, "Modern Racism: New Melody for the Same Old Tunes," *Episcopal Divinity School Occasional Papers* (1968): 6–12.

15. The criteria for cultural competence listed here are adapted from *The National Dialogues on Anti-Racism,* 127; Appendix.

16. For instance, see Mikel Hogan-Garcia, *The Four Skills of Cultural Diversity Competence: A Process for Understanding and Practice* (Pacific Grove, Calif.: Brooks/Cole, 2003).

17. Beverly Daniel Tatum, "Talking About Race, Learning About Racism: The Application of Racial Identity Development Theory in the Classroom," in *Facing Racism in Education,* ed. Tamara Beauboef-Lafontant and D. Smith Augustine (Cambridge, Mass.: Harvard Educational Review Reprint Series, 1996), 321–22.

18. These statistics are derived from Southern Poverty Law Center, "Ten Ways to Fight Hate," and "Population Profile of the United States: 2000" (Internet Release), U.S. Census Bureau.

19. Donald M. Chinula, *Building King's Beloved Community: Foundations for Pastoral Care and Counseling with the Oppressed* (Cleveland: United Church Press, 1997), 43.

20. Various developmental schema that correlate with stages of building multiracial community include Bailey W. Jackson and Evangelina Holvino, "Developing Multicultural Organizations," reprinted with permission from the authors, Brattleboro, Vermont, March 21, 1994; Norman Anthony Peart and John Perkins, *Separate No More: Understanding and Developing Racial Reconciliation in Your Church* (Grand Rapids: Baker Books, 2000). In addition, Crossroads Ministry has developed a six-stage "Continuum On Becoming An Anti-racist Multicultural Church," from the work of Jackson, Rita Hardiman, and it was further developed by Andrea Avazian and Ronice Branding.

21. Fumitaka Matsuoka, *The Color of Faith: Building Community in a Multiracial Society* (Cleveland: United Church Press, 1998), 104.

CHAPTER 1: ST. MATTHEW'S AND ST. PAUL'S
DELRAY BEACH, FLORIDA

1. Desmond Mpilo Tutu, *No Future Without Forgiveness* (New York: Random House, 1999), 196–97.

NOTES   **235**

2. William H. Stokes, Untitled Sermon, First Sunday of Lent, March 4, 2001.

3. Unless otherwise noted, quotations are from interviews conducted in January and August 2002 with William Stokes, Janet Aguhob, Tim Kilpatrick, Mary McCarty, Jeff Perlman, Rosalind Murray, Douglas Williams, Edie Quinn, Mike Brennan, Edward W. White, Jacqueline J. Lewis, Connie Impert, Sherry Fleming, Bonnie Davis, Keith Johnson, Mary Beth Wells, Chris Herin, Janet Davis, and Bob Chapin.

4. See Linda Reeves, "A Delray Teen's Interest in the Church Sparks a Growing After School Program," *Sun-Sentinel Community News,* Delray Beach Section, March 16, 2001, 6.

5. Planning and Zoning Department, Delray Beach, Florida; Housing Data, CACI Market Systems.

6. Leon Fooksman, "Crossing the Lines: Local Leaders Have Been Meeting in Discussions Intended to Bring Political Allies and Rivals Racism," *Sun-Sentinel Community News,* Delray Beach Section, June 19, 2000, 1–2.

7. Those who participated in the community dialogue along with members of St. Matthew's and St. Paul's included Palm Beach county commissioner Mary McCarty, executive director of MAD DADS of Delray Beach Charles Ridley, city commissioner Jeff Perlman, and the executive director of the Community Redevelopment Agency. William H. Stokes served as moderator.

8. Fooksman, "Crossing the Line."

9. Ibid.

10. *The National Dialogues on Anti-Racism* (New York: Episcopal Church Center, 1999; revised 2003).

11. Ibid.

12. *For Tomorrow's Harvest: St Paul's Episcopal Church in the Year 2006 Strategic Plan* (Boca Raton: Center for Strategic Planning, 2001).

13. See Elizabeth Clarke, "Blessed Are the Tolerant as Churches Share Staff," *The Palm Beach Post,* Accent Section, December 1, 2001, 1D, 6D.

14. Ibid.

15. William H. Stokes, "Proposal to Create a Team Ministry for St. Matthew's and St. Paul's Churches in Delray Beach, Florida"; also Mary W. Cox, "Clergy Team Helps Delray Parishes Bridge 'Racial Fault Line,'" *The Net* [Diocese of Southeast Florida], August 2001.

16. D. Aileen Dodd, "A Sanctuary of Many Voices," *Miami Herald,* Focus Section, May 20, 2001, 2L; also Clarke, "Blessed Are the Tolerant."

17. "Agreement between St. Matthew's and St. Paul's Churches in Delray Beach, Florida, to Create a Team Ministry."

18. Stokes, "Proposal to Create a Team Ministry."

19. See Clarke, "Blessed Are the Tolerant."

CHAPTER 2: QUINCY FIRST PRESBYTERIAN CHURCH
QUINCY, WASHINGTON

1. Virgilio Elizondo, *The Future Is Mestizo: Life Where Cultures Meet*, revised edition (Boulder: University of Colorado Press, 2000), 123. Both the terms "Hispanic" and "Latino/a" are used throughout this book, depending on the self-description of the people. Though in some contexts the terms are used interchangeably, they do convey different notions of identity. The term "Hispanic," derived from the Latin word *Hispania* is used to describe people who trace their origins to Spain and the Spanish-speaking countries of Latin America. "Hispanic" is also the term used by the U.S. Census Bureau. The term "Latino" includes also those whose ancestry is America Indian, African or Asian, as well as other Western speakers of Latin-derived languages, such as Brazilians and Haitians. Neither term represents a racial category; Hispanic and/or Latinos/as are members of all other racial groups. Though the Spanish language is the common cultural element shared by all Hispanic and/or Latino/a groups, not all people who are Hispanic or Latino/a speak it. Some speak English, Portuguese, or other Latin-derived languages. For further information, see *Facts about Americanos: Latino Life in the United States* (The Time Education Program, 1999); also, "The New Latinos: Why They Are, Where They Are," Lewis Mumford Center for Comparative Urban and Regional Research, September 2002.

2. Unless otherwise noted, all quotations from members of Quincy First Presbyterian Church are from interviews conducted in March, July, and October 2002 with Lynn Rowse, Mary Ybarra-Vega, Isabel Saldana, Lynn Snyder, Sally Curran, Roxa Kreimeyer, Candy Bennett-Houston, Mike Blakely, Jackie Flinn, Judy Bryant, Teri Wilson, Diana Santiago, W. Mark Koenig, Bill and Sylvia Wurl, Ellen Mead, Pat and Lea Patterson, and Marv Hinz.

3. Elizondo, *The Future is Mestizo*, xv.

4. Statistics for the state of Washington, Grant County, and Quincy, come from a variety of sources: *Quincy Washington Resource Guide*; Presbyterian Church Locator; Neighborhood Demographics Report Request, 2001; Grant County Health District; and the U.S. Census Bureau.

5. Becky Thompson, *A Promise and a Way of Life: White Antiracist Activism* (Minneapolis: University of Minnesota Press, 2001); Ruben Martinez, *Crossing Over: A Mexican Family on the Migrant Trail* (New York: Picador, 2001).

6. Ann Hinz, "Preaching as Weeping, Confession, and Resistance: Using Christine Smith's Metaphor of Preaching to Confront Issues of Individual and

Systemic White Racism Towards Spanish-Speaking People in a Local Congregation," (D.Min. thesis, San Francisco Theological Seminary, 2000), 6.

7. Ibid., 3, 8–9.

8. Ibid., 6–7.

9. For a related article, see Sheryl A. Kujawa, "Social Action Projects: A More Excellent Way," in *Resource Book for Ministries with Youth and Young Adults in the Episcopal Church* (New York: Episcopal Church Center, 1995), 264–65.

10. See also John D. Filiatreau, "Who, Me? Prejudiced? Presbyterians Are Committing Themselves to Rooting Out Racism," *Presbyterians Today,* September 2000.

11. For information on Crossroads Ministry and the consultation and training services offered, contact them at 425 S. Central Park Avenue, Chicago, IL 60624 (phone: 773/638-0166); or at 600 21st Street, Racine, WI 53403 (phone: 262/635-9737). The interfaith and community-based antiracism training organization offers new models to dismantle racism and build antiracist multicultural diversity in institutions and communities. The author wishes to express her thanks to Chuck Ruehle of Crossroads, who provided information on the organization.

12. Joseph Barndt, *Dismantling Racism: The Continuing Challenge to White America* (Minneapolis: Augsburg, 1991), 6–7.

13. Information from Crossroads Ministry.

14. Joseph Barndt and Charles Ruehle, "Rediscovering a Heritage Lost: A European-American Anti-Racist Identity," *Sojourners* (September 1995): 73–77.

15. Hinz, "Preaching as Weeping, Confession, and Resistance," part 3.

16. Barndt, *Dismantling Racism*, 160.

17. Ibid.

18. Update from Ann Hinz, "Letter to the Congregation," September 2002.

19. Ibid.

CHAPTER 3: CROSS LUTHERAN CHURCH
MILWAUKEE, WISCONSIN

1. *This Far By Faith: An African American Resource for Worship* (Minneapolis: Augsburg Fortress, 1999), Introduction.

2. Bob Helbig, "Blaze Guts Center of North Side Strength," *Milwaukee Journal,* February 5, 1995, 1.

3. *This Far by Faith*, Introduction.

4. Unless otherwise noted, quotations are from interviews conducted in May and September 2002 with Lois Glover, Ever Porter, Lula Williams, Jovanna Miller, Lisa Jacobsen, Kaylynn Blackwell, Gloria Wright, Betty Marx, Wayne Porter, Joseph W. Ellwanger, Khamphanh Bouakongxaya, Buonheua Bouakongxaya, Mary Steppe, Sammie Miller, Teri Woodley, Rick Cesar, Bradley Hauser, Lisa Quam, Ann Hogan, Fred Moss, Marty Schneider, Carolyn Jackson, Patsy Coleman, Katherine Wilcher, Guy Davis, Denise Davis, Johnson Hunter, Judi Hunter, Paulette Barr, Reynolds Honold, and Frances Bryant.

5. Statistics from the Evangelical Lutheran Church in America, 2001.

6. Eileen McClelland, "Sisterly Love: Lutheran Church Bridges Geographic Gap On Concert Tour," *Naples Daily News,* August 5, 1998; *www.naplesnews.com.*

7. Elizabeth Hunter, "Sisters By Choice," *The Lutheran* (October 2000): 2–3.

8. Hunter, "Sisters By Choice," 1.

9. Ibid., 2.

10. *City Vessel: An Outpouring of Ministries and Events of The Milwaukee Outreach Training Network* (Spring & Summer, 2002): 9.

11. "Resolution on Ministry to Gays and Lesbians," from the Northern Lakeshore Cluster, Greater Milwaukee Synod, ELCA; see also Sonia C. Solomonson, "ELCA Church Council Discusses Homosexuality," *The Lutheran* (September 2000).

12. McClelland, "Sisterly Love," 2.

13. Contact information on Crossroads Ministry can be found in chapter 2, n. 11, and in the Annotated Bibliography and Resource List in this book.

14. See *City Vessel.*

15. ELCA, "Building a Multicultural Church: Recommitment to a Strategy for Proclamation of the Gospel," *Multicultural Mission Strategy,* *www.elca.org.*

16. Elizabeth Hunter, "Seeing Our Racism," *The Lutheran* (February 2000): 15.

17. Ibid.

18. Ibid., 12–13.

19. ELCA, "Building a Multicultural Church."

CHAPTER 4: DELHAVEN CHRISTIAN CHURCH
LA PUENTE, CALIFORNIA

1. William Sloane Coffin, *The Heart Is a Little to the Left: Essays on Public Morality* (Hanover, N.H.: Dartmouth University Press, 1999), 60–70.

2. Unless otherwise noted, quotations are from interviews conducted in

December 2001 and in April and September 2002 with Marie Morgan, Roberta Harrison, Maurice Powell, Hank Smith, Kimberlie Manager, Richard Cantu, Pete Aranda, Shirley Aranda, Christine Cantu, Renee Cantu, Alice Peace, Bert DeYoung, Richard K. Miller, Roy Bullock, Gwen Gutierrez, Betty Franklin, Gayle Schoepf, Glenn Johnson, Art DeBry, Mark Carlock, Dierdre Carlock, Matthew Carlock, Britany Carlock, Gabrielle McClure, Dave Genung, Bob Cantrell, Doug Smith, Kate Moyer, Otis Landers, Mittie Hanson, Tom Nevarez, Kathy Cantu, and Mavis Davenport.

3. Charlotte D. Harris, presentation at Delhaven Christian Church, April 2002.

4. Marcus Borg, *Meeting Jesus Again for the First Time* (San Francisco: HarperSanFrancisco, 1995), 55–56.

5. Definition of "mulligan stew" from Dick Miller and *Random House Webster's College Dictionary,* 1992.

6. Dan B. Genung, *A Street Called Love: The Story of All Peoples Church and Center, Los Angeles, California* (Pasadena: Hope Publishing House, 2002), 4.

7. Genung, *A Street Called Love,* 5.

8. The history of Delhaven Christian Church was provided Gwen Guiterrez, Ray Walker, Helen Walker, Ollie Galloway, LouSeel Galloway, John Crist, Sam Steverson, Sam Steverson, Jr., Mildred Tolliver. See also, "Brief History of Delhaven Christian Church."

9. See "Journey Toward Becoming an Open and Affirming Congregation," Delhaven Christian Church.

10. Congregational history group in n. 8.

11. Edward Markham poem quoted by Richard K. Miller.

12. The Center for Progressive Christianity, "Statement of Purpose." See also Fred Plumer, "Study Guide for the Eight Points by Which We Define Progressive Christianity" (Cambridge: Center for Progressive Christianity, n.d.). Contact: The Center for Progressive Christianity, 99 Brattle Street, Cambridge, MA 02138 (phone: 617/441-0928), *www.tcpc.org.*

13. Plumer, "Study Guide," 9-10.

14. Ibid.

15. Anissa Vincente-Rivera, "Local Church Receives 'Disciple' Award: Group Cited for Inclusive Stance," *La Puente Highlander,* February 8, 2001, 1, 6.

16. Deirdre Carlock, "It (I Get It)," March 17, 2002.

17. Richard K. Miller, Sermon Notes, November 8, 2002.

18. Christian Church (Disciples of Christ), "Reconciliation Mission," *www.disciples.org*; see also "Initial Annual Report," Christian Church (Disciples of Christ), Pacific Southwest Region, Anti-Racism/Pro-Reconciliation Committee.

19. Charlotte D. Harris, presentation at Delhaven Christian Church, April 2002.

20. Information on training and consulting available from Crossroads Ministry is available from the organization. See chapter 2, n. 11, and the Annotated Bibliography and Resource List of this book for additional information.

21. Anthony Pappas, *Entering the World of the Small Church* (revised and expanded edition) (Bethesda, Md.: Alban Institute, 2000), 139.

22. Vincente-Rivera, "Local Church Receives 'Disciple' Award," 1, 6.

CHAPTER FIVE: CHURCH OF THE REDEEMER
MORRISTOWN, NEW JERSEY

1. Martin Luther King Jr., "Transformed Nonconformist," in *Keeping the Faith: African American Sermons of Liberation,* ed. James Haskins (New York: Welcome Rain, 2002), 195–96.

2. See the congregation's Web site, *www.redeemermorristown.org;* see also Errol Glee and James Broderick, "Holy Unique: Rejuvenated Mission Fills Church And Other Empty Spaces," *Morris Magazine* (October 2000): 7.

3. Church of the Redeemer, "Reconciliation Season" (2001): 1–2.

4. Colleen Hintz, "Cues for the Journey Are 'Hidden in Plain View,'" *The Voice* [Diocese of Newark] (March 2001): 12.

5. "Reconciliation Season," 1–2.

6. Darran Simon, "Church Focuses on Evils of Racism: 'Harriet Tubman' Addresses Congregation in Morristown," *Daily Record, Morris County,* January 29, 2001, A9, A11.

7. Unless otherwise noted, quotations are from interviews conducted in April 2001 and August 2002 with Phillip Dana Wilson, Carol King, Marcia Liotard, Larry Hamil, Richard Horsley, Charles Dickerson, Janice Paran, Kathy Seabrook, Bert Jones, and Traci C. West.

8. Glee and Broderick, "Holy Unique," 8.

9. John Shelby Spong, "The Bishop's Banner for Congregational Excellence," Convention of the Episcopal Diocese of Newark, January 1996.

10. Church of the Redeemer, "History," see the congregation's Web site.

11. Paul Wilkes, *Excellent Protestant Congregations* (Louisville: Westminster John Knox, 2001), 234–45.

12. John Zlock, "Study Lauds Morristown Church," *Daily Record: Morris County,* February 19, 2001, A7.

13. "Church of the Redeemer: Morristown: How One Community Lives Out Its Vision of Inclusivity," Episcopal Divinity School, February 8, 2000.

14. Lyle Timpson, "A Call for the Liberated to Become Liberators," *Crossroads* [Church of the Redeemer] (May 2002).

15. *The National Dialogue on Anti-Racism* (New York: Episcopal Church Center, 1999; rev. 2003).

16. Peggy McIntosh, "White Privilege: Unpacking the Invisible Knapsack," *Independent School* (Winter 1990).

17. Program overview from Charles Dickerson, September 2002.

18. Simon, "Church Focuses on Evils of Racism," A11; Phillip Dana Wilson, "What Does a White Person Have to Say about Racism," Church of the Redeemer, Martin Luther King Jr. Breakfast, January 21, 2002.

19. "Reconciliation Season," 2002, 12.

CHAPTER SIX: FIRST PARISH BREWSTER

BREWSTER, MASSACHUSETTS

1. Maya Angelou, "The Pulse of the Morning," in *The Collected Poems of Maya Angelou* (New York: Random House, 1994), 272.

2. "About First Parish Brewster." See the congregation's Web site, *www.fpbuu.org*; see also Jeanne Denike, "The Sea Captains and Slavery," October 24, 1999.

3. Denike, "The Sea Captains and Slavery."

4. Ibid.

5. Elaine Forman Crane, *An Independent People* (New York: Fordham University Press, 1985), 5, 9–10, 15, 33.

6. Denike, "The Sea Captains and Slavery."

7. First Parish Broad of Trustees, November 8, 2000.

8. First Parish Brewster, Unitarian Universalist, "Annual Report 2001–2001," 3.

9. "Justice Work Is a Major Focus at First Parish," *Interconnections* 5, no. 3 (summer 2002): 1; "Diverse Staff Helps Attract, Link People to First Parish," *Interconnections* 5, no. 3 (Summer 2002): 1–2.

10. "Statement to the First Parish Board of Trustees Concerning the Continuing Work at First Parish Towards Becoming an Anti-Racist Multicultural Church Community" (Fall 2001); "Growth Brings Financial Challenges for Brewster," *Interconnections* 5, no. 3 (Summer 2002): 2; Jeanne Denike, "Report to the Board of Trustees, Anti-Racism Task Force," November 14, 2001.

11. Statement by Dr. William Sinkford from the Web site of the Unitarian Universalist Association, *www.uua.org*.

12. "Statement of the Board of Trustees" (Fall 2001).

13. Unless otherwise noted, quotations are from interviews conducted in September and November 2002 and January 2003 with Frances Perkins, Mykel Johnson, David Billings, Carie Killam, Marilyn Watson, Jeanne Denike, William Gardiner, Joseph Daluz, Tom Wolfson, and Carlos Barbosa.

14. "Justice Work Is a Major Focus at First Parish," 1–2.

15. Ibid.

16. James Robinson, "Freedom," sermon preached at First Parish Brewster, 1996.

17. Ibid.

18. Ibid.

19. "All Church Racism Project," adopted unanimously, June 1996.

20. For information on Crossroads Ministry, see chapter 2, n. 11, and the Annotated Bibliography and Resource List in this book. "Continuum on Becoming an Anti-Racist Multicultural Institution," adapted from an original concept by Bailey Jackson and Rita Hardiman, and further developed by Andrea Avazian and Ronice Branding, available from Crossroads Ministry. See also *Journey Toward Wholeness Path to Anti-Racism,* materials available through the Unitarian Universalist Association, *www.uua.org.*

21. "Statement to the Board of Trustees" (fall 2001).

22. Ibid.

23. "Annual Meeting Motion and Background Information," passed by the congregation, June 2002.

24. "First Parish Brewster, Unitarian Universalist, Annual Report," 2–3.

25. Lori A. Nolin, "Ministry of Service: Pastor Applies Personal Values to Global Questions," *Cape Cod Times,* May 30, 1999, 1.

26. "One Earth One People Project," on the congregation's Web site, *www.fpbuu.org;* see also "Mashpee Wampanoag: A History," *Cape Cod Times,* June 16, 2002, 1–4.

27. James Robinson, "The Changing Face of Cape Cod," *The Angle,* June 6, 2001.

28. Ibid.

CONCLUSION

1. Martin Luther King Jr., "Address to the Southern Christian Leadership Conference," August 16, 1967.

2. Toni Morrison, Commencement Address at Duke University, Durham, North Carolina, June 1992.

3. Developed by Jayne J. Oasin, Social Justice Ministries Office, Episcopal Church Center, 2002.

BEN COHEN

AND

JERRY GREENFIELD

WITH MEREDITH MARAN

BEN&JERRY'S®

Double-Dip

How to Run a Values-Led Business

and Make Money, Too

SIMON & SCHUSTER PAPERBACKS
New York   London   Toronto   Sydney

SIMON & SCHUSTER PAPERBACKS
Rockefeller Center
1230 Avenue of the Americas
New York, NY 10020

For information about special discounts for bulk purchases,
please contact Simon & Schuster Special Sales:
1-800-456-6798 or business@simonandschuster.com.

SIMON & SCHUSTER PAPERBACKS and colophon are registered
trademarks of Simon & Schuster, Inc.

Designed by Karolina Harris

This book is manufactured in the United States on Totally Chlorine Free paper
made by Lyons Falls Pulp & Paper.

9   10   8

The Library of Congress has cataloged the hardcover edition as follows:
Cohen, Ben (Ben R.)
Ben & Jerry's double-dip : how to run a values-led business and make money, too /
Ben Cohen and Jerry Greenfield, with Meredith Maran.
p.   cm.
Includes index.
1. Ben & Jerry's (Firm)—History.   2. Cohen, Ben (Ben R.).   3. Greenfield, Jerry.
4. Businesspeople—United States—Biography.   5. Ice cream industry—United States.
6. Social responsibility of business—United States.   I. Greenfield, Jerry.
II. Maran, Meredith.   III. Title.
HD9281.U54B463   1997
338.7'6374'0973—dc21   97-9018
                                                                                              CIP

ISBN-13: 978-0684-83499-3
ISBN-10: 0-684-83499-5
ISBN-13: 978-0684-83855-7 (Pbk)
ISBN-10: 0-684-83855-9 (Pbk)

Acknowledgments

It's a funny thing, our names being the name of our company. For some strange reason people assume that we personally have had every great idea and done all the wonderful things that our company has accomplished. If only it were true. The simple truth is that the dedicated and hardworking folks at Ben & Jerry's have made our company what it is. It was many years ago when we first realized that part of our jobs was to accept credit for the work other people do. We are incredibly grateful to the entire group of people who have made Ben & Jerry's so successful. We are particularly appreciative of the members of our board for their wisdom, commitment, and perseverance.

When we got the opportunity to write a book, we thought we'd finally have to do something all by ourselves. Luckily, this wasn't true. It is our good fortune that once again we got lots of help. Jerry Welsh, the Primary Jerry, is truly a man of big ideas. Clichés notwithstanding, there wouldn't be this book without him. Yola Carlough, research assistant extraordinaire, and her able crew—Lee Holden, Diane Shea, and Heidi Nepvu—made sure all the facts were facts, and much, much more.

Thanks to Denise Dean for keeping it and us all together, as always. Liz Bankowski deserves enormous credit for providing us with the grounding and perspective we occasionally accept. And it's a good thing Duane Peterson arrived in time to help craft the military budget section, among other things.

Carol Niehus is not only a gifted, meticulous transcriptionist. She's also a warm, caring human being. Thanks, Carol.

Thanks to Students for Responsible Business for much of the information in the Resource Guide.

A big thank-you to our agent, Maria Downs. You owe us lunch.

Our editor, Bob Bender, and his assistant, Johanna Li, have been fabulous, not to mention flexible, which contributed greatly to the fabulousness of this book and the process of creating it. Thanks also to all the other folks at Simon & Schuster who did all the necessary work we barely knew about. You made it all look easy.

Did we mention Meredith Maran? Oh, she won't mind. We and Meredith don't need words anyway. Lest we forget to mention it, it was a privilege to work with Meredith. And that was the least of it.

Jerry's Dedication

For my parents: I'll never be able to thank you enough.

And for Elizabeth and Tyrone, who keep me waking up

every day.

Ben's Dedication

For my daughter, Aretha, and for those who are hurt by poverty,

ignorance, and injustice: "There but for fortune go I."

Contents

Introduction:

Being Here Now

Jerry: What's interesting about me and my role in the company is, I'm just this guy on the street. A person who's fairly conventional, mainstream, accepting of life as it is.

Ben: Salt of the earth. A man of the people.

Jerry: But then I've got this friend Ben, who challenges everything. It's against his nature to do anything the same way anyone's ever done it before. To which my response is always, "I don't think that'll work."

Ben: To which my response is always, "How do we know till we try?"

Jerry: So I get to go through this leading-edge, risk-taking experience with Ben—even though I'm really just like everyone else.

Ben: The perfect duo. Ice cream and chunks. Business and social change. Ben and Jerry.

Since the day we met in seventh-grade gym class at Merrick Avenue Junior High, we knew ours was a friendship made in Husky Heaven. We were the two slowest, fattest kids in the class. On the day we met we were lagging far behind the pack of runners on the school track. The coach yelled, "If you can't do the mile in under seven minutes, you're gonna have to do it again." Ben said, "But, Coach, if we can't do the mile in under seven minutes the first time, how are we gonna do it in under seven minutes the second time?"

All through junior high and high school we hung out—eating lunch together, sharing those one-calorie candies Jerry's mom used to stuff into his lunch box. (Attempting to lose weight by subsisting on those candies alone, Jerry keeled over at school one day.) During the summer we drove around in our parents' cars and worked for Ben's father, sorting direct mail by zip code. In our senior year Ben made what turned out to be a seminal career decision: he got a job driving an ice cream vending truck. The pitter-patter of little feet chasing the truck down the street, the happiness that lit up the children's faces when they took their first lick of an ice cream bar made a deep and lasting impression.

Like a lot of middle-class eighteen-year-old guys of our generation, we assumed we'd go to college—partly because it was the best way to avoid the military draft, and also to get out on our own. It was the sixties, a time when an unusually large number of young people were exploring and trying to find themselves. Jerry applied to several schools but was accepted only by Oberlin. Ben applied to just one college, Colgate University, because the brochure said it had fireplaces in the dorms. Surprisingly, Colgate accepted him. In the fall of 1969 we said our farewells, promised to stay in touch, and went our separate ways.

After several failed attempts at various universities to impersonate a serious student, Ben decided to devote himself to becoming a potter. He dropped out of college in 1972, moved to the East Village, in Manhattan, and soon proved himself unredeemably unemployable. He'd taken a series of "McJobs" to support his pottery apprenticeship—as a baker's helper, a short-order cook, a Yellow Pages deliveryperson, a garbageman, a hospital admissions clerk, and a night mopper, among other short-lived vocations. To qualify for one job Ben had to take a Minnesota Multiphasic Personality Inventory test, which labelled him as having "unresolved conflicts with authority." This came as no surprise to those who knew and loved him.

In 1974, in search of greener pastures, Ben found the one meaningful job he'd ever had (and kept): as a crafts teacher at a residential school for troubled teenagers, in the Adirondacks. The school's director, staff, and philosophy were as nontraditional and unstructured as Ben himself, and Ben was a big hit with the students and teachers. But then, in 1976, the school was shut down. Ben tried to make a living as a potter, failed, and was unemployed once again. Fully aware of his limitations as an employee, Ben started thinking about opening a business. He called Jerry and asked him to come back, to upstate New York and think about it with him.

The timing couldn't have been better. Having been rejected by every medical school he'd applied to for the second year in a row, Jerry had just given up his plan to become a doctor. After graduating from Oberlin, Jerry had moved to Manhattan, where he worked as a lab technician. There he and Ben made a happy home with their dog, Malcolm. Two years later Jerry left for Chapel Hill, North Carolina, to live with his girlfriend (and future wife), Elizabeth. He got a job as a lab assistant at UNC Hospital, where he was assigned the task of chopping off rats' heads. The job was a bit unappealing, so when Elizabeth broke up with him Jerry found himself fresh out of reasons to stay in North Carolina. He packed his belongings and headed to New York to see what Ben had in mind.

What Ben had in mind was finding a way for us to work together without having to work for someone else. A way for us to have a good time. And we shared a fantasy about earning $20,000 a year, which in those days seemed like a lot of money to us.

● Bagels, Ice Cream, or . . . Pizza?

One day in 1977 we found ourselves sitting on the front steps of Jerry's parents' house in Merrick, Long Island, talking about what kind of business to go into. Since eating was our greatest passion, it seemed logical to start a restaurant. Some people in that industry had told us that most restaurants fail, even more often than most small businesses, but the ones that are most likely to succeed are those with limited menus. So we were sitting there talking about fondue. Talking about crepes. Talking about kebobs. And then somehow we got focused on bagels or ice cream.

We wanted to pick a product that was becoming popular in big cities and move it to a rural college town, because we wanted to live in that kind of environment. We wanted to have a lot of interaction with our customers and enjoy ourselves. And, of course, we wanted a product that we liked to eat.

First we thought about bagels. We had this idea: UBS—United Bagel Service. We were going to deliver bagels, lox, cream cheese, and the *New York Times* to people's doors in the morning.

We stopped in at G&G Equipment, a used-restaurant-supply joint in Albany, New York, and priced used bagel-making equipment. We were talking to the owner, Lou G&G (as he came to be known). He drove a big Cadillac and smoked a big cigar. Lou kept saying, "You gotta have this. You gotta have this. If you're gonna make a real New York bagel, you gotta have that." The equipment came to $40,000.

That was more money than we thought we could ever get. We figured ice cream had to be cheaper. What do you need to make ice cream? An oversized homemade-ice-cream machine—how could that cost $40,000? We found an ad for a $5 ice-cream-making correspondence course offered through Penn State. Due to extreme poverty, we decided to split one course between us, sent in our five bucks, read the material they sent back, and passed the open-book tests with flying colors. That settled it. We were going into the ice cream business.

Ben: I used to have regrets because the ingredients in our products are so expensive. I mean, bagels! Flour and water, that's it.

Jerry: But bagels go stale really fast. Think about it, Ben. Ice cream—you freeze it and it lasts forever.

Ben: Pizza. That's gotta be a good one. Did you ever see a pizza place go out of business?

Jerry: I'm convinced we would have made a great bagel. We would have made a great pizza. It might not have turned into what Ben & Jerry's has turned into, but it would have been great, because we put our hearts and souls into it.

Ben: We'd have a lot more room for social-action messages on a pizza box than we have on pint containers. Think about *that*, Jer. We could print the whole Bill of Rights on the side of a pizza box.

Jerry: I think we're doing okay for now with ice cream, Ben.

Once we'd decided on an ice cream parlor, the next step was deciding where to put it. We knew college students eat a lot of ice cream; we knew they eat more of it in warm weather. Determined to make an informed decision (but lacking in technological and financial resources), we developed our own low-budget "manual cross-correlation analysis." Ben sat at the kitchen table, leafing through a U.S. almanac to research towns that had the highest average temperatures. Jerry sat on the floor, reading a guide to American colleges, searching for the rural towns that had the most college kids. Then we merged our lists. When we investigated the towns that came up we discovered that apparently someone had already done this work ahead of us. All the warm towns that had a decent number of college kids already had homemade-ice-cream parlors. So we threw out the temperature criterion and ended up in Burlington, Vermont. Burlington had a young population, a significant college population, and virtually no competition. Later we realized the *reason* there was no competition: it's so cold in Burlington for so much of the year, and the summer season is so short, it was obvious (to everyone except us) that there was no way an ice cream parlor could succeed there. Or so it seemed.

We found an abandoned gas station in downtown Burlington. It was only a block from Church Street, the main shopping street, right across from a park. Plus, there was some parking where the gas pumps used to be.

We had a few other potential locations, so before we made our final decision we bought a couple of little clicker-counters. We went from one location to the next, clicking and counting as people walked by. After we'd checked out all our other options, we stood outside the gas station for a couple of hours. "Seems like a lot of foot traffic to me, Ben." "Seems like a lot of foot traffic to me, Jerry." We headed off to rent the place.

● Starting Up Is Hard to Do

So there we were in the winter of '77, fixing up this broken-down gas station, trying out all these recipes for ice cream and crepes, renting somebody's summer house on Lake Champlain.

Jerry: In winter. In Vermont.

Ben: The place wasn't winterized. They used it themselves during the summer.

Jerry: And the wind whistled through. But it was a beautiful spot, right on the lake. The main thing was, it was a place we could afford.

Talk about living hand-to-mouth. We were eating saltine crackers and sardines from Woolworth's—three boxes for a dollar, three cans for a dollar, respectively. There was no heat in the gas station, so it was just as cold at work as it was at home. When we took the place over, there was a three-inch sheet of ice on the floor because the roof had failed. While we were working—and we were pretty much always working—we'd take breaks at the bus station down the street to go to the bathroom and warm up.

After months of frantic renovating, just before the grand opening, we gave the gas station its final touch: a fresh coat of orange paint on the walls and ceiling. Ben picked the color. The job took several people all day and night to finish. It came out looking like Grossman's Lumber. Gross. Garish. Not the warm peach color Ben had in mind.

Jerry: As soon as we finished painting, Ben stepped back and said we had to paint it again, a different color.

Ben: The gas station had very high ceilings, which were very difficult to paint.

Jerry: This was before we'd even opened, and already he'd changed his mind. That's one thing about Ben that drives people crazy: he's often said he needs to make a mistake first in order to make the right decision.

Ben: It was a bad decision to paint it that color orange the first time. But it was a good decision to change it.

Jerry: So it goes.

During those first few months there were really fun times, really bad times, really exciting times—not many relaxing times. Occasionally we made inedible batches of ice cream. We could afford to hire waitpersons only for the busiest times, so our customers had to stand in long lines at the counter. Even when there were waitpeople working, there were really long lines. Actually, we had no idea what we were doing. We had to fire people, the job we both detested most, for scooping too slowly or scooping overly large portions. We were paying ourselves $150 a week and working our tails off. Every piece of machinery we owned was breaking down, one after the other. Our checkbook was always empty, and our bills were piling up.

Still, we were having a great time. We were totally engaged in what we were doing. It was clear people loved our ice cream, and that felt really good. We weren't thinking about the future; we were just getting from one day to the next.

Of course, it helped that we shared this big delusion. We had thought there were maybe twenty things we didn't know how to do. Obviously, as soon as we figured out how to do them, we'd get out from under all these problems. Then things would run smoothly. The business would run itself. After about three years, however, we realized we'd been kidding ourselves—the business was never going to run itself. It was quite a disheartening revelation.

● Good Vibes, Good Business

During our first summer we were averaging about $650 a day in sales. We were still making all our ice cream in the four-and-a-half-gallon freezer; when we ran out we'd hang our international No Ice Cream sign (an ice cream cone inside a red circle with a slash through it) in the window. But even when we were sold out of ice cream, people still came into the shop. They drank the fresh-squeezed lemonade. They listened to Don Rose, a guy who would pound out his own ragtime tunes on our old piano in exchange for fresh-squeezed orange juice. Or they came in just to hang out.

Right from the beginning, even though the business wasn't making any money and we weren't making any money, we were always thinking up new excuses to give away ice cream. When we opened the gas station we had our Grand Opening Special: buy one, get one free. Then we started giving away cones at random to people waiting on the ice cream line. Then we had free cones for all mothers on Mother's Day. Visibly expectant mothers got two. To promote winter sales, we held the Penny Off per Celsius Degree Below Zero Winter Extravaganza (affectionately known as POPCDBZWE), thereby turning a liability (being located in a very cold winter town) into an asset.

At the end of the summer we threw a Fall Down Festival for the people of Burlington. There, Jerry finally got to make use of his college education. He had actually gotten a credit at Oberlin for taking a course entitled "Carnival Technique" from Bill Irwin, one of the foremost new vaudeville performers. Jerry would appear on the stage in his pith helmet while his partner—who assumed for the occasion his alter identity, that of noted mystic Habeeni Ben Coheeni—was carried out sitting on a platform, clothed only in a bedsheet, chanting himself into a metabolic trance. At the proper moment Coheeni, rigid as a board, would fall backward into a supine position. His dedicated followers would suspend him by his head and feet upon two properly spaced chairs. Then, with great dramatic flair, Jerry would place a real cinder block on Coheeni's bare stomach, raise a real sledgehammer high above his head, and bring it crashing down, smashing the cinder block into many real pieces. His incoherent chanting interrupted only by his periodic trance states, Coheeni would arise from amidst the rubble, tossing flower petals into the delighted, cheering crowd.

We'd always promised ourselves that if the business made it through its first year, we'd celebrate by giving away ice cream. So on our first anniversary, May 5, 1979, we started a ritual that's still with us today: Free Cone Day. On Free Cone Day every year, all Ben & Jerry's franchisees give away ice cream at their shops all day. All the scoopers come in; everybody works together. The line goes really fast because there's no money being exchanged. Last year on Free Cone Day the scoop shops gave away 358,850 cones. (You can get on line as many times as you want.)

That's one of the beauties of ice cream. We're not giving away cars. It's a comparatively inexpensive thing. There are disadvantages to ice cream, too: it doesn't have a very high ticket price. Our average sale is rather low. So why not take advantage of the good aspects? Who wants to have an ice cream parlor if you can't give away free ice cream every now and then? As we said on the flyer telling people about the first Free Cone Day:

"If it's not fun, why do it?" (Jerry).

And, "Business has a responsibility to give back to the community from which it draws its support" (Ben).

In the gas station, people used to come to the counter to order ice cream cones and we'd say, "How can we serve you better?" We really wanted to know.

Dear Ben and/or Jerry,

On Christmas Day of 1980 my intended and I arrived in Burlington, Vermont, where we were to be married the next day. We went downtown to have dinner but every place was closed.

Then we turned a corner and saw a gas station that was selling short-order food! We had our prenuptial supper there. A wise choice. You were so kind to us. Didn't you have a player-piano in your front room? We were the only customers, the food was good, you suggested ice cream, your specialty. We returned to our motel room happy and well-fed.

We've been married ever since. I'm seventy-one and my husband is sixty-nine. You've got millions of customers now. I thought you'd be interested in the brief résumé of a couple who you fed "when . . ."

Sincerely,
Freda B.

In the early days our major "marketing campaign" consisted of putting stacks of Ben & Jerry's bumper stickers on the counters in the store. Much to our surprise, a large percentage of people in Burlington started putting these bumper stickers on their cars. There wasn't any contest. There wasn't anything to gain. People didn't get any prizes for driving around with our bumper sticker. People were responding to a great product, genuine customer service, and genuine caring.

Jerry: People wanted us to succeed.

Ben: They wanted to help these two real guys who obviously needed a lot of help.

● Ice Cream for the People

We learned a lot, most of it the hard way. Being a small business, we had no human resources department and no human resources expertise, so we did a thoroughly amateur job of hiring and firing—perfecting our dysfunctional behaviors which persist to this day. (More about human resources in Chapter Six.) And then there was our famous pricing epiphany. We were working our hearts out for the first two or three years, and every year we just barely broke even. The first year we were thrilled to break even. We'd made our overhead; we could see the light at the end of the tunnel.

Then the next year came and we'd just broken even again, even though our sales had grown by $50,000. This went on for three years. Each year we would break even and say we needed only to do a little more business to make a profit. Then the next year we'd do a lot more business and still only break even. One day we were talking to Ben's dad, who was an accountant. He said, "Since you're gonna make such a high-quality product instead of pumping it full of air, why don't you raise your prices?"

At the time we were charging fifty-two cents a cone. Coming out of the sixties, our reason for going into business was that ours was going to be "ice cream for the people." It was going to be great quality products for everybody—not some elitist treat. We aren't just *selling* to people. We *are* the people! Ice cream for the people!

Ben said, "But, Dad, the reason we're not making money is because we're not doing the job right. We're overscooping. We're wasting ice cream. Our labor costs are too high—we're not doing a good job of scheduling our employees. We're not running our business efficiently. Why should the customer have to pay for our mistakes? That's why everything costs twice as much as it should."

And Mr. Cohen said, "You guys have to understand—that's human. That's as good as people do. You can't price for doing everything exactly right. Raise your prices."

Eventually we said, either we're going to raise our prices or we're going to go out of business. And then where will the people's ice cream be? They'll have to get their ice cream from somebody else. So we raised the prices. And we stayed in business.

● To Sell Out or Not to Sell Out

Nothing could have prepared us for how much work it was, running the company in the first few years. It's one thing giving birth (or so we're told). It's another thing giving birth for three or four years. It was a total commitment. We were living and breathing the business, working absurd hours, getting paid an extremely small amount of money.

In 1979 we started wholesaling two-and-a-half-gallon tubs. In 1980 we started wholesaling pints, which meant selling to distributors, calling on the buyers at supermarkets. We weren't shopkeepers in the store anymore, churning out a five-gallon batch of ice cream, scooping it to the customers, hopping over to the player piano every now and then. We'd become businesspeople: writing memos, doing correspondence, hiring and firing. The business had turned into more of a business. It was becoming a cog in the economic machine. For us, having grown up in the sixties, the idea of becoming real businesspeople running a real business had very negative connotations.

In 1982 we both decided we'd had enough. Jerry and Elizabeth were back together, and Elizabeth was moving to Arizona to go to graduate school. Jerry wanted to go with her. We'd never planned on being in business longer than a few years anyway.

Jerry: It sounded really nice to get away from working seven days a week, to go out to a nice, warm climate. Plus, I had issues about my personal identity versus my identity with the company—where did the company end and where did I begin?

> *Ben:* The thought of running the business without Jerry was quite daunting. I didn't know if I could do it.

So we put the company up for sale. A former executive with the M&M Mars corporation came forward to buy it. For a while we couldn't agree on the value of the business. Then we couldn't agree on the terms of the purchase. The Man from Mars, as we called him, wanted us to finance the sale. He said he'd pay us back out of profits over time—but the business wasn't profitable, and we didn't know if he would run it profitably. Essentially he was asking us to lend him the price of the company, with his ownership in some limited partnerships as our only security.

Since Jerry was planning to move to Arizona, he said the decision was up to Ben.

> *Jerry:* Ben kept changing his mind. I was trying to get him to decide what the heck he was gonna do. I said, "Keep it, sell it—I don't care. But let's get on with it."
>
> *Ben:* I was troubled by indecision.
>
> *Jerry:* Ben went to see Maurice Purpora, this eccentric eighty-year-old restaurateur-artist friend of his. Maurice told Ben he'd be crazy to sell. Luckily, Ben respected Maurice's opinion.
>
> *Ben:* Maurice said selling the business would be the worst mistake of my life. I said, "Maurice, you know what business does. It exploits the community, it exploits the employees, it exploits the environment." Maurice said, "Ben, you own the company. If there's something you don't like about the way business is done, why don't you just do it different?" That had never occurred to me before.

After Ben talked to Maurice he took the company off the market.

We'd always said we didn't want Ben & Jerry's to be a traditional business. Deciding not to sell sharpened our focus on exactly what kind of business we wanted it to be. Now we could articulate our purpose: to see whether a business could survive while being a force for progressive social change.

Ten years later we were introduced to the concept of values-led business. But at the company meeting we held in Ben's apartment in September of 1982, when we told our staff of eighteen that Jerry was leaving, we also talked for the first time about business as a vehicle for social change. It was a precursor of greater adventures to come.

● What a Long, Strange Dip . . .

It's been nearly twenty years since we started cranking the old four-and-a-half-gallon freezer in a renovated gas station in Burlington, Vermont. Since then we've seen a lot of changes—in us, in the company, and in the world.

We've put on a few pounds. Lost a little hair. Had a couple of kids. Shared a lot of tears and laughter. The company's bringing in more money every month than we ever thought we'd see in our lifetimes, with sales last year of over $160 million. We've got seven hundred employees, thirteen thousand stockholders, three plants, 132 scoop shops all over the United States, plus a few in Canada and Israel—and bigger challenges and problems to match.

The best news is, the idea of using the power of business to address problems in society isn't quite as radical as it was when we first started putting our hearts, skills, and resources into activities the "experts" said would put us out of business: showing free movies at the gas station, sending the Scoopmobile to an antinuclear demonstration, using the space on the packaging of our ice cream bars to advocate redirecting 1 percent of the U.S. military budget to peace-through-understanding activities during the middle of the Cold War.

We're not scooping cones, sleeping on the freezers, or eating leftover sundaes for dinner anymore the way we did when we were getting started. And we're not running the company single-handedly (double-handedly?) anymore, either. In the beginning there was Ben and there was Jerry, and we did it all: made all the ice cream and all the decisions, borrowed all the money, patched together all the broken-down equipment. That's one thing about starting a business: when you're an employee you can blame the boss for buying the wrong machine or making you work long hours. But when you're the boss, you have no one to blame but yourself. Darn—I bought the wrong equipment. Now I'll have to work all night. Again.

Another thing about starting a business: you get plenty of on-the-job training. Between us, over the years, we've been dilapidated-gas-station renovators; ice-cream-flavor inventors; short-order crepe chefs; hot fudge makers; ice cream scoopers; delivery persons; line workers; manufacturing overseers; vehicle, equipment, and facility procurers; circus-bus outfitters; ice cream distributors; and communications specialists. (Until about 1982, Jerry wrote a personal response to every person who sent a letter to the company.) And that just covers the first few years.

Later, we got to be salespersons. Then we got to be marketing guys. Then we got to be hardheaded founders.

Nowadays we're going through a transition in our relationship with the company. For many years other folks have been doing more and more of the work of running the business. Now we're collaborating with them to institutionalize the skills and values the two of us bring, making the company more about Ben & Jerry's and less about Ben and Jerry. Which is difficult in some ways, but mostly it's positive—for Ben, for Jerry, and for Ben & Jerry's.

There are some great benefits to having Ben and Jerry as your founders. And there are some less positive aspects, too. Like many people who start their own companies, we're both pretty headstrong. We tend to have incredibly high standards and to focus on at what goes wrong as opposed to feeling good about what goes right. That can be pretty hard on people.

On the other hand, what made the company possible was our partnership. From the beginning we had a commitment to each other as well as to the business. Each of us saw how hard the other guy was working, and neither of us would allow himself to let the other one down.

We made two deals early on. First—if one of us felt really strongly about something, he'd get his way. Second—neither of us would have to do anything he really, really didn't want to do. The consequence of that deal was that each of us has to take his responsibilities seriously. In the early days, Jerry wanted to be responsible for production, and Ben wanted to handle sales. So distribution was Ben's job, and if we had a funky truck with bad steering (which we did), Ben had to drive that truck. Jerry's job was making ice cream. If the cookies got stuck in the filling machine (which they did), Jerry had to clean out the machine.

Being old friends, we get along really well. We each have a great appreciation for the contributions the other one brings. Even more important, we have complementary skills *and* shared values.

Now the skills, talent level, and values congruity of the Ben & Jerry's staff are increasing. When we're not breathing down their necks, they're coming into their own. They're becoming the new leaders and, we hope, the new visionaries of the company. The business is getting ready to stand on its own.

These days the two of us don't have functional responsibilities, but we're still involved in many aspects of the company's operations: sales, marketing, quality, new-product development, and promotion. We're also involved with corporate governance: long-term strategic thinking, policy making—mostly on the conceptual level. Sometimes we get ideas about what the company should or shouldn't be doing and we'll go to the upper-level managers and gently foist our views upon them. Sometimes they listen, sometimes they don't—which is the way the process is supposed to work. Primarily we work with the board of directors, trying to help align the upper-level management group and the board around the concept of being a values-led business.

It's difficult to be involved in a business at a high level, to be the founders of a business, and not always to be in agreement with some of the decisions that your business makes. Friends who have teenage kids and teenage companies like ours tell us that the two experiences are a lot alike. For years you've got these children who are totally dependent on you, totally under your control. They wear the clothes you put on them and go wherever you take them. Then one day they're taller and stronger than you are. They're buying their own clothes and driving their own cars. They have their own ideas about everything, and a lot of them aren't the same as yours. This is something most founders go through. If there's a solution, we haven't found it yet.

One great thing about this recent period is that the two of us have been getting to spend a lot of time together. We can hang out on weekends, take family vacations. Aretha, Ben's daughter, and Tyrone, Jerry's son, get along really well. Tyrone's the only boy who'll play dolls with Aretha. She really likes that in a boy.

Ben moved into his new house, five minutes away from Jerry's, so we carpool to work a lot. We both bought Harleys, and in warm weather we go for rides through the Vermont countryside. And of course, as always, we spend a lot of time together eating.

Just like everyone else, we need to do what's fulfilling and self-actualizing for us. Just like everyone else, sometimes we can satisfy those passions in our day-to-day work within the company and sometimes we can't. When that happens, we take on special projects to keep ourselves juiced. Right now, for instance, Ben's working with Business Leaders for Sensible Priorities to move national budget priorities toward helping people out of poverty and away from Cold War military-expenditure levels.

What we're aiming toward is getting the company as a whole to embrace the idea of being a values-led business. It's going to take all of us at Ben & Jerry's working together—because integrating a social mission into the everyday actions of a business is new, uncharted territory. If everyone from top management on through the ranks starts choosing, in things we do on our jobs, those courses of action which integrate progressive social concerns into our day-to-day business activities— well, then we'll have a business that really is about social change.

The other thing we're working on is getting the company to be managed in an effective way. It's something the two of us haven't been good at ourselves. We need to adopt policies and structures that we're precise and clear about and that we hold ourselves accountable to. Without that, the company can't come close to reaching its potential. It's possible that it could survive, but it would not be a thing of beauty.

We're keeping the faith. The company is far from perfect, as are we. But quality is a process, not a place. If we keep going in a good direction, twenty years from now the company will be doing great, and still on a path to do even better. Our kids—our grandkids, maybe—will be eating Cherry Garcia. And the two of us will still be rocking (even if it's only in our rocking chairs).

Ben: We want the company to go on after our time. I mean, we'd want the company to operate with the same values it's always had if we were both hit by a car tomorrow.

Jerry: I think it would have to be a truck, Ben.

As the Cherry Garcia T-shirt says: "What a long, strange dip it's been."

1

What Do You Mean, Values-Led Business?

Ben: When we go out and speak to business groups, people ask what we mean by "values-led business." Sometimes they ask if we're talking about hippie values, or what. We say, "It's more like biblical values."

Jerry: Do unto others as you would have them do unto you. As you give you receive. Or, to put it in a more "businesslike" way: one hand washes the other.

Ben: When you're values-led you're trying to help the community. And when you're trying to help the community, people want to buy from you. They want to work for you. They want to be associated with you. They feel invested in your success.

Jerry: This isn't conventional business wisdom. It's Ben's business wisdom. But it works. That's one of the beautiful things about Ben. He questions everything, particularly conventional wisdom.

● Values-Led Business: An Overview

When we started making ice cream in 1978 we had simple goals. We wanted to have fun, we wanted to earn a living, and we wanted to give something back to the community. Only we didn't really know what that last item meant.

Then, as the business grew, our aspirations grew as well. We wanted to create a company we could be proud of. In order to do that, we—

and the like-minded companies we connected with along the way—had to find an alternative to the traditional business model. What evolved from that search is what Anita Roddick, founder of the Body Shop, called "values-led business."

Values-led business is based on the idea that business has a responsibility to the people and the society that make its existence possible. More all-encompassing and therefore more effective than philanthropy alone, values-led business seeks to maximize its impact by integrating socially beneficial actions into as many of its day-to-day activities as possible. In order to do that, values must lead and be right up there in a company's mission statement, strategy, and operating plan.

Let's say, for example, that we're looking at three possible new ice cream flavors. Being values-led means choosing the flavor that gives us the best opportunity to integrate our commitment to social change with the need to return reasonable profits to our shareholders. Assuming all three flavors are profitable, if we find out that we can make one of them using nuts from the rain forest (in order to increase economic demand for the living rain forest) and we can put the ice cream in a rain forest-themed container that raises awareness about the problem of rain-forest deforestation, we would choose that flavor. (That's exactly what happened with the development of our Rainforest Crunch flavor.) This is as opposed to making the decision based on what would be *most* profitable from a purely short-term financial perspective.

By incorporating concern for the community—local, national, and global—into its strategic and operating plans, the values-led business can make everyday business decisions that actualize the company's social and financial goals at the same time. Instead of choosing areas of activity based solely on its own short-term self-profitability, the values-led business recognizes that by addressing social problems along with financial concerns, a company can earn a respected place in the community, a special place in customers' hearts, and healthy profits, too.

Consumers are accustomed to buying products despite how they feel about the companies that sell them. But a values-led company earns the kind of customer loyalty most corporations only dream of—because it appeals to its customers on the basis of more than a product. It offers them a way to connect with kindred spirits, to express their most deeply held values when they spend their money. Unlike most commercial transactions, buying a product from a company you believe in transcends the purchase. It touches your soul. Our customers don't like just our ice cream—they like what our company stands for. They like how doing business with us makes them feel. And that's really what companies that spend huge amounts of money on advertising are trying to do —make their customers feel good about them. But they do it on a superficial level, with sexy women and cool cars.

Dear Jerry and Dear Ben:

Listening to my car radio on the way home, I heard you interviewed—and stopped to buy four different containers of your ice creams.

Not only am I in agreement with the political and humanitarian views you expressed and not only am I eager to encourage and support your work, but your ice creams turned out to be wonderful!

That's it, guys. I'm now brand loyal—and I'm yours.

Thank you from my head, from my guts and from my gut.

Bonnie S.
St. Louis, Mo.

Our experience has shown that you don't have to sacrifice social involvement on the altar of maximized profits. One builds on the other. The more we actualize our commitment to social change through our business activities, the more loyal customers we attract and the more profitable we become.

Ben: Being values-led is not an absolute. At Ben & Jerry's we're values-led to some extent. We're constantly seeking to be more so.

Jerry: The board and management of the company all agree that we want to be values-led, and we're doing what we can to move in that direction. It's an evolution. We're nowhere near there yet. But there is no disagreement within the company that that's where we want to be.

Ben: Becoming values-led takes a lot of people moving in the same direction to make it happen. I've been influential in that process. Jerry's been influential. People on the board have been influential. People in upper management, people throughout the company . . .

Jerry: But the impetus has been from you, Ben. Over time there have been influences from all those people—not insignificant influences—but the driving force behind it has been you.

Ben: Hmm. I guess so.

Jerry: And while we're on the subject of Ben's contributions, I do want to say, right from the outset, that anything in this book that appears harebrained or controversial is probably his idea.

Ben: Goes without saying.

● Cause-Related or Values-Led?

Over the past fifteen years, the success of Ben & Jerry's and other values-led companies has proved that there are plenty of customers who, when given a choice between products of equal quality, prefer to spend their money with companies whose values they share. Consequently, the idea that business should give back to the community started to seem less bizarre, and a lot more appealing, than it did when we were getting started. During the mid-eighties, the concept of "cause-related marketing" entered the mainstream corporate world.

Consultants started selling cause-related marketing campaigns to big corporations. Hershey's put Treats for Treatment coupons in Sunday newspapers and gave money to children's hospitals in exchange for each coupon redeemed. MasterCard started donating money with each transaction to anti-child-abuse organizations. Geo gave a fleet of fuel-efficient cars to TreePeople, a tree-planting group in Los Angeles, and planted a tree for each new car sold.

Cause-related marketing is a positive step. But it doesn't challenge the basic paradigms of conventional business and conventional marketing. It acknowledges that business has a responsibility to give back to the community, but it doesn't take advantage of the fact that the real power of business lies in its day-to-day activities. So a company that's doing cause-related marketing operates from a traditional, exclusively profit-maximizing motivation—then adds a charitable component almost as an afterthought. Instead of giving products a boost using a half-naked woman in a multimillion-dollar advertising campaign, cause-related marketing gives products a boost by associating them with compelling causes.

The basic premise of values-led business is to integrate social values into day-to-day business activities—into the very fabric of the business and its products. By contrast, the basic premise of cause-related marketing is to tack social values onto the marketing campaigns of a business that does not take social values into account in its other business activities.

At its best, cause-related marketing is helpful in that it uses marketing dollars to help fund social programs and raise awareness of social ills. At its worst, it's "greenwashing"—using philanthropy to convince customers the company is aligned with good causes, so the company will be seen as good, too, whether it is or not. Corporations know if they create the perception that they care about their consumers and the community, that's likely to increase sales. They understand that if they dress themselves in that clothing, slap that image on, that's going to move product.

But instead of just slapping the image on, wouldn't it be better if the company actually *did* care about its consumers and the community? Wouldn't it be better actually to *do* things that benefit people and society? That will also sell product—as well as motivate customers, employees, and investors. In most cases doing that doesn't cost any more. As a matter of fact, it may cost less.

Values-led business recognizes that the greatest potential a business has for benefiting society is in its operations—not in donating a small percentage of profits from its bottom line to charitable organizations.

Business has now become the most powerful force in society. We cannot solve social problems unless business accepts a leadership role. That in turn requires business to act in the interests of the common good. This is a very new role for business—one it is not used to or prepared for. The norm has been for business to be a special interest, and adversarial to the rest of society.

● Which Values Lead?

For the purpose of this book, the values we're talking about are what are often referred to as "progressive social values." We see our business, and values-led business in general, as promoting social progress for the common good: advocating for the many people in our society whose needs are not served by the status quo; giving a voice to the people who normally aren't heard; helping to address the root causes of poverty. That's why we've partnered with the Children's Defense Fund, whose purpose is to advocate the needs of children, and why we buy our brownies from a bakery that employs economically disenfranchised people, and why we're participating in the campaign to redirect a portion of the military budget to fund human services.

One of the most moving customer letters we ever got was about our Peace Pops and our involvement with One Percent for Peace. (More about these projects later.) The guy who sent the letter, a peace activist, wrote, "People who are out there working for peace are always viewed as being lefty hippies or bleeding hearts. They aren't taken seriously. They don't have much credibility. But when a company the size of Ben & Jerry's takes a stand for peace it legitimizes that stand in the public eye."

The central role business plays in our society means that business can give credibility to progressive causes in ways that social movements alone can't—much as the corporate world has lent credibility to conservative causes. Business is just a tool. It can be used to improve the quality of life in general or just to benefit business's narrow self-interest, that of maximizing profits.

Usually, when corporations are motivated strictly by financial self-interest, in order to meet their corporate goals they make decisions that don't serve the majority of the people. Tobacco companies oppose antismoking legislation. Manufacturing companies oppose antipollution legislation. Coal companies profit from strip-mining. Banks benefit from redlining in the inner city.

Those businesses are led by the values of short-term-profit maximization.

The thing is, most corporations don't make their values, their beliefs, or their political activities public. They don't put their politics on their packaging. Instead, they might pay lobbyists to oppose environmental legislation or to support corporate tax loopholes. They might make donations or fund politicians' campaigns.

Most corporations do what's become normal for businesses to do: they express their values covertly—using their customers' money to achieve political ends that many of their customers would probably disagree with if they knew where their money was going.

In 1776 the Scottish economist Adam Smith wrote in his book *An Inquiry into the Nature and Causes of the Wealth of Nations* that if individuals and organizations acted in their own interests, an "unseen hand" would guide them to the right moral choices, and benefits would flow indirectly to others in society. We seem to forget, however, that an integral part of Adam Smith's theory was free access to information, because he believed that if consumers and other actors in the economy had access to full information about the products and services they were purchasing, they would make the right choices.

Consumers can affect our collective quality of life by influencing one force that strongly controls it. And that force is business. We can influence business by "voting with our dollars": supporting companies that reflect our values. When we buy from the Body Shop, we oppose animal testing and support international human rights. When we spend our money with Patagonia, we help fund environmental initiatives. When we shop at local stores that support the community, we encourage other consumers and businesses to do the same.

That's why values-led businesses need to be public about their social activities. How can people know which companies to "vote" for if companies are secretive about their social stands and activities? When business acts covertly, it locks people out of the process. It deprives consumers of the opportunity to use their purchasing power to support social goals they believe in.

Dear Ben, Jerry, et al.:

Thank you for what I perceive as your corporate consciousness. I saw a television report about your "Peace Pop" and admire your overall efforts at helping/promoting worthy causes. You're a refreshing change in the "Me" age. Rest assured you'll continue to receive my support and my ice cream dollar(s). In fact, if you ever want a free actress for a commercial, let me know. I'm a writer/actress and I can't imagine a better way to express my support and use my abilities.

Sincerely,
Tara M.
Springfield, Ill.

Most of the methodologies we'll talk about in this book would also work for implementing conservative values—except for one thing: if you're out front with what you stand for and your beliefs are unpopular, you could end up turning off a whole lot of customers. We believe customers are more likely to support a company with progressive values because, as we've said, our definition of progressive values is that they serve people's desire to alleviate social problems. If you take the average person and put him in a room with both a starving child and a gun, and you give him $5 and say, "With this money you can either buy this gun, because someone may attack you, or you can feed this starving child," we believe most people would feed the child.

In the same way, most customers would rather do business with a company that shares those values.

Whose Values Lead?

In the case of Ben & Jerry's, the drive to make the company a vehicle for social change came mainly from the top—specifically, from Ben. That's often the case in small entrepreneurial companies. But in large corporations it's as likely to be the employees who push for social and environmental improvements.

Maybe an employee of the phone company goes to her division manager and says, "You know, I'm a member of Greenpeace, and they sent me this information about chlorine and how it creates dioxins, one of the most toxic chemicals known to humankind. And our Yellow Pages are printed on chlorine-bleached paper, and we go through five hundred thousand tons a year. What if we switched to chlorine-free?" Initially the manager says, "Sorry, no way we can do that." So the employee does a little research on her own, keeps the conversation going. Finally she convinces the manager to give unbleached paper a try. Sure enough— the company gets letters of praise from customers, and an award from an environmental group, and great press. And the customers feel good about the formerly anonymous phone company. The next time they get a call from the competitor offering them $50 to switch, they say, "No— I like my phone company."

So then the division manager tells another manager, "I've been able to source chlorine-free paper, and I'm psyched. We're reducing dioxins by five percent. We have the only Yellow Pages out there that's chlorine-free. The environmental community loves us. The general community loves us. Everybody loves us all of a sudden, and they used to hate us." Then the second division manager starts thinking about how he can incorporate social concerns into his business decisions. It goes on from there.

Once it's demonstrated that these changes can be made, and that they're having a positive effect on consumers, and that they're having a positive effect on employees (and therefore keeping them with the company), it becomes clear that integrating social concerns is good for business on many levels. But whether the impetus comes from the top, the bottom, or the middle—and no matter how big or small the company is—the social mission needs to be sold throughout the ranks if it's going to be brought to its full potential.

Let's say Joe, the purchasing guy, finds an unbleached cover stock for the same price, a little less, or even a little more than bleached stock. Joe then has to sell the idea to Sam, the marketing guy, because the cover stock's going to be tan now, not white. Then Sam's got to convince Mary, the creative director.

This doesn't happen just on environmental or social issues. In order for any change to be made inside a corporation, it has to be sold internally. The extent to which a company can be values-led depends on how completely the people in the organization have embraced, or bought into, the company's social mission.

Ben: Buy-in is especially important when it comes to the social mission. It's a new idea. People aren't convinced the company needs to make these changes in order to be successful.

Jerry: It's the same with any other business issue. The top person is crucial. If the top person doesn't believe in it, it won't happen.

Ben: I don't think it's the same as other business issues.

Jerry: It's just like having a quality perspective in your company. The top person has to be highly committed to quality for it to happen. And the top person's got to be highly committed to integrating social concerns for that to happen.

Ben: It depends somewhat on the size of the company. In a fifteen-person operation, the president is much more likely to be hands-on about the purchasing of paper. If you're at the phone company, the president doesn't even know who buys the paper.

Jerry: Ben—think about it. If the Yellow Pages suddenly comes out on a different-color paper, the president's gonna notice. She's gonna say something.

Ben: Hey. That's a thought. The Beige Pages. We'll give them that idea for free.

In a fifteen-person company, the top person is involved in nearly every decision. So if the top person is interested only in traditional business concerns, the person who's buying the paper has less freedom to integrate social values than he would if he were down in the bowels of some huge corporation. But either way, there's got to be someone in a decision-making position who's willing to take the initiative and look at things from a different, social-impact perspective.

● Innovation Is Failure (or, To Stumble Is Not to Fall but to Move Forward More Quickly)

Most new ice cream flavors never see daylight. A whole lot of new flavors that do see the light of day don't succeed in the marketplace. They end up in the Flavor Graveyard. (You can visit the graveyard in cyberspace at http://www.benjerry.com.)

The same dynamic exists in terms of social innovation and social integration. Most ideas you explore end up not being appropriate. Then you execute the ones that do seem appropriate—and some of them don't work.

Somehow when you fail with a new product or a new sales idea, it's okay, because everyone understands that that's normal business process: you try new things; they succeed or they fail. But when it comes to social innovation you have to have a firmer commitment, because when you go through the stumbling process there, there'll be a tendency for somebody—you or somebody else—to say, "We shouldn't even be meddling with this stuff."

You have to be firm in your resolve that being values-led is key to the success of your business, just as much as other essentials. Otherwise you'll find your values get sacrificed in a trade-off. As with most business decisions, each case is a judgment call. Sometimes you sacrifice short-term sales to advance your social mission; sometimes advancing your social mission drives sales. You don't know how it's going to work out until you try.

In 1992 we set up Action Stations in our scoop shops, with displays about the Children's Defense Fund and its grassroots lobbying campaign to pressure the government to meet children's needs. We gave away "Leave No Child Behind" brochures in our shops and at our music festivals, and installed special red phones in the scoop shops that our customers could—and did—use to call and join CDF. This collaboration was a success; we met our goal of signing up fifty thousand Ben & Jerry's customers as members of CDF.

Our public-interest marketing campaign to help save family farms was less successful. Our goal was to put consumer pressure on Congress to shift federal support from large factory farms to small family farms. We got an 800 number—1-800-E-I-O-FARM—and painted it on milk tanker trucks and barn silos. The campaign didn't generate a significant number of calls. But it certainly let people in Vermont know where Ben & Jerry's stood on the issue.

Values Are Built-Ins, Not Add-Ons

Business, like life, is full of trade-offs. Do you spend money to promote this new product, or that social cause? Do you allocate people to this project, or that one? If your social objectives aren't seen as an essential part of your business—like price and quality—chances are very good they'll be the first to go in a trade-off.

When your distribution manager has five trucks waiting at the dock to load up and he doesn't have enough product, it's not possible for him to think, "How can I load these trucks in a values-led kind of way?" That's why values integration can't start at the execution level. It has to be part of the strategy. It has to be part of the operating plan.

If the loading dock's plan doesn't include the actions necessary to reduce pollution by switching the truck fleet to run on propane instead of gasoline, the distribution manager can't realistically find the time to figure out how to convert to propane. He's trying to load the truck, and he gets a call from some guy who says, "Hi, Mike. Listen, I've got a business converting vehicles to run on propane. Can I have a meeting with you?" And Mike says, "Yeah, sure. I'll see you in six months, next time I have a free hour."

But if the department has a plan in place to convert all the trucks— even if it's not until two years from now—Mike doesn't have to take time out to think about it while the ice cream's melting; he's already planned for it.

Pick an Issue—Any Issue

In the early days of Ben & Jerry's, when we first started taking public social and political stands, lots of different groups with lots of different progressive agendas came to us wanting Ben & Jerry's to take a stand on their issues. They were asking us to support causes we wanted to support, causes that were in keeping with our values. So we started doing that.

After a while the board of directors became concerned that we were diluting our power and our voice. They said if we agreed to take stands on every progressive issue that came down the pike, we'd be reduced in the public eye to "one of the usual suspects" and we'd be less effective than we had the potential to be. Also, the board felt we needed to focus on which particular social causes we were advocating so we could have a significant, measurable effect, instead of making less significant contributions here and there.

Out of that discussion we came up with four focus areas: the environment, agriculture, economic opportunities, and children and families. After a while, we realized those areas were so broad that they essentially encompassed everything. So we cut it down to three, then two, and eventually one—which was, and still is, children and families. This was a several-year-long process.

Meanwhile we were coming around to the idea of values-led business. We came to believe that the best and highest use of the company was not just to take stands on social issues but to integrate the company's social mission into as many of its day-to-day operations as possible. We found there was a conflict between focusing on a single issue in our public stands, on the one hand, and maximizing the integration of the social mission into the company's activities, on the other.

Since the opportunities to implement the social mission within any particular department's day-to-day operations were so limited, a single-issue focus would limit them even more. If we told the departments they could do only things that benefited disadvantaged children, for example, they might miss an opportunity to help start a job-training program for homeless adults or to improve the company's recycling efforts. By imposing the same focus on the company internally as we'd imposed externally, we were actually decreasing the amount of progressive social integration that we could do.

The biggest breakthrough we had in this area came from Liz Bankowski, our social mission director and a board member. A few years ago she came up with what we now affectionately refer to as "Liz's Chart." The chart expresses the ways in which the social mission is (or can be) actualized at Ben & Jerry's: in the *quality of work life* and how employees are treated; in how the company's *business practices* are used to improve the quality of life in the community; in the impact Ben & Jerry's has on the *environment;* and in the company's *social-mission projects,* the efforts of the company to use its power to help solve social problems or advocate for particular social legislation.

Here are some comments on the accuracy of the chart, from the person who created it.

✳ We put the workplace on the chart to underscore that the social values expressed outside the company must exist within the company. We'll never be perfect. We'll never fully meet all the internal and external expectations of what we should be. Nonetheless a connection must exist between our external values as a company and what it's like to work here.

With regard to our workplace, we have excellent benefits. We provide what we regard as a livable wage at the bottom of our pay scale, based on what it really costs to live in Vermont (plowing, firewood, cable, etc.). We have pay equity and good representation of women in management positions. On the other hand, we have only one on-site day care center, which serves a very limited number of employees.

We have a stock purchase plan and in 1994 we made an across-the-board grant of stock options to everyone in response to our 1993 social-performance assessment, which highlighted the lack of employee-ownership strategies during the company's high-growth years.

Because the company concerns itself with creating economic opportunities where they haven't existed, we need to be really good at showing that people inside the company can advance. The model needs to be very entrepreneurial, very reliant on individuals taking a lot of responsibility for their careers. We have some great examples of people who went from making ice cream to management responsibilities and to whole new careers. But we have no formal programs in place. We are redesigning compensation at our plants, based on job knowledge. We are also creating more incentive-based pay at the senior levels, based on company performance across our three-part mission. Our CEO performance measures include social as well as financial performance.

With procurement we've made steady progress around values alignment but we have not articulated what we're trying to accomplish with some of our alternate supplier relationships. We also need to be careful that values alignment does not mean any political litmus test. Judging can become a slippery slope. In developing a values screen we need to have our own house in order, be clear about behaviors we're concerned with, and seek data or information that is meaningful around defined

WORKPLACE

Values

- Trust
- Walk the talk
- Building a caring community within the company
- Sharing the wealth
- Open/inclusive
- Opportunity to influence

How

- Compensation including
  —Livable wage
  —Benefits/profit sharing and employee ownership
- Family-sensitive policies/practices
- Pay equity
- Dispute Resolution Process
- Workplace safety/place/process/people
- Good communication down and up
- Organization design to support grass-root social mission efforts/projects. Examples are:
  —Green Teams
  —Community Action Teams
  —Joy Gang
  —Ben & Jerry's Foundation

BUSINESS PRACTICES

Values

- Caring Capitalism
- Including a concern for the community in our day-to-day business decisions
- Creating economic opportunity where it hasn't existed

How

- Social Performance Assessment/planning
  —Goals by department
  —Measures
- Management accountability
- Products
  —rBGH
  —Organic/Sorbet
- Social Ventures
  —Alternate suppliers
   i.e., Greyston, Aztec Harvests
  —Ingredient sourcing
   i.e., Rainforest Crunch
  —Social Ventures
   i.e., Russian Venture
  —PartnerShops
   i.e., Times Square, Larkin Street, etc.
- Cart Program
  —Youth entrepreneurial initiatives
- Decisions about where we build our plants
- Procurement consistent with our 3-part mission
- Natural ingredients
  —No rBGH
  —Organic/low pesticide
- Diversity in supplier, vendor, franchise, and marketplace strategies
- Philanthropy
  —Foundation promotions; sponsorships; donations (money and product)
- Ethical practices
- Compliance with laws and regulations
- What we do with our money
  —Investment in socially responsible funds
  —Affordable housing tax credits
  —Cards for Kids (1% of monthly charges to Vermont kids organizations)
  —Dairy premium to support family farms
  —401(K)

SOCIAL MISSION: "To operate the company in a way that actively recognizes the central role that business plays in the structure of society by initiating innovative ways to improve the quality of life of a broad community—local, national, and international."

ENVIRONMENT

Values

- Stewardship of natural resources
- Minimize the environmental impact of our business
- Support sustainable agriculture

How

- Adhere to CERES Principles
- Environmental Assessment
- Packaging Innovation

INTEGRATION ASSESSMENT

- Minimize impact on
  —Air via transportation
  —Water via dairy waste
  —Wastestream via packaging and paper, chemical use, manufacturing processes
- Achieve energy efficiencies via lighting, engines, building, and process design and innovation
- Reduce CFCs
- Procurement policies
  —What we buy, who we buy from: office supplies, ingredients, etc.
- Support for employee-led Green Teams
- Sustainable agricultural practices
  —rBGH
  —Organic
- Special Projects/innovation
  —Composting

SOCIAL MISSION PROJECTS

Values

- Improve quality of life of broad community
- Political activism/education
- Focus on children
- Support for progressive agenda
- Support for employee "grassroots" projects
- Support for community projects that have a measurable impact and sustainable results

How

- Marketing campaigns
- Position papers (education)
- Social audit/annual report
- Special events, i.e., festivals, bus
- Franchise promotions, i.e., Call for Kids, Head Start Book Drive
- Tour
- Packaging
  —Campaign for New Priorities
  —Saving Family Farms
  —"Call for Kids" 1-800-1BJ-KIDS
  —rBGH labeling

Focus on Children

- Vermont Children's Forum
- "Call for Kids"
- Vermont School Breakfast campaign
- Delegations to CDF conferences/other meetings
- Site children's projects
  —Christmas project, storytelling, Springfield haunted house, etc.

Community Outreach

- Site community projects, i.e., Springfield nature trail and science building

Taking a Stand

- rBGH, Hydro Quebec, Persian Gulf, Rainforest Action Network

Involvement with

- Business for Social Responsibility (BSR)
- Social Venture Network (SVN)
- Vermont Business for Social Responsibility (VBSR)

objectives that our suppliers would understand. It's a real challenge and a work in progress! To date we've not been successful in executing any real program around minority sourcing.

In terms of the environment our goal is very simply to diminish the environmental impacts of our business. We're doing innovative stuff like composting our dairy waste (it makes great fertilizer) but we're still shipping product mostly by truck across the country. Our focus now is on our packaging—it's core to who we are and what we are. I find it troublesome to talk about rain-forest preservation without addressing our own packaging impacts. We are putting great effort into developing a source of unbleached paper for our containers.

We've learned in our marketing campaigns that it works best to focus and not have a campaign of the week, to work with a very credible non-profit advocacy organization, and to hold our issue campaigns to the same high standards of any marketing campaign with clear messages, goals, excellent execution, and measurable results.

Danger also lies in feeling we have to be too perfect. If we have to be too perfect we wouldn't do any of this stuff. It's fraught with risk around things going badly for a supplier or social-mission partner, around being misunderstood in what we're trying to do, and in exposure to anyone who wants to say "Gotcha."

> —Liz Bankowski
> Ben & Jerry's Social
> Mission Director

Like everything else in business (not to mention life), the chart is a work in progress. But it's a good resource if you're thinking of starting or converting to a values-led business.

● Our Points (and We Do Have Them) Are . . .

In the chapters that follow we'll tell stories and share tips based on what we've learned from building Ben & Jerry's into what it is today. But before we get into specifics, we'll lay out the foundation here: the five main points we hope you'll take away from reading the book.

1. Business is the most powerful force in society. Therefore business has a responsibility for the welfare of society as a whole.

In 1988, we were surprised and delighted to be named U.S. Small Business Persons of the Year. When President Reagan presented us with the award he repeated the much-quoted phrase "The business of America is business."

Maybe that used to be the case. But now that business has become the most powerful influence in society, we believe business has to accept responsibility for the welfare of that society and the people in it. Or, as we'd say, "The business of business is America."

If we go back in time and look at societal structures around the world, we see that religion was originally the most powerful entity. Then power shifted, and nation-states became the institutions of greatest power. Today the most powerful force is business. This is a very new phenomenon, occurring only within our own lifetime. You can see this reality echoed in major cities around the world: the oldest big, ornate building is a religious institution. The second-oldest big, ornate building is a governmental institution. And today, the biggest, most ornate buildings being built are commercial.

In order to maximize its social responsibility, a company needs to put its social mission right up front. Values are either a forethought or an afterthought. There's no middle ground. In order to get values in the right place—in order to maintain the balance between your social mission and your financial mission—they have to start out in first place.

Understanding what it means to be a values-driven company has been an ongoing process at Ben & Jerry's. When the two of us started scooping ice cream in an abandoned gas station, we hadn't given much thought to business, let alone its role in society. We envisioned ourselves having a homemade-ice-cream parlor that we'd run for two or three years until we moved on to something else. Calling our business Ben & Jerry's, giving away ice cream, holding free movie festivals, doing things that were community related were just honest, true expressions of ourselves.

Later, when we decided not to sell the business, we consciously undertook an experiment: to find ways for a corporation to impact society positively. We dedicated ourselves to the creation and demonstration of a new corporate concept, of linked prosperity. The company developed a three-part mission statement that reflected our commitment to this conviction:

PRODUCT MISSION	SOCIAL MISSION	ECONOMIC MISSION
to make, distribute, and sell the finest quality product	to operate the company in a way that actively recognizes the central role that business plays in society, by initiating innovative ways to improve the quality of life of the local, national, and international communities	to operate the company on a sound fiscal basis of profitable growth

Business is the strongest influence in our society. It influences elections through campaign contributions; it influences legislation through lobbying; it influences the media through ownership; and it influences our everyday interactions as consumers and employees.

All of this is done in the narrow self-interest of business, without much concern for the welfare of society as a whole. And that is the major change. The purpose of the first two most powerful forces, religion and government, was to promote the general welfare. But promoting the general welfare has never been a part of business's reason for being.

If the most powerful force in society does not look out for the general welfare, society will be destroyed.

For us there isn't any road map to follow. We've had to make it up as we've gone along. We get a lot of support and good ideas from our friends in like-minded businesses, but each of us has to figure out how to apply the principles we share to his or her individual company. Even now, one of the biggest issues at Ben & Jerry's is that we haven't been able to articulate our objectives specifically enough so that everyone in the company is fully aligned. As a friend of the company's once said, "Everyone's heading west, but 'west' is a pretty broad description." But there's reason for optimism; just this past year, our board developed a much clearer vision of Ben & Jerry's social mission.

We have a progressive, nonpartisan social agenda.

We seek peace by supporting nonviolent ways to resolve conflict.

We will look for ways to create economic opportunities for the
disenfranchised.
We are committed to practicing caring capitalism.
We seek to minimize our negative impact on the environment.
We support family farming and sustainable methods of food production.

We're constantly in a process of clarification, of improving what
we're doing. But we do agree on one central point: the impact of business
is so far-ranging and all-encompassing that we can't shirk responsibility
for societal concerns. Incorporating that responsibility into a
business can make it a powerful, positive force for social change.

2. A values-led business can be a highly profitable business.

Businesspeople have traditionally said that business can't concern
itself with the needs of the broader society, because it won't be able to
survive. Our experience proves that's just not true.

So do the experiences of other companies. There are plenty of companies
that are thriving today—Patagonia, Inc. (clothing); Odwalla, Inc.
(juice); Tom's of Maine, Inc. (personal care products); the Body Shop
International Plc. (body care products); Blue Fish Clothing; Frontier
Cooperative Herbs; Working Assets Funding Service (credit cards and
long distance phone service); Rhino Entertainment (music); Tommy
Boy (music); Whole Foods Market; Just Desserts; Stonyfield Farm Yogurt;
Aveda Corporation (personal care products); and many more. Ask
their customers why they buy from those companies, and you'll probably
hear as much about how much they love the company as you hear
about how much they love its products. That's a reversal of the usual
situation—most consumers are buying from companies in spite of their
negative feelings about corporations in general.

In our early days in business, the two of us used to be a hot ticket on
the Rotary Club circuit in Vermont. They needed a speaker to lull their
members to sleep as they digested their rubber chicken. We'd give our
talk, they'd fall asleep. Then at the end someone would wake up, raise
his hand, and say, "All this stuff you're doing for the community—
you're just doing it because it's good for business, aren't you?" And we'd
say, "No. It's altruism."

When we get that question now, we say, "Altruism is the old answer.
The new answer is, it *is* good for business. If you want to be more
profitable, why don't you try it too?"

3. People can influence business—as investors, as employees, as consumers.

Business needs capital, so it needs people to invest in it. It needs labor, so it needs people to work at it. And it needs customers to purchase its products or services. So, people can greatly influence how business conducts itself by choosing which companies to invest in, to work for, and to support with their purchasing power.

Today over $1 trillion—almost 10 percent of all managed market investments in the United States—are invested in socially responsible investments. According to *Good Money* by Dr. Ritchie P. Lowry,

> ❋ The socially responsible investment movement is growing exponentially in numbers of individual and institutional investors participating, in the amount of money invested, and most importantly, in the movement's ability to persuade corporations to develop a sense of social responsibility in the conduct of their businesses.

As companies discover that their stock price is influenced by how much they integrate societal benefits into their business behavior, they'll be more and more motivated to do so.

Similarly, companies are discovering that they're better able to attract and keep the best employees if they factor social concerns into how they run their businesses. Employees are more motivated—and productivity is higher—when they bring their hearts and souls as well as their bodies and minds to work with them.

Today most people don't make those conscious choices. They don't consider a company's social values when they choose a company to interact with. But socially responsible business and socially responsible investing are growing at a tremendous rate. At the annual awards ceremony hosted by the Council on Economic Priorities, small, medium-sized, and large companies are honored for their environmental, social, and employee practices. There are surveys done by firms like Cone Communications in Boston and Roper Research in New York proving that more and more consumers are starting to factor in these concerns.

Here are some findings from a 1994 survey conducted jointly by Cone and Roper:

- Seventy-eight percent of adults said they were more likely to buy a product associated with a cause they care about.

- Sixty-six percent of adults said they'd be likely to switch brands to support a cause they care about.
- Fifty-four percent of adults said they'd pay more for a product that supports a cause they care about.
- After price and quality, 33 percent of Americans consider a company's responsible business practices the most important factor in deciding whether or not to buy a brand.

The number of people who want to "vote with their wallets" is growing toward critical mass. There's a paradigm shift occurring. As one indicator, the Council on Economic Priorities' handbook *Shopping for a Better World*, which rates the products available in supermarkets based on their degree of social responsibility, has sold over 1 million copies since 1991.

For employees to influence the company they work for is a little trickier, especially if they work for big corporations. When we give talks, people always ask us, "How do you influence the company you work for if it's Procter & Gamble, DuPont, or Exxon?" Certainly it's harder to make sweeping changes at a huge corporation than it is to make them at a small company. But sometimes it's actually easier to make small changes at a big corporation, because there's more distributed authority and autonomy. Of course, a small change in a big company—switching to chlorine-free paper, for example—usually has a greater impact than a big change in a small company.

More and more corporations are realizing that if they're going to attract the best employees and motivate the ones they have, they need to start dealing with this issue of values and social concerns. Just as consumers are loyal to companies whose values they share, when employees feel they're working for some higher purpose, as opposed to just trying to maximize the profits of the company they work for, they're more productive.

4. Ben and Jerry are two regular guys who succeeded in large part because we were true to ourselves.

We didn't plan on becoming captains of industry. And we still aren't. We approached our business in a nonbusinesslike fashion. We made flavors we liked to eat and eschewed traditional market research, mostly because we couldn't afford it. We viewed ourselves pretty much the way the average person on the street views herself or himself, except there are a lot more people viewing us on the lids of our ice cream containers.

Ben: And the average person on the street hates corporations.

Jerry: I think "hate" is too strong a word.

Ben: C'mon, Jer. Read the polls. Get the data!

Jerry: People think business acts only in its own self-interest without concern for anyone else.

Ben: Right.

Jerry: They think businesses will do anything they can, break any laws they can, to make as much money as they can.

Ben: Right.

Jerry: But people don't hate it. They just look at it as business as usual.

Ben: Okay, okay. They do not hold business in very high regard.

Jerry: Correct.

Somehow the two of us ended up being the guys on the lid of this company. So we approach our business as a person on the street would approach it if he'd been feeling taken advantage of by big corporations, and all of a sudden he was plopped in the director's chair, and he took his feelings and actualized them. If he said, "Here are all the ways that business doesn't act real nice to folks like me. Well, I'm running the show now, so why don't I run it in a way that's fair to people?"

Of course it's not possible to please everyone all the time. And even when we think we're being fair, our intentions aren't always perceived that way. In the past and in the present we've had disputes with organizations and people who feel Ben & Jerry's hasn't treated them fairly: for example, Reverend Carter of La Soule, who feels we didn't live up to our commitments to him, Amy Miller of Amy's Ice Creams in Texas, who believes we tried to make it difficult for her to distribute her ice cream, and some shareholders who felt we didn't disclose relevant information about construction of one of our plants.

A values-led business is still a business. You can't always please everyone. You have to make rules, make tough decisions, prioritize the things you want to do. No matter what you do, some people are always going to feel you're not treating them fairly.

But if you're thrown into the chair you can choose to be the same person you always were. You don't need to put on a suit and tie if you'd rather wear a T-shirt. You don't need to hire an ad agency if you want to tell your own truth. You can choose not to believe the so-called conventional rules of business, to trust your own reasoning and beliefs instead of—or along with—soliciting advice from lawyers, accountants, and other businesspeople. You can still lead with your values, even when the experts tell you what they told us so many times: "Nobody's ever done that before. You'd be crazy to do that. It won't work." But just because something's never been done doesn't mean it never can be.

That's why we're writing this book: to show that you can run a profitable company by doing things in a way that's true to you and to your values, as long as you also do a good job of paying attention to the business basics of manufacturing, customer service, human resources, sales, marketing, and finance.

5. *There's a spiritual aspect to business.*

Most people would agree that there's a spiritual part of our lives as individuals. Yet when a group of individuals gets together in the form of a business, all of a sudden they throw out that whole idea. We all know as individuals that spirituality—the exchange of love, energy, kindness, caring—exists. Just because the idea that the good you do comes back to you is written in the Bible and not in some business textbook doesn't make it any less valid. We're all interconnected. As we give we receive. As we help others we are helped in return. As your business supports the community, the community will support your business.

Most companies try to conduct their businesses in a spiritual vacuum. But it's absurd to think that just because spiritual connection isn't tangible or quantitatively measurable, it doesn't exist. When people are aware that there's a company that's trying to help their community, they want to support that company. They want to buy goods and services from that company. They want to be associated with that company. And that's what values-led business is all about.

But the reality is, we'll never actualize our spiritual concerns until we integrate them into business, which is where we spend most of our time, where our energy as human beings is organized in a synergistic way, and where the resources exist that allow us to be at our most powerful.

In a way, a values-led business is a self-marketing business. Just by the act of integrating a concern for the community into your day-to-day business activities—buying your brownies from a bakery run by a religious institution that puts economically disenfranchised people to work, and your coffee from a worker co-op that returns the proceeds to the farmers, for example—you're creating a spiritual connection between you and your customers. And that moves them to support you.

Some cynics ask, "How can you claim you have a spiritual connection to your customers? How do you know whether they buy your ice cream because they like the flavors or because they have a spiritual connection with you?" Spiritual connection is impossible to quantify. All we know is that when we meet people on the street, when people speak in focus groups, and when consumers write us letters about why they like Ben & Jerry's—and about fourteen thousand people a year do write us letters—they talk as much about what the business does as they do about the product we sell. They talk about a sense of meaning and interrelatedness and support for our efforts to help disenfranchised people.

This is a new role for business to play. A role it's not accustomed to and wasn't created for. That's why business has to re-create itself. Because if the most powerful force doesn't take responsibility for society as a whole, society—and eventually the business itself, which is dependent on that society—will be destroyed. Our country has now become the most unequal society in the industrialized world. Twenty years ago, the richest 1 percent of people in America owned 19 percent of the wealth. In 1992 (the most recent figures available) the richest 1 percent of Americans owned 37 percent—twice as much—of the nation's wealth. And the bottom 90 percent of the population owned just 28 percent of the nation's riches. If this trend continues we will not long endure.

There's so little in society these days that people can feel a part of or believe in. Politicians—forget it. Institutional religion isn't as relevant to most people as it used to be. School—not much. Families are in disarray. Business—it controls society and doesn't care about people. In the world in which we live, the spiritual has been taken out of our day-to-day life. So we go to work during the week and focus solely on earning our paychecks and maximizing profit. Then on the weekends we go to church or temple and devote what's left of our energy to the spiritual part of our lives. But the reality is that we will never actualize those spiritual concerns until we integrate them into business.

In the midst of this desolate landscape, when people find a company that cares, they want to connect with it. Doing business with that company is something they can feel good about.

● This Book's for You

When we first decided to open an ice cream parlor, our goals were pretty modest. With this book we admit to having greater aspirations. We're hoping that reading it will free up a lot of people to finally do what their hearts and souls have been aching to do—integrate social values into their daily business activities. If you're a businessperson reading this book, we hope to demonstrate that there's an alternative to the status quo. We hope you'll see that it's possible to run a business in a way that proactively supports society, and that as you integrate your values more and more, you'll be just as profitable, if not more so. If you're a shareholder, an employee, or a customer, we hope to convince you to bring those values to your interactions with business. We hope to help you become aware that there's a different, more caring way for business to be—and as employees, customers, and shareholders, to demand that business be that way.

Remember in 1988, when environmental groups exposed the fact that dolphins were getting trapped and killed in tuna-fishing nets? A lot of folks stopped buying tuna. Consequently the tuna companies changed the way they caught their fish, so they could print "dolphin-safe" on the labels and get their customers back. According to the *New York Times,* Heinz decided that changing their fishing methods and raising prices would cost the company less than the "social disapproval" they would face if they continued. In other words, the ethical choice had become the profitable choice.

The socially responsible business movement is in its early stages. It's at a critical point in its development. There's a lot of questioning going on—some of it cynical, some well intentioned—about where it's headed and whether it can actually work.

The same thing happened in the early days of the environmental movement. The mainstream pooh-poohed it. People called environmentalists "tree huggers" and "crazy hippies." Now there's curbside recycling in most major American cities. There's a steady stream of environmental legislation moving through Congress. Environmental considerations are a part of the normal planning process today. Many corporations have environmental coordinators on staff. Most Americans know there's no "away" to throw things. Concern for the environment doesn't seem so crazy anymore.

That's the way social movements change what the norms are. Our guess is, it'll be that way with values-led business. It won't be long before the idea that business should be a positive force in society won't seem crazy either.

We know the world won't change overnight. What we're talking about here is taking small steps. The important thing is to take them in the right direction—and in the company of a lot of good people.

2

Looking for Goods in All the Right Places:

Values-Led Sourcing and New-Product Development

Jerry: If we want our business to have a positive effect on society, we need to look at where we can have the greatest impact: how we source the things we buy.

Ben: Where you buy your office supplies, your furniture, your ingredients, your packaging—of all the money flowing through your company, that's by far the largest amount.

Jerry: The Ben & Jerry's Foundation gave away $420,000 in 1995 to nonprofit groups—seven and a half percent of our profits. Which is considered a huge percentage of profits to give away. And yet it's small compared to what we spend with our suppliers.

Ben: Cost of goods. That's the big lever. Ben & Jerry's spends $90 million a year on packaging and ingredients. If we can spend a major portion of that in ways that benefit the community, we'll accomplish a lot more than we can with philanthropy.

Jerry: And if we can combine that with philanthropy, Ben, we'll accomplish more still.

● Beggars Can't Be . . .

When we first started making ice cream, deciding where to get our ingredients was a pretty straightforward process. We used whatever free samples we could get from whichever businesses would send them to us.

We'd write away to companies whose names we got from trade magazines like *Dairy Field*. We'd say, "Hi. We're starting a homemade-ice-cream parlor, and we're considering using your flavorings. Would you send us some samples so we can evaluate them?" Most of them never responded to our letters. A few sent samples. Each sample was enough to make several batches of ice cream.

One day we came home at sundown after a day of fixing up the gas station and found a stranger in a bowler hat parked in front of our rented cabin in South Hero, Vermont. You don't see a lot of guys in bowler hats in South Hero. He said, "I'm Duncan. I'm from Virginia Dare." That was one of the flavor companies we'd written to. "I have your letter right here in my briefcase." He looked around at our humble abode. "You make ice cream out here?" He thought he was coming to an ice cream plant.

We told him what we were doing. He'd had his own homemade-ice-cream stand, so he understood our situation. "I can help you guys out," he said. "I can give you everything you need." It turned out Virginia Dare was a vanilla house. They had twenty different kinds of vanilla. He had all the samples with him. "Try Number Seven," Duncan said. "You won't go wrong with old Number Seven." So that's what we used. Number Seven vanilla from Duncan.

The fruit we got in the early days was cheap or free, too: cantaloupes, peaches, bananas that were about to turn. Luckily, those fruits are at their most flavorful just when they're about to go, so they were great for ice cream. Sometimes a friend would come in with a batch of rhubarb from her rhubarb patch, or a few buckets of strawberries from her garden. Nowadays, we buy our fruit from fairly large fruit processors because we don't have the capability to process it, but in the gas station days, Jerry used to chop up the cantaloupes and hull the strawberries himself. Being broke and being cheap were the key criteria that shaped our purchasing decisions.

When we were ready to open the gas station we had to find a way to make our mix (the fresh cream, milk, sugar, and egg yolks that make up the base for the ice cream). We didn't have the equipment to make it ourselves, and the volume we needed was so small we couldn't find a supplier who was willing to make it for us.

Jerry: You want how much? Two hundred gallons a week?

Ben: And you want me to store it for you and deliver it every other day?

Jerry: You're kidding, right?

Finally the University of Vermont's School of Agriculture said they'd make our mix in their teaching dairy plant. But pretty soon our business started to grow, and making the mix was interfering with their other processing, so they asked us to find a commercial supplier. We couldn't find anybody in Vermont. The only source available was Weeks' Dairy in New Hampshire.

That was our first sourcing conflict—which also led to our first bad press experience. It was important to us to be a Vermont company, to do business in Vermont. But if we didn't hire someone to make our mix soon, we wouldn't be doing business at all. So we went with Weeks'. And they did a great job.

In August of 1985, the *Vermont Vanguard* ran a front-page story about Ben & Jerry's. They said Vermont's finest was actually getting its milk from New Hampshire cows. That was true, of course. It wasn't the way we wanted it to be, but we couldn't do much about it at the time.

In 1984 we built the Waterbury plant. Then we could make our own mix. Once Waterbury was operational, we started buying all our milk and cream from the St. Albans Co-operative Creamery, a group of five hundred Vermont family dairy farmers. So we were 100 percent Vermont-dairy-made again.

● Be True to Your Sources, and They'll Be True to You

Ben & Jerry's didn't have a mission statement in the early years. We hadn't yet adopted the concept of values-led business. But we knew we wanted to help preserve Vermont family farms. And we knew the best way to do that was to provide a market for Vermont dairy products.

Family farms had always been the backbone of the state, and they were being forced out of business because of overproduction in the rest of the country, low government floor prices, and the dominance of corporate megadairies using federally subsidized water in the desert of the Southwest. Vermont dairy farms represent many of the values we believe in: decentralized agriculture as opposed to corporate agribusiness; decentralized economics as opposed to concentration of wealth; responsible stewardship of the land and responsible treatment of cows. Family farmers pasture their cows; corporate agribusiness farms tend to keep them tied to a stanchion in a barn all day and use large amounts of drugs to combat disease and increase milk production.

Our commitment to supporting family farms was clear. But the practicalities of doing that led to an interesting dilemma. By creating more demand for Vermont dairy products, we would be forcing up the value —and therefore the price—of the milk we were buying. In the traditional way of looking at it, we were working against ourselves. In our way of looking at it, we were in a long-term partnership with the farmers. As in any long-term relationship, there would be times when the relationship was more beneficial to one party than the other, and times when that dynamic would be reversed.

In 1991 the price of milk started dropping tremendously. Farmers were having to sell for below their cost of production. The standard business practice was for the processor to pocket the increased profits; that's what they'd always done, and that's what every other processor (except Ben & Jerry's) was doing in 1991. But our board of directors very easily decided to pay the same amount for milk that year that we'd paid the year before. Our thinking was, this year's milk isn't worth any less to us than last year's. We should pay the farmers, our partners, the same price. At a press conference to announce our decision, Ben said, "This will result in $500,000 coming out of our pockets—the processor's pockets—where it doesn't belong, and into family farmers' pockets, where it does belong." (See chart on next page.)

People in the company and the community felt good about us taking that stand. Besides supporting the farmers, who were members of our community, people also recognized that there was marketing value in being a Vermont-based and Vermont-made product. We didn't have that in mind when we started out, but we realized it along the way. If we needed a business justification for our position, that was it.

In 1995, while we were building our plant in St. Albans, we desperately needed extra manufacturing space. The St. Albans co-op gave us space rent-free in their building to set up a temporary manufacturing

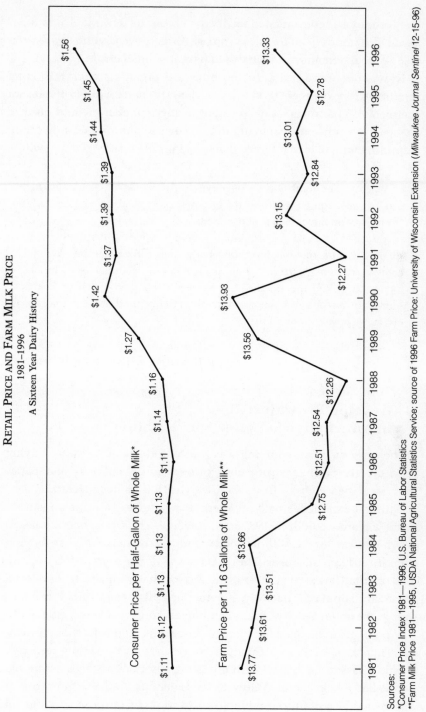

RETAIL PRICE AND FARM MILK PRICE
1981–1996
A Sixteen Year Dairy History

Consumer Price per Half-Gallon of Whole Milk*

$1.11 $1.12 $1.13 $1.13 $1.13 $1.13 $1.11 $1.14 $1.16 $1.27 $1.42 $1.37 $1.39 $1.39 $1.44 $1.45 $1.56

Farm Price per 11.6 Gallons of Whole Milk**

$13.77 $13.61 $13.51 $13.66 $12.75 $12.51 $12.54 $12.26 $13.56 $13.93 $12.27 $13.15 $12.84 $13.01 $12.78 $13.33

1981 1982 1983 1984 1985 1986 1987 1988 1989 1990 1991 1992 1993 1994 1995 1996

Sources:
*Consumer Price Index 1981—1996, U.S. Bureau of Labor Statistics
**Farm Milk Price 1981—1995, USDA National Agricultural Statistics Service; source of 1996 Farm Price: University of Wisconsin Extension (*Milwaukee Journal Sentinel* 12-15-96)

line—a major inconvenience for them—until our new plant was functional. If it hadn't been for the co-op's generosity, we wouldn't have been able to meet demand, and we would have lost business.

Nowadays, we're trying to move toward organic sourcing (finding vendors who grow their food or raise their livestock without the use of chemicals). That means our Vermont farmer suppliers would need to change from conventional to organic. Thanks to our long-term relationship with them, they're interested in working with us to make the switch.

✳   When you're in the conventional purchasing world and you're buying, you just buy. You go wherever the cheapest price is. You don't have a lot of loyalty. You buy it cheap, shove it out.

Values-led purchasing gives our suppliers a strong commitment to support us. Our relationship shows both sides of the equation. We both know we're in it for the long pull. If there's ever a shortage of materials, for instance, and the supplier has to decide whether to sell to Ben & Jerry's or someone else, there's no question in my mind they'll support us just as we have supported them.

—Todd Kane
Ben & Jerry's Purchasing Manager

● Greyston Brownies: An Alternative Supplier Success Story

In the early days our sourcing was pretty traditional. We were buying good quality products from conventional sources. Cones and paper from Sweetheart, Oreos from Nabisco, Heath Bars from Heath.

Our first experience with an alternative supplier came as a result of the new plant we built in 1987 in Springfield. The whole operation was dependent on the very thin, chewy, fudgy brownies we were buying from a fairly small baker. The bakery was doing a great job, but we realized that it was in the best interest of the company to develop a secondary supplier. That way, if something happened to our primary source, we could keep the plant running and our people working.

We looked and looked for someone else who could bake those brownies. Then Ben went to a Social Ventures Network meeting and met Bernie Glassman, a Jewish-Buddhist-former-nuclear-physicist-monk. Bernie had a bakery called Greyston in inner-city Yonkers, New York. It was owned by a nonprofit religious institution; its purpose was to train and employ economically disenfranchised people as well as to fund low-income housing and other community-service activities.

Ben said, "We're looking for someone who can bake these thin, chewy, fudgy brownies. If you could do that, we could give you some business, and you could give us the brownies we need, and that would be great for both of us."

Bernie understood exactly how great that would be, and he put a tremendous amount of effort—and time and money he didn't have— into developing a brownie to meet our specifications. Bernie's people made some excellent brownies, but they weren't exact duplicates of what we were getting. So we kept going back and forth, back and forth; tweak this, tweak that. Eventually they got it right and Greyston was approved as a secondary supplier.

The first order we gave Greyston was for a couple of tons. For us, that was a small order. For Greyston, it was a huge order. It caused their system to break down. The brownies were coming off the line so fast that they ended up getting packed hot. Then they needed to be frozen. Pretty soon the bakery freezer was filled up with these steaming fifty-pound boxes of hot brownies. The freezer couldn't stay very cold, so it took days to freeze the brownies. By the time they were frozen they had turned into fifty-pound blocks of brownie. And that's what Greyston shipped to us.

Ben: When the production people received those blocks they said, "We can't use this stuff. Pack it up. Send it back."

Jerry: I think we can say, Ben, that they were beside themselves.

Ben: So we called up Bernie and we said, "Those two tons you shipped us were all stuck together. We're shipping them back." Bernie said, "I can't afford that. I need the money to meet my payroll tomorrow. Can't you unstick them?" And we said, "Bernie, this really gums up the works over here."

Jerry: It was a real disaster. People were extremely upset that we were making them work harder, and we wouldn't just ship the brownies back. They said, "This is great for the social mission. But what about the quality mission? The product didn't meet spec. Why don't we ship it back as we would if it were any other supplier?"

We kept going back and forth with Greyston, trying to get the brownies right. Eventually we created a new flavor, Chocolate Fudge Brownie, so we could use the brownie pieces we ended up with when we broke up the brownie blocks. But we still had problems getting what we needed from Greyston. So we kept making our line workers work harder, and trying to explain to them why we were making an exception for this supplier. That explanation didn't go across too well. Working with Greyston didn't seem so socially beneficial to our production workers.

Finally we started having people from Greyston come and speak to our employees. They'd tell our people their histories and how Greyston was helping them and how our business was helping Greyston.

Jerry: What really made a difference was when the people from Greyston came and observed the people working in our plants . . .

Ben: . . . trying to deal with those brownie blocks they were shipping us.

Jerry: And then our people going to Greyston and seeing what it was like for them working there.

Ben: Everyone started understanding what we were putting one another through in order to get this thing right.

Now Greyston is one of our solid suppliers. The quality of the brownies they sell us is consistently excellent. They deliver on time. They do what they say they're going to do. And the benefit is mutual.

It took a lot to make Greyston a good supplier for us. We had our quality people working with them, our production people, our finance people. We fronted them money; we paid in advance for product. When they had management problems we sent people to help them with that. When they had quality problems, we worked with them instead of cutting them off.

In retrospect, we made a mistake in the way we presented Greyston to our employees. We told them Greyston was going to be just another supplier, that we'd treat them like any other supplier. They were our first alternative supplier, and we ourselves didn't know then that we needed to plan on treating those vendors differently. We need to give them more support and guidance at the beginning. A lot of times they're not geared up to make as much product as we need as fast as we need it.

If the company isn't convinced of the benefits of using alternative suppliers, there's less tolerance for the inevitable problems that arise, and more pressure to switch to a mainstream supplier when they occur. When we first started buying brownies from Greyston, we didn't have our production workers on board. It was a decision that came down from on high. We didn't adequately explain to people within the company how our decision was going to affect them. If we'd arranged exchanges between the two companies before we started doing business with Greyston, people's responses might have been different.

✳   I'd be lying if I said it's no extra trouble to do values-led sourcing. But one of the most powerful ways that Ben & Jerry's can influence the world is through our purchasing power. We're talking about $90 million a year of spending. That's worth some extra work up front.

—Debra Heintz-Parente
Ben & Jerry's Director of Materials

● More Trouble, and Worth It

Of course, there are always plenty of screwups, unexpected costs, and problems with mainstream suppliers too. For a protracted period of time, the company that makes our pint containers changed the glue they used on our lids, and the tops were coming apart. This was a very serious problem, of great magnitude, involving millions of lids and causing extreme customer dissatisfaction. We had trouble with our chocolate supplier, too: varying viscosities of fudge, burned-tasting chocolate. In both cases these large suppliers paid us money after the fact, but that didn't mean much to our unhappy customers.

The difference is, the smaller suppliers don't have the financial resources to fix things that go wrong. When something goes wrong with Greyston, they can't reimburse you the way a big supplier can. If your employees aren't committed to working with alternative suppliers, they'll be quick to point that out.

✳   Business has got to play a role in solving the problems of the urban centers in the United States today—which are caused in large part by the disappearance of quality blue-collar jobs from the inner city. The relationship between Ben & Jerry's and Greyston Bakery is a model for how that can happen.

Ben & Jerry's constitutes 75 percent of Greyston's business. Ben & Jerry's isn't the exclusive reason for Greyston's success, but it's certainly the dominant reason. Ben has always encouraged us to sell to other customers; he's prioritized the vision of Greyston above the exclusivity or ego of Ben & Jerry's. I've always thought that was quite enlightened of him.

Because we've developed these capabilities through our relationship with Ben & Jerry's, we have credibility as a supplier. Other companies approach us. We make six-inch cakes now for Whole Foods, and brownies for Stonyfield Yogurt. The volume of business has grown significantly. There was a time when we were proud to be doing two thousand pounds of brownies a day, and it was a struggle. Now we do six to seven thousand pounds a day.

The people at Greyston are reentering or entering the economic marketplace for the first time. These are people to whom that marketplace would not be otherwise accessible. Many of them had black holes in their résumés related to drugs or crime. Now we have this forty-five-person business in the community. People are going to work every day. They're able to provide for their families and be a model for their children.

These aren't just entry-level positions. All the supervisors, the purchasing manager, the human resources coordinator are all people who started on the Ben & Jerry's crew. But they're not high-paying jobs, either. The Greyston employees are working poor, but they're not destitute poor. We're not air-conditioned, so in the summer it's hot, hard work. But there's a sense of accomplishment and pride. They can have a nice place to live, good food, a few extras, and have their children see them go to work every day. For most people the real training is taking personal responsibility for their actions, showing up at work every day.

As our business has become profitable it's given space for some people to go on to the cake and tart crew, where people learn more—finished skills that can be taken on to other workplaces. For a lot of them this is permanent employment because there are no other jobs. But people who have been successful here have a good track record, so we can give them a good reference if they have an opportunity to move on. Recently we made a Social Venture Network connection: a young man was leaving Greyston to move to Boston. I made a call to an SVN friend, and he was able to get him a job at Reebok. The phone call was the introduction, but he earned that job on his own merit.

I describe this as a model of what other companies must do: take a risk and enter a partnership with a company like Greyston. It doesn't have to be a bakery. The product can be anything. It's a proactive way of dealing with the urban crisis in this country. The greatest gift Ben & Jerry's could have given is a sense of self-worth. And that's the most exciting thing about this partnership.

—Mac McCabe
CEO, Greyston Bakery

Candy from the Rain Forest

In 1989, at a Greenpeace party after a Grateful Dead benefit concert for the rain forest, the president of Greenpeace USA introduced Ben to Jason Clay from Cultural Survival. Cultural Survival is a Harvard-based anthropological organization that's dedicated to the preservation of indigenous cultures.

Cultural Survival was embarking on a project to create markets for sustainably harvested rain-forest products. Jason told Ben about a recent study that showed how the rain forest could be as profitable when it was sustainably harvested as when it was clear-cut for timber and turned into cattle ranches. Cultural Survival was beginning to market sustainably harvested rain-forest products to various companies, based on the idea that if the profitability of the living rain forest was increased, there'd be less incentive to destroy it. In addition to the intrinsic value of increasing demand for these products (and therefore for the living rain forest), they charged an environmental premium of 5 percent on the products they brokered. Then they used some of their profits to build a cooperative Brazil-nut processing facility, so that people who harvested the nuts could make the profits on the processing in addition to the selling price of the raw nuts.

Shortly after meeting Jason, in his "spare time," Ben launched a business called Community Products, Inc. (CPI). He wanted to create a business whose stated purpose from the outset was to do as much social good as possible by integrating social concerns into all its aspects. He decided to give away a substantial portion of profits to nonprofit organizations, and to create a mechanism that would provide no economic benefits to the owners of the business. He decided to create a product that would use Brazil nuts—which can't be cultivated but only grow wild in the rain forest—thereby providing an incentive to stop rain-forest deforestation.

Ben: The plan was that CPI's profits would be a means to an end—the end being social change. When people signed on as employees, they'd understand that social change was the purpose of the business. They'd understand we were hiring for alignment with those values.

Jerry: One of Ben's strengths is in starting from scratch, working by himself, not having to work within a larger organization. He chose a route that was more in line with his strengths and would allow him to accomplish his objectives.

Ben and his then wife, Cindy, went into their kitchen and set about inventing a candy recipe that would maximize the use of Brazil nuts. They studied cookbooks and did a lot of experiments, and finally came up with a butter toffee using Brazil nuts and cashews. (The cashews were from trees used to reclaim formerly deforested rain forests.)

Once he and Cindy had come up with the recipe for Rainforest Crunch, Ben bought ten tons of Brazil nuts for Community Products, Inc. Then, along with Irv Deutsch, a former Ben & Jerry's employee, he set up a Rainforest Crunch manufacturing facility.

Ben: The attempt was to integrate a concern for the community into as many of the day-to-day activities as possible. We had our long distance phone service with Working Assets, which donates over $2 million a year to activist groups chosen by its customers. We were giving away an amount equal to sixty percent of our profits to nonprofits ourselves. (Since its inception CPI has given away over half a million dollars.) That was modeled on Paul Newman's business—he gives away one hundred percent, but he doesn't have to reinvest profits in a manufacturing facility, because his products are manufactured under contract specifically for him.

Jerry: That is the lesson of Ben Cohen: total commitment. You get started, you don't know everything, you learn and improve as you go along. You try, you fail, you learn a little more and try again.

After CPI had been selling Rainforest Crunch candy in eight-ounce boxes for about a year, it became a runaway hit. CPI couldn't make

Rainforest Crunch is a registered trademark of CPI

TM ©1993 Ben & Jerry's Homemade, Inc.

HIS flavor combines our super creamy Vanilla ice cream with chunks of Rainforest Crunch, a cashew & Brazil nut buttercrunch made for us by our friends at Community Products in Montpelier, Vermont. The cashews & Brazil nuts in this ice cream are harvested in a sustainable way from tropical rainforests and represent an economically viable long-term alternative to cutting these trees down. Enjoy!

Ben & Jerry

The original Rainforest Crunch pint side bar

enough candy to fill its orders. Ben & Jerry's decided to make a new ice cream flavor based on the product. We put a sidebar on the pint about the social purpose behind the flavor—which also happened to taste great.

Rainforest Crunch ice cream took off like a rocket. The timing was excellent. *Time* magazine had recently made the Earth their Man of the Year. There was tremendous consciousness raising going on about the rain forest, and ours was one of the first rain-forest-related products on the market.

Dear Ben and Jerry:

I am basically a cheapskate and never buy anything unless it's 50% off, but *because of your efforts to save the rainforests I am now buying* your *ice cream. Keep up the good works! The planet needs more like you!*

—Martha S.
Montclair, N.J.

We didn't come out with Rainforest Crunch because we thought it would generate a lot of publicity or because we thought it would be a really hot-selling flavor. We did it because of the social values. But Rainforest Crunch ended up generating unprecedented publicity. It also became an incredibly profitable flavor. And along with the fifty or so other American companies who purchased sustainably harvested rainforest products—including Golden Temple Foods, the Body Shop, Whole Foods, the Nature Company, Dare Cookies, and Seventh Generation—Ben & Jerry's helped increase demand for Brazil nuts.

● Aztec Harvests Coffee

About ten years ago we got a letter from Bill Drayton of Ashoka, a foundation that gives fellowships to entrepreneurs in Third World countries who are working to solve social problems.

One of the programs Ashoka had going was the Aztec Harvests Co-op in Oaxaca, Mexico. The co-op was founded to provide more money and benefits to the peasant coffee farmers. Bill wanted to know whether we would start buying our coffee from Ashoka. That sounded great to us—especially after we tasted the coffee, which was delicious.

A few years after we started talking to Aztec Harvests, a guy named Dan Cox formed Coffee Enterprises and began purchasing and processing the coffee into an extract. Dan helped us work with Aztec Harvests until they were able to meet our quality specs. So, in 1990 we started getting our coffee from Aztec Harvests.

✳   A lot of companies were hesitant to get involved with Aztec Harvests because the co-op members didn't know American business. Ben just picked up the phone and asked if I could make it happen. Now Ben & Jerry's is Aztec Harvests' biggest customer. Ben & Jerry's has encouraged the co-op to get other customers, and they've done that. They also sell to Con-Agra (for their Healthy Choice frozen desserts) and some smaller companies. None of that would have happened without Ben.

When the co-op farmers were selling their coffee through normal channels, they were selling to big landlords and to "coyotes"—middlemen who pay below-market prices, cash on the spot. A lot of farmers couldn't afford to hold out, so they'd take the cash. When they don't have to sell to coyotes for below-market rates, they make more money. Plus, Aztec Harvests asks all its customers to pay a twenty-five-cent-per-pound premium so they can keep making improvements. Not all its customers agree to pay the premium, but Ben & Jerry's has paid over $200,000 in premiums since 1992.

A lot of people in the coffee industry think we're nuts for paying the premium and getting as involved as we have with the farmers. Our answer is, our customer doesn't want us to buy it elsewhere. Ben & Jerry's is committed to helping Aztec Harvests get what it needs to become a self-sufficient supplier.

—Dan Cox
CEO, Coffee Enterprises

● Switch to Values-Led Suppliers— or Help Traditional Suppliers Become Values-Led?

When we first heard about Aztec Harvests, we were getting our coffee from a traditional processor. We had to decide whether to buy our coffee direct from Aztec Harvests and have it extracted ourselves or have our existing processor buy it and extract it for us.

The bigger issue was, do you take your business away from a supplier who's treated you well, done everything you've asked of them, to switch to a supplier who's more aligned with your company's values?

We decided to have our processor buy the coffee and process it for us. Our hope was that our processor would start buying Aztec Harvests for its other customers as well.

But after many years of frustration, we realized that despite all the promises, our existing supplier was never going to buy beans from Aztec. Our processor wasn't used to dealing with one specific supplier. The normal way of choosing a supplier is to find out which suppliers offer the cheapest product, and buy from them. The processors aren't accustomed to the kind of one-to-one relationship we were asking our processor to establish with Aztec Harvests.

Also, Aztec Harvests wasn't as easy to deal with as a larger supplier. They couldn't afford to ship coffee unless it was prepaid. They didn't have expertise in dealing with processors. And they weren't a big enough player to make it worth the processor's while to work around the inconveniences. So we gave up and started buying our coffee direct from the co-op.

In the intervening years a discussion developed within the company about the best way to do socially responsible sourcing. The question was, is it more effective to help a new, values-led supplier to come into existence or to use our clout with bigger suppliers to get them to become more socially responsible?

Our experience has demonstrated how much more effective it is to help set up values-led suppliers than to try and change traditional suppliers' way of doing business. If you've got a market for a product, you can use your volume to help an alternative supplier grow and thrive.

For example, we have some of our T-shirts screened at City Works, a Washington, D.C., business whose mission is "to build a for-profit, inner-city business that offers high quality, environmentally responsible custom screen printing, while providing job opportunities and economic development."

City Works was established in 1994 in collaboration with Jubilee Jobs, a nonprofit employment agency for the poor and disenfranchised. The Body Shop gave City Works an interest-free loan to cover start-up costs, and an initial contract. In its first year City Works's sales were over $300,000. City Works employs about twelve people and now has a client list that includes not only Ben & Jerry's and the Body Shop, but Fannie Mae, Nations Bank, the Smithsonian Institution, Social Ventures Network, and Macy's.

● When the Marketing Mission Conflicts with the Social Mission (or Does It Ever, Really?)

In 1994 we created a new flavor for our chunkless Smooth line. We called the new flavor Aztec Harvests Coffee to help promote the brand, to give the co-op name recognition, and to help Aztec Harvests sell its coffee to other businesses. Our purpose in that relationship was to use the power of Ben & Jerry's to help the co-op. We had a panel printed on the pint container about the co-op and why we were supporting its work.

Ben & Jerry's has always had a hard time selling straight flavors like vanilla, chocolate, and coffee—and Aztec Harvests Coffee was no exception. It didn't sell very well. So then it became the job of the marketing department to figure out how to sell more of it. The solution they came up with was to rename the flavor Café Olé, on the theory that people couldn't tell it was coffee ice cream when the name was Aztec Harvests Coffee.

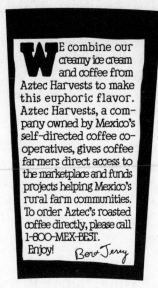

WE combine our creamy ice cream and coffee from Aztec Harvests to make this euphoric flavor. Aztec Harvests, a company owned by Mexico's self-directed coffee co-operatives, gives coffee farmers direct access to the marketplace and funds projects helping Mexico's rural farm communities. To order Aztec's roasted coffee directly, please call 1-800-MEX-BEST. Enjoy! *Ben&Jerry*

Ben: To say that I disagreed with that decision would be a huge understatement. If the people in marketing thought putting the name "Aztec Harvests" in front of "Coffee" was depressing sales, we should've called the flavor Coffee and put an Aztec Harvests star burst on the container.

Jerry: Well, Ben, let's say it does sell more as Café Olé. Let's say it sells fifteen percent more. Would you still disagree?

Ben: Then it should be "Café Olé made with Aztec Harvests Coffee." There should be a star burst on the label and an eight-hundred number people can call to order a pound of Aztec Harvests.

Jerry: But Ben, it may be too difficult to put all that on a pint container. The marketing department probably had to choose one or the other.

Ben: It doesn't help to have a socially responsible product if nobody's buying it. But it's not maximizing the benefit to Aztec Harvests to sell a lot of Café Olé ice cream if it doesn't build the Aztec Harvests brand and create more customers for their coffee beans.

● Screening Vendors for Values Alignment

Several years ago, we wrote a questionnaire to determine whether our suppliers were values-aligned with us and whether there was any social impact, negative or positive, resulting from our dealings with them. At the time other socially responsible companies—including Esprit, Smith & Hawken, and Working Assets—were using similar questionnaires.

Recently we've revived the idea of screening vendors' values alignment. Our director of operations, Bruce Bowman, is talking about including a review of vendors' social and environmental programs in our ingredients specifications. Bruce feels very positive about taking this step. It seems like a reasonable stance for Ben & Jerry's to take, and we hope to put it in place soon.

● Values-Led Purchasing: Define It, Staff It, Support It

✳   When I came to Ben & Jerry's, in 1994, the organization did not have a purchasing department. In their sixteen years in business they'd never had one.

The company actually had a belief that you shouldn't put anything down in writing with a supplier because then you'd get stuck with it. You wouldn't believe how much they got stuck with without putting things down in writing!

—Todd Kane

There are two key factors that affect a company's ability to do values-led sourcing. The first is the extent to which there is values alignment throughout the organization—especially in the purchasing department.

During the first several years of Ben & Jerry's existence, the common view of the social mission was that it took away from the company's profitability and caused extra work. Now there's a general understanding that what drives our financial success is being a different kind of company. People understand that the more kinds of values-led things we do, the more we contribute to that success.

The second factor is the extent to which you are well managed and well staffed.

Ben & Jerry's is doing more now in terms of alternative-supplier development and organic-supplier development than it's ever done before, because, starting about two years ago, we finally recognized the importance of our purchasing function and staffed it accordingly. Debra and Todd are 100 percent aligned with the company's values. They're also highly capable professionals.

✳   It takes a higher level of expertise to take the conventional sourcing model and change it. In the traditional companies where Todd and I used to work, what we'd look at was cost, quality, delivery. You'd actually prefer to go with a big supplier because they can give you high quality at low cost.

In its initial foray into values-led sourcing, Ben & Jerry's had some problems. We didn't look closely at cost or the supplier's ability to deliver. Instead of incorporating mission into the purchasing scheme, we just looked for mission. So some of our suppliers were negatively affecting our business.

To do values-led sourcing well, you need to consider three factors. One is the business concerns. One is the environmental concerns. And one is the social mission.

What we've learned is that if a supplier has a great social mission but can't deliver the business value, the model won't work long-term. What you're setting up is a dependent system. It's a false transfer of wealth. The supplier isn't really delivering the service you need, so they can't get other customers. You've gotten the supplier to be dependent on you. You're paying them for something they can't get anyone else to buy.

Even if the supplier's product is viable on the open market, if you're too high a percentage of their output, you really aren't doing them a favor. We encourage our suppliers to diversify their customer base, especially because our product demand has so much fluctuation. But if we can join with other companies to source them—as we did recently, when we turned Community Products, Inc. on to a Costa Rican organic vanilla we found—we are helping them become sustainable.

—Debra Heintz-Parente

✳   Greyston is a positive example of the model we're trying to build. They offer good quality and consistent delivery along with values alignment. We pay a slight premium on the cost, which adds just a few pennies to B&J's cost of producing a pint. They're diversifying, and they have other customers, because they have real value in the marketplace.

I go down to Greyston every couple of months and sit down with their business managers and provide them with a forecast. We'll adjust our schedules to suit their needs. We do a lot of added activity we wouldn't do with bigger, national bakeries if they were making the brownies. But that's a small price to pay for the values-led decision to work with Greyston.

—Todd Kane

We see Ben & Jerry's as this big circle that is a market for suppliers. And then there are these spokes coming out of the circle. At the end of each spoke is a little circle, which is an alternative supplier we've helped to set up. The model Todd and Debra have established is that then those little circles get bigger by adding other customers. And then there are more spokes coming out from those little alternative suppliers that are growing bigger, and the new spokes connect to new circles, which are new markets for their products.

Todd and Debra are looking for the big levers. They've analyzed the products we buy by the amount of money we spend on them, put them in priority order, and started looking for socially aligned suppliers for each of them.

✳ We buy Aztec Harvests Coffee through one co-op because we were able to ensure that most of the money is going right to the farmers. Although there was a push from the company to buy 100 percent of the co-op's output, we wanted to keep them level-loaded. So we bought about 50 percent of our requirements from them for two years. Then, this year, one of our major coffee flavors was discontinued. And we were able to continue to buy the exact same amount from them. We just reduced our order with our other supplier, who is larger and therefore could absorb the loss more easily. So the co-op felt no pain although we're buying 50 percent less coffee.

—Debra Heintz-Parente

● Sourcing Issues on the Horizon: Organics and Chlorine-Free Paper

As one of our board members said at a recent meeting, it's not getting to the heart of the matter for a values-led business to be values-led on the outside, in how it deals with the world, when its core product isn't consistent with its values.

Ben & Jerry's has taken stands on outside social and political issues. We've done partnershops to give nonprofit organizations a way to profit from our ice cream. (More about these in Chapter Four.) We've done supplier arrangements with Greyston and Aztec Harvests. Sourcing from a co-op is good. But now we've realized that conventional agriculture and chlorine-bleached packaging put toxins into the environment, which affect the health of everybody.

We haven't yet converted to organic sourcing for the major ingredients we buy: dairy products, sugar, cocoa, and vanilla. The conventional way that food is produced puts toxins into the food supply, the water supply, the air. That's not a sustainable form of agriculture. It's killing people. The cure for cancer isn't to treat it once it's in our bodies. The cure for cancer is to stop putting so many poisons into the environment.

There's evidence of this in *Our Stolen Future* by Theo Colborn, John Peterson Myers, and Dianne Dumanoski. Using decades' worth of wildlife studies, lab experiments, and human data, the authors—two environmental scientists and an environmental journalist—trace birth defects, sexual abnormalities, and reproductive failures in wildlife to synthetic chemicals that mimic natural hormones. Humans aren't immune to the effects of these "hormone disrupters." Sperm counts in men have dropped as much as 50 percent in the past few decades, and women have suffered a huge rise in hormone-related cancers, endometriosis, and other illnesses. From all of this the authors conclude that these chemicals may be invisibly undermining the future of the human species:

✻ Through the creation and release of billions of pounds of man-made chemicals over the past half century, we have been making broad scale changes to the Earth's atmosphere and even in the chemistry of our own bodies. Now, for example, with the stunning hole in the Earth's protective ozone layer, and it appears, the dramatic decline in human sperm counts, the results of this experiment are hitting home. From any perspective, these are two huge signs of trouble. The systems undermined are among those that make life possible. The magnitude of the damage that has already occurred should leave any thoughtful person profoundly shaken. . . .

As long as Ben & Jerry's uses conventionally produced agricultural goods, it's part of the problem. We're contributing to the destruction of the environment and the destruction of our customers' health. That's why we really have no choice but to make the switch to organic.

Dairy is our biggest issue. When we started trying to source organic milk, in 1993, we couldn't find a source we could afford. Then in 1996 we tried again, and found only an out-of-state source. We still couldn't find any organic milk that came from Vermont cows. The greater the market for organic products, the greater incentive dairy farmers have to switch from conventional methods. We wanted to buy the out-of-state milk for that reason, but we were committed to being "Vermont's Finest."

Then we learned that Stonyfield Farm Yogurt, a fellow values-led business and Social Venture Network member, had contracted to buy all the organic Vermont milk into the future. Recently we made an agreement with Stonyfield: since their selling proposition isn't predicated on Vermont dairy products, they've agreed to buy some of their milk from New York, so we can get ours from Vermont.

✱   I'm proud that Stonyfield is converting to organic. The majority of our ingredients are still conventional, but we're pretty concertedly converting. I don't know how long it'll take, but I'm confident we'll get there.

We're not leading the tide. We're being swept with the tide. Organic is here. It's not elite. It's mainstream. And that's incredibly exciting.

Stonyfield works with thirty-two organic dairy farmers. We and our partners at the Organic Cow converted most of them from conventional to organic. Seven have told us they'd be out of business if we hadn't become their customer and been willing to pay the higher price for organic.

Converting is important enough to us that we've built into our margin structure the ability to subsidize it, because using organic ingredients is not purely profitable. It's Robin Hood.

But there are some real cost benefits, too. My selling costs on organic are far less than my selling costs in conventional. I have lower slotting fees (the industry euphemism for extortion in exchange for getting your product on the shelves), which means lower cost of entry into supermarkets. It's an easier sale because organic is unique. It's directly targeted to the health-oriented customer. It takes a little more work to nail down my suppliers and get long-term contracts, but that's offset by a reduction of my selling expense.

There was this solar guru in the seventies, Steve Baer. He said, "One day we're going to wake up and see TV commercials for solar collectors. They'll be on sale at Sears. People will be driving around in their electric cars. It's all going to be so boring, so normal. And that's how we'll know that we've arrived."

That's what I'm looking forward to: the time when I can't compete based on organic anymore, because all my competitors are organic too.

—Gary Hirshberg
CEO and President, Stonyfield Farm Yogurt

A year ago, when we were developing our line of sorbets, we made a decision to use some organic fruits.

Our product-development and marketing groups had come up with flavor concepts in conjunction with the materials group. We all pushed for organic fruits. Debra and I knew there were organic ingredients out there. We presented it to the marketing group and they said, "Wow—what a great idea."

It's exciting because using organics in the sorbets is opening up doors to other organic sources, so we might be able to use organic products in our other finished goods down the road.

—Todd Kane

The transition to organic agriculture has a huge social impact—bigger, even, than coming out with a new flavor with a social-mission component. Buying organic is both environmentally and socially beneficial. Organic farms tend to be smaller than conventional corporate farms, and this contributes to economic decentralization—another value we support.

The importance of making this transition may not be as readily apparent as with some other things we do, but it's crucial for everyone's health. The problem isn't only trace poisons left on the food we eat. It's the huge quantities of poison that end up in the water supply, soil, and air that are killing us. And the intake of poisons from conventional agriculture isn't something consumers have a choice about. We can't just adjust our eating habits and avoid them. That's why food producers and food processors like Ben & Jerry's have a responsibility to address this issue and not leave it to consumers.

It's similar to the issue of children being shot in the inner city. Gun violence is currently the number one cause of death for African-American teenagers. But the government wouldn't fund programs to prevent shooting deaths because they said it wasn't a health problem. Which raises the question that's been asked many times: "If it's not a health problem, how come so many people are dying of it?" You could say the same thing about conventional agriculture.

Organic produce costs us about 25 percent more. But as more producers switch over to organic and more organic products come on the market, the price will decrease.

❋   People in the company embraced the idea of sourcing organics. Then we had to manage their expectations. Ben, whom we love dearly, said, "Great. Now let's make one hundred percent of our raspberries organic." We had to explain the reasons for moving more cautiously.

The supply chain in organics is so small that if you become totally dependent on it, one bad growing season will wipe you out. Also, a big player like Ben & Jerry's coming to the market could have caused premiums of multiple hundreds of percentages.

We don't do society any good if we, as a large producer, falsely drive the price up and create a demand the supply chain can't keep up with. If we convert farmers to organic with the expectation of a high price, and then they can't get that price, they'll go out of business.

The other thing that happens is that when you falsely drive up the price of organics, people start to falsify their products. They'll call it organic when it isn't. You drive a lot of bad behaviors when you create a market too quickly. You have to drive the demand up reasonably, at a pace the supply can stay close to.

Normally in a job like Todd's or mine, you don't have to think about such things. You just decide what to buy and buy it. But responsible, values-led purchasing means we don't just get organic at any price. It means we care about the supply chain and move in that direction responsibly.

—Debra Heintz-Parente

● Chlorine-Free Paper

McDonald's does not call itself a values-led company, but they're way ahead of Ben & Jerry's on paper. We're still using chlorine-bleached white napkins. McDonald's napkins are unbleached brown, and they're made from 100 percent postconsumer recycled paper. Ben & Jerry's napkins are made from at least 10 percent postconsumer waste and can be as high as 90 percent postconsumer, depending on what's available.

We've been grappling with how to switch to chlorine-free paper. Most white paper is bleached with chlorine, a process that releases dioxins—

among the most toxic chemicals known to humankind. Greenpeace has shared with us its expertise on the subject, which helped convince us of the urgency of making the transition.

✳   Clean, pure, and white. The first two words are the public expectation. Consumer products, particularly food, are presumed to be unadulterated and sanitary. And for the most part they would be, but for the third word —white.

White is the problem, particularly when it comes to paper. The white color often used in food packaging is thought to impart a sense of purity to the product it contains. The truth is far from that. Paper containers are made from wood pulp, and paper makers have traditionally made their wood pulp white by bleaching it with chlorine. In the process, chlorine reacts with organic, or carbon-based, chemicals present in the wood to form a group of pollutants known as organochlorines.

There are approximately three hundred different organochlorines in the chemical soup dumped by pulp mills into waterways. The most infamous among them is dioxin—one of the most potent poisons known to science. Dioxin and the other organochlorines dumped by pulp mills are not found in nature, and there are no natural processes for breaking down organochlorines.

These pollutants enter our environment from many different sources, but pulp and paper mills are the primary dischargers of organochlorines into water.

What's so different about organochlorine pollutants? Organochlorines are environmental poisons as a horror novelist might imagine them. As noted above, once produced they do not break down and are stable in the environment for decades. Second, they are bioaccumulative, which means that as they pass from the nonliving environment (air, soil, water) into the living environment (plants and animals) their concentrations are magnified by factors of thousands. While pulp and paper mills may be discharging organochlorines at relatively low levels, all of those organochlorines are passed up the food chain, with each level absorbing the collected organochlorines of the previous level. In the Great Lakes, organochlorines have been found to concentrate in fish at levels 150,000 times higher than in ambient water.

Once in the environment, organochlorines keep moving. They will not dissolve in water, but they will dissolve in fat. As a result, organochlorines keep moving through the food chain until they come to rest in fat. As mammals at the top of the food chain, this is bad news for humans.

Once in our bodies, these pollutants can poison their host. Organochlorines have been linked to cancer, birth defects, and a host of other maladies. Some of the current scientific thinking on the subject holds that organochlorines act as synthetic hormones in the human body, switching various functions on and off at random.

All of this trouble, just to make paper white, to give the false impression that the paper is "pure."

The connection between the chlorine used to bleach pulp for paper and organochlorine pollution was discovered in the early 1980s. Since then, a number of paper makers (most of them European) have switched bleaching chemicals to nonchlorinated alternatives. While that is a welcome and necessary step for printing and writing papers, a more direct alternative for nonprinting papers is to forgo bleaching altogether. Under the "reduce, reuse, recycle" paradigm, the best bleach is the one not used at all.

Coffee filters, toilet paper, women's sanitary products, and milk cartons (again, mostly European) are a few of the products that have switched from white to brown for environmental reasons.

Greenpeace has campaigned since 1987 for the elimination of all chlorine-based chemicals from the pulp and paper industry. We have lobbied governments, both local and national, worked with community activists in pulp mill towns for change in industrial processes and better protection for communities and the environment. We have worked with progressive paper makers and institutional paper buyers to bring innovative products to the market.

—Andre Carrothers
Greenpeace Board Member

Ideally, we'd like to switch to chlorine-free paper in all aspects of our operations—our offices, scoop shops, bathrooms, and everywhere else. But our greatest concern is in packaging, because that's where we use the most paper. When you talk about big levers, packaging is one of them. That's an area where our volume is sufficient to have an influence on the industry as a whole.

In terms of our pint containers, we haven't yet been able to come up with a container that's printed on unbleached, brown paper *and* meets our marketing and sales needs. The colors and design of our current packages don't show up as well against a brown background. There are plenty of opinions about how to solve the problem, but we all agree that purchasing paper and raw ingredients that are produced in ways that have a negative effect on the environment and on people's health is less than responsible when alternatives are available. That's why we're working to move toward purchasing chlorine-free paper and organic ingredients.

● Minority Sourcing

Choosing minority-owned vendors, which means supporting minority-owned businesses, is another factor to include in the matrix of values-led sourcing. Minority vendors provide economic opportunities to groups of people who have been systematically denied full economic opportunities. If you're in favor of equal opportunity for all, one way to express that is to direct some of your purchasing dollars to minority vendors.

Mainstream business has taken the lead on minority sourcing. Ben & Jerry's is lagging behind. In 1996, our purchasing group initiated a Supplier Diversity Program aimed at increasing purchases made from values-aligned businesses as well as those that are minority- and/or woman-owned. But most large corporations are involved with minority sourcing to one extent or another. If they're not, pretty soon they'll hear from an organization like the Reverend Jesse Jackson's P.U.S.H.—as well they should.

As with packaging, McDonald's does great work in this area. McDonald's Business Development Mission Statement is: "To grow and develop minority entrepreneurs who have the desire, ability, skills, and experience to capitalize on partnership opportunities; and to do business with existing companies who produce quality products and services at competitive prices." The company's franchisees represent the largest group of minority entrepreneurs in the United States; 65 percent of those now in training are minorities and women.

JCPenney has had a Minority Supplier Development Program since 1972. The program encourages buyers and managers to "take extra steps, provide guidance and assistance to help minority and woman-owned businesses make their products or services more attractive to JCPenney." Penney gives Minority Supplier Development Awards each year and helps minority suppliers develop business plans, gain access to capital, and develop products. In 1992 Penney was awarded the Minority Business Leadership Award by the National Minority Development Council for "demonstrating long-term achievements and growth in minority business development."

According to the National Minority Development Council, the companies that have the best minority-development programs are some of the country's biggest: AT&T, IBM, Nations Bank, and the Big Three automakers, who spend more than $1 billion a year *each* in purchases from minority suppliers.

The point is, size shouldn't be a barrier. Any company, small or large, can benefit from doing business with minority suppliers. What's difficult about opening your business to minority suppliers is the same thing that's hard about changing any supplier. Each supplier is represented by salespeople. Those salespeople have done their jobs very well. They have built relationships with your buyers. They have stroked, and schmoozed, and sent chocolates at Christmas, and made whatever accommodations they needed to make to stay in your buyers' good graces. So your buyers have to be very dedicated to the social mission if they're going to abandon those relationships. And the move needs to be made gradually, while the new relationships are beng established.

● Values-Led New Product Development

Ben: You could make a case that it's better to set up a new supplier for a flavor that's been a strong seller, that you know is going to be continued. There's less risk of the flavor not selling and the supplier going out of business than there would be with a new flavor.

Jerry: You could also make the case that going to an alternative supplier for a product that's necessary for the lineup, without being sure it's going to be done properly, is extremely risky.

Ben: We could switch to an alternative supplier for some but not all of the product, and make the transition gradually. So we're not putting the whole line at risk, and we're not putting this tremendous volume onto a new alternative supplier.

An important part of our business is coming up with new flavors and new products. We are constantly engaged in that process.

For most companies, new product development is an ongoing activity. For a values-led business, the R&D process represents a particularly significant opportunity.

Instead of taking a finished product and trying to figure out ways to add social value to it, the development process represents a chance to design a new product around its potential social value. We learned that when we developed Rainforest Crunch around socially beneficial ingredients. That's when you're establishing your specs, and choosing and working closely with your suppliers. That's when you have the most flexibility to create a product that will benefit society on as many levels as possible. Once you have a successful product that doesn't have social benefit, it's much more difficult to go back and retool or re-source it.

We've learned the importance of building values into the development process the same way we've learned a lot of other lessons: the hard way. Rainforest Crunch was the first time we consciously decided to create a product that served our social mission. Before that there were several times when we had to retrofit a successful product to bring it into alignment with our values.

The first time that happened was with our Oreo Mint ice cream, a perennial best-seller. At our annual meeting in 1988, our shareholders criticized us for using Oreo cookies because they're made by Nabisco, which is owned by R. J. Reynolds. The shareholders didn't like us doing business with a tobacco company. We were grateful to them for alerting us to that situation, and we re-sourced the cookies. But that meant we had to change the flavor name to Mint Chocolate Cookie, and we had to go through the difficult task of finding another cookie that tastes like an Oreo. If we'd been aware of the implications of using Oreos in the first place, we could have avoided the confusion and potential loss of sales.

The thing to do is to start by designing products for maximum social benefits, then work back from there to a product you can actually produce and sell. When we were developing our Wavy Gravy flavor, our intention was to use the maximum amount of Brazil nuts (for the same reasons we created Rainforest Crunch). The first few recipes we tried were overwhelmingly rejected by our customers because they essentially consisted of 100 percent Brazil nuts. The flavor was just too weird. We kept cutting back on the Brazil nuts until we finally came up with a recipe people really liked. The flavor has sold well for several years now, so we've ended up buying a lot more rain-forest nuts than we would have if we'd doubled the amount of Brazil nuts in the recipe but the flavor hadn't endured.

If you're lucky enough, as we are, to have people in your sourcing and purchasing functions who are highly capable and highly motivated by your company's values, after a while you'll find that they're initiating new products, or refining new products other departments initiate, because they're so committed to integrating the company's social values into new product development.

✳   We're always looking for socially responsible suppliers of ingredients that might be used in a frozen dessert. We keep a mental database, and we get references. We might read about someone, or one of our existing suppliers might mention someone, or sometimes new suppliers come to us. Debra and I are always keeping our eyes and ears open. So when someone at Ben & Jerry's comes up with a new flavor idea, we can get right to work making sure the social mission is built in from the start.

—Todd Kane

● Looking for Goods for All the Right Reasons

The process of values-led product development means looking for ingredients with positive social impact; then trying to make the best possible product using those ingredients; then testing it with consumers to see whether they like it; then offering it to consumers who you hope will choose to buy it. That's not the normal product development process. And that's not Ben & Jerry's product development process—yet. But we're moving in that direction, in many cases following the lead of other values-led companies.

The Body Shop has been a pioneer in the fields of values-led sourcing and product development. Patagonia now uses recycled plastic bottles to make some of its synthetic fabrics, and uses only cotton that's 100 percent organic. Just Desserts Bakery in San Francisco sponsors the Garden Project, which puts prison inmates and unemployable former inmates to work in a garden behind the bakery. Just Desserts buys some of its fruit from the garden, and when the inmates "graduate" from the project, some of them get jobs in the bakery. Chez Parnisse buys most of its vegetables from the garden.

Take the Lead Apparel is a less known but equally good example. Dominick Kulik looked around and saw that most socially responsible companies cater to high-end customers. He wanted to demonstrate that it's possible to be socially responsible and appeal to a broad mass market—and moreover, that the more people you appeal to, the more socially responsible you can be. He started developing 100 percent organic socks. Then he realized he couldn't hit the mass market price point with 100 percent organic, but if he blended in a percentage of organic and sold the socks for a lower price, he'd sell a lot more socks and provide more of a market for organic cotton.

Take the Lead donates some profits to nonprofit organizations, and they do joint projects with Little Souls Dolls, another values-led business. Little Souls hires culturally and economically disadvantaged girls and women—some of them former child prostitutes—around the world to make collectible dolls dressed in the clothing of the countries where they're made. "Little Souls, Inc., believes the end product is really the journey, the collaborative effort of interdependent peoples, ideas and solutions which ultimately creates a thing of beauty, no matter what the imagined boundaries," according to their mission statement.

Values-led sourcing gives your company a way to make a huge positive impact on society. So it motivates shareholders to invest with you, customers to spend their money with you, and employees to work for you.

＊ With my background, I wouldn't have come to work for Ben & Jerry's, except this is fun for me. Todd and I were both at a point in our careers where we needed to feel like our work contributed to positive change. We were looking for something different—a way to give back. And we found it.

—Debra Heintz-Parente

＊ I worked at a Fortune 500 corporation for ten years. What attracted me to Ben & Jerry's was that I believe in what Ben & Jerry's believes in. I thought it would be awfully nice to be able to live twenty-four hours a day with the same set of values, not have one set at home and a different set at work.

When I think back on the things I used to feel good about earlier in my career, it was always cost savings. On a Friday night I'd go home and say, "Boy I really saved the company a lot of money this week." The type of thing I feel good about now is when I walk out of Greyston Bakery after one of my visits and I realize, "Wow, what a difference we're making." There's been a huge shift in my values and in what makes me feel I'm being effective today.

—Todd Kane

Values-led sourcing and product development just means adding another box to your decision-making matrix. Instead of making sourcing decisions solely on the basis of cost and quality, you make them based on cost, quality, service, and impact on the community—negative or positive.

Sometimes values-led sourcing costs the same as traditional sourcing. Sometimes it costs more. Sometimes it costs less. But the benefits —measurable and intangible, financial and societal—make it well worth doing.

✳   What we're trying to do here is very holistic. The whole company has to believe in the mission, be integrated on the vision and on using it to leverage the company. When it's for real, the suppliers know it, the employees know it, and the customers know it. You can't buy the kind of loyalty that creates.

—Debra Heintz-Parente

Turning Values into Value:

Values-Led Finance

Ben: When we decided to go into business, the first thing we had to do was figure out how much money we'd need. Then we had to figure out how to get it.

Jerry: The bank wouldn't give us a loan without a business plan. A friend got us a copy of a plan from a pizza parlor in New York. We went through it and wherever it said "slice of pizza," we changed it to "ice cream cone."

Ben: Then we did our projections: how many cones per hour we'd have to sell, how much we'd have to pay for rent, ingredients, insurance, electricity.

Jerry: The projections showed there was no way the business could be profitable. I said, "Ben, the numbers say it's not going to work."

Ben: And I'm looking at the same numbers and I'm saying, "No problem. We'll just change the numbers."

Jerry: That turned out to be the right answer.

● Turning Values into Value

Profits and principles. Maximizing financial gain and contributing to the community. Doing well by doing good. These are concepts that are not commonly thought of as working well together. Most people think of finance as the area of business that most sharply clashes with values.

In fact, the realm of finance has incredible potential as a tool for social change.

✳   Money should never be separated from values. Detached from values it may indeed be the root of all evil. Linked effectively to social purpose it can be the root of opportunity.

> —Rosabeth Moss Kanter
> Harvard Business School Professor,
> Guggenheim Fellow, author of *World Class:*
> *Thriving Locally in the Global Economy*
> and eleven other books

There are as many ways to take advantage of that opportunity as there are ways to market, or source, or sell products in a values-led way. Depending on the nature and resources of the company, that might mean finding a creative way to engage in a conventional finance-related activity—like making it possible for members of the local community to get in on the ground floor with a direct public offering of stock. Self-underwritten direct public stock offerings can be used to make possible a low minimum buy, which in turn makes it possible for people who aren't wealthy and don't normally invest in the stock market to buy in.

Applying values to finance might mean making investments in companies that have a positive social impact. Or using investment tax credits to direct money into low-income housing. Or doing business with banks like South Shore Bank in Chicago, which invests in neighborhoods other banks abandon—"greenlining" low-income neighborhoods instead of redlining them.

✳   South Shore Bank's purpose is neighborhood economic development. The corporation exists to renew communities. Most neighborhood development initiatives are run by either government or nonprofits; there aren't many bank holding companies in the country with our agenda.

South Shore started in Chicago in 1973. Now we have banking operations in Detroit, Cleveland, the upper peninsula of Michigan, and the Pacific Northwest. We've served as advisors or as a model for the Southern

Development BanCorporation in Arkansas, Vermont National Bank, Community Capital Bank in Brooklyn, Community Bank of the Bay in Oakland, the new Louisville Development Bank, and several development banking initiatives abroad, including England, Pakistan, and Kenya.

You can't have a healthy neighborhood without a bank, but bank credit alone will not renew a community. You need programs that complement the lending activities of the bank. That's why we set up a holding company structure that originally had a bank and three nonbank companies: a real estate development company, a venture capital company, and a nonprofit to do housing and jobs work.

On the bank side, the beauty of it is that we can offer deposit accounts to people at the same rate and terms as any conventional financial institution. We raise money from all over the country by asking individuals and institutions to make deposits: institutional investors in NYC with seven-figure investments and forestry workers in the Pacific Northwest with balances of under a thousand dollars. We offer the same services as any other bank, except the people who invest in South Shore's Development Deposits^{sm} know what's happening to their money. It's going to rebuild inner-city neighborhoods. They get both a social and a financial return. If South Shore is profitable without generating development, it doesn't succeed. If it generates development without being profitable, it doesn't succeed. It's that rock-core combination that drives what we do.

Whereas most banks take your deposit and convert it to credit to fund real estate in an overdeveloped downtown area, for twenty-three years South Shore has been taking deposits and converting them to credit for development. Our depositors from all over the country—including Ben & Jerry's—put money in South Shore Bank because they care about what we're doing with their money.

—Joan Shapiro
Executive Vice President, South Shore Bank

＊ Currently we have a certificate of deposit with South Shore Bank for $1 million. We started this investment in 1989.

In addition to this investment, we worked with Joan Shapiro of South Shore to see if we could transition our overall corporate banking services to their bank. We found out that we needed a bigger bank to meet our line of credit and long-term debt needs. Joan researched whether she could put together a consortium of banks to give us a competitive rate for a $10 million line-of-credit facility. Unfortunately that didn't work out. But we're talking to Joan now about an increased deposit relationship.

Doing business with a bank like South Shore is very important to

Ben & Jerry's in terms of integrating our social mission with our financial management. So we'll keep trying to find innovative, secure, and mutually beneficial ways to expand our relationship.

—Fran Rathke
Ben & Jerry's CFO

As we discussed in previous chapters, turning values into value means integrating social values into the activities of a corporation, and in the process, creating financial value for shareholders. Companies that are values-led end up holding their financial value because they attract more productive employees and more loyal customers—which results in increased sales and profitability.

A company's financing mechanisms can be adapted to incorporate a values component while enhancing the company's profitability. For example, Ben & Jerry's initial public stock offering was not conventional, but it was successful.

● Raising Start-Up Money

When we decided to open a homemade-ice-cream parlor in Burlington, we went right to work trying to raise start-up capital. Jerry had about $4,000 in savings. Ben had $2,000. Ben's father had promised to lend us $2,000 more. We knew that wasn't enough money to open an ice cream parlor. We needed a bank loan, and to get a bank loan we needed a business plan.

So we sent away for some of the inexpensive little six-page brochures the Small Business Administration publishes. The brochures gave us formulas to figure out how much money we needed to start out with, and what our break-even point would be. Everything we needed, and in those days they cost only twenty-five cents each.

We used those brochures to fill in the blanks on the pizza parlor business plan we were using as a template. Unfortunately, we read one of the brochures wrong, which caused us to make a basic error in our planning. We thought you were supposed to double your cost of ingredients to come up with your retail price. In fact, for an ice cream parlor, you're supposed to triple it.

Also, the business plan called for us to estimate how many ice cream cones we were going to sell in an hour, a week, or a month. That stumped us. How were we supposed to know how many people were going to patronize a homemade-ice-cream parlor in a town that had never had one? There was no rational basis for coming up with an estimate of sales—but writing a business plan, applying for a bank loan, required us to do that.

There was a side benefit to that exercise. It taught us a new discipline: understanding how all the elements of a business are interrelated.

Later we realized that our initial calculations were based on sales projections that were unprojectable, on the wrong formula for figuring selling price, and on a huge underestimation of the number of ice cream cones we would end up selling in a typical day. Not surprisingly, our financial model showed the business couldn't be successful.

The numbers dictated one scenario, but our gut instinct dictated another. We had to decide which to act on. In those moments it helps to be a person like Ben, who realizes facts and figures don't tell the whole story—and may be downright misleading. But even if you're not quite that much of a free thinker, it's easier to go with your instincts when you're starting up, if you choose a business whose customers are people like you because you're operating so much from your gut anyway. You're more in touch with your market because you're selling your products to people like yourself. You don't have to hire consultants to get a handle on who they are demographically or psychographically. They're not just your customers; they're people like you.

But there's always that choice to make. You can just as easily say, "I don't believe the numbers," as, "I don't believe my own qualitative judgments based on my observations of the marketplace."

After all, it wasn't instinct alone that told us to go ahead despite the projections. We couldn't afford to hire anyone to do market research, so we'd done our own—visiting homemade-ice-cream parlors up and down the East Coast. We counted the revolutions per minute of the ice cream freezers at Steve's. We learned how other shops made ice cream. We saw ice cream parlors that were successful in towns similar to Burlington. We familiarized ourselves with the competition they faced, their pricing, the kind of products they were serving. We had reason to believe we could be successful too. So we changed the numbers to project first-year sales of $90,000 and a pretax net profit of $7,746.

Plan in hand, we went to Fred Burgess at the Merchants Bank in town and asked him for $18,000. Fred said he'd submit the loan to the Small Business Administration because the SBA would guarantee it. If we couldn't pay it back (which many small business start-ups never manage to do), the SBA would repay the bank 90 percent of what it had loaned us.

The SBA agreed to give us the $18,000 if we found a "suitable location" in Burlington. We thought the gas station was a fine choice, but the SBA didn't agree, because we couldn't get more than a one-year lease. When we went back for our loan, the SBA wouldn't approve it. Fred offered us $4,000 instead. We took it.

Fred's loan didn't seem like the greatest vote of confidence, but we weren't too proud to accept it. All we had was $8,000, and the extra $4,000 gave us just enough to open. Looking back on it now, it's clear that Fred didn't expect to get paid back. He probably thought it was worth the $4,000 just to watch how we spent it. Maybe he figured he'd get some amusing stories out of it.

When we were starting up we had two choices: take the bank loan, or look for someone to sell a share of the company to. Taking on an equity partner is risky business. We would have had to find someone we could really trust. We didn't want another owner. (Which was kind of academic, actually, since no one was exactly beating down our door with offers of start-up capital.)

● Too Much Money Can Be a Bad Thing . . .

Not having much money to start up actually helped us. A lot of people make the mistake of trying to start too high on the hog. They buy everything new instead of used, go first class all the way. Then the business fails because its debt load is too high.

Entrepreneurs who get too much money too fast don't go through the bootstrapping stage. There's a lot of learning that happens in the early, hands-on stages of a business. If we'd had money to throw at problems, we wouldn't have learned how to do things in the most cost-effective manner. Needless to say, that was one problem we didn't have.

● . . . Too Little Money Can Be a Bad Thing, Too

A couple of years after we got our first loan, we got another one, to buy a truck. Shortly thereafter we reached a point where we couldn't pay back our loan. We were really upset. We went to SCORE—Service

Corps of Retired Executives—a network of retired businesspeople who use their spare time consulting to struggling small businesses. After two bad matches, SCORE assigned us a business advisor named Rocky. He told us we should ask our bank for a moratorium on our loan until we could pay it back.

We couldn't believe it. Go to the bank and tell them we want to stop paying back our loan for a while? Rocky said, "It happens all the time. Just go in and tell them you'll start paying it back in another nine months." We were amazed, but we went into the bank, explained the seasonality of our business and why we wanted to pay the loan back in nine months. They said okay.

What we learned from that experience was, number one, stay on good terms with your loan officer. If you keep the people at the bank up-to-date, you're a lot better off than if you suddenly tell them you can't make your payments. It's best to keep them informed, via regular financial statements, and have a plan for how you're going to get out of whatever you've gotten yourself into. You don't want your banker to be nervous about you.

The other thing we learned was that it's actually good when you owe people money. That means they're invested in your company. They want you to succeed. If you don't make it, they don't get paid back. They'd much rather get paid back slowly than have to take over your business or take over your truck and try to sell it for you. When you don't have money and you're trying to borrow it, they have all the leverage. When you owe them, they have a lot more invested in your success.

● A Public Stock Offering

By 1983 the business had grown to $3 or $4 million in sales. We were bursting at the seams of our plant. Right about this time one of our early mistakes caught up with us.

When we'd done our projections for how much wholesale business we had to do to be profitable, we hadn't realized that the markups on the wholesale level are much lower than the markups on the retail level. And we were limited in what we could charge the grocers, based on what our competitors were charging.

This error had backed us into a difficult situation. We needed the business to become profitable so we could pay off our bank loans. But we were at maximum capacity in our building. Either we had to stop growing and try to become profitable at that level in that building, or we had to make a major investment and go on to the next level.

By then we'd determined that we wanted to use our business to address social issues. Our understanding of what that meant helped us make our decision. For one thing, the working conditions in the existing facility were primitive to say the least, definitely pre-ergonomic —which didn't correlate with our commitment to create a fun, stimulating, humane workplace. We knew we couldn't improve conditions without moving into a new building. And we couldn't move into a new building unless we expanded the business.

Even more important, at the time we believed that business was a machine for making money. Therefore we thought the best way to make Ben & Jerry's a force for progressive social change was to grow bigger so we could make more profits and give more money away. We'd decided to give away 10 percent of our profits every year. Ten percent of the profits of a $100 million company could do a lot more good than 10 percent of the $3 or $4 million we were currently doing.

For all those reasons we decided to go to the next level. Then the question was, how were we going to finance the expansion?

● . . . Sell Stock to Your Neighbors

When companies need to expand and grow, the most prevalent methods are either to sell out to a big corporation or to take in investment money from venture capitalists. In the first scenario the company can't be values-led unless the corporation that buys it shares its values. Also, the trend of small companies being swallowed up by big companies exacerbates the trend toward concentration of wealth in the hands of the few.

If, on the other hand, a values-led business takes in venture capital, the venture capitalists are unlikely to allow the company to maintain its social values, because most of them hold the mistaken belief that social values will make the company less profitable. The exceptions are the two or three socially responsible venture capital firms like Calvert Ventures, whose mission statement begins, "We believe that by providing financial and managerial support to young, socially responsible companies, a new generation of American business can be created— one that realizes the vision of simultaneously creating economic and social gains."

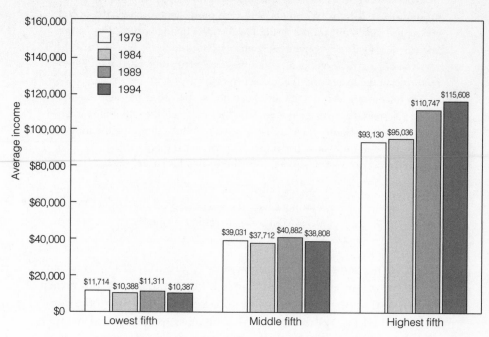

Average income of low-, middle-, and upper-income families, 1979–1994

Source: U.S. Department of Commerce, Bureau of the Census

✳   The Calvert Social Investment Fund was created in 1981, when a few investors got together to talk about what it means to be an investor in a world where we believe in working in an uplifting way to express our values. We decided to create a venture fund that got decent returns and also moved our collective agendas ahead. For example, we were the first fund not to invest in South Africa. After Mandela was elected, we went back to South Africa in a big way.

One activity we do is "Special Equities"—providing high-risk capital to propagate the companies of the future: the ones that make products to meet societal needs. We were investors in Earth's Best, the organic baby food company (which later was sold to Heinz). We helped fund the start-up of Ultrafem, a woman-owned company that makes a new kind of blood collector for women. Ultrafem went public; we made six times our money or more. We invested in Poland Partners after Lech Walesa made the call for people to start reinvesting in Poland. And a few weeks ago we bought a part of Real Goods, the alternative energy catalog company.

When we first started doing this high-risk investing, we wore our heart on our sleeve a little too much. We were more enamored of the social vision and didn't put on our usual hardheaded financial hats. But in the last five years we've become a lot smarter about that.

Over all, we're looking at a double-digit returning portfolio. That's factoring in the losers and the low returners.

I'm an entrepreneur—and my heart goes out to people who have a social vision and are struggling because they can't get the dollars together. The conventional venture capitalists just want to talk about the maximum return. We definitely look for return, but it isn't the only thing. We also look at how a product or service contributes to a better world.

> —D. Wayne Silby
> Founding Chair, the Calvert Social Investment Fund/
> Calvert Ventures/Emerging Europe Fund

When we needed to build our new plant, there were traditional venture capitalists who were interested in lending us the money. But rather than turn in that direction for a solution, Ben turned toward the community. He had always thought of the business as being held in trust for the community, so when the business needed money, it was a logical next step to offer the community an opportunity to own part of it. Ben suggested we hold a public stock offering for Vermont residents only.

The thinking behind Ben's idea was that in our economic system, the only people who achieve any degree of wealth are those people who have capital. Ben wanted to give people from most economic classes the chance to invest on the ground floor with a small minimum-purchase price—an opportunity that's rarely available to the average person, since initial public stock offerings are mostly sold within the financial community to good customers of the underwriters who can afford the usual minimum buys of $2,000 or more. The average person usually hears about a public offering only after it's over, when the underwriter runs the obligatory tombstone ad in the newspaper.

To research the logistics of his plan, Ben went down to see Harry Lantz, the securities administrator for the Vermont Department of Banking and Insurance, which controls stock offerings in the state. Although there had never been an in-state stock offering before, he found an obscure law that proved it was indeed possible to have one. Then he went to see a series of stockbrokers, every one of whom said the idea was doomed to fail. "You can't raise three quarters of a million dollars in hundred-dollar increments." "You can't afford to service shareholders who have bought only a hundred dollars' worth of stock." Naturally, this only strengthened Ben's resolve to pull it off. More determined than ever, he went to our lawyer and said, "We want you to help us sell the company to the community."

Like the bankers, our lawyer thought the plan was completely harebrained. "This plan meets the company's social objectives, and it'll accomplish our financial objectives, and it's legal. There's no reason not to do it," Ben insisted. Finally the lawyer agreed to go ahead. So we registered as stockbrokers with the state of Vermont and sold the stock ourselves.

> *Jerry:* Talk about swimming upstream, fighting against conventional thinking. It was a huge struggle to get this offering done. All the so-called professional experts highly recommended against it. Even within the company, some people thought it was a terrible idea, including some extremely rational people. Ben was betting the future of the company on this crazy scheme. But it was so important to him that he was willing to do that.
>
> *Ben:* Everybody said no one would buy any shares. And we sold them out.

The minimum purchase price we decided on was $126—twelve shares at $10.50 each. We encouraged people to form partnerships to purchase one minimum buy together. Our hope was that people would buy our stock in the same spirit they bought lottery tickets: thinking maybe it would pay off big. But the odds were against it.

To launch the stock offering, we took out ads in local newspapers under the headline "Get A Scoop Of The Action." We ran our ads in the front section, with the grocery coupons and clothing ads, not in the financial section, where the people we wanted to reach might not see them. We included an 800 number people could call to get a copy of the prospectus. When they called, we told them when our Traveling Public Stock Offering Road Show would be in their town.

Ben, Jerry, and then-CEO Chico Lager traveled around the state holding informational meetings about the stock offering. Chico had joined the company at the end of 1982 as general manager, and he began overseeing operations. It was not coincidence that the company began getting organized and first started making money after Chico's arrival. Chico brought with him not only excellent management skills but also a good marketing sense and a sense of humor only slightly dryer than Jerry's. It was under Chico's leadership that Ben & Jerry's would grow from under $2 million to more than $70 million.

In each town the three of us would tell people about the company, serve ice cream, and pass out copies of our prospectus. We told people the truth about the risks involved, and we also let them know what the company stood for and what it hoped to do with their money. We didn't want them investing based on false pretenses.

In the offering prospectus, in plain language, amidst all the legal gobbledygook, it said: IF YOU CAN'T AFFORD TO LOSE IT, DON'T DO IT. It's one thing to fail and lose the capital of a bunch of investors we'd never met. It's another thing to lose our neighbors' hard-earned $126. So the public offering gave us an extra incentive to do well financially, to make sure our neighbors' investment in us was to their advantage as well as ours.

The best-case scenario was that the offering would sell out. If that happened, we'd sell 17.5 percent of the company for $750,000. The worst-case scenario was that we'd raise less than $500,000—in which case we would have to return everyone's money, bury the in-state offering in the Not-So-Bright-Idea Graveyard, and go begging to the venture capitalists with our idealistic tails between our legs.

● Raising Capital the Values-Led Way

Within a month we'd hit the half-a-million mark. Then sales slowed and it looked like we weren't going to make it. Then it was down to the wire for another month, until July 2, 1984, the last weekend of the offering, when the bank called and told us we'd made it over the top.

The offering was oversubscribed. A hundred disappointed people got their money back. Nearly one in every hundred Vermont families— about eighteen hundred households—bought stock. A third of the people went for the minimum buy. The largest individual investment was $21,000.

The public offering accomplished our goals and then some. It raised all the money we needed. The people of the state of Vermont literally took on an ownership role in the company. They started seeing it as their own, because for a lot of them, a piece of it *was* their own.

January 14, 1989

Dear Ben and Jerry,

Your ideas for running a business different from most other businesses are great. You can show a good example of how a company can interact positively with its surrounding communities and still play the game on Wall Street according to the rules. What the heck! Why not!

When the company had to grow, the community was given a part of the company through stockholders. Also, making the stockholders feel like neighbors and friends was great. Redistributing the wealth was seen when Ben wanted to make the minimum buy price low. I wish all companies could allow participation like yours.

Cordially yours,
Wayne F.

P.S. Your prices are just a little bit higher than others. I wish they weren't.

What's unique about the shareholder base we built with the stock offering is that these people bought into Ben & Jerry's because of what the company stands for. Their commitment becomes apparent at each of our annual shareholder meetings, where our shareholders challenge us about the wheelchair accessibility of our scoop shops, our adherence to the CERES (Coalition for Environmentally Responsible Economies) environmental principles, the number of women and minorities on our board of directors, and other issues related to our social mission.

Thanks to the public offering and the way it was carried out, we have a very vocal and progressive group of shareholders who feel very tied to the values of the company. The feeling is mutual. We have a strong sense of responsibility to them.

The Vermont public offering was our first major effort to factor a concern for the community into our day-to-day decisions. The issue was, we needed to raise cash. In trying to solve the problem, we asked ourselves, how can we do that in a way that most benefits the community? In this case we were able to find a method that reflected our own style and values—an in-state public stock offering that was truly public.

Making the decision to do the offering in the face of all that opposition wasn't easy. The positive outcome of the offering strengthened our commitment to the principles of values-led business.

Since we did our offering in '84 there's been an increasing trend of what are now being called "direct public offerings." Companies sell stock on their own, not using an underwriter, in such a way that their customers become their major bloc of shareholders. Real Goods, an alternative energy company in California, had a successful direct public offering. Kinderworks tried it and failed. Blue Fish Clothing, Ben's personal favorite T-shirt maker, also did it successfully.

Most people, when they invest in the stock market, don't say, "I want to be an owner of this company. I want to be involved in developing this business." More often than not investors are just trying to make money. But there's value in feeling a sense of ownership in the company whose stock you own if the company is one whose values you agree with. So at the same time that you're making a good investment in terms of the numbers, you're making a good investment in terms of your heart and soul.

Unless you've got a few wealthy values-aligned private investors, one way for a values-led business to get expansion capital and maintain its values is to hold a direct public stock offering. You sell to the people who support your company, people who have been buying your products for years, people who believe in your values-led company and therefore aren't in it for the short term. They're people who want to combine their values with their wallets. They want to feel good about the company they own a part of, and not have to close their eyes to feel okay about an impersonal numbers transaction.

● The Ben & Jerry's Foundation

A year after the Vermont stock offering, we followed up with a national public stock offering to finance another round of construction and provide a market for the stock Vermonters had bought. This time we were working with underwriters, but once again we were trying to push the limits. Ben wanted to advertise the offering on the pints as we had for the Vermont offering. By selling stock "retail" to our customers, he hoped to increase the percentage of shareholders who were long-term investors aligned with the company's values. He wanted to use the same slogan we'd used the first time: "Get A Scoop Of The Action."

The head of the brokerage firm wasn't happy. He argued that the slogan made investing in the stock market sound like gambling. Ben said, "That's what it is, isn't it?" The broker said, "You don't understand, Ben. We're in the *securities* business."

The compromise solution was to advertise the offering on the pint containers with the slogan "Scoop Up Our Stock." We priced the stock at $13 a share. It quickly sold out; in fact, once again the offering was oversubscribed. Within a month the price had gone up to $21 a share. Eventually it settled at about $17. Since that time there have been several stock splits, and, of course, lots of price fluctuations.

Compared to our Vermont owners, our potential investors around the country didn't know as much about the company and our priorities. We wanted them to understand up front, and factor into their investment decision, that they were investing in a company that had decided to give away a sizable chunk of money each year. So we decided to set up the Ben & Jerry's Foundation to formalize our donations policy.

At that time—1985—we were still in the mind-set that business is a machine for making money, and the best thing we could do for society was to give it away. We thought of business as self-serving, and philanthropy as a way to counteract that. So, to make sure our charitable giving would exist in perpetuity, no matter what changes took place in the company in the future, we set up the foundation as a separate entity from the company, with a separate board of directors and a separate mission.

Ben endowed the foundation with fifty thousand shares of his stock. We wanted to fund it in the future with cash donations from the company, equal to 10 percent of our pretax profits. But the underwriters for our stock offering were resistant. They tried to convince us it was a mistake to take money out of a for-profit corporation to give to a nonprofit. They said we'd never be able to sell stock or finance our growth without keeping that 10 percent of the profits in the business. "Most companies give away one-point-five percent," they said. "If you want to do something big, why don't you give away three percent?"

The underwriters said they'd walk out on us if we stuck with 10 percent. We were with these high-powered Wall Street underwriters and their lawyers and accountants, in the bowels of the beast, determined to prove that a company can finance growth and give away money at the same time. The underwriters were determined to keep us from doing it. They reluctantly agreed to 5 percent. We insisted on 10 percent. To keep the deal from falling apart, we compromised at 7.5 percent.

As the foundation started giving away more and more money—in 1991, it gave away more than half a million dollars—we had more and more questions about how it could be most effective. Should it fund lots of small grants, or a few big ones? Should the foundation direct the funding, or be totally reactive to grant applications? Should it give new grants every year, or give multiyear grants?

In July of 1991 the foundation held a board retreat with experts in philanthropy, community activities, and progressive social change to try to answer these questions. The two things that came out of the meeting were, first, that it would be much more effective to have the foundation leverage the good name and power of the business—that the real power of the foundation was in its association with Ben & Jerry's. To maximize the effectiveness of the foundation, it had to work synergistically with the social initiatives of the company. And second, since we wanted the foundation to be about progressive social change and empowerment, we were missing a tremendous opportunity by not inviting the employees of the company—the people who were actually earning the money—to be involved in the foundation's activities.

The original idea was, the foundation would give away the money earned by a business with no social values through grants to progressive, values-led nonprofit groups. But as our understanding of values-led business evolved and we started trying to integrate our values into our everyday business activities, we realized that the foundation and the company could be a lot more effective in working for progressive social change if they worked together.

What we learned at the retreat changed the way we thought about corporate philanthropy. We decided to divvy up the 7.5 percent pool among three areas: the foundation, which is now entirely employee-run; corporate philanthropy, which is overseen by our social mission director, Liz Bankowski; and Community Action Teams, which exist at each employee site. Each CAT team gets a budget for each year and decides how to spend it—becoming involved in local activities or making donations to local groups, or whatever combination they come up with.

In the course of the discussion about whether the foundation should be run by employees, Liz Bankowski advanced a "ladder" theory. If we wanted the people who work at Ben & Jerry's to be interested in progressive social change, we needed to find ways for them to take gradual steps. Participating in an act of generosity could be a first step. An employee-led foundation created the opportunity for people in the company to study an important social or environmental problem, debate the best way to solve it, take a direct action to help, and feel the satisfaction of an act of generosity that would create ongoing action for social change.

Over the years, the priorities adopted by the CAT teams have shown that for the most part, our employees are more interested in funding local activities than they are in funding national organizations. That's fine with us. And now our employees have a way to actualize their priorities.

When we started giving away 7.5 percent of our profits, the pundits said, "How can you give away five times more than the average corporation and still survive? You'll never make it." But we always felt that if we set up our corporate philanthropy as a given, like our electric bill or our heating bill, we'd just pay it as a cost of doing business. If your electric bill goes up, you pay it. It's not an option. We look at our payments to the foundation as a higher electric bill. It's coming out of profits, so it's not preventing us from being profitable. And it's only a small percentage of profits, so it goes up only as our profits go up.

Integrating our values into our everyday business decisions yields the greatest impact, but we're extremely proud of the foundation and of the employees who run it.

We once heard Johnetta B. Cole, the president of Spelman College, give a speech at a conference. She said that in the African-American community it's understood that part of the cost of living on this Earth is helping people out. That's the way we look at running a values-led business. The money that runs through a company is in the hands of the company only because its customers, the people in the immediate and wider communities, put it there.

● Values-Led Investing

We were fortunate to hire Tom D'Urso as our treasurer three years ago. Along with our CFO, Fran Rathke, Tom is helping turn our corporate money into "the root of opportunity."

✱   Values-led investing takes a little more homework and a little more time, but you can come pretty darn close to the returns you'd get from conventional investments—without having to sacrifice the principles (or the principal) upon which the business is based.

For me personally it's been an evolutionary process. You come to Ben & Jerry's with an idea of what the company's values are about, but you don't necessarily land here and get it all at once. Nobody sits you down and gives you an orientation about how to integrate those values into your assigned tasks.

When I arrived at Ben & Jerry's, they were investing through Smith Barney, and so far we've continued with them. It seemed to me they had at least a piece of the message—they were using negative screens against investments in alcohol, tobacco, and defense. Rather than find a new firm, I thought I'd try to get them to invest more proactively on the municipal bond side. They've been very responsive. They do an awful lot of the legwork for us, without charging us an additional fee. They provide what I would consider to be a higher level of service than they provide for the normal corporate account, in order to help us perform the screens we use to determine where we'll put our money. There's a likelihood that, at a minimum, a chunk of the money will change at some point from Smith Barney to an even more socially responsible form of investment.

At Ben & Jerry's we have about $25 to $30 million to invest, depending on the season. Because a portion of that money was raised through a debt offering, the IRS requires us to invest a certain amount of that money in taxable instruments.

Working with a company our size and with our amount of cash, the primary principle I adhere to on the taxable side is not to put any of the money at risk. One thing I would not do is buy stocks, because those could descend in value 10 to 30 percent at the drop of a hat, and it would be very difficult to recover from those losses. So we always make sure the integrity of the principal is sound; then what we achieve as a return is interest, and the principal continues to be secure.

We have a corporate policy that we will not invest in an issue involved with gambling, alcohol, tobacco, weapons production, nuclear power, or environmental hazards. I call this a passive screen—meaning that we know these investments are not involved in anything we wouldn't want to be associated with, but we haven't aggressively investigated their employee practices, minority representation, and so forth.

We have a lot more flexibility with the money we can invest on the tax-free side. That's where we direct our funds toward investments that proactively help communities and various socially responsible organizations.

On the tax-free side we'll target municipal bond issues that support a hospital, or student loans, or public transportation. If we have a choice between a highway and a hospital, we'll target the hospital regardless of the yield. Currently our tax-free investment portfolio includes South

Carolina Educational Assistance; Michigan Higher Educational Student Loan Fund; Louisville, Kentucky, Hospital; and the Massachusetts State Health and Educational Facility.

We've also made some investments in housing issues directly. Thanks to investment tax credits allowed by the IRS for investments in low-income housing, we achieve benefits superior to most of our other investments. This is a real win-win scenario; the whole is greater than the sum of its parts. We get a dollar-for-dollar tax credit, and we also get to write off the depreciation of the real estate we invest in.

We've invested $774,000 in Housing Vermont, a statewide nonprofit that develops partnerships with local communities and the business sector to renovate abandoned houses and provide low-income, affordable housing. We anticipate an after-tax return on this investment of 12 percent a year.

In 1993 Ben & Jerry's made an investment in the restoration of the Times Square Hotel in Manhattan. The hotel now serves as affordable housing, with rents set at 30 percent of each resident's income. Residents are also offered on-site employment help, substance abuse counseling, and health care—and there's a Ben & Jerry's scoop shop in the lobby, operated by the organization that runs the hotel and staffed by its residents. Over the years of our commitment, the company will contribute a total of $1,276,000. The investment will result in a tax benefit of $1,943,000 over its 15 year life.

In addition to the short-term investments and direct housing investments, we also deposit funds into banks that actively support communities, mostly via lending for low-income housing and in support of small businesses. South Shore Bank is widely known for its support of the community and for low-income housing. We've invested $1 million with them, in a certificate of deposit. We also have a number of smaller deposits with other banks that have been identified as being supportive of the community.

Our corporate credit card is with Vermont National Bank's Card for Kids Program, under which 1 percent of monthly purchases is donated to children's organizations.

On a given day I may have $1 million to invest, and on that particular day there may not be an issue that's particularly appealing. Rather than put the money somewhere less than ideal, I might wait until the next day and see if something comes up.

I've never felt that I've been forced to invest our funds in something the company would be embarrassed to be associated with. My instructions are to make sure our money is invested in alignment with our values —not to achieve any particular yield or return.

In my previous experiences—my last job was with a technology company—the primary criterion was, seek the optimum yield without putting the principal at risk. That's really a pretty simple proposition. You have two Triple-A-rated issues; one is yielding 5.5 percent and one is yielding 5.6 percent—which do you pick? You could have a chimpanzee make that decision. That's not rocket science.

I took a pay cut and moved my family from Acton, Massachusetts, in order to join Ben & Jerry's. I thought it would be nice to be involved with a company with a broader horizon than just looking at maximum yield. I've never regretted my decision (once I got past the first couple of paychecks!). I have occasional interactions with Ben and Jerry, and that's a kick. Those folks are more complex to deal with and certainly a lot more fun than the engineers I used to work with.

I like the issues the company is involved with. That adds a dimension to the job that I haven't been exposed to before. The decisions I make here are more difficult and require more thought. Should we give up .10 yield to support a mental health facility instead of a turnpike? That's the kind of decision I'm supported to make. I feel good about that.

If we didn't take values into consideration, we could slightly improve the yield. But it's tough to say exactly how much. I don't believe it's a material difference. The market fluctuates so much day to day that you can't really make a judgment as to the best way to use the funds. I'm confident that the majority of our shareholders would be in tune with the concept that we're directing our funds in a way that's consistent with our corporate philosophy.

—Tom D'Urso
Ben & Jerry's Treasurer

Individuals and businesses have a certain amount of money to invest. A common investment strategy is to have a diversified portfolio—not only in terms of different stocks and industries, but also in terms of high-risk venture capital investments, medium-risk stock investments, and low-risk bond investments.

The next frontier for values-led investing is to take the money allocated for high-risk venture capital and put it into values-led ventures.

✳   If you buy publicly traded stocks or public investments, they're easier to deal with because they're liquid. With the high-risk investments we go into you can't sell the stock for a number of years. There's no market for it. The company hasn't proven out. On the other hand, they have a huge social benefit.

Oftentimes when we make investments of only a few hundred thousand dollars to get something worthwhile off the ground, our vote of confidence encourages other people to add money. That's what ends up making the venture happen.

Two years ago, for example, we heard about a man in Scotland who was working on a morphine suppository for children and adults who are in extreme pain and may be dying. The usual administration method, the morphine drip, is very clumsy, especially for babies. We kicked in a half million dollars and the man got his company started. Now other investors are seeing how much money there is to be made, so they've come in with about $15 million.

The key is balance. You've got to make secure, predictable investments and—if you're trying to make a contribution to the betterment of society —you've got to make some higher-risk, higher-social-yield investments too.

We've made twenty-five private equity investments of over $10 million and we have not lost a dime. Our investors may get a slightly lower rate of return but they're happy to know we're getting money to people who deserve it.

—D. Wayne Silby

By making values-led investments people can help values-led enterprises to start up, grow, expand. At the same time that you're accomplishing your financial objective of stock appreciation, you're accomplishing your social mission objective. That's what we mean by integrating social values into day-to-day business activities—in this case, turning money from the root of evil into the root of opportunity.

4

Franchises and Partnershops:

Values-Led Retailing

Ben: In terms of retail expansion, Jerry, how do you think we should decide on our priorities?

Jerry: On the basis of what's most profitable and what the company's managerial capabilities are. In other words, what we can actually do well.

Ben: Not what's most values-led? You mean any social benefit would be purely coincidental for you?

Jerry: Anything we'd even consider would have to have social benefit, Ben. Every undertaking, retail included, should have social programs associated with it. That's a given. So I'd look at our capabilities and decide from there.

Ben: That's a given? Since when?

Jerry: Well, it's more integrated into some areas of the company than others. But people do factor it in. They understand it's part of their job.

Ben: Wow. That's great news. Now I can sleep at night. I can rest easy.

Jerry: Ben, you'll never rest easy. When somebody comes up with a new retail campaign that has ten percent social content to it, you'll want a campaign with an eighty percent social content.

Ben: That Coheeni. Never satisfied.

● Early Adventures in Retailing

Our first shop, the gas station in downtown Burlington, was a down-home, comfortable, community based store. We had a community bulletin board, and Don Rose on the player piano (Don played some great boogie-woogie when the piano wasn't playing itself). People would come in to hang out and chat. The store supported local groups in various ways—giving away ice cream, sponsoring the occasional festival, publicizing events.

We did a good job of making customers feel at home, and a lousy job of managing the business. Our portion control was out of control; we were hiring our friends and then agonizing over supervising them; our financial records were usually located in the back pocket of Ben's jeans. We were having fun, but we weren't exactly mastering the art of retailing.

Then, in 1980, in response to requests from several restaurants, we got into the wholesale business. Instead of making ice cream in a home-made-rock-salt-ice-cream maker, we started manufacturing it on a larger scale, which naturally presented a new set of challenges. If we were going to be doing manufacturing, we needed to build the wholesale business up to the minimal level at which it would be profitable. That meant we needed more outlets. There were a few ways to do that: we could open other Ben & Jerry's stores and run them ourselves. We could sell our ice cream wholesale to existing ice cream parlors. Or we could sell franchises and have other people own and operate their own Ben & Jerry's shops.

We didn't have the money to set up more stores on our own. And in order to serve customers the way we wanted to serve them we felt a store needed an owner-operator on site. We didn't want the difficulty of dealing with cash control or other operational issues on an absentee basis.

First we tried selling tubs of our ice cream wholesale to other stores. But we quickly realized that once the product left our hands it was out of our control. We couldn't control how other stores handled our ice cream or the resulting quality of what they sold. So we sold our first franchise. The store opened in Shelburne, about ten miles down the road, in 1981.

Between 1981 and 1987, we'd opened about forty-one scoop shops. Between '87 and '88 we opened sixty more. In 1989 we declared a

moratorium on openings so we could evaluate our franchising processes and strategy, and figure out how we could better service the
stores we had. During the next few years we worked on understanding
retail fundamentals: target markets, ownership selection, location selection. We had another big retail expansion year in 1995, when we
opened forty-five new stores. By April 1997, Ben & Jerry's will have 168
scoop shops, including four in Canada and twelve in Israel.

When we first started franchising, we didn't recognize the power of
retailing to effect progressive social change. We saw the stores as a way
to sell ice cream and represent Ben & Jerry's to a broader segment of
the population.

As our franchise operations grew, so did our consciousness about
values-led retailing. We started to realize the potential impact of 156
shops serving several million people a year. They're not grocery stores;
we aren't selling packaged goods off a shelf. Every customer is waited
on personally. The quality of the interactions in the Ben & Jerry's scoop
shops is very personal.

Once we recognized the possibilities, we started trying to figure out
how to factor the social mission into our retail business.

● The Retail Store as Town Square

Our first companywide retail social-action campaign was in 1989, when
we started doing voter registration in scoop shops. Since voting is a
citizen's most basic way to participate in running our country, registering to vote should be easy. But, even with the new motor-voter laws,
registering is not something most people know how to do.

Many Americans feel disempowered and detached from the whole
process. They think their vote doesn't matter, or they don't like the
choices they're offered, or both. Consequently, the people who are
elected don't really represent the majority. Most presidents are elected
by about 25 percent of eligible voters (half of the 50 percent or so who
vote). We wanted to do what we could to make the government more
representative of the needs of the people, not the corporations and the
rich—both American and foreign—who fund politicians' campaigns.

So we put up big signs and banners outside the shops, offering a free
ice cream cone to anyone who came in and registered to vote. In order
to legally register people, we had to have at least one person in each
scoop shop notarized, so we did that.

Maybe it was the opportunity to participate in the electoral process; maybe it was the free ice cream; probably it was some of both—but we registered more than fifteen hundred Vermonters and thousands more voters in scoop shops across the country. From there we started registering voters at our festivals, and out of our ice-cream-sampling-and-voter-registration van. Other companies started registering people in their stores too. The Body Shop, for one, registered over forty thousand people in their U.S. shops in 1992.

We did voter registration to encourage people to participate in their government. But the campaign also had a nice side benefit for the scoop shops. Like every other business, we're always trying to find new customers, to let more people know where our stores are and how great our product is.

The next major campaign in our scoop shops was our alliance with the Children's Defense Fund, the preeminent child advocacy organization, which organizes in favor of a Healthy Start (health care for children and pregnant women); a Head Start (preschool, child care, and Head Start programs); a Fair Start (jobs for parents at decent wages); and a Safe Start (after-school and other preventive programs to keep children safe and challenged). In 1992 we set up Action Stations in the scoop shops, with displays and brochures about CDF and the situation of poor children in this country (such as the fact that one in five American children lives in poverty). The brochures had a tear-off card that people could send in to CDF to learn more. By return mail they received an informational packet which included the names and numbers of their elected representatives. We also gave the brochures away at our festivals.

The Action Stations had special red telephones our scoop shop customers could use to call CDF for free to join their grassroots lobbying campaign to get our government to meet children's needs.

So far, fifty thousand Ben & Jerry's customers have become members of CDF. And loyal, active members they've turned out to be. CDF tells us that of all their supporters, the Ben & Jerry's customers are the ones they can count on most to make phone calls, send letters, or take whatever action is needed.

A year later our involvement with children's rights led the company, mostly through our franchisees, to start working with the RCCP—Resolving Conflict Creatively Program. RCCP was initiated by Educators for Social Responsibility to help teachers train their students to use nonviolent conflict-resolution skills. The shop owners sent us the

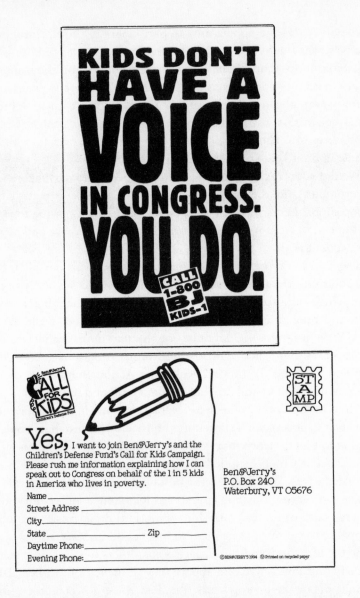

names and addresses of the schools closest to their shops, and we sent the principals an activities guide we'd designed for kids from kindergarten through twelfth grade. Eventually we sent the brochure to eight thousand schools in scoop shop neighborhoods. We also ended up taking a lot of calls from teachers throughout the country who'd heard about the activities guide but weren't located near a scoop shop. Of course, we sent them as many brochures as they wanted.

That same year we hooked up our franchisees with their local Head Start centers. The Head Start folks created lists of the types of books they needed, and the franchisees posted the lists in their stores. Customers got a free cone for every book they donated.

Over the years our shop owners have taken the lead in implementing the social mission in their own innovative ways.

＊   In 1993 we did a program with the D.C. government to immunize inner-city kids. The government had the vaccine, but they couldn't get the turnout. So I advertised in all the inner-city papers, offering a free cone to every kid who got a shot. We went to each immunization site and scooped ice cream. The government says five thousand kids were immunized that way who otherwise wouldn't have been.

—Dick Snow
Ben & Jerry's Franchisee,
Washington, D.C.

＊   When I was involved with the scoop shop in Providence, Rhode Island, we worked with the local blood center to make donating blood a more popular thing to do.

We set up a Ben & Jerry's kiosk at the blood bank with a waffle-cone baker, so as people were having their blood taken they could smell the cones baking. On their way out they'd get a warm cone full of ice cream and a big thank-you.

After we'd done this for two or three years it became known as the Ben & Jerry's Summer Blood Drive. People would commit to give blood every year because they knew we'd be there. We turned something that's usually an unpleasant hassle into a fun experience—and we also broke the blood bank's record by raising over eight hundred pints of blood in two days.

—Jim Ruggieri
Franchisee, Seattle, Wash.;
Former Franchisee, Providence, R.I.

＊   We have our biggest community event every year on Free Cone Day. The Celebrity Scoop is a fund-raiser for a local nonprofit called Christmas in April–San Francisco, which organizes volunteer projects that renovate homes and public facilities for elderly and disadvantaged San Franciscans.

Celebrities donate their time in our shops, as well as the Larkin Street partnershop—to scoop ice cream. Our guest scoopers have included Bob

Weir and Phil Lesh from the Grateful Dead, Wavy Gravy, Mayor Willie Brown, and many other local celebrities. While people are waiting on line for their free cones, we ask them for donations for Christmas in April. It's touching. People throw in pennies and dollars. Last year we raised $6,000 and had a great time doing it.

—Brian Gaines
Franchisee, San Francisco

Some scoop shops give free-pint coupons to local police departments, so the officers can give out the coupons to kids they "catch" wearing bicycle helmets. Some give coupons to local libraries for kids who read books and bring in book reports.

The power of retail is awesome. Retail is where a business has its most direct contact with its customers. That represents a tremendous opportunity for relationship building and values sharing. And our scoop shop owners are our liaison with the community. Each franchisee's interactions with his or her customers determines the quality of that customer's experience with Ben & Jerry's—which is one reason we're strongly biased toward owner-operated shops. An owner has more invested, not just financially but personally. She or he has a bottom-line perspective. It might be more expedient for us to work with large company franchisers, to have one master franchisee in each region, but we appreciate the personal touch an on-site owner-operator provides, and so do our customers.

We're extremely fortunate to have as our shop owners—and the folks they employ—people who are incredibly motivated and committed. Without them and the extra effort they put into their shops and communities every day, the good name of Ben & Jerry's would not be nearly as good.

✳ There's a lot of value in empowering your employees, and Ben & Jerry's commitment to community service helps me do that. I'm in a location that has high foot traffic and an element of tourism, so there's not much point in spending my marketing budget on local advertising. That frees me to use my budget to help out local organizations that my employees support.

At monthly meetings I encourage my staff to present the nonprofit groups they're working with; then I provide them with product, money, or coupons for those groups. There are lots of AIDS groups here, and some of my employees are closely tied to those organizations. Recently a scooper took it upon herself to provide the ice cream for a fund-raising picnic for gay youth. I set her up with coolers and everything she needed.

I was overwhelmed with applicants when I opened this store. Ben & Jerry's has a reputation for being a fun place to work, but I think the reputation for community involvement is a big factor too.

—Jim Ruggieri

* Our Haight Street store throws a Halloween party for the neighborhood kids every year. It's important, because parents don't let their kids go trick-or-treating anymore. We provide a safe environment for kids and their families to have fun. Our staff gets into it as well. They try to outdo each other with outrageous costumes. The kids get a free cone for being in costume and the winner gets an ice cream party. This year we got together with the other merchants on the street and organized a Halloween parade for the local grade school kids. It was quite a sight to see 350 kids marching down the street, in costume, with all the merchants out in front of their stores handing out candy.

—Brian Gaines

* The social mission motivates my staff. When the line has been out the door for twelve straight hours, I need a staff that's completely convinced they should go the extra mile for me. In another situation, the person might think, "Hey, I'm making six bucks an hour. The owner's already made enough money for today. Why am I busting my butt?" But my scoopers know that if the shop makes money, a good chunk of it goes to community projects that they help choose.

I try to make the job stimulating and fun. This year we're doing an exchange program with the new scoop shop in Sarasota, Florida. Their shop is busy in December, January, and February. We're busy in July and August. So I'm sending scoopers to Sarasota for the winter, and they're going to send scoopers to Washington for the summer. We're even providing housing. It's great for the scoopers, and it's great for the franchisees. A well-trained scooper is worth his or her weight in gold.

I get twenty applicants for every scooper position. In retail that's unheard of. I pay $5.50 an hour to start, so it's not the money those people are after. They want to work for Ben & Jerry's because it's socially responsible, and because it's a fun, friendly environment. We plan to keep it that way.

—Dick Snow

We could easily fill an entire book with stories of the activities that are initiated and carried out by Ben & Jerry's scoop shops and their owners.

● Social Action Drives Store Traffic

Great products, great customer service, and consumer alignment with the values of the company—as expressed, in part, via a social-action campaign—those are the factors that motivate people to patronize one retail store above another.

Like other marketing campaigns, the success of a social-action campaign is a function of how well it's embraced by the shop owners. If they're enthusiastic it makes a big difference.

To that end we have a lot of communication with our scoop shop owners. We hold annual franchise meetings and biannual regional meetings, and we have field representatives who meet with our shop owners on a regular basis. We give awards at our annual meetings, and not only to shops that do well in their operations. We also give out a social mission award so our shop owners are recognized within the franchise system for outstanding achievement in that area as well.

One contradiction we face in our franchise operations is that many socially aligned people tend not to have the money to open a franchised ice cream shop. Certainly people from the lower economic strata don't have access to that kind of financing. We've turned down a lot of highly qualified people because they couldn't come up with the down payment for the bank loan.

If we're going to use our franchise operations to help narrow the gap between rich and poor, we're going to have to get creative. In the beginning we didn't have the money to help finance our franchisees. Now we do. We're hoping that in the future we'll be able to set up a revolving loan fund for people who would make especially great, socially aligned, customer-service-oriented shop owners but don't have the money to get started. This would be similar to what colleges and universities do with their loan programs, and we would do it for the same reason.

Running a scoop shop is an especially good way for people to enter the realm of entrepreneurship, because it's possible to get into this business without a lot of previous experience. The franchisor (Ben & Jerry's) provides training and management support and an exclusive trading area.

Although it can't be the only qualification for shop ownership, it certainly helps when our franchisees agree with the company's social mission—because we don't require them to carry it out. Franchisees are independent businesspeople; they have a great deal of leeway in how they run their shops. The social-action campaigns we offer them have to motivate and appeal to their business sense as well as their hearts and minds.

✱   I have five extremely profitable scoop shops in the Washington, D.C., area, and I can honestly say that the social mission of Ben & Jerry's is largely responsible for my success.

The franchise agreement has a social-mission component built into it, which says we should spend 4 percent of sales either on advertising or community donations. It's our choice. Advertising is prohibitively expensive in Washington, and community donations are greatly needed. That's where I've always spent my money.

After eight years I've come to the conclusion that our involvement in the community has marketed my stores much better than advertising could.

For one thing, since our shop is known for community action, whenever there's a local news event the media flocks to our door. During Hurricane Fran, Old Town flooded twice in one year. There are hundreds of businesses in Old Town, but the press tracked me down. I was on all the networks; I was on the NBC national news. "Sure, there's a hurricane, but we're still making waffle cones!" At one point I was the *reporter* for the CBS affiliate. The whole time I was on-screen, the caption said, "Dick Snow of Ben & Jerry's Ice Cream." You can't buy that kind of coverage.

My philosophy, based on what I've learned as a Ben & Jerry's franchisee, is that the harder you try to blow your money on seemingly unprofitable community projects, the more money you end up making.

—Dick Snow

✱   There was a time when we were putting so much into the community that the bottom line suffered. We had to find a balance. We have to make the shops financially sustainable if we want to do the community activities we're in business to do. If you've got that balance right, you can really make a difference.

We've been in San Francisco since 1992, and everybody knows about Ben & Jerry's. Because they're familiar with our local programs, given the choice between Ben & Jerry's and Brand X, they'll choose Ben & Jerry's every time. People come into the shop and say, "I saw you at the AIDS Dance-A-Thon," or "I saw you at my kids' school." Customers appreciate it when we do something specific for their communities, and they let me know that on a regular basis.

—Brian Gaines

We can't point directly to extra traffic coming into the stores because we're doing voter registration or a CDF campaign. We've never tried to track those results. Even if we had, we probably wouldn't have seen an immediate increase in store traffic.

It's all the things we've done, including the social-action campaigns in the stores, that have built the spiritual connection consumers feel with Ben & Jerry's—which, along with great ice cream, is what makes people more likely to visit our scoop shops.

Of course, the stores also need product-marketing campaigns to bring in new customers and market new products. They can't rely on social-issue campaigns alone.

✳   When we were opening the Seattle store, it happened that Ben & Jerry's was just introducing sorbet. They'd allocated so many sorbet squeeze-ups to our region, and I said I have a good way to use them. Instead of advertising to promote the new product line, I called the Northwest AIDS Foundation and asked if we could give out free squeeze-ups at their annual AIDS Walk. We set up a cart where the walkers finish. It was a hot, sunny day, and at the end of a 10K walk the walkers were ready for something cool. Each person who passed us got a squeeze-up and a coupon for a free cone. That's how we let the community know that Ben & Jerry's was in Seattle. I coded those coupons, so I know I got at least three hundred new customers from that effort.

—Jim Ruggieri

✳   I do spend a small amount on advertising. There are things each year I need to promote: Valentine's Day cakes on Valentine's Day, Mother's Day cakes on Mother's Day. I spend money to promote Free Cone Day because I think it's a terrific promotion, and it gives the season a jump start.

But my 4 percent budget this year is about $80,000, and if I spend as much as $5,000 of it on advertising, I'll be surprised.

—Dick Snow

● Minority Franchise Ownership

Attracting and developing minority franchise owners is a significant step a company can take toward supporting groups that have been discriminated against and shut out of full participation in the economic system and consequently don't get a fair share of the economic pie.

When stores are locally owned, as they are in most affluent communities, the money goes around and around many times before it leaves. The guy who owns the stationery store pays rent to someone who lives in the neighborhood. He buys his gas at the local gas station and his groceries at the corner store. This helps the economic livelihood of these cities. In minority communities, since the majority of businesses are owned by people who don't live there, as soon as money is spent, it leaves the neighborhood. Minority franchise ownership could help solve both problems.

There are companies that do a good job of minority franchising. Unfortunately, Ben & Jerry's is not one of them.

Popeye's, for example, has 770 franchises, of which 50 are minority owned. Church's Chicken has 398 franchises, of which 37 are minority owned. McDonald's record is the best: 4.6 percent of their franchises are Latino-owned, and 11.9 percent are owned by African-Americans. McDonald's minority franchise program is designed to include Latino, African-American, Asian, and female franchisees in numbers that mirror the company's consumer base. Toward that end, they try to identify, then eliminate traditional barriers. For example, their financing program allows minority owners to acquire operating capital for three years through banks with which McDonald's makes special arrangements.

Of Ben & Jerry's 156 U.S. scoop shops, only two are owned by African-Americans. We're hoping to do much better in the future.

● Partnershops: Win-Win Retailing

Partnershops were the brainstorm of board member Jeff Furman. Ben and Jeff became friends in the seventies, when they both worked at the Highland Community School. Jeff has degrees in law and accounting. But undoubtedly Jeff's greatest claim to fame is that he's the one who gave us the original pizza parlor business plan—the one we used as a template when we applied for our first loan.

✳   In 1985 I was in charge of franchise development for Ben & Jerry's. I was living in Ithaca, New York, where I still live, a long way from the nearest scoop shop. I figured since I was responsible for franchises, I ought to see how a store actually operates. But I didn't want to become a franchisee myself. So I came up with the idea of franchising a scoop shop to the Learning Web, the nonprofit agency whose board I was on. The Web's purpose is to connect young people with businesspeople so they can learn the skills they need to make a living.

I thought if Ben & Jerry's would waive the franchise fee of $25,000, the Learning Web could probably raise the start-up money we'd need to set up a shop. Then the kids could get on-the-job training running it.

I went around the community and raised some money. The city put in a little from their community-development block grant. We set up the business as a corporation—Youth Scoops Incorporated—with our stock owned by the nonprofit. Once we found the right location we got the store built, hired a staff, and opened, in April of 1987.

The shop has been a huge success from every point of view. It's been solidly profitable, and it's paid back all the local people who loaned us start-up money—over $85,000.

We made about $15,000 profit last year. My goal is to make less. We pay taxes on profits. I'd rather use the money to offer more training, or hire extra kids. Sometimes we overstaff the store on purpose. A regular franchise owner wouldn't do that.

But for us, the real profit is the program. The money we make goes into the agency to run our programs with young people. Instead of constantly saying, "Where am I going to place my kids so they learn to run a business more cooperatively, do hiring and firing, pay their bills?"—we've got a place. We've got a self-sustaining program. I've always felt it's fine if the shop just breaks even, but as it turns out, we make a little extra money to help support the agency.

Over the years we've employed about two hundred kids. For maybe 15 percent the shop has made a radical, positive contribution to their lives. Some kids have gone on to get other jobs. Some who've dropped out of school drop back in. A couple have gone to work in other scoop shops. Certainly there's a bunch of kids we haven't helped at all.

There are particular kinds of kids this works for. We're not a drug rehab place, although we do deal with a lot of classified-as-at-risk kids. Other community agencies, a homeless-teen program for example, refer kids to us for jobs. The agencies work with the kids till they're job-ready, then we provide an opportunity for them to have their first job.

The young people run the store. They're not absentee owners, and this is not a top-down entity. We have management meetings with the kids on a regular basis. There's one adult manager, but the young people do all the bookkeeping, scooping, cleaning, hiring, and firing. You can walk into the store in the evening and there's just young people in the program here running it.

We're the largest employer of minority youth in the community. Ithaca has a black population of under 10 percent, and 25 percent of our staff is African-American. About 30 percent of our staff is nonwhite.

In many ways we're no different from any other business. We have a training program. We have excellent customer service. We have cash control systems. We do have a few issues that might be unique, like determining the appropriate number and placement of earrings. I can handle the ears. I've gotten to be okay with the nose. The belly button, that's covered up. But the scooper with the thing in the tongue—I can't deal with that!

We're not just providing job readiness here. We're actually providing an income, and training. The young people do the cash. They do the closeouts. They get supervisory experience. They're familiar with cost controls. They're honest and reliable. When they go out into the marketplace, they have a different level of skills than they'd have if they'd been slinging hamburgers at Burger King.

> —Jeff Furman
> Ben & Jerry's Board Member, Ithaca Partnershop Consultant

The Ithaca partnershop was our first. Since then we've opened one in Baltimore, three in New York City, and two in San Francisco—both run by Larkin Street, a nonprofit agency that works with street kids. Five out of seven of them have prospered; two closed for a number of reasons, the most significant of which was poor location.

Getting a partnershop up and running takes more effort from Ben & Jerry's than setting up a regular franchise shop does. The nonprofit groups that open partnershops need extra help with financing and management. But no matter how much we do, ultimately it comes down to the nonprofits doing the work. The people who run the organization need to learn a new skill set, just as any other franchisee does, but they also need to manage their program. That makes their job pretty complex.

● Finding the Right Partners

A big part of the learning curve for us was knowing how to choose the right partnershop partners—learning what a nonprofit has to have in order for it to succeed. The people who run the nonprofits that operate our most successful partnershops are MBAs who chose to work in the public sector. Having that professional expertise—a manager who really knows business, and a well-organized nonprofit—really helps.

For example, Sharon Wurtzel and Dianne Flannery, who ran the Larkin Street partnershop at the time, had the great idea, and the connections, to get a concession at Candlestick Park. So, besides running two stores in San Francisco neighborhoods, the young people in the Larkin Street program—many of them formerly homeless runaways—staff Ben & Jerry's carts at baseball and football games.

Most nonprofits don't have an MBA at the top of the organization. The normal way nonprofits work is that someone identifies a need for a program, say, to help wayward youth. Then the organization applies to funders for grant money to run that program. If the nonprofit gets all the money it applied for, it's able to do what it was planning to do. If the nonprofit gets half the money, it's able to service only half that number of kids. If they want to grow the program, the development director has to write more grant applications.

That's a very different mind-set from running a business—knowing that if you need money you have to earn it by making or buying something from one person and selling it to someone else at a profit.

Ben: I had a very telling conversation once with a partnershop manager. I was going over the financial statement with her, showing her the areas where they weren't controlling their labor costs. And she said, "I guess I'll just have to apply for a grant to make up for the operating losses."

The nonprofit attitude is very different from a business mentality. Nonprofit organizations are oriented toward getting people to give them money. Businesses are oriented toward making money. What's needed is to put the two together so social service agencies can learn to be more businesslike (which happens when they run a partnershop) and businesses can learn to be more socially beneficial.

✳   Being in business gives the nonprofit incredible credibility. It connects them to the business community as a full member, as opposed to their usual position of looking for handouts. Running the partnershop did an awful lot for the Learning Web in that regard. It made us a real player among the businesspeople in Ithaca.

—Jeff Furman

Location is another key factor in the success or failure of a partnershop. We learned that the hard way from our experience with the Harlem partnershop, which opened in 1992 and closed in 1996.

✳ Our franchise shop in Harlem was another experiment. It didn't work. The most significant reason was the location of the shop. Ninety percent of the sales of a franchise shop are a function of location. This partnershop was on the main drag, 125th Street, but it was too far from the Apollo Theatre area, where most of the neighborhood's foot traffic is at night. People weren't coming into the store, which is a disaster in the ice cream world, especially on weekends.

Another contributing factor was that the shop was run by a very small homeless men's shelter with only ten or fifteen people. That wasn't a large enough group to pick from to find the right people to work in the store. Still, the Harlem partnershop lasted for four years, which is better than 75 percent of the businesses that open in the United States.

—Jeff Furman

The partnershop we opened most recently is on Eighty-sixth Street in New York. It's run by an organization that serves the homeless mentally ill population. The homeless mentally ill adults from the program work in the store. This store represents another breakthrough for Ben & Jerry's in the realm of using retail stores to advance the social mission —in this case, hiring otherwise unemployable disabled people. The store is doing well, and it's offering a valuable employment experience to the people who work there.

● On Common Ground

One of our most successful partnershops is operated by Common Ground, the group that turned the Times Square Hotel into low-income housing (as we discussed in the finance chapter). The partnershop is in a storefront on the ground floor of the building on Forty-third Street and Eighth Avenue in Manhattan.

✳   In 1990, after I visited one of the other partnershops, I wrote a letter to Ben & Jerry's asking if we could open a shop that would employ tenants of the Times Square. Soon afterward Jeff Furman came to meet with me. I told him about Common Ground and the project. Forty-five minutes into the conversation Jeff said, "This is great. Count us in." I said, "Could you put that in writing?" I thought it was too good to be true. All the other companies we'd approached were all looking at each other like, "Is the water warm?"

We couldn't take possession of the store until 1994. But while we were fighting our way through every kind of bureaucracy, Ben & Jerry's invited us to their annual franchisees' meetings. We were welcomed into the family without even having a store in operation.

We got our start-up, build-out, and early training financing from the New York State Urban Development Corporation, the Robin Hood Foundation, Newman's Own, and some smaller foundations.

We finally opened in April of '94. We never in our wildest dreams imagined we'd be opening on Free Cone Day, but that's what happened. Our first day we served five thousand customers. It was a baptism by fire, and without the hands-on help from a lot of folks from Ben & Jerry's retail, I think we would've been ready to close the store that day out of sheer panic. They contributed an extraordinary amount of management support to get us off to a flying start. Dick Snow, a fellow franchisee from Washington, D.C., spent a lot of time with me and my coworkers from day one, going over everything we needed to know.

In the winter we have a staff of eight; in the summer we go up to sixteen. The manager and assistant manager are outside hires. Most of the other employees are residents of the Times Square or other nonprofit supportive-housing programs in the city.

The partnershop, in combination with the affordable housing and support services offered by the Times Square, offers an opportunity to do what a lot of us working with the homeless have always thought was necessary: linking housing, services, and jobs to make it possible for people to rebuild their lives and become self-sufficient.

Our training process starts with an assessment that's done by our social service partner, the Center for Urban Community Services. They evaluate our candidates' education level, work history, and other issues to find out what kind of on-the-job coaching might be necessary. That way we don't incorrectly assume that someone can go home and study the menu chart on his or her own.

After a few months in operation we realized we had to tailor our training process to meet the needs of our employees. Some of our more frail tenants, those with the greatest histories of disability, were getting wiped out by the customer service demand. We redesigned the jobs so they're smaller and more focused. We have the deliveryperson. The person whose job is to keep the tables clean. The person who's in charge of packing and decorating cakes. We have two job coaches who spend time with new hires, helping them get comfortable with the demands of their jobs.

We have to make sure the customers are well treated and that the store works from a business perspective. The store earned nearly $40,000 in profits in its first year, which went to support our economic development activities. Plus, it contributes $30,000 in rent to our program and distributes over $230,000 in wages to our tenants, which makes it possible for them to pay their rent.

A Starbuck's just opened in the storefront next door to the partnershop. As a term of their lease, they've agreed to hire our tenants. We wouldn't have been able to attract Starbuck's but for them looking at Ben & Jerry's and saying, "We can do this too."

Our opening the Ben & Jerry's scoop shop was the first positive retail development on our street in a generation. It confounded people's expectations about what it means to have affordable housing in their neighborhood. When we began, a lot of our neighbors were supportive but cautious; some were skeptical and just groaning. But now our project is seen as a benefit to the neighborhood, not just for the people who live at the Times Square.

The partnershop has opened doors for us and for other agencies working with the homeless. We don't have to make the case for funding our programs by anecdote. We can go to employers and say, "Give our tenants a chance. Look—they're working successfully at Ben & Jerry's."

It's made local and national companies think about how their employment goals could tie in with their social goals and serve these needy people. With such meanness afoot in the land with respect to services for the poor, this model serves as an example to hold out to businesses of goodwill who want to be community minded but haven't thought about how to do that.

—Rosanne Haggerty
Executive Director, Common Ground

Here's an editorial the *New York Times* published on April 23, 1994, about the Times Square partnershop.

Ice Cream Philanthropy

Lest readers perceive a hidden conflict of interest, this editorial concerns an ice cream shop that gave out free cones when it opened for business a few steps from the Times' front door. The cones were great. The shop's significance is greater.

It is a Ben & Jerry's "Partnershop," one of five that the ice cream producer has established with nonprofit organizations, where most or all of the profits go to the nonprofit's program. The oldest, Youth Scoops in Ithaca, New York, opened in 1987. The newest opened this month at the corner of Eighth Avenue and West 43rd Street, a block from Times Square in one of New York City's downscale neighborhoods.

Ben & Jerry's waives its $25,000 franchise fee for these shops. In addition to putting their profits into good works, the shops provide jobs and job training. Youth Scoops, for example, is part of a local youth development program; it employs more than 30 young people, ages 14 to 21, in jobs that range from scooper to assistant manager.

The new shop in Manhattan is on the ground floor of an old hotel refurbished by Common Ground Community Inc. as low-rent housing for single adults; the shop employs the hotel's tenants. Another New York City shop opened in Harlem two summers ago; it employs homeless men.

With flavors like Cherry Garcia, named after the world's most durable hippie rock guru, Ben & Jerry's manages to mix 60's ideals with profits.

● Bridging the Gap Between For-Profits and Nonprofits

Partnershops have a positive impact on their local communities and on the business community at large. They provide a model for bridging the gap between the for-profit and nonprofit worlds—a collaboration that's long overdue and is extremely helpful to the goal of meeting the basic needs of disadvantaged people, the financial needs of nonprofit organizations, and the sales needs for the retail ice cream outlets that sponsor them.

But the most moving thing about partnershops is the impact they've had on individual people's lives.

✳   Being a part of the scoop shop has been an incredible experience for every single tenant who's worked there. They've gained a sense that their skills, and their capacity to succeed, are much greater than they'd imagined. People who were just trying to stay sober two years ago have now shown up for work on time at Ben & Jerry's every day for a year. They're confident they're going to be sober. There's structure in their lives, and there's a community of support, and people they work with at Ben & Jerry's who rely on them and who they rely on. These are great human victories.

—Rosanne Haggerty

When we examine our options for retail expansion, there are different ways we could go, and different opinions within the company about how to go there. One extreme would be to sign up big deals with multi-regional master franchisees and blow the stores out.

The other end of the continuum, the option that would be values-driven, would be to decide that a huge percentage of our new franchises are going to be partnershops. (Jeff Furman believes it should be 90 percent.) That would mean devoting significant resources for that undertaking—staffing up our retail operations department, for starters.

It takes more energy at the front end for us to open partnershops. We do more research into the social and financial status of the partnering organization and often offer extra support in the form of Grand Openings, press conferences, and media coverage. Partnershop owners may also have a more labor-intensive opening process than traditional scoop shop owners. So if we determine, for example, that our resources allow us to open only twenty scoop shops next year, we could decide that they're all going to be partnershops, and open fewer shops overall. We certainly wouldn't have trouble finding organizations that want to open one; we currently have five hundred applications from nonprofits all over the country.

The five partnershops that we're currently operating tend to be slightly less financially profitable to the agencies that run them than privately owned scoop shops—although there's no difference to Ben & Jerry's. Some of the reason for that is the costs involved in providing additional services: job training, job coaching, and special services needed by the partnershop employees, many of whom are clients of the partnering organization. But the extra effort it takes to make these shops work in the short term is insignificant over the long run when one considers the benefits partnershop programs provide to the clients of each organization.

✳   If we weren't a partnershop we would sell less ice cream. But because we're very community-involved, people will come in to the store to support what we're doing. We get incredible amounts of free press and goodwill in the community.

—Jeff Furman

It's a wonderful thing to see nonprofits—who are working to alleviate the social problems our company wants to address—funding their human services programs by selling our ice cream. The real beauty of the partnershop model is that it doesn't depend on a company like Ben & Jerry's, or a product like ice cream. Any values-led company can make use of the partnershop concept to serve its own needs and the needs of the community that makes its existence possible.

Marketing for Real

Ben: Modern marketing is a process whereby faceless, nameless, values-less corporations hire marketers to determine what the customer would like one of their brands to be—then they fabricate an image for that brand that corresponds to what the customer wants.

Jerry: Couldn't you say, Ben, that traditional marketing is trying to appeal to the largest possible market?

Ben: Yes. So they adopt these middle-of-the-road, noncontroversial, innocuous identities.

Jerry: They want to sell as much product as they can. So they try not to alienate anyone.

Ben: But they still get only a slice of the market. Because whatever made-up story they've come up with usually doesn't end up appealing to the majority of the population any more than their competitor's made-up story does. With values-led marketing, you just go out there and say who you are. You don't have to fool people to sell them your product.

● Marketing for Real

Values-led marketing and traditional marketing are different in many ways, but they have this in common: the indicator of how well either type of marketing is working is whether people are buying the product that's being marketed.

In the gas station days we had virtually no marketing budget. Our business grew on word of mouth, based on three attributes: a great product; a fun, caring environment; and community involvement. Our marketing strategy is still based on these three attributes.

Marketing done well results in sales. Effective short-term marketing results in a short-term sales boost—a cents-off promotion or a six-week run of ads, for instance, can create a short-term lift. Long-term, image marketing results in ongoing, sustained sales. Image marketing is a slow build over time, and it's based on communicating the essence of the brand. The positioning statement of Ben & Jerry's—the essence of the brand—would be, "Two regular, caring guys living in Vermont, the land of the cows and green pastures, making some world-class ice cream in some pretty unusual flavors."

Both short-term and long-term marketing can induce customers to try a product—but neither approach can make people like it. Only the quality of the product and the resonance the customer feels with the company can generate repeat business and brand loyalty.

Traditional marketing falsely attributes "desirable" qualities—sexiness, wealth, coolness, power—to products and brands through the use of techniques (like advertising) that have no real value to people or to society.

Values-led marketing, on the other hand, promotes products and brands by integrating social benefits into many different aspects of a business enterprise. Instead of advertising, which adds no value, we do things that actually provide a service to people and society: putting on music festivals, opening partnershops that benefit nonprofit groups, buying goods and services from alternative suppliers, moving to chlorine-free paper, using more organically grown ingredients, doing advocacy for nonprofit community groups.

Some of these activities aren't marketing per se, but they result in marketing benefits. Either way, instead of arising from an ad executive's imagination as a cute way to push product, values-led marketing arises from the day-to-day activities of a values-led business.

That's why writing a chapter on marketing for a book about values-led business is almost a contradiction in itself—because part of the beauty of being values-driven is that every values-led activity your company does helps market the company.

Much of traditional marketing consists of throwing billions of dollars and tremendous human resources at creating what often amounts to fairy tales that are of no intrinsic value, outside of possible entertainment, to anyone. With all the pressing social needs going unmet every day, can we afford that waste?

We don't think so. That's why we've built a $150 million company, for the most part, without it. And that's why we advocate values-led marketing, which is the antithesis of traditional marketing.

Traditional marketing takes a product and attempts to slap an image onto it that's usually unrelated to the company that makes it and is oftentimes unrelated to the product itself.

Values-led business uses the power of a business to meet social needs that a large segment of the community is interested in getting met. And that has the effect of making consumers want to support that business by buying its products.

When you're running a values-led business—when each person in your company is looking for ways to integrate a concern for the community into his or her daily business decisions—innovative and (most importantly) socially beneficial marketing opportunities constantly present themselves (although not always in easily recognizable form). Oftentimes the most significant marketing activities originate outside the marketing department.

For example, it wasn't a marketing strategy that led us to start buying what is now a million dollars' worth of brownies each year from a bakery that employs and trains formerly unemployable people, or to partner with Vermont dairy farmers to save family farms, or to create flavors like Rainforest Crunch, which provides a market for rain-forest nuts. But we got more than delicious brownies, fresh Vermont cream, and popular flavors as a result of those decisions. We also got a lot of loyal customers.

We didn't pay a public relations firm to tell us to put up billboards protesting the Seabrook nuclear power plant ("We Want to Keep Our Customers Alive and Licking") or to sign an ad with other companies urging a diplomatic solution to prevent the Gulf War. But doing those things made our position on the issues clear and made us popular with the many people who shared that position.

It's controversial for a business to take stands that aren't in its own self-interest, because that's not the norm. We've learned that some people are going to be tremendously impressed by our positions and buy more ice cream. A very small number of people are going to be tremendously impressed and buy less. Some people will be completely unaffected. Anything that's not pabulum is going to alienate some people. And that goes for traditional marketing as well.

But compared to anything Ben & Jerry's has done (supporting family farms, opposing nuclear power, advocating children's rights), the normal mode of corporate behavior (lobbying against environmental protection, against an increase in the minimum wage, and against health care reform) has alienated a lot more people.

Vote for Values

Doing values-led marketing alters the role of a company's marketing and communications departments. At Ben & Jerry's, the most significant "marketing" we do consists of integrating social values into as many aspects of the business as possible. So the job of the marketing department, oftentimes, is to respond to projects initiated by other departments. How can we tell the story of the Greyston Bakery on a pint container? How can we promote the Children's Defense Fund at a festival? How can we communicate that we've come up with a new ice cream flavor based on alternatively sourced ingredients? How can we explain to our customers why we're working on converting to chlorine-free paper in our packaging?

Values-led marketing is a lot like what politics used to be. In the old days, politicians used to stand up and say, "These are my values. This is what I believe in. If elected, I will do this. All those who support what I believe in, vote for me."

Then politicians started hiring marketers, who managed the politicians the same way they managed packaged goods. The marketers told the politicians that in order to garner the most votes, they needed to do some research and determine what the electorate wanted—then espouse those views to make the product (themselves) into what the research called for. This is traditional, mainstream packaged-goods marketing.

Ben & Jerry's and other values-led companies market themselves in the same way that politicians used to attract voters. We stand up and tell people what we believe in and ask those people who agree to "vote for us" by trying our products. If you've got values that are aligned with the values of your potential customers, you don't have to create a phony image. You just have to show consumers who you are.

The task of a values-led marketing department is not to create a false identity for a corporation. Its task is to advance the social mission at the same time it's selling products. Our consumers love our ice cream, but that's not all they need. We meet their needs more holistically by addressing their social concerns as well as their taste buds.

The kind of marketing you do determines the kind of people you need to do it. We market experientially—mostly through sampling, plant tours, newsletters, our Web site, and special events—as opposed to media buys. Our marketing task is to distribute samples of frozen desserts and explain who we are, not to invent a cute TV ad campaign. Marketing people accustomed to traditional advertising techniques may lack the skills necessary to pull off values-led marketing, which is more like grassroots campaigning or circus promotion.

Of course, sometimes there's a short-term, product-specific marketing project to be done that requires us to use a conventional method. When we launched our Smooth line, we needed to let a lot of people who weren't our current customers know—in a very short time span— that we were coming out with a new line: chunkless ice cream flavors. We decided the best way to do that was via traditional advertising. But we still wanted to tweak the medium a bit, to inject some social content into the campaign. What we came up with was an ad honoring progressive social activists, showing them eating different flavors of our new Smooth ice creams.

Ben: I don't see that campaign as a great example of values-led marketing. I don't think it served the community.

Jerry: It was something we had to do. One of those trade-offs.

Ben: I'm not sure it served the interests of the business, either. The customers we were trying to communicate to were largely Häagen-Dazs customers. Some people felt those customers were turned off by progressive activists.

Jerry: Oddly enough, though, the Smooth introduction was one of our most successful.

Ben: Go figure.

● Values-Led Marketing Is Honest Marketing

"Honesty is the best policy" has always been our marketing approach— starting with our name. Our competitors were superpremium ice cream companies with phony, foreign-sounding names like Häagen-Dazs, La Glace de Paris, Alpen Zauber, Perche No? and Frusen Glädjè—all manufactured in the United States, all trying to pretend they came from foreign countries.

Into this elite, cosmopolitan fray came Ben & Jerry's. Our name made us stand out in the crowd and conveyed down-home authenticity. We were "two real guys."

Honest marketing wouldn't work for many corporations, because their values aren't aligned with those of their potential customers. For example, the lumber industry fights legislation that would protect ancient forests and stop clear-cutting. Retailers oppose returnable-bottle legislation. The auto industry resists safety and fuel-efficiency standards. The health and insurance industries fight single-payer health insurance. Manufacturers oppose pollution regulations. Most business associations lobby to keep the minimum wage down.

Those corporations keep their values and activities covert for good reason: they know if they went public with them, they'd lose some support from their customers. They'd lose sales.

There are two paths for corporations like that to pursue. One is to keep doing what they're doing, and use traditional marketing to create an image that conceals their values and activities.

The other path a corporation can take is to transform its operating philosophy from a win-lose scenario—business versus the consumer, business versus the environment, business versus employees—to a win-win scenario in which business is working in partnership with those other entities for their mutual benefit. This requires a company to examine not only its operations but its core product in terms of impact on society and the environment.

The Monsanto Corporation, for example, is working toward zero emissions in terms of the by-products of its manufacturing process. That's a worthy goal. But many of Monsanto's core products, such as Round-Up weed killer, are toxic chemicals. A big market for Monsanto is the agriculture business. The values-led—and long-term-profits-led —direction for that company would be to start to transform its business to technology that supports sustainable organic food production.

That kind of transition might originate at the top of the organization (as it did when Yvon Chouinard, the founder of Patagonia, decided the company would use only organic cotton, despite the additional cost to the company and its customers). It might come from employees at any level, or from shareholders. Our shareholders consistently challenge us on our business practices, from the suppliers we use to the number of women and minorities on our board.

Or changes might originate with customers. After massive numbers of consumers protested Coors' homophobic hiring policies, the company reversed them.

● The Ultimate U.S.P.

The good news is, being values-led requires no sacrifice of marketing power. In fact, it gives you what every marketer seeks: a genuine point of differentiation from its competitors, a "unique selling proposition" (U.S.P.).

Competing with other businesses by convincing customers to line our pockets with their money instead of somebody else's pockets was not a selling proposition that would have worked for us. When Ben was working his way through his spotted college career selling Pied Piper ice cream off a vending truck, his competitor was the Good Humor man. One day the Good Humor man stopped Ben and his partner and said, "You're cutting into my business. You're college kids, just earning some extra money. I'm trying to support my family doing this."

Ben thought, "The guy has a point."

Years later, when we were deciding where to set up our homemade-ice-cream parlor, Ben thought back on this situation. We went to great pains not to locate where there already was a homemade-ice-cream parlor, because Ben couldn't justify competing with an existing business. And when we started competing on the freezer shelves with other pints, Ben felt there had to be some social benefit to Ben & Jerry's to justify asking people to buy our ice cream instead of someone else's.

He couldn't feel good about asking his customers to buy his products instead of the competition's if it was just a matter of giving their money to his company versus the competitor's. But if the money they gave him was also helping to solve problems in the larger society, then he felt fine about asking his customers to choose Ben & Jerry's.

Being in business necessarily means competing—taking sales from other companies. Doing that makes sense to us if our business benefits society. In today's business climate, that approach constitutes a unique selling proposition.

Part of creating a U.S.P. is infusing your product with benefits for the customer. Some are intangible, like a personality, brand imagery. Some are tangible, like chunks, unusual flavors, and service to the community. You can come up with the most creative ad there is, but if you're just doing traditional advertising, you're less able to break through the clutter.

✳   In New York City, Stonyfield is number two in sales at full price behind Dannon, and we're pushing Dannon. We're ahead of Yoplait, Colombo, and Breyers when all brands are "off deal" (full price). When four national brands are on sale and the fifth one is at full price and it's Dannon, Dannon doesn't sell. When the fifth one is Stonyfield, Stonyfield's sales don't dip at all.

The trade has told us that if we're ever out of stock, nobody screams louder than our customers. I know taste is the primary reason. But I know the other big reason is that our customers like what we stand for.

What I'm finally figuring out after thirteen years in this business is that the reward for corporate responsibility is not necessarily that you get on the shelves. It's not even necessarily that you get the first consumer trial. But it is the repeat buy. It's that your customers become fiercely loyal.

—Gary Hirshberg
CEO and President, Stonyfield Farm Yogurt

Jerry: The medium is the message. To the extent that you market using run-of-the-mill methods, you'll be seen as a run-of-the-mill company.

Ben: You won't just be seen as run-of-the-mill. You'll *be* run-of-the-mill. A business is defined by what it does. And marketing is a major component of what every business does.

● As You Give You Receive

When we started our company we had the same feelings about corporations that most Americans share. We felt business was taking from the community and not giving back. We felt business was avaricious, out for profit at the expense of people and society. Ben's background was in social services. His only real job had been as a counselor for troubled teenagers. Jerry had planned to be a doctor. Being in business solely to maximize profit was not a motivation that worked for us.

Our commitment to giving back to the community dovetailed with another, equally compelling factor. We were broke. We didn't have the option of hiring image consultants and market researchers and ad agencies and public relations firms to create an image for our product. Any promotion we undertook had to meet one of two criteria. It had to be free, or it had to be dirt cheap.

We did what we could afford to do. As Greyston Bakery's founder, Bernie Glassman, says in his book *Instructions to the Cook,* you see what you've got in the cupboard, then you make the best meal possible. The strategy that evolved from that approach turned out to be a lot more worthwhile than advertising. We gave away ice cream cones to good customers waiting on line in our shop. (Nowadays, that's considered a mainstream marketing technique: "rewarding frequent buyers." For us it was personal—the proprietor of the ice cream parlor comes out and recognizes a loyal customer. It was a surprise, a treat for people we cared about.)

We gave away bumper stickers. We threw a free festival for the people in the community. Fall Down cost us about $300. How much advertising space can you buy for $300? People got a lot more out of Fall Down than they would have gotten from an ad, and Ben & Jerry's made a much bigger impression than a $300 ad would have made. People appreciated Ben & Jerry's for sponsoring it.

We did Free Cone Day. We figured if we were able to stay in business, we could afford to give away ice cream cones once a year to our customers and would-be customers. We put on free movie festivals for the city of Burlington. We borrowed a projector and put up posters announcing that we'd be showing movies on the blank wall alongside the gas station one night a week all summer—free, bring your own chair. At first City Hall wouldn't let us do it. So we wrote a petition and asked the other businesses in the neighborhood to sign it. After the city officials saw the petition they gave us permission to show the movies. That was the first time we experienced the power of businesses united for the common good. It made quite a lasting impression. And the whole series cost us a thousand bucks, because we rented the movies off-season, when the colleges weren't using them.

Eventually we got other businesses to cosponsor the movie festivals, which made them even cheaper for us to do. This wasn't a flash-in-the-pan thing. We still show free movies one night a week in the summer at our plants in Waterbury and Springfield, and so do some of the local Ben & Jerry's shops. Now that we've got all these different locations, the movie festivals aren't exactly the same as they used to be. Ben isn't the projectionist anymore. Jerry isn't the security guard. But people still love going. And by the way, on those nights we also sell a lot of ice cream.

The business pundits, lawyers, accountants, and advisors all said the social mission was going to be Ben & Jerry's undoing. They said it was not financially viable for a business to be profitable and to serve the needs of the community at the same time. Now that we've proved that's not true, they ask, how do you know that giving back to the community has improved your bottom line?

How does any business know that its marketing activities have improved its bottom line?

If you run a short-term advertising campaign that yields a quick boost, you can say it succeeded. But you can't predict what the long-term effect will be. You can see the positive: a momentary increase in sales. But you can't see the negative: the potential denigration of your brand equity (the value of your brand in the marketplace). You run the risk of cheapening your reputation and hurting your brand imagery by couponing and by running inconsistent ad campaigns.

✱   Advertising can be 7 to 8 percent of a company's gross. When you're Procter & Gamble that's pretty significant dollars.

When I translate what my market research has told me—that my customers buy Stonyfield for taste first, and social responsibility a close second—what that logically means is that I should discount less and put my money into additional socially responsible activities.

If you're a major player looking to have a point of difference—and you know these guys fight over a quarter point of share—I offer to you this possibility: the 7 percent of your gross that you spend on advertising could be reduced and reapplied in ways that will gain you much more than a quarter point of share. And that's return on investment.

—Gary Hirshberg

Some of our marketing efforts are more effective than others. In that regard it's just like traditional marketing. As the old saw says, "I know half of the money I spend is wasted. I just don't know which half." It's also true that some of our values-led activities are more effective than others at delivering social value.

● Lead with Your Values and Your Customers Will Find You

In 1990, when we were about to launch our Light ice cream, we asked ourselves how we could integrate our social mission with our business objectives. We needed to spread the news about Light, and we needed to do some sampling (give people free tastes of the new product).

In order to do national sampling the way we wanted to do it, we needed to have mobile ice cream vending capability. So we created a "marketing vehicle"—a truck with solar-powered freezers—that would demonstrate the benefits of solar energy (another form of "Light") while spreading the word about our new Light line. We wanted to counter the common misconceptions that solar power doesn't really work and that it's too complicated or expensive to be practical. The truth is, when you factor in the environmental and military costs of oil-based and nuclear power, the cost of solar energy is many times cheaper. A Greenpeace report determined that the federal government subsidized the civilian nuclear power industry to the tune of $96 billion from 1950 to 1990. The federal government's sponsorship of research and development into clean and renewable energy has been one-sixty-eighth of what it has lavished on the nuclear industry—$1.4 billion.

So we bought a panel truck, then hired a solar-power installation company to fit it out so the freezers could be powered by photovoltaic collectors on the roof. The panels collected enough power that the fully charged batteries could keep the ice cream frozen for up to four days without additional sunlight. We put a sign on the truck explaining how photovoltaics work. When people got their ice cream samples, they also got information about the benefits and viability of alternative energy. We called the truck the Solar Roller.

The response to the Solar Roller was so positive that a year later we bought a used Silver Eagle bus; outfitted the roof with solar panels to power onboard freezers, lights, appliances, and sound system; painted the bus in Ben & Jerry's style; hired a troupe of vaudeville performers; and sent the Ben & Jerry's circus bus out on the road for a national tour. The bus had a solar-powered inflatable canopy that covered the stage. The stage itself pulled out from under the chassis. Setting up the bus for a performance was a living demonstration of solar power.

When the circus bus came to town—and it came to more than 150 towns across the country—jugglers and magicians performed onstage, then people in the bus scooped our new Light ice cream. Sometimes we gave ice cream away; sometimes we partnered with local-community-based nonprofit organizations and gave the money from ice cream sales to them.

The circus bus drew attention wherever it went. It generated tens of thousands of dollars, which in turn funded the important work of activist groups. The circus bus made a much more positive impression on people than any advertising campaign could have.

To help spread the word about the new Light line, we also came up with a campaign called A Thousand Pints of Light. George Bush had issued his promise to solve all social problems with "a thousand points of light." The phrase sounded inspirational and beautiful, but when you tried to analyze it, nobody—including President Bush—seemed to understand what it actually meant.

We sent out a press release that said Ben & Jerry's had hired a team of audio experts to analyze the president's speech, and that by using computer modeling and advanced audio-analysis techniques, these experts had discovered that what the president had actually said was that the cure for the country's ills was a thousand *pints* of light. So Ben & Jerry's had come out with this product in order to help the president accomplish his agenda for the country.

We announced that we'd bestow a thousand pints of Light on individuals who were working for progressive social change in their local communities. Essentially, we'd be throwing big ice cream parties all over the United States.

Giving out the thousand pints of Light was a wonderful experience. We went to Miami and honored an AIDS activist, a really controversial guy. We went to Philadelphia and saluted Maggie Kuhn from the Grey Panthers, a senior citizens' advocacy group. We went to Cabrini Green public housing in Chicago to recognize a high school girl who was doing antigang organizing in her school.

We'd bring a thousand pints of Light and pile them into a giant pyramid. The people who'd won would have a party and invite some local nonprofits or the groups of their choice and give it all away. In terms of combining product, and fun, and a social message, and a community celebration, and local media, it was a very well coordinated and holistic campaign.

The Thousand Pints of Light was a great success. The product itself, however, was a dismal failure—not because people didn't try it but because they didn't like it. Which proves that even if you do the marketing side well, if the product isn't right, marketing can't make the product succeed.

● Gross Rating Points Are Gross

The standard way to measure the cost effectiveness of a marketing program is by the cost per impression. Marketers assign CPM (cost per thousand) based on circulation, viewership, or numbers of listeners divided by the cost of an ad in print, TV, or radio. Individual shows are assigned "gross rating points" based on what percentage of households watching TV are watching that particular show.

Conventional wisdom holds that the more people you reach within your target demographic for the least amount of money, the more effective your media buy is.

We believe it's the quality, not the quantity, of interaction that engenders customer loyalty. That's why we'd rather spend our marketing budget on community activities like music festivals than on TV ads.

In 1991 we threw the first in a series of Ben & Jerry's free music festivals. As the flyer announcing the first One World, One Heart Festivals in Stowe (Vermont), Chicago, and San Francisco said, "The nice thing about becoming bigger is that you can throw bigger parties. This festival is a time to play and celebrate together—it's also an opportunity to take the first step in a sustained effort at working together for a more just world."

When we throw a festival we don't just make an impression on the people who walk through the gates. We reach a lot more people through the publicity and media coverage surrounding the festival. People who come get to sample our ice cream and interact with our company, which makes a lot stronger impression than watching a thirty-second TV commercial. People who don't come hear about the festival and about Ben & Jerry's from their friends and from the media before and after the event.

Along with games like Tug-of-Love, great music, great food, and dancing, the festivals featured ice cream Action Stations, where people got free cones for writing postcards to their legislators. Billboards explained where Americans' tax dollars were going: the billions of dollars being spent on military hardware versus what that money could buy if

POLITIC$ $TAND

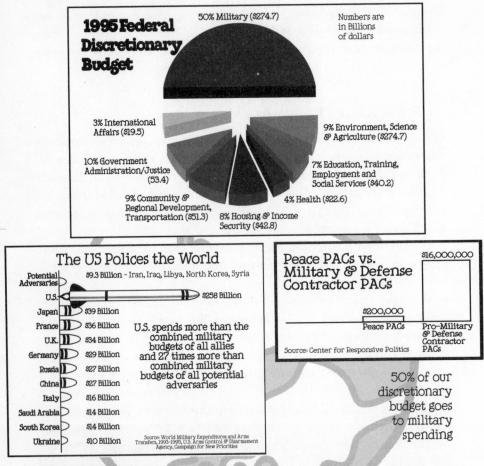

1995 Federal Discretionary Budget

Numbers are in Billions of dollars

50% Military ($274.7)

3% International Affairs ($19.5)

10% Government Administration/Justice (53.4)

9% Community & Regional Development, Transportation ($51.3)

8% Housing & Income Security ($42.8)

4% Health ($22.6)

7% Education, Training, Employment and Social Services ($40.2)

9% Environment, Science & Agriculture ($274.7)

The US Polices the World

Potential Adversaries: $9.3 Billion - Iran, Iraq, Libya, North Korea, Syria

U.S.	$258 Billion
Japan	$39 Billion
France	$36 Billion
U.K.	$34 Billion
Germany	$29 Billion
Russia	$27 Billion
China	$27 Billion
Italy	$16 Billion
Saudi Arabia	$14 Billion
South Korea	$14 Billion
Ukraine	$10 Billion

U.S. spends more than the combined military budgets of all allies and 27 times more than combined military budgets of all potential adversaries

Source: World Military Expenditures and Arms Transfers, 1993-1995, U.S. Arms Control & Disarmament Agency, Campaign for New Priorities

---

Peace PACs vs. Military & Defense Contractor PACs

$16,000,000

$200,000

Peace PACs

Pro-Military & Defense Contractor PACs

Source: Center for Responsive Politics

50% of our discretionary budget goes to military spending

Organizations:

20/20 Vision —A national network of citizens engaging in effective action to protect the environment and promote peace. 1828 Jefferson Place N.W., Washington, DC 20036. (202) 833-2020.

Minnesota COACT - Builds community, social and economic justice, and empowers people to take action in the democratic process. 2233 University Avenue W., Suite 300, St. Paul, MN 55114. 645-3733.

U.S. Public Interest Research Group - Non-partisan consumer watchdog group operating in defense of clean air, water, and a free and vigorous democracy. 201 Main Street S.E., Suite 228, Minneapolis, MN 55414. 379-3022.

Woman's Action for New Directions - Empowers women to act politically to reduce violence, militarism and to redirect military resources toward human and environmental needs. 110 Maryland Avenue N.E., Washington, DC 20002. (202) 543-8505.

we were using it to meet the needs of children and families; the relative size of our military budget versus those of our "enemies."

At the 1996 Ben & Jerry's festival in Minneapolis, fifty thousand people hung out in the sun with their friends, listening to Arlo Guthrie, JJ Cale, the Robert Cray Band, and Toad the Wet Sprocket; playing games created jointly by Concerts for the Environment and local non-profit groups; and eating ice cream. The challenge was to give people a good time and a good amount of information at the same time.

Each concertgoer received a Festival Passport where they could record the number of points (or "chunks") they got for participating in the games. A certain number of chunks could be redeemed for free ice cream.

Jerry was initially concerned that the games were going to be kind of dry and lame, but every booth was mobbed all day. People had a great time playing If a Tree Fell (tossing beanbag animals through a hole in a cardboard old-growth tree) and spinning the Wheel of Action, a giant wheel divided into categories of issues specific to the Minneapolis area: taxes, food, housing, solid waste.

At the computerized Politics Stand, players divided federal budget spending as they saw fit, then compared their priorities to the government's.

Your **PASSPORT** to:

BEN&JERRY'S®

ONE WORLD • ONE HEART
FESTIVAL
MINNESOTA • SEPTEMBER 14, 1996

The
CHUNK TRUNK

Scoop 1	Scoop 2	Scoop 3	Your Passport to FREE Ben & Jerry's Ice Cream!
			Take an action in the Children's Forum
			Take an action in the Politics Stand
			Take an action in the Community Corner
			Take an action in the Green Scene
			Take an action in the Voter Registration Station
FREE ICE CREAM!	FREE ICE CREAM!	FREE ICE CREAM!	Go to Station/Cart

Visit the New Flavors Sampling Station to try our new Euphoric flavors and register to win a weekend for 2 at the Hyatt, a Trek Bike, a six foot Subway sub, or a year supply (52 pints) of Ben & Jerry's.

Hyatt logo   Trek logo   subway logo   **BEN&JERRY'S**

Imagine A Billion Dollars

This bag holds 100,000 grass seeds. It will take 10,000 bags to hold the one billion seeds from the Ben & Jerry's One World, One Heart Festival.

For most of us, a large purchase is several hundred dollars. We think in terms of thousands only when we're talking about our house or our car. A person would have to win a $1 million lottery 1000 times to have $1 billion.

The U.S. military budget is $300 billion. The Center for Defense Information tells us we can defend ourselves for half that amount —a plan which is endorsed by *The New York Times*.

It's time to think about security in more human terms.

One B-2 Stealth Bomber costs $860 million. For $860 million an additional 225,000 children could be in the Head Start program.

Twenty-nine Seawolf Nuclear Attack Submarines cost $44 billion. For $20 billion we could lift every American child out of poverty.

For $142 million we could buy one MX missile or provide prenatal care for 236,000 expectant mothers.

It's up to us to plant the seeds of change. The money this country needs to remain strong is there. We just need to get it planted in the right places.

BEN&JERRY'S.
VERMONT'S FINEST ALL NATURAL ICE CREAM™

At several festivals we had a huge truck come in and dump a billion seeds of grass. A billion seeds makes a nice, big, soft pile, and people have a lot of fun rolling around in it. We dump the seeds to demonstrate how many a billion is, to help people understand the magnitude of the numbers that get tossed around when we read about federal programs in the newspaper. Here's the bag we hand out at the festivals.

Fifty thousand people attended the Minneapolis festival, but it made 9 million impressions through advertising, articles in newspapers, and radio and TV coverage. It cost us $150,000, or 17 cents per thousand impressions. A thirty-second TV commercial on the WCCO Minneapolis evening news costs $1,800 and reaches 260,000 people, for a cost of $6.92 per thousand impressions. A full-page ad in the *Minneapolis Star*

Tribune costs $13,917 and reaches 407,504 people, at a cost per thousand impressions of $34.15.

The goal of the One World, One Heart Festivals is to provide consumers with something of value. They get great entertainment. They also get information and inspiration that encourages them to take part in the political process. At the same time, they're experiencing and participating in the totality of who and what Ben & Jerry's is, getting to know the company and getting to try our products. We get to interact with 50,000 of our customers and potential customers for six hours. That's worth a lot more than a thirty-second TV commercial.

● Relationship Marketing

Our early experience with the movie festivals taught us that by providing service to the community, we could do more than have fun, do some good, and save money on advertising. We could also build extraordinary relationships with our customers. So we kept on doing that.

June 26, 1995

Dear Ben and Jerry,

I'm writing to thank you guys for yet another foot stomping, socially conscious, educational, environmentally aware, dance your butt off, sweat generating, mind opening, mmm mmm good time at this past weekend's One World, One Heart Festival at Sugarbush.

This is the third year in a row I have attended the festival. I live about six hours away but it's worth every mile to come every year.

> *Signed, a Ben & Jerry's junkie,*
> *Tracie B.*
> *Middlebury, Conn.*

P.S. I know Ben & Jerry won't actually see this letter, but maybe you (whoever you are that is reading this) could pass it along?

June 26, 1995
Dear Ben and Jerry,
*Thanks so much for the wonderful day we had at your
festival. We had fun, ate ice cream and loved the music. Your
staff was not only helpful and smiling all the time but made the
bus ride enjoyable and they never lacked enthusiasm.*

> *Good luck in your next year—we'll keep on eating!!*
> *Dave, Margo and Todd H.*
> *Waitsfield, Vt.*

March 20, 1995
Dear Ben and Jerry,
*I just found out that your festival this year will only be one
day short! I had such a great time last year that I've planned to
make your festival an annual event in my life, and to think now
you've reduced the fun in half . . .*
*Last year you had great fun events, terrific music, awesome
local vendors for food as well as the BEST ICE CREAM IN THE
WORLD!*
*What can we, the visitors, do to help extend the fun? Pay a
nominal admission? Pay a nominal fee for ice cream?*
*My family and I will be there this year, but I wish it were for
the whole weekend!*

> *Most sincerely,*
> *Lois N.*
> *Chilmark, Mass.*

When traditional grocery marketers think about growing sales, they
think about coupons and price reductions. We don't believe that trying
to motivate sales through couponing or cents-off promotions is a rela-
tionship-building activity. Couponing and cents-off promoting are very
short-term undertakings. They'll bump up sales this quarter; they'll provide a lift for the next few weeks. But they don't grow sales among
loyal customers. They grow sales among bargain hunters—who are fine
people, but the least loyal customers. Bargain hunters are brand

switchers. They're not interested in forming a long-term relationship with a company.

Sales gained through couponing are ephemeral and fleeting. They do nothing for the brand long-term. Couponing and cents-off promotions do get people to try your products, but those people are motivated by price-off coupons, so if your competitor offers one, they'll switch. That might make sense for undifferentiated commodity products like laundry detergent and canned green beans, but it's the least effective form of marketing for premium-quality specialty products.

That's not to say that Ben & Jerry's doesn't do cents-off price promotions. We do them because we must: supermarkets base their marketing on those promotions and strongly encourage us to participate. But generally what we're doing is much more long-term oriented.

Jerry: And slower.

Ben: And more durable.

Jerry: People talk about brand building. What we're trying to do is along those lines, but it's relationship building through the vehicle of the brand.

Ben: In our case the brand is the company. The brand and the company are synonymous.

In marketing lingo, what we do is what would be known as corporate-image marketing, or institutional marketing. It's designed to be a long, consistent, slow build.

A lot of companies lose potential marketing equity because their marketing isn't consistent. They change their image fairly frequently; they change their advertising campaigns. A new marketing director comes in; she wants to leave her mark, so she switches ad agencies. Then the product isn't selling, so she switches agencies again. The new agency comes up with a totally different ad campaign, one that doesn't synergize with the last campaign. So maybe there's a bump in sales initially, but then sales go back down because the new campaign doesn't build on the last one.

Incredibly, marketers point to a scenario like this and say, "We did a great job. We moved the needle. What we did increased sales." But despite all that effort and all those resources spent, what they're doing isn't developing progressively deeper relationships with their customers.

The Cone-Roper survey we mentioned in Chapter One, as well as other surveys—including the 1994 Walker Information on Corporate Character Study and the 1995 two-year Measuring Corporate Citizenship Project, which was funded by sixteen multinational corporations—show that consumers are more likely to patronize a company that provides social benefit to the community. Many companies that aren't values-led run helter-skelter, hither and yon coming up with one short-lived ad campaign after another. These campaigns reveal that the company has no soul. No realness. No integrity. And those are the values people are yearning to connect with.

If your company has values, an essence, you need to capitalize on that strategic advantage and make sure your marketing expresses your values and your essence. A company with values is a company with soul. When you've got a soul, you can market from your values.

If a traditional marketing campaign is really well done it makes people say, "Great ads. I like those ads."

Values-led marketing evokes a different reaction. People say, "Great company. I love that company."

Which response is likely to foster a more long-lasting relationship?

Selling your product is an essential part of any business. It's a means to an end, a way of accomplishing an objective. For a conventional business, the objective is maximizing short-term profitability. For a values-led business, the objective is to build long-term relationships with customers—so we can work together for the greater common social good and make money as well. Building long-term relationships helps both parts of the bottom line. Loyal customer relationships help us to be effective in the community and help us sell our product. Our experience—and the experiences of other values-led companies—shows that we can be just as profitable as conventional businesses, while also using the power of business for the common good.

● The Downside

The quality of our products and our fun-loving, down-home, values-led business philosophy: those are the factors that lead people to buy our ice cream. Apart from the contact we've had with people at our festivals and through our ice cream donations, our plant tours, our newsletter, and our Web site, most of what people know about Ben & Jerry's comes from the articles they've read about us. Most of those articles weren't pushed through our PR department. The news media usually comes to us because we do things that aren't traditionally done.

That said, it's also true that being a values-led company and doing values-led marketing has its downside. In a word (in two words, actually), the negative aspect is the phenomenon of elevated expectations.

When you set yourself up as a model, when you say you're trying to do things in a different and a better way, you set yourself up for criticism. No one expects Chevron to do much for society. But people expect a lot from Ben & Jerry's. They have come to want us to be all good things to all people. When we don't achieve our aspirations, we're criticized for being hypocritical. It comes with the territory.

For example, a reporter with an agenda who's trying to show that Ben & Jerry's is hypocritical can do that very easily. Sometimes, the same set of facts can make the company look great or terrible, depending on how it's presented. That set of facts can make customers want to be associated with the company, and they can just as easily make customers feel they've been lied to. Here's an article that was printed in the *Boston Globe,* followed by Ben's op-ed response.

Ben & Jerry's Shelves Inaccurate Rainforest Pitch

JEFF GLASSER

Nuts! And you thought you were helping forest peoples in the rainforest.

After all, the label on Ben & Jerry's Rainforest Crunch ice cream claimed for five years that "money from these nuts will help Brazilian forest peoples start a nut-shelling cooperative."

The truth is, Ben & Jerry's Homemade Inc. purchased 95 percent of the nuts for Rainforest Crunch ice cream from Brazilian agribusinesses and less than 5 percent from the little nut-shelling cooperative in western Brazil. And recently, the Xapuri cooperative got out of the nut business entirely, forcing Ben & Jerry's to quietly remove the helping-the-forest-people pitch from its crunch containers.

It's not exactly a scandal to rival Watergate—or even Whitewater. But it's also not the type of thing one would expect from a poster child for the socially conscious business movement. . . .

The Brazil nut brouhaha is is the latest in a series of

recent setbacks for self-described "socially responsible" businesses. . . .

"Being socially responsible in sourcing is very complex when you're dealing with international markets," notes analyst Matt Patski, who follows Ben & Jerry's for Boston's Adams Harkness.

The company has discovered just how complicated.

Ben & Jerry's began producing Rainforest Crunch in 1989, after cofounder Ben Cohen met with Jason Clay, who was then directing a nonprofit Cambridge outfit called Cultural Survival Inc. At a Grateful Dead benefit concert for the rainforest, Clay made the pitch that, by helping poor rainforest people derive economic benefit from the harvesting of rainforest products, nut purchases could combat both poverty and the clear-cutting of rainforests for very profitable timber sales.

Cohen bit, and a new flavor, now one of the company's top 10, was born. Through Cultural Survival, the nuts would come from the Xapuri cooperative.

But, almost immediately, the company knew its nut purchases were not solely going to help forest peoples.

"We always knew we were not sourcing all of the nuts from the cooperatve," admits Alan Parker, head of investor relations and special projects for Ben & Jerry's.

That didn't stop the ice cream maker from touting its rainforest aid to eco-friendly customers. Ben & Jerry's displayed a mural of the cooperative at its corporate headquarters in Waterbury, Vt. And Cohen, in speaking tours around the country, continues to tell audiences that the company "had made a difference" in helping forest peoples.

Meanwhile, nut-supplier Cultural Survival was having increasing problems supplying the nuts. The Xapuri co-op could not produce enough nuts with low enough coliform-bacteria counts to meet US commercial standards.

In fact, the first supply of nuts the Xapuri sent through Cultural Survival to the United States came, not from forest peoples, but from the notorious Mutrans's, a wealthy agribusiness family convicted of killing labor organizers in Brazil.

Ben & Jerry's—actually, an independent company called Community Products, founded by Cohen—quickly ended its relationship with the Mutrans. But the company had to purchase more and more nuts on the open market as demand grew in direct proportion to the popularity of Rainforest Crunch.

"The demand was much higher than the supply," says Geraldo Marques of Cultural Survival. "The cooperative couldn't keep up."

In 1994, the cooperative decided to put its nut business on ice, saying it could not make a profit under current market conditions. Several months later, Ben & Jerry's began quietly removing the claims from its Rainforest Crunch labels.

"It would be misleading at this time to imply that 100 percent of the profits from 100 percent of the nuts would be used to help Xapuri," Cohen admitted in a recent interview.

That is surely an understatement. Ben & Jerry's purchased more than 1 million pounds of nuts through Community Products, and the cooperative processed only 50,000 pounds that met US standards.

The Xapuri cooperative also saw very little of the $3.02 million in profits on the 140,000 gallons of Rainforest Crunch Ben & Jerry's has sold. . . .

Cohen chafes at the suggestion of wrongdoing. "I would do it just the way I did if I had to do it again," he says, claiming his company at least "created demand" for rainforest products. . . .

The forest people may yet see some cash for the crunch. Cohen's Community Products is working on a purifying process to lower coliform counts in nuts. With such a process, the company could make the Rainforest Crunch with nuts only from cooperatives or other enterprises deemed to be eco- and labor-friendly.

"For us, that would be revolutionary," says Community Products chief executive Mark Sherman, who hopes to reach agreement with indigenous organizations by summer's end.

Parker says Ben & Jerry's will be more cautious before making new claims about saving the rainforest. "We recognize that issues are always more complicated than they look at first blush."

Defending Ben & Jerry's Efforts to Aid Brazilian Forest People

BEN COHEN

There's been a false implication of deception related to Ben & Jerry's rain forest efforts, as reported in Thursday's Globe. It involves critics inventing "goals" for the company's undertaking then berating Ben & Jerry's Homemade Inc. for the "scandal" of not accomplishing those fictitious objectives. Rather than respond to the inaccuracies point by point, I think it's better to just tell the story of why we make Rainforest Crunch ice cream.

Here's what really happened.

In 1989, my friend Jeff Furman and I started a company called Community Products Inc. Ben & Jerry's already donates 7½ percent of its profits to nonprofit organizations—the highest percentage of any publicly held US company, but I wanted to take the Ben & Jerry's model one step further by making "the social mission" supreme.

At Community Products, we were emulating Newman's Own—a company that gives 100 percent of its profits to charity.

From the outset, 60 percent of Community Products profits have gone to nonprofit groups working for progressive social and environmental change. Another 10 percent of the profits go to employee profit sharing. And, while Newman's Own has products manufactured for it, Community Products does its own manufacturing, so the remaining 30 percent of profits is reinvested in the business.

The idea for making Rainforest Crunch, a cashew–Brazil nut buttercrunch, was born at the 1988 Grateful Dead Rainforest Benefit Concert. I met Jason Clay, an anthropologist who had published a study on the rain forest.

Jason told me the fruits, nuts, plants and medicinal herbs that grow wild and are gathered by forest dwellers could create a living, sustainable-harvested rain forest that would be more profitable than burning the forest down to create cattle ranches. Increasing market demand for sustainably harvested rain forest products would increase demand for the living rain forest.

Jason wondered whether Ben & Jerry's might use any such products. I told him that Community Products was thinking about making a gourmet nut brittle. Jason said funny you should mention that, because not only does the rain forest have lots of Brazil nut trees growing wild, but Brazil nut trees have never been successfully cultivated anywhere.

Increase demand for Brazil nuts, he said, and you increase demand for living rain forests!

So that's when our goal of helping to preserve the rain forest by selling Rainforest Crunch was born. And that has remained our goal to this day.

Toward that end I developed a gourmet nut brittle maximizing use of Brazil nuts. Community Products bought Brazil nuts through Cultural Survival, a nonprofit organization, then affiliated with Harvard University, for which Jason Clay worked. Cultural Survival is dedicated to helping indigenous peoples enter the world economy on terms that preserve their own cultural integrity.

Community Products agreed to pay a premium of 5 percent above the market rates. Cultural Survival's profits, including the 5 percent premium, were to be used to help start a nut-processing cooperative for the nut harvesters.

In September, 1989, Community Products began selling Rainforest Crunch Brazil Nut Buttercrunch. In 1990, Ben & Jerry's introduced Rainforest Crunch ice cream.

Against the odds, and thanks to a lot of dedicated people, Community Products survived and, despite some ups and downs, is still in business.

By the end of 1992, the company had given over $484,000 to nonprofit organizations such as Working Assets Funding Service, Cultural Survival and 1% for Peace. We had also become one of 50 companies using their purchasing power to increase demand for rain forest products.

We used Rainforest Crunch packaging to help educate people about what we were doing, and to accurately inform them that money from the purchase of these nuts would help Brazilian forest people start their own nut-shelling cooperative.

Have we made a difference? The Xapuri Brazil nut-processing co-op was created, and despite some difficulties, is still in operation. In fact, from 1989 to 1993, other new nut cooperatives were formed, the price paid to nut gatherers in Brazil rose, and US demand for Brazil nuts rose 50 percent!

We now find ourselves assailed by critics who talk of deceptive advertising, broken promises and false claims of rain forest assistance.

Yes, some governments may try to use our work as an excuse to shirk their responsibility to preserve the rain forest. But such cynicism should not and will not stop us from doing what's right.

And yes, there are sincere critics who believe introducing indigenous people to a cash economy helps destroy their culture. But the modern world is already encroaching upon them. Perhaps by being respectful of ecologies and local people, we can find a way to preserve more of both.

The critics also fault us for buying only 5 percent of the nuts from the Xapuri Co-op. But it should be pointed out that we never made any claims about sourcing the nuts from the co-op.

In fact, Cultural Survival bought all the nuts the co-op could produce.

The matter of Rainforest Crunch was fully addressed by Paul Hawken in our Social Performance Assessment, which appears in our 1994 Annual Report.

No business that attempts to redefine the social and environmental role of business is going to have an easy time of it. The issues of social justice and commerce are complex.

This does not mean we should not keep trying.

> Those who cynically slash at any effort in this direction do a disservice to more than their targets. They contribute to the erosion of the public's hope that together we can make the world a better place.

In 1985, when we moved into our new plant in Waterbury, we were limited in the amount of wastewater that we could discharge into the municipal treatment plant. As sales and production skyrocketed, so did our liquid waste, most of which was milky water. Gail Mayville, assistant to the president, Chico Lager, was asked to help figure out how to dispose of it.

Gail made a deal with Earl, a local pig farmer, to feed our milky water to his pigs. (They loved every flavor except Mint with Oreo Cookies. Cherry Garcia was their favorite.) Earl's pigs alone couldn't handle our volume, so eventually we loaned Earl $10,000 to buy two hundred piglets. As far as we could tell, this was a win-win solution to a tricky environmental problem. The pigs were happy. Earl was happy. We were happy. The community was happy.

But one writer saw it differently. He fabricated and published a ridiculous fairy tale in which Ben & Jerry's milky water was responsible for causing pigs to die before their time of hardening of the arteries. We had to go so far as to get a letter from Earl the pig farmer to prove that that never happened.

✳ August 15, 1995
To whom it may concern:

My name is Earl Mayo. I am a pig farmer from Craftsbury, Vermont. I feed my pigs waste ice cream from the Ben & Jerry's plant in Waterbury, Vermont. I have done so for over seven years.

A couple of months ago, I got a telephone call from [a reporter], who said he was doing an article about Ben & Jerry's. He had heard that the pigs I own were getting some kind of heart disease from eating the ice cream I feed them. I told him that this wasn't true. He said that he had first heard about this from some college professor. The only college professors who have ever been to my farm are researchers with the University of Vermont's College of Agriculture. They concluded that my pigs were very healthy. . . .

[My] pigs live as long and are as healthy and productive as the pigs I kept before I started feeding them waste ice cream. Pigs do die sometimes before they are ready for market, but it's usually because of the heat or because they catch cold or something like that. I work hard to keep them healthy because it's the right thing to do for the animals and the right thing for my business.

If [the Reporter] would like to call me again, I can tell him again what I said the first time. I really don't appreciate his suggestion that I would mistreat my animals. A good farmer doesn't do that.

Sincerely,
Earl Mayo
Craftsbury, Vt.

The launch of Rainforest Crunch ice cream, in 1990, along with the efforts of many other companies, helped increase demand for sustainably harvested rain-forest products and an economic incentive to preserve rain forests. Rainforest Crunch had a positive effect on our business. But it also had one negative side effect: the media and the population at large generalized from that one project and bestowed on Ben & Jerry's an inflated reputation as a leader on all environmental issues.

✳ We've been criticized for the fact that only a small portion of the nuts in Rainforest Crunch come directly from a co-operative. The point is, we are purchasing everything they can supply, but our needs exceed their capacity. All the nuts come from the rain forest.

I wonder what most businesses would think of this type of criticism. They'd be scratching their heads saying, "What's the charge? They didn't source all the nuts from a co-operative?" It probably makes them think the whole community of socially responsible people is a bit, well, nutty.

—Liz Bankowski
Ben & Jerry's Social Mission Director

When Ben & Jerry's released its 1992 social audit, *Newsweek* published an article about the company, based mostly on quotes taken directly from our own report (published as part of our annual report). That's another downside of elevated expectations: the media can use your self-disclosures against you.

✳ The negative of having a mission-driven business is the elevated expectations, not just on the part of your team members but very much on the part of your customers. It gives everyone license to criticize.

This year we got picketed in Austin by the farmworkers because we were selling grapes. The grapes were 100 percent certified organic. The grower pays his farmworkers $6 an hour and gives them health benefits. But they're not union-picked grapes. Everyone in the picket line is going to shop at Central Market, where they sell nonorganic, non-union-picked grapes, but Whole Foods is the one that gets targeted.

The larger you get, the bigger the target becomes. Whole Foods is going to do over a billion dollars next year and we're hitting at this whole new level of expectation. I'll admit it's creeping into our consciousness. We're starting to think, "What if we do this and someone comes and attacks us for it?"

For example, we've never sold cured meats because they contain sodium nitrate. We've been working on it and we've found that spinach is a natural source of nitrate. You can put it in a salami and it does the same thing as the sodium nitrate—but it's not quite as effective. We were talking about it and someone said, "Somewhere along the line someone's going to claim they got sick off our salami and these freaks put spinach juice in it."

Every single one of us is a human being. No way is Whole Foods without flaws. But when you put yourself out there, and especially when you get bigger, those flaws become magnified and people attack you.

—Peter Roy
President, Whole Foods Market

  ✳   When you say you're for something, you're demanding, not inviting, cynicism and criticism. None of us can be perfect environmentally. I produce millions of plastic cups. At the same time, I'm trying to educate my customers about the problems of solid waste and potential toxins. We're inciting demand for alternatives, which is great, but we're also inciting a "question authority" mentality on the part of our own customers. In a way, it's counter to loyalty building.

Ben & Jerry's problems with the media were critical evolutionary growing pains for a concept that hadn't yet had its first test. We need to institute into the fabric of business some kind of third-party bullshit detection. That's why I believe we're in the Age of the Social Audit.

We need to ensure that when the inevitable scrutiny comes, we'll stand up to an audit. If we're not inviting measurement or corroboration of our claims, we should just stop making them. Because it's all about measurement.

—Gary Hirshberg

It's crucial that when you do values-led marketing, you maintain a high level of consistency throughout your company. You can't be a values-led marketer if your company isn't values-led. It can't just be a marketing feature. If there are inconsistencies between what you say and what you do, ultimately your customers will know your efforts aren't thoroughgoing.

The pressure doesn't come just from outside. Those of us inside Ben & Jerry's are probably more impatient with and intolerant of inconsistencies than any of our critics could be.

*   In 1995, we built our St. Albans plant. St. Albans is an area of Vermont where there's a community of indigenous people—the Abenaki Indians. As a group they have high rates of poverty and unemployment. We thought we could have some effect on this social problem.

The reality of our hiring Abenaki turned out to be quite different from our expectations. Our director of manufacturing at the time was very committed to the notion of a high-performance workplace and team design. There's nothing wrong with that, but it requires a skilled and educated workforce. Many of the local Abenaki did not have the skill set our jobs required.

There was disconnect between our motivation and what we were actually able to do.

We did end up hiring some Abenaki. But if you were to ask them, I'm afraid you'd hear they're pretty disappointed about what they thought having Ben & Jerry's in their community would mean for them.

—Liz Bankowski

• Continuous Improvement

American consumers are a suspicious and cynical group. And they have good reason to be. They've been abused and lied to by government and business. No wonder they instinctively don't trust what they hear, see, or read. But over time, as more people have more direct, positive experiences with values-led businesses, they'll come to trust them.

The only solution for a company that's sincere about using its power to change society for the better is to keep doing more and more activities that integrate a concern for the community. You have to try to reach people deeply and touch people's lives. That's the only way to transform cynicism into hope—and involvement.

We continually challenge ourselves to improve the extent to which we are able to integrate our values into every aspect of the company. We create our own pressures to do so via our social audit.

Jerry: Values-led marketing is much more difficult than simply hiring an ad agency and writing a check. As Ben is so fond of saying, "It's easy to do it lousy. It's hard to do it right."

Ben: I don't know if I agree that it's harder. I definitely agree that it's not easier.

Jerry: What could be easier, Ben, than writing a check?

Ben: I think what makes it hard is that the kind of marketing we do is so activity-intensive. It's people-intensive. It's not media-intensive.

Jerry: The marketing people need to be values-aligned so they're motivated to do this kind of work.

Ben: But values-led marketing gives marketing people an opportunity to actualize themselves. They're not just putting in their time, picking up a paycheck. They're combining their hearts and souls—and they're creating innovative, socially beneficial marketing campaigns.

Jerry: That's all true, Ben. I just think we need to acknowledge that off-the-shelf marketing solutions are easier to come up with than the stuff we do.

Ben: I guess so. But they're not anywhere near as effective —or as much fun to do.

● In Order to Get Values in the Right Place, They Have to Start Out in First Place

The Solar Roller, the circus tour, and the festivals wouldn't have happened if we hadn't factored our social concerns in at the beginning of the planning process. If all we'd thought about was the quantity of contacts instead of the quality and the social impact of those contacts, we would have hired sampling agencies and ad agencies instead.

Building values in at the beginning, instead of tacking them on at the end, is not something you can do just once. It's a process of continual improvement.

For example, last year we needed to give away a million samples of our new sorbet very quickly. The original concept was to work with kids from inner-city schools in Chicago, Los Angeles, San Francisco, and New York to do the sampling. We did a full-day session at each school to give the kids a little bit of marketing training and business education, then sent them out for a few hours after school to give out tastes of sorbet on the street. We made a gift of $10,000 to each of the schools that participated, so the kids would get an educational experience and the schools would get some badly needed funds.

It was a great idea. But since we hadn't planned it out ahead of time, when we ran into procedural and policy problems with some of the school boards, we didn't have time to solve them. We were able to do only a fraction of the sampling we'd planned with the young people. We had to turn to sampling agencies to complete the task—the off-the-shelf, traditional, default solution. The samples were distributed; we accomplished our business objectives. But our social objectives were not accomplished as well as they would have been if we had had students do all the sampling.

Every year we get thousands of requests from nonprofits that want us to donate ice cream. Each of those organizations has lots of contributors, volunteers, and employees. What ended up happening this year was that at the same time we were telling them we didn't have enough money in the donations budget to give away ice cream, another department in the company was hiring sampling agencies at thirty cents a sample to give away ice cream.

One possible solution is to combine the two groups within the company and start thinking of the nonprofits who ask for donations as "no-cost sampling agencies." Then we'll have found a way to integrate our concern for the community into our sampling program.

Our Newport, Rhode Island, shop owners did that last summer when they were asked to help protect the Narragansett Bay by donating ice cream for a Save the Bay fund-raiser. The scoop shop donated a large amount of ice cream. Forty volunteers from the nonprofit group made a three-hundred-foot banana split, which was then sold to the public in human-sized portions. The volunteers had fun, the people attending the event had a great sundae, the group made a bunch of money, and we made some new friends, thanks to the generosity of our shop owners.

Every business grapples with the balance between planning ahead, on the one hand, and being flexible enough to respond successfully to unpredictable market forces and opportunities, on the other. When you're committed to leading with your values, planning ahead takes on greater significance.

Let's say the marketing department determines that this year they need to increase sampling by 500 percent. So they start researching ways to do that. They start executing their plan. Then they realize it doesn't have a social component. So they say, "We need to integrate social concerns into our plan." Doing that becomes additional work, a burden that makes their jobs more difficult.

But by integrating the social mission into the marketing-planning process, we change the decision-making matrix. Instead of factoring in only cost and reach, we factor in cost, reach, and impact on the community. Instead of taking out ads and hiring sampling agencies, we send a traveling circus bus across the country, entertaining people, winning loyal customers, and promoting our brand at the same time. Instead of just increasing customer visits to our stores, we find ways to use our shops to educate and motivate and activate people on social issues concerning children.

Unorthodox marketing solutions like these won't occur naturally. They have to emerge from a strategic direction from the top, at the beginning of the planning process.

Our execution in this arena can always be improved, just as every aspect of our business can always be improved. But more and more, our employees understand and embrace the idea that a significant part of their jobs is to promote the social agenda. A couple of years ago we started building the social-mission objectives into the yearly operating plan. Before that, they were always seen as an add-on.

● Lead with Your Values

If product quality is equal, people are going to select one brand or another based on marketing imagery—your ads, the color of your package, or your values. You're going to get only a slice of the market anyhow, whether it's the yellow package lovers or the people with progressive social values.

We're not saying traditional marketing doesn't work. It can be very effective. But no matter what kind of marketing you do, there are going to be more people who don't buy your product than people who do. You might as well get your share of the market by leading with your values, appealing to the people who share them, and actively helping to meet basic human needs while you're at it.

6

People Power:

Values-Led Human Resources

Jerry: Screening for values. Hiring for values. It's a thorny issue, isn't it, Ben?

Ben: Thorny as all hell.

Jerry: Everyone agrees the company would be much better off to have people working within it who agree with the company's values.

Ben: But it's tricky. Because it's not the norm in business to hire people based on their alignment with a company's social mission. . . .

Jerry: And also, Ben, because some people don't think it's legal.

Ben: Unless the criteria are relevant to the job.

● Values-Led People Power

There's nothing more important to a business than its people and how they are managed. And there are a limited number of ways we can influence that dynamic. There are three intervention points. First, in order to get the best people on our team we need to become highly skilled and efficient at selecting the right people. Second, we need to become really good at educating those people about how to do their jobs well. Third, we have to motivate them to want to do their jobs well.

If we blow it on selection, it's really tough to make up for it on education and motivation.

But if we've selected people who have great potential for doing the work, and we've done a great job of training them, and we've motivated them to want to do what they've been hired to do—that's good management. We're not there yet at Ben & Jerry's.

● Hiring Is Everything

The first major influence on the organizational effectiveness of a business is whom we hire.

We choose the people we think would be best to work for us. But people don't come with a set of specs that you can look over and read. It's very difficult to understand the qualities, strengths, and weaknesses of a person based on talking to that person for a few hours and reading her résumé. We know what she's done in her life, a little bit of her history. And based on that, we're supposed to determine whether this is a person who's going to be a good fit for the job we want her to do and for the culture of our company.

But it's very difficult to know if a person will make a good accountant until you've seen him account for you, or a good manager until you've seen how she manages.

In the early days, we didn't have much of a method for determining whom to hire. Somebody would come in and apply for a job. He'd say he likes to scoop ice cream. We had no idea whether that person was a high-energy, fast-working kind of person or a slow, low-energy, tranquil kind of person. Both kinds of people are wonderful. But we should have been screening for people who like to move at a rather rapid pace. We didn't know how to do that.

We didn't check references, either. We figured no prospective scooper would give us the name of anyone who wouldn't give him or her a good reference—so what was the point? Also, a reference wouldn't indicate how well the person would do at figuring out how much four ounces is (without weighing it) and making it look appetizing. That's manual dexterity. It's spatial relations. It's hard to get a reliable reference on that.

Our hiring process was purely a matter of chance. When we were interviewing people for a scooper opening one time, a guy said, "What are you looking for? I mean, you like me, right?"

And we said, "Sure. You seem like a fine person."

"So why don't you hire me?" he said.

We said, "Well, we need to interview all the other people who applied."

And he said, "Why? What's the difference?"

It occurred to us that maybe he was right.

Our job requirements back then were pretty simple. We needed people to be friendly, warm, and genuine with our customers, but not to have extended conversations with them. We needed them to scoop quickly and also scoop accurately.

If they weren't doing that, we had to give them feedback, to help them to understand their shortcomings and help them improve. If they *were* doing that, we had to give them feedback, praise them, encourage them, motivate them.

Ben: I was always really bad at giving positive feedback. I felt that if I told someone I thought she was doing a good job and then tomorrow she did something wrong, she'd still think she was doing a good job.

Jerry: A problem that persists to this day.

Ben: But I also didn't like giving people negative feedback. Jerry was really good at being positive, but I don't think he was good at giving negative feedback either.

Jerry: I was worse. I thought if I said something critical to someone, they wouldn't like me.

The method we used for establishing our employees' schedules wasn't exactly based on how well they were performing. We'd say, here's this college kid who's applying for this job. He needs to make X amount per week in order to meet his expenses. So we're going to guarantee him twenty hours a week, or thirty hours a week, whatever he needs. We'd give people short shifts because it was hard for people to keep up a high energy level for eight hours.

Ben: When I was sixteen I got my first job, at McDonald's. The way they started you was, they gave you two four-hour shifts a week. If they saw you were doing a good job, they gave you more shifts. If they saw you weren't doing a good job, they gave you fewer shifts.

> *Jerry:* Fewer shifts than two a week?
>
> *Ben:* They essentially suggested to you that you weren't going to get a whole lot of work there. And they posted a new schedule every week. If you couldn't make the slots they fit you into, they'd find someone who could. It was definitely a less employee-friendly setup than ours.

We had a training process that was limited exclusively to scooping ice cream. People would go to work for us and they'd just kind of be how they were. People who were spacey and warm and loving would be that way. They'd relate well to the customers, but they'd scoop really slowly and not particularly accurately. Some people would scoop slowly and quite accurately. But that wasn't good enough, either.

At some point we'd say to each other, "Joe isn't cutting the mustard. I'm afraid he's not gonna make it." The two of us would try working with the person, talking to him. If the situation didn't improve we'd say to each other, "The Monster is hungry. The Monster must eat." We couldn't stand to fire people, so we had to create a persona—the Monster—to do it for us.

Jerry was (and still is) so conflict-avoidant that Ben always played the role of the Monster. He would say to the guy, "You're a wonderful person. We really like hanging out with you. But you don't scoop fast enough. Therefore, you shouldn't take this personally, but you can't work here anymore."

The person would be really bummed. Some of them would cry. We'd say, "Look—you're in college. You're looking to become a philosophy major. Scooping quickly is not a skill you need for what you're trying to do with your life." But no matter what we said or how nicely we tried to say it, the whole process took a lot out of us. Not to mention what it took out of them.

One day before we opened the gas station, we were talking to our landlady-to-be about what running a business was going to be like. She said the hardest part of business was managing people, human resources. When she left we said to each other, "That's not going to be a problem for us. We're going to be really good at that. We'll have employee meetings weekly. We'll talk with everyone about what's going on, and they'll feel a part of the business. It's not going to be a hierarchical thing. It's going to be a team thing."

We had great and noble intentions. But we learned pretty quickly that our landlady was right. Managing people well is the hardest part.

● The Potential and Pitfalls of Values-Led Management

One of the greatest potential levers of a values-led business can be an incredibly motivated workforce. If people understand that the work they do produces more than just profits, and they're in alignment with the values of the company, there's no end to what they can contribute.

❋ Values-led businesses have a lower human resource cost because you have a growing group of long-term employees who are totally invested in the success of the company. You can access what Bob Rosen (author of *The Healthy Company*) calls "discretionary effort." The employee decides how far open to turn the valve. The employee decides how much effort she's going to give to each task and to every day of her employment.

If you create an environment that motivates employees to turn the valve on full throttle, you can outperform any competitor any day of the week. Because when you boil it down, it's the creativity, the ingenuity, the longevity, the loyalty of the employee base that makes it all happen.

—Helen Mills
Senior Vice President, AON Consulting;
Franchisee, the Body Shop;
Cochair, Businesses for Social Responsibility

It's like the difference between working for a for-profit company and for a nonprofit social-service agency. Most people who work at nonprofit agencies take those jobs—despite the fact that they earn less money than they would in the private sector—because they're highly motivated by what the agency does. Their work has meaning for them because they're addressing an issue they're concerned about.

❋ The most intriguing thing I learned from my survey work with Ben & Jerry's is that when you look at the factors that are most closely associated with people's involvement or identification with the organization, the number one predictor is the social mission of the company. In other words, if I know how an employee feels about the social mission, I know how that person feels about Ben & Jerry's.

Even in well-managed companies, the number one predictor is usually the challenge and meaning of an employee's individual job. At Ben & Jerry's that came second.

What makes people feel good about Ben & Jerry's is the company's social mission. The significance of that is enormous. That's the huge distinction—they've fundamentally changed the consciousness of the people who work there.

> —Phil Mirvis
> Organizational Psychologist,
> author of *The Cynical Americans* and *Managing the Merger*

Employees can bring the same passion that's usually reserved for nonprofits to a for-profit workplace, if they see the work they're doing as supportive of goals and values they believe in.

✳ I've been here for eleven and a half years. When I came here there wasn't a social mission in full force as there is now. We didn't even have a social mission written down. I got the job because I wanted to do something in the food industry. My husband and I had farmed for many years, so I knew about sanitation and milk testing. That's how I came into the lab.

It's everybody's job here to think about what we do and see if there's a way to do it that might help other people. I've been working on the diversity team, looking at minority suppliers. My job is to ask the place where I purchase my lab supplies if they use anything from these other diverse people. The idea is to help companies develop on their own, like Greyston. It's a little more work for me, but eventually there might be something good coming out of it, like helping some minority companies get started.

I get satisfaction from the other things the company does, like the Children's Defense Fund program. The QA lab is on the tour route, and when we interact with the visitors, they say they're glad we're doing things to help children. That's an impact and a half for me.

> —Cathy Fuller,
> Quality Assurance Coordinator, Waterbury plant

✳ The social mission was definitely a plus in my decision to come to Ben & Jerry's. I'm very drawn to those values. I believe business does have a responsibility to give back to the community. One of our goals at St. Albans is to incorporate that into our daily happenings.

Sometimes in all the busyness you lose sight of the big picture: that even if you're on the floor making ice cream, what you're doing is making money for the company, which enables us to give back to the community —not just money, but in a lot of different ways. If I worked for a company without those values it would be a lot less motivating.

—Jesse Metcalf
Ben & Jerry's Production Worker, St. Albans plant

✳   I came to Ben & Jerry's nearly twelve years ago, when the Vermont economy wasn't doing real well. I didn't know anything about the company, but I needed a job. So I've been here since before the social mission.

I think Ben & Jerry's has some real good ideals, especially their thought process on trying to spread money around. We give away a lot of money to a lot of good organizations. I get to be a part of that by making ice cream. There's certainly nothing adverse about it. I think more businesses should be doing it.

—David "Wilbur" Wright
Lead Mix Maker, Waterbury plant

Corporate executives are always saying, "People are our most important asset. There's nothing more valuable to our business than people." For a lot of companies, that's just talk. They don't treat their employees as respectfully as they treat their other assets. Values-led management aspires to respect employees and seeks to meet their needs as well as the needs of the company. It's not an autocratic, command-and-control method, but instead uses a consultative, participative, non-hierarchical approach—one that utilizes employees' hearts and minds as well as their hands. It solicits input from employees and offers benefits that reflect the importance of staff well-being to corporate well-being.

Whom we hire and how our people are managed determines the success of a business more than any other factor. That's why most of the business books in the bookstores are about how to manage people more effectively. Because doing that is so hard. And so important.

✳   We do something at Tom's of Maine that I think is unique: we have a curriculum for teaching our mission within the company. Once every three months the whole company gets together for this purpose. We spend the morning together focusing on one aspect: profitability, diversity, the environment—values we've held up in our mission. It costs us about $75,000 each time in lost production, and it's worth every penny.

Our managers and staff come away from those experiences with recommendations, which then are gathered and taken to the appropriate department heads. So we take the fruits of a very intentional learning environment and transfer them into a very practical environment. Doing this helps improve everyone's consciousness about having our practicalities reflect our values. It's a morale booster for everyone and helps build fellowship and team skills. It shows the company is serious about walking its talk.

We also have benefit programs that reflect our commitment to helping people lead balanced lives. Everyone gets 5 percent of their time—about two hours a week, paid—to volunteer in the community. And when a mother, father, or adoptive parent has a baby, they get a full month of paid leave. We only have 80 employees; we're too small to have a day care center or an elder care center. But we subsidize those services for people who need them. And we have a liberal flex-time program—about one-third of the staff is either on flex-time or a compressed work week.

The analysts wonder what effect this has on our bottom line. When we need to call upon the reserves of our people—to dig in deeper, meet extraordinary goals—we can expect it here. It's a give-and-take relationship such that we're giving to our people the benefits tangible and intangible, and they're giving us their highest performance, their greatest ideas on how to solve problems.

This also extends to hiring and retaining people. We're in a small town in a remote location, but when we put out a notice that we're looking to hire, we get a lot of highly qualified people applying for these positions. We're able to keep and attract good people because we offer something they can't get somewhere else.

—Tom Chappell
Cofounder and CEO, Tom's of Maine

The thing I'm proudest of is that we're a high-growth company and we have a harmonious workplace. I'm not saying it's stress-free, but we have 110 people and we work as a real team.

Stonyfield essentially doesn't advertise. Our growth has been fueled by quality. Taste is number one. And quality and taste are direct results of our investments in our employees. You can't have a quality product without the kind of employee participation and benefits programs we've implemented.

I know that, because I have an excellent recipe and I've tried it in two copacking locations where I paid people a lot of money to make my yogurt, and they couldn't make my yogurt. They could make it occasionally. They couldn't make it day after day after day, because they didn't

have profit sharing. They didn't have stock options. They could occasionally peak to perfection, but the mandate of perfection for every batch,
every day is a whole other drill. And it's the environment at Stonyfield
that makes that happen.

—Gary Hirshberg
CEO and President, Stonyfield Farm Yogurt

Managing people is essential to implementing both our social and
financial missions. During those times when we're well managed, we're
doing a good job at both parts of the bottom line. During those times
when we're poorly managed, we're doing a lousy job at both parts of
the bottom line.

✳   The gain from having a mission-driven business is certainly very prevalent with your employee base. It's a major magnet to attract people to
your business. I believe that 85 percent of the people who work for Whole
Foods wouldn't be working in a supermarket if they weren't working
for us. The things our team members do on a day-to-day basis are not
substantially different from what the employees are doing at Safeway.
What makes it okay for our people to be at Whole Foods cleaning lettuce
is our mission. That's what gives their work meaning.

—Peter Roy
President, Whole Foods Market

Theoretically, if everybody's values are aligned and we're all working
together toward a higher purpose, we'll all be more motivated to reach
that common goal. In order to maximize the strength of that lever, two
things need to happen.

One, the company needs to be managed in a values-led way, and
managed well.

Two, the company needs to be staffed with people who are aligned
with the social mission. How to accomplish this is a controversial issue,
both at Ben & Jerry's and within socially responsible business as a whole.

● Do As We Say, Not As We Do

✳   Many socially responsible companies don't do well on the whole in
terms of human resources. Most of them are smaller companies, so they
can't always put in the range of benefits and support structures that some
bigger companies can afford. If you're at that size, you're paying a lot of

attention to other things: how to make the ice cream better, how to market it better. So those things get more attention than the care and feeding of employees.

Also, socially responsible companies tend to be disorganized and chaotic. Employees don't know where they stand. The companies don't have the formal procedures that some bigger companies have. They don't set up the communications processes that allow employees to talk back.

I think the main reason is that these companies think, "We're trying to save the world." They forget they have to take care of business.

—Milton Moskowitz
Coauthor of *The Hundred Best Companies to Work for in America*

The halls of corporate America are full of management consultants who talk a great game. Corporate America is paying millions of dollars a day for consultants to tell them how to manage their businesses well.

Ben: We've paid hundreds of thousands of dollars to people who talked really well about how to manage. Hasn't helped much, has it?

Jerry: It's easier to talk about it than it is to do it.

Ben: I can talk about it pretty well, actually.

Jerry: We could probably consult about it ourselves.

Developing a healthy, well-functioning organization has probably been the hardest thing for Ben & Jerry's. Over the years there have been times when we've been better functioning or less well functioning, but overall, management has been an incredible challenge for us.

In the mainstream world, especially in older, established large corporations, in order for them to become better managed they need to break down the walls between departments and become less rigid and hierarchical.

But—because neither of us ever liked being supervised himself and therefore assumed no one else would, either—the opposite is true for Ben & Jerry's. In order for Ben & Jerry's management to become more effective, we need to become *more* structured.

We conduct an employee survey every eighteen months, and in each survey our employees have told us that the most important factor in determining job satisfaction is how well they're supervised. For the most part, they don't feel they're supervised well.

In 1994 only about half of the five hundred Ben & Jerry's employees who filled out the survey felt their supervisors were good at planning and organizing, set a good example, and let employees know how they were doing. Only 29 percent said, "Things run smoothly in the company."

✱   One dimension that's contributed to our organizational confusion is actually a wonderful thing: we have a very familial environment at Ben & Jerry's. We've struggled with whether the model for our organization should be family or community. In family, someone's got to be the mom and someone's got to be the dad. And the kids—they might get in trouble, but you don't send them out the door. That's the way we've been. When people went through hard times they were fully supported by the company. People would take one another's children, take one another to alcohol-treatment facilities . . . there's nothing people wouldn't do for one another.

That's still a strong ethic at Ben & Jerry's, but the company doesn't play the role of benevolent parent as much as it used to. As you get bigger, you just can't have that happening the way you could at one site with fifty people. You can't keep people who need to go, and you can't fire people for not meeting expectations when you haven't been clear with them about what your expectations are.

For a long time it was unclear why people got fired at Ben & Jerry's. There's a real sense of not knowing what the rules are around here. The performance-review process is still broken. People don't have confidence in it. They don't feel it tells them what they're doing well and not doing well.

The crux of the matter is, the company has never said clearly to the organization what we're managing toward, so we're not good at management training. We haven't made clear what we want it to be like to work here.

We've put a lot of effort recently into getting clarity about job descriptions, whom people report to, what's expected of them. In many parts of the company we've finally created some structure. Finance is very well thought out now in design and organization. We've made real strides in operations. The improvement process isn't moving as quickly as any of us would like, but we're plugging away at it.

—Liz Bankowski
Ben & Jerry's Social Mission Director

A company can have the best benefits in the world—as many external ratings have indicated Ben & Jerry's does—but that doesn't satisfy the employees if your core management system isn't helping them work to their potential.

Employee Benefits

Health coverage	Free to employee, subsidized 90 percent to partner/family
Dental coverage	Free to employee, subsidized 90 percent to partner/family
Life insurance	Free at two times annual salary, available at cost up to five times
Disability insurance	Free short- and long-term coverage
Family leave	Two weeks paid for mother or father employees
Retirement plan	Up to 2 percent contribution matched by company
Stock purchase	Available twice yearly at 85 percent of previous six-month low
Holidays	Eight paid holidays
Education	Up to $2,000/year paid job-related or degree courses
Health club	Free membership for employees
Vacation	One day/month worked until three years, 1.5 days/month after, to maximum of 36 days/year
Sick time	Six paid days/year
Domestic partner	Health, dental, life insurance, and family leave available for domestic partners no matter marital status or gender
Profit sharing	Five percent aftertax profits distributed to employees

You can give your employees parental leave, beautiful cafeterias, domestic partnership benefits, a child care center—but if they're not managed well, their perception of the quality of their work life will be that it is poor.

Ben & Jerry's has won recognition and awards for its progressive benefits package and family-friendly workplace. But some of our employees don't feel well treated, so we're obviously not conveying to them how important their well-being is to us. Liz and Chuck Lacy came up with a document called "Our Aspirations" that describes how we want to treat one another. (Chuck Lacy became president of Ben & Jerry's in 1989. The company continued to undergo tremendous growth under his leadership—from $58 million to $149 million—thanks in large part to the introduction of Chocolate Cookie Dough ice cream and also frozen yogurt. Chuck was instrumental in institutionalizing the social mission in the company. He brought the understanding that the question was not whether the company would undertake social initiatives but rather how we would do that. This was a big step forward for Ben & Jerry's.)

We have high hopes of making this document represent the way Ben & Jerry's actually operates. Right now it's just aspirations. It hasn't even been distributed to the company yet. Now we've got to get our programs aligned with these aspirations. That's our intention.

✳ We're in business to make and serve the best all natural ice cream, frozen yogurt, and sorbet, to provide fair economic return to our staff and our shareholders, and to include an active concern for the community in our day-to-day decisions. As a company

---

we have a progressive, nonpartisan social agenda
we seek peace by supporting nonviolent ways to resolve conflict
we will look for ways to create economic opportunities for the
    disenfranchised
we are committed to practicing caring capitalism
we seek to minimize our negative impact on the environment
we support sustainable methods of food production and family farming
        There will always be differences of opinion about how we
    actualize our mission, but a commitment to the intent of our mission
    is an essential part of membership at Ben & Jerry's. No amount of
    expertise can compensate for a lack of commitment to our mission
    and to our aspirations. In calling these "Our Aspirations" we are
    mindful that we will constantly be striving to reach these ideals.

✳   **OUR ASPIRATIONS**

TO BE REAL: We need to be who we say we are, both inside and outside the company. We are all custodians of the reputation of Ben & Jerry's. We will strive to put into practice the words we use to describe ourselves: Friendly, Enthusiastic, Exciting, Caring, High-Quality, Progressive, Offbeat, Innovative, Cutting-Edge, Funny, Lighthearted, Encouraging, Informal, Activist, Honest, Childlike, Down-Home.

TO BE THE BEST: If our customers are euphoric about our products, we will prosper. Our future together depends upon our ability to outperform the competition. That's our business strategy. We want to be the best ice cream company in the world. We want to be viewed as master ice cream makers. We are passionate about giving customers what they want, when they want it, every single time.

TO IMPROVE CONTINUOUSLY: Every time we do something, we should be checking to see if our methods worked and figure out how we can do it better the next time. From the minute we join the company we are responsible for helping to shape and improve what goes on around us.

TO LEARN CONTINUOUSLY: We want people to have the opportunity to develop their potential to contribute to the company. We'll need to keep growing skills in three areas: technical skills to achieve excellence in day-to-day work, personal skills to give life and vitality to these aspirations, and business knowledge to understand the companywide implications and importance of what each of us does.

TO BE INCLUSIVE: We embrace individual differences. The right to be ourselves contributes to our sense of ownership. We perform better and serve the marketplace better when men, women, gays, lesbians, and people of different races, nationalities, ethnicities, and backgrounds work together. Building a diverse staff contributes to excellent performance, not just to societal good.

TO BE CREATIVE: Our creativity is our strength. We want to see beyond conventional thinking and come up with ideas that work, that excite our customers and reflect our values.

TO BUILD COMMUNITY: No one at Ben & Jerry's should feel alone or apart. When one of us needs help, we reach out to help. People from outside feel our energy when they visit us. We have a zest for life, a sense of humor, and we enjoy one another's company. We share the excitement of succeeding at the game of business and we'll try to have fun while we do it.

TO BE OPEN AND TRUSTING: Rationales, strategy, and the truth should be shared. We want to be open about our concerns and admit our mistakes and failings. We need to make sure people feel safe to speak up about things they care about. If we trust one another's good intentions, we'll feel better about trying new things and about speaking up about things that concern us. It's expected that we'll all do the right thing even when nobody is looking.

TO CELEBRATE AND TO GIVE MEANINGFUL RECOGNITION: When we reach or exceed our targets, we should cheer. Celebration establishes a sense of accomplishment, which leads to more accomplishments. Celebrations don't need to be elaborate. Recognition is the currency of leadership. We should make recognition a contagious part of everyday life.

TO USE CONSULTIVE DECISION MAKING AND ACTIVE LISTENING: When making decisions we'll involve people with special expertise and people likely to be affected. We'll also give those with a contrary point of view an opportunity to be heard. However, Ben & Jerry's is not a democracy. Leaders need to make calls based on facts, data, and input. In order to practice consultive decision making and to create the conditions for people to contribute their best thinking, we must be active listeners.

TO HOLD OURSELVES ACCOUNTABLE: We all need to do what we said we were going to do and be clear about who's responsible and what's expected. When we don't do our part it affects everybody. We put the company at risk when we tolerate poor performance.

TO BE GREAT COMMUNICATORS: Leaders are responsible for effectively and consistently communicating pertinent information in a timely way. Good leaders have well-informed teams. We're each responsible for absorbing the information offered through company communication vehicles like postings, staff meetings, and *The Rolling Cone*.

TO BE UP-FRONT: People aren't going to do better unless they understand what they need to do to improve. Good straight feedback is essential to improvement. Talking about someone's performance to people other than the person does harm to the individual and to the company.

TO BE PROFITABLE BY BEING THRIFTY: We believe in investing wisely and with a sense of frugality. When we save the company money, we do a service to our shareholders and ourselves.

We're the first to admit that our performance doesn't always live up to our aspirations.

✳   When we were compiling the list for *The Hundred Best Companies to Work for in America,* we used six criteria: pay and benefits; opportunities for advancement; job security; pride in the work and in the company; openness and fairness; and camaraderie and friendliness. We visited each company we rated and interviewed employees at all levels; our results weren't based on questionnaires.

Ben & Jerry's made the list in 1992 and 1994. We have a tag line on each company to summarize its biggest plus and minus. For Ben & Jerry's the biggest plus was, "Save the World While Making Ice Cream." The minus was, "You Need Good Humor to Tolerate the Chaos."

Just before we went to press in 1994, Liz Bankowski called and asked us to take Ben & Jerry's off the list. She said morale was poor, they were having safety problems at their second plant, and they thought they didn't deserve to be included.

I told Liz that the very fact that they'd admit morale was bad put Ben & Jerry's way above most companies. I also said I thought it was a disservice to the employees and the shareholders to be so publicly self-critical. So we included them in the book.

Because Ben & Jerry's has been so well publicized, they're more vulnerable than other companies. When they do one little thing wrong they're immediately subject to attack. I think they feel their lapses more keenly than other companies might. That's part of their culture.

—Milton Moskowitz

● Values Begin at Home

Ben & Jerry's has tried to focus its efforts on building a state-of-the-art workplace as much as it has focused its efforts on building a state-of-the-art relationship with the outside world. We've been less successful with the former than the latter.

> *Jerry:* We're well-intentioned, yet we're not able to make it happen. So our employees wonder, "How can they make these external things happen and not make the internal things happen? Where's the will, the commitment?" And it's a legitimate question.
>
> *Ben:* The real answer is that it's a very different capability to manage a seven-hundred-person organization than it is to identify a source of vanilla beans that's environmentally and socially beneficial and buy them there instead of from the mainstream supplier.

Because Ben & Jerry's hasn't made the progress we'd like to make in improving the way people are managed internally, what employees notice is the effort and resources we put out externally. They see the $170 million a year that comes into the company. And they see the corporate largesse—the money given away by the foundation, the grants, the resources we devote to our partnershop partners and our alternative-supplier partners. One thing that's been brought up in the past is the fact that our foundation receives 7.5 percent of the pretax profits, whereas profit sharing is 5 percent. Somehow that's come to be symbolic. People see that the company is spending a tremendous amount of money to help the external community, but they feel their needs are not being taken care of.

The reality is that the amount of money the company spends on employee benefits and profit sharing far exceeds the money that's spent on the outside community. But we haven't managed expectations well, so some employees don't perceive it that way. If we had an open-book management system, like the one instituted by Jack Stack at Springfield Remanufacturing, the employees would better understand the flow of money in and out of the company.

We're currently considering switching to open-book management, whereby various departments would review their own profit-and-loss statements on a weekly or monthly basis, and would be taught to read and understand financial statements. Being trained in financial literacy and further understanding the financial workings of the company—being able to read balance sheets, understand cash flow, et cetera—gives employees an ownership perspective on the workings of their own departments.

(This ownership method is described in Jack Stack's book *The Great Game of Business,* which we highly recommend.)

Some people at Ben & Jerry's say, "Why should the company be spending money to improve the quality of life for people out in the community when I'm an employee of the company and I don't have enough money to buy a new car?"

* Before I came here I'd heard the company did a lot for the community. But I didn't know how much they went outside the community. They do give money to good causes. But I think they should concentrate on their own people first.

For one thing, the pay stinks around here. Here we are, fighting to get decent wages, wages that we deserve, and the higher-ups are giving all this money away. I think they could do more for their employees before they look outside.

—Daisy Sweet
Ben & Jerry's Shipping and Receiving Team Member, St. Albans plant

✳   As far as spending outside the company, I think they're worthy causes. I don't have a problem with that. Here at Ben & Jerry's we're paid based on our knowledge, and the company helps us better ourselves by paying for us to take classes so we can increase our knowledge. I'm taking a class in nutrition and they're paying for that.

What they do with their money is good. Where else are these children going to get things coming in if nobody steps forward? Any company should do that.

I don't think there's too much controversy about the company spending money elsewhere. We did have an issue recently because we wanted to upgrade some production equipment and it took a while to get approved. But that's happening now. One nice thing is that management doesn't make that decision alone. They take a couple of people who work on that line and ask if the machinery they've got in mind is feasible. They don't just put it in and tell us, "This is what you're going to use."

—Cathy Fuller

✳   I make pretty good money and I'm treated well here. We get a lot of thanks from the community, which makes it worthwhile.

I just went and painted a fire station as a project through my CAT team. The company sent me away on a day's work; I was on the clock. It wasn't like making ice cream. I can look back and see the final product. When you make ice cream it's just gone.

They sent me to Europe for three weeks on an employee exchange with the Body Shop. Four Body Shop employees came over here, four of us went over there. I had a blast. I spent two weeks in England, and one week in Europe on my own. I never would have made it to Europe if that hadn't happened. I got to see the Eiffel Tower.

It has occurred to me that I might make more money if the company gave away less money. But I can't complain. Ben & Jerry's takes care of me very well.

—David "Wilbur" Wright

This raises an interesting question: what level of our own needs should we meet before we start helping others? If we say that we'll devote all of our resources to meeting our own needs until we've reached a particular level, and *then* we'll devote ourselves to helping others, there's a good chance that we'll keep raising the level we're trying to reach. We'll never get there.

The answer is the same for a business as it is for an individual.

People donate to causes they believe in—whether it's a dollar they drop into the Salvation Army bucket at Christmastime or a check they send every month to Greenpeace—even when they haven't completely met their own or their family's needs. In fact, poorer Americans tend to give a higher proportion of their resources to charity than wealthy people do.

Businesses can never meet all of their own needs, those of their employees, or those of the community. We need to do some combination of all three at the same time.

✳ Doing good should not be seen as a luxury, affordable only after being earned, but rather as a way of life which integrates our values with our work. I had looked up "philanthropy" in the dictionary, and in seeing it defined as "the effort to increase the well-being of mankind," had decided that making money by any means and then donating the excess change to charity did not truly fit the definition. Have we been improperly measuring philanthropy by how much money we give away at the end of the year or at the end of our careers, rather than considering how we earned that money in the first place? Do we take too much credit for the volunteer hours we may give once a month, rather than honestly examining how the work we do 40 or more hours a week actually benefits mankind? Should we not also consider how we spend our earnings and our tax dollars toward the best interests of the common good?

An acquaintance who works for the foundation of a major corporation recently confided in despair that all the money that would ever be given by her foundation could not begin to make up for the environmental and social damage caused by the funding corporation in the process of making that money in the first place. Doing well, or making a profit, should never be separated from doing good. Increasing profit while not increasing the well-being of mankind has led to most of society's major problems —from poverty, crime, and addiction, to ignorance, war, and environmental destruction. On the other hand, it's the combination of profit and goodness which is perhaps our most powerful tool for solving these very problems, while also providing livelihoods which bring fulfillment and happiness. In fact, is there really any other way that we can create a peaceful and healthy world where everyone can profit?

—Judy Wicks
Owner, White Dog Café, Philadelphia,
in *Tales from the White Dog Café*, Winter 1997

● Employee Benefits

✳   Unless we recognize the needs of families, we're going to have a less productive workforce. Companies that address those needs will have a competitive advantage.

Stride Rite has had that advantage from early on. Shortly after I became president in 1971, we set up a child care center and an inter-generational center at our Cambridge location. We provided a place for people in the community and people in the Stride Rite workforce to bring their children and their older dependents. Instead of being put in nursing homes or left at home alone to become isolated, the elders in our program could work and play with children who needed their care.

Although many people in the workforce and in the community didn't have those needs themselves, it gave them a perception of Stride Rite as a company that cared about people. That reduced turnover, which in turn yielded great economic gain for the company. We could always attract the best people. We didn't have the cost of training new workers to bring them up to the same level of productivity as the seasoned workers.

The Conference Board estimated that it costs an average of $21,000 a year to attract, train, and bring a new employee up to the level of productivity of a departed employee. That's an enormous cost. And it can be avoided by simply providing the family benefits that so many people in the workforce need today.

> —Arnold Hiatt
> Chairman, Stride Rite Foundation;
> Former CEO/President/Chairman, Stride Rite Corporation

Ben & Jerry's is known for its "progressive" benefits, but there are many other companies—values-led and traditional, well known and unknown—that are innovators in that realm. To name just a few:

H. B. Fuller, a multinational specialty chemical company, has a Bridge to Retirement program that lets employees volunteer at community-service organizations for a year before they retire—with full pay and benefits. Because the work at Fuller is often too physically taxing for its older employees, this gives them a way to bridge the gap between their last full-time paycheck and their first Social Security check.

Shaman Pharmaceuticals, a medicinal-plant firm founded by Lisa

Conte, provides free food at all times of the day and night for its employees. The program started with groups of workers getting together to shop for and cook food paid for by the company. Nowadays the shopping and cooking are hired out, but the employees still eat for free. CEO Lisa Conte says the meal program gives people from all levels of the company a chance to sit down and eat together, and also makes it easier for people to work their own hours without having to stop to go out for meals.

Herman Miller Furniture helps employees who have been disabled or unemployed for other reasons to get back into the workforce. The company consults with its disabled employees' doctors and helps them return to work by purchasing or designing special equipment, providing rehabilitative training, or transferring them to another position. If medical restrictions force a job change to what would be a lower-paying position, the pay stays the same.

If you've ever wondered why your Federal Express deliveryperson is so friendly and efficient, it's because the company knows how to treat its employees. Among other things, FedEx has an extremely effective grievance procedure. If you think you've been treated unfairly, you can follow a line of appeal up to the top, where the CEO will sit in on a meeting to hear your complaint. At the very end, a five-member panel of employees is appointed to decide the issue. Three of those panel members are selected by the employee who filed the complaint.

Some of our fellow Social Ventures Network companies are quite innovative in the human-resources area, too.

✳   We do what we call labor-gain sharing, which allows our team members to directly affect their compensation by increasing labor productivity. If they increase sales per labor hour, the gain goes directly to them. The company paid out over $4 million in gain-sharing bonuses last year. The bonus can be anywhere from 10 to 50 percent of someone's income.

We're the largest supermarket chain in the country that offers discounts to its team members. It's unheard of in the industry, but we give all our team members a 20 percent discount because we believe in the value of organic food and we want our people to try the products. We gave our employees 4 million bucks' worth of discounts last year.

Our benefits program is very untraditional in mainstream business, too. It's based totally on freedom of choice—cafeteria-style, with a range of everything from tofu to prime rib on the cafeteria line. Each employee gets to pick. We enacted a domestic partners program pretty early on, and we have tremendous diversity in our team-member base in terms of sexual orientation, dress codes, lifestyles, all of that.

I don't really think of our human-resource policies as coming from social values. They're just commonsense business values. You could be a John Bircher and recognize the value of an effective employee-incentive program.

—Peter Roy

● Managing Expectations: If It's Not Fun . . .

People come to Ben & Jerry's with extremely high expectations. There's a widespread impression outside the company that the quality of work life at Ben & Jerry's and other values-led companies is wonderful, perfect, hunky-dory.

When an employee goes to work for a company that is driven solely by profit, he doesn't think that company is going to care about him. He thinks, "I'm here to maximize profit. That's all the company is interested in. That's how I'm going to be rated. That's the contract." So his expectations are not high.

But when a company has as part of its mission that it supports the community, it makes sense for the workforce to see itself as a primary part of that community. It's understandable for employees of Ben & Jerry's to feel that when the company talks about improving the quality of life, that improvement should extend to their lives.

＊　When I first came to work at Ben & Jerry's I was astounded at what a terrific workplace it was. I heard people who'd been here awhile complaining about the lack of organization and direction, the pay, the uncertainties. Most of them had never worked anyplace else. I kept finding myself telling people, "You guys don't know how good you have it. You don't know how it is out there. No matter what company you work for, they all have problems."

—Tom D'Urso
Ben & Jerry's Treasurer

Jerry's quote "If it's not fun, why do it?" has been taken literally by some of our employees. Ben & Jerry's projects a fun image externally, and a lot of employees believe that working at the company is supposed to be that much fun. And it's still work.

✳   IF IT'S NOT FUN, YOU DO IT.

WE'RE PUTTING THE FUN BACK INTO DYSFUNCTIONAL.

—signs seen in two different cubicles in our marketing department

Some people at Ben & Jerry's have unrealistic expectations because those of us at the top of the organization have not been clear in stating what a realistic set of expectations would be. It's our responsibility to articulate our contract with our employees. We need to say, "We will do these things; we will not do those things. Here's a list of things you will get from working at Ben & Jerry's. If that's what you're looking for, you'll be happy here. On the other hand, these are the things you will not get from working at Ben & Jerry's. If those things are extremely important to you, this is the wrong place for you to be working."

It all comes down to leadership, and conscious culture creation. During times when Ben & Jerry's has been well managed, there's been more of both. During times when we're poorly managed, we've had too little of both.

If we're not consciously creating our culture, it devolves into cynicism. Cynicism is the prevailing mode of the national culture. If we're not working at shaping our company's culture, there's reason for cynicism. We're not addressing people's concerns. We're not talking openly with them about what's going on, what it's like in the company, what our problems are, how we're going to fix them. It takes good managers and good management structures to address employees' concerns and fix them.

Good managers and good management structures, in turn, depend on a recruitment process that can bring good people in.

● Values-Led Recruitment

Over the years we've been around and around on the issue of how to recruit people who have expertise in a given area and who share our values as well.

Once we developed our mission statement in 1988, and started defining the purpose of the company, we mostly depended on self-selection for new employees. People who agreed with the values were drawn to the company. That worked to some extent, but it wasn't enough to rely on as the company grew.

In 1985, around the time we set up the Ben & Jerry's Foundation, we implemented a five-to-one salary ratio, which limited top salaries to five times the lowest salary. The idea was brought to us by Jeff Furman. Jeff had read about the Mondragón co-op in Spain, an association of one hundred separate businesses and community-based ventures that employs over twenty-five thousand people and has sales of over $2.6 billion a year. At Mondragón the top managers are paid no more than three times what the lowest-paid workers earn. The idea, which we strongly agree with, was that as the company prospers, everybody in the company should prosper.

The compressed salary ratio dealt with an issue that's at the core of people's concerns about business and their alienation from their jobs: the people at the bottom of the ladder, the people who do all the actual physical work, are paid very poorly compared to the people at the top of the ladder.

When we started our business we were the people on the bottom. That's whom we identified with. So we were happy to put into place a system whereby anytime the people on the top of the organization wanted to give themselves a raise, they'd have to give the people on the bottom a raise as well.

The salary ratio was seen by our employees as a strong statement of commitment to improving their quality of life. It was clear and simple and quantitative. It stood out in stark contrast to the normal business paradigm. They loved it. It became a touchstone of our culture.

But as the company grew, the salary ratio became problematic. Some people in upper-level management believed that we couldn't afford to raise everyone's salaries, and the salary ratio was therefore limiting the offers we could make to the top people we needed to recruit. Other people—Ben included—thought money wasn't the problem, and that we'd always had problems with our recruitment process. Ben points out frequently that eliminating the salary ratio, which we did in 1995, has not eliminated our recruiting problems.

Between our less-than-perfect recruitment practices and our desire to employ values-aligned people, we've had an increasingly difficult time hiring as the company has grown.

We've also been plagued by job turnover in the human-resources department. People would submit unsolicited résumés for positions that weren't open at the time, and we'd send them the standard "We'll keep it on file" letter. Then when we had a position open we'd advertise to fill it, instead of calling the people who'd already applied. Maybe by then we'd lost their applications; maybe we'd just forgotten we had them. In any case, we failed to connect with a significant number of highly qualified people who very much wanted to work for Ben & Jerry's.

If you're not values-led, it doesn't matter so much if you lose people's résumés, because there are so many potential employees out there for you. You put out the call; lots of qualified people respond. Or you hire a headhunter and they put on your desk the résumés of twenty people who meet your criteria exactly. But when values alignment is an issue, you have a much smaller pool to draw from. It's hard to know where to find the people who make up that pool. You can't go out and find them, because you don't know who they are.

For years we had several crucial positions unfilled at a time. So, out of desperation, we started using outside recruiters. From this experience we learned that when you use recruiters and you don't advertise, you have a small chance of finding people who are values-aligned. You need to advertise so that a broad number of people know there's an opening in this values-led company. That way the people who are values-aligned can self-select for the position.

With a few notable exceptions, recruiters are inexperienced at finding people with a particular set of values. That's not their skill set. One way around that problem is to have an in-house recruiter who has all the connections and expertise of an outside recruiter but who's committed to the social mission of the company.

Another lesson we learned from our recruiting mistakes is that a values-led company needs to take advantage of the opportunity *whenever it arises* to hire highly qualified people who are aligned with the company's values. Some companies have a policy of hiring great people when they find them, whether they have a specific job opening at the time or not. The person works in different areas of the company until it becomes clear where he or she can make the greatest contribution. Someone at the top of the organization takes that person under his or her wing and says, We'd like you to be in charge of creating safety teams in manufacturing. Or, We'd like you to select students at ten universities who'll be Ben & Jerry's reps, to organize sampling and sell Ben & Jerry's at the various concessions on campus.

For a values-led company, hiring people who have been schooled for ten or twenty years in the traditional way of doing business can be a real negative. Also, when we hire from outside we're hiring an unknown quantity. Many times these people don't work out. When we promote from within we know what we're getting.

Staples, Inc., does hire new MBAs they don't have particular jobs for and lets them work in different departments until they're acclimated to the company. That's what we should do, too. Until the graduates are trained and we have a specific job for them, they'll be performing valuable work; two years later, when we have a job for them, they'll be ready. This is in contrast to what happens now: we suddenly have an opening; we go out and get a recruiter and pay the recruiting fee; we get someone cold, who's been working in traditional industry and getting industry experience but not values-integration experience.

This strategy does require planning ahead, because it might take the young people three or four years to grow into the job. But it's worth it to hire people who are smart and have the right values orientation, to get them used to the company and have them learn the business. When the time comes, there'll be a job for them.

● Hiring for Values Alignment

Five or six years into the business, before we'd adopted our mission statement, Ben got up at a staff meeting one day and said he thought Ben & Jerry's should start screening prospective employees for social values. It didn't go over real well. People completely rejected that notion. They felt it was totalitarian mind control. They thought it was a statement that they themselves didn't have the "right" values, that they didn't fit.

Later we realized that because we hadn't started the company with the social mission, the people who worked there hadn't signed on for that. We had some long-term employees who'd taken the job because they liked ice cream, or because it was the best job they could get, or for any number of other reasons. The company didn't have well-defined values when they were hired. Before we had the mission statement, there was no justification for hiring people with a particular set of values.

But even since we've had the mission statement there's been resistance to the idea of hiring for values alignment. The argument is that people need to be hired and evaluated not on what they believe but on their ability to perform the job, which includes implementing all three parts of our mission. The argument on the other side is that employees who don't believe in the social mission won't be as motivated to do their jobs to the best of their ability.

Everyone agrees that it's best for the company to be staffed with people who are motivated by the social mission. The question is, how

do you get there? Do you screen potential employees for values alignment? Do you make your company's values public and let people self-
select for alignment with them? Or do you hire people regardless of
their beliefs and then try to win them over?

There's no precedent for hiring for values alignment in a for-profit
organization. Most companies don't have a social mission; therefore
they don't attempt to hire people who are aligned with it. There is a
model for values-alignment hiring—in the nonprofit sector, where the
only mission of the enterprise is a social mission.

Ben: No one would expect a nonprofit that works with the
homeless to hire people who believe homeless people
deserve to be on the street. Greenpeace doesn't hire
people who don't care about the environment to go
door-to-door trying to get donations.

Jerry: But we're not a nonprofit, Ben. I'm sure there are
people at Ben & Jerry's who disagree wholeheartedly
with what we believe and what we do. And that's okay,
as long as they're doing their jobs.

Ben: How far would you take that idea? What if an employee
is bad-mouthing gays or people of color?

Jerry: It's a value of the company that we don't support that.
While you're at work you can't bad-mouth any group of
people.

Ben: I guess it's true—we don't control your whole life. Go
home and bad-mouth gays or people of color, but not
while you're in our workplace.

Jerry: We don't control your beliefs. It's your job
performance, which incorporates the economic,
quality, and social missions. And that's all we have the
right to comment on.

✳   I think you need to interview for values because somebody coming
into a company wants to know what the company's about. But I don't
think you have to insist that they buy into the whole political mission.
You want someone with the competence to do the job. With a company as
well known as Ben & Jerry's, I don't think you have to fear that prospective
employees won't know what the mission is.

When Ben & Jerry's was looking for a chief financial officer (before
they hired Fran), they conducted a frantic search. They ran ads describing

who they were, what they were, and what they were looking for. They had a hard time finding someone because they were insisting on values alignment. Especially when you're hiring a top management position like CFO, you should hire for competence and skills first.

—Milton Moskowitz

We've tried it both ways. We've tried hiring people for their expertise, being less concerned about their values alignment. We've tried hiring people for their values alignment, being less concerned about their expertise. It's a dicey game either way. Going forward, we're going to hire at the top of the company only people who agree with our progressive social values.

Our last two hires for the CEO position have taken values into account quite profoundly. In 1994 we had a well-publicized search, from which we chose Bob Holland. In addition to his business expertise and experience, Bob had demonstrated a passion for social concerns through his work with nonprofits and with Spelman College, a historically African-American women's college in Atlanta. It was under Bob's leadership at Ben & Jerry's that the social mission was first fully integrated into the operating plan of the company.

Perry Odak is our current CEO. Perry sought out the company because of his excitement about combining social endeavors with a growing, profitable business. Perry's previous position was at a gun company, and the media made a flap about the apparent conflict with Ben & Jerry's stand in favor of reducing gun violence. What the media neglected to mention was that Perry had been a consultant at that company for nine months out of a twenty-five-year career, and they made hunting rifles, not handguns. We spent a great deal of time talking with Perry about our company's values, and we were as excited about his alignment with the company's mission as we were about his business acumen. As Ben said, "Anytime you can change someone from making guns to making ice cream, you've done a wonderful thing for the world."

Jerry: I think it's good for the company to get people in who are enthusiastic about the social mission. But I'm not sure that people's beliefs are any business of an employer.

> Ben: So you don't agree with the idea of hiring people for values alignment?
>
> Jerry: The issue should be who can do the best job.
>
> Ben: How can someone do a great job if they don't agree with the mission? Where's their motivation?
>
>   It's the same as the financial mission or the quality mission. We shouldn't hire people who believe that corporate profits are a rip-off. We shouldn't hire people who don't care about quality. Ideally we want a hundred percent of our people to have a hundred percent alignment with all three missions.
>
> Jerry: I agree we want our employees to be aligned. The question is how to get them aligned.
>
> Ben: Hire them that way.
>
> Jerry: Or educate them once they're here.
>
> Ben: I've read a lot of research that shows people's values are a core part of their identity, something that is very difficult to change.

● Hiring from Within

Improving our recruitment process is necessary, but it's not the ultimate solution to our staffing needs. The best way for a values-led company to improve the expertise level of its staff is to develop it from within.

What happens at Ben & Jerry's also happens at a lot of high-growth companies: as the business matures, the people who have done a fine job at one level don't necessarily have the skills to rise to the next level. So we're forced to hire out-of-house, which in turn creates the problem of culture clash and lack of values alignment. It would be preferable to place somebody in-house in a new job and mentor him or her one-on-one. That way, people are continually being groomed for positions of greater responsibility. While that's being put into motion, it might be helpful to try to control the company's rate of growth so it matches the pace at which people can be developed to go to the next level of business.

Although we've never succeeded in putting ongoing training programs in place, we have had a couple of notable training successes. One was Fran Rathke, who's now our CFO. When the position came open in 1990, Fran was our controller. Fran didn't have the level of expertise required for the CFO position, but we decided that instead of hiring an outside person for the top job, we'd hire an outside mentor to help Fran develop the skills she needed. That's what we did, and it's worked out wonderfully.

We did the same thing with Wendy Yoder, whom we promoted to plant manager at our St. Albans plant. Wendy had been with the company for a long time. The plant manager job was going to be a big stretch for her; she needed a lot of support in order to be able to do it. We provided the support, and she rose to the occasion. Everyone won: Wendy got her promotion, and we got a plant manager who knows and is deeply committed to the company's culture and values.

● Orientation

When a person first comes to our company, we have a unique opportunity to get that person started on the right track. That's the time to present management's perspective on where we want the company to go, how it should be run, how employees should be treated, how they should deal with particular contingencies that come up, what they should do if they think their manager's not treating them right. That's the time to lay out the responsibilities of the company to the employee, the employee's responsibilities to the company, and the basis on which the person will be evaluated.

Orientation is especially important in a values-led company because values-led business is not yet familiar to most people. New employees are coming out of a society and out of businesses that don't, as a rule, uphold those values. The mission of the company is fundamentally different from what they've experienced in traditional business. It needs to be laid out and explained. That's a tremendous shift for people to make, and we need to help them make it.

This is also the time to explain to people how different functions throughout the company integrate the social mission into the things they do. We can talk to a new employee in purchasing about how to factor the social mission into their truck-buying decisions, to get them acclimated to the idea of considering the environmental and social implications of what they do. We tell them, "In your previous job, your decision-making matrix was cost and functionality. Now it's cost, functionality, and social impact. When your suppliers are making their pitch to you, you tell them, 'Along with your pitch about how great this truck is and how much money you'll save me, I need to know the environmental impact of driving your truck versus driving your competitor's truck.' "

That's why it's a major plus to hire people who are motivated by the social mission. Instead of seeing the social mission as extra work, they say, "Oh, great—I can factor in my social values on my job!"

● Believe It or Not

In any values-led company there's always a range of employee responses to the social mission.

✳ I don't feel pressured at all to participate in the mission activities. That's all strictly volunteer. I volunteered to be on the Safety Team. There are some other things I'd like to volunteer for, like the foundation, but I'd like to give other people a chance. It's nice that I can tell other people on the Community Action Teams and the Green Teams what I think, and they take my input back to their committees. I don't have to personally go.

There have been times when the company has tried to get people to take part a little more. There's E-mail, there are sign-ups on the bulletin board. It's offered, it's out there, but you don't have to say yes, you'll do it.

—Cathy Fuller

✳ There's too much pressure to participate in the social mission. You're supposed to do so much every year; it's in your review. At every company function we have, social mission is all the time pressed on us. Every time you turn on your computer it's on your E-mail: we need help for this and that. You feel guilty if you don't do something.

People don't mind helping people. But people want to be home with their families. You're so stressed out from working here all day, you don't want to do any more for Ben & Jerry's than you have to.

I love my job. I love what I do. But in how they deal with the social mission, I think there's definitely room for improvement.

—Daisy Sweet

✳ Being production workers, the only pressure we get is to make the best ice cream in the world. That's our pressure. We like getting off the production floor once in a while to do a social-mission thing, like painting the firehouse.

I bounce in and out of a lot of the committees. I was on the employee foundation group when it started. I didn't know how I got on there, but they picked me. All of a sudden I was giving away the company's money. That was pretty cool.

—David "Wilbur" Wright

One thing that helps build a sense of unity and internal community within the workforce—while directly serving the outside community—is to make it easy for employees to get directly involved in the company's social-mission activities.

✳   Whole Foods donates 5 percent of after-tax profits to community organizations. The vast majority of that money is allocated at the store level. Each store decides what the groups and causes are that are important to the people in that store. Berkeley got involved with a battered women's shelter. New Orleans contributes to the SPCA. Palo Alto does the Little League and the senior center. This local, real community-based philanthropy program works really well.

—Peter Roy

In 1991, a production worker from our Waterbury plant, Mary Messier, approached Liz Bankowski. Mary asked, "If Ben & Jerry's cares so much about indigenous peoples, and the rain forest, and other environmental issues, why aren't we worried about the construction of the James Bay hydroelectric plant?" The plant, which was sited on James Bay, an Indian reservation in Quebec, would have wreaked havoc on the natural environment. It would have flooded an area the size of Connecticut and wiped out the hunting lands, and eventually the culture, of the Inuit and Cree Indians who lived in the area. There was a big debate in Vermont about whether or not the state should purchase power from the project.

Liz said, "Good question, Mary."

The Hulbert Center, a Burlington group, was organizing trips to James Bay so people could see for themselves what was going on. We decided to send a team of seven employees. They were all line workers; they had a great, eye-opening trip. When they came back they advocated that the company take a stand opposing construction of the plant. They also decided they wanted to write an open letter to the community about their experience and how it affected their opinions on the issue. So the company paid for a full-page ad and printed the letter, which helped mobilize opposition in Vermont. The ad read:

It doesn't make sense.

This past September, a small delegation of Ben & Jerry's employees were offered a rare opportunity. We were asked by our company to go to Northern Quebec to spend a week living with the Cree Indians and to bring back a firsthand account of the effects of Hydro Quebec development.

Two of our new friends, William and Margaret Connerty, who are trying to hold on to the old ways, are standing in front of their cooking tepee.

Looking back, we realize we had been naive in our thoughts of the traditional Indian world we thought still existed. We were expecting tepees and lodges. We thought our meals would be of wild game and fresh fish caught earlier that day. We were going to experience the spirit of the Indian. As soon as we arrived, these notions quickly disappeared.

In the small village of Chisasibi, we were not prepared to see a community of Cree Indians living close together in a modern concrete town handed to them by their government. Rather than living in lodges, Cree families now live in modern cluster housing complete with running water, television, and four-wheel drives. We were surprised to learn they pay more for their electricity than we do in Vermont. Instead of hunting as they used to, they buy their food from convenience stores. We learned they could no longer fish in their traditional fishing spots. Land flooded by dam construction had poisoned the lakes with mercury.

In exchange for their land, they were told by their government that this new lifestyle would be good for them. Walking around Chisasibi, we saw a community that felt betrayed, sold out, and isolated from its past pride and traditions. Many families in Chisasibi are struggling with the new sedentary lifestyle, while others are beginning to refuse it and are heading back to the bush to regain what traditional way of life they can.

Later in the week we spent a day touring Hydro Quebec. We were in awe of the size of the project and the amount of land that has already been flooded. We walked along one of the project's spillways and went 500 feet underground into one of the power houses. This project is huge. The technology and manpower involved was exciting to witness. Later in the day that excitement faded. Our tour ended at a memorial site where a small stone monument stands in dedication to the Cree people who lost their hunting grounds to the project.

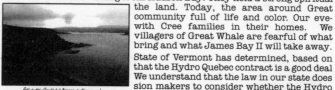

A spillway at Hydro Quebec.

Our stay ended with a visit to the small community of Great Whale, the proposed site of James Bay II. We had to fly into Great Whale, since the closest road is about 120 miles away. From the plane, we could see huge light-green patches of cari-bou moss, food which helps support caribou herds. Families of Great Whale still spend many months hunting geese in the bush and fishing from Hudson Bay. They hold a strong spiritual connection with the land. Today, the area around Great Whale is an active community full of life and color. Our eve-nings were spent with Cree families in their homes. We learned that the villagers of Great Whale are fearful of what the future may bring and what James Bay II will take away.

Recently, the State of Vermont has determined, based on financial analysis, that the Hydro Quebec contract is a good deal for Vermonters. We understand that the law in our state does not allow for deci-sion makers to consider whether the Hydro Quebec contract is a good deal for the Cree or for the environ-ment, but after visiting James Bay and experiencing firsthand the effects of Hydro Quebec, some things don't make sense.

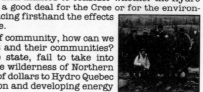

A shot of the Great Whale River. Under the proposed James Bay II Contract nominated this river will disappear.

Living in a state that exemplifies the value of community, how can we not extend that same value to the Cree Indians and their communities? How can we, an environmentally progressive state, fail to take into account the impact this contract will have on the wilderness of Northern Quebec? Why is Vermont willing to send millions of dollars to Hydro Quebec instead of putting our resources into conservation and developing energy sources here at home?

A group shot, up in Great Whale. Us and our guides out in the bush.

Kevin D. Corliss
Production

Andrew S. Fellows
Maintenance

Gary Audy
Facilities

Mike Noury
Shipping & Receiving

Ray Stapleton
Production

Tom Burrows
Shipping & Receiving

Brent D. Campbell
Community Services

BEN&JERRY'S.
VERMONT'S FINEST • ICE CREAM & FROZEN YOGURT™   **We are proud to support this statement from our employees.**

The James Bay project was an example of the company taking action on an issue that bubbled up from within the organization as well as from outside. Since the power purchase was being sold as essential to future economic development in the state, it was a business issue that we as a company could not sit out. Mary and others in the company were also telling us that we couldn't sit this one out despite any interest we might have in cheaper electricity. The pros and cons of this complex matter were debated over a couple of board meetings. We finally reached the conclusion that it was not good economic development policy for Vermont to be exporting the social and environmental costs of meeting its energy needs to indigenous people in northern Canada. We also felt there was a lot more that could be done through conservation to meet the state's energy needs. So we opposed the contract. As it turned out, Vermont did not need the additional power and the utilities needed to restructure their contract with Hydro Quebec.

Each year during the time we were working with the Children's Defense Fund, we sent a delegation of employees to the CDF annual meeting in Washington, D.C. Ours was the only corporate delegation; the others were all from nonprofit organizations. People in the company applied to go by writing a paragraph about what they thought they'd get out of the experience. The delegations always came back incredibly inspired and pumped. A couple of delegations came back and organized teams at the job sites to work on local children's issues.

One of our most successful experiences with employee involvement was the Campaign to End Childhood Hunger in Vermont. We found out that there were federal funds available to provide free breakfast for schoolchildren. All the communities needed to do was ask, but most of them didn't know the program existed. So we identified each town in Vermont that wasn't getting free breakfasts, and then we identified the employees who lived in those towns and invited them to get involved. People signed up. We provided educational training around the programs. They became captains in their towns; they went to their school board meetings and blitzed them. Tens of thousands of children in Vermont now get school breakfast because their towns got signed up.

✳   Recently we instituted Making a Difference Day, where the employees are paid to work in the community doing some kind of social service. We're also just starting an adopt-a-school program, which the employees are very enthused about.

When the social mission is abstract, it's easy to reject—especially here in New Hampshire, where 70 percent of the population and about 70 to 80 percent of Stonyfield's workforce is conservative and Republican. Our challenge is to make the social mission real and acceptable to our employees first, so we can convey it to our customers most effectively.

—Gary Hirshberg

*   I know some people feel the social mission is imposed on us from above. I've never felt that way. It usually changes once people start understanding what the mission is all about. I can think of a couple of people right off the top who didn't want anything to do with it when they got here. Then they got involved. Now they're committed.

I'd say about half the people here at St. Albans are actively in support of the company's values. I think the social mission is great. We have the potential to do a lot more. If more places did what Ben & Jerry's does, we'd have a better planet.

—Jesse Metcalf

Mixing Business and Politics:

Taking Stands on Social Issues

Ben: What's odd and scary to many people is that Ben & Jerry's takes stands that aren't in its own narrow self-interest but in the interest of the community as a whole.

Jerry: I think it's more than that, Ben. I think it's scary because taking those stands has the potential to alienate customers.

Ben: Most businesses take political stands. They just do it covertly. So their customers never know what they're up to.

Jerry: I don't disagree with that. But our stands are quite outspoken, aren't they?

Ben: Some of them are. Yes.

Jerry: So our customers *do* know about them. And that's what makes it risky.

Ben: But mostly our customers agree with our stands, and instead of feeling alienated actually feel closer to us.

● Business As Usual?

Long before the advent of the corporation, the purpose of business was to meet people's needs. Businesses were small and community based. Society was most strongly influenced by two entities whose reason for being was the good of society: religion and the nation-state.

It is just within our lifetimes that business has become the most powerful force in society. And since the goal of the corporation is to maximize profits, not social good, business often ends up advocating for legislation that is harmful to the rest of society. That's a by-product of business looking out for its own interest, which is what it's set up to do.

✱ The well-being of a company is tied directly into the well-being of a community. If people in the community live below the poverty line, they can't afford to purchase the products that business produces or the services business renders.

Something like 38 million people in this country are living below the poverty line. That's an enormous market—equivalent to the combined populations of Scandinavia, Holland, Belgium, and Luxembourg. Look how hard we in business try to develop markets abroad, yet we have a market in this country that we're neglecting.

I don't know how you can separate the well-being of the one from the other. The community is where your employees come from. If they're well schooled, given an opportunity, they can develop a learning capacity and skill levels that allow them to be productive employees. If they're without that kind of exposure, they become like many young people in the inner city, who don't even have the attention span to learn anymore. They've never worked, they've dropped out of school, they have all kinds of social problems. They become tax consumers instead of tax producers.

Corporations pay taxes that are used to try to remedy situations that may not even be remediable anymore. Look at the cost of unemployment, drug addiction, teen pregnancy. All those problems come with a price tag, which is estimated to be $750 billion. And that doesn't include lost wages. Prevention would cost infinitely less.

Another compelling reason to invest in the community is to help the United States be competitive in the global market. We won't do very well against the Japanese, Germans, or French as long as their children have infinitely more opportunity from preschool on through the upper grades and university.

It's not just a moral imperative for business to become committed to and invested in the community. It's an economic imperative. Even the

Milton Friedman school of business would find it hard to turn away from the economic implications of not investing in the community.

> —Arnold Hiatt
>   Chairman, Stride Rite Foundation; Former CEO/President/
>   Chairman, Stride Rite Corporation

Unfortunately, it's unusual for a company to recognize and address the basic social, human, and environmental needs in our society that are going unmet, as Stride Rite does. Meeting human needs is not tops on government's agenda, either. One major reason is that it is business that, to a great degree, finances the campaigns of the politicians who run the government, so the politicians are invested in business's agenda. And business finances most of the lobbyists, who influence legislation as well.

Business speaks in its own short-term interest. No one is speaking for the disenfranchised, so the country underinvests in the disenfranchised by default. That's how we've ended up with a set of national budget priorities that underinvests in human needs and overinvests in the military.

To varying degrees, people understand this. They certainly understand that the powers that be aren't set up to tend to their needs. People are tired of special-interest groups and elected officials being in it for themselves, fighting environmental regulations and proconsumer regulations. People are tired of being mistreated as employees and as consumers.

We've come to expect business to try to manipulate the government and the political process for its own benefit. As the most influential and pervasive entity in society, business sets an example of what constitutes acceptable behavior. By its actions, business has helped create a culture in which we expect entities to act solely in their own self-interest, often to the detriment of the community as a whole. Business has modeled that behavior for us, as Michael Lerner has described.

✱   The competitive market teaches us to see other human beings as means to achieving our own advancement, and teaches us that "looking out for number one" is the highest goal of life. We believe, on the other hand, that human beings are intrinsically to be revered and cherished, and that without that attitude, families and loving relationships tend to fall apart.

Changing the bottom line must start in our own personal lives. We are aware, however, that individual change is not enough. We live in a society whose economic institutions massively reinforce selfishness and materialism and marginalize all those who think that love and caring can be the basis of public decision making. Hence, we are committed to challenging the ethos of the competitive market, and to insisting that corporations themselves must be changed to incorporate a new bottom line.

We are encouraging people in every workplace and profession to re-vision what their work world could look like if the bottom line were shifted to enhance caring and ethical and spiritual sensitivity. We are calling on corporations to issue an annual ethical-impact report, and we are calling on consumers to use their buying power to reward corporations that demonstrate a history of social responsibility.

> —Michael Lerner
> Clinical Psychologist, Rabbi, Editor of *Tikkun* magazine and
> Coauthor of *Jews and Blacks: Let the Healing Begin*

People understand that to a much larger extent than any other entity in society, business influences elections and legislation, through campaign contributions and lobbying. They understand that business is lobbying against the minimum wage, fighting environmental regulations and consumer-protection legislation.

In this environment, when a business stands up for the good of the general population, people are very attracted to that business. People think government should care for people. They think religion should care for people. Business is not expected to care for people. So it's all the more striking when business does act for the common good.

There is a range of ways for business to do that. The easy thing to do is donate some money to disadvantaged kids, donate some money to sick kids, donate some money to the orchestra—essentially to try to fill in some of the gaps that are left by government's failure to address the needs of the people.

Charity is fine, but it's dealing with the symptoms and not the root cause of the problem. It's just plugging the holes in the dike while the water rises around us.

Also, making charitable donations can be somewhat hypocritical. At the same time that a corporation is trying to shoot down environmental regulations—which has the effect of increasing the amount of toxins in the environment, which has the effect of making kids sick—that corporation donates some money to taking care of sick kids, which is presented as an act of generosity.

In order for business to sincerely effect any structural change in society, it has to engage in the political realm. And that's where people start to get scared. They say business has no right to be involved in the political realm. Business will offend potential customers if it's involved in the political realm.

And yet the reality is that business is steeped in the political realm— but not, for the most part, in the interests of the majority of people and not, for the most part, openly. Business is an extremely political animal. It's just that the way business has traditionally been involved in politics is in a covert way. If you don't tell anybody what you're doing, how can it be controversial?

Taking a position on a controversial issue is fundamentally different from, say, buying brownies from a nonprofit organization that employs economically disenfranchised people. That's not going to alienate any-one. Who's going to disagree with supporting an organization like Greyston Bakery?

If we want to help solve the problems we're addressing by buying our brownies from Greyston, we can accomplish that on a significant scale only when we get the government involved in teaching people to fish—helping people get out of poverty, giving them job training. That's what Greyston is, essentially: a job-training program. But saying that the task of getting people out of poverty is solely in the hands of private enterprise is an abdication of government's responsibilities. And that goes counter to what the general population wants. We Americans do care about our neighbors and we do care about people who are suffer-ing. That's why Americans give a tremendous amount of voluntary con-tributions to charitable organizations every year. But we also want our government to help look after people's needs.

Recently there was a survey conducted on people's attitudes about welfare. The survey showed that people aren't against welfare because of how much it costs. They're against welfare because it's not helping people get out of poverty. Eighty-five percent of the population is in favor of spending money on welfare on the condition that the recipients are required to do some kind of work in order to get their checks.

When a business—which has tremendous credibility in the society, as compared to nonprofit activist groups—lends its credibility and mus-cle and voice to supporting a cause, people are more likely to support that cause. This is not always the case when a nonprofit is involved. An advocacy group like the Children's Defense Fund points out that Head Start saves $5 for every dollar spent. Despite the fact that this social program is actually profitable, that message is given short shrift. CDF is marginalized and portrayed as a special interest group.

But when a business is advocating for an issue that is not in its own interest, that helps cut through people's cynicism. Business has a high degree of credibility where money is concerned. People believe that businesspeople understand money, that business is financially conservative and rational because it's focused on financial results.

Business Is Credible

People's beliefs are based on their knowledge. How do you convince someone of something? You give him or her information. If they're someone who's looking to restrict children's access to Head Start— which has been shown to be the most cost-effective social program we have—while increasing the military budget, what can we say to them except, "Look at the facts. The Cold War is no longer. We don't need to be spending the same amount of money we spent when we were fighting another superpower.

"And our kids are being shortchanged. We're not providing them with the skills and knowledge they need to succeed in their early years. Because of that they need extra help at school, they drop out, they get in trouble, they get pregnant, and all the remedial social services that are then necessary cost us five times more than what it would have cost to get those kids on the right track in the first place."

That's why we try to put out the facts at our festivals. The interesting thing about doing that is, the facts turn out to be real news to many people. Because they don't get them otherwise.

The knowledge that's made available to us by the mainstream media doesn't amount to much. Unless it's a big plane crash or O.J.'s trial, we're not going to learn about it on the six o'clock news. The day-to-day federal budget decisions aren't reported on, because they're a little on the dry side. But it's the budget that tells us what our country's priorities are.

We don't believe those priorities are in sync with those of the majority of the population. We say, get the facts, then make your own decisions. If you agree with how the country is using its resources, don't work to change that. If you disagree, get involved. That's what we did when we set up Action Stations in our scoop shops so our customers could join the Children's Defense Fund.

Recently Business Leaders for Sensible Priorities did some focus groups on the issue of taking money out of the military budget to fund domestic needs. The participants were given a list of ten different categories of people and asked which category they'd find most credible on the subject. The groups included military people, businesspeople, college professors, doctors, lawyers, economists, actors, and a few others.

The focus groups said the number one credible source on the budget issue was military people. The number two credible source was businesspeople. The other categories weren't even on the chart.

Since business has now become the most powerful force in society, it's incumbent upon us businesspeople to consider the greater good when we do the things we do.

● Business Unusual

In the early days of the gas station we had no concept of trying to impact social issues. All we knew was that we were trying to be a community-based business.

Ben: That was Jerry's idea.

Jerry: Ice Cream for the People!

Ben: I had no idea what he meant. I went along with it.

Then, in 1984, when Häagen-Dazs (which was owned at the time by Pillsbury, which has subsequently been gobbled up by Grand Metropolitan) tried to keep our distributors from carrying Ben & Jerry's, we had our first experience with using our business to activate our customers to take a stand on an issue. A small company fighting for survival against a $4 billion corporation wasn't a political issue per se, but it did teach us that our customers could be mobilized into a powerful force for action.

We believed that Pillsbury's actions were illegal under federal antitrust law, which states that a company that controls a major share of a given market cannot use its power and economic strength to keep other companies out of the market. But we knew that in a strictly legal fight we'd run out of time and money long before Pillsbury did. Our only option was to rely on our customers and the media to pressure Pillsbury into backing off. So we started printing the slogan "What's the Doughboy Afraid Of?" on our pint containers, along with an 800 number for the Doughboy Hotline. Everyone who called got a Doughboy Kit, with protest letters addressed to the Federal Trade Commission and the chairman of the Pillsbury board, and a bumper sticker.

This David-versus-Goliath story ran in the *New York Times*, the *Wall Street Journal*, the *San Francisco Chronicle*, and the Sunday *Boston Globe*. Calvin Trillin wrote a long article about it in the *New Yorker*. Soon, four hundred people a week were calling the Doughboy Hotline. Eventually, Pillsbury agreed to stop trying to block sales of our products. The thousands of customers who'd contributed to that outcome shared in its reward: we stayed in business; they could still get their Ben & Jerry's.

One year later, when we formed the Ben & Jerry's Foundation, our thinking was that business was a machine for making money, and the best thing a business could do for the community was to make as much money as possible and to subsequently give away as much money as possible. But as soon as it was established, the foundation was flooded with applications from incredibly worthwhile groups that were performing much-needed services for people who were disadvantaged, abused, neglected, or shut out of the economic and social mainstream. We discovered that we couldn't fund even a small percentage of the groups that applied. All the foundations in the country were in the same position—there were so many groups that needed money, they couldn't fund more than a small fraction of them.

We began to wonder why there were so many unmet needs in society. When you look at the federal budget, it becomes clear that the majority of the discretionary budget goes to the military. That's why there isn't enough money available to meet basic needs. The Cold War was going on at the time, and we were in an arms race to be able to blow up the world more times than the Soviet Union could. It occurred to us that only by ending the Cold War could we eliminate the public's willingness to put so much money into the military. And we could achieve true security by teaching people that we had more things in common with the Russian people than differences.

With that goal in mind, in 1988 Ben organized a group called One Percent for Peace, whose goal was to help people in the two countries get to know each other so they wouldn't want to blow each other up.

● **One Percent for Peace**

Since the Cold War justified the arms buildup, One Percent for Peace began by working for an end to the Cold War. This would be accomplished by redirecting one percent of the military budget to peace-through-understanding activities such as citizen exchanges.

> *Ben:* A few years after we started the organization, the Cold
> War ended. Remarkable what a few well-intentioned
> people can accomplish, isn't it?

There was tremendous opposition at the company to Ben's insisting that the company be involved in One Percent for Peace—especially when Ben proposed renaming our ice cream bars Peace Pops and printing a message supporting One Percent for Peace on the wrapper.

This was the first time Ben & Jerry's had ever considered taking a public stand on a government policy. Some of our managers felt this would turn off our customers. They said, "Customers are going to protest. They're not going to buy our products. The conservatives are going to picket the stores. We've just invested money in a new factory to make ice cream pops. If the product is pulled off the shelves it will put our people out of work and result in disaster for the company. It's not right to take a stand against the government. Businesses don't do that."

The other question this raised was, whose company is it? Chico Lager was president at the time, and he'd set up a management team that was overseeing the different departments in the company. People said, "Is Ben meddling in places he shouldn't be? Is Ben dictating to management?"

> *Jerry:* Ben creates this organization One Percent for Peace.
> Then he comes to the company and says, "There's this
> organization and I think we ought to come out with this
> item called the Peace Pop so we can support it."
>
> *Ben:* Mom, it followed me home. Can I keep it?
>
> *Jerry:* There was a question as to whether One Percent for
> Peace was a legitimate organization, or just Ben and
> his friends. After all, OPP had a seven-person board of
> directors that included Ben, Jeff Furman, and me. The
> board of directors of Ben & Jerry's had seven people
> that included Ben, Jeff, and me.
>
> *Ben:* But the real issue was whether or not Ben & Jerry's
> should be speaking out about something like the
> military budget.

> *Jerry:* Everyone's for peace. But should Ben & Jerry's be attacking the business of the United States government?
>
> *Ben:* That could conceivably be seen as unpatriotic.

The process of deciding whether or not to do Peace Pops was not an easy one. It was a difficult, painful time at Ben & Jerry's. The dissension took its toll on personal relationships as well as the functioning of the business. There was a lot of discussion on the board, and a lot of head banging at the management level. Ben and Jeff had a history of operating on the outside, as opposed to working with people within the company. Even if the issue itself had been less controversial, it would have been heated because it was "another one of Ben's ideas."

> *Jerry:* Ben, for all his wonderful qualities, is not really big on process.
>
> *Ben:* I think I've gotten much better.
>
> *Jerry:* At that time he was not that much into process. Ben kept upping the stakes with the things he wanted the company to get involved with.
>
> *Ben:* It's that hairy line between cutting-edge innovation and failure.
>
> *Jerry:* But we eventually shoved Peace Pops down the company's throat.
>
> *Ben:* The only problem with shoving something down the company's throat is that it has a tendency to come back up.
>
> *Jerry:* It taught me never to shove it down again. The process was too hard.
>
> *Ben:* It taught me that anytime you do something cutting-edge, the company doesn't go for it at first.

Ultimately the Ben & Jerry's board of directors decided to support Ben and proceed with the Peace Pops. The marketing director at the time, Alan Kaufman, came up with some great copy for the package. Lyn Severance did some incredible inside-wrapper graphics, presenting serious subject matter in a whimsical way.

Chico started wearing a "One Percent for Peace" button to work as a signal that we were all united and going forward with the project. Jerry wore his "Peace Is Patriotic" button. And Ben initiated his infamous Parking Lot Bumper Wash: he and another One Percent for Peace supporter stood in the employee parking lot one morning, offering to wash people's bumpers and put a One Percent for Peace bumper sticker on their cars.

Ben: I thought it was a good, creative marketing stunt.

Jerry: Some of the staff felt that because it was Ben, the head of the company, they were being pressured.

Ben: There were sure a lot of people who didn't seem to cave in to the pressure.

The Peace Pops episode was destructive in certain immediate ways, but overall its effects were constructive. It was a watershed event in the life of Ben & Jerry's. Once the company took that stand, it was easier to take political stands in the future—because it proved that doing could have positive effects.

The response from customers was overwhelmingly positive. Over the years we've received a few negative letters from customers about the One Percent for Peace message on the wrapper, but the damaging response some people were worried about has never materialized.

March 23, 1989

Dear Ben & Jerry's,

Just a note to say "Thank You" for your Peace Pops! I work full-time, teach AIDS education, volunteer with people with AIDS, raise money for hunger, and participate in our church's peace program. I have little time to read labels and boxes. This week our college kids were all home on break and they were pleased to see your "Neat!" message. I said, "What message?" Now I know. And now I want to thank you for spreading the word and providing us with info and the opportunity to participate.

Blessings and peace,
Cindy B.
Cape Elizabeth, Maine

July 5, 1996

Dear Ben & Jerry,
I am a big fan of your ice cream products—not only because of their delectable taste and innovative flavor combinations, but because of your commitment to bettering the world through direct action, One Percent for Peace, and environmentally sound packaging.

Sincerely,
Laura S.
Brooklyn, N.Y.

The company's involvement with One Percent for Peace and Peace Pops, in turn, evolved into the next level of activity.

● Act Now

Since 1988 Ben had been participating in a group of socially concerned businesspeople called the Social Venture Network. At SVN conferences company leaders got together to share their experiences in trying to run values-led businesses.

Within SVN there was a subgroup of about twelve companies that wanted to move from talk to action. The group named itself Act Now. The unifying idea was the belief that the best way to contribute to progressive social change was to take united actions as businesses.

Act Now recognized that our greatest strength was in how many customer interactions we collectively had per year. If we could tag some social or political message onto all those interactions—when people visited our shops, or received our packages, or saw our trucks driving by—we'd be using our businesses as a kind of alternative media to help change laws and policies.

We agreed that the key to Act Now's success would be for all the companies to take the same action at the same time. But first we had to agree on what that action was going to be. We went around the room and it turned out that everybody had the same ten items on their list. The problem was, they were all in different order. We couldn't agree on which action to do first.

After many meetings, in 1991 we finally decided to take on the issue of automobile fuel efficiency. There was a bill before Congress, the Bryan Bill, that would require automobile manufacturers to meet "corporate average fuel efficiency" standards—the cars and trucks they sold had to achieve an average fuel efficiency of forty miles per gallon by the year 2001. This goal was intended to reduce our country's dependence on foreign oil, and reduce pollution by reducing auto emissions.

All the participating companies—Smith & Hawken, Esprit, Rhino Entertainment, Stonyfield Farm, Seventh Generation, the Body Shop, the *Utne Reader,* Working Assets, Calvert Funds, and Ben & Jerry's— agreed to use their packaging and communications to encourage customers to send postcards to their elected officials expressing their support for the Bryan Bill. Smith & Hawken included postcards in all its outgoing mail orders. Esprit stuffed them into shopping bags. Rhino enclosed them in their CD cases.

All told, Act Now received three hundred thousand postcards. The leaders of the group, including Jerry, brought the cards to Washington, D.C., in big mail sacks. We had a press conference in East Front Room 100 of the Capitol Building. The press conference was great because we had a mix of environmental groups, businesspeople, politicians—even David Zucker, the director of *Naked Gun 2½*. The media wanted a photo, and we all looked really dumb just standing there. So they got a great action shot of us throwing the three hundred thousand post-cards up in the air. Then we picked up the cards and carried them through the halls of Congress, distributing them to the appropriate legislators.

Act Now had some level of success for a first shot. The Bryan Bill didn't pass, however, and Act Now had significantly less impact than its members had hoped for, especially considering the amount of work we'd all put into it. Act Now pretty much fizzled after its first act. But working together helped strengthen the connections between the Act Now companies, many of which ended up participating in the next action.

● Opposing the Gulf War

One lesson from Act Now was that it's less efficient to gather a group of like-minded companies for joint political action on as yet undefined issues than it is to develop an ad hoc group that's united around a particular political issue to begin with.

In 1990, when it appeared that President Bush would decide to go to war in the Persian Gulf, Ben decided to organize a group of business leaders to take out a full-page ad in the *New York Times* asking the president to find a diplomatic solution. Ben and Liz Bankowski spent a week or so telephoning and faxing a draft of the ad around to the members of Act Now and SVN, and to others they thought might share their point of view. Before the ad was published, a real effort was made to explain to the company what we were doing and why. In the end, nineteen companies signed the ad.

The unique thing about the Gulf War ad was that it wasn't signed by business leaders as individuals—it was signed by the companies themselves. For the first time, businesses took a unified stand on a social and political issue that wasn't in their own short-term self-interest. The ad was surprisingly well received; most companies that signed it reported far more positive than negative feedback from their

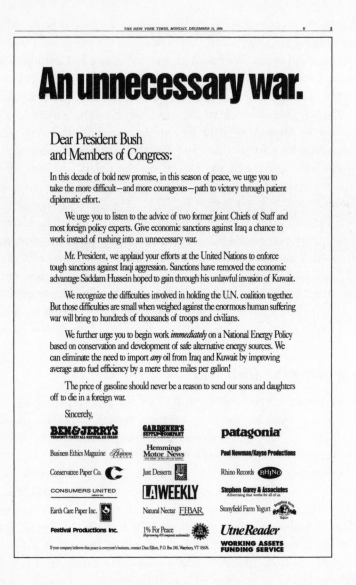

customers. The response of Ben & Jerry's customers was about nine to one in support of our participation in the ad.

● In Good Company

In the early years, before SVN was formed and we started meeting other people with a similar business philosophy, we felt like a lone voice in the wilderness. When everyone around you is telling you you're crazy, it's hard to keep on doing what you're doing.

But once Ben started going to SVN, he met businesspeople with similar values who were trying to accomplish many of the same objectives. Twice a year at SVN conferences, Ben discusses these issues with other business leaders facing many of the same challenges—including the dicey realm of taking stands on political issues.

✳   In Austin, where we're headquartered, we got further out on a political issue than we ever have before. Whole Foods was the major corporate sponsor of the Save Our Springs referendum, an initiative to save Barton Springs, a beautiful swimming hole in central Austin. We decided to do it because it was a local issue, and because we felt that, with us being in the food business, the environment is something we should take a strong stand on. We were going up against George Bush's cronies and the developers who'd bought land in central Austin. The measure passed.

We've taken a lot of heat for our role in that victory. A year after the vote Whole Foods decided to build a major new downtown store, and the developers came out big-time to try and block our permits. It took us a long time to get that building built.

But I have no regrets. We helped save a natural treasure in our hometown. The hassles we experienced because of the stand we took are insignificant compared to the customer appreciation and loyalty we gained.

—Peter Roy
President, Whole Foods Market

Judy Wicks is modest about her accomplishments, but she, her restaurant, and her company have won a long list of awards, including the Business Enterprise Trust Award, the American Jewish Congress Award, the Women in Leadership Award, the UNICEF Award for Mother-Friendly Business, and the Human Rights Award from the Philadelphia Commission on Human Relations. Judy's also on the board of the Social Ventures Network.

✳   I always joke that I'm not really in the restaurant business. What I really do is use good food to lure innocent customers into social activism. I use food as a way of bringing people together.

We take groups of customers to visit countries like Vietnam and Cuba. We call it the Eating with the Enemy Program. The idea of going to eat food in Vietnam attracts people who aren't necessarily activists, so we're not just preaching to the converted. While we're over there we visit hospitals and schools. We find out who owns the land, how it's farmed, how U.S. foreign policy affects the lives of the people—a farm-to-table review of the country. Through that perspective you can get a lot of understanding of political issues as well as the basic commonalities between people of all nations.

We also do a dinner series where we have speakers from underrepresented perspectives tell their stories. We do Tales from Jails with ex-convicts. We have senior citizens—African-American women from the South who migrated North. We have graffiti writers along with members of a neighborhood group that's organized to try and stop graffiti.

Once I put a message about military spending on the check stub: "Cut killing, fund healing, reduce military spending." I got some flak about that. I decided to take it off because I felt the customers didn't have a choice about reading it. When they paid for their meals it was almost like I was forcing them to condone my message. I thought they might feel cornered. So I changed it to "Blessed are the peacekeepers." No one can argue with that, right?

You can't please everyone in terms of the politics. I've been called a communist for some of the things I've done. But for the most part what I hear from people is that they might not believe in the same things, but they respect me for putting out my beliefs. The activist programs we do make the business more interesting, more human. That definitely draws a lot of business and gets us a lot of attention, as well as educating the people who participate.

—Judy Wicks
Owner, White Dog Café, Philadelphia

One Percent for Peace had its problems—one of which was that Ben & Jerry's was the biggest company in it. The organization was never able to attract larger, more influential businesses. But OPP led to the next step, which was Act Now; and Act Now eventually evolved into Businesses for Social Responsibility (more to come about these groups in Chapter Nine). Some of the Act Now companies are continuing their social activism in Act Now–like ways. As we're writing this, Richard Foos of Rhino Entertainment is putting together an Act Now–type collaboration among companies to put a message in their packaging that advocates redirecting money out of the military budget into social spending.

● Process and Politics

Starting with One Percent for Peace and the Peace Pops, and continuing on with his efforts to fund basic human needs by redirecting money out of the military budget, Ben was continually frustrated by what he perceived as a lack of enthusiasm within Ben & Jerry's for his political undertakings. And the people in the company were continually frustrated with what they perceived as a never-ending stream of crazy ideas from Ben.

Ben: After a lot of valiant and beyond-the-call-of-duty effort from Jerry and Liz—and some lessons I learned from the Body Shop's experiences—I finally came to understand that no matter what kind of stand the company is taking, if the people in the company don't support it, Ben & Jerry's is not going to be an effective agent for change.

Jerry: Initially there was some talk about letting the whole company decide what the social mission of the company was going to be. We considered letting everybody vote.

Ben: I was concerned that since the people in the company are a cross section of the general population, if we asked them to decide on what social actions to take, what would come out would be the political views of a cross section of the population—which was not necessarily going to move the company, or the country, away from the status quo.

We didn't know how to give the employees more ownership of the social mission. We didn't have a system for encouraging people to come up with ideas, and we didn't have a system for deciding which ideas to act on. Some people felt it was management's prerogative to make those decisions. Ben thought it was the board's.

The company finally decided that it was the board that should make decisions about which social-political stands the company was going to take. (This is one of the many reasons that it's crucial to be sure the board of directors is composed of values-aligned people.) Our activity in this regard breaks down into two categories: first, positions the board initiates and adopts in formal statements; second, various progressive campaigns that we endorse by lending them our name. So far we have acted in only a few instances in the first category to create policy statements and direction for the company. These include the opposition to the Hydro Quebec James Bay Contract, which also committed the company to energy-reduction goals; opposition to rBGH (the synthetic growth hormone given to cows to increase milk production); support for an rBGH-free label on our products; and a commitment to moving toward organically produced ingredients in our products.

More frequently we have added our names to social campaigns initiated by other progressive businesses or by various nonprofits. These can originate from people anywhere in the company, and they do. Our guidelines are that the issue needs to be within one of our broad social mission focus areas and that the practices of our company be consistent with the action we are advocating.

A good recent example was the request we received in 1996 from the Rainforest Action Network to sign a letter protesting the Mitsubishi Corporation's tree harvesting practices in the forests of the Northwest. Because our own packaging is reliant on virgin paper (by FDA standards), we felt we needed to look at that issue. We involved our director of natural resources use, Andrea Asch, and our packaging coordinator, Michael Brink, in a review of our practices and the drafting of a letter to Mitsubishi.

Anyone anywhere in the company can initiate a discussion about the company's taking a stand on an issue, but ultimately the board has the prerogative to make the decision.

In 1992, as we were putting together the year's marketing plan, we decided to ask our employees which of our issue areas they would like us to concentrate our social mission marketing around. It turned out people in the company wanted us to work on children's issues. This didn't surprise us. People are incredibly motivated to take care of kids. In a survey reported on by the Center for Defense Information, when asked to "imagine that the President and Congress decided to cut defense spending by 20%," 56 percent of respondents said they would support that move. When it was specified that the money would be directed "to improving education, fighting crime and cutting the deficit," 72 percent supported the reduction.

In response to the employees' wishes, the company decided to start working with the Children's Defense Fund. That made Ben happy, too, since CDF's mission is to take care of the needs of our poorest children by changing federal budget priorities.

CDF is located in Washington, D.C., and lobbies Congress on behalf of children. It was becoming clear that they needed a much larger grassroots support network around the country to reach members of Congress, so when they were trying to convince Congressman X to allocate money to Head Start, not only would he have the CDF staff in Washington at his door but he'd have his constituents and neighbors at home telling him the same thing and how it mattered in their community.

● The Children's Defense Fund

In Ben & Jerry's collaboration with CDF, we tried to conduct more of a coordinated campaign than we'd ever done before. We tried to integrate the needs of CDF into as many of the company's activities as possible and make the most of the particular capabilities that Ben & Jerry's brought to the table.

During the height of the budget debate in 1994, CDF very effectively created telephone trees with our customers to lobby members of the Budget Conference Committee to save important children's programs like Head Start. The staff at CDF told us they were getting calls from Capitol Hill saying, "Call your people off."

We printed an 800 number on the pints, set up Action Stations at our franchise shops, and set up an Action Station on the Waterbury plant tour. Our objective was to get forty or fifty thousand new grassroots supporters for CDF and to raise public consciousness about the plight of America's kids. We were successful, for the most part, on both fronts. We did get fifty thousand new members for CDF, and we followed up by participating in CDF's campaign to reduce gun violence.

We lost some customers over that one. The National Rifle Association people took exception to that particular campaign. They circulated our name on their boycott list. We received fifty-four letters about our stance on gun control. Fifty-one opposed it.

July 25, 1995

Dear Sirs,

    Politics and business don't mix. Sometimes, even though you love something, you have to give it up for a more important cause. This is the conclusion that I have regretfully arrived at,

after delighting on your absolutely fabulous English Toffee
Crunch "Peace Pop" *and then reading the lies being spread about
guns by your package wrapper, and by the "Children's Defense
Fund" in their "Cease Fire! Campaign."*

*The same Constitutional right that permits you to spout
anti-self-defense/anti-gun propaganda on your packages and in
the media gives me the right to vote with my wallet. As much as I
love your products, and I truly do, I choose to no longer enjoy or
recommend your products.*

> Sincerely,
> Richard B.
> New York, N.Y.

Our friends at Stonyfield Farm Yogurt did a little antigun slinging
too—and got the same reaction from the NRA, as well as some very
positive results.

＊   I was watching the news one night and I heard about yet another kid
getting caught in the street-fight cross fire. I just melted down. I went in
and lay down next to my kids and kissed them. I thought, "How can I go
on and not do something about handguns?" I knew the statistics—fifteen
kids under the age of nineteen are killed by gunfire every day. But I
thought, "What can I do? I'm a yogurt manufacturer."

I got involved with a group called Stop Handgun Violence. I went with
them instead of an antigun group—which I personally support—because
I wanted something my employees would support. We're in New Hampshire, the NRA capital of the USA.

At work I announced a meeting to discuss the idea of putting out a
million yogurt lids that said, "We support our friends at Stop Handgun
Violence. For more information call . . ." Every NRA member in the company came to the meeting. I said, "I feel that I can't not use my company
to bring attention to this issue. I want to know where I cross your line of
acceptability."

What came back was, if we okay trigger locks today, then tomorrow
we're going to say "fewer guns." We went back and forth. Finally I watered
down the message so much that the only way they could have been
against it would be to support the murder of children. It was a lower
common denominator than I wanted it to be, but it was a hell of a lot
better than not doing anything.

What we did turned out to be quite risky anyway. We put out a million lids with the gun-safety message, and we got some flak. One supermarket buyer said, "How dare you use my store as a podium?" He demanded that we fly in replacement lids, which we did.

But in the end we received countless letters of support. Stop Handgun Violence got two or three thousand calls and lots of money. And because of their and our efforts, a major billboard company in Rhode Island agreed to put up fifty billboards for free, replicating the message on our yogurt lids. They saw potential advertisers, commercial entities, rather than a bunch of activists, using a million little billboards to get out this message. It caused them to say, hey, we've got a responsibility here too.

—Gary Hirshberg
CEO and President, Stonyfield Farm Yogurt

● Pick Your Battles Wisely

One thing we've learned from taking stands on political issues is that we need to be clear from the outset about what our objectives are and whether it's possible to accomplish them.

This is a basic marketing tenet. But when we first started out we didn't apply it to our social activism. Every progressive group was trying to get Ben & Jerry's support. We attempted to do that. Finally we realized that we were watering down our ability to impact any issue. We were becoming just another one of the usual suspects.

Now we're trying to be more effective with what we do. There are a limited number of activities that a company can be involved in. As with any business decision, we want to choose efforts that aren't going to be wasted. We want to maximize our movement toward the goal.

Liz Bankowski has always said that it is important to base our involvements on what Ben & Jerry's is good at. We're not particularly good at affecting legislation when we work on our own. We've learned that in order to maximize our effectiveness we need to partner with existing advocacy organizations. When we did the campaign with CDF we tried something we thought we would be good at—communicating directly with customers, getting them signed up for CDF's citizens' army.

As a company, we've taken stands in more ways than just taking positions. We withdrew from the state Chamber of Commerce some years ago because their lobbying—which, as expected, represented business's narrow interest—was incompatible with our broader environmental and social interests. We withdrew from a local business group at our Waterbury plant when they were calling for the removal of members of the state's Environmental Board because they felt they were too pro-environment. And perhaps the hardest thing we did was remove ourselves from the International Ice Cream Association, a huge trade group, because of their advocacy for the use of rBGH. Many people in manufacturing felt there were important benefits that came from our membership in this group. No doubt there were, but we couldn't be standing against rBGH and with the International Ice Cream Association at the same time.

With the failure of the FDA to provide any national standard for an rBGH label, leaving the matter to the individual states, we've embarked on a legal strategy to bring suits in those states—Illinois, Nevada, Hawaii, and Oklahoma—where we were precluded from saying anything about rBGH on our package. Here's what we want to say on our packaging:

✳ We oppose the use of recombinant bovine growth hormone (rBGH). The family farmers who supply our milk and cream pledge not to treat their cows with rBGH. The FDA has concluded that no significant difference has been shown, and no test can now distinguish, between milk from rBGH-treated and untreated cows.

This isn't the first time we've used a legal strategy to achieve a social mission goal. A few years ago Kayne Strippe, an administrative assistant in our central support department, staffed the voter registration booth at our Vermont One World Festival. She signed up lots of new voters. After the festival she had to sort the forms by town and get them to all the town clerks. It turned out that some of them didn't get to the clerks in time, and a couple of people we registered were told they couldn't vote in the primary election. This did not strike us as fair. Needless to say Kayne was feeling really, really bad. We checked around and talked to the lawyer in the secretary of state's office. He agreed it wasn't fair, so we sued the state of Vermont, saying they were making it too hard for people to vote. The judge agreed with us.

● Why All This Focus on the Military Budget, and What Does It Have to Do with Business, Anyway?

When we think about all of the unmet human needs in our society, we realize that business alone does not have the resources to meet those needs. The real money lies in the federal budget. And for the last seventeen years, 50 percent of the discretionary federal budget has been spent on the military. This continues to be the case despite the fact that the Cold War is over and the enemy (the Soviet Union) is no more.

We believe in a strong military. We support our men and women in uniform. We believe that the United States should continue to be the most powerful military force in the world. But some significant things have changed.

In the old days, when the Cold War was going on, our government leaders used to tell us that they wanted to take care of social needs but they just couldn't because the money wasn't available after we spent it all defending ourselves from the Soviet Union.

Well, the Cold War is over. Thankfully, so too is the threat of war with the Soviet Union. But you wouldn't know it by looking at what we're still spending on defense. During the Cold War, the United States and the Soviet Union each spent about an average of $285 billion annually on the military. Russia now spends about $80 billion on defense. But—despite recently published reports on base closings—the U.S. still spends about $260 billion every year. For us, it's as though the Cold War had never ended.

Spending what we need to in order to maintain the world's strongest defense is something we support. Spending tens of billions above and beyond that is unconscionable.

This should be the golden age of America. We could be investing in our country, in our infrastructure, in our people. If we did that, we'd be breaking through the cycle of poverty with education, good nutrition, decent housing, and good health care. We'd have clean streets, a sufficient number of police, less crime. Each year we'd have fewer homeless people, and fewer people being abused at home, because we'd be investing in programs that keep people from living in desperate circumstances.

But because the United States has disinvested in our workforce, in our children, in education, in our industries, society is getting worse instead of better. And the United States is at a competitive disadvantage with the very nations—Germany and Japan—that the United States spends a total of $9.2 billion a year to defend militarily.

Those countries don't need to spend a tremendous proportion of their national budgets on defense, because they're provided for by the United States. So they can (and do) invest instead in becoming more economically competitive. They have a tremendous economic advantage because we're using our resources to defend them militarily, instead of investing in our own economic competitiveness. We're footing the bill for the military defense of our economic competitors.

Initially there was a good reason to prevent these countries from having a military buildup: so they wouldn't rearm themselves after World War II. But this strategy has continued far beyond its usefulness. Since the end of the Cold War the market for weapons has been shrinking, so weapons manufacturers are trying to create demand, as any business would. They're doing that by upping their sales effort to Congress (otherwise known as lobbying), looking for new markets, and upping their advertising efforts, which take the form of full-page ads in periodicals like *Roll Call* magazine, *The Hill,* and other publications aimed at senators and congresspeople.

Here's a good example of how this all plays out: General Dynamics (since swallowed up by Lockheed Martin) sold over $40 billion worth of F-16 fighter planes to the U.S. Air Force. Then (with our government's aid and support), the arms contractor sold over 1,700 of the same F-16s to other countries around the world. Then Lockheed Martin bid on a brand-new, improved model plane, the F-22, costing $96 billion for the whole system, and went to Congress to sell them the new generation fighter by telling them that the U.S. no longer had technological air superiority and backed it up by showing a map of the world, color-coded to indicate which of Lockheed Martin's other customers around the world—now referred to as potential trouble spots—already had last year's model.

This is just what happened when the United States sold planes to Iran in the mid-1970s.

General Dynamics was just a business operating with the same mentality as any other business. They and the other military contractors just happen to be in the business of war.

How can we look a hungry child in the face who has just come home from a disintegrating, ill-equipped school down a garbage-strewn street in a neighborhood where gunshots are an everyday occurrence, and say that we don't have the money to feed that child, repair that school, or police those streets? It's not true.

Late in 1996, the *New York Times* published a column by Bob Herbert that read, in part, "Two-thirds of the boys who reach the age of 15 in Harlem can expect to die in young or mid-adulthood—that is, before they reach the age of 65." They will die not because of the "tabloid image of gun and needle . . . think instead of severe and unrelenting stress, cardiovascular disease and cancer." These kids will die from the physical effects of living in a subhuman environment.

We as businesspeople with influence, credibility, and a voice that can be heard need to act. After Congress slashed domestic spending by $17 billion and showered the military with $10.5 billion for projects it didn't even ask for, some of us businesspeople began looking into this gulf between unmet human needs at home and actual expenditures. What we found disturbed us.

● The New Threat

Since 1948 we've had twelve aircraft-carrier battle groups to counter the Soviets on the high seas. After the fall of communism, a much heralded Bottom Up Review was undertaken by the Pentagon to redefine our post–Cold War military needs. They recommended the same twelve carriers even though there is no longer any other global navy challenging U.S. seagoing superiority.

The *Bulletin of the Atomic Scientists* reported that the Russians are lucky to field one or two missile-carrying submarines on patrol at any given time, yet the United States still is budgeted for eighty-eight attack submarines to track the shrunken Russian fleet. Keeping those aircraft-carrier battle groups and attack submarines chasing their phantom targets will cost $40 billion annually.

Our military planners now say that they need to maintain the identical force once needed to fight the Soviets in order to fight other "rogue" states. Congress has accepted the idea that now we must be able to fight two regional wars simultaneously without any help from allies. The latest assumed threats are North Korea and countries in the Middle East, each requiring the United States to single-handedly come to the rescue.

Retired air force chief of staff Merrill A. McPeak argues that "neither our historical experience nor common sense leads us to think we need to do this."

The United States and its allies spend almost $500 billion annually on "defense." The nations that are our potential adversaries, now described as "the rogue states," spend a total of $15 billion combined. Cuba spends less than $1 billion annually on its military, Iran and Iraq less than $3 billion each, Libya and Syria not even that, and North Korea barely $5 billion. We no longer are in an arms race with other aggressor nations. We are in an arms race with ourselves.

If Ben & Jerry's market competitor, Häagen-Dazs, were spending $15 billion on sales and marketing to compete with us, it would be crazy for us to spend seventeen times that to counter that commercial threat. That would be corporate malpractice for us just as it is governmental malpractice for our federal government to react so irrationally to un-identified military threats.

● Cooler Heads Could Prevail

Don't take the word of a couple of ice cream salesmen. Distinguished military planners have concluded that our national security would be more than adequate if we reduced our defense spending by $40 billion to $100 billion annually.

Lawrence Korb, who served as assistant secretary of defense under President Ronald Reagan, argued in the distinguished journal *Foreign Affairs* that "with the demise of the Soviet threat and the merging consensus on the need to deal with the deficit, one might have expected defense spending to bear some portion of the reductions, or at least not be increased." He then goes on to detail how we could trim $40 billion annually from the military budget, still leaving the United States with "the wherewithal not only to defend itself but to play the role of world leader."

Rear Admiral Eugene Carroll, Jr., U.S. Navy (ret.), said:

✳ The Cold War is over. We have no enemies capable of threatening America, its citizens, or its interests abroad. Nevertheless, we go on spending at near Cold War levels, preparing to fight World War III against nonexistent adversaries. We can safely make substantial reductions in military spending as part of the effort to balance the federal budget, and, at the same time, tailor our defense forces to address valid security requirements in the twenty-first century.

This comes from Colonel David Hackworth, U.S. Army (ret.), America's most-decorated living combat soldier and now a best-selling author:

✳ Insane spending has turned our military machine into a gadget-loaded truck with a hundred more gold-plated cylinders than it needs . . . This massive post–Cold War spending places an unacceptable burden on the American economy and saddles the nation with a military force that is far too powerful in some respects and too weak in others. The Japanese and Germans spend a fraction of their GNP defending themselves. Why shouldn't they? We do it for them while they clean our clocks on the economic front . . . Where are our priorities, especially when you consider that for the moment we have no serious enemy threatening us?

● What Could Be

Greg Speeter, author of *America's Heart and Soul,* suggests that we cut back unnecessary Pentagon spending and reinvest in our children. He calculates that we could make modest cuts in the Pentagon budget over the next five years, as proposed by Congressman Peter DeFazio (D-OR). We'd still be spending $210 billion a year, many times more than our potential adversaries. But with the money saved we could provide health care for all 10 million children who have none, remedial education and Head Start for all eligible children, four computers for every classroom in America, and have tens of billions of dollars left over to provide real job training, affordable housing, and thousands of jobs rebuilding the infrastructure. Now, that sounds like real security.

As businesspeople, we understand investment. In business, you learn that spending money to address potential problems before they crop up is a lot cheaper than trying to fix the problems later. That's why you invest in your company. If we didn't invest in our people and our infrastructure, we wouldn't have a company. And yet our country is not willing to do that.

There are business leaders, us included, who believe that our money could be better spent. We believe that the best way to protect the well-being of the United States is to redirect unnecessary money out of the military budget in order to feed, clothe, educate, heal, and shelter the people who live in our country. Some of us have joined together in Business Leaders for Sensible Priorities.

For its first public action, BLSP took out a full-page ad in the *New York Times* before the 1996 presidential election.

After running the ad, BLSP was swamped by individuals, organizations, businesses, and professional groups wanting to know more. For the first time in U.S. history, the end of a war has not been accompanied by conversion to a peacetime economy. That serves the defense contractors well—to the detriment of the rest of society.

It's time America's last sacred cow shared the burden of budget cuts.

Dear President Clinton and Senator Dole:

As the two American leaders most responsible for setting our national agenda, we strongly urge you to put the Pentagon back on the table when considering cuts in next year's budget.

Deep cuts are proposed for education, nutrition, and medical programs for poor children. But the Pentagon — which represents over half of discretionary funding — may get $14 billion *more* than was asked for by the military.

Our armed forces are by far the most powerful on earth and account for a full 40% of the world's military spending. We spend more today in inflation adjusted dollars than President Nixon spent in the 1970s at the Cold War's height.

We support a strong defense, but we are deeply troubled that America has the highest child poverty rate in the industrialized world, and the lowest per capita spending on poor children.

Building a truly strong America requires insuring children get a fair start — with adequate medical care, nutrition, and education. Our military pre-eminence abroad won't last if we fail to provide for the next generation at home. Surely, giving poor children the hope of lifting themselves out of poverty would solve many other national problems.

We urge you to take a hard look at Pentagon fat and waste.

> "*E*very gun that is made, every warship launched, every rocket fired signifies, in the final sense, a theft from those who hunger and are not fed, those who are cold and are not clothed.
>
> *This world in arms is not spending money alone.*
>
> *It is spending the sweat of its laborers, the genius of its scientists, and the hopes of its children.*"
>
> **— President Eisenhower**
> **April 16, 1953**

Former CIA Director William Colby and Reagan Defense Planner Lawrence Korb agreed we could cut $40 billion from defense — and still have the world's best military. The G.A.O. reports that Pentagon departments cannot be audited for lack of even "rudimentary bookkeeping." Conservative Senator Charles Grassley warns of "financial chaos," and the National Reconnaissance Office has discovered $4 billion in misplaced funds.

We ask you both to lead the fight to reduce this wasteful Pentagon spending that threatens America and to support programs providing every American child with a fair start.

● Does Society Exist to Serve Business—or Does Business Exist to Serve Society?

The growing gap between rich and poor makes U.S. society the most unequal of any industrialized nation. In 1980, 29.3 million Americans were living below poverty level; in 1993, the number was up to 39.3 million. In 1996, the richest one percent of Americans (with assets averaging $2.3 million) owned 39 percent of the nation's wealth. The bottom 90 percent owned just 29 percent. In addition to the most obvious reason for business to help reverse this trend—caring about the well-being of our fellow human beings—business has a lot of reasons to get involved.

Widespread poverty is bad for business. It means there are millions of people who cannot afford to buy our goods and services. As the educational system declines, there are fewer people capable of making up a high-powered workforce. We aren't giving our citizens the tools they need to earn a living.

The lack of investment in our economic infrastructure—nonmilitary research and development, job training, education—is making American business uncompetitive in the global environment. Germany and Japan spend nearly 3 percent of their gross national product on civil research and development. The United States spends only 1.9 percent.

Jerry: Some businesspeople would say it's better to have more rich people, more profitable businesses, and rich people paying smaller taxes, because that helps create more jobs. A rising tide lifts all ships, et cetera. They think that's the best way to create a better society.

Ben: I don't believe that's true. The huge proportion of wealth in this country is owned by an extremely small minority of the population. Some people believe it's fine for this trend to continue. I don't think the majority of people agree with that.

It's incredible that we still need to talk about the perceived risk to a business of taking humanistic stances when the result of doing that is anything but risky. In all these years we've alienated a very small percentage of people. Our customers love Ben & Jerry's because it stands for humanistic values, in contrast to what they regard as the narrow, self-interested behavior of typical corporations.

A business can win in the short term at the expense of society. But that is not a sustainable position. When society falls apart, business is going to fall apart as well. Alternatively, business can win in the long term along with society.

8

International Growth

Ben:　The best way to integrate social values into international expansion is to choose those countries where we can find a social-mission-driven organization to partner with us as our distributor, franchisee, or licensee.

Jerry:　You wouldn't choose based on where we'd be most profitable?

Ben:　I wouldn't enter a country if it's not going to be profitable. But I wouldn't choose based solely on which would be most profitable. We have to factor in the receptivity of the population to our values proposition and our ability to integrate a concern for the community into our day-to-day operations.

Jerry:　What about the size of the population, or the competition, or the available distribution partners?

Ben:　Yeah. All that counts, too. But our values are so tied up with our identity, it would be a huge marketing mistake not to lead with our values in other countries—unless we decided that in Europe we won't be the same Ben & Jerry's we are in the United States.

● Values-Led Growth Options

In terms of size, there are only three possible ways for a company to go. It can get bigger. It can stay the same size. Or it can get smaller.

Getting smaller isn't really a workable option. As a company decreases in size, it's no longer able to employ the same number of people, which means layoffs. And as its market share decreases, its product becomes less able to compete in the marketplace.

Staying the same size is a possibility, but if a company plans to stay the same size and falls short of its sales objectives (as so often happens), the company ends up getting smaller. Even if the internal direction is set up to maintain the business at the same size, it's impossible to control external forces to ensure that outcome.

Also, if the external marketplace is growing—as the frozen dessert market has been doing since we've been in it—and a company stays the same size, the company loses market share. If Ben & Jerry's market share dropped below a certain level, we'd no longer be a valuable partner to our retailers. Supermarkets would lose interest in putting our products on their shelves.

As a public company, we have a responsibility to our shareholders, our investors, to grow profits. We need to be increasing dividends or increasing the stock price or both.

Growing is clearly our best choice. But with a values-led company like Ben & Jerry's, our mission calls for increased value in terms of the social mission. So we need to grow in ways that increase both shareholder financial value and social value.

In the beginning, Ben & Jerry's grew very rapidly by going into new geographical markets domestically. In addition, there used to be several brands that shared the superpremium market; Ben & Jerry's grew its sales by taking market share from these other brands, as well as from its major competitor, Häagen-Dazs. We integrated values into our growth as we could.

Then, about four or five years ago, our growth began to slow. We ran out of new territories for our pint sales. Also, the superpremium frozen dessert market was pretty much reduced to two major players—Ben & Jerry's and Häagen-Dazs. So there weren't a lot of other companies from which to take market share.

At the present time, these are our options for growth: coming up with new frozen dessert products (novelties like Brownie Bars); selling more of our existing products in existing territories; coming up with new, nonfrozen dessert products; growing our ice-cream-by-the-scoop sales—by opening more franchises and selling to restaurants and other outlets that scoop ice cream; and expanding international sales.

In order to choose between these opportunities, we first must decide which factors to consider in planning how to grow. We create a matrix that includes amount of growth, amount of profitability, implications for management, investment required, synergies with our existing business. Being values-led, we consider the additional factor of social concerns.

Assuming that all of the above options would provide the necessary level of return on investment (ROI)—the amount of profit that's derived from an activity as a percentage of the money that's invested in the activity—we should make our choice based on which growth strategy yields the best combination of factors mentioned above, including the highest possible social value.

For example, if we were to increase our franchise operations, we could integrate social values by making sure that a healthy percentage of our new scoop shops are partnershops. If we were to expand our line of novelties, we could design the new products around ingredients sourced from Greyston or other alternative suppliers.

Talking about international expansion is a good way to talk about integrating our values into the growth of our company—so we'll do that here. International expansion presents a unique set of challenges. For one thing, we have different arrangements in each of the countries we're in: as licensor, as importer; as exporter. Also, different countries have different social needs, so the application of our social mission requires some translation.

● בּלידת בּן&גּ'ר'ס

Our first foray outside of the United States market was kind of an accident. In 1986 Avi Zinger, a friend of a friend of Ben's who was attached to the Israeli embassy, went to Ben and said he wanted to sell Ben & Jerry's ice cream in Israel. Without giving the matter a great deal of thought, Ben said go ahead, sell ice cream in Israel. We'd never even contemplated the possibility of selling ice cream outside the United States.

We gave Avi a license, and he set up a scoop shop in Tel Aviv in 1988. Luckily Avi knew what he was doing, even if we didn't. He now has fourteen scoop shops all over Israel. Since 1994 he's also been selling pints of Ben & Jerry's through the two Israeli supermarket chains and smaller grocery stores. He sells about $5 million worth a year and supports several children's organizations with the proceeds.

● Бен энд Джерриз Айс Крим

In 1988 Vermont Governor Madeleine Kunin invited Ben along on a delegation to the Karelian Republic in the Soviet Union, which had been designated as Vermont's sister state. The trip was a peace-through-understanding project, designed to set up business, cultural, educational, and governmental relationships between the people of the United States and the people of the Soviet Union.

On that trip, Ben met some people who were interested in opening a Ben & Jerry's scoop shop in Karelia. The idea appealed to us. We figured the best contribution we could make to ending the Cold War was to help build bonds of friendship between the Soviet and American peoples. One way to do that was to create U.S.-Soviet joint ventures.

Our scoop shop in Karelia was a social mission-driven undertaking. There was no expectation that we'd see profits. In fact, we couldn't exchange rubles for dollars, so we agreed that the profits in rubles, if there were any, would be used to fund exchange programs between the United States and the Soviet Union. Ben & Jerry's invested about $250,000 in equipment. Our hope was to be repaid for that investment, whether through barter or hard currency, at a later date.

After many adventures more bizarre than we could have imagined, we finally formed Iceverk, a joint venture between Ben & Jerry's Vermont and Karelia Ice Cream. The Karelia scoop shop, which opened on July 2, 1992, became one of the first joint Soviet-American manufacturing ventures. Although the political and business climate in the region has been extremely unstable, the Karelia shop has been quite successful. It serves over two thousand customers daily, and we've been able to organize several exchanges between American and Russian scoopers.

Recently Ben & Jerry's transferred its stock in Iceverk to the City of Petrosovosk—which allows the business to be 100 percent owned by the local community. Iceverk will continue to operate its ice cream manufacturing plant and eight scoop shops in Karelia and Moscow.

We decided to transfer our shares to the city because we found it difficult to oversee this venture due to the frenetic rate of change in Russia. Also, we felt we'd reached our goals in setting up Iceverk in the first place: local people learned to make great ice cream, and we helped foster peace through understanding and entrepreneurism—as well as providing 100 jobs that would not otherwise exist.

British Ben & Jerry's

Over the years we'd been receiving a huge number of inquiries from people in about two-thirds of the countries in the world who wanted to sell Ben & Jerry's in their countries. Except for Avi Zinger in Israel, we'd always put them off because we didn't want to set up manufacturing operations overseas, and we didn't have the capacity in this country to meet any more demand.

But as we started building our manufacturing capacity, we felt ready to respond to the demand. In 1994 we made our first deliberate effort to expand into international sales and our first effort to export ice cream overseas by opening operations in England.

Jerry: We picked England because we thought the language and cultural differences would be less of a problem.

Ben: And because when you decide to cross the Atlantic, it's one of the first countries you run into. Besides, Sainsbury's, a big English supermarket chain, really wanted us in their stores.

Jerry: As Ben always says, it's a lot easier to sell product in places where they're ready for it than trying to sell it to people who don't yet know they want it. It's a theory of yours, isn't it, Ben?

Ben: It is. I pushed for our entry into England because I was the guy who was most sick of the idea that we were getting tons of inquiries from people who were ready to sell our ice cream and we weren't taking advantage of all those opportunities.

Jerry: Coheeni can't stand to see a good opportunity go to waste.

Trying to do values-led business is different in other countries. Most of our values-led activities here in the United States, except for partnershops, occur before the point of distribution. So the only available social mission activities we can do when we export internationally are partnershops, marketing, and partnering with the distribution system.

When we went into England we were selling our ice cream, which was already made, to a distributor, who sold it to retailers. The distributor we found didn't have any particular social mission alignment. We couldn't figure out how to factor in the values. So we reverted to the fallback scenario. We insisted that the distributor donate 1 percent of his gross purchases to some socially beneficial organization in England.

> *Ben:* Why was the charge into England not values-led?
> Because Coheeni, sometimes he doesn't think. He
> knew he wanted to do it, but he couldn't figure out how
> to do it values-led.
>
> *Jerry:* It was not intuitively obvious.

Then we ran into problems with that distributor—he wasn't meeting the business objectives we'd agreed to. So we switched distributors, and in the process we lost the 1 percent donation. We do sell our product in England currently, in increasing amounts, and there's not yet much social benefit to those sales—with the exception of the flavor we're putting out in support of Comic Relief, the nationwide British fundraiser that supports development projects throughout the United Kingdom and Africa. Some donations were made also to A Place 2 Be, a nonprofit organization working with troubled children.

Here are a few highlights of what the British media had to say about us. The BBC Greater London radio said, "If Häagen-Dazs is the ice cream you have after sex, Ben & Jerry's is the ice cream you have instead of sex."

The *London Evening Standard* said, "The world is divided into two kinds of people: those who love Ben & Jerry's and those who have yet to taste it."

> *Ben:* The England experience convinced me that in order to
> maximize the social benefit in other countries we
> needed to choose values-led business partners in
> those countries. We needed to find distributors who
> wanted to use the activities associated with
> distributing our ice cream to help solve social
> problems.

● French Ben & Jerry's

At a meeting of the Social Ventures Network Europe, Ben met Jean-Marie Deberdt from the Auchan supermarket chain in France. A year or two later, an associate of Jean-Marie's called Ben and said, "We want to introduce your ice cream to France, and it's our twenty-fifth anniversary, and we want to do it now, now, now."

At the time we joined them, Auchan was supporting the Banque Alimentaire, a worldwide food bank. Our copromotion generated a donation of one franc from Ben & Jerry's and one franc from Auchan for each pint sold.

This was a positive action, but as we've said, philanthropy alone does not match our ideal of integrating the social mission into the company's day-to-day business operations. Besides generating this donation, we weren't able to take full advantage of the values alignment we shared with Auchan—in part because the people in our international department were new to the company. They'd come from traditional business environments, so they weren't used to integrating social values into their work.

At the same time we were entering France, there was an international outcry going on because France had resumed nuclear testing. Many people inside Ben & Jerry's felt we shouldn't sell our ice cream in the country for that reason. They saw it as supporting the French government.

Jerry: Ben, on the other hand, saw this as an opportunity for Ben & Jerry's to take a stand on the issue as we were entering a new market. He wanted the company to use its power, credibility, and visibility as a business to help change the French government's decision.

Ben: We could have piled up a bunch of ice cream in front of some French governmental building. We could have stickered our pints to help Greenpeace rally support to end the testing. But some people felt it would have a negative effect on our entry and on our sales.

Jerry: It was a lively debate.

Ben: I acknowledge it was a tricky situation. Here's an ice cream company from the United States introducing its product in a new country by saying that country's government is wrong.

But I think it could have been done, because the majority of the French people were against nuclear testing. It would have raised public awareness on the issue and brought public pressure to bear on the French government. It would have perfectly positioned us as a values-led company. Everybody in France would have heard of us. I think it would have sold product.

Later we did set up a sampling program with a nonprofit organization called Parene that works with troubled teenagers. Parene trained the teenagers in basic work skills. A five-restaurant chain agreed to hire two kids per location to give free samples of Ben & Jerry's to people in the restaurant as well as to people walking by on the street. Then they'd scoop ice cream to the restaurant customers if they wanted to order some. The idea was to give the young people training in social skills, communication skills, and selling skills, and at the same time meet a business need of Ben & Jerry's. The program was small in scope, but several of the young people have found permanent jobs as a result of their involvement. And it was a significant step toward establishing a Ben & Jerry's social mission in France.

Jerry's niece lives in France and was supposed to help train the teenagers, but by the time we were ready to implement the program she was unavailable. The two of us were in France for the launch, so we were recruited for the training, which we did using our high school French. We learned three phrases, and we repeated those three phrases all day, every day: *"La glace gratuite"* (free ice cream); *"Régalez-vous"* (treat yourself); *"Nous sommes les hommes de la glace"* (we are the ice cream guys).

Overall, Ben & Jerry's business in France is good. After we'd been in fifty Auchan stores for a while, we started working with three other supermarket chains. All told, our products are in more than four hundred stores throughout France.

Our plan is to expand sampling and special events next year, employing the Parene scoopers and a scoop truck we're refurbishing for the French streets.

● Benelux Ben & Jerry's

On the plane ride back from the same SVN Europe conference in 1994 where he met Jean-Marie, Ben happened to sit next to Hamilton Fish. Ham works with Human Rights Watch, an international organization that deals with human rights abuses in countries all over the world. Ben told Ham what a hard time we were having trying to figure out how to factor our social mission into our European expansion. And Ham said that HRW had just been looking for ways to get involved in some business that could raise money for their organization.

Ben said, "Why don't we make Human Rights Watch the distributor for our ice cream?" Soon after that we were contacted by Jan Ooster-wijk, a founding board member of SVN Europe, who was also the Body Shop franchisee in the Benelux countries (Belgium, the Netherlands, Luxembourg). Jan was in the process of forming a values-led venture capital group called PYMWYMIC—Put Your Money Where Your Mouth Is Company. His idea was to have PYMWYMIC invest in businesses, give a percentage of each of them to a nonprofit organization, and eventually sell the ownership to employees. PYMWYMIC would have its exit strategy, and then set up another venture.

Jan and Ben talked about giving PYMWYMIC the rights to Ben & Jerry's in the Benelux countries. We'd make HRW an equity owner, but HRW wouldn't have to pay any money for the equity. The investors in PYMWYMIC would put up 100 percent of the money to start the business, but they'd only end up with 70 percent of the equity because they'd give 30 percent to HRW.

PYMWYMIC presented us with a business plan and a person they planned to employ as manager of the business. They did this about three times. Each time there was a problem with the business plan as it was presented. The discussion got pretty drawn out. During the process the 30 percent ownership by HRW decreased to 15 percent. But finally, together, we made it happen.

The Benelux arrangement has a different structure than our other European operations. In England and France, Ben & Jerry's U.S. is responsible for distribution, sales, and marketing. In the Benelux countries, PYMWYMIC is responsible for that.

There was some concern at Ben & Jerry's that we'd still have to help them a lot, but we're seeing that PYMWYMIC is doing an excellent job holding up its end in the Benelux countries. They're an in-country entity that imports the ice cream, distributes it, markets it.

● The Challenges of International Expansion

As a result of the Benelux experience, Ben concluded that we should choose which countries in Europe we're going to go into, and when, and in what order, based on finding values-aligned partners in those countries.

Our experiences in Europe in general have taught us that there are particular challenges to doing values-led business in foreign countries. We're not manufacturing in those countries, so we have to integrate our social values into the areas of distribution and marketing.

The starting point is the same as it is for doing values-led business within the United States: put values on the screen from the word "go" and let all of your decisions flow from that.

Now we're considering expanding into Japan—the largest superpremium ice cream market outside the United States. We're learning that being values-led has a different meaning there because the government takes better care of its people than the U.S. government does. So being values-led needs to be tailored to match Japanese society, which we don't yet understand. We're looking for a Japanese partner—someone who shares our view of business and its role in society, and also knows Japanese culture.

As Ben & Jerry's has expanded beyond the boundaries of the U.S. market, we've had a steep learning curve and a lot of challenges. The greatest challenge has been figuring out how to implement our values in different countries.

We've found some models that work. One is the Benelux model, in which partial ownership in the in-country licensee is donated to a nonprofit organization. Another is the French model, where we partner on the operations level with a nonprofit organization, as we did with Parene. The third option is to open partnershops in other countries, based on the model of U.S. partnershops.

Our goal is to offer our international customers the same things we offer our U.S. customers: great ice cream, fun, and an opportunity to support their social values with their purchases.

The Future of Values-Led Business

Traditionally business is defined as an entity that produces a product or provides a service. At Ben & Jerry's we're starting to define it differently. The new definition is that business is a combination of organized human energy and money—which equals power. It's the most powerful force in the world.

* My dream for Whole Foods Market is that we can continue to grow and still remain true to our values. Some people think that's impossible. When we went from one to two stores, the number one concern was, we're going to lose what's special. Lo and behold, we pulled it off. Now we're going from sixty-nine to seventy stores, with ten thousand employees, and the naysayers are sure this will be the one that puts us over the edge.

Yet the company is still true to its vision. Which proves that what's special about Whole Foods Market, what's special about Ben & Jerry's, what's special about mission-driven business has nothing to do with size. It has everything to do with values.

Ben & Jerry's is influencing the mainstream. Stonyfield Farm is influencing the mainstream. The Body Shop is influencing the mainstream. Whole Foods Market is influencing the mainstream. Consequently, what's considered mainstream is changing quickly. Case in point: when I was growing up, organic foods were off-the-wall. Recycling was unheard of. But for my kids, organic foods and recycling are the default mode.

The socially responsible business trend is having a powerful impact. It's changing business for the better. I believe it's going to change society for the better in the process.

—Peter Roy
President, Whole Foods Market

● Values-Led Business into the Mainstream

Seven or eight years ago we were invited to a conference for the CEOs of some of the largest corporations in the United States. Kmart was there, Home Depot, UPS, the Chicago Bears, the World Bank. We were the smallest company represented. We weren't even sure why we were invited.

We discovered that the people running those big companies were wonderful, caring people. They had social values. They cared about social problems and the state of our society and the world. In their private lives, they made donations and volunteered their time to organizations that help disadvantaged people.

So the question arose in our minds: if the people running these companies are good people with caring social values, why aren't their companies helping to address social issues?

We believe the answer comes in two parts. The first is that you get only what you measure. If you're trying to lose weight, you weigh yourself fairly frequently to see how well you're doing. You might even keep track of exactly what you're eating and how much exercise you're getting. By measuring your progress, you're motivated to continue your good work or change your behavior so you can make more progress. In business the only way we measure success is by how much money we make—in other words, profit. Since that's the only measure of success and the only basis on which people are evaluated and bonuses handed out, that's the only thing that businesspeople are motivated to pursue.

After getting a chance to know some mainstream businesspeople, we've realized that many of them feel their lives are bifurcated. They see themselves as having to be cutthroat in business; then they go home and behave in a caring manner. And they don't feel particularly good about being cutthroat in business.

Which leads to the second reason that businesses don't often behave in accordance with the values of the people who run them: the compartmentalization of our lives. We live in a society in which we try to take care of our spiritual needs on the weekend, in temple, church, or mosque. We try to deal with our social concerns by donating time or money to whatever nonprofit organization knocks on the door. And we deal with our financial needs by going to work, which is where we spend most of our time.

❋   When I speak at different conferences and schools, tremendous numbers of people come up to me or write me and say, "I want my life to be driven by values, too. How can I make that happen?"

In the general public there's a sense that work as it's been defined is not fulfilling. Even when people make as much money as they'd hoped to make, they're not happy.

I think that's why this philosophy of business is growing. The alliance between for-profits and nonprofits is growing. The involvement of young people is growing. The Social Ventures Network and Business for Social Responsibility are bringing along young people, with Students for Responsible Business. The next generation of MBAs won't have the same mind-set as the previous one.

The time is right for people to be searching for a different way of addressing work and business. Maybe I'm an incurable optimist, but I believe we're going to find it.

—Judy Wicks
Owner, White Dog Café, Philadelphia

What we need to understand is that we'll never actualize the spiritual values we practice in church or temple until we integrate them into our day-to-day activities. And we'll never be able to solve the social problems we contribute money and time to until those issues are integrated into the day-to-day activities of the businesses we work for—because business is where our energy as human beings is organized in such a way that we're at our most powerful. And it's in the business world that we spend most of our time.

❋   In the business of managing time, money, and people, it's essential that spirituality be step one. Spirituality says the world is bigger than our balance sheet, bigger than the walls of Tom's of Maine. You have to be intentional about integrating spirituality with business. That's what our mission does. Our Statement of Beliefs says, "We believe that both human beings and nature have inherent worth and deserve our respect."

Setting this value out in our mission gives people in the company permission to use their whole selves—to have more than just their minds or hands on their work, but also their souls and their spirits. We try to be open to the head, heart, and the hands here. The more people are freed up to be their best selves, the easier it becomes for them to provide our customers with good products, our owners with good rates of return, and our community with a sensitive, responsible corporate partner.

✳   Companies like Ben & Jerry's and Tom's of Maine provide validation that a company can integrate broad expectations of both goodness and performance. We're helping create a new mind-set: that responsible practices and profitable practices are one and the same. It's more difficult to manage responsibly and profitably, but it's within our human means. It just takes being intentional about being good as well as being successful.

—Tom Chappell
Cofounder and CEO, Tom's of Maine

More and more mainstream businesses are realizing the responsibility that business has to give back to society—and the benefits, to business and society, of acting on that responsibility.

✳   I've been sitting in roundtables lately with the CEOs of some of the largest corporations in America. And these people spend most of their time at these luncheons asking me questions about my little $30 million business.

The fact that I'm even at the table is a statement in itself. But the fact that they're asking the questions is an even more important statement about the changing role of socially responsible companies in the business world. Mainstream corporations are recognizing that we're on to something—that it's to their competitive advantage to take the needs of people, not just their own profits, into account.

—Gary Hirshberg
CEO and President, Stonyfield Farm Yogurt

● Mobilizing the Power of Business

✳ All truth passes through three stages. First, it is ridiculed. Second, it is violently opposed. Third, it's accepted as being self-evident.

—Arthur Schopenhauer
German philosopher, 1788–1860

When we started looking for ways to integrate concern for the community into our business activities, we felt alone, out on a limb. The "experts" said we were crazy. The pundits said our business couldn't survive if we were going to focus energy on helping to solve social problems.

That's why joining the Social Venture Network, and especially meeting and talking with Anita and Gordon Roddick from the Body Shop were such wonderful experiences. Once we saw that we weren't the only ones with those crazy ideas, we realized the ideas weren't so crazy after all.

✳   When I met Ben, five years ago, I was doing a lot of social activism with my business, but I didn't really see the big picture of what I was doing. I didn't have the language for it. I sometimes doubted my own sanity. My husband used to tell me I was nuts. Every time I came into the office and said, "I have a new idea," my staff would say, "Oh no!" I was working in a vacuum.

So when Ben, who's a successful businessperson, saw the things I was doing and said, "That's great!"—and when he introduced me to SVN and other kindred spirits—I felt legitimized. It strengthened my conviction that we *can* use business to change the world

—Judy Wicks

Business is a powerful tool, but it's just that—a tool. It can be used to build or destroy. It can build walls of separatism or bonds of cooperation.

In the past ten years or so the idea of socially responsible, or mission-driven, or values-led, business has grown from an isolated phenomenon into a recognized business practice. The subject of socially responsible business and case studies of socially responsible companies are now included in college textbooks, business books, and business school classes. And since the original organization, Social Venture Network (SVN), started in 1987, there are now several organizations that are consolidating and mobilizing the power of business to make positive changes in society.

In 1992, an organization called Business for Social Responsibility was formed. BSR's stated purpose is "to help companies implement responsible business policies and practices." Today BSR is a national association with over eight hundred members and affiliates, including large companies such as AT&T, Federal Express, Hallmark, Hasbro, Levi Strauss, Polaroid, Reebok, Starbucks, and Time Warner.

BSR serves large corporations as well as small companies that are interested in exploring and adopting methods of operation that are beneficial to their employees and the community at large.

✳   On June 12, 1992, we had one hundred people jammed into a hotel room in Washington, D.C., to launch this fledgling organization with fifty-four members. Clearly the concept has hit a nerve. There's incredible momentum to find a better way to do business. Now BSR has nearly a thousand members and a staff of thirty people. We'll have a budget of over $4 million next year. Large and small, from Ben & Jerry's to Time Warner, the demand is great, and that's just on U.S. soil. Wait till we go international!

I think BSR will grow by geometric proportions every year and that as we do, the concepts it embodies will become more mainstreamed and deeply ingrained in the ethos of corporate behavior. It will increase the competition to be a better and better company, raise more and more questions, improve corporate behavior more and more.

—Helen Mills
Senior Vice President,
AON Consulting; Franchisee,
the Body Shop; Cochair,
Business for Social Responsibility

In 1993, Students for Responsible Business was formed under the auspices of SVN. SRB's mission is "to promote social responsibility among business students and alumni . . . who believe that business is not only a means to financial success, but also a powerful force to create a more just, humane and sustainable world." SRB has over five hundred members at forty business schools nationwide.

Besides SVN, BSR, and SRB, there are other business organizations that take stands on crucial issues. Business Executives for National Security is helping the Pentagon to reduce waste by becoming more cost effective and running more like a business.

The American Small Business Alliance was founded in 1996 by Joel Marks and Eric Sklar. (Eric is cofounder of the Burrito Brothers restaurant chain.) The American Small Business Alliance is a national nonprofit organization committed to investing in workers and communities as the best way to grow the business. The nonpartisan group's focus on issues like increasing the minimum wage, providing universal health care, and creating a fairer tax system has set it apart from business lobbies that seek influence in the narrow interest of their corporate members.

Business Leaders for Sensible Priorities uses the marketing and budgeting expertise of business leaders to campaign for redirecting U.S. federal budget priorities away from Cold War military-expenditure levels and toward meeting the basic human needs of our citizens. BLSP urges that the national budget meet basic human needs rather than the needs of the military-industrial-political complex.

For any businessperson who's interested in effecting social change, joining one of these organizations is an important step to take. They make it possible for like-minded businesspeople to learn from one another, work together, speak together with one voice, and wield substantially more power.

✳   Our mission is to convert Dannon and Monsanto, because that's where we're going to get a grip. To do that we have to be deeply humble. In our language and in our actions we need to acknowledge that without the entertainment industry, without the leading suppliers of agrigoods in America, without the supermarket chains, without—to use a terrible expression—the captains of industry, we won't accomplish our life's work, which is to put business in service to humanity.

—Gary Hirshberg

● You Get Only What You Measure

We've seen what happens when business measures its success solely by the financial bottom line. So at Ben & Jerry's we decided many years ago that if we changed the way we measure our success, that would help us change what we do. If we want to integrate social concerns into our day-to-day business activities, we need to measure our success in the social as well as the financial realm.

We changed our one-part bottom line to a two-part bottom line. Instead of measuring just our profitability at the end of the year, we decided to measure also how much we've helped to improve the quality of life in the communities of which we're a part. Around the same time Dave Barash, one of our managers, coined the phrase "linked prosperity," which meant that as the company grew, its financial success would benefit not only our shareholders but our employees and the community as well.

In 1985 we went to our staff and said, in effect, "We're changing the rules. Instead of having a one-part bottom line, we're going to have a two-part bottom line. We expect you, our managers, to do both things: improve the quality of life in the community and make a reasonable profit."

Jerry: People stood up and applauded.

Ben: Yeah. Then a couple of months later they started coming back to us and saying, "Hey, Ben. Hey, Jerry. This sounded like a really good idea. But we've found that when we put our energy and time and money into helping the community, it takes away from the energy and time and money we can put into increasing profits. And vice versa."

Jerry: Being reasonable people, we said, "Hmm. That sounds like a problem, all right."

We thought about this dilemma for quite a while. Then we realized that the solution was to choose those courses of action that have a positive effect on both sides of the bottom line.

When you first hear that idea it sounds impossible, airy-fairy, pie-in-the-sky. After all, we've been brought up to believe that it's impossible for a business to concern itself with social needs and still be profitable. It's been drummed into our heads that if a business concerns itself with social needs, it'll go broke. We're used to relying on nonprofits and social-service agencies to deal with social needs, and businesses to deal with money.

When Ben & Jerry's adopted the two-part bottom line we needed a way to measure both sides of it. We already had a way to measure the financial side: an audited financial statement. Just as the audited financial statement helps us manage the company in order to accomplish our financial objectives and report our progress to our shareholders, we needed a way to measure the social bottom line and report on it to our stakeholders, including the community.

As is true of our financial mission, if we don't track how well we're implementing our social mission, it's much more difficult to achieve our objectives. We need a feedback loop. We don't know if we're accomplishing our goal unless we're measuring our progress.

Measuring the social bottom line also ensures that we'll devote the same rigor to it that we devote to our financial results. It makes the social mission more of an integral part of the company and encourages people to take it seriously.

The Social Audit

Measurement is a key tool to convince boards of directors and core executives that the socially responsible company is a sound business strategy. As companies make more data from their efforts available, the story becomes more compelling. BSR data from the social investment arena shows that more dollars are coming in every day and the funds are starting to outperform the S&P. Data shows that socially responsible companies have lower human-resource costs because they have a growing group of long-term employees who are totally invested.

And now there is the social audit, which is a huge breakthrough. It's a new standards-setting tool and management document. I look forward to the day when the social audit automatically gets included in an annual report and it's unacceptable when a company doesn't do it. That day is coming. We could get there in ten years' time. And ten years is a minute increment when you look at the history of the industrialized world.

A lot of companies, including some in BSR and SVN, are trying to be socially responsible but are not comfortable with putting their flaws in the public eye. It's a scary thing to do. When you're shareholder owned, you have to think about the marketplace ramifications. Some shareholders don't want to know the dirt, because it's going to impact their share price. But if you don't get it on the table, you can't fix it. You can't improve the company.

Ben & Jerry's has laid the foundation for all of us to build from. They've challenged people. Maybe they haven't fully met their vision of where they want to be or who they hope to be, but at least they've put a marker down and said, "That's how far I'm jumping today." And then they move the marker.

Anyone who wants to get into business or is in business and wants to try and meld principles and profits has someone to learn from, because Ben & Jerry's has been so open about the things they've done right and wrong. To advocate transparency in business and for all of us to ascribe to that—that's the ultimate acid test.

I see socially responsible businesses as being at the beginning of a continuum of awareness, knowledge, and wisdom. While we're gathering data, which we didn't have before, we're gaining more tools for measurement, demonstrating that pursuing socially responsible business practices generates superior outcomes and long-term financial performance.

My dream is that in all our activities around decision making, businesspeople will start considering who is the beneficiary and who is the loser in the decision, because there is almost always someone who wins and someone who loses. I hope we'll be evaluating those choices and their ramifications with much greater care as we go forward.

—Helen Mills

When we started looking for models of how to do a social audit, we found only one. ARCO had done a report a number of years ago. The report was printed on tan paper with brown ink. You couldn't really read it. We felt that was indicative of the quandary ARCO was in about whether to publish the thing.

Ben & Jerry's first "social-performance report" was published in our 1989 annual report. The report was prepared by a volunteer committee of employees and reviewed by William Norris, founder and chairman emeritus of Control Data Corporation. We gave Bill and each successive auditor access to the information and people they needed. We agreed to publish each report in its entirety, edited only for corrections of fact. The topics Bill's report covered were

- Social Activism
- Customers and Their Needs
- Environmental Awareness
- Supplier Relationships
- Use of Financial Resources
- Financial Support for Communities
- Quality of Work Life

The report concluded:

> As employees of Ben & Jerry's, we believe that we are doing a good job of developing the social conscience of this company. Our shortcomings and failures are many. . . . We commit to celebrating our successes without self-righteousness, and facing our deficiencies without fear.

Bill Norris wrote a couple of paragraphs verifying what the employees had found.

We've done a social audit each year since 1989. The format has gone through a lot of evolution and revisions. In 1991, for example, we hired Milton Moskowitz, a pioneering reporter in the field of corporate social responsiblity and author of many books on the subject, to write the report. That year the topics were

- Nutrition and Health
- The Social-Mission Agenda
- A Dissident Voice from Waterbury
- Charitable Contributions
- The Workplace
- The Company As Big Daddy
- Equal Employment Opportunity
- Workplace Safety
- Coping with Change
- Environmental Protection
- Franchises

In Milton's summary, he wrote:

> The argument made by Nobel laureate Milton Friedman and other traditional economists is that the social responsibility of companies is to increase profits and that any programs mounted to redress social ills are nothing more than theft from the shareholders. . . .
>
> At Ben & Jerry's, though, there is no hypocrisy about social responsibility. It was always designed to be part of the fabric of the company. . . .
>
> So they are serious here about making good ice cream and helping the world become a better place, *Barron's*, *Forbes* and *Fortune* notwithstanding.

Here are excerpts from some Ben & Jerry's social audits from years past.

✳ 1990
Taking a Stand

In 1990, the company also lent its name and support to these current issues:
- Support for legislation guaranteeing workplace rights for people who test positive for the AIDS virus, and adoption of this policy in our workplace.
- A boycott of Salvadoran coffee, profits from which support a repressive regime in El Salvador.
- Support for federal legislation that would guarantee unpaid parental leave for new parents as passed by the Congress and vetoed by the Bush administration.

1991
Equal Employment Opportunity

Vermont is 98.6 percent white, and Ben & Jerry's has done nothing to change that picture. At the end of 1991, only three of its 349 employees were black. Opinions are mixed as to whether the company can make a difference here. One high-ranking Ben & Jerry's manager told me that the company's tepid approach to recruiting blacks has been disappointing, but one director said he couldn't imagine why blacks would opt to live in Vermont. However, the board of directors is about to be desegregated. Frederick A. Miller has been invited to join the board as the company's first black director, and his nomination will be presented to shareholders at the annual meeting in June.

Ben & Jerry's workforce is 40 percent female—and women have been rising in the ranks here. Three of the six senior managers (department heads) are women, and females hold five of the twelve positions on the new Quality Council.

1993
Administrative

In many areas of the company, hiring of key personnel has been slow, even nonexistent. For example, the company needed a sales director and was unable to hire one for two years. Because of this, sales leadership has been provided by a troika of officers including the president, the CFO, and Jerry. Some feel that the relatively low management salaries paid by the company, while they may be viewed as very equitable, have been an obstacle to hiring.

The Customer

Ben & Jerry's is actively committed to working with farmers to produce milk without the use of rBGH (recombinant Bovine Growth Hormone). The synthetic hormone, developed by Monsanto, can increase milk production by as much as 20 percent when injected into cows. Ben Cohen testified at FDA hearings in May 1993 against FDA approval of rBGH or, assuming FDA approval, for full disclosure to the consumer. The company's opposition to rBGH is based on concerns about its effect on the health of dairy cows and on an expected adverse impact on the economic viability of small family farms if rBGH comes into use.

1994
Community

Locally, the company is still meeting some resistance to its plans to expand its Waterbury tour site to include more amusements for visitors and children. Objections include traffic, noise, and fear of its becoming part amusement park. These objections have arisen despite the fact that the company shelved far more ambitious plans to expand the site. At present, plans to expand in Waterbury are on hold.

1995
Staff

In 1995, the effective ratio between the highest and lowest salaries was 14.5:1, excluding the value of stock options. Including options, based on Ben & Jerry's stock price at the end of 1995, the ratio was 18:1.

Suppliers

In 1995 Ben & Jerry's made purchases of $26.5 million, or roughly 26 percent of total raw material and packaging purchases, from suppliers it deemed to operate with specific social goals the company wished to support, of which approximately $21 million was from St. Albans Co-operative Creamery.

In 1992 and 1993 our social auditor was Paul Hawken, cofounder of Smith & Hawken and author of *Growing a Business* and *The Ecology of Commerce.*

✳   When I did the first Ben & Jerry's audit, I found some of the people I interviewed to be somewhat cynical. They'd had a different auditor every year and they felt that not much had come of it. There was also a certain amount of fear. By the second year people realized there'd been no retribution, so they were a lot more open. It helped that Ben and Jerry were personally so courageous about pursuing the truth. They were right there, unflinchingly supportive of the process.

Doing a social audit has a bit of a Rashomon quality to it. You hear three or four different sides of every issue. You have to pick your way through. Higher up in the organization, people are fairly voluble; they feel more secure. As you go away from top management, people are much less willing to talk.

I found nothing at Ben & Jerry's you wouldn't expect to find in a company that was growing at 40 percent a year. There were some management issues: cases where the company outgrew the person, that kind of thing. People who had a clear understanding of certain problems felt frustrated, not listened to. And there were safety problems, mostly in manufacturing.

At Ben & Jerry's I believe the audits have saved fingers and limbs and backs. They've also helped temper some of the marketing fervor— encouraged the company to understate instead of overstate their accomplishments. There were always forces in the company who urged temperance, so it wasn't just my voice speaking up on that issue. We did follow-up interviews in successive years and found that employees were quite pleased by the changes in some areas.

The social audit serves a highly constructive function. It's useful to have someone who's outside the company, but invested in the outcome, take a close look at what's going on.

The only problem with Ben & Jerry's being so public about their intentions and flaws is that other companies aren't doing the same thing. We have all these corrupt corporations that no one says "boo" to. Then someone finds a nickel in a pint of Ben & Jerry's and everyone goes ballistic. But if five hundred companies every year released their social audits at the same time, you wouldn't have this feeding frenzy in the media. You'd say, "Oh my God, isn't this amazing? Five hundred companies have been really candid."

That would improve all the companies' performances because it would lead to better understanding of what's being measured and how to measure it. That's where I hope we're heading.

I wish that somehow SVN and BSR and other companies would link arms and stand together to make the social assessment a requisite part of doing business. The first time a company does it, it's going to hurt. But it's like putting off going to the dentist—if you don't go for ten years, that doesn't keep your teeth from falling out. The social assessment is a really good corrective tool that helps develop people, criteria, and standards for each business and for business overall.

> —Paul Hawken
> Cofounder, Smith & Hawken;
> author of *Growing a Business*
> and *The Ecology of Commerce*

Internally the social audit is our best way of keeping true to our mission. When the audit identifies a problem, we have a way to see whether we're solving it. When we track the amount of energy consumed or of waste put out each year, that information is staring us in the face. If we didn't do a social audit, the issue might disappear into the vapor.

Social audits are a mix of quantitative and qualitative measurements. We can easily quantify what percentage of our ingredients are sourced in a way that adds some social benefit. We know we buy $90 million worth of raw ingredients in a year, so we can say, today 20 percent is sourced from socially beneficial entities; if it's 20 percent this year, it should be higher next year. We can quantify our environmental impacts and what percentage of our employees are people of color.

But the nonquantitative aspects are important too, because a lot of social issues—such as community relations and social impact—aren't quantitatively measurable. We can't use the level of exactitude we expect in a financial report as the standard for a social audit. Many of the important things to measure are the most difficult to measure precisely. But if we measure only that which is easily measurable, we miss the most important things.

It's like a story we heard from Ram Dass, author of several books, including *Be Here Now*, and founder of the Hanuman Foundation. There's a drunk man walking back and forth, back and forth under a streetlight at night. A guy comes up to the drunk and says, "What are you doing?"

The drunk says, "I lost my keys. Will you help me look for them?"

The guy says, "Sure," so then they're both walking back and forth looking for the keys. After a while, the guy says to the drunk, "Are you sure you dropped them here?"

The drunk says, "No. I dropped them two blocks up the street."

"Then why are you looking for them here?" the guy asks.

The drunk answers, " 'Cause this is where the light is."

When you read your financial audit, you're looking at your beauty marks and your warts. You may see that you're doing a mediocre job of controlling your ingredient costs; your cost of goods sold may have improved considerably; your balance sheet may be awful; your production costs may be increasing; the company may be overleveraged; its GS&A (general sales and administration) may be way above industry norms. The financial audit has the potential to expose at least as many negatives as a social audit.

The difference between the financial audit and the social audit is, only financial experts and businesspeople can read financial reports. Social audits are written in English. They're accessible to the general population, including consumers, which is why a lot of companies are afraid to do them. The norm up to now has been for companies to hide their social impact, because for the most part, those impacts haven't been too positive.

Ben: I happen to be very familiar with the auditing process because my father, Irving J. Cohen, spent most of his life working for the New York State Department of Audit and Control, and his life was devoted to assessing the veracity of financial statements of school districts around upstate New York.

Jerry: You know, Ben, I've always wondered: what was the *J* for?

Ben: In my father's high school there were two young boychiks named Irving Cohen. My father took the name of the high school, Jefferson High, as his middle name, in order to differentiate himself from the other young boychik.

The social audit is useful to shareholders or prospective shareholders. Theoretically those folks are reading the company's financials. If a shareholder is interested in investing her money based on social criteria as well, she should be able to read the company's social audit and make her investment decision based on being able to compare different investment opportunities.

More and more companies are doing social audits in one form or another. The Body Shop and Whole Foods Markets do social-performance reports similar to what Ben & Jerry's does. Other companies publish environmental-impact disclosures and statements of social responsibility: Patagonia, Reebok, British Airways, Volvo, Philips Electronics, Sony, Compaq, Intel, and IBM, among others.

As the social audit becomes more popular, the methodology of doing it is becoming more refined and defined. It's tricky, though, because the proper social report for one company is different from the proper social report for another.

● Taking Accurate Measurements

The way a company's degree of social responsibility should be measured is as a percentage of the potential of social benefit that company is able to provide. A $200,000 single-store operator should be measured very differently from the way a $7.8 billion corporation should be measured. Companies need to be measured differently, too, based on the industries they're in. A service company like Federal Express would be evaluated very differently than a manufacturing company.

When a huge company like the Union Pacific Corporation gives away a total of $7.3 million to charity—as it did in 1994—that's often perceived as an incredibly generous contribution. But Union Pacific's donation comes to .6 percent of its pretax earnings. If the $200,000 single-store owner made a profit of $5,000 and gave away $1,000 that would be 20 percent of profits. The single-store owner would be more socially responsible in terms of philanthropy than Union Pacific, and that's the basis on which social audits need to report. But people don't get that information in context. They say, "Wow, $7.3 million. Union Pacific is fantastic." And then they hear, "$1,000," and they say, "Oh, that company didn't do much."

Jerry: I'm not sure I agree that the purpose of social audits is to compare businesses to one another, or to themselves at different stages.

Ben: It's a tangential effect. But that's not the reason to do it.

Jerry: Right. What we're trying to let businesspeople know is that you can integrate values and still be as profitable. The social audit serves that purpose. It's a tool for a business to use to help manage itself and make values a functional part of the business.

Ben: But businesses are always watching percentages, because absolutes aren't as good an indicator of trends.

It does cost money to do a social audit. It does take more effort. And it is difficult to sit there every year in a board meeting and look at all the information we're about to publish, including the places where we fall short. Our 1996 social-performance report points out that "we have not yet established sufficient measurements of environmental performance for both on-site and off-site activities," among other things. That's a hard thing to make public. It's a bit like airing your dirty laundry.

We've been experimenting at Ben & Jerry's and finding more and more ways to integrate our financial and social missions. We've been struggling, innovating, failing, learning. Trying again, failing, learning, trying again. The social audit has helped keep us moving forward, and it's also resulted directly in improvements in the company, particularly in the area of safety.

Both Milton Moskowitz and Paul Hawken criticized the company's failure to measure its environmental impacts, which then contributed to the company's developing specific targets. This led to greater accountability. And Milton pointed out that we had a lack of focus for the social mission, which ultimately helped us consolidate our efforts around children's needs and the Children's Defense Fund.

● The Future of Ben & Jerry's

At some point in the future, Ben and Jerry will not be at Ben & Jerry's. It's a fact of life, a natural law—when we're busy pushing up daisies, if not sooner. There are a few things we look forward to seeing happen before then.

Much of Ben & Jerry's social mission-driven activity has been around the perimeters of its business. Now we need to move away from the externals, from the periphery, and get to the core—the products we make and the ways in which we make them.

● The Core Product

For Ben & Jerry's, two top priorities are the transition to organic ingredients and the transition to chlorine-free packaging and paper throughout the company. The Ben & Jerry's board authorized the transition to organics before we had a full understanding of the financial implications, and with the understanding that management would find ways to make it profitable. That's as it should be. It's a values-led decision.

The same is true of our packaging. The paper we use for our containers is a major ingredient of our core product. Since we now know that the method of producing it creates toxic by-products and we know there's a potential alternative, our values dictate that we make use of that alternative—even if it means helping to create it ourselves, since there's currently no comparable food contact package in the United States that's produced from non-chlorine-bleached stock.

We're hoping also that a higher and higher percentage of our ingredients will be what we call alternatively sourced—that is, sourced in a way that helps deal with social problems or has a positive environmental impact. We hope that more and more of our money will be invested according to social screens. And we want a higher and higher percentage of our scoop shops to be partnershops. That's a values-led innovation that works. It's tried and proven.

● When Ben & Jerry's Speaks . . .

Now that Ben & Jerry's is publicly held and does over $160 million a year in sales, the things the company does and the stands the company takes have more of an impact. When we do something new, it's taken more seriously than it was when we were a smaller player. The impact of Ben & Jerry's transitioning to organic or to chlorine-free paper is greater than when a niche health-food company does that.

Ben: I feel quite certain that Ben & Jerry's making those changes will advance the pace and lend a lot more credibility to the trend toward organic and chlorine-free—

Jerry: If we can pull it off.

Ben: —just as it advances the pace when businesses join together to promote redirecting national priorities.

A factor we need to consider in pushing forward with our social mission is that our growth has slowed. We're in a much more competitive marketplace than we were in when we were a small player. We're a publicly held company that has not offered great financial returns for its shareholders in the recent past. Consequently there's a lot of questioning in the external world about whether the time has finally come when Ben & Jerry's has to abandon its values, as the cynics always said we would.

When we're under financial pressure as we are now, taking bold, values-led steps, like switching to organics and chlorine-free paper, has greater meaning. We're not in our earlier days of meteoric growth, when we could do anything willy-nilly and not worry about the implications.

Our former president Chuck Lacy used to say that people looked at

Ben & Jerry's and thought, "That's a company that is just lucky. They don't know what they are doing. It's either a fluke or a fake." As we've hit these difficult business conditions, outside people keep suggesting that Ben & Jerry's needs to become more businesslike and give up its so-called extraneous activities. The implication, of course, is that being values-led is what leads to being in a noncompetitive position.

But our experience has shown that being values-led is actually a tremendous competitive advantage. It has contributed greatly to our financial success. Eliminating our values-led activities would make us less, not more, profitable. Ben & Jerry's customers, shareholders, investors, and employees have made it abundantly clear that the values we share are a big part of the connection they feel to the company.

The fact is, Ben & Jerry's is at a crossroads—but it's an issue of business processes, not a crisis of values. Within the company we know that what's making competing difficult for us is the way we're structured and managed. The problem is not with the values we hold. And the company has done a better job this past year of integrating social concerns into the annual planning process than it's ever done in the past.

● In Conclusion, Let Us Say . . .

We were born in 1951. We remember going to elementary school and learning about the threat of the Russians, crouching under our desks during air raid drills. We went to sleep at night thinking about the Russians bombing us. Then a huge military buildup and the demise of the Soviet Union made the United States the world's last remaining superpower. (That buildup resulted also in the accumulation of incredible debt, which our grandchildren will be paying for.)

But now the Cold War is over. Our enemies have vanished. We no longer have to borrow and spend like crazy to fund the military at Cold War levels. We currently have 25 percent of our children living in poverty. For $62 billion—less than 25 percent of the military budget—we could lift every one of those children out of poverty and create more than a million family-supporting jobs. We could fully fund Head Start, which saves $5 dollars for every dollar spent and still be the most powerful military force in the world. That's just a good business investment.

We are capitalists. The American economy has been very, very good to us. We lead good lives and we are grateful. We believe in a strong

America. But we also believe in an America that meets the needs of its people.

Our country—the last remaining superpower on earth—needs to learn to measure its strength not by the number of people it can kill but by the number of people it can feed, clothe, house, and care for. We believe business has a responsibility to help accomplish that.

✳   There are lots of reasons why business has to address problems that in the past were not its concern. If companies are going to be highly productive—especially in this part of the world, where labor costs tend to be higher—they need to have a skilled, committed workforce that can offset the labor cost differential with productivity gains.

I think business as a whole has every reason to end up being values-driven, although it may not be defined in those terms. In the future, what we now call "values-driven" may simply be called "well run"; that is, responsive to the company's various constituencies.

Consumers now play a critical role. They're more discriminating. They voice their approval and disapproval by the way they purchase products. Studies have shown that 70 percent of all consumers would prefer buying from a company they perceive to be socially responsible; an even larger percentage would avoid buying from companies that have a reputation for being insensitive—like those led by "Chainsaw Al" Dunlap. The changing role of consumers will help to sensitize the leadership of companies to this broader perspective. They can't afford to be indifferent to concerns that in the past they had no need to be aware of.

—Arnold Hiatt
Chairman, Stride Rite Foundation;
Former CEO/President/Chairman,
Stride Rite Corporation

Martin Luther King said:

✳ The stability of the large world house, which is ours, will involve a revolution of values to accompany the scientific and freedom revolutions engulfing the earth. We must rapidly shift from the thing-oriented society to a person-oriented society. When machines and computers, profit motives, and property rights are considered more important than people, the giant triplets of racism, materialism, and militarism are incapable of being conquered. A civilization can flounder as readily in the face of moral and spiritual bankruptcy as it can through financial bankruptcy.

Lily Tomlin said, "The problem with being in the rat race is, even if you win, you're still a rat."

Like a civilization, business, too, can flounder when it's spiritually bankrupt. What we continue to learn at Ben & Jerry's is that there's a spiritual aspect to business, just as there is to the lives of individuals. We're all interconnected. As we give we receive. As we help others we're helped in return. For people, for business, for nations, it's all the same.

✳   A man is granted permission to see both heaven and hell while he is still alive. First he goes to visit hell. He goes down, opens up this big door, and sees a huge banquet hall. There's a long table in the center of the room, with people seated on both sides. The table is laden with every imaginable delicacy: crispy roast suckling pig, apricot-glazed goose, candied yams, butter-drenched green beans, piping-hot bread spread with fragrant jam, warm pies topped with Ben & Jerry's ice cream. As he's looking at this scene the man sees that the people seated at the table are crying and wailing and in terrible pain. He looks a little closer and sees that the utensils the people have to eat with have such long handles that it's impossible for them to get the food into their mouths.

Depressed, with heavy heart, the man goes to visit heaven. He opens the door and sees virtually the same huge banquet room—the same long table covered with the same delicious food, and people sitting on both sides of the table with the same long-handled utensils.

But instead of crying in pain and hunger, these people are laughing, singing, and rejoicing. The man looks closer and sees that the people in heaven, instead of trying to feed only themselves, are feeding one another.

—Ancient Eastern parable

Appendix A
The Social Performance
Report

The 1996 social performance report for Ben & Jerry's is being written as this book goes to press, so we can't include it here. What follows is a hypothetical report for a diversified food and beverage manufacturer, Tastes Good, Inc., intended to show the range of issues that such a report might include. The issues are real; the data in this model report are not.

As much as possible, the data are presented in relation to the output of the fictitious company. Of course, inputs and outputs will increase as the scale of the enterprise grows. But just presenting raw numbers would give no information about the company's relative success or failure in addressing social issues. For example, a raw number like 2 billion BTUs of energy used for a given year may have little meaning to most readers. By presenting such data as a function of the pounds of food produced, the company can measure its efforts against a meaningful constant over time.

Also, wherever possible, the data are compared with external benchmarks, like industry standards or other comparable companies, in order to give a frame of reference for the company's performance. Those issues that can be presented only in narrative are described that way.

• Review of Past Issues

We begin with an assessment of how the company addressed issues raised in previous social-performance reports.

In 1994, the report described the company's wastewater treatment plant as being out of compliance with the discharge permit on thirteen occasions. After a two-year project costing $314,000, the situation is remedied. The company had no violations of its discharge permit in 1996.

In 1992, the board's ethnic composition was noted as 92 percent white. Efforts since then to recruit a more diverse board have resulted in a current ethnic makeup of 67 percent white, 16 percent African-American, 8 percent Asian, and 8 percent Latino—all with significant experience in business and nonprofit organizations committed to social change.

The reports from 1991 through 1995 repeatedly revealed no clear career-growth program for employees to enhance their job skills and for promotion within the company. No such plan was begun in 1996.

Production

SOLID WASTE

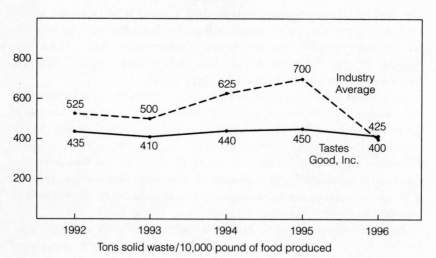

Tons solid waste/10,000 pound of food produced

ENERGY USED

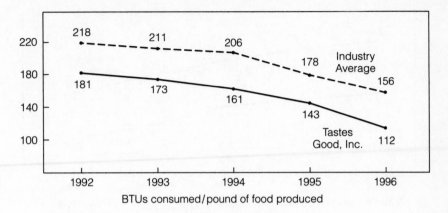

BTUs consumed/pound of food produced

WASTEWATER STRENGTH

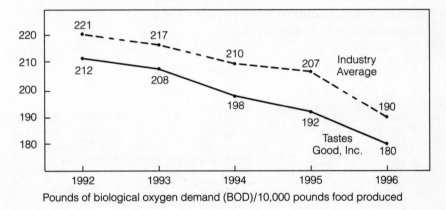

Pounds of biological oxygen demand (BOD)/10,000 pounds food produced

CLEANING CHEMICALS

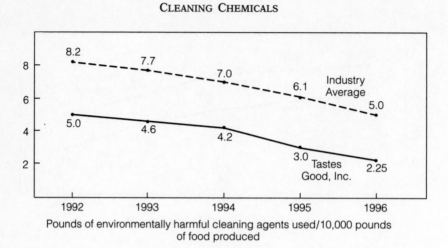

Pounds of environmentally harmful cleaning agents used/10,000 pounds
of food produced

The company uses environmentally benign cleaning agents (like baking soda)
wherever possible. Measured above are those chemicals which are not biode-
gradable or otherwise benign to nature.

TRANSPORTATION ENERGY

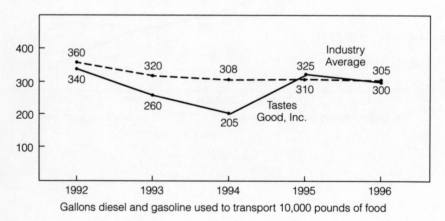

Gallons diesel and gasoline used to transport 10,000 pounds of food

SOCIALLY BENEFICIAL SUPPLIERS

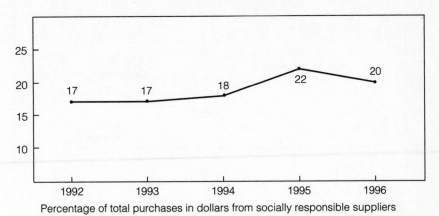

Percentage of total purchases in dollars from socially responsible suppliers

The company buys all its milk from a cooperative creamery, owned by family farmers, which has committed to forbidding the use of bovine growth hormone (rBGH) by its member farmers. The pastries used in our products come from a bakery that hires disadvantaged people and provides them job and life skills. Vanilla extract is purchased from Mexican cooperatives, which allows farmers to get more money for their beans.

WOMAN/MINORITY-OWNED VENDORS

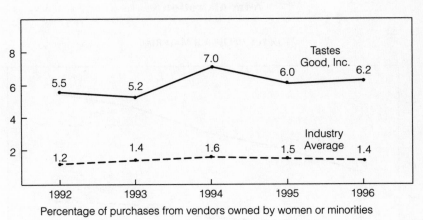

Percentage of purchases from vendors owned by women or minorities

ORGANIC INGREDIENTS

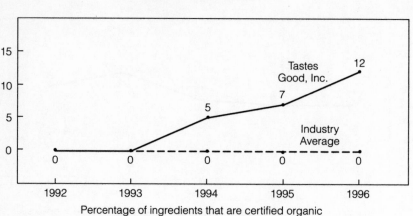

Percentage of ingredients that are certified organic

TAMPER-EVIDENT PACKAGING

Even though a design exists for tamper-evident packaging that would use no additional material, the company has chosen the industry standard, which is a thin film of plastic covering the product inside the pint lid. This choice has required the use of 4,500 pounds of nonrecyclable plastic for the first year of implementation, 1996.

Administration

RECYCLED OFFICE MATERIAL

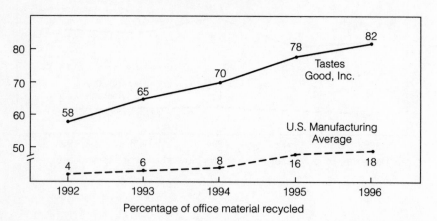

Percentage of office material recycled

RECYCLED CONTENT

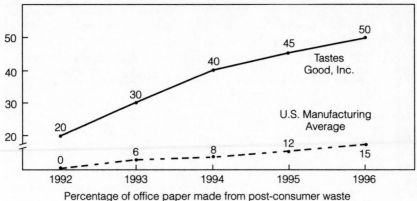

Percentage of office paper made from post-consumer waste

CHLORINE-FREE PAPER/PACKAGING

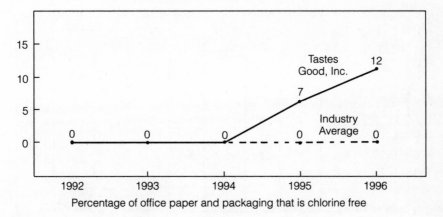

Percentage of office paper and packaging that is chlorine free

• Human Resources

Companies increasingly are hiring temporary workers to reduce the amount of benefits they pay employees. Tracking the use of temps can reveal if this is occurring in Tastes Good, Inc.

WORKER SAFETY

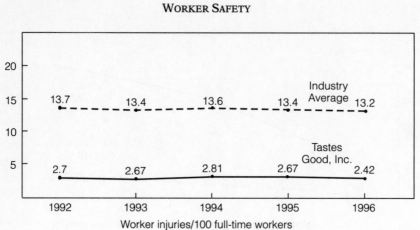

Worker injuries/100 full-time workers

TEMPORARY WORKERS

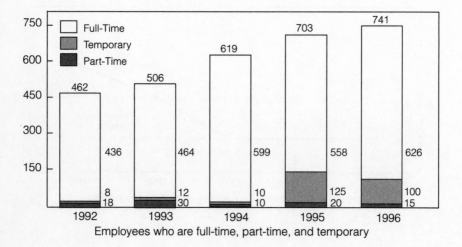

Employees who are full-time, part-time, and temporary

GENDER MIX

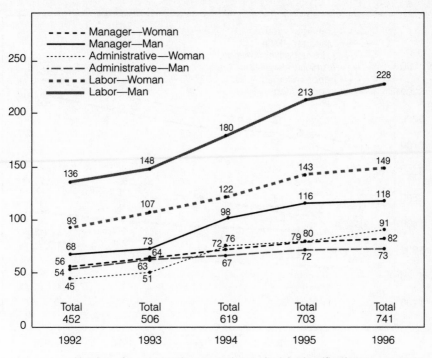

Number of women and men employees by job classification

ETHNIC MIX

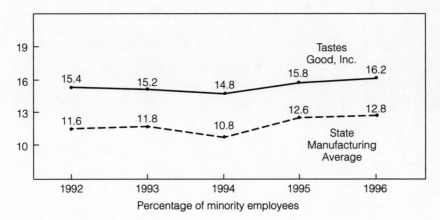

Percentage of minority employees

GENDER PAY EQUITY

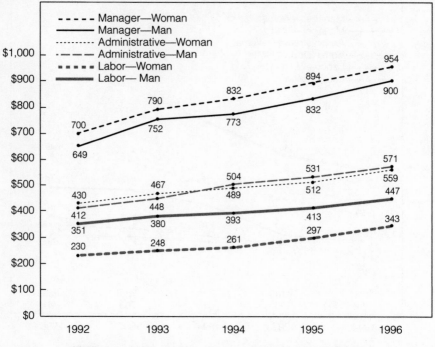

Median weekly income for women and men by job classification

PAY AND BENEFITS

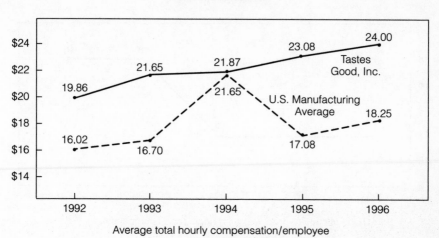

Average total hourly compensation/employee

To treat employees with respect and value, the company had relied on paying workers more than their counterparts in the industry or in the local community. But we realized that an arbitrary marginal increase over the norm did not necessarily guarantee that workers could live on that wage. So we sought to calculate a livable wage, what an average person living in our community needed to earn to adequately fund his or her life (rent, utilities, health and dental care, transportation, nutrition, recreation, and savings). For 1995, that came to $8.42/hour for a single person, so we pegged our entry-level wage at $8.50 and recalculated the pay scale above that accordingly.

PAY RATIO

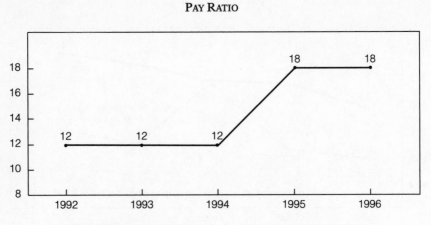

Ratio of highest- to lowest-paid (includes all compensation)

EMPLOYEE STOCK OWNERSHIP

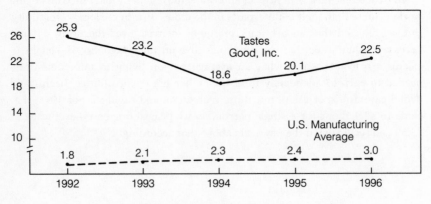

Percentage of company employees who own stock

EMPLOYEE WORK LIFE SURVEY

Beginning in 1992, the company surveyed employees to understand their views about the company so these views could be compared over time. These are highlights of those surveys, in percentage of company respondents who *agreed* with the statements. Industry benchmark comparisons follow the slash.

	1992	1994	1996
Company effectively meets social responsibilities	90/NA	88/NA	92/NA
Company treats people with dignity and respect	73/41	66/38	69/33
Company respects home and family responsibilities	72/38	66/36	58/32
Employee satisfied with pay and benefits	64/40	76/31	78/28
Employee satisfied with job security	75/62	80/55	85/47
Employee satisfied overall with job	80/67	82/62	85/58

EMPLOYEE BENEFITS

Health coverage	Free to employee, subsidized to partner/family
Dental coverage	Free to employee, subsidized to partner/family
Life insurance	Free at two times annual salary, additional available at cost
Disability insurance	Free short- and long-term coverage
Family leave	Two weeks paid for mother or father employees
Retirement plan	Company matches 50 percent of employee's contribution
Education	Company will reimburse for job-related or degree courses
Vacation	Two weeks for up to five years' service; three weeks for five to ten years' service; four weeks thereafter
Sick time	Six paid days/year
Domestic partner	Health, dental, life insurance, and family leave available for domestic partners no matter marital status or gender

CODE OF CONDUCT

The company does not have a code of conduct to address office demeanor, conflicts of interest, or acceptance of gifts from vendors.

• Finance

The company typically maintains cash reserves in the tens of millions of dollars, invested short-term. None of the company's money is invested in banks, corporate or government bonds, or other financial instruments that promote tobacco, nuclear power, oil exploration, military contractors, jails or prisons, or resource exploitation. This policy provides what is known as negative screens. Positive screens involve our search for investments that promote values we support,

such as affordable housing, education, environmental restoration, and job training, or other socially responsible businesses.

SOCIALLY RESPONSIBLE INVESTMENTS

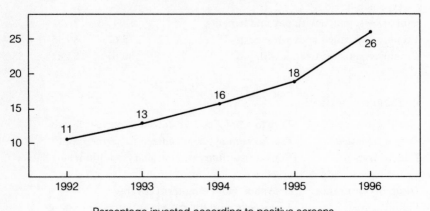

Percentage invested according to positive screens

Retail Operations

FRANCHISES OWNED BY NONPROFIT ORGANIZATIONS

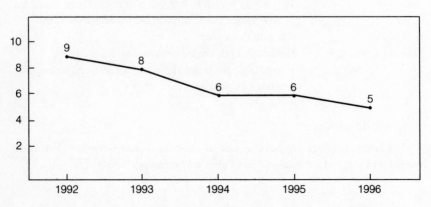

Percentage of franchises that are community-sponsored franchises owned
by nonprofit organizations

FRANCHISES OWNED BY NONPROFIT ORGANIZATIONS CLOSED

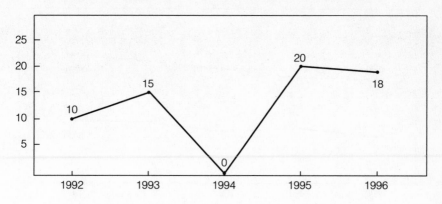

Percentage of franchises owned by nonprofit organizations that failed

FRANCHISES OWNED BY NONPROFIT ORGANIZATIONS BENEFITS

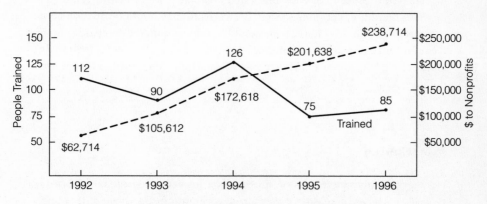

People trained and employed, dollars earned by nonprofits

FRANCHISE OWNERSHIP BY WOMEN AND MINORITIES

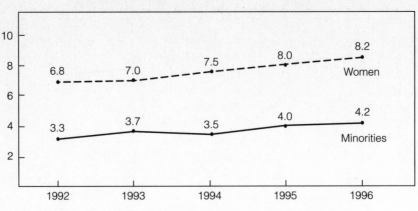

Percentage of franchises woman- or minority-owned

The company makes social action campaigns available to its franchisees, who are welcome to participate in the efforts at the store level. Typically, signage promotes the cause and leads interested customers to an action center that provides literature, petitions to sign, postcards to mail, and information about volunteer opportunities in the community consistent with the campaign. Examples of recent campaigns include Cease Fire, to reduce gun violence; It Shouldn't Hurt to Be a Kid, to prevent child abuse; Clean Our Community, to reduce toxic pollution of neighborhoods.

• Marketing

How a company markets its products tells a lot about its values. Advertising typically enriches increasingly centralized corporations that have little connection to communities or their social values. We've chosen to avoid those channels, instead focusing on marketing efforts that add value to people's lives. For example, the company produces a series of outdoor festivals around the country, typically attended by forty thousand people each, for a free day of live music and information, with volunteer-recruitment booths from nonprofit organizations. Lots of food is given away. We have a traveling bus that creates a minifestival in communities, with a portable music stage, scooping equipment, and booths.

Packaging is used to promote ideas and sell product at the same time. Our snack bar is called KidsBars, with packaging that educates the consumer about congressional underfunding of programs that help kids stay healthy, learn, and grow into responsible adults. Programs like Head Start have been shown to save billions by preventing delinquency and encouraging learning, but it and others have been slashed to fund other budget items supported by influential lobbyists. The KidsBars wrapper encourages customers to write their congress members to ask for a shift in budget priorities, and informs them that 5 percent of the purchase price will be donated to organizations seeking such a humane budget. This campaign both promotes an idea and serves to differentiate the product in the marketplace—yielding a very loyal customer base that appreciates the social mission. Other socially responsible methods of distribution can draw attention to our products as well. For example, we maintain seventeen solar-powered carts from which snack bar samples are given away free. People see the solar panels with our colorful logo and stop to investigate. They are served a sample of free snack bars. This is a way to recruit new customers while promoting alternative-energy use.

• Social Activism

The same skills and resources that the company brings to bear to sell its product can be used to promote an issue campaign. While cause-related marketing can help sell product, social activism is not intended to sell food but to promote a cause.

One such campaign is the company's support for political reform. During the 1996 elections, over $2 billion was raised by federal candidates from special interests who typically want some government action in return. This pay for play system alienates the average citizen whose only resource, his or her vote, is drowned by money that drives our political process. But expecting those who have succeeded within the system to reform it is foolhardy. Instead, political reform is bubbling up from the grassroots in local communities and at the state level. The company has used its packaging to educate customers on the issues, and through an 800 number allowed them to request information about their representatives' campaign donors and votes while providing customers with an avenue to get active in reform efforts in their own communites.

Philanthropy

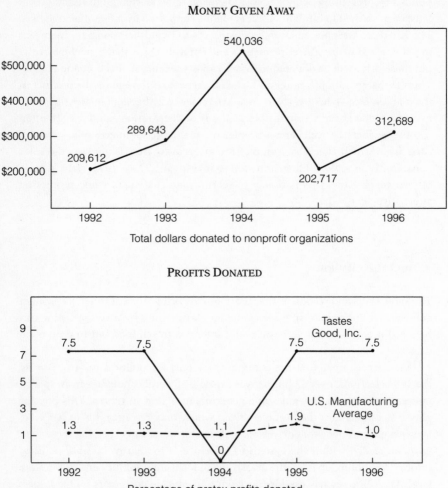

MONEY GIVEN AWAY

Total dollars donated to nonprofit organizations

PROFITS DONATED

Percentage of pretax profits donated

Examples of nonprofit organizations that have received company funding are Citizens' Clearinghouse for Hazardous Waste, to assist building local community organizations to fight for environmental justice; Healing Our Mother Earth (HOME), which organizes community members in the cancer-cluster town of McFarland, California, to protect them from local health risks; Center for Better Living, which assists homeless and formerly homeless residents to develop business opportunities for personal and community growth.

Appendix B
Resource Guide

- **Organizations That Promote Sustainable Business Practices**

American Small Business Alliance
3421½ M St. N.W.
Washington, DC 20007
(202) 337-0037

The Business Enterprise Trust
204 Junipero Serra Blvd.
Stanford, CA 94305
www.betrust.org
(415) 321-5100

Business for Social Responsibility

National offices:
    1030 15th St. N.W.,
       Suite 1010
    Washington, DC 20005
    (202) 842-5400

    1683 Folsom St.
    San Francisco, CA 94103
    (415) 865-2500
    www.bsr.org

Regional offices:
Arizona
    Dorice Exline
    Blue Wolf Marketing
       Communications Inc.
    4690 W. Tulsa St.
    Chandler, AZ 85226
    (602) 940-7627

Southern California
Jessica Laufer
Laufer Associates
12100 Wilshire Blvd.,
    19th Floor
Los Angeles, CA 90025
(310) 826-8826
Laufer@primenet.com

Bay Area
Tom Flynn
Tom Flynn, Inc.
10 Willow Ave.
Larkspur, CA 94939
(415) 924-8050

Colorado
Katherine Ott
Marketing Works
2845 Wilderness Pl., Suite 200
Boulder, CO 80301
(303) 413-5050
jkott@ix.netcom.com

District of Columbia
Mary Fehlig
The Fehlig Group
2 Pueblo Court
Gaithersburg, MD 20878
(301) 948-6978
fehlig@mail.erols.com

Massachusetts/Boston Area
Laury Hammel
The Longfellow Group
524 Boston Post Rd.
Wayland, MA 01778
(508) 358-7355

Connecticut River Valley
Dan McKenna
Principle Profits Asset
    Management
P.O. Box 2323
Amherst, MA 01002
(413) 256-1528
ppam@prdigy.com

Maine
295 Forest Ave., Suite 972
Portland, ME 04101
(207) 761-4300

Upper Midwest
Danie Watson
The Watson Group
339 Barry Ave. So.
Wayzata, MN 55391
(612) 472-2230
dwatson@millcomm.com

New Hampshire
Lindsay Shearer
Healthsource New Hampshire
54 Regional Dr.
Concord, NH 03301
(603) 229-2186
jlshearer@aol.com

Northwest
Kristin DeVoe
P.S.U. School of Business
P.O. Box 751
Portland, OR 97207
(503) 725-3000
kristind.sba.pdx.edu

Philadelphia
John O'Donnell
Renewable Energy
  Development Corp.
223 Chesire Circle
West Chester, PA 19380
(610) 940-1994
Odonnelljp@aol.com

Vermont
Jane Campbell
Vermont Businesses for
  Social Responsibility
30 Community Dr.
So. Burlington, VT 05452
(802) 862-8347
VBSR@together.org

**Business Leaders for
  Sensible Priorities (BLSP)**
885 2nd Ave., 7th FL
New York, NY 10017
(212) 207-9237

**Canadian Centre for Ethics &
  Corporate Policy**
50 Baldwin St.
Toronto, ON M5T 1L4
(416) 348-8689

Caux Round Table
1156 15th St. N.W., Suite 910
Washington, DC 20005-1704
(202) 872-9007

**Center for Ethics,
  Responsibilities, and
  Values**
College of St. Catherine
2004 Randolph Ave.
St. Paul, MN 55105
(612) 690-6646

**Coalition for
Environmentally
  Responsible Economies
  (CERES)**
711 Atlantic Ave., 5th Floor
Boston, MA 02111
(617) 451-0927

**Council on Economic
  Priorities (CEP)**
30 Irving Pl.
New York, NY 10003
(212) 420-1133
http://www.2.realaudio.
  com/CEP

Healthy Companies
1420 16th St. N.W.
Washington, DC 20036
(202) 234-9288

**Interfaith Center on
  Corporate Responsibility**
475 Riverside Dr., Rm. 566
New York, NY 10115
(212) 870-2293

**Minnesota Center for
  Corporate Responsibility**
1000 LaSalle Ave.
Minneapolis, MN 55403-2005
(612) 962-4120

**National Institute for a New
  Corporate Vision**
Box 523
Mansfield Center, CT 06250
(860) 456-1153

New Careers Center
1515 23 St.
Box 339 Ct.
Boulder, CO 80306
(303) 447-1087

New Consumer Institute
700 No. Milwaukee Ave.,
Suite 204
Vernon Hills, IL 60061
(708) 816-0306

The Rocky Mountain
   Institute
1739 Snowmass Creek Rd.
Old Snowmass, CO 81654
(303) 927-3851
www.rmi.org

Social Banking Programs,
   Inc.
14 Elliot St.
Brattleboro, VT 05301

Social Ventures Network
1388 Sutter St., Suite 1010
San Francisco, CA 94109
(415) 561-6501
www.svn.org

Students for Responsible
   Business
P.O. Box 29221
San Francisco, CA
   94129-0221
(415) 561-6510
www.srbnet.org

• Books

CAREER DEVELOPMENT

Everett, Melissa. *Making a Living While Making a Difference*. Bantam Books, 1995.

Jankowski, Katherine. *The Job Seeker's Guide to Socially Responsible Companies*. Gale Research, 1994.

Levering, Robert, and Milton Moskowitz. *The 100 Best Companies to Work for in America*. Currency, 1993.

Lydenberg, Steven, Alice Tepper Marlin, Sean O'Brien Strub, and Council on Economics Priorities. *Rating America's Corporate Conscience*. Addison-Wesley, 1986.

Morgan, Hal, and Kerry Tucker. *Companies That Care: The Most Family-Friendly Companies in America—What They Offer, and How They Got That Way*. Fireside, 1991.

Moskowitz, Milton, Robert Levering, and Michael Katz. *Everybody's Business: A Field Guide to the 400 Leading Companies in America*. Doubleday Currency, 1990.

Nader, Ralph, and Donna Colvin (editors). *Good Works: A Guide to Careers in Social Change*. Barricade Books, 1994.

O'Neil, John. *The Paradox of Success*. Jeremy P. Tarcher, 1994.

Sinetar, Marsha. *Do What You Love, the Money Will Follow*. Dell, 1987.

ECONOMICS

Breton, Denise, and Christopher Largent. *The Soul of Economics: Spiritual Revolution Goes to the Marketplace.* Idea House Publishing Company, 1991.

Heilbroner, Robert L., and Lester C. Thurow. *Economics Explained.* Simon & Schuster, 1987.

Henderson, Hazel. *Paradigms in Progress: Life Beyond Economics.* Knowledge Systems, Inc., 1991.

Meeker-Lowry, Susan. *Economics As If the Earth Really Mattered.* New Society, 1988.

Zelizer, Viviana A. *The Social Meaning of Money.* Basic Books, 1994.

ENVIRONMENT/SUSTAINABILITY

Ashworth, William. *The Economics of Nature: Rethinking the Connections Between Ecology and Economics.* Houghton Mifflin, 1995.

Ausubel, Kenny. *Seeds of Change: The Living Treasure. The Passionate Story of the Movement to Restore Biodiversity and Revolutionize the Way We Think About Food.* HarperSanFrancisco, 1994.

Brown, Lester. *Building a Sustainable Society.* W. W. Norton, 1981.

Ernest Callenbach, et al. *Eco-management: The Elmwood Guide to Ecological Auditing and Sustainable Business.* Berrett-Koehler, 1993.

The Earthworks Group. *50 Simple Things Your Business Can Do to Save the Earth.* EarthWorks Press, 1991.

Hawken, Paul. *The Ecology of Commerce: A Declaration of Sustainability.* Harper Business, 1993.

Hollister, Benjamin, et al. *Shopping for a Better World.* Sierra Club Books, 1994.

Makower, Joel. *The E Factor: The Bottom Line Approach to Environmentally Responsible Business.* Times Books, 1993.

———. *The Green Consumer.* Penguin Books, 1993.

Meeker-Lowry, Susan. *Economics As If the Earth Really Mattered.* New Society, 1988.

INVESTING

Alperson, Myra, Alice Tepper Marlin, et al. *The Better World Investment Guide.* Prentice-Hall, 1991.

Brill, Jack A., and Alan Reder. *Investing from the Heart.* Crown Publishers, 1992.

The Council on Economic Priorities. *The Better World Investment Guide.* Sierra Club Books, 1994.

Domini, Amy, and Peter Kinder. *Ethical Investing.* Addison-Wesley, 1986.

Harrington, John C. *Investing with Your Conscience.* John Wiley & Sons, 1992.

Judd, Elizabeth. *Investing with a Social Conscience.* Pharos Books, 1990.

Kinder, Peter D., et al. *The Social Investment Almanac.* Henry Holt, 1995.

Kinder, Peter, Steven D. Lydenberg, and Amy L. Domini. *Investing for Good: Making Money While Being Socially Responsible.* Harper Business, 1993.

Lowry, Richie P. *Good Money: A Guide to Profitable Social Investing in the '90s.* W. W. Norton, 1991.

Meeker-Lowry, Susan. *Invested in the Common Good.* New Society Publishers, 1995.

Miller, Alan J. *Socially Responsible Investing.* New York Institute of Finance/ Simon & Schuster, 1991.

Rosenberger, Jr., Claude. *Wealthy and Wise: How America Can Get the Most Out of Your Giving.* Little, Brown and Company, 1994.

Zelizer, Viviana A. *The Social Meaning of Money.* Basic Books, 1994.

SOCIALLY RESPONSIBLE BUSINESS

Block, Peter. *Stewardship: Choosing Service Over Self-Interest.* Berret Koehler, 1993.

Carson, Patrick, and Julia Moulden. *Green is Gold: Business Talking to Business About the Environmental Revolution.* Harper Business, 1991.

Chappell, Tom. *The Soul of a Business: Managing for Profit and the Common Good.* Bantam, 1993.

Collins, James, and Jerry Porras. *Built to Last: Successful Habits of Visionary Companies.* HarperCollins, 1994.

Donaldson, John. *Key Issues in Business Ethics.* Academic Press, 1989.

EarthEnterprise. *Tool Kit: Markets, Financing, Technology, New Business Practices.* International Institute for Sustainable Development, 1994.

Freudberg, David. *The Corporate Conscience: Money, Power, and Responsible Business.* Amacon, 1986.

Garfield, Charles. *Second to None: How the Smartest Companies Put People First.* Business One Irwin, 1992.

Huselid, Mark. *Human Resource Management Practices and Firm Performance.* Rutgers University, 1993.

Lager, Fred "Chico." *Ben & Jerry's: The Inside Scoop. How Two Real Guys Built a Business with a Social Conscience and a Sense of Humor.* Crown Publishing Group, 1995.

Leibig, James. *Business Ethics: Profiles in Civic Virtue.* Fulcrum Publishing, 1991.

Lydenberg, Steven, Alice Tepper Marlin, Sean O'Brien Strub, and Council on Economic Priorities. *Rating America's Corporate Conscience.* Addison-Wesley, 1986.

McGuire, Jean, et al. *Corporate Social Responsibility and Firm Financial Performance.* University of Massachusetts.

Makower, Joel. *Beyond the Bottom Line: Putting Social Responsibility to Work for Your Business and the World.* Simon & Schuster, 1994.

Navran, Frank. *The 1993 Desktop Guide to Total Ethics Management.* Navran Associates, 1992.

Ray, Michael, and Alan Rinzler, eds. *The New Paradigm in Business.* Jeremy P. Tarcher/Perigree, 1993.

Reder, Alan. *In Pursuit of Principle and Profit: Business Success Through Social Responsibility.* G. P. Putnam & Sons, 1994.

———. *Seventy-Five Best Business Practices for Socially Responsible Companies.* Jeremy P. Tarcher, 1995.

Roddick, Anita. *Body and Soul.* Crown Publishers, 1994.

Rosen, Robert. *The Healthy Company: Eight Strategies to Develop People, Productivity and Profits.* Jeremy P. Tarcher, 1992.

Scott, Mary, and Howard Rothman. *Companies with a Conscience: Intimate Portraits of 12 Firms That Make a Difference.* Citadel Press, 1992.

Shames, Laurence. *The Hunger for More: Searching for Values in the Age of Greed.* Times Books, 1989.

Shore, William H. *Revolution of the Heart.* Riverhead Books, 1995.

Shrivastava, Paul. *Greening Business: Profiting the Corporation and the Environment.* Van Nostrand Reinhold, 1995.

Sonnenberg, Frank. *Managing with Conscience: How to Improve Performance Through Integrity, Trust and Commitment.* McGraw-Hill, 1993.

Stack, Jack. *The Great Game of Business: The Only Sensible Way to Run a Company.* Doubleday, 1994.

• Periodicals

Business and Society Review
(212) 399-1088

Business Ethics Magazine
(612) 962-4700

Co-op America's Green Pages
Co-op America's Quarterly
(202) 872-5307

Green Business Letter: The Hands-on
   Journal for Environmentally
   Conscious Companies
(800) 955-GREEN

Perspective
(415) 393-8251

*Who Cares: A Journal of Service and
    Action*
(800) 628-1692

• Related Programs

Initiative for a Competitive Inner
    City
1 MetroTech Center No., 11th Floor
Brooklyn, NY 11201
(718) 722-7376
initiative@aol.com

Kenan Institute of Private
    Enterprise
Urban Enterprise Corp.
University of North Carolina
    at Chapel Hill
Campus Box 3440, The Kenan
    Center
Chapel Hill, NC 27599-3440
(919) 962-8201

• Education/Curriculum-Development Programs

Center for Business Ethics
Bentley College
175 Forest St.
Waltham, MA 02154-4705
www.bentley.edu
(617) 891-2981

Center for Corporate Community
    Relations
Boston College
6 College Rd.
Chestnut Hill, MA 02167
(617) 552-2555

Lemelson National Program in
   Invention, Innovation, and
   Creativity
Hampshire College
Amherst, MA 01002-5001
www.hampshire.edu
(413) 582-5613

Management Institute for
   Environment and Business
World Resources Institute
1709 New York Avenue, N.W.
Washington, DC 20006
(202) 638-6300

New Academy of Business
University of Bath
3/4 Albion Pl.
London W6OLT
United Kingdom
101572.3506@compuserve.com

Students for Responsible Business
P.O. Box 29221
San Francisco, CA 94129-0221
webmaster@SRBnet.org
(415) 561-6510

- **Socially Responsible Investing Organizations**

Catalyst, Inc.
P.O. Box 1308
Montpelier, VT 05602
Newsletter: *Catalyst: Economics
   for the Living Earth*
(802) 223-7943

Council on Economic Priorities (CEP)
30 Irving Pl.
New York, NY 10003
Newsletter: *CEP Newsletter*
(212) 420-1133

Data Center
464 19 St.
Oakland, CA 94612
(510) 835-4692

GOOD MONEY Publications
Box 363
Worchester, VT 05682
(802) 223-3911

INFACT
256 Hanover St.
Boston, MA 02113
(617) 742-4583

Investor Responsibility Research
    Center
1350 Connecticut Ave., N.W.
    Suite 700
Washington, DC 20036
(202) 833-0700

Management Reports, Inc.
101 West Union Wharf
Boston, MA 02109
Journal: *Business and Society
    Review*

Social Investment Forum (SIF)
430 First Avenue North, No. 290
Minneapolis, MN 55401
Newsletter: *FORUM*
(612) 333-8338

The Social Responsibility
    Investment Group, Inc.
The Chandler Building, Suite 622
127 Peach St., N.E.
Atlanta, GA 30303
(404) 577-3635

Index